ALSO BY GERALD MARTIN

Men of Maize
(translation and critical edition of Miguel Angel Asturias,
Hombres de maíz)

*Journeys Through the Labyrinth:
Latin American Fiction in the Twentieth Century*

Gabriel García Márquez

Gabriel García Márquez

 A LIFE

Gerald Martin

Alfred A. Knopf New York

2009

THIS IS A BORZOI BOOK
PUBLISHED BY ALFRED A. KNOPF

Originally published in Great Britain by
Bloomsbury Publishing Plc., London, in 2008

Maps by John Gilkes

All permissions to reprint previously published material
can be found on page 642.

Library of Congress Cataloging-in-Publication Data
Martin, Gerald.
Gabriel García Márquez : a life / by Gerald Martin.—1st U.S. ed.
p. cm.
"This is a Borzoi book."
Includes bibliographical references and index.
ISBN 978-0-307-27177-8 (alk. paper)
1. García Márquez, Gabriel, 1928– 2. Authors, Colombian—
20th century—Biography. I. Title.
PQ8180.17.A73Z718 2009
863'.64—dc22
[B]   2009003806

Manufactured in the United States of America
First United States Edition

In Memoriam:

George Edward Martin and Sheila O'Keeffe,
Dennis Shannon and Dorothy May Owen.
And to their granddaughters
Camilla Jane and Leonie Jasmine.

Contents

Acknowledgements

ONE OF THE BURDENS of researching a biography is that so many favours have to be asked of so many people, most of whom respond with generosity and goodwill even though they have absolutely nothing to gain from their endeavour. Rarely can a researcher have been indebted to so many people or, indeed, so deeply and hopelessly indebted to a significant proportion of them—even if, of course, the eventual shortcomings of the book are mine alone.

First and foremost, in England (and in the United States), I thank my wife Gail, who over eighteen years has helped me research the book, prepare the book and write the book, with extraordinary generosity, dedication and (for the most part) patience; it is also her book and I would still be years away from finishing it without her assistance. And I also thank my daughters Camilla and Leonie, who have never complained at our occasional neglect of them and their families, whom we love so much. Second, my dear friend John King, of the University of Warwick, who has read both versions of this book, including the longer one, but has read them at the time and in the way necessary to ease my neuroses and maximize my time and effort; I will always be grateful to him.

Gail Martin, Andrew Cannon and Leonie Martin Cannon (literary lawyers both), Liz Calder and Maggie Traugott all read the manuscript and made many invaluable suggestions. Camilla Martin Wilks gave critical help with family trees at a difficult moment.

I could not be more grateful to Gabriel García Márquez and Mercedes Barcha. Few couples have more public and private commitments than they do and yet they have treated me with courtesy, generosity and good humour over almost two decades despite our shared awareness, never spelled out, that few invasions of privacy are more exasperating—or indeed far-reaching—than the repeated and always unpredictable requests and requirements of a biographer. Their sons Rodrigo and Gonzalo (and Gonzalo's wife Pía) have also been friendly and helpful. Their secretaries, especially Blanca Rodríguez and Mónica Alonso Garay, have always assisted me on request, and their cousin Margarita Márquez Caballero, their secretary in Bogotá, has been not only charming but efficient and helpful beyond the call of duty. Carmen Balcells, García Márquez's agent in Barcelona, has talked to me at length on several occasions and has enormously facilitated this undertaking both at the beginning and at its end. Jaime Abello, the Director of the Foundation for a New Ibero-American Journalism in Cartagena, has been most supportive in recent years, as has his colleague, my inimitable and unforgettable friend Jaime García Márquez; and without Alquimia Peña, Director of the Foundation for New Latin American Cinema in Havana, I might never have met Gabriel García Márquez in the first place. Later, Antonio Núñez Jiménez made his unique knowledge of the relationship between García Márquez and Fidel Castro available to me as well as the facilities of his foundation, the Fundación de la Naturaleza y el Hombre in Havana.

In Colombia my *cachaca* friend Patricia Castaño's generosity, knowledge of the country and networking skills gave me advantages and resources invaluable to a foreign researcher; not only would this have been a different book without her help and advice but the research and preparation would have been much less interesting and enjoyable without her friendship and hospitality and that of her husband Fernando Caycedo. Gustavo Adolfo Ramírez Ariza has contributed to my understanding of García Márquez's relationship with the capital city (despite being a *costeño*) and has given me crucial and judicious assistance with illustrations and other details (my thanks also to his mother, Ruth Ariza); Rosalía Castro, Juan Gustavo Cobo Borda, Margarita Márquez Caballero and Conrado Zuluaga all opened their personal archives in Colombia to me with unhesitating generosity and gave me indispensable source material. Heriberto Fiorillo has kindly made the resources of the new "La Cueva" available to me and Rafael Darío Jiménez has guided me around Aracataca with great insight and good humour.

Also in Colombia I have been privileged to meet not only Gabriel

García Márquez's mother, Luisa Santiaga Márquez Iguarán de García, on several occasions, but have been treated almost as one of the family ("el tío Yeral") by his relatives, especially his brothers and sisters and their spouses and children. It would be individious to try to single anyone out but I am grateful to them all, not just for the information but for the extraordinary human experience they have given me both individually and collectively: Margot García Márquez; Luis Enrique García Márquez and Graciela Morelli and their children; Aida Rosa García Márquez; Ligia García Márquez (the family genealogist, literally a "godsend" to all researchers); Gustavo García Márquez and Lilia Travecero with their son Daniel García Travecero; Rita García Márquez and Alfonso Torres, Alfonsito and all the rest; Jaime García Márquez and Margarita Munive; Hernando (Nanchi) García Márquez and family; Alfredo (Cuqui) García Márquez; Abelardo García and family; Germaine (Emy) García; and last but certainly not least, the unforgettable and much missed Eligio (Yiyo) García Márquez, his wife Myriam Garzón and their sons Esteban García Garzón and Nicolás García Garzón. I hope to give more of a "biography of the family" in a later volume.

Among members of the extended family, I have met and been generously assisted by the writer José Luis Díaz-Granados and his son Federico, his mother Margot Valdeblánquez de Díaz-Granados (another indispensable family memorialist), José Stevenson, another distinguished writer and good friend, whose knowledge of Bogotá has been invaluable, Oscar Alarcón Núñez (yet another writer; the family boasts several), Nicolás Arias, Eduardo Barcha and Narcisa Maas, Miriam Barcha, Arturo Barcha Velilla, Héctor Barcha Velilla, Heriberto Márquez, Ricardo Márquez Iguarán in Riohacha, Margarita Márquez Caballero (mentioned above), Rafael Osorio Martínez and Ezequiel Iguarán Iguarán.

In Paris, Tachia Quintana de Rosoff has always been helpful and welcoming, as was her late husband Charles Rosoff; I feel privileged to have known her.

Worldwide, as well as those mentioned above, my interviewees have included Marco Tulio Aguilera Garramuño, Eliseo (Lichi) Alberto, Carlos Alemán, Guillermo Angulo, Consuelo Araujonoguera ("La Cacica"), Germán Arciniegas, Nieves Arrazola de Muñoz Suay, Holly Aylett, Carmen Balcells, Manuel Barbachano, Virgilio Barco, Miguel Barnet, Danilo Bartulín, María Luisa Bemberg, Belisario Betancur, Fernando Birri, Pacho Bottía, Ana María Busquets de Cano,

Antonio Caballero, María Mercedes Carranza, Alvaro Castaño and Gloria Valencia, Olga Castaño, Rodrigo Castaño, José María Castellet, Fidel Castro Ruz, Rosalía Castro, Patricia Cepeda, Teresa (Tita) Cepeda, Leonor Cerchar, Ramón Chao, Ignacio Chaves, Hernando Corral, Alfredo Correa, Luis Carmelo Correa, Poncho Cotes, Luis Coudurier Sayago, Claude Couffon, Antonio Daconte, Malcolm Deas, Meira Delmar, José Luis Díaz-Granados, Eliseo Diego, Lisandro Duque, Ignacio Durán, María Jimena Duzán, Jorge Edwards, María Luisa Elío, Rafael Escalona, José Espinosa, Ramiro de la Espriella, Filemón Estrada, Etzael and Mencha Saltarén and family in Barrancas, Luis and Leticia Feduchi, Roberto Fernández Retamar, Cristo Figueroa, Heriberto Fiorillo, Víctor Flores Olea, Elida Fonseca, José Font Castro, Marcos María Fossy, Alfonso Fuenmayor (I owe Alfonso an unforgettable tour of old Barranquilla), Carlos Fuentes, José Gamarra, Heliodoro García, Mario García Joya, Otto Garzón Patiño, Víctor Gaviria, Jacques Gilard, Paul Giles, Fernando Gómez Agudelo, Raúl Gómez Jattin, Katya González, Antonio González Jorge and Isabel Lara, Juan Goytisolo, Andrew Graham-Yooll, Edith Grossman, Oscar Guardiola, Tomás Gutiérrez Alea, Rafael Gutiérrez Girardot, Guillermo Henríquez, Jaime Humberto Hermosillo, Ramón Illán Bacca, Michael Jiménez, José Vicente Kataraín, Don Klein, Maria Lucia Lepecki, Susana Linares de Vargas, Miguel Littín, Jordi Lladó Vilaseca, Felipe López Caballero, Nereo López Mesa ("Nereo"), Alfonso López Michelsen, Aline Mackissack Maldonado, "Magola" in the Guajira, Berta Maldonado ("La Chaneca"), Stella Malagón, Gonzalo Mallarino, Eduardo Marceles Daconte, Joaquín Marco, Guillermo Marín, Juan Marsé, Jesús Martín-Barbero, Tomás Eloy Martínez and Gabriela Esquivada, Carmelo Martínez Conn, Alberto Medina López, Jorge Orlando Melo, Consuelo Mendoza, Elvira Mendoza, María Luisa Mendoza ("La China"), Plinio Apuleyo Mendoza, Domingo Miliani, Luis Mogollón and Yolanda Pupo, Sara de Mojica, Carlos Monsiváis, Augusto (Tito) Monterroso and Barbara Jacobs, Beatriz de Moura, Annie Morvan, Alvaro Mutis and Carmen Miracle, Berta Navarro, Francisco Norden, Elida Noriega, Antonio Núñez Jiménez and Lupe Véliz, Alejandro Obregón, Ana María Ochoa, Montserrat Ordóñez, Jaime ("El Mono") Osorio, Leonardo Padura Fuentes, Edgardo ("Cacho") Pallero, James Papworth, Alquimia Peña, Antonio María Peñaloza Cervantes, Gioconda Pérez Snyder, Roberto Pombo, Eduardo Posada Carbó, Elena Poniatowska, Francisco ("Paco") Porrúa, Gertrudis Prasca de Amín, Gregory Rabassa, Sergio

Ramírez Mercado, César Ramos Hernández, Kevin Rastopolous, Rosa Regás, Alastair Reid, Juan Reinoso and Virginia de Reinoso, Laura Restrepo, Ana Ríos, Julio Roca, Juan Antonio Roda and María Fornaguera de Roda, Héctor Rojas Herazo, Teresita Román de Zurek, Vicente Rojo and Albita, Jorge Eliécer Ruiz, José ("El Mono") Salgar, Daniel Samper, Ernesto Samper, María Elvira Samper, Jorge Sánchez, Enrique Santos Calderón, Lászlo Scholz, Enrique (Quique) Scopell and Yolanda Field, Elba Solano, Carmen Delia de Solano, Urbano Solano Vidal, José Stevenson, Jean Stubbs, Gloria Triana, Jorge Alí Triana, Hernán Urbina Joiro, Margot Valdeblánquez de Díaz-Granados, Germán Vargas, Mauricio Vargas, Mario Vargas Llosa, Margarita de la Vega, Roberto de la Vega, Rafael Vergara, Nancy Vicens, Hernán Vieco, Stella Villamizar, Luis Villar Borda, Erna Von der Walde, Ben Woolford, Daniel Woolford, Señor and Señora Wunderlisch, Martha Yances, Juan Zapata Olivella, Manuel Zapata Olivella, Gloria Zea and Conrado Zuluaga. I am grateful to all of them and would like to be able to detail exactly what each of these interlocutors has done for me or taught me, but this would take a book in itself.

Others to whom I am grateful for information, conversations and other forms of assistance or hospitality include: Alberto Abello Vives, Hugo Achugar, Claudia Aguilera Neira, Federico Alvarez, Jon Lee Anderson, Manuel de Andreis, Gustavo Arango, Lucho Argáez, Ruth Margarita Ariza, Oscar Arias, Diosa Avellanes, Salvador Bacarisse, Frank Bajak, Dan Balderston, Soraya Bayuelo, Michael Bell, Gene Bell-Villada, Giuseppe Bellini, Mario Benedetti, Samuel Beracasa, John Beverley, Fernando Birri, Hilary Bishop and Daniel Mermelstein, Martha Bossío, Juan Carlos Botero, Pacho Bottía, Gordon Brotherston, Alejandro Bruzual, Juan Manuel Buelvas, Julio Andrés Camacho, Homero Campa, Alfonso Cano, Fernando Cano, Marisol Cano, Ariel Castillo, Dicken Castro, Juan Luis Cebrián, Fernando Cepeda, María Inmaculada Cerchar, Jane Chaplin, Geoff Chew and Carmen Marrugo, William Chislett, Fernando Colla and Sylvie Josserand, Oscar Collazos and Jimena Rojas, Susan Corbesero, Antonio Cornejo Polar, Sofía Cotes, Juan Cruz, George Dale-Spencer, Régis Debray, Jörg Denzer and Leydy Di, Jesús Díaz, Mike Dibb, Donald Dummer, Conchita Dumois, Alberto Duque López, Kenya C. Dworkin y Méndez, Diamela Eltit, Alan Ereira, Cristo Figueroa, Rubem Fonseca, Juan Forero, Fred Fornoff, Norman Gall, Silvia Galvis (whose book on *Los GM* is indispensable), José Gamarra, Diego García Elío, Julio García Espinosa and Dolores Calviño, Edgard García Ochoa ("Flash"), Verónica Garibotto, Rosalba Garza, César Gaviria and Ana Milena Muñoz, Luz Mary Giraldo, Margo Glantz, Catalina Gómez, Richard Gott, Sue Harper Ditmar, Luis Harss, Andrés Hoyos, Antonio Jaramillo ("El Perro Negro"), Fernando Jaramillo, Carlos Jáuregui, Orlando and Lourdes Jiménez Visbal, Carmenza Kline, John Kraniauskas, Henry Laguado, Patricia Lara, Catherine LeGrand, Patricia Llosa de Vargas, Fabio and Maritza López de la Roche, Juan Antonio Masoliver, Tony McFarlane, Pete McGinley, Max and Jan McGowan-King, María del Pilar Melgarejo, Moisés Melo and Guiomar Acevedo, Oscar Monsalve, Mabel Moraña, Patricia Murray, Delynn Myers, Víctor Nieto, Harley D. Oberhelman, John O'Leary, William Ospina, Raúl Padilla López, Michael Palencia-Roth, Alessandra María Parachini, Rafael Pardo, Felipe Paz, Conchita Penilla, Pedro Pérez Sarduy, Carlos Rincón, Manuel Piñeiro ("Barbarroja"), Natalia Ramírez, Arturo Ripstein, Jorge Eduardo Ritter, Isabel Rodríguez Vergara, Jorge Eliécer Ruiz, Patricio Samper and Genoveva Carrasco de Samper, Emilio Sánchez Alsina, Noemí Sanín, Amos Segala, Narcís Serra, Donald L. Shaw, Alain Sicard, Ernesto Sierra Delgado, Antonio Skármeta, Pablo Sosa Montes de Oca, Adelaida Sourdis, David Streitfeld, Gustavo Tatis Guerra, Michael Taussig, Totó la Momposina, Adelaida Trujillo and Carlos ("Caturo") Mejía, Carlos Ulanovsky, Aseneth Velázquez, Ancizar Vergara, Erna Von der Walde, Dan Weldon, Clare White, Colin White, Edwin Williamson, Michael Wood, Anne Wright and Marc Zimmerman. Again I would like to be able to detail each of their contributions, many of them considerable, some immense. To those I have overlooked I sincerely apologize.

I also thank Roger MacDonald, Librarian at the University of Portsmouth, England, for his assiduous help at the beginning of this project, and the legendary Eduardo Lozano, Latin American Librarian at the University of Pittsburgh.

Dean Peter Koehler and Dean John Cooper of the Faculty of Arts and Sciences, University of Pittsburgh, both gave me invaluable support over many years.

I must also thank Neil Belton, editor extraordinary, whose original idea this book was; we had good times together.

My agent Elizabeth Sheinkman came into my life at a providential moment and has been enterprising, decisive and warmly supportive at all times; she has my grateful thanks.

Finally the team at Bloomsbury—Ruth Logan, Nick Humphrey,

Phillip Beresford, the judicious and resourceful Emily Sweet, and the imperturbable Bill Swainson, whose diplomatic skills and inspired editorial work were absolutely crucial—treated their reprobate author with patience and consideration beyond any call of duty; the book is much the better for their unstinting efforts and I sincerely thank them all, as well as Diana Coglianese of Knopf, who has helped me undergo my transatlantic makeover with sympathy and tact.

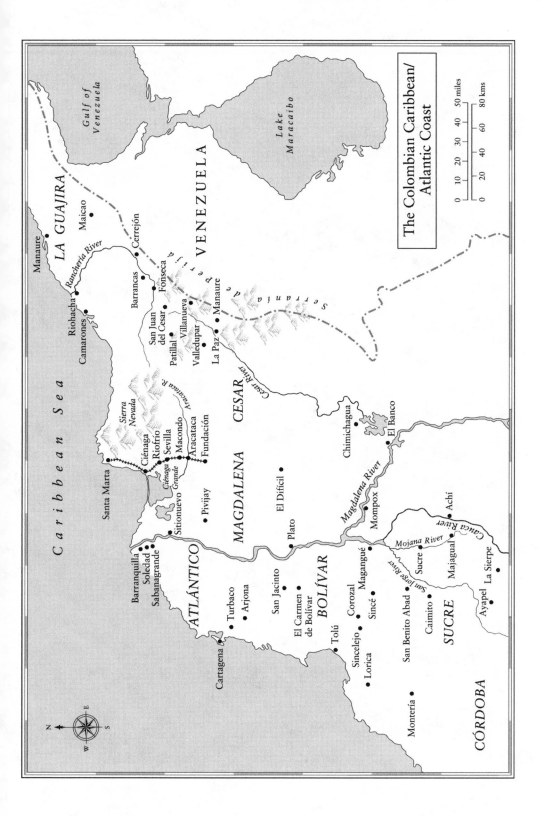

The Colombian Caribbean/
Atlantic Coast

Caribbean Sea

Gulf of
Venezuela

Lake
Maracaibo

VENEZUELA

LA GUAJIRA

Manure

Maicao

Cerrejón

Rancheria River

Riohacha

Camarones

Barrancas

Fonseca

San Juan
del Cesar

Villanueva

Patillal

Valledupar

Manaure

La Paz

Serranía de Perijá

Sierra
Nevada

Ciénaga

Riofrío

Sevilla

Macondo

Aracataca

Fundación

Santa Marta

Ciénaga
Grande

Sitionuevo

Aracataca R.

Cesar River

CESAR

MAGDALENA

Pivijay

El Difícil

Plato

Chimichagua

El Banco

Magdalena River

Mompox

Achí

Cauca River

Barranquilla

Soledad

Sabanagrande

ATLÁNTICO

Turbaco

Arjona

San Jacinto

El Carmen
de Bolívar

Tolú

BOLÍVAR

Corozal

Magangué

Sincé

Mojana River

Sucre

Majagual

La Sierpe

Sincelejo

Lorica

San Benito Abad

Caimito

SUCRE

Ayapel

San Jorge River

Carragena

Monteria

CÓRDOBA

N
W E
S

0   10   20   30   40   50 miles
0   20   40   60   80 kms

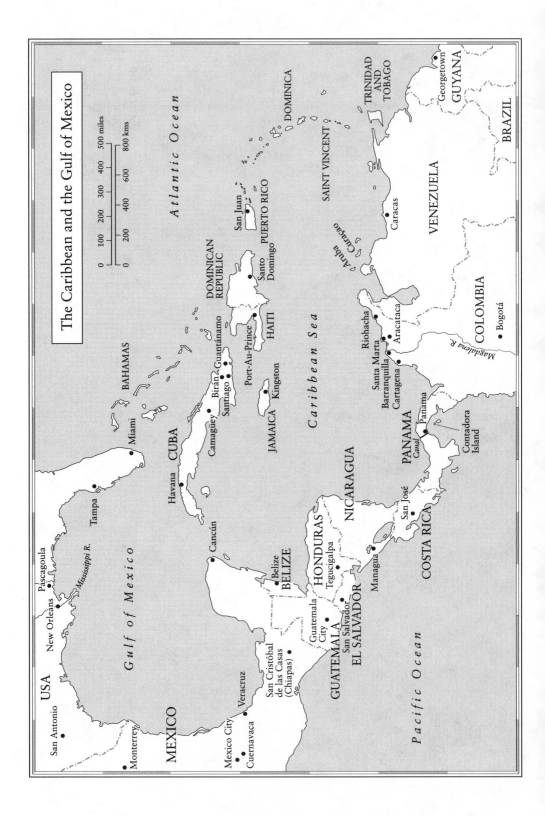

The Caribbean and the Gulf of Mexico

Foreword

GABRIEL GARCÍA MÁRQUEZ, born in Colombia in 1927, is the best-known writer to have emerged from the "Third World" and the best-known exponent of a literary style, "magical realism," which has proved astonishingly productive in other developing countries and among the novelists who write about them—like Salman Rushdie, to quote just one obvious example. García Márquez is perhaps the most widely admired and most representative Latin American novelist of all time inside Latin America itself; and even in the "First World" of Europe and the United States, in an era in which universally acknowledged great writers have been difficult to find, his reputation over the last four decades has been second to none.

Indeed, if we look at the novelists of the twentieth century we discover that most of the "great names" on which critics currently agree belong to its first forty years (Joyce, Proust, Kafka, Faulkner, Woolf); but in the second half of the century perhaps only García Márquez has achieved true unanimity. His masterpiece, *One Hundred Years of Solitude*, published in 1967, a book which appeared on the cusp of the transition between "modernist" and "postmodernist" fiction, may be the only novel between 1950 and 2000 to have found large numbers of enthusiastic readers in virtually every country and culture of the world. In that sense, in terms of both its subject matter—broadly, the clash between "tradition" and "modernity"—and its reception, it is probably not an exaggeration to claim that it was the world's first truly "global" novel.

In other ways, too, García Márquez is a rare phenomenon. He is a serious but popular writer—like Dickens, Hugo or Hemingway—who sells millions of books and whose celebrity approaches that of sportsmen, musicians or film stars. In 1982 he was the most popular winner of the Nobel Prize for Literature in recent times. In Latin America, a region that has never been the same since García Márquez invented the small community of "Macondo," he is known everywhere by his nickname, "Gabo," like silent cinema's "Charlie" or soccer's "Pele." Although one of the four or five biggest personalities of the twentieth century in his continent, he was born in the proverbial "middle of nowhere," in a town of less than ten thousand mainly illiterate inhabitants, with unpaved streets, no drainage and a name, Aracataca, aka "Macondo," which makes people laugh when they first hear it (though its closeness to "Abracadabra" should perhaps make them cautious). Very few famous writers from any part of the world have come from such a small-town background, and yet fewer have lived their era, both culturally and politically, as fully and intimately as this one.

García Márquez is now a wealthy man, with seven homes in glamorous locations in five different countries. In recent decades he has been able to demand (or, more usually, refuse) $50,000 for a half-hour interview. He has been able to place his articles in almost any newspaper in the world and receive huge sums for them. Like those of Shakespeare, the titles of his books appear in ghostly fashion in headlines all over the planet ("one hundred hours of solitude," "chronicle of a catastrophe foretold," "autumn of the dictator," "love in the time of money"). He has been forced to confront and endure an astonishing level of celebrity for half a lifetime. His favours and his friendship have been sought by the rich, the famous and the powerful—François Mitterrand, Felipe González, Bill Clinton, most of the recent presidents of Colombia and Mexico, and many other celebrities besides. Yet despite his dazzling literary and financial success, he has remained throughout his life a man of the progressive Left, a defender of good causes and a constructor of positive enterprises, including the founding of influential institutes of journalism and film. At the same time his close friendship with another political leader, Fidel Castro, has been a constant source of controversy and criticism for more than thirty years.

I have been working on this biography for seventeen years.* Con-

---

* I had reached over two thousand pages and six thousand footnotes when I finally realized that perhaps I would never finish the project. What lies before the reader, then, is the abbreviated version of a much longer biography, almost completed, which I intend to publish in a few more years, if life is kind. But it seemed sensible to delay that gargantuan task and to distil my discoveries and such knowledge as I have accumulated into a brief, relatively compact narrative while the subject of this work, now a man past eighty, is still alive and in a position to read it.

trary to what I was told by everyone I spoke to in the early days ("You'll never get to see him and if you do he won't cooperate"), I got to meet my man within a few months of starting work and, although he could not be said to have been brimming with enthusiasm ("Why do you want to write a biography? Biographies mean death"), he was friendly, hospitable and tolerant. Indeed, whenever I have been asked if my biography is an authorized one my reply has always been the same: "No, it is not an authorized biography, it's a tolerated biography." Yet to my mingled surprise and gratitude, in 2006 García Márquez himself told the world's press that I am his "official" biographer. Probably that makes me his only officially tolerated biographer! It has been an extraordinary privilege.

As is well known, the relationship between biographer and biographee is invariably a difficult one, but I have been extremely fortunate. As a professional journalist and a writer who himself uses the lives of those he has known in the elaboration of his fictions, García Márquez has been forbearing, to say the least. When I first met him in Havana in December 1990, he said that he would go along with my proposal on one condition: "Don't make me do your work." I think he would agree that I have not made him do my work and he has responded by helping when I have really needed his assistance. I have carried out some three hundred interviews in order to produce this biography, many of them with crucial interlocutors who are no longer with us, but I am aware that Fidel Castro and Felipe González might not have been among the list if "Gabo" had not given some sign to say that I was "OK." I hope he still thinks I am OK now that he is in a position to read the book. He has always declined to give me the kind of "heart to heart" that biographers inevitably dream of, on the grounds that such interaction is "indecent," yet we must have spent a total of one full month together at different times and in different places over the past seventeen years, in private and in public, and I believe that few other people have heard some of the things that he has said to me. Yet he has never tried to influence me in any way and he has always said, with the combined ethic and cynicism of the born journalist: "Just write what you see; whatever you write, that is what I will be."

This biography was researched in Spanish, the works all read in Spanish, most of the interviews conducted in Spanish, yet it has been written and is now published in English (though the Spanish translation will appear in 2009). Moreover, it goes without saying that the more normal procedure is for a biography, especially the first complete biography, to be written by a compatriot who knows the country of origin as well as the subject himself and who understands the smallest nuances of every communication. That is not my case—besides, García Márquez is an international figure, not just a famous Colombian— but, as the man himself, perhaps not altogether sincerely, once sighed when my name was mentioned in conversation: "Oh well, I suppose every self-respecting writer should have an English biographer." I suspect that my only virtue in his eyes was my obvious lifelong love for and attachment to the continent in which he was born.

It has not been easy to find my way through the multiple versions that García Márquez has given of almost all the important moments in his life. Like Mark Twain, with whom he can profitably be compared, he loves a good yarn, not to mention a tall tale, and he likes a story to be satisfyingly rounded off, not least the formative incidents that make up the story of his own life; at the same time he is also playful, anti-academic and strongly in favour of mystification and downright mis-chief-making when it comes to putting journalists or professors off the scent. This is part of what he calls his *mamagallismo* (more of this later; for the moment one may discreetly translate it with the British term "piss-taking"). Even when you can be sure that any particular anecdote is based on something that "really" happened, you still cannot pin it down to a single shape because you find that he has told most of the well-known stories about his life in several different versions, all of which have at least an element of truth. I have personal experience of this mythomania, by which I too have become joyfully infected (in my own life, though not, I hope, in this book). The García Márquez family were always impressed by my tenacity and preparedness to engage in the kinds of investigation to which only mad dogs and Englishmen would resort. Thus I have found it quite impossible to kill off the myth which García Márquez himself has disseminated, and evidently believes, to the effect that I—and this is apparently characteristic of my manias—once spent a rain-drenched night on a bench in the square at Aracataca in order to "soak up the atmosphere" of the town in which my subject was, reputedly, born.

After so many years I can hardly believe that the book finally exists and that I am here writing its preface. Many burned-out biographers much more illustrious than I have concluded that the time and effort invested in such a labour are not worth the candle and that only the foolish and the deluded would begin such a task, led on, perhaps, by the possibility of communing and identifying with the great, the good or the merely famous. I might have been tempted to agree with this conclusion; but if ever a subject was worth investing a quarter of one's own life in, it would undoubtedly be the extraordinary life and career of Gabriel García Márquez.

Gerald Martin, July 2008

Gabriel García Márquez

From Origins Obscure

1800~1899

ONE HOT, ASPHYXIATING MORNING in the early 1930s, in the tropical coastal region of northern Colombia, a young woman gazed through the window of the United Fruit Company train at the passing banana plantations. Row after row after row, shimmering from sun into shade. She had taken the overnight steamer, besieged by mosquitoes, across the great Ciénaga swamp from the Caribbean port city of Barranquilla, and now she was travelling down through the Banana Zone to the small inland town of Aracataca where, several years before, she had left her first-born child Gabriel with her ageing parents when he was still a baby. Luisa Santiaga Márquez Iguarán de García had given birth to three more children since that time and this was her first return to Aracataca since her husband, Gabriel Eligio García, took her away to live in Barranquilla, leaving little "Gabito" in the care of his maternal grandparents, Tranquilina Iguarán Cotes de Márquez and Colonel Nicolás Márquez Mejía. Colonel Márquez was a veteran of the bitter Thousand Day War fought at the turn of the century, a lifelong stalwart of the Colombian Liberal Party and, latterly, the local treasurer of the municipality of Aracataca.

The Colonel and Doña Tranquilina had angrily disapproved of Luisa Santiaga's courtship with the handsome García. He was not only a poor man, and an outsider, but also illegitimate, a half-breed and perhaps worst of all, a fervent supporter of the detested Conservative Party. He had been the telegraphist of Aracataca for just a few days when his eyes first fell upon Luisa, one of the most marriageable young women in the town. Her parents sent her away to stay with relatives for the best part of a year to get the wild infatuation with the seductive newcomer out of her head, but to no avail. As for García himself, if he was hoping that his marriage to the Colonel's daughter would make his fortune he was disappointed. The bride's parents had refused to attend the wedding he eventually managed to organize in the regional capital of Santa Marta and he had lost his position in Aracataca.

What was Luisa thinking as she gazed out of the train window? Perhaps she had forgotten how uncomfortable this journey was going to be. Was she thinking of the house where she had spent her childhood and youth? How everyone would react to her visit? Her parents. Her aunts. The two children she hadn't seen for so long: Gabito, the eldest, and Margarita, his younger sister, also now living with her grandparents. The train whistled as it passed the small banana plantation named Macondo which she remembered from her own childhood. A few minutes later Aracataca came into view. And there was her father the Colonel waiting in the shade . . . How would he greet her?

No one knows what he said. But we do know what happened next.[1] Back in the old Colonel's Big House, the women were preparing little Gabito for a day he would never forget: "She's here, your mother has come, Gabito. She's here. Your mother. Can't you hear the train?" The sound of the whistle arrived once more from the nearby station.

Gabito would say later that he had no memory of his mother. She had left him before he could retain any memories at all. And if she had any meaning now, it was as a sudden absence never truly explained by his grandparents, an anxiety, as if something was wrong. With him, perhaps. Where was grandfather? Grandfather always made everything clear. But his grandfather had gone out.

Then Gabito heard them arrive at the other end of the house. One of his aunts came and took his hand. Everything was like a dream. "Your mamma's in there," the aunt said. So he went in and after a moment he saw a woman he didn't know, at the far end of the room, sitting with her back to the shuttered window. She was a beautiful lady, with a straw hat and a long loose dress, with sleeves down to her wrists. She was breathing heavily in the midday heat. And he was filled with a strange confusion, because she was a lady he liked the look of but he realized at once that he didn't love her in the way they had told him you should love your mother. Not like he loved grandpa and grandma. Not even like he loved his aunts.

The lady said, "Aren't you going to give your mother a hug?" And then she took him to her and embraced him. She had an aroma he would never forget. He was less than a year old when his mother left him. Now he was almost seven. So only now, because she had come back, did he understand it: his mother had left him. And Gabito would never get over it, not least because he could never quite bring himself to face what he felt about it. And then, quite soon, she left him again.

LUISA SANTIAGA, the Colonel's wayward daughter, and mother of little Gabito, had been born on 25 July 1905, in the small town of Barrancas, between the wild territory of the Guajira and the mountainous province of Padilla, to the east of the Sierra Nevada.[2] At the time of Luisa's birth her father was a member of a defeated army, the army of the Liberal Party vanquished by the Conservatives in Colombia's great civil war, the War of a Thousand Days (1899–1902).

Nicolás Ricardo Márquez Mejía, Gabriel García Márquez's grandfather, was born on 7 February 1864 in Riohacha, Guajira, a sun-baked, salty, dusty city on the north Atlantic coast of Colombia and diminutive capital of its wildest region, home to the redoubtable Guajiro Indians and refuge for smugglers and traffickers from colonial times to the present day. Little is known about Márquez's early life except that he received only an elementary education but made the most of it and was sent westward, for some time, to live with his cousin Francisca Cimodosea Mejía in the town of El Carmen de Bolívar, south of the majestic colonial city of Cartagena. There the two cousins were brought up by Nicolás's maternal grandmother Josefa Francisca Vidal. Later, after Nicolás had spent a few years wandering the entire coastal region, Francisca would join his family and live under his roof, a spinster for the rest of her life. Nicolás lived for a time in Camarones, a town by the Guajira shoreline some fifteen miles from Riohacha. Legend has it that he was a precocious participant in one or more of the civil wars that regularly punctuated nineteenth-century life in Colombia. When he returned to Riohacha at the age of seventeen he became a silversmith under the tutelage of his father, Nicolás del Carmen Márquez Hernández. It was the traditional family occupation. Nicolás had completed his primary education but his artisan family could not afford for him to go further.

Nicolás Márquez was productive in other ways: within two years of his return to the Guajira, the reckless teenage traveller had fathered two illegitimate sons—"natural sons," they are called in Colombia—José María, born in 1882, and Carlos Alberto, born in 1884.[3] Their mother was an eccentric Riohacha spinster called Altagracia Valdeblánquez, connected to an influential Conservative family and much older than Nicolás himself. We do not know why Nicolás did not marry her. Both sons were given their mother's surname; both were brought up as staunch Catholics and Conservatives, despite Nicolás's fervent Liberalism, since the custom in Colombia until quite recently was for children to adopt the political allegiance of their parents and the boys had been brought up not by Nicolás but by their mother's family; and both would fight against the Liberals, and thus against their father, in the War of a Thousand Days.

Just a year after the birth of Carlos Alberto, Nicolás, aged twenty-one, married a girl his own age, Tranquilina Iguarán Cotes, who had been born, also in Riohacha, on 5 July 1863. Although Tranquilina was born illegitimate, her surnames were those of two leading Conservative families of the region. Both Nicolás and Tranquilina were, visibly, descendants of white European families and although Nicolás, an incorrigible Casanova, would dally with women of every race and colour, the essential hierarchies from light to dark would be implicitly or explicitly maintained in all their dealings both in the home and in the street. And many things were best left in obscurity.

And thus we begin to grope our way back into the dark genealogical labyrinths so familiar to readers of Gabriel García Márquez's best-known novel, *One Hundred Years of Solitude*. In that book he goes out of his way not to help his readers with reminders about the details of family relationships: usually only first names are given and these repeat themselves obsessively down through the generations. This becomes part of the work's unspoken challenge to the reader but it undoubtedly reproduces the confusions and anxieties experienced by its author when, as a child, he tried to make sense of the tangled historical networks of family lore.

Take Nicolás, who was born legitimate but brought up not by his parents but by his grandmother. Of course there was nothing unusual about this in a frontier society underpinned for security by the concept of the extended family. As we have seen, he had two illegitimate sons before he was twenty. There was nothing unusual about that either. Immediately thereafter he married Tranquilina, like Altagracia, a woman from a higher class than himself, although, to balance things up, she was illegitimate. Furthermore, she was also his first cousin; this too was common in Colombia and remains more common in Latin America than most other parts of the world though of course, like illegitimacy, it still carries a stigma. The couple had the same grandmother, Juanita Hernández, who travelled from Spain to Colombia in the 1820s, and Nicolás descended from her original legitimate marriage whereas Tranquilina came from her second, illegitimate relationship, after she was widowed, with a Creole born in Riohacha called Blas Iguarán who was ten years her junior. And so it transpired that only two generations later two of Juanita's grandchildren, Nicolás Márquez Mejía, and Tranquilina Iguarán Cotes, first cousins, were married in Riohacha. Even though none of their surnames coincided, the fact was that his father and her mother were both children, half-brother and half-sister, of the adventurous Juanita. You could never be sure who you were marrying. And such sinfulness might bring damnation or, worse—as the Buendía family members fear throughout *One Hundred Years of Solitude*—a child with a pig's tail who would put an end to the family line!

Naturally the spectre of incest, whose shadow a marriage like that of Nicolás and Tranquilina inevitably raises, adds another, much darker dimension to the concept of illegitimacy. And later Nicolás spawned many, maybe dozens more illegitimate children after he was married. Yet he lived in a profoundly Catholic society, with all the traditional hierarchies and snobberies, in which the lowest orders were blacks or Indians (to whom, of course, no respectable family would wish to be related in any way despite the fact that, in Colombia, almost all families, including the most respectable ones, have such relations). This chaotic mixture of race and class, with so many ways of being illegitimate but only one straight and narrow path to true respectability, is the same world in which, many years later, the infant García Márquez would grow up and in whose perplexities and hypocrisies he would share.

Soon after his marriage to Tranquilina Iguarán, Nicolás Márquez left her pregnant—from the patriarchal point of view, always the best way to leave a woman—and spent a few months in Panama, which at that time was still part of Colombia, working with an uncle, José María Mejía Vidal. There he would engender another illegitimate child, María Gregoria Ruiz, with the woman who may have been the true love of his life, the beautiful Isabel Ruiz, before returning to the Guajira shortly after the birth of his first legitimate son, Juan de Dios, in 1886.[4] Nicolás and Tranquilina had two more legitimate children:

Margarita, born in 1889, and Luisa Santiaga, who was born in Barrancas in July 1905, though she would insist until near the end of her life that she too was born in Riohacha because she felt she had something to hide, as will be seen. She too would marry an illegitimate spouse, and would eventually give birth to a legitimate son called Gabriel José García Márquez. Little wonder illegitimacy is an obsession in the fiction of Gabriel García Márquez, however humorous its treatment.

Nicolás's illegitimate children did not die dreadful deaths in the civil war, as the Colonel's favourite grandson would later fantasize in his novel (in which there are seventeen of them).[5] For example, Sara Noriega was the "natural" daughter of Nicolás and Pacha Noriega, and she too became known as la Pacha Noriega, married Gregorio Bonilla and went to live in Fundación, the next stop down the line from Aracataca. In 1993 her granddaughter, Elida Noriega, whom I met in Barrancas, was the only person in town who still had one of the little gold fish which Nicolás Márquez had fashioned. Ana Ríos, the daughter of Arsenia Carrillo, who was married in 1917 to Nicolás's nephew and close associate Eugenio Ríos (himself related to Francisca Cimodosea Mejía, who also lived with Nicolás), said Sara looked very like Luisa, "skin like a petal and terribly sweet";[6] she died around 1988. Esteban Carrillo and Elvira Carrillo were illegitimate twins born to Sara Manuela Carrillo; Elvira, Gabito's beloved "Aunt Pa," after living with Nicolás in Aracataca, eventually went to Cartagena near the end of her life, where her much younger half-sister, the legitimate Luisa Santiaga, would "take her in and help her to die," according to Ana Ríos. Nicolás Gómez was the son of Amelia Gómez and, according to another informant, Urbano Solano, he went to live in Fundación, like Sara Noriega.

Nicolás's eldest son, the illegitimate José María Valdeblánquez, turned out to be the most successful of all his children, a war hero, politician and historian. He married Manuela Moreu as a very young man and had a son and five daughters. The son of one of them, Margot, is José Luis Díaz-Granados, another writer.[7]

Nicolás Márquez moved from the arid coastal capital Riohacha to Barrancas, long before he became a colonel, because his ambition was to become a landowner and land was both cheaper and more fertile in the hills around Barrancas. (García Márquez, not always reliable in these matters, says that Nicolás's father left him some land there.) Soon he bought a farm from a friend at a place known as El Potrero on the slopes of the Sierra. The farm was called El Guásimo, named after a local fruit tree, and Márquez set to cultivating sugar cane from which he made a rough rum called *chirrinche* on a home-made still; he is thought to have traded the liquor illicitly, like most of his fellow landowners. Later he purchased another farm closer to the town, beside the River Ranchería. He called it El Istmo (The Isthmus), because whichever way you approached it you had to cross water. There he grew tobacco, maize, sugar cane, beans, yucca, coffee and bananas. The farm can still be visited today, half abandoned, its buildings decayed and in some cases disappeared, an old mango tree still standing like a dilapidated family standard, and the whole tropical landscape awash with melancholy and nostalgia. Perhaps this recollected image is just the visitor's imagination, because he knows that Colonel Márquez left Barrancas under a cloud which still seems to hang over the entire community. But long before even that happened, the Colonel's sedentary existence would be overshadowed by war.

EVEN LESS IS KNOWN about the early life of Gabriel García Márquez's father than that of his grandfather. Gabriel Eligio García was born in Sincé, Bolívar, on 1 December 1901, far beyond the great swamp, far even beyond the Magdalena River, during the great civil war in which Nicolás Márquez was actively distinguishing himself. García's great-grandfather was apparently called Pedro García Gordón and was said to have been born in Madrid early in the nineteenth century. We do not know how or why García Gordón ended up in New Granada, or who he married, but in 1834 he had a son called Aminadab García in Caimito, Bolívar (now Sucre department). According to Ligia García Márquez, Aminadab "married" three different women and had three children by them. Then, "widowed," he met María de los Angeles Paternina Bustamante, who was born in 1855 in Sincelejo, twenty-one years his junior, and they had three more children, Eliécer, Jaime and Argemira. Although the couple were not married, Aminadab recognized the children as his own and gave them his name. The baby girl, Argemira García Paternina, was born in September 1887, in Caimito, her father's birthplace. She was to be the mother of Gabriel Eligio García at the age of fourteen and thus the paternal grandmother of our writer, Gabriel García Márquez.[8]

Argemira spent most of her life in the cattle town of Sincé. She was what in Hispanic culture used to be called a "woman of the people." Tall, statuesque and fair-skinned, she never married but had relationships with numerous men and gave birth to seven illegitimate children by three of them, particularly a man called Bejarano.[9] (Her children all carried her name, García.) But her first lover was Gabriel Martínez Garrido, who by then was a teacher, though he was heir to a line of conservative landowners; eccentric to the point of delirium, he had frittered away almost all of his inheritance.[10] He seduced Argemira when she was just thirteen and he was twenty-seven. Unfortunately Gabriel Martínez Garrido was already married to Rosa Meza, born in Sincé like her husband: they had five legitimate children, none of whom was called Gabriel.

Thus Gabriel García Márquez's future father was known throughout his life as Gabriel Eligio García, not Gabriel Eligio Martínez García.[11] Anyone who cared at all about these things would have worked out almost at once that he was illegitimate. In the late 1920s, however, Gabriel Eligio would make up for these disadvantages. Just as Nicolás Márquez had acquired an important military title during the war, becoming a "colonel," so Gabriel Eligio, a self-taught homeopath, started to add the title "doctor" to his name. Colonel Márquez and Doctor García.

PART I

Home: Colombia

1899-1955

1

Of Colonels and Lost Causes

1899~1927

F IVE HUNDRED YEARS after Europeans stumbled across it, Latin America often seems a disappointment to its inhabitants. It is as if its destiny had been fixed by Columbus, "the great captain," who discovered the new continent by mistake, misnamed it—"the Indies"—and then died embittered and disillusioned in the early sixteenth century; or by the "great liberator" Simón Bolívar, who put an end to Spanish colonial rule in the early nineteenth century but died dismayed at the newly emancipated region's disunity and at the bitter thought that "he who makes a revolution ploughs the sea." More recently the fate of Ernesto "Che" Guevara, the twentieth century's most romantic revolutionary icon, who died a martyr's death in Bolivia in 1967, only confirmed the idea that Latin America, still the unknown continent, still the land of the future, is home to grandiose dreams and calamitous failures.[1]

Long before the name of Guevara circled the planet, in a small Colombian town which history only briefly illuminated during the years when the Boston-based United Fruit Company chose to plant bananas there in the early twentieth century, a small boy would listen while his grandfather told tales of a war that lasted a thousand days, at the end of which he too had experienced the bitter solitude of the vanquished, tales of glorious deeds in days gone by, of ghostly heroes and villains, stories which taught the child that justice is not naturally built in to the fabric of life, that right does not always triumph in the kingdom of this world, and that ideals which fill the hearts and minds of many men and women may be defeated and even disappear from the face of the earth. Unless they endure in the memory of those who survive and live to tell the tale.

AT THE END of the nineteenth century, seventy years after achieving independence from Spain, the republic of Colombia had been a country of less than five million controlled by an elite of perhaps three thousand owners of large haciendas, most of whom were politicians and businessmen, and many also lawyers, writers or grammarians—which is why the capital, Bogotá, became known as the "Athens of South America." The War of a Thousand Days was the last and most devastating of more than twenty national and local civil wars which had ravaged Colombia during the nineteenth century, fought between Liberals and Conservatives, centralists and federalists, bourgeoisie and landowners, the capital and the regions. In most other countries the nineteenth century gradually saw the Liberals or their equivalents winning the historical battle, whereas in Colombia the Conservatives were dominant until 1930 and, after a Liberal interlude from 1930 to 1946, took charge again until the mid-1950s and remain a powerful force to the present day. Certainly Colombia is the only country where, at the end of the twentieth century, the general elections were still being fought out between a traditional Liberal Party and a traditional Conservative Party, with no other parties gaining a lasting foothold.[2] This has changed in the last ten years.

Although named the "War of a Thousand Days," the conflict was really over almost before it began. The Conservative government had vastly superior resources and the Liberals were at the mercy of the eccentricities of their inspirational but incompetent leader Rafael Uribe Uribe. Nevertheless the war dragged on for almost three years, increasingly cruel, increasingly bitter and increasingly futile. From October 1900 neither side took prisoners: a "war to the death" was announced whose sombre implications Colombia is living with still. When it all ended in November 1902 the country was devastated and impoverished, the province of Panama about to be lost for ever and perhaps a hundred thousand Colombians had been slaughtered. Feuds and vendettas resulting from the way the conflict had been fought were to continue for many decades. This has made Colombia a curious country in which the two major parties have ostensibly been bitter enemies for almost two centuries yet have tacitly united to ensure that the people never receive genuine representation. No Latin American nation had fewer coups or dictatorships in the twentieth century than Colombia but the Colombian people have paid a staggeringly high price for this appearance of institutional stability.

The War of a Thousand Days was fought over the length and breadth of the country but the centre of gravity gradually shifted north to the Atlantic coastal regions. On the one hand the seat of government, Bogotá, was never seriously threatened by the Liberal rebels; and on the other hand, the Liberals inevitably retreated towards the coastal escape routes which their leaders frequently took in order to seek refuge in sympathetic neighbouring countries or the United States, where they would try to raise funds and buy weapons for the next round of hostilities. At this time the northern third of the country, known as *la Costa* ("the Coast"), whose inhabitants are called *costeños* (coast-dwellers), comprised two major departments: Bolívar to the west, whose capital was the port of Cartagena; and Magdalena to the east, whose capital was the port of Santa Marta, nestling beneath the mighty Sierra Nevada. The two major cities either side of the Sierra Nevada—Santa Marta to the west and Riohacha to the east—and all the towns in between as you rode around the sierra—Ciénaga, Aracataca, Valledupar, Villanueva, San Juan, Fonseca and Barrancas—changed hands many times during the war and provided the scenario for the exploits of Nicolás Márquez and his two eldest, illegitimate children, José María Valdeblánquez and Carlos Alberto Valdeblánquez.

Some time in the early 1890s Nicolás Márquez and Tranquilina Iguarán had moved with their two children Juan de Dios and Margarita to the small town of Barrancas in the Colombian Guajira and rented a house in the Calle del Totumo, a few paces from the square. The house still stands today. Señor Márquez set up as a jeweller, making and selling his own pieces—necklaces, rings, bracelets, chains and his speciality, little gold fish—and establishing, it seems, a profitable business which turned him into a respected member of the community. His apprentice and eventual partner was a younger man called Eugenio Ríos, almost an adopted son, with whom he had worked in Riohacha, having brought him from El Carmen de Bolívar. Ríos was the half-brother of Nicolás's cousin Francisca Cimodosea Mejía, with whom Nicolás had grown up in El Carmen and whom he would later take with him to Aracataca. When the War of a Thousand Days began, after many years of Liberal frustration and bitterness, Nicolás Márquez was, at thirty-five, getting a bit old for adventure. Besides, he had established a comfortable, productive and agreeable life in Barrancas and was looking to build on his growing prosperity. Still, he joined the army of Uribe Uribe, fought in the Guajira, Padilla and Magdalena provinces and there is evidence that he fought harder and longer than many others. Certainly he was involved from the very start when, as a *comandante*, he was part of a Liberal army which occupied his native city of Riohacha, and he was still involved at the conclusion of the conflict in October 1902.

By the end of August 1902 the recently reinforced Liberal army, now under the command of Uribe Uribe, who had recently made one of his frequent unscheduled reappearances, had marched its way westward around the sierra from Riohacha to the small village of Aracataca, already known as a Liberal stronghold, arriving on 5 September. There Uribe Uribe held two days of talks with Generals Clodomiro Castillo and José Rosario Durán and other officers, including Nicolás Márquez. And it was there, in Aracataca, that they made the fateful decision to fight one more time which would lead to their disastrous defeat at the Battle of Ciénaga.

Uribe advanced on Ciénaga in the early morning of 14 October 1902. The battle went badly for the Liberals from the moment that a government warship began to shell their positions from the sea. Uribe Uribe was shot from his mule and several bullets that pierced his jacket miraculously missed his person (not for the first time). He exclaimed, as García Márquez's Colonel Aureliano Buendía might have done: "How many changes of uniform do these damned Goths think I have!" ("Goths" was the Liberal name for the Conservatives.) Nicolás Márquez's teenage son Carlos Alberto died a hero's death; his elder brother José María, fourth in command of the Conservative army's "Carazúa Division," survived.

Two days later, shattered by the death of Carlos Alberto, José María rode out of Ciénaga towards the encampment of the defeated Liberals, where his father, among others, was nursing his wounds. José María was carrying a peace offer from the Conservatives. As his mule approached the tents of the defeated Liberals an advance party intercepted him and he rode in blindfolded to present the Conservative terms to Uribe Uribe. What took place between the nineteen-year-old illegitimate son and his rebel father on an historic occasion overshadowed for both of them by the death of the younger son, we shall never know. Uribe Uribe discussed the Conservative proposal with his senior officers. They decided to accept. The young messenger rode back to

Ciénaga and arrived late at night at the railway station, where he was greeted by a delirious crowd and carried aloft to deliver the joyful news. Ten days later, on 24 October 1902, Conservative leaders and Uribe Uribe met with their respective chiefs of staff at a banana plantation called Neerlandia not far from Ciénaga, to sign the peace treaty. It was little more than a fig leaf concealing the bitter truth: that the Liberals had suffered a disastrous defeat.

LATE IN 1902, Nicolás Márquez went back to Barrancas and his wife Tranquilina and picked up the threads of his life. In 1905 their third child, Luisa Santiaga, was born and things appeared to have returned to normal.[3] But in 1908 Nicolás was involved in a violent encounter which would change his family's destiny for ever and he was forced to leave Barrancas. Everyone still knew the story when I passed through Barrancas eighty-five years later in 1993. Unfortunately everyone told a different version. Still, no one denies the following facts. Around five o'clock on the rainy afternoon of Monday 19 October 1908, the final day of the week-long Festival of the Virgin of Pilar, whilst the procession carrying her image was proceeding to the church just a few streets away, Colonel Nicolás Márquez, a respectable local politician, landowner, silversmith and family man, then in his forties, shot and killed a younger man called Medardo, the nephew of his friend and comrade in arms General Francisco Romero. Something else that no one denies is that Nicolás was a "ladies' man" or, more bluntly, a philanderer. To readers from some other parts of the world this quality might seem to conflict with his image as a man of dignity and good standing among his neighbours. But there are at least two sorts of renown which a man prizes in such a society: one is his "good reputation" as such, the conventional respect, always mingled with fear, which he should know how to impose; and the other is his reputation as a "Don Juan" or a "macho," which others will happily circulate for him, usually with his complaisance. The trick is to ensure that these reputations mutually reinforce one another.

The first version I heard was as convincing as any that followed. Filemón Estrada had been born in the very year the events took place. He was now completely sightless, and that long-ago story had retained for him a vividness which other testimonies had lost. Filemón said that Nicolás, who already had several illegitimate children, seduced Medarda Romero, the sister of his old friend General Romero, and then bragged about it over drinks in the square. There was a lot of gossip, most of it at Medarda's expense but some of it involving Tranquilina. Medarda said to her son, "This slander must be washed clean with blood, my son, there's no other way. And if you won't see to him I'll have to put on your trousers and you can put on my skirts!" Medardo, a skilled marksman who had ridden with Nicolás in the war, and now lived in nearby Papayal, repeatedly and publicly challenged and insulted his former commander, who took the warnings seriously and some time later lay in wait for the younger man. Medardo rode in to town on the day of the fiesta, dressed up in a white gabardine raincoat, and took a short cut down an alleyway that no longer exists. As he got down from his horse with a bunch of grass in one hand and a lighted pilgrim's candle in the other, Nicolás said, "Are you armed, Medardo?" Medardo said "No." "Well, you remember what I told you"—and Nicolás fired one, some say two shots. An old woman who lived down that alleyway came out and said, "So you finally killed him." "The bullet of right has prevailed over might," said Nicolás. "After that," said blind Filemón, "old Nicolás Márquez charged off down the street, leaping over puddles, with his gun in one hand and his umbrella in the other, and looked for Lorenzo Solano Gómez, his *compadre*, who went with him to give himself up. He was jailed but later his son José María Valdeblánquez, who was very smart, and almost a lawyer, got him out of jail. Medardo being illegitimate, it wasn't certain whether his surname was Pacheco or Romero, so Valdeblánquez said it wasn't clear who exactly had been killed; it was a technicality, see, and that's how Valdeblánquez got him off."

None other than Ana Ríos, the daughter of Nicolás's partner Eugenio, who surely had better reason to know than most, told me that Tranquilina was closely involved in the entire tragedy.[4] She recalled that Tranquilina was intensely jealous, and with good reason because Nicolás was always deceiving her. Medarda was a widow and there is always talk about widows in small towns. It was widely rumoured that she was Nicolás's regular mistress. Tranquilina became obsessed with this possibility, perhaps because Medarda was from a higher class, and therefore more dangerous, than his other conquests. It was said that Tranquilina consulted witches, brought water from the river to clean her threshold and sprinkled lemon juice around the house. Then one day—it is said—she went out into the street and shouted, "There's a fire at widow Medarda's place, fire, fire!," whereupon a boy she had paid to wait in the tower of the the church of San José began to ring the alarm bells, and shortly thereafter Nicolás was seen sneaking out of Medarda's house in broad daylight (presumably while his friend the General was away).

When he gave his statement to the authorities Nicolás Márquez was asked whether he admitted killing Medardo Romero Pacheco, and he said: "Yes, and if he comes back to life I'll kill him again." The Mayor, a Conservative, resolved to protect Nicolás. Deputies were despatched to collect Medardo's body. He was placed face down in the rain and his hands were tied together behind his back before they carried him away. Most people accept that Medardo sought the confrontation and "asked for" what happened; this may be, although the bare facts seem to demonstrate that it was Nicolás who chose the time, the place and the manner of the final showdown. There is not enough information to appreciate how justified or reprehensible his action may have been; what is crystal clear is that there was nothing remotely heroic about it. Nicolás was not some sedentary farmer but a seasoned war veteran; and the man he killed by stealth was both his military inferior and his junior.

Many in Barrancas saw it as fate. The Spanish word for such an event is a *desgracia*, closer to bad luck than to disgrace, and it is said that many of Medardo's family sympathized with the Colonel in his misfortune. Still, there was talk of a lynching and fear of a riot so as soon as it was safe to extricate him, they sent Nicolás under armed guard to Riohacha, his home town. Even there he was not considered secure and was moved to another prison in Santa Marta, on the other side of the Sierra Nevada.[5] It seems an influential relative of Tranquilina's got the sentence reduced to just a year in jail in Santa Marta with "the city as his prison" for the second year. Tranquilina, the children and other family members followed him there some months later. Some say he managed to buy his release with the proceeds of his craft; that he worked at his jewellery inside the jail and made fish, butterflies and chalices for sale and then bribed his way out. No one has yet found any documents relating to the case.

The García Márquez family never faced up to the full implications of this event and a sanitized version of the story was adopted. According to this version at some point a rumour emerged that Medarda, who was no spring chicken, was once more "doing some local man a favour." One of Nicolás's friends commented on this piece of gossip while they were drinking in the main square and Nicolás said, "I wonder if it's true?" Medarda heard the story in a form which suggested that Nicolás himself had been peddling the rumour, and asked her son to defend her honour. In later years Luisa would often recall that in alluding to the almost unmentionable episode Tranquilina would say, "And all over a simple question." In this version the gunfight is a "duel," the dead man gets what he deserves and the killer becomes "the real victim" of the murder.[6]

In 1967, in the immediate aftermath of the success of *One Hundred Years of Solitude* (in which García Márquez gives a less idealized version of the murder than the rest of his family), Mario Vargas Llosa asked its author who the key person was in his childhood. García Márquez replied: "It was my grandfather. And note that he was a gentleman that I found afterwards in my books. He had to kill a man when he was very young. He lived in a town and it seems there was someone who was always bothering him and challenging him, but he took no notice until the situation became so difficult that he simply put a bullet in him. It seems that the town was so much in agreement with what he did that one of the dead man's brothers slept that night in front of the door to the house, in front of my grandfather's room, so that the dead man's family would not come to avenge him. So my grandfather, who could no longer bear the threat that existed against him in that town, went elsewhere; that is to say, he didn't just go to another town; he went far away with his family and founded a new town. Yes, he went and founded a town; yet what I most remember about my grandfather is him always saying to me, 'You don't know how much a dead man weighs.' "[7] Many years after that García Márquez would say to me: "I don't know why my grandfather had to be caught up in all that and why it all had to happen but they were tough times after the war. I still believe he just had to do it."[8]

It may just be a coincidence but October would always be the gloomiest month, the time of evil augury, in Gabriel García Márquez's novels.

MYSTERY SURROUNDS Nicolás Márquez's movements after his ignominious departure from Barrancas.[9] García Márquez's mother Luisa gave different versions to different interlocutors.[10] She told me that she and Tranquilina sailed from Riohacha to Santa Marta a few months after Nicolás was transferred to the prison there (Luisa was only four), that he was released after a year and the family then moved to nearby Ciénaga for a further year, arriving in Aracataca in 1910. This had become the official story. But people in Ciénaga insist that Nicolás and family spent three years there after his release from prison, from 1910 to 1913, and only moved to Aracataca in 1913.[11] It may be that Nicolás used Ciénaga as a base from which to scout the region for new opportunities; if so, he might have begun to develop political and commercial interests in Aracataca, a mainly Liberal town, before moving his family there. It also seems likely however that one reason for staying in Ciénaga, whether for one year or three, was the fact that Ciénaga was now the home of Isabel Ruiz, whom Nicolás had met in Panama in 1885, around the time of his marriage to Tranquilina, and who had given birth to his daughter María Gregoria Ruiz in 1886.

Ciénaga, unlike colonial Santa Marta, was modern, commercial, raucous and unrestrained; it was also a hub for regional transportation. It too is on the shores of the Caribbean; it was the connection with the Ciénaga Grande, or Great Swamp, across which steamboats travelled to make contact with road traffic heading either for the Magdalena River and Bogotá or for the rapidly growing commercial city of Barranquilla; and the first railway in the region ran from Santa Marta to Ciénaga after 1887 and then was extended between 1906 and 1908 to run down the spine of the Banana Zone to Aracataca and Fundación.

The Banana Zone is situated south of Santa Marta, between the Ciénaga Grande and the Magdalena River to the west, the Caribbean or Atlantic Ocean to the north, and the great swamp and the Sierra Nevada, whose highest peaks are called Columbus and Bolívar, to the east.[12] In the broad plain between the western side of the mountains and the great swamp lay the small settlement called Aracataca, the birthplace of Gabriel García Márquez. Up above it rose the Sierra Nevada, home of the reclusive, peace-loving Kogi Indians. The first founders of Aracataca were quite different people, the warlike Chimilas, an Arawak Indian group. The tribe and its chief were called Cataca, "clear water." Thus they renamed the river Cataca, and so their village was called Aracataca ("ara" being river in Chimila), the place of diaphanous waters.[13]

In 1887 planters from Santa Marta introduced banana cultivation into the region. In 1905 the Boston-based United Fruit Company moved in. Workers migrated from all over the Caribbean, including *cachacos* (the derisive *costeño* name for their compatriots from the interior of the country, especially Bogotá),[14] and others from Venezuela, Europe, and even the Middle and Far East: the so-called "leaf-trash" vilified by the protagonists of García Márquez's first novel *Leaf Storm*.

Within a few years Aracataca was transformed from a small settlement to a thriving township, a "Wild West boom town," in García Márquez's phrase. It became a municipality, a fully functioning part of Colombia's national political system, in 1915.

The real leader of the town was not Colonel Márquez, as his grandson would frequently claim, but General José Rosario Durán.[15] Durán had several large plantations around Aracataca; he had led the Liberal forces in regional wars for two decades and was the effective leader of the Aracataca Liberals for almost half a century. Nicolás Márquez had been one of his close military subordinates, and became perhaps his most trusted political ally in Aracataca, during the 1910–13 period. It was Durán, then, who had helped Márquez to get installed in the town, to buy land out at Ariguaní and other properties in the town itself, and to acquire the posts of departmental tax collector and later municipal treasurer.[16] These responsibilities, added to his military reputation, made Colonel Márquez undoubtedly one of the most respected and powerful members of the local community, though he was always dependent on Durán's goodwill and subject to pressures from the Conservative government's political appointees and the managers of the United Fruit Company.

García Márquez's mother Luisa told me that Nicolás was named "departmental tax collector" of Aracataca early in the century,[17] possibly in 1909, but did not take his family there immediately because of the poor sanitary conditions in the newly developing tropical boom town, at that time a village of fewer than two thousand people. Still, let us imagine them all arriving—Colonel Márquez, Doña Tranquilina, their three legitimate children, Juan de Dios, Margarita and Luisa, his illegitimate daughter Elvira Ríos, his sister Wenefrida Márquez, his cousin Francisca Cimodosea Mejía, and his three Indian servants, Alirio, Apolinar and Meme, bought for 100 pesos each in the Guajira—on the banana company's yellow-painted train, full of optimism, on an exploratory visit, in August 1910. Unfortunately the zone around Aracataca was still unhealthy and plagued by disease, and tragedy struck the new arrivals almost immediately when twenty-one-year-old Margarita died of typhoid. Always pale, with her fair hair in two plaits, she was the Colonel's pride and joy and he and his superstitious family may have interpreted her death as some kind of further punishment for his sins in Barrancas. Now she would never make the kind of marriage her parents were no doubt envisaging, and all their hopes would rest on little Luisa. Family tradition tells that shortly before she died, Margarita sat up in bed, looking at her father, and said: "The eyes of your house are going out."[18] Her pale presence would live on in the collective memory, especially, paradoxically, in a picture taken when she was ten years old; and the anniversary of the day she died, 31 December, would never again be celebrated in the large, comfortable house which the Colonel began to build near the Plaza Bolívar.

Nicolás Márquez, though never wealthy, and always hoping in vain for the pension promised to all veterans of the civil war, became one of the makeshift community's local notables, a big fish in a small pool, the eventual owner of a large wooden residence with cement floors which in Aracataca would be considered—not least by his grandson Gabriel—a veritable mansion by comparison with the shacks and hovels that housed most of their fellow townsfolk.

THE COLONEL'S DAUGHTER Luisa was almost nineteen and her father had already turned sixty when in July of 1924 a new telegraphist named Gabriel Eligio García arrived in town from his native Sincé.[19] By that time Aracataca had been enjoying the *jai lai* or "high life" for several years. Luisa had been sent to the Colegio de la Presentación, the most respected convent school in stuffy Santa Marta, though she had left at seventeen due to her delicate health. "She never went back because our grandparents said she looked very thin and worn and they were afraid she would die like her sister Margarita," her daughter Ligia recalls.[20] Luisa could sew and play the piano. She had been educated to embody the improvement in station that Nicolás and Tranquilina were looking for as consolation when they moved from the Guajira to the Banana Zone. So the Colonel was thunderstruck at the idea that his carefully groomed daughter might be falling in love with a dark-skinned no-account telegraphist from elsewhere, a man with no father and few prospects.

Nicolás Márquez and his daughter's suitor, Gabriel Eligio García, had very little in common when they met except, ironically enough, a matter which is a recurrent theme of Gabriel García Márquez's work: a collection of illegitimate children. Although Nicolás had been born in wedlock and Gabriel Eligio out of wedlock, each had engendered more than one illegitimate child by the time they married in their early twenties.

Gabriel Eligio had spent his childhood and youth in poverty, though little is known in detail of his early life—indeed, little detail seems to have been asked of him even by his children: it was always the Márquez side which counted, and the Guajira connection.[21] We do know that he had half-brothers and half-sisters named Luis Enrique, Benita, Julio, Ena Marquesita, Adán Reinaldo and Eliécer. We also know that, with the help of relatives, he completed his secondary education—a notable achievement anywhere in the world in those days—and we hear that in the early 1920s he managed to begin some courses in the medical school of the University of Cartagena, but was soon forced to abandon them. He would later tell his children that his father, a teacher, had undertaken to fund his training but ran into financial problems and had to renege on his promise. Without the means to sustain his studies, he left home and looked for work in the Caribbean provinces of Córdoba and Bolívar, working mainly as a small-town telegraphist but also as a homeopathic physician, and travelling the entire frontier region of rivers, swamps and forests. He became possibly the first telegraphist of Magangué, then worked in Tolú, Sincelejo and other towns. At that time the position of telegraphist was undoubtedly reputable among the lower classes, depending as it did on modern technology in the machinery and literacy in the operator. It was also hard, demanding work. In Achí, a small town on the River Cauca, south of Sucre, the first of his four illegitimate children, Abelardo, was born, when Gabriel Eligio was just nineteen, and in 1924 he ran into more trouble in Ayapel, on the border of Córdoba province and what is now Sucre province, on the edge of a vast swamp. There, in August 1924, he asked his first true sweetheart, Carmelina Hermosillo, to marry him after she gave birth to another child, Carmen Rosa. During a trip to Barranquilla to make the arrangements, he was apparently dissuaded by his relative Carlos Henrique Pareja from such a naive decision,[22] and fled to the plantation town of Aracataca, where he again found work as a telegraphist. By then he was a practised seducer, hungry for sexual conquest wrapped up in poetry and love songs. Or, as his famous son would later put it, "a typical Caribbean guy of the era." Meaning, among other things: talkative, extrovert, hyperbolic and dark or very dark of skin.

He arrived in Colonel Nicolás Márquez's house in Aracataca with a letter of recommendation from a priest in Cartagena who had known Colonel Márquez in earlier days. For this reason, according to Gabriel Eligio's own version, the Colonel, famous for his hospitality, greeted him warmly, invited him to eat, and the next day took him to Santa

Marta, where his wife Tranquilina and their only daughter Luisa were spending the summer by the seaside. At the station in Santa Marta, the Colonel bought a lark in a cage and gave it to Gabriel Eligio for him to give it in turn to Luisa as a present. This—which sounds frankly implausible—would have been the Colonel's first mistake, even though, again according to Gabriel Eligio, he did not fall for Luisa at first sight. "To be honest," he would recall, "I was not at all impressed by Luisa, even though she was very pretty."[23]

Luisa was no more impressed by Gabriel Eligio than he was by her. She always insisted that they met first not in Santa Marta but in Aracataca at the wake of a local child and that as she and the other young women sang to send the child on its way to a better place a male voice joined the choir, and when they all turned to see who it was they saw a handsome young man in a dark jacket with its four buttons done up. The other girls chorused, "We're going to marry him," but Luisa said that to her he seemed like "just another stranger."[24] Luisa, who was no pushover despite her lack of experience, was on her guard and for a long time she would rebuff each and every one of his advances.

The telegraph office was opposite the church, behind the main square in Aracataca, close to the cemetery and just a couple of blocks from the Colonel's house.[25] The new arrival had a second letter of recommendation, this one to the parish priest. Whether the good Father noticed that the new arrival received frequent female visitors at advanced hours of the night we do not know but it is said that Gabriel Eligio had not only a hammock for himself but also a well-oiled bed for his lovers in the back room of the telegraph office. He was a talented amateur violinist whose party piece was "After the Ball," the bittersweet waltz from America's Gilded Age that exhorted young lovers not to miss their opportunities, and the priest invited him to play his violin with the choir of the so-called Daughters of the Virgin. This was like setting the fox to play with the chickens. One of his courtships involved a newly qualified local primary school teacher, Rosa Elena Fergusson, with whom a marriage was rumoured, so much so that at a party in Luisa's house he joked with the Colonel's daughter that she would be his principal matron or godmother. This joke, no doubt calculated to make Luisa jealous if she were in any way attracted to Gabriel Eligio, allowed them to call one another "godmother" and "godson" and to cloak their growing intimacy under the guise of a fictitious formal relationship which neither took seriously.

Gabriel Eligio was a man who had a way with women and was

good-looking to boot. Though far from cynical, he was shameless, and far more confident than anyone with his background, qualifications and talents had any right to be. People from his part of the country, the savannahs of Bolívar, were known as outgoing and rumbustious, in stark contrast to the apprehension, introspection and downright suspiciousness of those who hailed, like Nicolás Márquez and Tranquilina, from the frontier lands of the Guajira, still considered Indian territory in the early twentieth century. The Colonel's affability in public belied a deep-rooted Guajiro clannishness, an attachment to old ways and places, and a wariness of outsiders. Besides, the last thing he needed was an unqualified son-in-law who would be an extra burden when he was surely looking for a successful union with a family much better heeled and at least as respectable as his own.

Luisa was somewhat delicate and a little spoilt, the joy of her father's life. Legend depicts her, perhaps exaggeratedly, as "the belle of Aracataca."[26] In fact she was not conventionally pretty but she was attractive, vivacious and refined, though perhaps a little eccentric and certainly rather dreamy. She was imprisoned in her house and social class by a father and mother whom she loved and respected but whose concern for her sexual and social security was neurotically reinforced by her own father's wayward history.[27] Moreover, as Gabito himself would note, the family was already nurturing a long, paradoxically "incestuous" tradition of rejecting all outside suitors, which turned the men into "furtive street hunters" and condemned the women, frequently, to spinsterhood. At any rate, Luisa was infinitely less experienced than the man who, eight months after his arrival in Aracataca, would fix his attention firmly upon her and set out to make her his wife.

They started exchanging ardent looks at Sunday mass and in March 1925 Gabriel Eligio looked for a way to convey his feelings and ask her to marry him. He would pause beneath the almond trees in front of the house, where Luisa and her aunt Francisca Cimodosea Mejía would sit and sew at siesta time or in the early evening; occasionally he would get a chance to chat beneath the great chestnut tree inside the garden, with Aunt Francisca, scourge of Luisa's several suitors, hovering close in chaperone mode, like the unfortunate Aunt Escolástica in *Love in the Time of Cholera*.[28] Eventually, beneath that monumental tree, he made one of the least gallant proposals recorded in romantic folklore: "Listen, Señorita Márquez, I was awake all night thinking that I have a pressing need to marry. And the woman in my heart is you. I love no other. Tell me if you have any spiritual feelings towards me; but don't feel you have to agree because I am certainly not dying of love for you. I will give you twenty-four hours to think it over."[29] He was interrupted by the redoubtable Aunt Francisca. But within twenty-four hours Luisa sent a note with one of the Indian servants proposing a secret meeting. She said she doubted his seriousness, he seemed so flirtatious; he said he would not wait, there were other fish in the pond. She asked for reassurance and he swore that if she accepted he would never love another. They agreed: they would be married to one another and to no other. "Only death" would stop them.

The Colonel soon saw worrying signs of mutual infatuation and decided to nip the relationship in the bud, not realizing that by now it was fully in bloom. He closed his house to the telegraphist and refused to speak to him again. García's courtship of their daughter was a bitter pill that Nicolás and Tranquilina were not prepared to swallow. On one occasion, when the Colonel was hosting a social event from which Gabriel Eligio could not be excluded, he was the only person in the room not invited to sit down. So intimidated was the young man that he even bought himself a gun. But he had no intention of leaving town. Luisa's parents told her that she was too young, though she was twenty by then and Gabriel Eligio was twenty-four. No doubt they also pointed out that he was swarthy, illegitimate, a public employee attached to the odious Conservative regime against which the Colonel had fought in the war, and a member of the "leaf-trash," the windblown human garbage from out of town. Still, the courtship continued clandestinely: outside the church after mass, on the way to the cinema, or at the window of the Colonel's house when the coast was clear.

Aunt Francisca told her cousin the Colonel about these new manoeuvres and he now took radical measures. He sent Luisa, escorted by Tranquilina and a servant, on a long journey to the Guajira, staying with friends and relatives along the way. Even today this remains an uncomfortable and arduous trek by road, because no modern highway has been completed. In those days much of it involved narrow pathways overlooking the precipices of the lower slopes of the Sierra Nevada, and Luisa had never previously ridden a mule.

The Colonel's plan failed completely. Luisa outwitted Tranquilina as easily as he himself had always done. The veteran of numerous battles had not counted on Gabriel Eligio working out his own "campaign strategy" and should not have underestimated the resources of a telegraphist. *Love in the Time of Cholera* recounts the entire story of the coded messages passed on by sympathetic telegraphists in every town the mother and daughter passed through. Ana Ríos recalled hearing that the telegraph communication was so effective that when Luisa was invited to a dance in Manaure she asked her prospective husband for permission to go; the reply, in the affirmative, came back the same day and she danced until seven in the morning.[30] It was thanks to the solidarity of his fellow telegraphists that, when mother and daughter arrived on the shore in Santa Marta early in 1926, Gabriel Eligio was waiting to greet his beloved as she stepped off the boat in a "romantic" pink dress.

Luisa evidently refused to go back to Aracataca and stayed in Santa Marta with her brother Juan de Dios and his wife Dilia in the Calle del Pozo. What this defiance cost in terms of family dramas may well be imagined. Dilia herself had already been through the horrors of the Márquez Iguarán family's clan-like hostility to outsiders and was only too happy to help out her sister-in-law, though Juan de Dios kept a watchful eye on both women on his father's behalf. Gabriel Eligio would visit Luisa at weekends, under conditions of relative freedom, until in due course he was transferred to Riohacha, which was too far away for weekend visits. Luisa spoke to the parish priest of Santa Marta, Monsignor Pedro Espejo, formerly of Aracataca, who was a good friend of Colonel Márquez. The priest wrote to the Colonel on 14 May 1926 to persuade him that the two were hopelessly in love and that a marriage would avoid what he darkly termed "worse misfortunes."[31] The Colonel relented—he must have been aware that Luisa was only a few weeks away from her twenty-first birthday—and the young couple were married in the Cathedral of Santa Marta, at seven in the morning on 11 June 1926. It was the day of the Blessed Heart, emblem of the city.

Gabriel Eligio would say he had refused to invite his new parents-in-law to the wedding because of a dream. It seems more likely that they had refused to attend. Mario Vargas Llosa, who received most of his information directly from García Márquez around 1969–70, says that the Colonel himself insisted that the couple should live "far from Aracataca."[32] When reminded of this, Gabriel Eligio always retorted that he had been more than happy to oblige. He confessed to his bride as they sailed, both seasick, to Riohacha, that he had seduced five virgins in his first years as a country Casanova and that he had two illegitimate children. Whether he told her anything about his mother's record in the sexual arena we must doubt but this admission from her new husband about his own misdeeds must have come as a deeply unpleasant surprise. Nevertheless Luisa would for the rest of her days remember the months she spent with Gabriel Eligio in the house they rented in Riohacha as one of the happiest times of her life.[33]

Luisa may have become pregnant on the second night after the wedding—if not before the wedding—and family legend has it that the news of her condition promised to thaw the icy relationship between Gabriel Eligio and the Colonel. It is said that presents were sent via José María Valdeblánquez. Still, Gabriel Eligio would not relent until one day Juan de Dios arrived from Santa Marta to say that Tranquilina was pining for her pregnant daughter and Gabriel Eligio allowed her to travel back to Aracataca for the confinement.[34]

TWENTY-ONE-YEAR-OLD LUISA arrived back in her home town of Aracataca one February morning, without her husband, after almost eighteen months away. She was eight months pregnant and seasick, after another turbulent voyage to Santa Marta by boat from Riohacha. A few weeks later, on Sunday 6 March 1927, at 9 a.m., in the midst of an unseasonal rainstorm, a baby boy, Gabriel José García Márquez, was born. Luisa told me that her father had left early on his way to mass when things were going "very badly" but when he got back to the house the whole thing was over.

The child was born with the umbilical cord around his neck—he would later attribute his tendency to claustrophobia to this early misfortune—and weighed in, so it was said, at a substantial nine pounds and five ounces. His great-aunt, Francisca Cimodosea Mejía, proposed that he be rubbed with rum and blessed with baptismal water in case of further mishap. In fact, the child would not be officially baptized for almost three and a half years, together with his sister Margot, who by then had also been sequestered with the grandparents. (Gabito would remember the baptism clearly. It was officiated by Father Francisco Angarita in the church of San José at Aracataca on 27 July 1930 and the godparents were the two witnesses at his parents' wedding, his uncle, Juan de Dios, and his great-aunt, Francisca Cimodosea.)

Colonel Márquez celebrated the birth. His beloved daughter had become another lost cause but he determined to consider even that setback to have been just a battle and resolved to win the war. Life would go on and he would now invest all his still considerable energies in her first child, his latest grandson, "my little Napoleon."

2

The House at Aracataca

1927-1928

"MY MOST CONSTANT and vivid memory is not so much of the people but of the actual house in Aracataca where I lived with my grandparents. It's a recurring dream which persists even now. What's more, every single day of my life I wake up with the feeling, real or imaginary, that I've dreamed I'm in that huge old house. Not that I've gone back there but that I *am* there, at no particular age, for no particular reason—as if I'd never left it. Even now in my dreams that sense of night-time foreboding which dominated my whole childhood still persists. It was an uncontrollable sensation which began early every evening and gnawed away at me in my sleep until I saw dawn breaking through the cracks in the door."[1]

Thus, half a century later, talking to his old friend Plinio Apuleyo Mendoza in Paris, would Gabriel García Márquez recall the dominant image of his "prodigious" childhood in the small Colombian town of Aracataca. Gabito spent the first ten years of his life not with his mother and father and the many brothers and sisters who regularly followed him into the world, but in the big house of his maternal grandparents, Colonel Nicolás Márquez Mejía and Tranquilina Iguarán Cotes.

It was a house full of people—grandparents, aunts, transient guests, servants, Indians—but also full of ghosts (above all perhaps, that of his absent mother).[2] Years later it would continue to obsess him when he was far away in time and space, and the attempt to recover it, re-create it and master his memories of it was a large part of what would make him a writer. It was a book he carried inside him from childhood: friends recall that when Gabito was barely twenty years of age he was already writing an interminable novel he called "The House." That old lost house in Aracataca remained in the family until the late 1950s, though it would be rented to other households after Gabriel Eligio took his wife and children away from Aracataca again in 1937. It eventually reappeared, intact yet somehow hallucinatory, in García Márquez's first novel, *Leaf Storm*, written in 1950, but only later, in *One Hundred Years of Solitude* (1967), did the obsession fully realize and exhaust itself, and in such a way that Gabito's vivid but anguished and often terrifying childhood could become materialized for all eternity as the magical world of Macondo, at which point the view from Colonel Márquez's house would encompass not only the little town of Aracataca but also the rest of his native Colombia and indeed the whole of Latin America and beyond.

After Gabito's birth, Gabriel Eligio, still working in Riohacha, and still sulking, waited several months to make his first journey back to Aracataca. He resigned from his job in Riohacha, gave up telegraphy for ever and hoped to earn his living from homeopathic medicine in Aracataca. But since he had no qualifications and equally little money, and since, despite family legend to the contrary, it appears he was not made welcome in the Colonel's house, he eventually decided to take Luisa off to Barranquilla and, through some obscure negotiation, it was agreed that Gabito would remain with his grandparents.[3]

Of course such arrangements as the two couples agreed were so common as to be almost normal in traditional societies with large extended families; but it is still hard to understand Luisa leaving her first child behind at an age when she could have continued to suckle him for many more months. What seems certain is that her commitment to her husband was more than tenacious. For all the criticisms of her parents, for all Gabriel Eligio's flaws and eccentricities, she must have really loved her man and she gave herself, apparently without hesitation, into his keeping. Above all, she put him before her first-born son.

We will never know what Luisa and Gabriel Eligio were thinking or what they said to one another as they took the train out of Aracataca heading for Barranquilla, having left their first baby behind. We do know that the young couple's first foray was a financial failure yet within months Luisa was pregnant again and returned to Aracataca to have her second child, Luis Enrique, on 8 September 1928. This means that she and the second baby were in Aracataca during the period leading up to the massacre of the banana workers in Ciénaga in December of that year and the many killings in and around Aracataca itself that followed. One of Gabito's own first memories was of soldiers marching past the Colonel's house. Curiously, when Gabriel Eligio came to take the mother and her new son back to Barranquilla in January 1929, the baby was hurriedly baptized before the departure, whereas Gabito was not baptized until July 1930.[4]

Let us look at the face of the small child, just one year old, reproduced on the cover of García Márquez's memoir *Living to Tell the Tale*. His mother had left him with his grandparents several months before the picture was taken and now, several months after it was taken, she had returned, only to be trapped by the drama of the strike and subsequent massacre. This massacre was not only a hugely, even crucially, important event which would change Colombian history by leading directly to the return of a Liberal government in August 1930 after half a century of civil war and exclusion, thereby uniting the small boy with his nation's history; it also coincided with the moment when the boy's mother could have taken him back to Barranquilla with her. Instead she took another child, her new baby, Luis Enrique, newly baptized, and left Gabito behind in the big house with his grandparents, thereby ensuring that he would have to assimilate this abandonment, live with this absence, explain this unexplainable sequence of events to himself and, through the elaboration of such a story, somehow forge an identity which, like all identities, would connect his own personal circumstances, with all their joys and all their cruelties, to the joys and cruelties of the wider world.

DESPITE HIS MEMORIES of solitude Gabito was not the only child in the house, though he was the only boy. His sister Margarita also lived there from the time Gabito was three and a half and his adolescent cousin Sara Emilia Márquez—the illegitimate child of Uncle Juan de Dios, rejected by his wife Dilia (some say Dilia argued that the girl was José María Valdeblánquez's daughter, not her husband's)—was also brought up there with the two of them. Neither was the house the mansion that García Márquez has sometimes claimed.[5] In fact, in March 1927, rather than one house it was three separate buildings mainly of wood with some adobe plus a number of outhouses and a large area of land at the back. By the time Gabito was born these three main buildings had American-style brushed cement floors, steel windows with gauze screens against mosquitoes and red zinc gabled roofs, though some of the outhouses still retained the more traditional Colombian palm leaf roofs. There were almond trees outside the property, sheltering the entrance. By the time of García Márquez's earliest memories, there were two buildings on the left-hand side as you entered the property, the first the Colonel's office, with a small reception room adjoining, followed by a pretty patio and garden with a jasmine tree—this garden, a profusion of brilliant roses, jasmines, spikenards, heliotropes, geraniums and astromelias, was always full of yellow butterflies—and then a further suite of three rooms.

The first of these three private rooms was the grandparents' bedroom, completed as late as 1925, where Gabito was born just two years later.[6] Next to that room was the so-called "room of the saints," where Gabito would actually sleep—in a hammock after he outgrew his cot—during his ten years with his grandparents, accompanied, variably but sometimes simultaneously, by his younger sister Margarita, his great-aunt Francisca Cimodosea and his cousin Sara Márquez, together with an unchanging pantheon of saints, all illuminated day and night with palm oil lamps and each charged with the protection of one particular member of the family: "to look after grandpa, to watch over the grandchildren, to protect the house, for no one to fall ill, and so on—a custom inherited from our great-great-grandmother."[7] Aunt Francisca spent many hours of her life praying there on her knees. The last room was the "room of the trunks," a lumber room full of ancestral possessions and family souvenirs brought in the exodus from the Guajira.[8]

On the right-hand side of the property, across a walkway, was a suite of six rooms fronted by a verandah lined with large flower pots which the family called the "verandah of the begonias." Going back to the entrance-way, the first three rooms of the building on the right constituted, together with the office and reception room opposite, what might be called the public side of the house. The first was the guest room where distinguished visitors stayed, including, for example, Monsignor Espejo himself. But family and war comrades from all over the Guajira, Padilla and Magdalena were lodged there, including Liberal war heroes Rafael Uribe Uribe and General Benjamín Herrera.[9] Next to it was the Colonel's silversmith's workshop, where he would continue to practise his craft until shortly before he died, though his municipal duties obliged him to turn his prior profession into a hobby.[10] Then came the large dining room, the effective centre of the house, and even more important to Nicolás than the workshop along-side; open to the fresh air, the dining room had space for ten people at the table and a few wicker rocking chairs for drinks before or after dinner when the occasion arose. Then came a third bedroom, known as "the blind woman's room," where the house's most celebrated ghost, Aunt Petra Cotes, Tranquilina's sister, had died some years before,[11] as had Uncle Lázaro, and where now one or other of the aunts would sleep; then a pantry cum store room where the less distinguished guests could be placed, at a pinch; and finally Tranquilina's great kitchen, with its large baker's oven, open to all the elements like the dining room. There grandmother and aunts made bread, cakes and sweets of every kind both for their guests to enjoy and for the household Indians to sell in the street and thus supplement the family income.[12]

Beyond the rooms of the saints and the trunks was a further patio with a bathroom and a large water tank where Tranquilina bathed Gabito with part of the five barrels' worth of water that haulier José Contreras delivered every day. On one unforgettable occasion little Gabito was up above climbing on the roof when down below he saw one of his aunts, naked, taking a shower. Instead of shrieking and covering herself up, as he expected, she simply waved to him. Or so the author of *One Hundred Years of Solitude* would recall. The patio by the bathroom looked out, on the right, to a yard where the mango tree stood, with a large shed over in the corner which served as a carpenter's workshop, the base from which the Colonel carried out his strategic renovations of the household.

And then, at the very back of the property, beyond the bathroom and the mango tree, the new, fast-growing town of Aracataca, which this large household's wealth and ambition ostentatiously represented, seemed to fuse back into the countryside in a large semi-wild space called La Roza (The Clearing).[13] Here were the guava trees whose fruit Tranquilina would use to make sweets in a huge steel pail and whose fragrant aroma Gabito would forever associate with the Caribbean of his childhood. Here loomed the huge, now legendary chestnut tree to which José Arcadio Buendía would be tied in *One Hundred Years of Solitude*. Beneath this spreading chestnut tree Gabriel Eligio García had asked Luisa for her hand while the "guard dog," Aunt Francisca, growled at him from the shadows. In these trees there were parrots, macaws and troupials, and even a sloth up in the boughs of the breadfruit tree. And by the back gate stood the stables where the

Colonel kept his horse and mules, and where his visitors tied their own mounts when they arrived not just for lunch, when they would leave them out in the street, but for a longer stopover.

Adjacent to the house was a building which the children would always think of as a house of horrors. They called it the "Dead Man's House" and the entire town told blood-curdling stories about it because a Venezuelan called Antonio Mora went on living there after hanging himself and could clearly be heard coughing and whistling inside.[14]

At the time when García Márquez's earliest memories were fixed, Aracataca was still a dramatic, violent frontier town. Almost every man carried a machete and there were plenty of guns. One of the boy's earliest memories was of playing in the outer patio when a woman walked past the house with her husband's head in a cloth and the decapitated body carried behind. He remembers being disappointed that the body was covered in rags.[15]

Daytime, then, brought a vivid, varied, ever-changing world, sometimes violent, sometimes magical. Night-time was always the same, and it was terrifying. He recalled: "That house was full of mysteries. My grandmother was very nervous; many things appeared to her which she would tell me about at night. When she talked about the souls of the dead she would say 'they are always whistling out there, I hear them all the time.' In each corner there were dead people and memories and after six o'clock in the evening you just couldn't move around in there. They would sit me in a corner and there I would stay, just like the boy in *Leaf Storm*."[16] Little wonder the child saw dead men in the bath and in the kitchen by the stove; once he even saw the devil at his window.[17]

Everyday life was dominated inevitably by Tranquilina, or "Mina," as her husband and the other women called her, a small, nervy woman with grey, anxious eyes and silver hair parted down the middle which framed an unmistakably Hispanic face and ended in a bun on her pale neck.[18] García Márquez recalled: "If you make an analysis of how things were, the real head of the household was my grandmother, and not only her but these fantastic forces with which she was in permanent communication and which determined what could and could not be done that day because she would interpret her dreams and organize the house according to what could and could not be eaten; it was like the Roman Empire, governed by birds, and thunderclaps and other atmospheric signals which explained any change of the weather, change of humour; really we were manipulated by invisible Gods, even though they were all supposedly very Catholic people."[19] Dressed always in mourning or semi-mourning, and always on the verge of hysteria, Tranquilina floated through the house from dawn to dusk, singing, always trying to exude a calm and unflustered air, yet always mindful of the need to protect her charges from the ever-present dangers: souls in torment ("hurry, put the children to bed"), black butterflies ("hide the children, someone is going to die"), funerals ("get the children up, or they'll die too"). She would remind the children of those dangers last thing at night.

Rosa Fergusson, García Márquez's first teacher, recalled that Tranquilina was very superstitious. Rosa and her sisters would arrive in the early evening and the old lady might say, "Do you know I heard a witch last night . . . it fell up there on the roof of the house."[20] She also had a habit of recounting her dreams, like many of the female characters in García Márquez's novels. Once she told the assembled company that she dreamed that she felt a crowd of fleas, so she took her head off, put it between her legs, and began to kill the fleas one by one.[21]

Aunt Francisca Cimodosea Mejía, known as Aunt Mama, was the most imposing of the three aunts who were present in the house during Gabito's childhood and, unlike Tranquilina, was reputed not to be afraid of anything either natural or supernatural. Half-sister of Eugenio Ríos, the Colonel's partner in Barrancas, brought up with the Colonel, her cousin, in El Carmen de Bolívar, she moved from Barrancas to Aracataca with him after the killing of Medardo. She was dark in complexion, strong of physique, with black hair like that of a Guajiro Indian, combed in plaits which she tied in a bun to walk in the streets. She dressed all in black and wore tightly tied boots, smoked strong cigarettes, was permanently active, shouting questions, giving orders in her loud, deep voice, shaping and organizing the children's days. She looked after everybody, the family members, all the waifs and strays; she cooked special sweets and fancies for guests; she bathed the children in the river (with carbolic soap when they had lice), took them to school and to church, put them to bed, and made them say their prayers, before abandoning them to Tranquilina's nocturnal postscripts. She was trusted with the keys of the church and the cemetery and dressed the altars on holy days. She also made the wafers for the church—the priest was a frequent visitor to the household—and the children looked forward excitedly to eating the blessed left-overs. Aunt Mama lived and died a spinster. And when she thought she was going to die she began to sew her own shroud, like Amaranta in *One Hundred Years of Solitude*.

The aunt next in importance to the children was Aunt Pa, Elvira Carrillo, who was born in Barrancas at the end of the nineteenth century. She was one of the Colonel's natural children, the twin sister of Esteban Carrillo. She moved to Aracataca when she was twenty. Despite the inevitable initial tensions, Tranquilina treated her as one of her own and she in turn cared for Tranquilina until her death in Sucre many years later. She was sweet-tempered, self-effacing and hard-working, always cleaning, sewing and making sweets for sale, though she herself preferred not to venture into the street.

Another aunt, Wenefrida, "Aunt Nana," Nicolás's only legitimate sister, was also a constant presence, though she lived in a house of her own. She had moved to Aracataca with her husband Rafael Quintero, and she would die there in Nicolás's house—she spent her last days in his office—shortly before the Colonel himself.

There were also numerous female servants, mostly part-time workers who cleaned around the house, and washed the clothes and dishes. It was indeed a house full of women, a fact which destined Gabito on the one hand to an especially close and indeed decisive relationship with the only other male, his grandfather, and on the other to an ease with women, and a dependence on them, which would last the rest of his life. Men, for Gabito, were either to emulate, like his grandfather, or to fear, like his father. His early relationships with women were far more varied and complex. (There were several Indian servants in the house who were effectively slaves; the boy, Apolinar, hardly counted as a male because he did not count as a full human being.)

When García Márquez read fairy stories he must have been struck by the fact that many of them involved a boy and a girl and grandparents—always grandparents. Like him, Margot, Nicolás and Tranquilina. Psychologically it was a complex world, which he later explained to his friend Plinio Mendoza. "The strange thing was that I wanted to be like my grandfather—realistic, brave, safe—but I could not resist the constant temptation to peep into my grandmother's territory."[22] Leonine and magnificent in the memory of his grandchildren, "Papa Lelo" imposed order and discipline upon a pride of females, a houseful of women whom he had brought to Aracataca through his search for security and renewed respectability. He was bluff and forthright, with decisive, straightforward opinions. Gabito evidently felt like his direct descendant and his heir.

The Colonel took his young grandson everywhere, explained everything to him and when in doubt took him home, took down the family dictionary and underlined his own authority with the definition he found there.[23] He was sixty-three when Gabito was born, quite European-looking, like his wife, stocky, of average height with a broad forehead, balding and with a thick moustache. He wore gold-rimmed glasses and by that time was blind in the right eye because of glaucoma.[24] On most days he would wear a spotless white tropical suit, a panama hat and brightly coloured braces. He was a direct, good-hearted man of easy, confident authority leavened by a twinkle in the eye which showed that he understood this society he was living in and did his best in all the circumstances but that morally he was no prude.

Many years later, when García Márquez managed to reconstruct these two ways of interpreting and narrating reality, both of them involving a tone of absolute certainty—the worldly, rationalizing sententiousness of his grandfather and the other-wordly oracular declamations of his grandmother—leavened by his own inimitable sense of humour, he would be able to develop a world-view and a corresponding narrative technique which would be instantly recognizable to the readers of each new book.

ALTHOUGH DEFEATED in the War of a Thousand Days, Colonel Márquez had managed to prosper in the peace. After the end of hostilities the Conservative government had opened the republic to foreign investment and during and after the First World War the national economy expanded at an unprecedented rate. U.S. financiers invested intensively in petroleum exploration, mining and bananas, and the U.S. government eventually paid the Colombian government $25 million in compensation for the loss of Panama. This was invested in a range of public works designed to modernize the country. More borrowing followed, and all those dollars and pesos swirled around and around, creating a kind of financial hysteria that Colombian historians call the "dance of the millions." These brief years of easy money would be remembered by many as a time of unparalleled prosperity and opportunity on the Caribbean coast.

The banana is a tropical fruit which takes seven to eight months to grow and can be harvested and shipped at almost any time of year. It carries its own packaging and, with modern methods of cultivation and transportation, would help transform the dietary and economic habits

of the world's great capitalist cities. Local landowners, belatedly opening up Colombia's northern coastal region, were overtaken by events.
In the mid-1890s American entrepreneur Minor C. Keith, who already
owned huge tracts of land in Central America and Jamaica, had begun
to buy land around Santa Marta. Then in 1899 he founded the United
Fruit Company (UFC), with its offices in Boston and its main shipping
port in New Orleans. At the same time as he bought land Keith also
bought shares in the Santa Marta railway and eventually the fruit company not only ran the railway but owned 25,500 of its 60,000 shares.[25]

One critic has said that Minor C. Keith's holdings in Colombia
amounted to a "pirate's charter."[26] By the mid-1920s the zone was the
third largest exporter of bananas in the world. More than ten million
bunches a year were leaving the UFC wharves in Santa Marta. Its railway ran sixty miles from Santa Marta to Fundación, with thirty-two
stations along the way. It had a near monopoly of land, irrigation systems, exports by sea, transport out of Santa Marta and across the Ciénaga Grande, the telegraph system, cement production, meat and
other foodstuffs, telephones and ice.[27] By owning the plantations and
the railway the UFC effectively controlled the nine towns in the zone.
It also indirectly controlled the local police, local politicians and
press.[28] One of the largest farm properties belonging to the UFC was
called Macondo, 135 acres on the banks of the River Sevilla, in the
corregimiento of Guacamayal.

The top echelons of the Santa Marta ruling class already had links
to New York, London and Paris, and were culturally sophisticated,
albeit politically conservative. But now the UFC's Great White Fleet
brought daily contact with the USA, Europe and the rest of the
Caribbean for everyone. At the same time migrants both from other
parts of Colombia, including the Guajira Peninsula and the old run-
away slave regions of Bolívar, and from other parts of the world, came
to work on the banana plantations or to set up small businesses serving
the farms and the people who laboured in them. Artisans, merchants,
boatmen, prostitutes, washerwomen, musicians, bartenders appeared.
Gypsies came and went too, but in a real sense almost all the inhabitants of the Banana Zone were gypsies in those days. These growing
communities became plugged in to the international market for goods,
with cinemas which changed their movies two or three times a week,
Montgomery Ward catalogues, Quaker Oats, Vicks Vaporub, Eno
Fruit Salts, Colgate Dental Creme, indeed many of the things by then
available in New York or London.

Aracataca's population had been a few hundred in 1900, dispersed around the countryside and concentrated on the river banks; by 1913 it had risen to three thousand and it soared thereafter to perhaps ten thousand in the late 1920s. As the hottest and wettest place in the entire zone, it also produced the biggest bananas; their production required a daily epic struggle by the workers, since for most mortals even sitting or lying down in the Aracataca heat is arduous. By 1910, when the Colonel had begun to move his family there, the railway track already ran all the way down from Santa Marta through Ciénaga and Aracataca to Fundación, the last town in the zone. Banana plantations grew up on either side of the tracks for a distance of almost sixty miles.

Aracataca was a boom town with boom-town excitements. A lottery was held on Sundays as a band played in the main square. The Aracataca carnival, first held in 1915, was a particular draw, with the square occupied annually by improvised cantinas, stalls, dance floors, traders, healers, herbalists, women dressed in exotic costumes and masks, and the local men swaggering by in khaki trousers and blue shirts, all in a cloud of cigar smoke, rum and sweat blown about by the salt breeze sweeping in from the Ciénaga Grande. It was said that in those golden years almost everything was for sale: not only consumer goods from all over the world but dance partners, political votes, pacts with the devil.[29]

Even at its height the town was only ten blocks in either direction. Were it not for the searing heat, any moderately fit person could walk it end to end in less than twenty minutes. There was only a handful of cars. The UFC company offices were directly opposite the house of Colonel Nicolás Márquez, close to the pharmacy of his Venezuelan friend Doctor Alfredo Barbosa. On the other side of the railtrack was another community, the American company administrators' camp, alongside a country club with recreational lawns, tennis courts and a swimming pool, where you could see "beautiful languid women in muslin dresses and wide gauze hats cutting the flowers in their gardens with golden scissors."[30]

During the banana era Aracataca was a territory with only limited respect for God or law. In response to a request from the local citizens the diocese of Santa Marta had sent Aracataca's first priest, Pedro Espejo, from Riohacha, on a part-time basis. It was he who initiated the building of the parish church, which took more than twenty years.[31] It was he too who famously levitated one day during mass. He became a close friend of the Márquez Iguarán family and stayed with them whenever he was in Aracataca. Now, many years later, the street in which that old house stood is called "The Street of Monsignor Espejo."

LATE IN 1928 Aracataca's golden age came to a violent end. The UFC needed labour to build railways and irrigation canals; to clear land, plant trees and harvest the fruit; and to load the trains and ships to carry the bananas away. At first it had managed to divide and rule the workers with ease but gradually they organized into unions over the course of the 1920s and in November 1928 they put in a wide-ranging demand for more pay, a shorter working day and better conditions. The management rejected these demands and a strike of the thirty thousand workers in the Banana Zone was declared on 12 November 1928. The infant García Márquez was twenty months old.

Strikers moved in to occupy plantations that same day. The government of Conservative President Miguel Abadía Méndez responded by sending General Carlos Cortés Vargas to the zone as Civil and Military Leader the following day, accompanied by 1,800 troops from the highlands. When Cortés Vargas arrived in Santa Marta he and his officers were feted by the UFC management and the soldiers were housed in UFC barracks and warehouses all over the zone. It was said that UFC officials gave the officers riotous parties at which local ladies were abused and insulted and that prostitutes rode naked on military horses and bathed naked in the company's irrigation ditches.[32]

At dawn on 5 December 1928 three thousand workers arrived in Ciénaga to occupy the square and, by controlling Ciénaga, to control railway communications throughout the region. Together with Ciénaga, Aracataca was one of the zones of strongest support for the strike; like the merchants of Ciénaga, local storekeepers and landowners gave significant material assistance to the strikers right up to the day of the showdown.[33] General José Rosario Durán had a reputation as a decent employer who tried to have good relations with the union; indeed, many Conservatives felt he was overly friendly to "socialists."[34] At midday on 5 December General Durán, described in military communiqués at the time as "the Liberal leader of the entire region,"[35] sent a telegram to Santa Marta requesting a train to take him and his associates to Santa Marta where he hoped to mediate between the workers and the company with the help of Governor Núñez Roca. Cortés Vargas agreed, no doubt reluctantly, and the train was duly sent.[36] Durán and his delegation, including Colonel Nicolás Márquez, eventually arrived in Ciénaga at nine that evening. The workers greeted them with enthusiasm and they continued to Santa Marta to negotiate a settlement, only to find themselves arrested on arrival. The Conservative administration, the UFC and the Colombian army all seem to have been intent on a salutary piece of bloodletting which would teach the workers a lesson.

Back in Ciénaga the crowd confronting the army was of more than three thousand people.[37] Each of the soldiers had a rifle and bayonet, and three machine guns were set up in front of the station. A cornet sounded and an officer, Captain Garavito, stepped forward and read out "Decree no. I": a state of siege was in force, a curfew was declared with immediate effect, no groups of four or more would be permitted and if the crowd did not disperse in five minutes it would be fired upon. The crowd, which had at first cheered the army and chanted patriotic slogans, now burst into boos and insults. After some time Cortés Vargas himself stepped forward and appealed to the crowd to move or be shot. He gave them one further minute. At that point a voice from the crowd shouted out the immortal rejoinder, recorded for ever in *One Hundred Years of Solitude*: "You can have the other minute on us!" "Fire!" shouted Cortés Vargas, and two of the three machine guns (the third one jammed) and two or three hundred rifles resounded around the square. Many people fell to the ground and those who could run, ran.[38] Cortés Vargas later said the fusillade lasted a few seconds. Salvador Durán, the General's son, who was in his house adjoining the square, reported that it lasted five full minutes; after it everything was so quiet he could hear the mosquitoes buzzing in his room.[39] It was said that the army finished off the wounded with bayonets.[40] It was also said that Cortés Vargas had threatened all the soldiers with summary execution if they did not obey orders that night.[41] Only at six in the morning did the authorities begin to dispose of the bodies, stating officially that there were nine dead and three wounded.

How many died? Forty years later, in *One Hundred Years of Solitude*, García Márquez would invent a figure of three thousand, a total which many of his readers would take at face value. On 19 May 1929 *El Espectador* of Bogotá said there were "more than a thousand" dead. Likewise the U.S. representative in Bogotá, Jefferson Caffery, said in a letter dated 15 January 1929, but not released until many years later, that, according to Thomas Bradshaw, Managing Director of the UFC, there were "more than a thousand dead." (In 1955 the then Vice-President of the UFC would tell a researcher that 410 were killed in the massacre and more than a thousand in the following weeks.)[42] The statistics are still discussed and bitterly disputed to this day.

Gabriel Eligio García was away working in Barranquilla unable to communicate with his family, though the telegraphist of Aracataca wired him that everyone was safe and well. Luisa had recently given birth to Luis Enrique and Gabriel Eligio was making plans to move them back to Barranquilla. He always sided with government estimates, and even apologized for Cortés Vargas, arguing that the husband of a great-aunt of Gabito's in Ciénaga told him there could not have been more than a few casualties since "no one was missed."

Prisoners were summarily executed in the days after the massacre. One army detachment guided by UFC officials went through Aracataca "firing everywhere and against everyone."[43] In one night 120 workers disappeared in Aracataca and parish priest Father Angarita was woken up by soldiers who took his set of keys to the cemetery.[44] Father Angarita stayed up the whole of the next night to ensure that another seventy-nine prisoners would not be executed.[45] During the three months after the massacre, the authorities and leading residents of Aracataca, including treasurer Nicolás R. Márquez and his friends Alfredo Barbosa the pharmacist and exiled Venezuelan General Marco Freites, as well as the entire municipal council, were persuaded to send letters declaring that the military had behaved impeccably during the state of siege and had worked for the good of the community.[46] This must have involved painful moral somersaults and an almost unbearable sense of humiliation. The ensuing state of siege lasted three months.

The strike and its bitter aftermath scarred the region and it remains one of the most controversial events in Colombian history. In 1929 Jorge Eliécer Gaitán, the politician whose assassination would spark the brief but devastating civil insurrection known as the *Bogotazo*, became a national leader, at the age of twenty-six, through the passionate parliamentary campaign he initiated against the government, the military and the UFC. After visiting the site of the massacre and talking to dozens of people, he made a report to the House of Representatives back in Bogotá, talking for four days in September 1929. His most dramatic pieces of evidence were the fragment of a child's skull and an accusatory letter from Father Angarita, the man who would baptize Gabriel García Márquez just a few months later.[47] As a result of Gaitán's sensational testimony, the prison sentences handed down to workers in Ciénaga were quashed. The Liberals, although still weak and disorganized nationally, were galvanized into action, began to gain the upper hand politically and started their rise to power, coming into government in 1930. The end of that period would be marked by Gaitán's assassination in April 1948, the most important and far-reaching event in Colombia's twentieth-century history.

The deterioration in the relations between the UFC and its workers and the impact the massacre had on the Banana Zone would be overtaken by the Great Depression, which was about to engulf the region and the entire global trading system. The devastating slump caused the company to severely contract its operations. Executives and administrators left and Aracataca began its long and unstoppable decline, a period whose beginning would coincide precisely with García Márquez's childhood and the last years of his grandfather's life.

3

Holding His Grandfather's Hand

1929~1937

ALTHOUGH THE SEEDS of Aracataca's decline were sown, it took years before the full implications became clear, and life in the Colonel's household went on much as before. Across the Great Swamp, in Barranquilla, Gabriel Eligio was working by day in a hardware store run by the Singer company, but had recently opened his first modest pharmacy, which he attended in the evenings and at weekends, assisted by Luisa. The young couple endured grinding poverty, and the pampered Luisa, used to the attentions of a mother, aunts and servants, must have found life desperately hard.

The Colonel and Tranquilina took Gabito to Barranquilla in November 1929, after the birth of Luisa's third child, Margarita, on the 9th of that month. Just two and a half, the boy's main memory was of seeing traffic lights for the first time. His grandparents took him back to Barranquilla again in December 1930 for the birth of Aida Rosa and he saw his first aeroplane in a city which pioneered air travel in Colombia.[1] He also heard the word "Bolívar" for the first time because Aida Rosa was born on 17 December, exactly a hundred years to the day after the great Liberator died and Barranquilla, like the whole of Latin America, was commemorating his death. Gabito would retain no firm memories of either his mother or his father but these visits must have been intensely troubling to a child trying to make sense of the world and his place in it.[2] It was on this last occasion that Tranquilina, seeing that little Margarita was a sickly, withdrawn child who needed urgent attention beyond her harassed young mother's

45

means, insisted on taking her back to Aracataca to be brought up with Gabito.[3]

The formative period in Gabito's development thus stretched from the age of two, when his mother went away for the second time, to almost seven, when his parents and siblings returned to Aracataca. Those are the five years whose memories really form the basis of the mythological Macondo which readers the world over have come to know. And although it is not true that he had no contact with his birth parents, it is certainly true that he had no sustained contact with either them or his new brothers and sisters after 1928 and no reason therefore to have any enduring memories of them. His only parents were his grandparents and his only sibling was Margarita, now called Margot, who would not become a satisfying companion until she was three or four, by which time the rest of the family would be making their return to Aracataca towards the end of 1933. Nicolás and Tranquilina evidently decided that between incessantly having to explain that his parents had gone away (and why, and if and when they would ever return) and drawing a veil of silence over his origins, the latter would be less painful in the long run. Of course other children must have asked questions and García Márquez could not possibly have been as ignorant as he has always maintained. It is difficult to imagine that Luisa was never remembered at bedtime prayers, for example. But clearly the matter of his mother and father was a taboo area which he learned to approach as little as possible.

In Spain and Latin America women traditionally belonged in the house and men in the street. It was his grandfather, the Colonel, who gradually rescued him from that feminine world of superstition and premonitions, those stories that seemed to spring from the darkness of nature itself, and who installed him in the man's world of politics and history; took him out, so to speak, into the daylight. ("I would say that the relationship with my grandfather was the umbilical cord that kept me in touch with reality until I was eight years old.")[4] In later life, with touching naivety, he would remember his grandfather as "the natural patriarch of the town."[5]

The truth is that the men who were really powerful, like the large landowners, rarely occupied regional political positions like treasurer or tax collector, preferring to leave them to less important relatives or to middle-class political representatives usually ignorant of the law.[6] Mayors were appointed by governors who were named by politicians in Bogotá in association with local interests, and Liberals like Nicolás

Márquez had to transact, usually in quite humiliating ways, with the Conservative Party and other local forces such as the UFC. The whole political system was grossly corrupt, resting on personal relations and various forms of patronage. Significant local personalities like Márquez got UFC perks such as fresh meat and other desirable luxuries at the company store, and in return could be relied on to maintain the system. Many of the most vivid memories of both Gabito and Margot were of their grandfather's expeditions to the store, which was just over the road from their house. It was like an Aladdin's Cave from which the Colonel and Gabito would return triumphantly to surprise and enchant Margot with magical commodities manufactured in and imported from the USA.[7]

The municipal treasurer and tax collector would mainly be involved in extracting municipal—and in some cases personal—income from the only significant form of taxation in existence at the time, namely liquor consumption, meaning that the Colonel's own income depended heavily on the financial well-being, physical intoxication and resultant sexual promiscuity of the much-despised "leaf-trash." How conscientiously Nicolás himself carried out his duties we cannot know but the system was not one which left much freedom for personal probity.[8] After 1930, with the Liberal Party coming to power for the first time in fifty years, things should have got better for Nicolás, who was actively involved in the campaign to elect Enrique Olaya Herrera, the Liberal candidate, but all the information we have suggests that they gradually got worse.

García Márquez has recalled: "He was the only person in the house that I was not afraid of. I always felt that he understood me and cared about my future vocation."[9] The Colonel adored his little grandson. He celebrated his little Napoleon's birthday every month, and yielded to his every whim. But Gabito would not himself be a warrior nor even a sportsman, and he would be governed by terrors—ghosts, superstitions, the dark, violence, rejection—all his life.[10] All of them originated in Aracataca, during his anguished, troubled childhood. Still, his intelligence and sensitivity, and even his frequent tantrums, confirmed his indulgent grandfather in the belief that this child was worthy of him and was, perhaps, destined for greatness.[11]

The boy was certainly worth educating; it was he who would inherit the old man's memories, his philosophy of life and political morality, his view of the world; the Colonel would live on through him. It was the Colonel who told him about the War of a Thousand Days, his own deeds and those of his friends, heroic Liberals all; and it was the Colonel who explained the presence of the banana plantations, the UFC and its company houses, stores, tennis courts and swimming pools, and the horrors of the 1928 strike. Battles, scars, gunfights. Violence and death. Even in the relative safety of Aracataca the old man always slept with a revolver beneath his pillow, though after the killing of Medardo he had stopped carrying it in the street.[12]

By the time Gabito was six or seven, then, he was already a fully fledged Colombian. He thought his grandfather was a hero, but even this hero was clearly subject to the whims of American managers and Conservative politicians. He had lost the war, not won it, and even the small boy must have divined, dimly, that perhaps the gunfight was not the unblemished act of heroism he had been led to believe. Years later one of the family's favourite stories was about Gabito sitting listening to his grandfather, blinking incessantly and forgetting where he was.[13] Margot recalls: "Gabito was always by my grandfather's side, listening to all the stories. Once a friend came from Ciénaga, one of those old men who were in the War of a Thousand Days with Grandpa. Gabito, all ears as usual, stood beside the gentleman and it turned out the leg of the chair they'd given the old man trapped Gabito's shoe. He just kept quiet and put up with it, staying quite still until the visit ended, because he thought, 'If I say something they'll notice me and throw me out.' "[14]

Late in her own life his mother would tell me that "Gabito was always old; when he was a child he knew so much he seemed like a little old man. That's what we called him, the little old man." Throughout his life most of his friends would be significantly older and more experienced than he was and despite his Liberal and eventually socialist politics, he would always be drawn, consciously or unconsciously, to combinations of wisdom, power and authority in his preferred associates. It is not fanciful to conclude that one of the strongest impulses in García Márquez's later life was the desire to restore himself to his grandfather's world.

Most lastingly and decisively of all, Colonel Márquez was involved in providing a number of symbolic adventures, memorable incidents which would remain fixed in his grandson's imagination until, many years later, he would fuse them into a definitive shaping image in the very first line of his most celebrated novel. Once, when the child was still very small, the old man took him to the company store to see the fish frozen in ice. Many years later García Márquez would recall: "I touched it and felt as if it was burning me. I needed ice in the first sentence of [*One Hundred Years of Solitude*] because in the hottest town in the world, ice is magical. If it wasn't hot the book wouldn't work. That made it so hot it was no longer necessary to mention it again, it was in the atmosphere."[15] Similarly: "The initial image of *One Hundred Years of Solitude* was already in 'The House' [his first attempt at a novel] and then in *Leaf Storm*. Every day was a discovery, both through visits to the banana company and visits to the railway station. The banana company brought the cinema, radio and so forth. The circus arrived with a dromedary and a camel; complete fairs arrived with wheels of fortune, roller-coasters, carousels. My grandfather always took me by the hand to see everything. He took me to the cinema and although I don't remember films I do remember images. My grandfather had no notion of censorship so I saw every kind of image. But the most vivid of all of them and the one that is always repeated is that of an old man leading a child by the hand."[16] Eventually, in that first line of his most famous novel—"Many years later, as he faced the firing squad, Colonel Aureliano Buendía was to remember that distant afternoon when his father took him to discover ice"—the author would turn the different images of his expeditions with his grandfather into a self-defining experience that a fictional son has with his father, thereby subliminally confirming that Nicolás was not only his grandfather but also the father he felt he never had.

Thus for almost a decade the child lived with the old man and on most days he would walk around the town with him. One of their favourite walks was on a Thursday to the post office to see if there was any news about the Colonel's pension from the war twenty-five years earlier. There never was, a fact which made a big impression on the child.[17] Another was to the station to collect the day's letter from the Colonel's son Juan de Dios, Uncle Juanito, because the two men wrote to one another every day—mainly about business matters and the movements of relatives and mutual acquaintances.[18] From the station they would walk back down the short boulevard named for the country's national day, Camellón 20 July, where the Montessori School was (Nicolás's good friend General José Durán had donated the land);[19] then down the Street of the Turks, past the Four Corners and the pharmacy of Alfredo Barbosa and back to the house on Carrera Six between Calles 6 and 7; or they might go on past the house and the Liberal Party headquarters to the parish church of Saint James of the Holy Trinity, which was still a work in progress, with three small naves, thirty-eight wooden seats, many plaster saints and a great cross with a skull and crossbones at its base. (Gabito was an altar boy there, always went to mass and was closely connected to church matters throughout his childhood.)[20] Then they would walk across Bolívar Square, where vultures sat on the surrounding buildings, to the telegraph office where Gabriel Eligio had worked—though whether this fact was ever mentioned we cannot know. Not far beyond here was the cemetery along an avenue of palm trees—buried there now are General Durán, local trader José Vidal Daconte and Aunt Wenefrida—and what had only recently been open countryside, once forests, then cattle pastures, now closed off by the interminable, perfectly geometrical banana plantations.

Gabito had actually been assisted into the world by a Venezuelan woman, Juana de Freites, the wife of exiled General Marcos Freites who had fallen foul of the dictator Juan Vicente Gómez. He became the UFC warehouse manager and his house was a part of the UFC office complex. Not only was Señora Freites an invaluable presence at Gabito's birth but she later told him and his little friends a series of classic fairy stories—all set in Caracas!—which would contribute to his lifelong affection for Venezuela's capital city.[21] Another Venezuelan who lived across the mud road from Gabito's house was of course the pharmacist Alfredo Barbosa, also a victim of Gómez. He acted as the town doctor after his arrival just before the First World War and married a local woman, Adriana Berdugo. His was the town's leading pharmacy during the banana boom but by the end of the 1920s he was subject to fits of depression and passed long idle days swinging in his hammock.[22]

A cooler, more distant presence was that of the "gringos" who worked for the UFC and lived inside what García Márquez would later call the "electrified henhouse" of the company compound with their air-conditioned houses, swimming pools, tennis courts and manicured lawns. It was these other-worldly creatures who had diverted the course of the river and unleashed the 1928 strike and ensuing massacre. It was they who built the canal between two rivers which, during the rainstorms of October 1932, contributed to the devastating floods on which the five-year-old Gabito gazed, mesmerized, from the verandah of his grandfather's house.[23]

The Italian Antonio Daconte Fama had arrived after the First World War. He brought the silent movies through his cinema the Olympia, the gramophone, the radio and even bicycles which he hired out to the astonished population. Antonio Daconte lived alternately with two sisters, one of whom bore him only sons, the other only daughters.[24] Many Dacontes live in Aracataca to this day.

Some of Gabito's most enduring memories were of "the Frenchman," really a Belgian, known as Don Emilio, who also arrived after the First World War, on crutches, with a bullet in his leg. A talented jeweller and cabinet maker, Don Emilio would play chess or cards with the Colonel of an evening until the day he went to see *All Quiet on the Western Front* and went home and killed himself with a slug of cyanide.[25] The Colonel arranged the funeral and the whole episode ended up in *Leaf Storm* (where he is "the Doctor," fused in part with the depressive Venezuelan pharmacist Alfredo Barbosa) and *Love in the Time of Cholera* (where he is Jeremiah de Saint-Amour). García Márquez recalls, "My grandfather was given news of his suicide one August Sunday as we came out of eight o'clock mass. He almost dragged me to the Belgian's house where the mayor and two policemen were waiting. The first thing that struck me in the untidy bedroom was the strong smell of bitter almonds from the cyanide he had inhaled in order to kill himself. The body was lying on a camp bed covered with a blanket. By his side, on a wooden stool, was the tray in which he had vaporized the poison and a piece of paper with a message carefully written with a brush: 'No one is to blame, I'm killing myself because I am no good.' I can remember as if it were yesterday when my grandfather removed the blanket. The body was naked, stiff and twisted, the skin without colour, covered by a sort of yellow gauze and the watery eyes looked at me as if they were still alive. When she saw the look on my face as I returned to the house, my grandmother predicted: 'This poor child will never again sleep in peace for the rest of his life.' "[26]

There is reason to believe that the corpse of Don Emilio did indeed haunt the imagination of the susceptible boy throughout his childhood and fused with other corpses seen or only imagined; that it looms large in his very first published story, which is a meditation about his own status as a potential corpse (or possibly as an ex-corpse); and that even after *Leaf Storm*, where its much contested burial is the central drama of the novel, it would rise again and again from beneath the surface of his traumatized consciousness. Perhaps it is the screen concealing the corpse of the Colonel himself, which Gabito would never see.

Sometimes the Colonel would take Gabito out for a last "turn" before his bedtime: "My grandmother would always interrogate me when I got home after my evening walks with my grandfather; she would ask me where we'd been and what we'd done. I remember one night passing a house with other people and seeing my grandfather sitting in the parlour; I saw him from a distance, sitting there as if it was his own house. For some reason I never spoke about it to my grandmother, but I know now that it was the house of a lover, a woman who wanted to see him when he died and my grandmother wouldn't let her in, saying that corpses were only for legitimate wives."[27] The woman whom his grandmother would not let in to see Nicolás's corpse was almost certainly Isabel Ruiz, who seems to have moved to Aracataca in the 1920s.[28] And there was even a girl in his class at school whom Tranquilina told him he should have nothing to do with: "You and she must never marry." But the boy was unable to make sense of this warning until much later in life.[29]

While Gabito and the Colonel were out on their walks, greeting the Colonel's comrades and acquaintances, the women back at the house were permanently involved in arranging hospitality, some of it relating to the arrival of dignitaries, the Colonel's old war comrades or his Liberal Party cronies; much of it involved them dealing with the human products of his past misdeeds, who would usually arrive on mules, tie them out back and sleep in hammocks out in "The Clearing."[30] However most guests arrived by train: "The train arrived at eleven every morning and my grandmother would always say, 'We have to prepare fish and meat because you never know if those who are coming would prefer meat or fish.' So we were always excited to see who would be coming."[31]

But by the early 1930s everything was beginning to change. The banana strike and massacre, combined with the great depression of 1929, had set everything in reverse and Aracataca's brief period of prosperity gave way to the beginnings of a steep decline. Despite the massacre and the resentment felt by many at the general arrogance of the banana company, its stay in Aracataca was remembered with nostalgia for the next half century; many a conversation would speculate about the possibilities of it returning and with it the good old days of easy money and constant excitement.[32] Nicolás's income from liquor and other sources was catastrophically reduced and before long the steady stream had become a trickle. In the case of the Márquez Iguarán family, then, the permanent sense of loss which was the aftermath of the move from the Guajira was now supplemented by the sense that Aracataca's best days were also behind it, and Nicolás and Tranquilina, pensionless, began to stare poverty in the face as they entered an uncertain and intimidating old age.

. . .

EARLY IN 1934 Luisa returned to Aracataca to see her eldest son and daughter and to talk to her parents. It cannot have been an easy encounter from any point of view. She had never been forgiven for disobeying and shaming her parents and for bringing an unacceptable son-in-law into the family. By early 1933 things were getting hopeless in Barranquilla and she had probably persuaded Gabriel Eligio to let her negotiate their return to Aracataca. She arrived late one morning on the train from Ciénaga. Margot was terrified of her unknown mother and feared she would take her away.[33] She hid in her grandmother's skirts. Gabito, who would have been six, going on seven, was utterly perplexed by the arrival of this stranger and then embarrassed when he saw five or six women in the room and had no idea which one was his mother until she gestured that he should approach.[34]

By the time he was reacquainted with Luisa, Gabito had started his education at the new school—named after Maria Montessori and loosely based on her methods—near the railway station on Boulevard 20 July. The Montessori system, limited to kindergarten activities, was felt to do little harm as long as a good Catholic education was then instilled at primary level. The method stresses the child's creative potential, innate desire to grow and learn, and individuality; it teaches initiative and self-direction through the medium of the child's own senses. García Márquez would later say that it was "like playing at being alive."[35]

As it happened, Gabito's first teacher, Rosa Elena Fergusson, had been his father's first love in Aracataca (or so Gabriel Eligio claimed) and perhaps it was as well that Gabito did not know this. Rosa Elena, who had been born in Riohacha, was said to be a descendant of the first British consul in that city and to be related to Colonel William Fergusson, an equerry of Bolívar. She studied at the teachers' college in Santa Marta and followed her family to Aracataca. There her father and grandfather worked for the UFC, one of her relatives became Mayor,[36] and there the Montessori school opened in 1933. Gabito had to repeat the first grade because the school closed for operational reasons halfway through the year, and so he did not learn to read and write until he was eight years old, in 1935.

Rosa Elena, who was graceful, gentle and pretty, was twice crowned carnival queen of Aracataca. She was devoted to Spanish Golden Age poetry, which would be a lifelong enthusiasm of her precocious pupil.[37]

She was his first infant love—he was simultaneously thrilled and embarrassed to be physically close to her—and she encouraged him to appreciate language and verse. Sixty years later Rosa Elena had a particularly vivid memory of her famous ex-pupil: "Gabito was like a doll, with his hair the colour of whipped brown sugar and his skin all pale and pink, an odd colour in Aracataca; and he was always carefully washed and combed."[38] For his part, García Márquez said that Miss Fergusson "imbued in me the pleasure of going to school just to see her."[39] When she put her arms around him to guide his hand in writing, he would get some inexplicable "funny feelings."[40] Miss Fergusson recalled: "He was quiet, he hardly spoke, he was very, very shy. His class mates respected him for his application, tidiness, and intelligence, but he never liked sports. He took great pride in being the first to carry out an instruction."[41] She taught Gabito two key work habits, punctuality and producing pages with no errors, which would be lifelong obsessions.

Gabito had previously shown no precocity in reading and writing and failed to learn at home.[42] But long before he started to read he had taught himself to draw and this remained his favourite activity until he was thirteen years of age. When he was very small the old man had even allowed him to draw on the walls of the house. Above all he loved to copy comic strips—little stories—from his grandfather's newspapers.[43] He also retold the plots of the movies the Colonel took him to see: "He used to take me to every kind of picture, I particularly remember *Dracula* ... The next day he would make me tell him the film to see if I had been paying attention. So I not only fixed the films very clearly in my mind, but was also concerned to know how to narrate them because I knew he would make me tell him the story step by step to see if I had understood."[44] Thus the movies transported the young child; and he was, of course, a member of the first generation in history for whom the cinema, including talking films, was an experience prior to that of written literature. Later it was the Colonel who taught him respect for words and for the dictionary, which "knew everything" and was more infallible than the Pope in Rome.[45] The permanent sense of exploration and discovery encouraged by the Montessori system must have been the perfect complement to Nicolás's more traditional sense of certainty based on authority and personal empowerment.

But now came a jarring change in the lives of Gabito and Margarita. Gabriel Eligio, always energetic but always an improviser, with no head for finance, was never much of a bet to be able to start from scratch in a big bustling city like Barranquilla, in its first flush of prosperity when he moved there. So things were even more likely to go downhill once the depression began to bite in Colombia. He had managed to acquire a pharmacist's licence, leave his job in the hardware store and establish not one but two drugstores in the centre of the city, "Pasteur I" and "Pasteur 2."[46] This venture failed and the family retreated to Aracataca in disarray. Luisa arrived first with Luis Enrique and Aida, and stayed at the Colonel's house. Although she did in fact have a three-year break between pregnancies after giving birth to four children in less than four years by the time Aida Rosa was born in December 1930, Luisa was now pregnant again. Gabriel Eligio, who always had other "business" to attend to, was away for many more months and eventually returned on his birthday, 1 December 1934, long after the birth of the fifth child, Ligia, in August.[47]

His arrival is one of the few dates from these early years that can be fixed precisely, because García Márquez vividly remembers the arrival of a stranger: a "slim, dark, garrulous, pleasant man in a white suit and straw hat, every inch a Caribbean of the 1930s."[48] The stranger was his father. The reason he is able to date it precisely is that someone wished Gabriel Eligio a happy birthday and asked how old he was and Gabriel Eligio, born on 1 December 1901, responded, "the same age as Christ." A few days later the boy's first expedition with this new father was to buy Christmas presents at the market for all the other children. Gabito might have chosen to feel privileged by this experience; but what he vividly remembered instead was his feeling of disillusionment at realizing that it was not Baby Jesus or even Santa Claus or Saint Nicholas who brought presents at Christmas but one's own parents.[49] The father would regularly disappoint his son in the years—and decades—to come. Their relationship would never be either easy or close.

Now Gabriel Eligio set up his new pharmacy, "G.G." ("Gabriel García"), early in 1935 and managed to persuade the departmental medical authorities to award him a limited licence to practise homeopathic medicine, which allowed him to diagnose and treat patients and also to prescribe and sell his own quack remedies as the only appropriate cure for the complaints he identified. He had been combing magazines and medical journals and carrying out his own, often hair-raising experiments. Soon he invented a "Menstrual Mixture" under the brand name "GG," a wheeze worthy of José Arcadio Buendía in *One Hundred*

Years of Solitude, that incompetent dreamer who unmistakably bears numerous traces of García Márquez's own idiosyncratic, impractical but irrepressible progenitor. Economic survival was never more than precarious, and continuing subsidies from Colonel Márquez, himself increasingly impoverished, were humiliating but necessary. Before Gabriel Eligio's return Luisa had moved in temporarily with her parents in the absence of her eccentric and wayward husband.[50] Rosa Elena Fergusson even remembered that Nicolás began to expand the house to fit the new arrivals—perhaps hoping that his unloved son-in-law would not be returning.[51] After Gabriel Eligio did return, he and Luisa rented a house a couple of blocks from the Colonel's home, and it was there that a sixth child, Gustavo, was born on 27 September 1935.

In the household of their youthful, struggling parents, though truth to tell more in the yard and street than in the house, Luis Enrique and Aida both grew up as normal, healthy, unruly children, active, outgoing and without obvious complexes. Meanwhile, Gabito and Margot were being brought up by old people and had developed quite a different world-view, obsessive, superstitious, fatalistic and fearful but also diligent and efficient; both were perfectly behaved, rather timorous, spending more time in the house than in the street.[52] Gabito and Margarita must have felt at once inexplicably abandoned by their parents—Why me? Why us?—yet privileged to be cared for in the house of the much-respected and much-loved grandparents. It was these two outsiders, Margot and Gabito, who, in later life, would keep the García Márquez family's collective head above water.

Adjustment to the new situation was extremely difficult.[53] Aida remembers that Gabito was very jealous of the affection of his grandparents and watched everything and everybody when his siblings visited the house, trying to make sure they stayed as little as possible. No one was to come between him and his grandfather. Antonio Barbosa, the son of the pharmacist, who lived opposite, and was ten years older than Gabito but a good friend of the family, remembers him as a cissy or "petticoat-hugger" who played with tops and kites but never played football with the street children.[54]

Perhaps because he was not encouraged to become personally adventurous Gabito developed an active imagination—through drawing, reading, visits to the cinema and his own interactions with grown-ups. He seems to have become something of a show-off, always trying to impress the visitors with his fancy ideas and amusing anecdotes, tales which had to become ever taller in order to achieve the desired effect. Tranquilina was convinced he was a clairvoyant. Inevitably some adults interpreted his love of story-telling and fantasy as a tendency to dishonesty, and for the rest of his life García Márquez would have trouble with other people's questioning of his veracity.[55] Perhaps no modern writer's work raises so compellingly, indeed mysteriously, the relation between truth, fiction, verisimilitude and sincerity as his.

The two eldest children remained the property of their grandparents, as an eloquent anecdote from Margot demonstrates: "Grandfather didn't allow anyone to tell us off. Once, I remember, when we were older, they gave us permission to go to my mother's house by ourselves. When we set off, at about ten in the morning, my grandmother was cutting up a cheese and we asked for a piece. We arrived at the house and it turned out Luis Enrique and Aida were fasting because they'd taken medicine against parasites and couldn't eat for a few hours. Naturally they were starving and when they saw the cheese they asked for some. When my father found out he was furious and started to shout insults at us. Gabito said, 'Run, Margot, he's going to hit us,' and he took my hand and we made a run for it. We arrived home all frightened, and me crying. When we told Grandpa what had happened he went to tell my father off: why had he shouted at us, why had he threatened us."[56]

In 1935, however, the old world really did start to come to an end. One day, at six o'clock in the morning, Nicolás, by now over seventy, climbed a ladder at the side of the house to retrieve the family parrot, which had become caught in the sacking placed over the huge water tanks on the roof to prevent the leaves from the mango trees dropping in. Somehow he missed his footing and fell to the ground, and was left scarcely able to breathe. Margot remembers everyone screaming, "He's fallen, he's fallen!"[57] From that moment the old man, who was still enjoying reasonably good health, went into a sharp physical decline. It was now that Gabito, spying on the occasion of a doctor's visit, saw a bullet scar close to his grandfather's groin, the undeniable mark of a warrior. But after his fall, the old warrior was never the same again. He began to walk with a stick and to suffer from a series of ailments that would lead, before long, to his death. After the accident the walks around the town came to an abrupt end and the magic of the child's relationship with his grandfather—based above all on security—would begin to fade. The Colonel even had to ask Gabriel Eligio and Luisa to collect taxes and other payments on his behalf, which must have been a demoralizing blow to his pride.

In early 1936 Gabito moved to the public school in Aracataca.[58] He had suddenly become an obsessive reader. His grandfather and Miss Fergusson had already opened his eyes to learning, and the dictionary had begun to lay down the law; but the book which most stimulated his imagination was *The Thousand and One Nights*, found in one of his grandfather's old trunks, which seems to have conditioned his interpretation of much of what he experienced in the Aracataca of those days, part Persian market, part Wild West. For a long time he was unaware of the book's title because the cover was missing; when he did discover the title he must surely have made a connection between the exotic and mythological "Thousand and One Nights" and the more local, historical "War of a Thousand Days."[59]

Now that the Colonel was a virtual invalid, Gabriel Eligio felt able to reassert his rights to his two fostered children. Thus Gabito had no sooner learned to read and write, with all its wonders, than his own adventurous, restless father decided to take the family away to Sincé, where he himself had been born. And this time Gabito too would be included, taken away from his home, his grandparents and his sister Margot by this man he hardly knew, who had already decided that his son's main character trait was that he was a born liar, a kid who would "go somewhere, see something and come home telling something completely different. He exaggerated everything."[60] In December 1936 this frightening father, a born fabulator himself, took Gabito and Luis Enrique on an exploratory expedition to Sincé, to see if prospects there were better than the increasingly grim reality of Aracataca.[61]

Gabriel Eligio enrolled the boys to study with a local teacher, though the classes would not be recognized by the authorities and Gabito would lose yet another school year. Little wonder he eventually decided to adjust his age downwards to make up for all the school years he had lost! Now the two boys got to know their colourful paternal grandmother, Argemira García Paternina, still unmarried in her forties. She had given birth to Gabriel Eligio at the age of fourteen and thereafter had at least six children by at least three other men. "She was an extraordinary woman, I now realize," said García Márquez sixty years later, "the freest spirit I've ever known. She had an extra bed ready at all times for whoever wanted to sleep with someone. She had her own moral code and she didn't give a fuck what anyone else thought about it. Of course we thought it was quite normal at the time. Some of her sons, my uncles, were younger than I was, and I used to play with them, we'd go off and hunt birds and things like that; I never thought twice about it all, it was the social world we lived in. Of course the landowners would seduce or rape thirteen-year-old girls in those days and then just cast them aside. My father went back to see her when he was grown up with a family and she was in her forties and he was outraged to find her pregnant again. She just laughed and said, 'What's it to you, how do you think you came into the world?' "[62]

Gabito's recollections of this stay were fragmentary and no doubt painful, despite his jokes in later life. It is not difficult to imagine the anguish at leaving his sick grandfather and the culture shock at meeting the less respectable side of the family. Like Aracataca, Sincé was a small compact town with an even larger central square, the usual wedding-cake church, the usual statue of Bolívar, and a population of perhaps nine thousand inhabitants. Its economy was based principally on cattle, rice and maize and, like most cattle areas, its politics were essentially conservative. Grandmother Argemira, known as "Mama Gime," lived in a little sloping square well away from the main plaza in a tiny two-room wooden house, painted white, with a palm thatch roof. It was there she had all her children.[63] The experience must have shown Gabito a different world. He was no longer the protected child of Colonel Márquez and must have had to adjust to the wilder ways of his illegitimate uncles and cousins, not to mention his own rebellious and increasingly reckless younger brother, Luis Enrique.

Meanwhile, back home in Aracataca life had been getting harder. The culmination came early in March 1937 when, two years after his accident, Colonel Márquez died in Santa Marta of bronchial pneumonia. He had never recovered from the effects of his fall from the ladder in 1935. The old man had already been emotionally devastated by the death of his sister Wenefrida in his own house on 21 January 1937 and we can only imagine what the departure of his beloved "little Napoleon" had done to the old soldier's morale. His son Juan de Dios moved the Colonel to Santa Marta early in 1937 for a throat operation. In March he contracted pneumonia and died on the 4th of that month at the age of seventy-three, in the city where another warrior, Simón Bolívar, had died and in whose cathedral he had been laid to rest.

Colonel Márquez was buried that same day in the Santa Marta city cemetery and the newspaper *El Estado* recorded his death in a brief obituary. Margot vividly recalls the funeral in Santa Marta. "I cried and cried the whole day. But Gabito was away with my father and Luis Enrique in Sincé on another of his adventures. Gabito didn't get back for months, so I don't remember his reaction. But it must have been one of deep sadness, because they adored one another, they were inseparable."[64]

Gabito, in Sincé, learned about the death indirectly through over-hearing a conversation between his father and grandmother. Many years later, he would say that he was unable to cry at the news, and only realized the old man's importance to him after he had grown up. He even made light of the moment: "I had other worries. I recall that at that time I had lice and it used to embarrass me terribly. They used to say that lice abandoned you when you died. I remember being very worried: 'Shit, if I go and die now, everyone'll know I have lice!' So in those circumstances I can't have been much affected by my grandfa-ther's death. My main worry was the lice. In fact I only started to miss my grandfather later when, grown up, I couldn't find anyone to replace him, because my father was never a proper substitute."[65] The quirky recollections and provocative hyperboles, the typically indirect com-munication of personal emotions and implicit denials, conceal a sim-pler, more brutal fact: the boy was never able to grieve for the being he loved most during a painful and often incomprehensible childhood, the one who was the fount of all wisdom and the foundation of all secu-rity. Surrounded now by the members of his own nuclear family, his real family, the family who had left him when he was a baby, little Gabito was bereft. In April 1971, in answer to a reporter's question about his grandfather's death, and in front of his own biological father, García Márquez stated, with characteristic and in this case cruel hyper-bole: "I was eight when he died. Since then nothing important has hap-pened to me. Everything has just been flat."[66]

Gabriel Eligio took the two boys back briefly to Aracataca to per-suade Luisa to join them in Sincé. Luisa was decidedly unenthusiastic about the expedition. In 1993 she told me, "I didn't want to go, just imagine, a young family and all our things. Train to Ciénaga, boat to Cartagena and road to Sincé. But I always did what he wanted, and he was a great traveller, an adventurer. We hired two trucks, with Luis Enrique and Gabito in the first one and their father behind in the sec-ond one, which overturned once on the way."[67] Only their cousin Sara Márquez, recently married, stayed behind in the old house in Araca-taca with Tranquilina and Aunt Francisca.

Margot's response to all these changes in the family's fortunes was a bitter one: "We lived in my grandmother's house until the money started to run out and she had to live on what Uncle Juanito sent her; so then it was decided that Gabito and I should move to my father's home in Sincé . . . It was terrible. To move from a quiet environment to live with those devils, my brothers and sisters, added to the character of our father, who was rough and noisy. He never let anything go. He used to give Aida some tremendous thrashings and she would take no notice. I thought, 'If he ever touches me, I'll throw myself in the river.' Neither I nor Gabito ever stood up to him, we always did as we were told."[68]

But things went badly in Sincé. Gabriel Eligio had invested in livestock, notably a herd of goats, but the venture turned out disastrously and the family returned to Aracataca within a few months. Gabriel Eligio did not accompany his wife and children all the way but stopped off in Barranquilla where he began to find the means to set up yet another pharmacy. In Aracataca the rest of the family burned the Colonel's clothes in the courtyard of the house and Gabito somehow saw the old man alive again among the flames. Gabito tried to come to terms with the loss of his grandfather, the collapse of his grandmother, who, already losing her eyesight, was inconsolable without her husband of over fifty years, and the simultaneous decline of the redoubtable Aunt Francisca, who had been with Nicolás even longer than his wife had. For Gabito, it was the end of an entire world. Immersed in this grief that he was unable even to recognize, and wholly in the hands, now, of the family that had abandoned him so many years before, he was reluctant to reintegrate into the life of the other children in Aracataca.

Luis Enrique, less reflective and with none of his brother's painful psychological baggage to carry, threw himself back into the life of their Caribbean home town, the life which the hypersensitive Gabito would only be able to appreciate many years later, as he looked back with rueful nostalgia not only on the world he had lost but the fun he had missed. Both went back to the public school for boys. Luis Enrique recalls that the gypsies and the circus soon stopped passing through and, like the García Márquez family, lots of people were preparing to leave: "Even the prostitutes went away, the ones who practised their trade in 'The Academy,' as the house of pleasure was known . . . Naturally I never [went inside] but my friends told me all about it."[69]

For many, many years Gabito would see Aracataca far more darkly than his reckless and rumbustious younger brother, as his first literary portrait, *Leaf Storm*, would illustrate. Although, much later, he would talk somewhat warmly about the town, he would always be afraid to go back. Not until he was forty years of age would he achieve the distance to view it through the picaresque filter Luis Enrique had already developed as a boy.

The end had arrived for all of them and Gabito, now eleven, was about to leave "that hot dusty town where my parents assure me I was born and where I dream that I am—innocent, anonymous and happy— almost every night. In which case I would not perhaps be the same person I am now but maybe I would have been something better: just a character in one of the novels I would never have written."[70]

4

Schooldays:
Barranquilla, Sucre, Zipaquirá

1938-1946

GABRIEL ELIGIO took Gabito alone with him to Barranquilla
to set up the pharmacy and their new life. It took them two
months. Eleven-year-old Gabito found his father treated him
better when there was no one else to show off to. But he was also left
alone a lot of the time and Gabriel Eligio often neglected to feed him.
One time the boy even found himself sleepwalking along an avenue in
the centre of the city, suggesting a serious emotional disturbance.[1]

Barranquilla stood on the Magdalena River at the point where it
begins to open out to the Caribbean Sea. In half a century it had been
transformed from a mere hamlet lying between the historic colonial
harbours of Cartagena and Santa Marta to become perhaps the most
dynamic city in the nation. It was the hope of Colombia's shipping
industry and the home of its aviation. It was the only conurbation with
significant immigration from abroad, which made it in a way like a capital city with a strong sense of its own somewhat makeshift modernity
compared to Bogotá's gloomy Andean traditionalism and the conservatism of its more aristocratic neighbour Cartagena. It was full
of foreign and national import-export businesses, factories and
workshops—a German airline, Dutch manufacturers, Italian food producers, Arab stores, American developers—and a plethora of small
banks, commercial institutes and schools. Many of the firms were
founded by Jews who had migrated from the Dutch Antilles. Barran-

quilla was the point of entry for travellers from abroad and the point of departure for travellers to Bogotá, whether by river or by air. Its carnival was the most famous in the country and many *barranquilleros* still live the whole year in impatient expectation of that week in February when their already vibrant community will once again explode.

In Sincé and during the brief return to Aracataca relationships had been diluted to some extent by the presence of numerous members of the respective extended families. But when they arrived in Barranquilla late in 1938, leaving Tranquilina and the aunts behind in Aracataca, the members of the García Márquez nuclear family found themselves alone together for the very first time. Gabito and Margot, silently mourning their grandfather and the absence of their now ailing grandmother, found the adjustment almost too difficult to bear. But bear it they had to. Each knew that the other was suffering but they never spoke about it. Besides, their mother was suffering similar grief and had moved back to Barranquilla with great reluctance and visible resentment. The new pharmacy was down in the town centre and the new house was in the Barrio Abajo or Lower Quarter, perhaps the best-known popular district of Barranquilla. The house was small but surprisingly pretentious; Gabriel Eligio had realized that Luisa, expecting another baby, was in no mood for stoicism. Although it only had two bedrooms, the main living room had four Doric columns and on the roof was a small mock turret painted red and cream. Locals called it "the castle."

It became clear almost at once that the new pharmacy was to be another disastrous failure. Overwhelmed by his misfortunes, Gabriel Eligio set off once more for greener grasses, leaving his pregnant wife with no way of supporting herself and the children. Now came the family's worst days. Gabriel Eligio travelled up and down and around the northern reaches of the Magdalena River, treating patients ad hoc, taking on temporary jobs and looking for new ideas. Luisa must often have wondered if he would ever be coming back. Her seventh child, Rita, would be born in July 1939; Aunt Pa travelled to Barranquilla to assist Luisa in the absence of Gabriel Eligio, and García Márquez notes in his memoir that the child was named Rita in honour of St. Rita of Cascia whose claim to moral fame was "the patience with which she bore the bad character of her wayward husband."[2] Luisa Santiaga would have four more children, all of them boys.

She was forced to rely on the generosity of her brother Juan de Dios, an accountant in Santa Marta, who was already supporting Tranquilina and the aunts in Aracataca.[3] It turned out that Luisa had resources of resilience, practicality and common sense which Gabriel Eligio never managed to develop. She was a quiet, gentle woman who could seem passive and even childlike, yet she found a way to bring up and protect eleven children without ever having enough money to feed, clothe and educate them in comfort. Where Gabriel Eligio's sense of humour was somewhat broad and always eccentric, Luisa had an incisive sense of irony—which again she kept under tight rein—and a sense of humour that ranged from the wry to the openly festive and which has been immortalized in a number of her son's female characters, most notably the unforgettable Ursula Iguarán in *One Hundred Years of Solitude*. The period in Barranquilla, during which Gabito and his mother fought together against real poverty, established a new link between them which would never be broken: García Márquez, stressing its importance to him but concealing his hurt, would say that his relationship with her was "a serious relationship . . . probably the most serious relationship I've ever had."[4]

Despite the hardships Luisa decided to enrol Gabito in school so that he could complete his primary education. He was the eldest and academically the brightest and as such he represented the family's best hope for the future. The headmaster of the Cartagena de Indias school, Juan Ventura Casalins, took a protective attitude to his new pupil and the encouragement of a sympathetic adult male must have been providential. Even so, García Márquez's reminiscences of his schooldays are of loneliness and of overcoming great trials and tribulations. He immersed himself in books such as *Treasure Island* and *The Count of Monte Cristo*.

He also had to look for real work and earned a few pesos painting signs for a store named El Toquío which stood—and still stands—next to the old house. The boy would paint messages from the shopkeeper such as "If you don't see it, just ask," or, "The man who gives the credit is out looking for his money." On one memorable occasion he was paid twenty-five pesos for painting the sign on the local bus. (Colombia's buses are the gaudiest in Latin America.) On another he entered a radio talent contest in which he remembers singing "The Swan," a well-known waltz, but unfortunately he came second and he also remembers that his mother, who had alerted all her friends and relatives and was not unnaturally hoping for the five-peso prize, found it hard to conceal her disappointment. He also got a job with a local printer which included hawking samples around the streets. He abandoned the job after meeting the mother of one of his friends from Aracataca, who shouted after him: "Tell Luisa Márquez she should think what her parents would say if they saw their favourite grandson handing out leaflets to consumptives in the market."[5]

Gabito himself was a sickly child at this age, pale, underfed and physically underdeveloped. Luisa tried to protect him from tuberculosis by giving him Scott's Emulsion, the famous brand of cod liver oil, while her husband was away and Gabriel Eligio would say that when he got home from his travels Gabito "stank of fish." One of the boy's most chilling childhood memories was of a dairywoman who often called at the house saying crassly one day to Luisa Santiaga in front of the child himself, "I hate to say it, ma'am, but I don't think this boy of yours is going to make it to grown-up."[6]

During one of the family's occasional telephone calls to the long-lost head of the family, Luisa said she didn't like the tone of his voice and during the next call she exhorted him to come home. The Second World War had just broken out and perhaps she was feeling especially insecure. Gabriel Eligio sent a telegram which simply said, "Indecisive." Smelling a rat, she gave him a blunt alternative: either he came home at once or she would take all the children to wherever he was. Gabriel Eligio caved in and was back in Barranquilla within the week. In no time at all he began dreaming about new ventures. He recalled nostalgically a small river town called Sucre, which he had visited as a very young man. No doubt there was a woman somewhere in his mind's eye. Once again he acquired a loan from a pharmaceutical wholesaler whose drugs he undertook to purvey and within a couple of months the family was on its way from the most modern city in Colombia to a small rural backwater.

As usual Gabriel Eligio went on in advance to the new destination and left Luisa, pregnant once more, to move or sell the family effects— this time she sold most of them—and bring the seven children. Gabito, who had already been given tasks beyond his years when he went on ahead to Barranquilla with his father a year and a half before, now found himself in an enhanced role as man of the family. He made almost all the arrangements, including the packing, booking the removal truck and buying the steamer tickets to take the family up-river towards Sucre. Unfortunately the ticket clerk changed the rules in mid-transaction and Luisa found herself without enough money because the company said that all the children had to pay full fare. Desperate, she carried out a one-woman sit-in and won the day. Years later, Luisa herself, chatting to me in Barranquilla when she was eighty-eight, remembered that odyssey: "At the age of twelve Gabito had to organize the journey, being the eldest. I can still see him standing on the deck of the river steamer counting the children and suddenly panicking. 'There's one missing!' he said. And it was him. He hadn't counted himself!"[7]

The river-boat took them south to Magangué, the largest town on the northern Magdalena. From there they had to switch to a launch which would take them up the smaller San Jorge River and then along the much narrower Mojana, with swamps and jungle on either side, a great adventure which opened wide the children's imagination. Gustavo, the youngest son, was only four years old and the arrival in Sucre in November 1939 is one of his most vivid early memories: "We went to Sucre by launch and stepped down from the boat along a plank. The scene is imprinted on my mind: my mother walking down the plank, dressed all in black, with pearl buttons on the sleeves of her dress. She must have been about thirty-four. I remembered that episode many years later, when I was thirty myself; it was as if I was looking at a portrait and I realized she had a look of resignation on her face. It's easy enough to understand because my mother had been educated in a convent school and had been the favourite child of one of the most important families in the town; an indulged little girl who had painting and piano lessons and who, all of a sudden, had to live in a town where the snakes came into the houses and there was no electric light; a town where the floods were so bad in winter that the land disappeared beneath the water and clouds of mosquitoes appeared."[8]

Sucre was a small town of about three thousand inhabitants with no road or rail access to anywhere. It was like a floating island lost in a lattice-work of rivers and streams amidst what had once been dense tropical jungle, now thinned out by constant human endeavour but still covered by trees and undergrowth with large clearings for cattle, rice, sugar cane and maize. Other crops included bananas, cacao, yucca, sweet potato and cotton. The landscape was constantly changing and shifting between scrub forest and savannah, depending on the season and the height of the rivers. Immigrants had come from Egypt, Syria, Lebanon, Italy and Germany between 1900 and the mid-1920s. The more prosperous inhabitants lived around the large plaza, which was not a conventional square but an area more than a hundred and fifty yards long and perhaps thirty yards wide, with the river at one end, the church at the other and a row of brightly painted two-storey houses on either side. This was where Gabriel Eligio had rented his new house, with the pharmacy set up on the ground floor.

Soon after their arrival Luisa insisted on raising the question of Gabito's secondary education and persuaded her reluctant husband that he should be sent to the San José College back in Barranquilla, about which she had made enquiries before her departure. "They make governors there," she said.[9] Gabito himself may have felt that he was being rejected again but decided to put a brave face on things: "I thought of school as a dungeon, I was appalled at the very idea of living subject to a bell, but it was also my only hope of enjoying a free life from the age of thirteen, on good terms with my family but away from their control."[10]

A friend has described his appearance in those days: "He had a large broad head, and wiry unkempt hair. He had a rather coarse nose, long as a shark's fin. He had a mole starting to grow to the right of his nose. He looked half Indian and half gypsy. He was a thin, taciturn boy who went to school because he had to."[11] He was almost thirteen and his education was well behind schedule. During his first fifteen months back in the big coastal city he stayed with José María, one of his Valde-blánquez cousins, his wife Hortensia and their baby daughter. He slept in the lounge on a sofa.

Despite his own self-doubts and the competition from other talented boys, Gabito's performance in school was consistently excellent across the board. He became celebrated for his literary exercises entitled "My Foolish Fancies," humorous satirical poems about his schoolmates and about severe or silly school rules, which, when they came to the attention of his teachers, he was regularly asked to recite.[12] He also published a number of other short pieces and poems in the school magazine *Juventud (Youth)* and was given a series of positions of trust and responsibility during his three years at the school. For example, the boy with the best grades of the week would raise the national flag before classes in the morning and this was a task Gabito had to himself for long periods of the school year. There is a picture of him in the school magazine with his medals; he is looking slightly sideways at the camera and somewhat shamefaced, as if he has reason to doubt the justice of his success. This was a feeling which would pursue him down the years.

At the end of the first year the adolescent García Márquez returned home for the annual two-month vacation in December and January. Inevitably another child had been born, and prematurely at seven months: his baby brother Jaime, destined to be sickly for seven years;

Gabito became his family godfather and much later in life Jaime would become Gabito's closest sibling. By now the family was established in the new environment and Gabito, as always, had a lot of catching up to do. His brothers and sisters came to view him as a sort of occasional brother, who turned up every so often, quiet, shy and somewhat solitary—the oldest and the most distant. These regular absences, at the very outset of adolescence, deepened the gulf between the boy and his father, who never understood him and seemed not to try. But he never forgot about his sister Margot, who was equally afraid of their father, while their mother could never find time for her. She missed him terribly. ("We were almost like twins.") Aware of her solitude, Gabito wrote to Margot religiously every week he was away.[13]

He dreaded going home. If in order to learn about Sucre we had to rely upon statements made by García Márquez between 1967 and his 2002 autobiography we would have known next to nothing apart from the indirect evidence of novels such as *In Evil Hour* and *No One Writes to the Colonel*, written in the 1950s, and *Chronicle of a Death Foretold*, written at the beginning of the 1980s. Such grudging statements as he did make merely confirmed the grim and sombre impression left by those novels. Sucre was the anonymous *pueblo* (small town), the dark and evil twin of Macondo; he would not even refer to it by name, just as he rarely mentioned his father, with whom it was so closely identified in his mind. (The original title for *In Evil Hour* was *This Shit-Heap of a Town*.) Yet for the younger children, particularly for Rita and the four who were born there, it was a tropical paradise of river, jungle, exotic animals and freedom.

This was also Gabriel Eligio's most successful period as a pharmacist and homeopathic practitioner and he not only worked on his own account but was connected to the local clinic. For such perks it was helpful to be a Conservative, for Sucre, unlike Aracataca, was a largely Conservative town. At the same time, violence was never too far below the surface. On the day Jaime was christened a local trumpeter had his throat slit at the very moment he was straining to blow the highest, wildest note. Some said the blood soared three metres. Luis Enrique heard about the incident immediately and raced off to see but by the time he arrived the unfortunate man was almost out of blood, though the body was still palpitating.[14] Nothing quite so dramatic would happen again in public until a family friend, Cayetano Gentile, their next door neighbour, was murdered in front of the whole town in January 1951 and all their lives were irremediably changed.

For Gabito there had been a jarring alteration in the family arrangements brought about by his errant father. As he walked up from the launch on his return to Sucre at the end of 1940 he was embraced by a vivacious young woman who announced herself as his sister Carmen Rosa; the same evening he would discover that his other half-sibling Abelardo was also in town, working as a tailor. The presence of Abelardo must have come as a particular shock. Gabito's only consolation for being with this almost unknown family had been that he was the eldest and this consolation had now been taken away from him: he was not his father's eldest son, only his mother's.

Gabriel Eligio's career frustrations and professional inferiority complex account for part of the problem between him and Gabito, who was always looking at him with an outsider's eye. Most of Gabriel Eligio's children took his stories about his medical expertise and achievements at face value.[15] Gabito, who had already seen far more of the world, was undoubtedly more sceptical than his brothers and sisters. Gabriel Eligio evidently read a lot and knew a lot; he also had a lot of brass neck and the fortitude to follow his own intuitions while his patients took the risks. He had qualified as a homeopathic doctor in Barranquilla and while he worked as a pharmacist there he struggled part-time to earn a qualification through the University of Cartagena to secure full recognition as a doctor; eventually, after prolonged negotiations, he was granted the title "Doctor of Natural Sciences," but he called himself "doctor" long before that.[16] It seems doubtful Gabito ever took his father's assumed title very seriously; besides, "Colonel" was a title he undoubtedly much preferred. Gabriel Eligio himself often boasted that his techniques were far from orthodox: "When I used to go and see a sick person the beating of his heart would tell me what was wrong with him. I used to listen with great care. 'This is a liver problem,' the heart would . . . say to me, 'This man's going to die talking,' so I'd say to his relatives, 'This man is going to die talking' and the man would die talking. But afterwards I lost the knack."[17]

Not surprisingly, *teguas* (*tegua* is a pejorative word meaning anything between a Western quack doctor and an Indian herbalist), indeed all homeopathic doctors, had a reputation for sexual profligacy in Colombia in those days. After all, they were travelling experts, with no ties to most of the places they passed through, with unrivalled access to members of the opposite sex and a ready explanation for any disconcerting behaviour. A woman in a nearby settlement hired a lawyer who accused Gabriel Eligio of raping her while under anaesthetic and although he denied the more serious charge of rape he admitted that he was indeed the father of her child.[18] This too—having sexual relations with a patient—was a criminal offence, but he managed to extricate himself from what was perhaps the most perilous moment of his career, when he could have lost everything. Later another woman came forward to say that her granddaughter too had been made pregnant by Doctor García and that she could not look after her. Luisa, after the inevitable quarrels and recriminations, did the same as her mother before her and accepted that her husband's offspring were also hers. As García Márquez himself said, "She was angry, yet she took the children in and I actually heard her say that phrase: 'I don't want the family blood going wandering around the world.' "[19]

During the first annual vacation Gabito not only had to assimilate the appearance of Abelardo and Carmen Rosa, and the darkly whispered news about yet another illegitimate half-brother; another traumatic experience awaited him. He took a message from his father to what turned out to be the local brothel, "La Hora" ("The Hour"). The woman who opened the door looked him up and down and said, "Oh, sure, come this way." She led him to a darkened room, undressed him and, as he put it the first time he ever mentioned it in public, "raped" him. He would later recall: "It was the most awful thing that ever happened to me, because I didn't know what was going on. I was absolutely certain I was going to die."[20] To add insult to injury, the prostitute rather brutally told Gabito he should ask his younger brother, evidently already a regular, for lessons. He must have blamed his father for this sordid, frightening and humiliating experience. Indeed, it is more than likely that, in time-honoured Latin American tradition—what the Brazilians used to call "sending a boy to buy candy"—Gabriel Eligio actually set it up.

The second year at San José started like the first. García Márquez remained the literary star of the lower school and enjoyed a quiet popularity. He wrote an entertaining report on a school excursion to the seaside in March 1941 which is a pleasure to read, overflowing with good humour, youthful enthusiasm and sheer verve and nerve: "On the bus Father Zaldívar told us to sing a devotion to the Virgin and we did so despite the fact that some boys proposed instead a *porro*[21] (an Afro-Colombian song) like 'The Old Cow' or 'The Hairless Hen.' " The chronicle ends, "Whoever wants to know who wrote these 'foolish fancies' should send a letter to Gabito." He was one of the swots, allergic to sports and fighting, and used to sit reading in the shade during break time while the others were playing football. But like many other stu-

dious and non-sporting students before and since, he learned to be
funny and to defend himself with his tongue.

Yet there was much more to this enigmatic adolescent than met the
eye. Gabito's blossoming education was interrupted in 1941 by a
lengthy absence from San José when he missed the second half of the
academic year through an emotional disorder which came to a head in
May. The ever indiscreet Gabriel Eligio discussed it in an interview in
1969, soon after his son became famous: "He had something like a
schizophrenia, with terrible temper tantrums and such like. Once he
threw an inkwell at one of the priests, a well-known Jesuit. So they
wrote to say they thought I should take him out of school, which I
did."[22] It is rumoured in the family that Gabriel Eligio intended to
trepan his son's head "at the place where his consciousness and memory were situated" and that only Luisa's threat to make the plan public
restrained him.[23] It is not hard to imagine what effect such a plan may
have had on a boy who had no faith in this home doctor anyway and
who must have been petrified at the thought of his father literally getting inside his head.

When the wretched Gabito arrived in Sucre his half-brother
Abelardo said bluntly that what he needed was to "get his leg over" and
provided him with a stream of willing young women who gave him
early sexual experiences while the other boys back at San José were
busy praying to the Holy Virgin. These precocious adventures gave
García Márquez, who until that time evidently felt less of a male than
other males in a profoundly macho society, the sense of being a sexual
insider, which never left him whatever his other complexes and sustained him in the face of numerous other anxieties and setbacks.[24]

It was at this point that a mysterious character called José Palencia,
son of a local landowner, appeared on the scene. Like Gabito's brother
Luis Enrique, Palencia was a talented musician and a great *parrandero*
(drinker, singer, seducer) who would remain a good friend of Gabito's
through his time at Bogotá. He was also handsome, and an accomplished dancer, a skill which Gabito, an excellent singer, had not yet
mastered. Palencia would be the protagonist of numerous picaresque
and even melodramatic anecdotes down the years before an untimely
but not unexpected demise. Acquiring such a friend was another shot
in the arm for a growing adolescent.

On his return to school in February 1942 the young García
Márquez was warmly greeted by both pupils and teachers. Although he
makes light of the experience in his memoirs, he must have felt embar-

rassed and humiliated by his absence and the explanations he had to invent. His father was given much credit for his "cure." He no longer stayed with José María and Hortensia Valdeblánquez, who now had two children, but with his father's uncle, Eliécer García Paternina, a bank clerk known for his probity and generosity whose great passion in life was the English language. Eliécer's daughter Valentina was, like Gabito, a great reader and took him to meetings of the local "Arena y Cielo" ("Sand and Sky") group of poets.[25]

One day, while he was waiting in the house of one of the poets, a "white woman poured into a mulatta's mould" came to visit. Her name was Martina Fonseca and she was married to a black river pilot well over six feet tall. Gabito was just fifteen and very small for his age. He talked to her for a couple of hours as they waited for the poet. Then he saw her again waiting for him—he says—on a park bench after they had both been to church on Ash Wednesday. She invited him home and they embarked on an intense sexual affair—"a secret love that burned like a wild fire"—which lasted the rest of the school year. The pilot was frequently away for twelve days at a time and on the corresponding Saturdays Gabito, who had to be back at Uncle Eliécer's by eight o'clock, pretended to be at the Saturday afternoon performance at the Rex Cinema. But after a few months Martina said she thought it would be better if he went somewhere else to study because "then you will realize that our affair will never be more than it has already been."[26] He left in tears and as soon as he got back to Sucre he announced that he was not returning either to San José or to Barranquilla. His mother, according to this version, said, "Then you'll have to go to Bogotá." His father said there was no money for that and Gabito, suddenly realizing that he wanted to go on studying after all, blurted out, "There are scholarships." A few days later came the pay-off: "Get yourself ready," said Gabriel Eligio, "you're going to Bogotá."[27]

GABITO SET OFF for the capital in January 1943 to try his luck. Even this was a risk for the family because the journey to Bogotá was an expensive investment for a boy who might easily fail the entrance examination. Bogotá was, in effect, another country, and the journey there was long and intimidating. His mother adjusted one of his father's old black suits and the whole family saw him off at the boardwalk. Never one to miss the chance of a trip, Gabriel Eligio began the journey with Gabito in a small launch which took them along the rivers Mojana and San Jorge and then down the great Magdalena to the city of Magangué. There Gabito said goodbye to his father and took the river-boat *David Arango* south to the port of Puerto Salgar, a voyage which normally lasted a week but sometimes three if the river was low and the steamer was stranded on a sandbank. Although he wept during the first night, what had seemed daunting in prospect became a revelation.[28] The boat was full of other young *costeños*, hopeful first-timers like him looking for grants, or more fortunate schoolboys and university students already enrolled and returning after the long vacations. He would come to remember these journeys as floating fiestas during which he, with the rest of the young men, sang *boleros*, *vallenatos* and *cumbias* to entertain themselves and to earn a few pesos, on that "wooden paddle-wheeler that went along leaving a wake of piano-player waltzes in the midst of the sweet fragrance of gardenias and rotting salamanders of the equatorial tributaries."[29]

A few days later, as Gabito was leaving the river-boat at journey's end his more experienced companions, jeering at a tropical bundle his mother had forced upon him—a palm-leaf sleeping mat, a fibre hammock, a coarse woollen blanket and an emergency chamber pot—wrested it from him and threw it in the river to mark the accession to civilization of this *corroncho*—the deprecating Bogotá word for a *costeño*, which implies that all of them are coarse and ignorant and incapable of discriminating good behaviour from bad.[30] It was as if nothing he knew or possessed would be of use to him in Bogotá, among the devious and supercilious *cachacos*.

At Puerto Salgar, at the foot of the Eastern Andes, the passengers boarded the train which would take them up to Bogotá. As the locomotive climbed into the Andes the mood of the *costeños* changed. With each twist of the line the atmosphere grew colder and thinner, and breathing became more difficult.[31] Most of them started to shiver and developed headaches. At 8,000 feet they reached the Meseta and the train began to accelerate towards the capital city across the Sabana de Bogotá, a plateau 300 miles long and 50 miles wide, a gloomy dark green beneath the year-round rains but a brilliant emerald colour when the high Andean sun shone down from its cobalt sky. The Sabana was dotted with small Indian villages of gray adobe huts with thatched roofs, willow trees and eucalyptuses, and flowers decorating even the humblest dwellings.

The train arrived in the capital at four o'clock in the afternoon. García Márquez has often said it was the worst moment of his life. He was from the world of sun, sea, tropical exuberance, relaxed social customs and a relative absence of clothing and prejudices. On the Sabana everyone was wrapped up tight in a *ruana* or Colombian poncho; and in rainy and grey Bogotá, backed up against the Andean mountains at a height of 8,660 feet, it seemed even colder than on the Sabana; and the streets were full of men in dark suits, waistcoats and overcoats, like Englishmen in the City of London; and there were no women anywhere to be seen. Reluctantly, with a heartfelt sigh, the boy put on the black trilby hat he had been told everyone wore in Bogotá, got down from the carriage and hauled his heavy metal trunk on to the platform.[32]

No one was waiting for him. He realized that he could hardly breathe. Everywhere around him was the unfamiliar smell of soot. As the station and the street outside became deserted, Gabito wept for the world he had left behind. He was an orphan: he had no family, no sunshine, and no idea what to do. Finally a distant relative arrived and took him off in a taxi to a house near the town centre. If outside in the streets everyone wore black, inside they all wore ponchos and dressing gowns. When García Márquez got into bed that first night he jumped straight out again and shrieked that someone had soaked his bed. "No," he was told, "that's what Bogotá's like, you'll have to get used to it." He lay awake all night weeping for the world he had lost.

Four days later, early in the morning, he was standing in line outside the Ministry of Education on Jiménez de Quesada, the great avenue named after the Spanish conqueror of Colombia and founder of Bogotá.[33] The line seemed interminable; it started on the third floor of the ministry building and stretched two blocks along Avenida Jiménez. García Márquez was near the end of it. His despair deepened as the morning wore on. And then some time after midday he felt a tap on his shoulder. On the steamboat from Magangué he had met a lawyer from the Costa, Adolfo Gómez Támara, who had been devouring books throughout the journey, including Dostoyevsky's *The Double* and Fournier's *Le Grand Meaulnes*. Gómez Támara had been impressed by García Márquez's singing and had asked him to write out the words of one of the *boleros* so he could sing it to his sweetheart in Bogotá. In return he had presented him with his copy of *The Double*. The shivering youth blurted out his perhaps hopeless purpose: to win a scholarship. Incredibly, it turned out that the elegant lawyer was none other than the national director of educational grants, who at once led the stupefied applicant to the front of the line and into a large office. García Márquez's application was registered and he was entered for the examination, which took place at the College of San Bartolomé, the academy in old Bogotá where upper-class Colombians had been educated since colonial days. He passed and was offered a place in a new school, the National College for Boys in nearby Zipaquirá thirty miles away. García Márquez would have preferred to be at the prestigious San Bartolomé in Bogotá but struggled to conceal his disappointment.

He had neither the time nor the money to go home and celebrate with his proud and excited family. He had never heard of Zipaquirá but he headed straight there, arriving by train on 8 March 1943, two days after his sixteenth birthday. Zipaquirá was a small colonial city, typically Andean, with the same climate as Bogotá. It had been the economic heart of the Chibcha Indian empire, based on the salt mines which even today are the main attraction for tourists. The imposing main square was surrounded by huge colonial houses with blue balconies and heavy, overhanging red-tiled roofs, and was fronted by a great pallid cathedral with double towers which seemed too big for what in those days was really little more than a large village. Zipaquirá was full of small workshops with black chimneys processing salt by evaporation, after which the product would be sold back to the government. Particles drifted down all over the small community like ash. For a boy from the Costa the climate and environment were cold, dismal and oppressive.

The school was newly established but housed in an old colonial building. Formerly the College of San Luis Gonzaga, it was an austere two-storeyed edifice which dated back to the seventeenth century and was organized around an inner courtyard lined with colonial arches.[34] The premises comprised the rector's study and private quarters, the secretariat, an excellent library, six classrooms and a laboratory, a storeroom, a kitchen and refectory, toilets and showers and a huge first-floor dormitory for the eighty or so boarders who slept at the school. Winning a grant for Zipaquirá, he would later say, was like "winning a tiger in a raffle." The school was "a punishment" and "that frozen town was an injustice."[35]

Although he did not appreciate it at the time, García Márquez benefited from two circumstances unique in the history of Colombia. The Conservatives had abandoned state secondary education in 1927 and handed it to the private sector, essentially the Church, but when Alfonso López Pumarejo was elected President in 1934 he declared a

"Revolution on the March." For the only time in the nation's entire history a government, inspired in part by the Mexican Revolution and by the precarious reforms of the socialists in Republican Spain, set out to unify and democratize the country and create a new type of citizen. One of the main instruments for this transformation was to be a truly nationalist education system and the first "national college" to be founded was, precisely, the National College of Zipaquirá. At this time there were only forty thousand secondary students in the whole of Colombia and that year barely six hundred of them graduated from high school (of whom only nineteen were women). Most Colombians had only a vague idea of the regional complexity of their country but in Zipaquirá boys from every region were thrown together.[36]

The teachers at Zipaquirá were outstanding. Many of them had been rejected by other schools because of their progressive orientation. They tended to be hard-working idealists of a radical Liberal or even Marxist persuasion, and were sent to Zipaquirá to prevent them from polluting the minds of the upper-class boys in Bogotá. They were all specialists in their subjects, most of whom had passed through the Higher Normal School under one of Colombia's great educators, the *costeño* psychiatrist José Francisco Socarrás, a relative of one of Colonel Márquez's old war comrades and indeed of the Colonel's wife Tranquilina.[37] Socarrás believed that young Colombians should be exposed to all ideas, not excluding socialist currents. Many of the teachers were recent graduates and established relaxed and informal relationships with the pupils.

The school day was demanding. The wake-up bell was at six and by half past six García Márquez had taken a cold shower, dressed, cleaned his shoes and fingernails and made his bed. There was no school uniform but most students wore blue blazers with grey trousers and black shoes. García Márquez had to do the best he could with hand-me-downs from his father and would be embarrassed for the next few years by badly frayed jackets with extra-long sleeves, which did at least help him keep warm in the unheated school. At nine o'clock at night, after the school day and homework were behind them, the boys went up to the dormitory, where a memorable school tradition was instituted soon after García Márquez's arrival. There was a small cubicle for the teachers to sit dozing in the dormitory and from there before lights out a teacher would sit reading to the boys from his window as they fell asleep—usually some popular classic like *The Man in the Iron Mask* but sometimes an even weightier work like *The Magic Mountain*.[38] According to García Márquez the first of the authors was Mark Twain, an appropriate recollection for a man destined to be—among other things—the Mark Twain of his own land: symbol of the country, definer of a national sense of humour and chronicler of the relation between the provincial realm and the centre. The dormitory had iron beds with planks and these planks were the item mainly stolen by one boy from another. García Márquez became famous for terrifying dreams in the middle of the night which made him wake the entire dormitory with his screams. He had inherited this tendency from his mother Luisa; his worst nightmares "did not occur in terrifying visions but in joyful episodes with ordinary persons or places that all at once revealed sinister information in an innocent glance."[39] His recent reading of Dostoyevsky's *The Double* can surely not have helped.

On Saturdays there were classes until midday, after which the boys were free until six to wander the town, attend the cinema or organize dances—if they were lucky—at the houses of local girls. On Saturday they could play soccer, though the *costeños* preferred baseball. Sunday was totally free until six and, although the school did have religious instruction by a priest, there was no daily service and attendance at church was not mandatory even on Sunday—though García Márquez used to attend, perhaps so that he would not have to lie to his mother in his letters home. Such freedom was extraordinary for Colombia in the 1940s. And, as García Márquez would later reflect, with three square meals a day and more freedom—a sort of "supervised autonomy"—than in one's own home, there was much to be said after all for life at Zipaquirá.

He would always be grateful to the school for the grounding it gave him in Colombian and Latin American history, but literature, inevitably, was his favourite subject and he studied everything from the Greeks and Romans up to recent Spanish and Colombian texts. His spelling was, then as now, surprisingly erratic (though not as poor as his abject mathematical skills); he consoled himself with the thought that the great Simón Bolívar was also rumoured to have been a poor speller. He would later say that his best teacher of spelling was his mother Luisa; throughout his schooldays she would send his letters back to him with the spelling corrected.

At weekends he would play games, a bit of football with his friends in the grounds of the school, go to the cinema or walk the streets and highland meadows of Zipaquirá beneath the eucalyptus trees. Sometimes on a Sunday he would take the train to Bogotá, thirty miles away, to visit *costeño* relatives; on one such occasion he was introduced by a friend in the street to a distant cousin, Gonzalo González, who worked for the newspaper *El Espectador*. González, who had also been born in Aracataca, left a rare snapshot of the young man that García Márquez then was: "He must have been about seventeen and weighed no more than fifty kilos. He did not approach me. He said nothing before I spoke and I at once suspected that this boy was a methodical fellow, thoughtful and disciplined. He didn't move from where he was, with one old but clean shoe on the sidewalk and the other down on the asphalt of Seventh Avenue at Sixteenth Street in Bogotá. Maybe he was a timid person who did not show his fear. Circumspect, almost a bit sad, and in any case lonely and unknown. Once his initial reserve was overcome, he began to communicate and to put on the sort of controlled effusiveness that I later heard him call his 'nice guy show.' Within a minute or two he was talking about books . . ."[40]

Reading was this evasive young man's principal activity in Zipaquirá. In Barranquilla he had read every cheap Jules Verne and Emilio Salgari novel he could find as well as enough lowbrow poetry for a lifetime, together with the classics of the Spanish Golden Age. He knew many of these poems by heart. Now the lonely adolescent set to reading every book he could lay his hands on. He went through the whole library of literature, then turned to books of history, psychology, Marxism—mainly Engels—and even the works of Freud and the prophecies of Nostradamus. At the same time he was bored by the demands and rigours of his formal education and spent his time daydreaming, so much so that he was in real danger of losing his grant. Yet with just a week or two of study he astonished both his classmates and his teachers by getting straight fives and becoming "top boy."

In late 1943 Gabito returned again to Sucre. He would travel back to this remote river town from school in Barranquilla and Zipaquirá, from university in Bogotá, and from his jobs in Cartagena and Barranquilla until the family moved to Cartagena in 1951. Here, or in other nearby towns, he would meet the models for many of his best-known characters, including "innocent Eréndira" from the book of that name and the prostitute he would call María Alejandrina Cervantes in *Chronicle of a Death Foretold*. While he had been away this first year in Zipaquirá the ninth child, Hernando ("Nanchi"), had been born at the end of March, and while his wife was pregnant Gabriel Eligio's philandering ways had got him into hot water once more, with the birth of yet another illegitimate child. This time both Luisa and her eldest daughter Margot had been filled with womanly outrage, and for quite a while even Gabriel Eligio thought he might have gone too far; but as usual he talked them round.[41]

During this vacation García Márquez had another torrid sexual experience, this time with a voluptuous young black woman he calls "Nigromanta" (the name he would give a similarly sensuous black woman in the penultimate chapter of *One Hundred Years of Solitude*), whose husband was a policeman. Luis Enrique has told part of the story: "One day at midnight Gabito met a policeman on the Alvarez bridge in Sucre. The policeman was going to his wife's house and Gabito was coming from the policeman's wife's house. They greeted one another, the policeman asked after Gabito's family and Gabito asked after the policeman's wife. And if that's a story my mother tells you can imagine the ones she knows and doesn't tell. And she doesn't tell that one complete either because the end of the story is that the policeman asked Gabito for a light and as he drew near the policeman made a face and said, 'Shit, Gabito, you must have been in "La Hora" because there's a smell of whore on you even a billy-goat wouldn't jump across.'"[42] Weeks later—according to García Márquez's own version—the policeman caught him in bed with his wife (he had unfortunately fallen asleep) and threatened him with a round of Russian roulette with him, Gabito, as the only player. The lawman relented not only because he had the same political proclivities as García Márquez's father but also because he recalled with gratitude a recent occasion when Gabriel Eligio had cured him of a bout of gonorrhoea which no other doctor had been able to shift.[43]

Gabito was growing older, finally beginning to look his age. Contemporaries at Zipaquirá remember him at this time as thin, wild-eyed, always shivering and complaining about the cold; his previously combed and parted hair gradually turned to wire wool, never to be fully controlled again.[44] He stopped trying to look like the *cachacos*—sombre, tidy clothes; hair greased and combed at all times—and began to make a virtue of who and what he was. A wispy *costeño* moustache appeared on his adolescent lip and was left to wander where it would. The previous rector had been replaced by a young poet, Carlos Martín, only thirty years of age and as handsome as a matinée idol. He was a member of the fashionable "Stone and Sky" movement in poetry which was all the rage in Bogotá. These poets, who had taken their name from the work of the Spaniard Juan Ramón Jiménez, would not have been thought revolutionary in most other Latin American republics at the time. But Colombia, always a home of poetry rather than prose—except for speeches, another national speciality—was also a home of literary conservatism. Its poetic tradition is very rich, one of the strongest in a continent of great poets, but operates within an unusually narrow, subjectivist vein, and the nation's social and historical reality was almost completely absent from its literature in those days. New Colombian poets such as Eduardo Carranza, Arturo Camacho Ramírez, Jorge Rojas and Carlos Martín mirrored the works of Jiménez and the later Spanish 1927 Generation, together with Latin American avant-garde poets such as Pablo Neruda, who had visited Bogotá and made contact with the group in September 1943.

For the next six months the poet Martín replaced the self-effacing teacher Carlos Julio Calderón Hermida as García Márquez's Spanish literature professor. García Márquez was already writing poetry under the pseudonym "Javier Garcés." Martín concentrated especially on the works of Rubén Darío, the great Nicaraguan who had almost single-handedly revolutionized the poetic language of both Spain and Latin America between 1888, when his *Blue (Azul)* appeared, and 1916, when he died. Darío, whose childhood had been eerily similar to García Márquez's, would become one of the principal gods of the young Colombian's poetic Olympus.[45] He began to compose poems "after the manner of . . . ," technical pastiches of the great Spaniards such as Garcilaso de la Vega, Quevedo and Lorca, and Latin Americans such as Darío and Neruda. He wrote sonnets on request for boys to take to their girlfriends and once he even had one of them recited back to him by the unwary recipient.[46] He also wrote love poems on his own account, inspired by his relationships with local girls. The older García Márquez has always been curiously embarrassed by these early efforts to the point of denying authorship of many of them.

The *costeño* students organized dances in the town whenever they could. By this means, and others, he met numbers of young women. One of them, Berenice Martínez, was his partner in a brief but evidently impassioned romance towards the end of his stay in Zipaquirá. She was born in the same month as García Márquez and she recalled in 2002, by which time she was a widow with six children and living in the United States, that she and García Márquez fell in love "at first sight" and that their principal shared enthusiasm was the *boleros* then in vogue, snatches of which they would sing to one another during their romance.[47] Also unforgettable was Cecilia González Pizano, "who was no one's love but the muse of all the poetry addicts. She had a swift intelligence, personal charm and a free spirit in an old Conservative family, plus a supernatural memory for poetry."[48] Cecilia was called "the little One-Arm" ("La Manquita"), in that rather brutal Hispanic way, because she only had one hand and covered up its absence with a long sleeve. She was a pretty and vivacious blonde girl with whom Gabito constantly talked about poetry. Most boys assumed she was his girlfriend.

And there were other adventures, nocturnal escapades to the theatre, boys lowering others by knotted sheets to make their getaway in the dark for some illicit rendezvous. The school porter never seemed to catch anyone absconding and the boys concluded that he was their tacit accomplice. García Márquez struck up a relationship with an older woman, the wife of a physician, and during her husband's absences made nocturnal visits to her bedroom at the end of a labyrinth of rooms and corridors in one of Zipaquirá's old colonial houses. This experience, worthy of a story by Boccaccio, is recalled in the unforgettable scene early in *One Hundred Years of Solitude* in which the young José Arcadio has his first sexual experience, after feeling his way in the dark through a house full of sleeping bodies in hammocks.[49]

Carlos Martín knew all the leading poets of his generation and, a few months after his arrival, he invited the two most influential among them, Eduardo Carranza and Jorge Rojas, to speak at Zipaquirá. García Márquez and a friend had the honour of interviewing them in the great lounge of the colonial house Martín had rented in the main square of the town. This was his first contact with living literature at the highest level and he was at once delighted and embarrassed when Martín introduced him to the two celebrity visitors as "a great poet."[50] Unfortunately a magazine the boys founded, *La Gaceta Literaria*, became an improbable victim of national political developments and also García Márquez's first experience of the violence threatening the new Colombia that President López Pumarejo was trying to fashion. On 10 July 1944 López Pumarejo, two years into his second term, was kidnapped in the town of Pasto in a coup attempt supported by the arch-Conservative politician Laureano Gómez, known to Liberals as "the Monster." López Pumarejo, under increasing stress, would resign on 31 July 1945 and another Liberal, Alberto Lleras Camargo, would serve the last year of his term in a climate of increasing tension. Carlos Martín as headmaster had sent a telegram of support to the government palace some days after the attempted coup. Shortly afterwards, the Conservative Mayor of Zipaquirá arrived at the school with a police detachment and confiscated the entire first issue of the *Gaceta Literaria*, which had been specially printed at a workshop in Bogotá. A few days later the new rector was telephoned by the Minister of Education, summoned to his office, and asked to resign.

García Márquez returned to the classes of Señor Calderón Hermida and went on with his own reading. He has remarked that he found Freud's works as speculative and imaginative as those of Jules Verne,[51] and they inspired him to present a composition entitled "Obsessive Psychosis" ("Sicosis obsesiva"), written, ironically enough, in detention.[52] It was about a girl who turned into a butterfly, flew far away and underwent a series of extraordinary adventures. When García Márquez's classmates jeered at such pretentiousness the teacher hastened to support and encourage him and gave practical advice about the organization of his prose and the rhetorical instruments he might use. The story was passed around the school until it reached the school secretary who said, prophetically, that it reminded him of Kafka's "The Metamorphosis."

This is a striking detail because García Márquez has always said that he first heard of Kafka in Bogotá in 1947 and that the impact led directly to his first published stories.[53] Yet it seems he may have read Kafka at school. Interestingly, *The Double*, given him by Gómez Támara, is not only one of Dostoyevsky's strangest books, as the donor himself observed at the time, but also one of the least known. Someone who had read it, however, was Franz Kafka. The idea that we all have more than one personality, more than one identity, must have been extremely consoling and in every way therapeutic for a young man like García Márquez, who was much more troubled than he seemed, who had already been through quite serious emotional problems at his previous school and was now confronted not only with a much greater challenge to his confidence and sense of self in general but also with a need to respond to the dusty conventions of Bogotá as regards authority, taste and civilization. Señor Calderón later claimed that he told his talented pupil, who was thought by most observers at the time to be an even better graphic artist than writer, that he could become "the best novelist in Colombia."[54] Such moral support was surely priceless.

Despite his extra-curricular antics and only intermittent attention to his academic obligations, García Márquez's prestige in the school continued to grow. On the last day of 1944, at the end of his second year there, *El Tiempo*, Colombia's most important newspaper, would publish one of his poems in its literary supplement, under his pseudo-

nym, Javier Garcés. This has been a source of profound embarrassment to its author for almost sixty years but at the time it must surely
have seemed a wonderful piece of recognition for a seventeen-year-old
who was still two years away from completing secondary school.[55] The
poem, "Song," was dedicated to a friend, Lolita Porras, who had died
tragically not long before. It had an epigraph from a poem by Eduardo
Carranza, the leader of the Stone and Sky group, and began as follows:

SONG

"It is raining in this poem"
E.C.

It is raining. The afternoon
is a blade of cloud. Raining.
The afternoon is soaked
in your sadness.
At times the wind comes
with its song. At times . . .
I feel my soul pressed
against your absent voice.

Raining. And I'm thinking
of you. And dreaming.
No one will come this afternoon
to my grief, shut tight.
No one. Only your absence
that pains me hour by hour.
Tomorrow your presence
will return with the rose.

I think—the rain falls—
of your tender gaze.
Girl like fresh fruit,
joyful as a fiesta,
today your name is twilighting
here in my poem.[56]

García Márquez would judge of the verses he wrote during his
schooldays, "They were mere technical exercises without inspiration

or aspiration, to which I assigned no poetic value because they had not come out of my soul."[57] In fact a first reading of the poem—not to mention its subject—would surely suggest that the emotional charge is rather strong. The technical aspect, though promising, is admittedly derivative—it is a pastiche, and not a bad one, of 1920s Neruda—but surely secondary. The truth seems to be that García Márquez is embarrassed not only, in the most "poetic" of Latin American republics, by the wholly understandable technical shortcomings of his early poetic beginnings but also, and much more strongly, by the otherwise unexpressed emotions he felt when he was an adolescent.

His growing literary prestige, a continuation of his juvenile prowess in Barranquilla, must explain why García Márquez gave the ceremonial graduation speech on 17 November 1944 in which he bade farewell to the boys in the class two years above him. The chosen theme of the speech was friendship, one of the leitmotifs of his future life.

IN 1944 THE JOURNEY home took him only as far as Magangué. The García Márquez family had been happy and—so they thought—settled in Sucre but happiness was always a transient experience for Gabriel Eligio, who suddenly decided to move his reluctant dependants downriver to Magangué, a hot, sprawling, flat city, surrounded by marshes, on a promontory above the Magdalena, the most important river town between Barranquilla and Barrancabermeja and the principal road link between the Magdalena and the west of the country. There is reason to believe that Gabriel Eligio was fleeing the site of his own sexual misdemeanours and embarrassments, but this had not stopped him taking a punitive view of the misdeeds of his second son, Luis Enrique, who had been sent away to a reform school in Medellín for eighteen months.

It was in Magangué that Gabito's sisters remember meeting his future wife Mercedes Barcha. García Márquez himself has always claimed that she was nine when he met her, which would place their first meeting somewhere between November 1941 and November 1942—even before he left for Zipaquirá—and that he knew even then (at the age of fourteen) that he would marry her.[58] Mercedes herself, who claims to remember "almost nothing about the past," has confirmed that she first met her future husband when she was "just a little girl."[59] Now, in early 1945, he wrote a poem entitled "Morning Sonnet to an Incorporeal Schoolgirl" and there is good reason to assume that the schoolgirl in question was none other than Mercedes Barcha. She was just finishing her last year of primary school. The poem circulated both in Zipaquirá and Magangué and is another enthusiastic pastiche of the poetry of Neruda. The extant version is entitled simply "Girl" and is signed by "Javier Garcés":

GIRL

She greets me as she passes and the air
breathed from her early morning voice
blurs not the four-sided light of my window
'gainst its glass but my own breath, my very soul.

She is early like the morning,
as unbelievable as any story,
and as she cuts her way through the moment
the morning sheds drops of pure white blood.

If dressed in blue she goes to school,
none can tell whether she walks or flies,
so light she treads, so like the breeze

that in the morning blue no one can say
which of the three that pass may be the breeze,
which the girl and which the morning.[60]

If the sonnet is indeed for Mercedes it is one of the very few things García Márquez has ever said about her in public without a humorous or ironic edge to it.

He must have returned to school with mixed emotions in February 1945. He had taken to smoking up to forty or fifty cigarettes a day, a habit he would maintain for the next three decades.[61] During classes he would find frequent cause to take refuge in the lavatories and break time was anxiously awaited. He acted in part like a rebel let down by the system, and in part like a kind of *poète maudit* whom no system would ever satisfy. He began to affect boredom in all his classes except literature and found it almost intolerable to have to work at subjects that did not interest him. He has always expressed astonishment at his academic success and speculated that his teachers graded him for the presumed intelligence of his personality and not his actual achievements.

Despite his sense of alienation, his behaviour and record were such that he was one of three boys chosen to accompany the rector when he travelled to the National Palace in Bogotá to request funding from President Lleras Camargo, López Pumarejo's emergency replacement, for a study visit to the Costa. Lleras not only agreed but attended the school's graduation ceremony at the end of the year. García Márquez would get to know this consummate Liberal politician quite well in years to come and establish with him one of his curiously ambivalent relationships with the great and powerful of Bogotá. Certainly eighteen was a precocious age at which to have one's first audience with a president and one's first access to the seat of government. It was during this year that García Márquez made his most successful speech of all— and the only one he ever improvised. When the Second World War ended there was euphoria at the school and he was asked to say a few words. He declared that Franklin D. Roosevelt had been able, like the great Spanish hero the Cid, to "win victories even after his death." The phrase was celebrated not only in the school but throughout the city and García Márquez's oratorical reputation was further enhanced.[62]

In late 1945 he returned to Sucre. His father had closed the pharmacy in Magangué and returned for several months to his wandering ways, leaving Luisa, pregnant yet again (when she was not pregnant she was hardly let out of the house), to cope with her large family in a large rambling house. On his return he moved the family back to Sucre, to a different house a few blocks from the square, renounced pharmacy and devoted himself full-time to homeopathy. The tenth child, Alfredo ("Cuqui"), had been born in February and was effectively being brought up by Margot.

Gabito now allowed himself to be thoroughly led astray by his good-natured but incorrigible younger brother. He immediately joined Luis Enrique's musical group, stayed out all night, frequented the local brothels and spent his share of the money the band earned drinking riotously for the first time in his life. Over Christmas, instead of making his usual contribution to the rival floats during the end-of-year festivities, he disappeared to the nearby town of Majagual for ten days and lived it up in a whorehouse: "It was all the fault of María Alejandrina Cervantes, an extraordinary woman whom I met the first night and over whom I lost my head in the longest and wildest binge of my life."[63]

After many sighs and silences, Luisa finally asked her eldest son what was going on and he replied: "I've had it up to here, that's what's going on." "What, with us?" "With everything." He said he was sick of his life, sick of school, sick of the expectations placed upon him. This was not an answer his mother could pass on to Gabriel Eligio so she processed it for a while and finally suggested that the solution was for Gabito, like almost all other ambitious young men in Latin America in those days, to study law. "After all," she said shrewdly, "it's a good training for writing, and people have said that you could be a good writer." According to his memoir, Gabito's first response to his mother on the subject was negative: "If you're going to be a writer it has to be one of the greats and they don't make them any more." The reader is confronted by the astonishing realization that, although the young man had not yet read Joyce or Faulkner, he was not interested in being the kind of writer these poor twentieth-century also-rans might represent: in his immature heart of hearts he wanted to be Dante or Cervantes! Luisa was not deterred by his demurral and over the next few days she achieved a brilliant negotiation without father and son even discussing the issue face to face: Gabriel Eligio accepted, albeit tragic of demeanour, that his son would not follow him into medicine; and Gabito accepted that he would not only finish off the baccalaureate but would also go on to study law at the National University. Thus were a major teenage rebellion and a disastrous family crisis averted.[64]

García Márquez, now something of a sexual reprobate, must have been astonished, as Christmas approached, to find that the incorporeal schoolgirl from Magangué had moved to Sucre. Her full name was Mercedes Raquel Barcha Pardo, the child, like him, of a pharmacist, one whom Gabriel Eligio had known for many years since he was a young man travelling the rivers and jungles of the Magdalena basin in the early 1920s. She had been born on 6 November 1932. Like Gabito she was also the eldest child, mysteriously pretty, with high cheekbones and dark oblique eyes, a long slim neck and an elegant bearing. She lived in the main square, opposite Gabito's good friend Cayetano Gentile, who in turn lived next to the house the García Márquezes had lived in before their move to Magangué.

Mercedes's mother Raquel Pardo López was from a cattle ranching family, as indeed was her father; but he, Demetrio Barcha Velilla, was of partly Middle Eastern stock, though he had been born in Corozal and was a Catholic. Demetrio's father, Elías Barcha Facure, hailed from Alexandria, probably out of Lebanon: hence, presumably, Mercedes's "stealthy beauty, that of a serpent of the Nile."[65] Elías had acquired Colombian nationality on 23 May 1932, six months before

Mercedes was born. He lived to be almost one hundred and read people's stars in coffee grains. "My grandfather was a pure Egyptian," she told me. "He used to bounce me on his knee and sing to me in Arabic. He always dressed in white linen, with a black tie, a gold watch and a straw hat like Maurice Chevalier. He died when I was about seven."[66]

Mercedes Raquel, named after her mother and grandmother, was the eldest of the six children of Demetrio and Raquel. The family moved to Majagual after she was born, then back to Magangué and finally to nearby Sucre. Demetrio had various businesses, including general provisions, but like Gabriel Eligio García, he specialized in pharmacy. Mercedes had just spent her first year at the Franciscan convent school of the Sacred Heart in Mompox, across the river from Magangué. It was only one block from the famous octagonal tower of the church of Santa Barbara in the main square of what is perhaps Colombia's most perfectly preserved small colonial city.[67]

In Magangué a childhood friend told me, "Mercedes always attracted a lot of attention, she had a good figure, tall and slim. Though to be fair, her sister María Rosa was even prettier. But Mercedes always got more compliments."[68] She would help in the family pharmacy in those days and the García Márquez children would see her often when they were running errands for their father. They were all aware, then and later, that Mercedes had a strong sense of herself and a quiet authority. Gabito, who rarely went about anything directly, would often hang around talking to Mercedes's father, Demetrio Barcha: he always preferred older men and Demetrio had the great virtue of being a Liberal, despite his friendship with Gabriel Eligio. Mercedes herself has always insisted that she was blissfully unaware of her lovesick admirer's intentions. Usually she would not even acknowledge Gabito's presence and her father would look over his glasses as she stalked past and gently reprove her: "Say hello." She told Gabito that her father always said that "the prince who will marry me has not yet been born." She told me that for many years she thought that Gabito was in love with her father!

Over the course of that Christmas vacation, 1945–6, he had an opportunity to get closer to this cool, distant girl when they coincided at parties. In *Chronicle of a Death Foretold* the narrator recalls, "Many people knew that in the heat of one party I asked Mercedes Barcha to marry me, when she had scarcely finished primary school, as she herself reminded me when we did marry fourteen years later."[69] Days after the party he saw her in the street walking two small children and she laughed, "Yes, they're mine." He took this grown-up joke, from such an enigmatic young person, as a secret sign that they were on the same wavelength. It would keep him going for years.

García Márquez's return to Zipaquirá for the final year began on a glamorous note. He had undertaken to somehow get his madcap friend José Palencia enrolled at the National College, Palencia having failed the final grade at his school in Cartagena. In return Palencia bought him an air ticket and they flew to Bogotá in an unpressurized DC-3, a journey which took four hours instead of eighteen days.[70] Palencia rented a large room in the best house in the square, with a view of the cathedral from his window. This would provide García Márquez with a useful bolthole in which to enjoy his senior status as a twelfth grader. Palencia bought him a dark suit to express his gratitude. García Márquez's embarrassment at his dishevelled, hand-me-down clothes, which had dogged him throughout his schooldays, was at an end.

Early in this last year at school García Márquez reached the age of nineteen. He was a published poet, with considerable prestige among his classmates, whom he would regularly amuse with comical or satirical verses, with the poems written especially for their girlfriends, or with the caricatures he drew of his classmates and teachers. Even at this age he was still prey to nightmares which terrified his dorm mates and teachers almost as much as himself and for this final year he was moved to a smaller dormitory where fewer people would be disturbed by his shrieks.

The whole of Colombia was now on edge. The Conservatives had predictably defeated the divided Liberal Party in the national elections and by the time García Márquez graduated in November 1946 they were already taking sinister revenge on their political enemies and their supporters, particularly in the rural areas where the peasants had been given some reason to hope that land reform might be on the political agenda. That was never going to happen. The Conservative rollback was given an added tinge of hysteria by the growing popularity of the ever more strident Jorge Eliécer Gaitán, now the undisputed leader of the Liberals and already their proclaimed candidate for the 1950 elections. The *Violencia*, the horrific wave of violence that would kill a quarter of a million Colombians from the late 1940s to the 1960s, is usually dated from April 1948 but it was well under way during García Márquez's last years in Zipaquirá.

Nervous about his examinations and desperate to carry out his promise to his mother, García Márquez eventually achieved the excellent result in the final examination that his talent evidently merited. But he was fortunate. During the revision period before the exam he and Palencia stayed out all night and got rolling drunk. They were in serious danger of expulsion and were suspended from taking the examinations, which meant that they would not be able to graduate as "bachelors" for another year. However, the principal, realizing that it would be embarrassing and anyway regrettable if his best student were to end his career in this way, reversed the decision and personally escorted the two delinquents to take the examinations belatedly in Bogotá.[71] Later García Márquez would acknowledge, "Everything I ever learned was thanks to the baccalaureate I took in Zipaquirá."[72]

So home went the hero, still convinced that his achievements were one large confidence trick, and therefore somehow lacking in confidence for that very reason; yet also dimly aware that to hoodwink everyone as he felt he had done probably meant that he was even more talented than they all thought he was; determined, finally, despite all his feelings of guilt, to go on deceiving the family, to pay lip-service to the project of getting a law degree whilst in reality following his own chosen path through life.

Quite soon after the return to Sucre from Magangué Gabriel Eligio, while renting yet another house some distance from the town square, had set about building a house of his own, an ambitious one-storey utopia among the mango trees, some fifty yards from the Mojana, on its northern bank. Could it be he had finally resolved to put down roots? The family would come to call their new home "La Casa Quinta," the country house, but Gabito, for whom there was only one house in the whole wide world, would call it "the hospital," because his father had his consultancy and laboratory there and because it was painted white; and because he begrudged the man even the smallest of achievements.

Yet the new house was surprisingly large by Sucre standards, though it hardly compared with the relatively majestic residences in the town square. Jaime García Márquez remembers a fine house, though with no electricity, which there had been in Aracataca; and no running water or proper sanitation (there had been a fully functioning septic tank in Aracataca). The family used oil lamps, which were always swarming with tropical insects. Snakes were often found coiled on the window sills at night. A neighbour, Miss Juana, used to cook and clean, play with the children and tell them terrifying stories, inspired by local legends.

There had been another big change in the family circumstances, as Ligia recalls: "Grandma Tranquilina and Aunt Pa, my mother's half-sister, came to live at the new house with us. Aunt Pa could predict the droughts and rains, because she knew all the secrets of nature, learned from the Guajiro Indians. We all loved her because she helped bring us up. She's the one who told me all the stories about the family ancestors . . . When our grandmother died, our mother made a beautiful garden and planted roses and daisies to take to her tomb."[73] García Márquez recalls that Tranquilina was blind and demented and would not undress while the radio was on because she imagined that the people attached to the voices she heard might be watching her.[74]

There is, undoubtedly, a poignant story relating to the new house. Gabito was especially embarrassed by the celebrations surrounding his return to Sucre late in 1946. Here was his father, with whom he had a difficult relationship, and whom he was intending to deceive and disappoint in the immediate future and for the long term, at a moment of great mutual triumph: Gabito was a "bachelor," a rare achievement in those days even among the middle classes; and Gabriel Eligio had built a fine new house and was determined to remind everyone of that achievement at the same time as he celebrated his son's academic success. Aida Rosa recalls, "I'll never forget the party Dad put on in Sucre when Gabito graduated from high school. Don Gabriel Eligio really went to town. He invited the whole of Sucre, had a pig killed, there were drinks for everyone and we danced all night."[75]

García Márquez spent as much time away from the family as possible during this transitional vacation and ended it as soon as he could. He had completed his secondary schooling and had accumulated, although he could not have guessed it, as much formal education as he was going to need in life. He was still not sure what he was going to do but what lay ahead was a return to the lugubrious Andean city of Bogotá and years of study for a university degree and a profession from which he felt profoundly alienated in advance and which he hoped never to have to practise.

5

The University Student and the *Bogotazo*

1947-1948

GABRIEL GARCÍA MÁRQUEZ enrolled at the National University of Colombia on 25 February 1947. This meant four or five years in Bogotá, which must have seemed a depressing prospect indeed for a young man who already knew that he hated the place. The epic journey from Sucre to the highland capital by river steamer and railway was not the fiesta filled with anticipation which he had experienced on previous occasions. Colombia itself was in a state of grim apprehension, with a minority Conservative government newly elected and determined to hold on to power, and the Liberal majority in a paroxysm of frustration at its party's miscalculation in allowing two candidates, Turbay and Gaitán, to go forward against the Conservative Ospina Pérez.

Gabriel Eligio had wanted his son to be a doctor; and if not a doctor, a priest or a lawyer. He had sent him to study in the capital city for social distinction, and for financial gain. With the Conservatives in power there would surely be fortunes to be made. Literature was just a risky sideshow. Gabito had managed to avoid a showdown for the time being; but the much-debated law degree was now a pretext and Gabito would be forced at last to become the liar his father had always said he was.

Set in a mountain paradise of salt, gold and emeralds, the mythical home of El Dorado, Bogotá was founded on 6 August 1538 by the Andalusian explorer Gonzalo Jiménez de Quesada. He named the city

Santa Fe. It was known first as Santa Fe de Bacatá, then Santa Fe de Bogotá. For many decades the Santa Fe was dropped but was briefly restored late in the twentieth century, as if the religious title might somehow redeem the city and raise it once more above the savage country over which it presides from its emerald green throne. Historically Bogotá has always been right, the rest of the nation always wrong; yet at 8,000 feet above sea level, this often cold and usually rainy city makes a strange capital for such a varied, essentially tropical country. In 1947 it had a population of 700,000 inhabitants: the *cachacos* (which could be translated as fops or dandies).[1]

Bogotá has traditionally considered itself the home of the "purest" Spanish spoken anywhere in the world, not excluding Spain itself.[2] In the 1940s almost all the politicians of Colombia were lawyers and many of them, particularly the Liberal lawyers, taught in the National University. The new university city, a landmark in Art Deco architecture, opened in 1940 and more or less complete by 1946, stood on the very outskirts of Bogotá, with the great savannah beyond. In García Márquez's time there were more than four thousand students, half of whom were from the provinces. The political right considered the university a hotbed of communism.

The new student had found a boarding house in the former Florián Street, now Carrera 8, near the corner of Avenue Jiménez de Quesada; a house where numerous *costeño* students lived. Florián Street was one of the oldest and best-known in the city, running parallel to the best-known of all: "Séptima," Seventh Avenue. García Márquez's *pensión* was perhaps three hundred yards from the intersection of Seventh and Jiménez de Quesada, generally considered the strategic centre of the city and even exalted by some local patriots as the "best street corner in the world."

Up on the second floor of his boarding house García Márquez shared a room with a number of *costeño* students, including the irrepressible José Palencia. The rooms were comfortable though not luxurious but despite the economical cost of bed and board García Márquez found it hard to get by. He would always be short of money: "I always had the feeling I was short of the last five centavos." He has never made too much of the more painful aspects of this theme but despite Gabriel Eligio's exertions, which meant that his family were always above the peasants and proletarians, poverty and its humiliations were a constant feature of Gabito's childhood and youth. And beyond.

His anguished recollections about this time remind one of Kafka's comment that studying law was "like living, in an intellectual sense, on sawdust, sawdust which had moreover already been chewed for me in thousands of other people's mouths."[3] The teachers included an ex-president's son, Alfonso López Michelsen, himself a future president. In that first year García Márquez would fail statistics and demography and scrape through constitutional law, which he took with López Michelsen, who said to me forty-five years later, "No, he wasn't a good student. But because of my *costeño* family background all the students from Padilla and Magdalena would take my course; they knew I was sure to pass them."[4]

A classmate, Luis Villar Borda, recalls, "I met Gabo in the very first days. There were maybe a hundred new students in law—only three of them women—organized in two alphabetical groups. Gabo was in the first and I was in the second. I was very interested in the subject but Gabo never was. He started to miss a lot of classes quite early on. We used to talk about literature: Dos Passos, Hemingway, Faulkner, Hesse, Mann and the Russians. Colombian literature hardly at all, just a few poets like Barba Jacob, De Greiff, Luis Carlos López. At midday we would move back to the city centre and sit in the cafés, which is where we all studied. If you lived in a *pensión* there was nowhere to work. The café owners would let the students take over a corner just like the regular customers."[5]

Sometimes García Márquez and his *costeño* friends would organize impromptu Saturday night dances. Then on Sunday mornings at nine o'clock the young *costeños* would walk up to Seventh Avenue and 14th Street to the radio station that broadcast "The *Costeño* Hour" and they would dance outside in the street. By now García Márquez was a proud representative of his culture and compensated for his poverty by dressing in an even more garish manner than he had started to do at the Colegio San José. It was the first great era of "Latin" music and García Márquez lived it from the inside.[6]

He also made friends among the uptight *cachacos*, some of whom would play an important role in his future. One of them was Gonzalo Mallarino, whose mother would develop a soft spot for this sad little *costeño* Chaplin figure.[7] Others were Villar Borda, Camilo Torres, who would later achieve continental fame as a martyred guerrilla priest,[8] and one of the great buddies of his life, Plinio Apuleyo Mendoza, son of a leading politician from Boyacá, Plinio Mendoza Neira—by then perhaps Gaitán's closest political ally—and a few years younger than García Márquez.

Some of García Márquez's contemporaries contemplated him, it seems, with a mild dose of pity. Plinio Mendoza says many viewed him with contempt, as a "lost cause." He recalls the day Villar Borda introduced him in the Café Asturias to a young *costeño*, who "made his way between the crowded tables and black hats, stunning us with the lightning flash of his cream-coloured tropical suit." But he was also shocked by the newcomer's general demeanour and behaviour. When the waitress approached the table the *costeño* gazed at her, all of her, and whispered suggestively: "Tonight?," after which he placed his hand on her posterior. She pushed him away and flounced off in theatrical disgust.[9]

Behind the colourful costumes, the *costeño mamagallismo* (piss-taking),[10] and the adolescent pride ("Problems, me?" "Lonely, me?"), García Márquez was a deeply solitary young man with very contradictory feelings about his self-worth. His life now, despite the friendships, was one of loneliness, alienation, disorientation, and a lack of vocation. But also defiance: it was to protect himself that he played the effervescent *costeño*. Fleeing his solitude on Sundays, he would take endless tram rides through the grey, monotonous city, reading and reflecting.[11] Sometimes he would take up an invitation from Gonzalo Mallarino, also a friend of both Camilo Torres and Villar Borda. Mallarino had been born only four days after García Márquez, of illustrious parentage. He told me: "The Bogotá weekends could be very long for a stranger. Gabo often used to visit me at home on a Sunday. We would always have chocolate and *arepas* [corn-cakes]. My mother, who was widowed when I was nine, felt sorry for him; he always seemed lonely to her, and she was always kind to him. She was from the provinces, like he was, and they instinctively knew how to talk to one another."[12]

From the very start of his university studies, as both Mallarino and Villar Borda perceived, García Márquez, behind his protective *costeño* persona, was developing his literary vocation, even if he was reluctant to admit to such ambition in case he failed. Certainly between the attractions of the law and literature it was no contest. He was a fish out of water with his long anarchic hair, his tatty coloured trousers and his bizarre checked shirts, rebelling self-consciously with every awkward move he made.

Villar Borda and Camilo Torres edited a literary page called "University Life" ("La Vida Universitaria"), a Tuesday supplement of the newspaper *La Razón*, which published two of García Márquez's "Stone and Sky"–style poems.[13] "Poem from a Seashell" ("Poema desde un caracol") appeared on 22 June, only a few weeks before Torres took the fateful decision to abandon the university and become a priest.[14] Two of its stanzas read:

VIII

For my sea was the sea eternal,
sea of childhood, unforgettable,
suspended from our dream
like a dove in the air . . .

XII

It was the sea of our first love
in those autumnal eyes . . .
One day I wished to see that sea
—that sea of childhood—I was too late.[15]

It was a poem by a boy profoundly aware not only that he has lost his childhood but also that he has lost his other homeland, the Caribbean coast, the land of sea and sun.

Something like Kafka was what García Márquez was looking for in that ghostly highland city and Kafka is what he eventually found. One afternoon a *costeño* friend lent him a copy of *The Metamorphosis*, translated by an Argentine writer called Jorge Luis Borges.[16] García Márquez went back to the boarding house, up to his room, took off his shoes and lay on his bed. He read the first line: "As Gregor Samsa awoke one morning from uneasy dreams he found himself transformed in his bed into a gigantic insect." Mesmerized, García Márquez recalls saying to himself: "Shit, that's just the way my grandmother talked!"[17]

Kafka undoubtedly opened wide his imagination (including his ability to imagine himself as a writer) and showed him for the long term that even the most fantastic episodes can be narrated in a matter-of-fact way. But what García Márquez first took from Kafka seems to have been something rather different from what he has said in retrospect. First, evidently, Kafka addressed the alienation of urban existence; but beneath the surface, suffusing everything he wrote, was his terror of another authority, his father: his simultaneous loathing and veneration of his tyrannical progenitor.

García Márquez had read Dostoyevsky's *The Double*, set in an even more repressive St.Petersburg, four years before, on his arrival in

Bogotá. Kafka's vision is a direct descendant of that novel and its impact on the young writer is not in doubt. García Márquez had discovered European modernism; more, he had discovered that far from being merely complex and pretentious, the innovations of modernism had emerged from the spirit of the age, from the structure of reality as currently perceived, and could be directly relevant to him—even in his remote capital city in Latin America.

The protagonists of both *The Double* and *The Metamorphosis* are victims of a split personality, characters who are hypersensitive and terrified of authority, and who, by internalizing the distortions of the outside world, conclude that it is they themselves, finally, who are sick, deformed, perverted and out of place. Many young people are beset by conflicting impulses and defensive–aggressive perceptions of their abilities and their relations with others; but the gap between García Márquez's self-confidence, bordering on unusual and sometimes startling arrogance (he was the Colonel's grandson and clever with it), and his simultaneous sense of insecurity and inferiority (he was the quack doctor's son and had been abandoned by him but maybe took after him), is undoubtedly unusual and it created a dynamic that allowed him to develop a hidden ambition which would burn within him like a fierce, sustained flame.

The very next day after reading *The Metamorphosis* García Márquez sat down to write a story, which he would entitle "The Third Resignation." It was his first work as a person prepared to think of himself as an author with something serious to offer. It already sounds something like "García Márquez" and is strikingly ambitious, profoundly subjective, suffused with absurdity, solitude and death. It initiates what will be a constant in García Márquez: building a story around the initial motif of an unburied corpse.[18] Eventually his readers would discover that García Márquez has lived with three interconnected but also impossibly contradictory primordial terrors: the terror of dying and being buried oneself (or, worse, being buried alive); the terror of having to bury others; and the terror of any person remaining unburied. "A dead person can live happily with his irremediable situation," declares the narrator of this first story, a person who is unsure whether he is living, or dead, or both at the same time or successively. "But a living person cannot resign himself to being buried alive. Yet his limbs would not respond to his call. He could not express himself, and that was what terrified him; it was the greatest terror of his life and of his death. That they would bury him alive."[19]

By way of compensation García Márquez's story appears to propose some new American telluric—historical genealogy founded on the conception of a family tree:

> He had been felled like some twenty-five-year-old tree . . . Perhaps later he would feel a slight nostalgia; the nostalgia of not being a formal, anatomical corpse, but an imaginary, abstract corpse, living only in the hazy memory of his relatives . . . Then he would know that he would rise up through the blood vessels of an apple and find himself being eaten by the hunger of a child some autumn morning. He would know then—and this thought really did make him sad—that he had lost his unity.[20]

Evidently the horror of being trapped in a house, between life and death, as in a coffin (as in memory, perhaps), is here mitigated by the idea of one's lost individuality fusing into a tree as symbol both of nature and history (the generational family tree). The poignancy of such a genealogical impulse in a young man separated soon after birth from his natural mother and father and the brothers and sisters who would follow him requires no elaboration. And there is no need to have a qualification in psychoanalysis to question whether this young writer did not unconsciously feel, as he looked back on his early life, that his parents had buried him alive in the house at Aracataca; and that his real self was buried inside a second self, the new identity that he had had to build, Hamlet-like, to protect himself from his true feelings about his mother and his perhaps murderous feelings about the usurper, Gabriel Eligio, who belatedly claimed to be his father—when he, Gabito, knew perfectly well that his real father was Colonel Nicolás Márquez, the man who, admired and respected by all who knew him, had presided benignly over his early years. And then disappeared. There follows what may either be a piece of literary bluster (a form of wish-fulfilment) or a genuine sense that the writer has achieved wisdom (and "resignation"?): "All that terrible reality did not give him any anxiety. Quite the opposite, he was happy there, alone in his solitude."

Clumsy though the story is, it has a curiously hypnotic effect and is narrated with an unmistakable confidence that is more than just literary, and a resolution surprising in a novice writer. The ending is pure García Márquez:

> Resigned, he will hear the last prayers, the last phrases mumbled in Latin and clumsily responded by the altar boys. The cold of the cemetery's earth and bones will penetrate to his own bones

and may dissipate somewhat that "smell." Perhaps—who knows!—the imminence of that moment will force him out of that lethargy. When he feels himself swimming in his own sweat, in a thick, viscous liquid, as he swam before he was born in his mother's womb. Perhaps at that moment he will be alive.

But by then he will be so resigned to dying that he may die of resignation.[21]

Readers of *One Hundred Years of Solitude*, *The Autumn of the Patriarch* and *The General in His Labyrinth*, written twenty, twenty-five and forty years later, will recognize the tone, the themes and the literary devices. It is, palpably, and contradictorily (given the morbid nature of the narrative voice), a bid for authority.

On 22 August, a week or two after he had written this story, he read in Eduardo Zalamea Borda's daily column, "The City and the World," in *El Espectador*, that Zalamea Borda was "anxious to hear from new poets and storytellers, who are unknown or ignored due to the lack of an adequate and just publication of their works."[22] Zalamea Borda, a leftist sympathizer, was one of the most respected of newspaper columnists. García Márquez sent his story in. Two weeks later, to his joy and stupefaction, he was sitting in the Molino café when he saw the title of his piece covering a whole page of the "Weekend" supplement. Flushed with excitement, he rushed out to buy a copy—to discover as usual that he was "short of the last five centavos." So he went back to the boarding house, appealed to a friend, and out they went to buy the paper—*El Espectador*, Saturday 13 September 1947. There on page twelve was "The Third Resignation" by Gabriel García Márquez, with an illustration by the artist Hernán Merino.

He was euphoric, inspired. Six weeks later, on 25 October, *El Espectador* published another of his stories, "Eva Is Inside Her Cat" ("Eva está dentro de su gato"), again on the theme of death and subsequent reincarnations, about a woman, Eva, who, obsessed with the desire to eat not an apple but an orange, decides to transmigrate through the body of her pet cat, only to find herself, three thousand years later, trapped—buried—in a new and confusing world. She is a beautiful woman, desperate to escape the attentions of men, a woman whose physical allure has begun to pain her like a cancer tumour. She has become aware that her arteries are teeming with tiny insects:

She knew that they came from back there, that all who bore her surname had to bear them, had to suffer them as she did when insomnia held unconquerable sway until dawn. It was those very insects who painted that bitter expression, that unconsolable sadness on the faces of her forebears. She had seen them looking out of their extinguished existence, out of their ancient portraits, victims of that same anguish . . .[23]

Both the genealogically obsessive *One Hundred Years of Solitude* and its primitive version, "The House" ("La casa"), soon to be conceived (perhaps already conceived), can be divined in this remarkable passage.

Only three days after the publication of this second story his unexpected literary patron announced in his daily column the arrival of a new literary talent upon the national scene, one who was in his first year as a student and not yet twenty-one. Zalamea declared unequivocally: "In Gabriel García Márquez we are seeing the birth of a remarkable writer."[24] One side effect of the confidence being placed in him was that García Márquez felt ever more justified in the neglect of his studies and in his obsessive love of reading and writing. More than half a century later the world-famous writer would comment that his first stories were "inconsequential and abstract, some absurd, and none based on real feelings."[25] Once again a reverse interpretation suggests itself: that he hated his poems and early stories precisely because they *were* "based on real feelings" and that later he learned to cover up—but not entirely suppress—the callow romanticism and emotionalism which left him exposed in all his vulnerability and might later give him away. It may also be the case that he is unwilling to give Bogotá the credit for his having become a writer.[26]

García Márquez stayed in Bogotá for the Christmas 1947 vacation. It was expensive to remain in the *pensión* but it was more expensive to find the fare to return to Sucre. Mercedes remained oblivious to his overtures. Besides, his grandmother was dead and his mother was just about to have yet another baby. Above all, though, despite having scraped through the examinations, failing only statistics and demography, he knew by now that he was not going to dedicate himself to the law and he was reluctant to confront Gabriel Eligio on this matter. The success of his first two stories suggested that there might be another path through life for him and he preferred to make the most of his perhaps temporary independence.

It was probably during this vacation that he began his next story, "The Other Side of Death" ("La otra costilla de la muerte"). If the first story was a meditation on one's own death, this was more a reflection on the death of others (or perhaps on the death of one's own other, one's double, in this case a brother). Appropriately, therefore, the narrative voice alternates modernist-style between a "he" and an "I." Again we are implicitly in a city but now the themes of the twin, the double, identity, the mirror (including that internal mirror, the consciousness) predominate. This brother, who had died of cancer, and of whom the narrator has a mortal terror, is now metamorphosed into another body

> that was coming from beyond his, that had been sunken with him in the liquid night of the maternal womb and was climbing up with him through the branches of an ancient genealogy; that was with him in the blood of his four pairs of great-grandparents and that came from way back, from the beginning of the world, sustaining with its weight, with its mysterious presence, the whole universal balance ... his other brother who had been born and shackled to his heel and who came tumbling along generation after generation, night after night, from kiss to kiss, from love to love, descending through arteries and testicles until he arrived, as on a night voyage, at the womb of his recent mother.[27]

This genealogical, dynastic obsession and the parallel exploration of the entire universe (time, space, matter, spirit, idea; life, death, burial, corruption, metamorphosis) is a structure of thought and feeling which, once explicitly explored and elaborated, will apparently disappear from García Márquez's work but will in fact become implicit and its manifestations used sparingly, strategically, for maximum effect. This first García Márquez, qua literary persona, is anguished, hypersensitive, hypochondriac—Kafkaesque: far from his later, carefully constructed narrative identity, which will be closer to that of, say, Cervantes. Apparently with very little help from Colombian or other Latin American writers—the best-known of whom he appears hardly to have read—the early García Márquez attacks the essential Latin American questions of genealogy (*estar*, existence, history) and identity (*ser*, essence, myth). They make up, without doubt, the essential Latin American problematic of that era: genealogy is inevitably a crucial matter in a continent that has no satisfactory myth of origin, where everything is up for grabs. This García Márquez has not yet got on to the question of legitimacy (which is what is *really* tormenting him and is certainly implicit here). Nevertheless, this narrator is also, clearly, a problem *unto himself*.

The long vacation eventually came to an end and things finally looked up. At the start of the new university year in 1948 Luis Enrique arrived in Bogotá, in theory to continue his secondary education; in practice he took up a job with Colgate-Palmolive that Gabito had secured for him and then devoted himself to the usual hell-raising in his spare time. By now their Uncle Juanito (Juan de Dios), following the death of his mother, Tranquilina, had moved to Bogotá to work for the national bureaucracy. Luis Enrique brought with him a secret present which he was supposed to have saved for Gabito's twenty-first birthday on 6 March, but when his brother and his friends told him at the airport that they had no money with which to celebrate, Luis Enrique slyly revealed that the surprise inside his package was a new typewriter: "The next step was a visit to the pawnshop in the centre of Bogotá, and the guy opening the case, turning the handle and pulling out a piece of paper. I remember he looked at it and said, 'This must be for one of you.' One of our friends took it and read it out loud: 'Congratulations. We're proud of you. The future is yours. Gabriel and Luisa, Sucre, 6 March 1948.' Then the pawnshop assistant asked, 'How much do you need?' and the owner of the typewriter replied, 'As much as you can give me.' "[28]

With Luis Enrique's new income and some additional money that Gabito himself was earning by providing newspaper illustrations through a friend, the standard of living improved markedly in the following weeks—adventures involving wine, women and song ensued—and Luis Enrique renewed his vagabonds' alliance with the madcap José Palencia. Meanwhile, Gabito, by now the most prestigious of the university's many students with pretensions to literary status, was missing even more classes as he devoted himself ever more zealously to reading and writing literature, including reading another modernist masterwork, James Joyce's *Ulysses*.

At that very moment political storm clouds were gathering rapidly over Colombia and heading directly for Bogotá. Jorge Eliécer Gaitán, an outstanding lawyer who had imbibed a potent political cocktail offered by the Mexican Revolution, Marxism and Mussolini, was the most charismatic politician in twentieth-century Colombian history and one of the most successful political leaders in Latin America in an era of populist politics. He was the hero of the rising proletarian classes and of many lower-middle-class inhabitants of the rapidly growing cities. García Márquez knew that he had first come to national attention in 1929 when he took up the case of the banana workers massacred in Ciénaga in December 1928. García Márquez did not know that among his key informants was Father Francisco Angarita, the man who had baptized him in Aracataca, and possibly also Colonel Nicolás Márquez. Gaitán had grown ever stronger despite the electoral setback caused by his own division of the Liberal Party, had soon captured the leadership and began to conduct a style of politics never before seen in one of the most conservative republics in Latin America. Some called him "The Tongue," others "The Throat," such was the power of his oratory and of the voice that delivered it. García Márquez has almost never spoken of Gaitán in public interviews until very recently, most likely because his own politics have always been well to the left of any Latin American populism since the early 1950s and also in part, no doubt, because in April 1948, although instinctively attached to the Liberals, his political consciousness was still largely undeveloped.

In April 1948 the ninth Pan-American Conference was taking place in the centre of Bogotá and the Organization of American States was in the process of being set up at the behest of the United States. On Friday the 9th, just after 1 p.m., Gabriel García Márquez was sitting down to lunch in his boarding house in Florián Street with Luis Enrique and some of his *costeño* friends. Jorge Eliécer Gaitán was at that moment leaving his law office to walk down Seventh Avenue to lunch with his Liberal Party colleague Plinio Mendoza Neira and other associates. As he reached number 14–55, between Avenida Jiménez and 14th Street, an unemployed worker called Juan Roa Sierra walked across from the Black Cat café and fired at him three or four times from point-blank range. Gaitán fell to the pavement, just a few yards from "the best street corner in the world." It was five past one. Before they lifted him from the ground, sixteen-year-old Plinio Apuleyo Mendoza, who had come to meet his father, bent over and gazed with horror into the dying leader's face. Gaitán was rushed to the Central Clinic in a private car and pronounced dead soon after arrival, to the inconsolable dismay of the large crowd that gathered outside the clinic.

That was the murder. Now came the *Bogotazo*.[29] A wave of fury and hysteria swept through the city immediately. Bogotá was in uproar. An afternoon of riots, lootings and killings ensued. The Liberal mob took it for granted that the Conservatives were behind the assassination: within minutes Roa had been murdered and his battered body was dragged naked through the streets towards the government palace. The centre of Bogotá, all of it the very symbol of Colombia's reactionary political system, began to burn.[30]

García Márquez ran out immediately to the site of the murder but Gaitán's dying body had already been rushed to the hospital—weeping men and women were soaking their handkerchiefs in the fallen leader's blood—and Roa's corpse had already been dragged away. Luis Villar Borda remembers meeting García Márquez between two and three o'clock in the afternoon just a few steps from where Gaitán had fallen: "I was very surprised to see him. 'You've never been a fan of Gaitán,' I said. 'No,' he said, 'but they've burned down my *pensión* and I've lost all my stories.'"[31] (This much-exaggerated tale would gain mythical status down the years.) During this same excursion García Márquez encountered an uncle, the law professor Carlos H. Pareja, in 12th Street as he hastened back to finish his lunch in the—still intact—*pensión*. Pareja stopped his young nephew in the street and urged him to hurry to the university and organize the students on behalf of the Liberal uprising. García Márquez reluctantly set off but changed his mind as soon as Pareja was out of sight and made his way back through the chaos—Bogotá was now a mortally dangerous place—to the *pensión* on Florián.

Luis Enrique and the other *costeños* were having a kind of apocalyptic celebration. Behind their din, on the radio, Uncle Carlos could already be heard, together with the writer Jorge Zalamea (destined to become, like his first cousin Eduardo Zalamea Borda, another significant figure in García Márquez's life), both urging the Colombian people to rise against the dastardly Conservatives who had assassinated the country's greatest political leader and only hope for its future. Pareja, whose own radical bookstore was a victim of the flames, thundered that "the Conservatives will pay for Gaitán's life with many other lives."[32] Gabito, Luis Enrique and their friends heard his call to arms on the *pensión* radio but they did not answer the appeal.

Not far away another young Latin American aged twenty-one was also beside himself, but with joy and excitement. Fidel Castro was a Cuban student leader who had travelled to Bogotá as part of a delegation taking part in a student congress set up in opposition to the Pan-American Conference. Castro forgot all about the Congress of Latin American Students and took to the streets, attempting to impose some sort of revolutionary logic upon the violently erratic actions of the popular uprising. Only two days before, he had interviewed the now martyred leader in his office in Carrera 7 and had apparently impressed the Colombian politician. Incredibly, they had agreed to meet again at 2 p.m. on 9 April: the name Fidel Castro was found pencilled in Gaitán's appointment book for that day. Little wonder the Colombian Conservative government and right-wing press were soon claiming that Castro was involved either in the plot to murder Gaitán

or in the conspiracy to subvert the Pan-American Conference and provoke an uprising, or both. At times, Castro must have been no more
than a couple of hundred yards from his future friend García Márquez.[33] In retrospect the *Bogotazo* would be as crucial to Castro's understanding of revolutionary politics as later events in Guatemala in 1954
would be to his future comrade Che Guevara.[34]

As Castro began to organize for a revolution that never came, García Márquez sat mourning the loss of his typewriter—the pawnshop
had been looted—and rehearsing his explanation for his parents. However, when smoke began to waft through the walls of the boarding
house from the burning Cundinamarca state building behind it, the
García Márquez brothers organized their friends from Sucre and set
off for their Uncle Juanito's new house, which was only four blocks
away. The band of friends and brothers joined in the generalized looting and Luis Enrique made off with a sky-blue suit which his father
would wear for years to come on special occasions. Gabito found an
elegant calfskin briefcase which became his proudest possession. But
the most prized piece of plunder was a large fifteen-litre flagon into
which Luis Enrique and Palencia poured as many varieties of liquor as
they could find before bearing it off in triumph to Uncle Juanito's.

Margarita Márquez Caballero, then twelve years old, today García
Márquez's personal secretary in Bogotá, vividly remembers the arrival
of her favourite cousin, his brother and their friends. The house was
full of refugees from the Costa and in the evening, drunk on their illicit
liquor, the young men joined Uncle Juanito on the roof of the building
and gazed with stupefaction at the burning city centre.[35] Meanwhile,
down in Sucre the family feared the worst, as Rita recalls: "The only
time I ever saw my mother cry when I was a child was 9 April. Then I
could tell that she was very upset because of Gabito and Luis Enrique
being in Bogotá at the time Gaitán was assassinated. I remember that
at about three in the afternoon the next day she got dressed all of a sudden and went out to the church. She was going to give thanks to God
because they'd just told her that her sons were safe. I was struck by it
because I wasn't used to seeing her go out, she was always at home
looking after all of us."[36]

In Bogotá, the young *costeños* stayed indoors for three days. The
government had imposed a state of siege and snipers were still sporadically picking off those who ventured out. The city centre continued to
smoulder. The university was closed and much of old Bogotá was in
ruins. But the Conservative government had survived and the leading
Liberal politicians had reached an unsatisfactory agreement with the

unexpectedly valiant President Ospina Pérez which put some of them back in the cabinet but would effectively leave them out of power again as a party for another decade. As soon as they felt it was safe to return to the streets the two brothers, whose parents had urged them to fly down to Sucre, began to hustle for tickets to travel back to the Costa. Luis Enrique had decided to try his luck in Barranquilla, where the latest love of his life was waiting for him, and Gabito had decided to pursue his law studies in the University of Cartagena; or at least, he had decided to pretend to do so. A little over a week after the disastrous events of 9 April, Gabriel García Márquez, his brother Luis Enrique and the young Cuban agitator Fidel Castro Ruz set off from Bogotá on different planes towards their different historical destinies.

As for Colombia, it has become a historical cliché, but nonetheless true, that the death of Gaitán and the ensuing *Bogotazo* divided the nation's twentieth-century history in two. What Gaitán might or might not have achieved lies in the realm of speculation. No politician has since excited the masses as he did and Colombia has moved further away from solving its real political problems with every year that has passed since he died. It was the crisis following his death which gave rise to the guerrilla movements that continue to compromise political life in the country until this very day. If it can be said that the War of a Thousand Days showed the upper classes the need to unite against the peasantry, the *Bogotazo* similarly showed the danger represented by the urban proletarian masses. Yet it was in the rural areas that the reaction would be most brutal, beginning twenty-five years of one of the world's most savage and costly civil wars: the *Violencia*.

As for García Márquez, it can fairly be said of him, unlike most other people caught up in the events, that the *Bogotazo* was one of the most fortunate things that ever happened. It interrupted his law studies in the most prestigious university in the country and gave a shot in the arm to a young man looking for some further excuse to abandon his education; and it gave him an irrefutable pretext for abandoning a place he hated and for returning to his beloved Costa, but not before he had acquired a familiarity with the capital city which would be crucial in giving him a wider national consciousness. Never again would he take the two ruling parties entirely seriously. Slow as he was to develop a mature political consciousness, there were significant lessons that García Márquez had now assimilated about the nature of his country; as he had lost or abandoned most of his material possessions, these new lessons were perhaps the most important things the young man took with him on the plane to Barranquilla and Cartagena.

6

Back to the Costa:
An Apprentice Journalist
in Cartagena

1948~1949

ARCÍA MÁRQUEZ LANDED in Barranquilla in a Douglas
DC-3 aircraft on 29 April 1948, two days after his brother
Luis Enrique. Luis Enrique stayed on in Barranquilla and
started looking for employment; he would soon land a job with the airline company LANSA and would work there for the next eighteen
months. Meanwhile all the transport systems of the country remained
in chaos in the aftermath of the *Bogotazo* and Gabito, with a heavy suitcase and a similarly heavy dark suit, found himself perched on top of a
postal truck in the searing heat of the Caribbean coastlands, heading
for Cartagena.[1]

Cartagena was the merest shadow of its former self. When the
Spaniards arrived in 1533, it became a vital bastion of the colonial system linking Spain to the Caribbean and South America and, before
long, one of the most important cities for the delivery and sale of slaves
in the entire New World. Despite this grim antecedent it had also
become (and has remained) one of the most gracious and picturesque
cities anywhere in Latin America.[2]

But after independence in the nineteenth century Barranquilla
expanded to become the large trading city that Colombia required and
Cartagena stagnated, nursed its wounds and its grievances, and con-

soled itself with the knowledge of its glorious past and its ravaged beauty. This decadent city was García Márquez's new home. He was back in the Caribbean, back in a world where the human body was accepted for what it was, in its beauty, its ugliness and its fragility, back in the realm of the senses. He had never before visited the heroic city and was struck, simultaneously, by its magnificence and its desolation. It had not entirely escaped the effects of the *Bogotazo* but, like the Costa as a whole, it had quickly returned to a somewhat uneasy normality despite the state of siege, the curfew and the censorship. The young man went straight to the Hotel Suiza in the Calle de las Damas, which doubled as a student residence, only to find that his wealthy friend José Palencia had not arrived. The owner would not give him a room on credit and he was forced to wander the old walled city, hungry and thirsty, and eventually to lie on a bench in the main square and hope that Palencia would soon turn up. Palencia didn't. García Márquez fell asleep on his bench and was arrested by two policemen for breaking the curfew, or possibly because he didn't have a cigarette to give them. He spent the night on the floor in a police cell. This was his introduction to Cartagena and the auguries were not good. Palencia finally turned up the next day and the two young men were admitted to the residence.[3]

García Márquez went to the university, just a couple of blocks away, and managed to persuade the authorities, who examined him in front of his prospective classmates, to take him on for the remainder of the second year of the law degree, including passing the subjects he had failed in year one. He was a student again. He and Palencia took up where they had left off in Bogotá, went drinking and partying despite the curfew and generally acted like the kind of upper-class student layabout that Palencia actually was and that García Márquez could hardly afford to be. This idyllic state of affairs was brought to an end after just a few weeks when the restless Palencia decided to move on and García Márquez moved up to the collective dormitory, which cost thirty pesos a month for full board and laundry.

Then fate took a hand. As he wandered down the Street of Bad Behaviour (Mala Crianza) in the old slave quarter of Getsemaní, adjacent to the walled city, he came across Manuel Zapata Olivella, a black doctor he had known in Bogotá the year before. The next day Zapata, a well-known philanthropist to his many friends and later one of Colombia's leading writers and journalists, took the young man to the offices of the newspaper *El Universal* in San Juan de Dios Street, just round the corner from his student *pensión*, and introduced him to the managing editor, Clemente Manuel Zabala. As luck would have it, Zabala, who was a friend of Eduardo Zalamea Borda, had read García Márquez's short stories in *El Espectador* and was already an admirer. Despite the young man's timidity he took him on as a columnist and, without discussing terms or conditions, said he looked forward to seeing him the next day and to printing his first article the day after that.

At the time García Márquez seems to have conceived journalism only as a means to an end and as an inferior form of writing. Nevertheless, he had now been taken on as a journalist precisely because of his pre-existing literary prestige, just past his twenty-first birthday. He contacted his parents immediately to tell them that he would now be able to support himself through his studies. Given his intention to give up those studies as soon as he could, and certainly never to practise law even if he qualified, the message significantly eased his conscience.

El Universal itself was a new paper. It had been founded only ten weeks before by Dr. Domingo López Escauriaza, a patrician Liberal politician who had been state governor and a diplomat and now, in the light of growing Conservative violence, had decided to open a new front in the propaganda war on the Costa. This had been a month before the *Bogotazo*. There was no other Liberal newspaper in that very conservative city.

Everyone agrees that Zabala was the newspaper's trump card. Such was the managing editor's dedication and lucidity that *El Universal* emerged, despite its unprepossessing offices, as a model of political coherence and, by the standards of the time, good writing. The good writing would be providential for the new recruit. Zabala was a slight, nervous man in his mid-fifties, born in San Jacinto, with "Indian" features and hair. Dark in complexion, with a slight paunch, he always wore glasses and was rarely seen without a cigarette in his hand. He was also, it was rumoured, a discreet homosexual, who dyed his hair black to defy the advancing years and lived alone in a small hotel room. He had been a political associate of Gaitán. It was said he had been private secretary to General Benjamín Herrera in his youth and he had worked on the General's newspaper *El Diario Nacional*. In the 1940s he had worked in the ministry of education and later he had collaborated closely with Plinio Mendoza Neira's magazine *Acción Liberal*.

Zabala introduced García Márquez to another recent recruit, Héctor Rojas Herazo, a young poet and painter of twenty-seven from the Caribbean port of Tolú. He did not recognize García Márquez but he had briefly been his art teacher eight years before at the Colegio San José in Barranquilla. It was another of the extraordinary conjunctions which were already punctuating García Márquez's life; Rojas Herazo was himself destined to be one of the country's leading poets and novelists as well as a widely admired painter.[4] Craggy and leonine, he was louder and larger, more dogmatic and apparently more passionate than his new friend, expansive and prickly at one and the same time.

Well after midnight, when Zabala had checked and corrected every article on every one of the newspaper's eight pages, he invited his two young protégés out to eat. Journalists were exempt from the curfew and García Márquez now embarked on a new life, which was to last many years, in which he worked through much of the night and slept, when he slept at all, during much of the day. This would not be easy in Cartagena where law classes began at seven in the morning and García Márquez arrived home at six. The only place open so late at night was a restaurant and bar nicknamed "The Cave" on the waterfront behind the public market, run by an exquisitely beautiful young black homosexual called José de las Nieves, "Joe of the Snows."[5] There the journalists and other night owls would eat beefsteak, tripe, and rice with shrimp or crab.

After Zabala had returned to his solitary room, García Márquez and Rojas Herazo began to wander the port area, beginning at the Paseo de los Mártires, where nine busts commemorate the deaths in 1816 of some of the first rebels against the Spanish empire.[6] Then García Márquez went home to work. After an anxious few hours, but infatuated with his own rhetoric, he trotted off to show his first column to the boss. Zabala read it and said it was well enough written but wouldn't do. Firstly, it was too personal, and far too literary; and secondly, "Haven't you noticed that we are working under a regime of censorship?" On Zabala's desk was a red pencil. He picked it up. Almost immediately the combination of García Márquez's own inborn talent and Zabala's professional zeal produced articles which were readable, absorbing and patently original from the very start.[7] All García Márquez's signed columns in *El Universal* appeared under the byline "New Paragraph" ("Punto y Aparte"). The first, the one that received most attention from the editor, was a political piece about the curfew and state of siege, cunningly disguised as a general meditation on the city. The young writer asked prophetically how, in an era of political violence and dehumanization, could his generation be expected to turn out as "men of good will." Evidently the novice journalist had been abruptly radicalized by the events of 9 April. The second article was equally remarkable.[8] If the first was implicitly political in the traditional sense, the second was almost a manifesto about cultural politics: it was a defence of the humble accordion, a vagabond among musical instruments but an essential element in the *vallenato*, a musical form developed in the Costa by usually anonymous musicians and, for García Márquez, a symbol of the people of the region and their culture, not to mention of his own desire to challenge ruling-class preconceptions. The accordion, he insisted, is not only a vagabond but a proletarian. The first article had been a rejection of the kind of politics coming from Bogotá; the second embraced the writer's newly recovered cultural roots.[9]

For the first time the future of Gabriel García Márquez was moderately assured. He was doing a job, and one that other people recognized he was good at. He was a newspaperman. He would continue to study the law sporadically and unenthusiastically, but he had found his way out of the legal profession and into the world of journalism and literature. He would never look back.

In the next twenty months he would write forty-three signed pieces and many times that number of unsigned contributions for *El Universal*. Mostly this was still a noticeably old-fashioned journalism of commentary and literary creation, more for entertainment than political information, closer indeed to the genre of daily or weekly "chronicles" which would not have been out of date in a Latin American newspaper of the 1920s. On the other hand, one of García Márquez's tasks was to sift through the cables coming off the teletype machine in order to select news items and propose topics for the commentary pieces and literary extrapolations that were so important in the journalism of those times. This daily practice must have given him an experience of the way in which the events of everyday life are transmuted into "news," into "stories," that immediately demystified ordinary reality and provided a powerful antidote to his recent excursions into the works of Kafka. Journalists almost everywhere at this time were obliged to adopt the hands-on, sleeves-rolled-up approach of U.S. journalistic practices and from the beginning García Márquez took to this like a duck to water. It would make him a very different sort of writer from the majority of his Latin American contemporaries, for whom France and French ways of doing things were still the models to follow in an age when France itself was beginning to lose its grip on modernity.

Much though he had to learn, the new columnist's originality was obvious from the start and must have been a joy to the editor who hired him. Just three months later, in his article on the Cartagena Afro-Colombian writer Jorge Artel, he was implicitly calling for a literature at once local and continental which would represent "our race"—an astonishing perspective for Colonel Márquez's grandson to adopt at the age of twenty-one—and to give the Atlantic Coast "an identity of its own."[10]

In mid-July of that first year Conservative police massacred Liberal families in El Carmen de Bolívar, the town where García Márquez's grandfather had been brought up with Aunt Francisca. El Carmen had a long and glorious Liberal political tradition. It also happened to be the nearest large town to Zabala's place of birth, San Jacinto, so both men took a special interest in events there and between them carried out a campaign based on the slogan, "What happened in Carmen de Bolívar?" Zabala's grim joke, whenever he renewed the campaign, in the face of government denials and inertia, was to end with the words, "No doubt about it, in Carmen de Bolívar absolutely nothing happened."[11] This is almost exactly the phrase García Márquez would later use about his invented town of Macondo in a celebrated section of *One Hundred Years of Solitude* after the pivotal episode of the banana-workers massacre.

In one sense there could have been no worse time to become a journalist in Colombia. Censorship was imposed immediately after the events of April 1948, though less brutally on the coast than in the interior of the country. García Márquez began to practise journalism because of the *Violencia* but the *Violencia* severely limited what a journalist could do. For the next seven years, under Ospina Pérez, Laureano Gómez, Urdaneta Arbeláez and Rojas Pinilla, albeit with variable intensity, government censorship would be continuously active. All the more significant, then, that the first article of García Márquez's career, dated 21 May 1948, had implied a clear left-of-centre political position. He would never diverge from this broad perspective; yet it would never, in the last instance (as the Marxists used to say), constrain or distort his fiction.

Only two weeks after starting with *El Universal* García Márquez asked for a week's holiday and travelled across to Barranquilla, up to Magangué and then on to Sucre to see his family. Whether he stopped off at Mompox to get a glimpse of Mercedes we do not know. By the time he set off he must have realized that his new salary was not what he had given his parents to believe but he evidently did not have the heart to disabuse them. This was not only his first visit since the *Bogotazo* but the first time he had been home since he travelled to Bogotá at the start of his university studies in February 1947, more than a year before. It was therefore the first time he had seen his mother since her own mother had died and the first time he had seen the last of his brothers and sisters, Eligio Gabriel, named, like himself only more completely, after their father. In later life García Márquez, who was twenty years older than Eligio Gabriel, would often jokingly tell the story that the new child was so named because "my mother had lost me but she wanted to be sure there was always a Gabriel in the house." In fact when he personally delivered Eligio Gabriel, whom the family would call Yiyo, in November 1947, Gabriel Eligio declared: "This baby looks like me; Gabito is not at all like me so we'll call this one after me, only the other way round—Eligio Gabriel!"[12]

Back Gabito went to Cartagena. It was only now, on 17 June, that he formally registered at the university, though he had passed the interview weeks before. Professionally things were going well but economically disaster stared the young writer in the face. Despite being, effectively, a staff journalist, García Márquez was paid by the piece. Although he himself was never much of a mathematician and was relatively indifferent to budgetary questions, a friend, Ramiro de la Espriella, later calculated that he was paid thirty-two centavos, a third of a peso, for each article, signed or unsigned, that he wrote, and virtually nothing for his other duties. This was below any imaginable minimum wage. By the end of June he had been thrown out of the *pensión* and had taken to sleeping on park benches again, in the rooms of other students or, famously, on the rolls of newsprint in the office of *El Universal*, one place that never closed. One evening, as he walked with colleagues in the Centenary Park, where they would sit on the steps of the Noli Me Tangere monument and drink, smoke and talk, another journalist, Jorge Franco Múnera, asked how his lodgings were turning out and García Márquez confessed the truth. That same night Franco Múnera took him to his family home in Estanco del Aguardiente Street on the corner of Cuartel del Fijo, near the Heredia Theatre in the old city. The family embraced the hungry, homeless student, especially Jorge's mother Carmen Múnera Herrán.[13] Other people's mothers always took to him. He would board with her on and off, trying to appease his conscience by eating as little as possible, for the rest of his stay in Cartagena.

So at this time García Márquez was living a life even more desperate than his time in Bogotá and he now habituated himself to a virtual
disregard for his own bodily needs. Even here on the Costa he was
famous for his ghastly multi-coloured shirts—usually he owned only
one at a time—and checked jackets, worn over black woollen trousers
from some old suit, canary yellow socks which hung around his ankles
and dusty moccasins which he never cleaned. He had a tentative wispy
moustache and curly, untidy black hair which rarely saw a comb. Even
after getting the Franco Múnera room he slept wherever fatigue and
the approaching dawn caught him. He was thin as a rake and friends,
touched by the fact that he remained eternally cheerful and never ever
seemed sorry for himself or appealed for help, repeatedly clubbed
together to buy him meals by day and include him in their night-time
excursions.

The opinions of friends and acquaintances varied. Many people,
especially social conservatives, thought him eccentric to the point of
lunacy or, not infrequently, homosexual.[14] Even friends like Rojas
Herazo say in retrospect that he was something of a cissy ("such a *good*
boy").[15] Both Rojas and another friend, Carlos Alemán, remember
García Márquez's boyishness, his bouncy gait—which he has never
lost—and his tendency to dance with glee when someone gave him a
new idea or he was excited about one of his own ideas for a story.[16]
Acquaintances remember him always drumming his fingers on the
table as he waited for his lunch, or on anything else to hand, singing
quietly or noisily, music always somehow wafting through him.[17]

García Márquez learned everything his new friends and colleagues
had to teach him. He also developed some key ideas about his vocation
at an astonishingly early age. For example, he picked up George
Bernard Shaw's declaration that he was going to devote himself henceforth to advertising slogans and making money; García Márquez commented that this was food for thought for those, like himself, who were
"resolved not to write for commercial reasons and yet find ourselves
doing it out of vanity instead."[18]

Life settled into a routine in Cartagena. He missed most of his
classes but not all professors took an attendance list and the Liberal
teachers sympathized with the young man's journalistic skirmishes
with the censors and with the authorities in general, who more than
once sent military detachments to the newspaper offices to intimidate
the staff. Among his most important relationships was that with Gustavo Ibarra Merlano, a student of the classics who had graduated from

the Bogotá Normal School and now taught in a local college a few yards from the *El Universal* office. Ibarra Merlano was already a good friend of Rojas Herazo's. To amble about with these two cost García Márquez no money—nor involved him in receiving any charity— because they did no drinking or partying and mainly discussed lofty matters related to poetry or religious philosophy.[19]

García Márquez also had other friends whose inclinations were less austere. Principal among them were the De la Espriella brothers, Ramiro and Oscar, whom he met occasionally in 1948 and more frequently in 1949, whose interests were not only much more political— in the arena of radical Liberalism and even Marxism—but also far more worldly. With them and others García Márquez would spend time drinking and going to brothels. Three surprisingly provocative articles printed in July 1948 suggest that at the time García Márquez may have been enamoured of some young woman of the night and may, right then, have been evolving the attitudes towards sex and love which would characterize his later work. The first has him quite explicitly inventorying the body of a young female while musing, "And to think that all this one day will be inhabited by death," then ending the first paragraph, "To think that this pain of being inside you and far from my own substance will one day find its definitive remedy."[20] It is as well that the reactionary Catholic matrons of Cartagena would no more have opened the pages of *El Universal* than walk naked through the Plaza Bolívar.

By the time of the third article the young writer has discovered one of his key ideas, later given classic form in the novel *Love in the Time of Cholera*: that love can last for ever but is much more likely to flower and die in the briefest of times, like a sickness.[21] Few male visitors will quickly forget their first sight of the voluptuous, under-dressed women of Caribbean harbour towns like Cartagena or Havana, and García Márquez lived on the Costa as a young man in the heyday of the Caribbean prostitute. But as for serious, respectable girlfriends, Ramiro de la Espriella remembers him mentioning only one, Mercedes, by then a sixteen-year-old schoolgirl. "Though what she saw in him I can't imagine: he was just a kid, insignificant, pimply, malarial, he looked puny, without any physical presence . . . If you saw him in the street you'd have taken him for a messenger boy."[22]

Mercedes's family and most of García Márquez's were still down in Sucre. But Luis Enrique was living in Barranquilla and would often travel across to Cartagena at weekends and over holiday periods:

"Gabito was in Cartagena doing the same as in Bogotá, pretending to study law but really writing."[23] It was the era of the great Latin American *bolero* singing trios such as Los Panchos and Luis Enrique's dream was to set up his own trio—"my father would have been even more horrified by that than he was by Gabito's writing."[24]

Around this time Zabala received a message from Zalamea Borda in Bogotá asking what was happening to his young protégé's literary activities. García Márquez had actually given up on his stories at this time but could never say no to Zalamea and quickly revised another, "The Other Side of Death" ("La otra costilla de la muerte"), which was published in *El Espectador* on 25 July 1948. It must have been flattering and profoundly comforting to know that an important and influential personage was still thinking about him and furthering his interests up in Bogotá.

On 16 September 1948 García Márquez travelled to Barranquilla on newspaper business and instead of taking the bus straight back to Cartagena he decided to look up some fellow journalists recommended by his friends in Cartagena. It was another historic decision. He headed for the offices of *El Nacional*, where Germán Vargas and Alvaro Cepeda were then employed. They were part of a loose bohemian fraternity which would eventually be known as the "Barranquilla Group."[25] García Márquez's passionate yet judicious contribution to the literary discussions that first evening impressed the third member of the group, Alfonso Fuenmayor, who was the assistant editor of the Liberal newspaper *El Heraldo* and asked García Márquez to look him up before returning to Cartagena.

García Márquez was delighted to discover that these apparently hard-bitten journalists knew him by his reputation and he was embraced like a long-lost brother, introduced to the local literary guru, the Catalan writer Ramón Vinyes, and then taken off on a bar and brothel crawl which ended up in a legendary establishment called "Black Euphemia's," which would later be immortalized in *One Hundred Years of Solitude*. There García Márquez sealed his own personal triumph and his bond with the group by singing *mambos* and *boleros* for more than an hour. He stayed overnight at the home of Alvaro Cepeda, who, unlike the others, was the same age as he was and had similar tastes in flowered shirts and artist's smocks, had even longer hair and wore sandals, like a pioneer hippy. Cepeda was loud, bombastic and dogmatic. He showed García Márquez a wall of books, mainly North American and English, and roared: "These are the best books going, the only ones worth reading by the only people who know how to write. You can borrow all of them if you want."

The next morning, according to the memoir, García Márquez was sent off with a novel called *Orlando* by a writer he had never heard of, Virginia Woolf, whom Cepeda seemed to know personally since he always called her "old Woolf," just as the entire group evidently also had an intimate relationship with their favourite writer, William Faulkner, whom they usually called "the Old Man."[26] After all these years the enthusiasm displayed by these tough guys for the work of the demure Mrs. Woolf remains astonishing. Friends recall that García Márquez was particularly struck at the time by an apparently unlady-like line he claimed to have read in one of her novels: that "love is taking your knickers off," a somewhat "loose" translation of "love is slipping off one's petticoat" from *Orlando*.[27] This quotation may have had more impact on his view of the world than may appear to be the case at first sight. At any rate, he told everyone that "Virginia" was "a tough old broad."[28]

The time for the second-year examinations approached and García Márquez was desperate. His attendance had been more than erratic—fifteen absences officially noted down—and he had absorbed little of what he had heard. A classmate from that era recalls that García Márquez "worked until three in the morning at the newspaper, then slept on rolls of newsprint until seven o'clock when our classes began. He always said he would have to bathe later because he had no time to wash before arriving at the university."[29] He passed the year overall but a failure in Roman law would come back to haunt him several years later and may even have been decisive in ensuring that he would never qualify as a lawyer.

Meanwhile his contact with the Barranquilla Group had inspired him—and given him the confidence—to begin work on his first novel, which he entitled "The House" ("La casa"). It was a novel about his own past—possibly, indeed, a novel which he had been nurturing for a long time. He worked on this novel initially in the second half of 1948 and then more intensively in early 1949. His friend, Ramiro de la Espriella, and his brother Oscar lived in their parents' large nine-teenth-century house in the Segunda Calle de Badillo in the old walled city. García Márquez was a frequent visitor, often eating there and even sleeping there on occasion. The house had a large collection of books and García Márquez would often be found reading Colombian history in the library. Oscar, the older of the two brothers, remembers:

"My father called him 'Civic Valour' because he said it took a lot of nerve to dress the way he did ... My mother loved him like a son ... He would turn up with his great roll of papers tied up with a necktie, it was what he was writing, and so he'd unwrap his stuff and sit down and read it to us."[30]

From the extracts that survived and were later published in *El Heraldo* of Barranquilla we can see that the novel was set in a house something like the house of García Márquez's grandparents and was faintly reminiscent of Faulkner in theme though not in manner; it was interesting and had potential but it was rather flat and none of the extant extracts from it suggest the influence of Faulkner or Joyce or indeed Virginia Woolf. It involved characters something like his grandfather and grandmother and their ancestors, a place something like Aracataca, a war like the War of a Thousand Days, but at this time he never managed to go beyond a rather episodic, one-dimensional and somewhat lifeless narrative. It seems García Márquez could not escape from the house. Or to put it another way, he could not separate "The House" from the house, the novel from its inspiration. Still, it is impossible to doubt that here, to an astonishing degree, are the germs of *One Hundred Years of Solitude*, with the themes of solitude, destiny, nostalgia, patriarchy and violence all waiting for the distinctive tone and perspective that were still more than a decade away from discovery. The truth in part is that García Márquez could not yet fully ironize his own culture; it was inconceivable in those days that anything connected to Nicolás Márquez could be ludicrous or even funny. Ironically enough, then, it had not yet occurred to him to connect the fantastic world of Kafka with the real world of his memories.[31]

In March 1949, suddenly, he fell seriously ill. According to his own testimony, it was a political confrontation with Zabala which triggered the crisis. One night towards the end of March García Márquez was sitting in "The Cave" with Zabala as the editor ate his late-night supper. García Márquez had been behaving increasingly badly since his trips to Barranquilla, working erratically at *El Universal* and showing signs of an unfocused adolescent rebellion brought on by his contact with Alvaro Cepeda. Zabala stopped eating his soup, looked over his glasses and said acidly, "Tell me something, Gabriel, in the midst of all your stupid antics, have you noticed that this country is going down the pan?"[32] Stung, García Márquez went on drinking and ended up fast asleep on a bench in the Paseo de los Mártires. He woke up next morning at the end of a tropical downpour with his clothes sodden and his lungs shot. He was diagnosed with pneumonia and so he went back to Sucre for however long it might take to convalesce at his parents' house—not necessarily the ideal destination for a bronchial invalid because the waters around Sucre had risen higher than ever and the town was flooded as it would so often be in *In Evil Hour* or *Chronicle of a Death Foretold*.

This would turn out to be an important return home. García Márquez has said that he half expected the stay to last six months, though in the event it was not much more than six weeks. But not only was it the longest time he had spent with the family for some years but it was also a visit where he knew in advance that he would be house-bound for a long time. He didn't realize it at the time but a quiet unconscious revolution would begin to work inside him now that several of his brothers and sisters were growing up, a revolution too slow to take immediate effect but crucial in the longer term to his literary and historical imagination and perspective. One might say that he would begin to add living people to the dead people who already haunted his imagination.

Now that he was a journalist García Márquez also began to notice Sucre. One of the most interesting local legends in the region was that of the Marquesita de La Sierpe, a blonde Spanish woman who was supposed to have lived in the remote settlement of La Sierpe (a *sierpe* is a serpent) and never married or engaged in sexual congress with any male. She had magical powers, a hacienda as big as several municipalities and lived for more than two hundred years. Each year she would tour the region curing the sick and dispensing favours to those she protected. Before she died she had her cattle parade past the house, which took nine days until so much trampling in wet earth eventually formed the Swamp (Ciénaga) of La Sierpe, south-west of Sucre, between the San Jorge and Cauca rivers. She then buried the rest of her most precious possessions and treasures in the Swamp together with the secret of eternal life, and distributed her remaining wealth among the six families who had served her.[33]

This legend, told to García Márquez by his friend Angel Casij Palencia, José Palencia's cousin, together with others he would collect himself, helped not only to form the basis of a series of brilliant articles he would write three or four years later but also to inspire his own fabulous literary creation "Big Mama" (la Mamá Grande), which would be the first unmistakable sign of the mature García Márquez style, in the late 1950s. Another ingredient was a wealthy resident of Sucre, who lived next door to the family's friends the Gentile Chimento family. She was called María Amalia Sampayo de Alvarez, a woman who sneered at education and culture and bragged endlessly about her wealth. When she died in 1957 she was given a grotesquely extravagant funeral.[34] Another equally extraordinary story was that of an eleven-year-old girl who was forced into prostitution by her grandmother; many years later she would become several fictional characters, notably the famous "Eréndira."[35]

In fact, the matter of his development as a narrator was now called into question in the most dramatic fashion. García Márquez had hinted in a letter to his friends in Barranquilla that a shipment of books would be welcome to counteract the wilderness of Sucre and the uncouthness of his parents' home.[36] The books duly arrived. They included Faulkner's *The Sound and the Fury*, *The Hamlet*, *As I Lay Dying* and *The Wild Palms*, Virginia Woolf's *Mrs. Dalloway*, Dos Passos's *Manhattan Transfer*, Steinbeck's *Of Mice and Men* and *The Grapes of Wrath*, Nathan's *Portrait of Jenny* and Huxley's *Point Counter Point*. Unfortunately the result of reading these scintillating works of modernist literature was that work on "The House" slowed almost to a halt.[37] Moreover as he began to recover his health he also began to return to leisure activities. He never made it to La Sierpe but he got back into his relationship with the voluptuous Nigromanta (who by then had lost her husband), much to Luisa Santiaga's disgust. He also made some new friends. One, Carlos Alemán, from Mompox, who had already been elected to the departmental assembly, remembers arriving at Sucre in May 1949: "In the midst of the crowd greeting our arrival from the huts there stood out a man in exotic garb: he had peasant sandals, black trousers and a yellow shirt. I said to Ramiro, 'Who's that parakeet?' and he replied, 'That's Gabito' . . . He stood right out in those clothes of his, with everyone else there dressed in khaki."[38]

So García Márquez, still supposedly convalescent, joined the group with his friend Jacobo Casij, another Liberal militant, and they sailed on around the entire Mojana region in three launches, each with Liberal flags, barrels of rum and a brass band. Liberal supporters cheered from the river banks and local bosses, usually Liberal landowners, would organize fiestas and meetings wherever they landed. Oscar de la Espriella later reflected, "Really we were all Marxists in those days, all waiting for the revolution, but Carlos Lleras would never give the order."[39]

By the middle of May García Márquez felt well enough to return to his activities in Cartagena. As a newly elected member of the departmental assembly, his friend Carlos Alemán was not noticeably more aware of his self-importance than before but used his new status and budget to organize frequent binges which usually gave his poorer friend enough to eat to last him a week and invariably ended up in a brothel.[40]

When García Márquez got back from Sucre and wrote his next signed article—by then an extremely rare phenomenon—about the elections for student beauty queen, he signed it not Gabriel García Márquez but "Séptimus," inspired by the character of that name in Virginia Woolf's *Mrs. Dalloway*.[41] This first Séptimus article, "Friday," is notable for its confident, almost arrogant tone, and includes the following defiant statement: "We are the students and we have discovered the formula for the perfect state: concord between the different social classes, fair salaries, the equal distribution of surplus value, the dissolution of salaried parliaments and total and collective abstention from elections."

García Márquez had seriously neglected his legal studies before he fell ill and neglected them even more determinedly afterwards. He was well known for proclaiming his loathing of the law and for organizing impromptu football games in the university's august corridors. The danger was that if he qualified as a lawyer he might be tempted—or forced, either by his family or his conscience—to practise it. Law studies in Cartagena were even more tedious than in Bogotá. In the end he failed both medical law (one in the eye for Gabriel Eligio?) and the seminar in civil law, scraped through civil law itself and passed five other subjects. Even this was a miracle in view of his numerous absences. But he did not retrieve Roman law and thus carried three failures into the fourth year.[42]

On 9 November in Bogotá, sensing the divisions and weaknesses within the Liberal leadership, the existing Conservative government reimposed the state of siege and closed the Congress—the so-called "institutional coup." An eight o'clock curfew was decreed a few days later. The Liberal failure to react encouraged the Conservatives to cast off all restraint and the *Violencia*—redoubled—filled the entire country with corpses, above all in rural areas, though as usual less in the northern coastlands than elsewhere.

Internationally, this period—1948-9—was also an extraordinary time, one of the most intense and decisive moments of the entire twentieth century. García Márquez had been in Bogotá while the new inter-

American system was being created there—largely in the interests of the United States, which had only recently dominated discussions in Europe about the establishment of the United Nations and had arranged, symbolically enough, to move the new organization's meetings from London to New York. President Truman, who had taken the decision not long before to drop two atomic bombs on Japan, had now declared a worldwide crusade against communism—the CIA had been set up in 1947 as part of the anti-communist struggle—and the Pope had tacitly supported the American line; Truman had got himself re-elected on the strength of this position. The state of Israel had been founded with the full support of the Western nations and NATO had been established; the USSR had imposed a blockade on Berlin and the USA had responded with an airlift; the USSR had then tested its own atom bomb and on 1 October 1949 the People's Republic of China had been founded. By the time García Márquez finally made the decision to take hold of his own life and move on from Cartagena, the new international system which would run the world throughout the recently declared Cold War and beyond was firmly in place. This was the context of his adult life and time.

It was at this moment that Manuel Zapata Olivella, the black vagabond, writer, revolutionary and doctor, crossed García Márquez's path again—as he would on further occasions in the future. Now he took him off for his first encounter with the old province of Padilla, the stamping ground of Colonel Márquez during the Thousand Day War. Zapata Olivella had just graduated from the National University in Bogotá; although a native of Cartagena, he was travelling to practise his new profession in the small town of La Paz, in the foothills of the Sierra Nevada, about twelve miles from Valledupar. Zapata invited García Márquez to go with him to his new place of residence and the young man leaped at the chance. There, for the first time, in La Paz and Valledupar, he met the singers of *vallenatos* and *merengues* in their natural habitat—in particular the influential Afro-Colombian accordionist Abelito Antonio Villa, the first man to record *vallenato* music.[43]

By the time he got back to Cartagena he had finally made up his mind: it was time to leave. Barranquilla would be a much more convenient place from which to look back upon his cultural heritage. His last public appearance in Cartagena was at a party on 22 December to celebrate the publication of his seventeen-year-old friend Jorge Lee Biswell Cotes's novel, *Blue Mist (Neblina azul)*, which he damned with faint praise in a patronizing and deprecating review in *El Universal*.

Oscar de la Espriella recalls García Márquez singing what he announced as "the first *vallenato* I ever learned," whose first line went, "I'll give you a bunch of forget-me-nots, so you'll do as their name tells you."[44] The line has been used implicitly by writers from Cartagena to insinuate that García Márquez has unfairly "forgotten"—indeed, repudiated—not only the city, with its admittedly snobbish and reactionary upper-class values, but the friends who helped him, the colleagues who inspired him and, above all, the editor who loved and instructed him: Clemente Manuel Zabala, whom García Márquez almost never mentioned publicly until the prologue of *Of Love and Other Demons* in 1994.[45]

The young man would indeed be ostensibly ungrateful to specific individuals in later life and he has consistently played down the contribution of the Cartagena period to his development; but it is also clear that Cartagena writers now claim too much for the impact of the city and its intellectuals on the budding novelist and underestimate how much he suffered through his treatment there. García Márquez was a poor boy during his seven years at school, dependent on grants and the benevolence of others. In Bogotá he was always short of money and in Cartagena—and later Barranquilla—he would be close to indigent. Somehow he managed to smile and nearly always be positive during these years; friendly and unfriendly witnesses alike confirm that he virtually never expressed pity for himself or asked for favours. How he maintained his equanimity, how he held on to his confidence, how he built his resolve and managed to fashion and fortify a vocation in these arduous circumstances, with a family of ten other children beneath him also living in relative poverty, is something that can only be explained by words like courage, character and unshakable determination.

Barranquilla, a Bookseller and a Bohemian Group

1950~1953

"MAN, I THINK he went to Barranquilla looking for fresh air, more freedom and better pay."[1] Thus, more than forty years later, did Ramiro de la Espriella explain his friend's decision to move from the historic city of Cartagena to the bustling seaport of Barranquilla, eighty miles to the east. When García Márquez left Cartagena towards the end of December 1949 the curfew was in place again and it was not easy to reach Barranquilla by the late afternoon before it came into effect. He had 200 pesos secretly smuggled to him by his mother Luisa in his pocket and an unspecified sum from one of his university professors, Mario Alario di Filippo. He was carrying the draft of "The House" in the leather briefcase he had looted in Bogotá and, as usual, was much more anxious about losing that than he was about the possibility of losing his money. And he was euphoric, despite the fact that he would be spending yet another Christmas holiday alone. After all, as even a Cartagena aficionado would later concede, "Arriving in Barranquilla, in those days, was like returning to the world, the place where things were really happening."[2] And García Márquez had a promise from Alfonso Fuenmayor that he would move heaven and earth to get him a job on *El Heraldo*.

Barranquilla was a place with almost no history, with almost no distinguished buildings; but it was modern, entrepreneurial, dynamic and hospitable, and far from the *Violencia* which was ravaging the interior of the country. Its population was approaching half a million. "Barran-quilla enabled me to be a writer," García Márquez told me in 1993. "It had the highest immigrant population in Colombia—Arabs, Chinese and so on. It was like Córdoba in the Middle Ages. An open city, full of intelligent people who didn't give a fuck about being intelligent."[3]

The spiritual founder of what would later be known as the Barran-quilla Group was the Catalan Ramón Vinyes, destined to become the wise old Catalan bookseller of *One Hundred Years of Solitude*.[4] Born in the mountain village of Berga in 1882, he was brought up in Barcelona and established a minor reputation in Spain before migrating to Cié-naga in 1913. Rumours that he was homosexual persist in Barranquilla to this day and appear well founded. Thus it turns out that both García Márquez's crucial mentors during his Caribbean period, Zabala and Vinyes, were probably homosexuals. When García Márquez got to know him—and it was only briefly—Vinyes was in his late sixties. He was slightly portly, had a shock of white hair and an uncontrollable quiff like that of a cockatoo. He managed to look both intimidating and benevolent. Though not himself a great drinker, he was a great conversationalist and had a delicate but acid humour; on occasion he could be brutally frank.[5] He had huge prestige among the group. He knew he was not a great writer but he was widely read and had a view of literature which was both catholic and shrewd. He never had much money but was always relaxed about it. It was Vinyes who gave the group cohesion and the confidence to believe that even in an unknown, apparently uncultured city, with no history, no university and no culti-vated ruling class, it was possible to be educated. And easy to be mod-ern. One of his sayings that García Márquez never forgot was, "If Faulkner lived in Barranquilla he'd be sitting at this table."[6] It was probably true. One of his key themes was that the world was becoming a "universal village," many years before Marshall McLuhan came up with the idea.

Alfonso Fuenmayor, born in 1917, and son of the respected writer José Félix Fuenmayor, was the quietest and perhaps the most serious of the younger members, but he was also the most pivotal. First, because of his direct connection to the older generation. Second, because he was the one who had brought all the others together through his own prior relationships. Third, because it was he who had first suggested to García Márquez that he should move to *El Heraldo*, where Fuenmayor himself worked for twenty-six years. Widely read in Spanish, English and French, he was myopic in appearance, quiet and judicious, but a

well-practised drinker like the rest of them, and a determined lubrica-
tor of the collective wheels. He had a serious stutter which rum or
whisky tended to ameliorate. And he had a penchant for classical literature and for dictionaries, and was, without doubt, the most genuinely
erudite and the most widely read of the group.

German Vargas was Fuenmayor's close friend and associate, born in
Barranquilla in 1919. Tall, with piercing green eyes, he was an insatiable reader, but slow and careful in everything he did, and with a hard
edge to him. If Fuenmayor, despite his seriousness, was unavoidably
bumbling, untidy, funny, Vargas was always neat, white-shirted, prudent—though occasionally savage—in his judgements,[7] and reliable.
(He was the one García Márquez would later send his manuscripts to
for a first impression and he was the one García Márquez would write
to for relief packages of books or for money.) He smoked heavily, the
blacker the tobacco the better, and he and Fuenmayor, despite being
the most sedentary, were the biggest drinkers among the gang, special-
izing in a potion whose main ingredients were "rum, lemons and
rum."[8]

Alvaro Cepeda Samudio was the energetic motor of the group,
handsome, rakish, with the widest flashing smile in the world, irresistible to women—he had well-publicized affairs with some of the
leading female artists in Colombia—yet a man's man; and, because of
his early death in 1972, he has become a Barranquilla legend.[9] He was
born in the city on 30 March 1926, though he always claimed to have
been born in Ciénaga, where the banana massacre had taken place,
because he wished his birth to be associated with that tragic historical
event in which the abominable *cachacos* had murdered innocent *costeños*.
His father, a Conservative politician, went insane and died when
Alvaro was a child, leaving a whiff of tragedy about the boy, belied by
his expansive and unforgettable adult personality. Cepeda was a mass
of contradictions which he resolved with uproarious bluster. He
looked like a vagabond but had come into money while away in America in 1949–50 and always had close links with local aristocrats, including Barranquilla businessman Julio Mario Santo Domingo, briefly a
member of the group and later the wealthiest man in Colombia and
one of the wealthiest in Latin America.

Even more suicidally turbulent was Alejandro Obregón. He too
was away from Barranquilla when García Márquez arrived and indeed
Obregón was in Europe most of the time García Márquez was in
Barranquilla; nevertheless he made occasional visits and he was an

essential member of the group both before and after García Márquez's sojourn. Obregón was a painter, born in Barcelona in 1920. His family owned the Obregón textile factory in Barranquilla and the city's luxury hotel, the Prado. Married and divorced several times, and as much of a magnet for women as Cepeda, Obregón was the archetype of the impassioned painter and by the mid-1940s his reputation was on the rise.[10] In the second half of the century he became the best-known painter in Colombia, before the rise of Fernando Botero, and undoubtedly the most loved and admired. His usual dress was a pair of shorts and nothing else. His exploits are legendary in Barranquilla: taking on several U.S. marines single-handed after they had mistreated a prostitute; eating a fellow drinker's large trained cricket in one mouthful; breaking open the door of his favourite bar with an elephant hired from a local circus; playing William Tell with his friends and using bottles instead of arrows; shooting his favourite dog in the head when it became paralysed after an accident; and dozens more.

These, then, were the central players in what would later be known as the Group of Barranquilla, organizers of the permanent fiesta to which García Márquez was invited in early 1950. There were many others, almost all of them colourful and individualistic. Germán Vargas, writing in 1956 and referring to the group's heterogeneous enthusiasms, talked about his friends in terms that were "postmodern" *avant la lettre*: "They can consider with the same interest and without prejudice phenomena as different as Joyce's *Ulysses*, Cole Porter's music, Alfredo di Stefano's skill or Willie Mays's technique, Enrique Grau's painting, Miguel Hernández's poetry, Réné Clair's judgement, Rafael Escalona's *merengues*, Gabriel Figueroa's photography or the vitality of Black Adán or Black Eufemia."[11] They considered friendship even more important than politics. As for the latter, they were almost all Liberals though Cepeda tended towards anarchist postures and García Márquez towards socialist ones. García Márquez would later say that between them his friends had every book you could wish for; they would quote one at him in the brothel late at night and then give it to him the next morning and he would read it while he was still drunk.[12]

The group seemed anti-bourgeois but really they were more anti-aristocratic; Cepeda and Obregón were linked to some of the most important political, economic and social interests in the city. Their most striking posture—extraordinarily rare in Latin America at this time—was their sympathy for many things North American; while Bogotá, and most of Latin America, was still in thrall to European culture, the Barranquilla Group identified Europe with the past and with tradition, and preferred the more straightforward and modern cultural example of the United States. Naturally this preference did not apply to political questions, nor was it uncritical; but, for good or ill, it placed the group a good twenty-five years ahead of almost every other significant literary or intellectual movement in Latin America.

Of course the posture also made them anti-*cachaco*, none more so than Cepeda, who was both a great believer in Caribbean—as against Andean—popular culture and a great modernizer. He would later advocate the creation of a Caribbean Republic. In a 1966 interview with the Bogotá journalist Daniel Samper he would assert that *costeños* "are not transcendentalists . . . don't invent mysteries. We are not liars and hypocrites like the *cachacos*."[13] Samper, a *cachaco*, had no idea any of his fellow Colombians could be like that and was infatuated with such a larger-than-life personality. Cepeda was one of the first enthusiasts for cut-the-crap North American writers like Faulkner and Hemingway and the number one exponent of the Group's favourite pastime, *mamagallismo*.

Their stamping ground was a few blocks in central Barranquilla. García Márquez would later say that "the world began in San Blas Street" or 35th Street as the more recent denomination has it.[14] In fact, on just one block of San Blas, between Progreso (Carrera 41) and 20 de Julio (Carrera 43) was where the Librería Mundo stood, the Café Colombia, the Cine Colombia, the Café Japy and the Lunchería Americana; a block to the north stood América Billares and a block to the east was the Café Roma, on Paseo Simón Bolívar. And just beyond was the Colón Park, where Vinyes lived, by the open street market, with a view of San Nicolás church, known as the "cathedral of the poor," a few steps away from the offices of *El Heraldo*.[15]

The Librería Mundo belonged to an ex-communist called Jorge Rondón Hederich and was seen as the spiritual successor of Vinyes's own bookshop, which had been destroyed by fire in the distant 1920s.[16] It was the place García Márquez headed for whenever he arrived in the city and the place where his mother would find him when she came to look for him a few weeks after his arrival.[17] If the drinking went on to midnight or beyond, the group would usually adjourn to one of Barranquilla's many brothels, often in the so-called Chinese Quarter, though the favourite destination was Black Eufemia's place, then on the edge of the city more than thirty blocks away.[18]

García Márquez was the youngest of the entire group, the most naive and inexperienced—according to Ibarra Merlano, García Márquez not only did not swear in Cartagena but didn't like others swearing either. He was never a great drinker and certainly no fighter, though there is evidence that he was a discreet but regular fornicator. Germán Vargas later remarked, "He was shy and quiet, like me and Alfonso; that was understandable because he was the most small-town of all of us . . . He was also the most disciplined."[19] He was still, as he would be for many years, the one without a house, the one without money, the one without a wife or even, for most of these years, a proper girlfriend. (His semi-fictional relationship with Mercedes saved him from the fate of having to find a real, steady girlfriend.) He was like some eternal student or bohemian artist. He would say later that although he was happy at the time, he never expected to survive it.[20]

He could not afford to pay a proper rent. He ended up living for almost a year in a brothel which went under the name Residencias New York, in a building nicknamed "The Skyscraper" by Alfonso Fuenmayor, because it was four storeys high, unusual for Barranquilla at that time. Situated in the Calle Real, known popularly as "Crime Street," it was almost opposite the *El Heraldo* office and very close to where Vinyes lived in the Plaza Colón. The ground floor of the building was given over to notaries and other offices. Up above were the prostitutes' quarters, tightly administered by the madam, Catalina la Grande.[21] García Márquez rented one of the rooms at the very top of the building, for one peso fifty a night. The room was three square metres, more like a cubicle. A prostitute called María Encarnación used to iron his two pairs of trousers and three shirts once a week. Sometimes he would not have the money to pay the rent, and then he would give the doorman, Dámaso Rodríguez, a copy of his latest manuscript as a deposit.[22]

He lived in those conditions, between the uproar from the street and the diverse noises, business discussions and catfights of the brothel, for almost a year. He made friends of the prostitutes and even wrote their letters for them. They lent him their soap, shared their breakfast with him, and occasionally he would reciprocate by singing them the odd *bolero* or *vallenato*. He was especially grateful when, a few years later, his one-time idol William Faulkner declared that there is no better place for a writer than a brothel: "In the mornings there is peace and quiet, and in the evenings there are parties, liquor and interesting people to talk to."[23] García Márquez heard many illuminating conversations on the other side of his insubstantial wall and would make much of them in literary episodes to come. Other times he would take aimless nocturnal rides with a taxi driver friend, "El Mono" Guerra. Thereafter he would always consider taxi drivers to be paragons of common sense.

He continued with the pseudonym "Séptimus" which he had assumed in Cartagena, and he entitled his daily column "The Giraffe" ("La Jirafa"), a secret tribute to his adolescent muse, Mercedes, noted for her long slim neck. From the very start these columns carried a new radiance, even if—there was still a censorship regime in place—they were often very low on content.

García Márquez nevertheless maintained his political perspective—and impertinence—as far as possible. At the very start of his career in *El Heraldo*, he showed that he was not susceptible to the Peronist populism which was tempting other Latin American leftists. Of Eva Perón's visit to the old continent he wrote: "The second act was Eva's foray into Europe. In an ostentatious act of international demagoguery, she squandered on the Italian proletariat—more as a spectacle than as an act of charity—almost an entire ministry of finance. In Spain the state comics welcomed her with the enthusiasm of magnanimous colleagues."[24] On 16 March 1950 he got away with an article that noted the extraordinary opportunity open to the barber who shaved the President of the republic every day with an open razor;[25] on 29 July 1950 he would write nonchalantly, as if he were a personal acquaintance, about a visit to London by Ilya Ehrenburg, one of the Soviet Union's most effective propagandists;[26] and on 9 February 1951 he would state baldly that "no political doctrine is more repugnant to me than falangism."[27] (At the time Colombia was run by a regime, under Laureano Gómez, which was the first in Latin America to restore full relations with Franco's Spain, despite United Nations warnings to the contrary, and which would clearly have liked to run a similar administration to Franco's.)

If one of his main problems was censorship, one of his main topics was the search for a topic. And both concerns are humorously addressed in an article entitled "The Pilgrimage of the Giraffe" about his daily chore:

The giraffe is an animal vulnerable to the slightest editorial movement. From the moment the first word of this daily column is conceived—here, at the Underwood . . . until six in the morning the next day, the giraffe becomes a sad, defenceless animal who can break a joint as he turns any corner. In the first place, one has to bear in mind that this business of writing fourteen centimetres of foolishness every day is no joke however temperamentally foolish the writer may be. Then there's the matter of the two censors. The first, who is right here, at my side, blushingly sitting by the fan, ready to stop the giraffe having any colour other than the one he is naturally and publicly allowed. Then there is the second censor, about which nothing can be said without danger of the giraffe's long neck being reduced to the absolute minimum. Finally the defenceless mammal reaches the dark chamber of the linotypists where those much-maligned colleagues labour from sun to sun converting what was originally written on light and transitory leaves into lead.[28]

In many of these articles we can feel not only the "joy of living" but the joy of writing. It was in these early weeks of 1950 that he first experienced this pleasure over a sustained period of time.

Just as García Márquez was getting used to his new life, he received an unexpected visit. At lunchtime on Saturday 18 February, on the eve of Carnival, his mother Luisa Santiaga, who had travelled down-river from Sucre, found him in the Mundo Bookshop. His friends had been discreet enough not to direct her towards the "Skyscraper." This moment is the one that would be chosen by García Márquez to initiate his autobiographical narration in *Living to Tell the Tale*. The family were running short of money again and Luisa Santiaga was on her way to Aracataca to begin the process of selling her father's old home. The journey the mother and her son were about to make was exactly the same journey Luisa had made alone more than fifteen years earlier when she went back to Aracataca to meet a small boy she had left several years before and who had forgotten her. Now she was back again, a couple of weeks before Gabito's twenty-third birthday.[29]

He finished his article for the following day's paper and then he and Luisa travelled on the seven o'clock launch across the great swamp to Ciénaga, a journey recaptured unforgettably in the memoir. From Ciénaga they went on to Aracataca in the same yellow train that had run between the two towns all those years before. They arrived in Aracataca and walked through the empty streets trying to shelter in the shade of the walnut trees.[30] García Márquez considers this visit the single most important experience of his entire life, attributing to it the definitive confirmation of his literary vocation and the catalyst for what he regards as his first serious piece of writing, the novel *Leaf Storm*. That is why it is this episode that initiates *Living to Tell the Tale*, and not the moment of his birth; and it is, without a doubt, a narrative tour de force which gives life to the entire memoir.

The effect of this return to things past was stunning. Every street seemed to funnel him backwards in time towards the house where he was born. Was this the Aracataca of his childhood, these ramshackle houses, these dusty streets, this crumbling toy-sized church? The busy green avenues of his memory were deserted and looked as if they would never be animated again. Everyone and everything he saw seemed covered in dust and had aged to a degree he could not have imagined; the adults all looked sick, weary and defeated, his contemporaries aged beyond their years, their children listless and pot-bellied; stray dogs and vultures appeared to have taken over the town.[31] It was as if everyone else was dead and only he and his mother were alive. Or as if, as in a fairy tale, he himself had been dead and only now had come back to life.

When the two travellers reached the corner diagonally across from the grandparents' old house, on Monsignor Espejo's Avenue, Luisa and Gabito stopped at the old dispensary of the Venezuelan doctor Alfredo Barbosa. Behind the counter, his wife Adriana Berdugo was working at her sewing machine and Luisa blurted out, "*Comadre*, how are you?" The woman looked round, stupefied, tried to reply but couldn't; the two embraced without a word and wept for several minutes. García Márquez looked on, stunned by the confirmation that it was not only distance that had been separating him from Aracataca but time itself. He had once been frightened of the old pharmacist, now a pitiful sight, thin as a dry withered stick, sparse of hair and with most of his teeth missing. When they asked how he was, the old man stammered, almost accusingly, "You cannot imagine what this town has gone through."[32]

Years later García Márquez would say, "What really happened to me in that trip to Aracataca was that I realized that everything that had occurred in my childhood had a literary value that I was only now appreciating. From the moment I wrote *Leaf Storm* I realized I wanted to be a writer and that nobody could stop me and that the only thing left for me to do was to try to be the best writer in the world."[33] Adding to the ironies involved in all returns, the visit itself was a complete failure: his mother was unable to reach agreement with the sitting tenants.

Indeed, the entire journey had been made on the basis of a misunder-standing and anyway Luisa herself was in two minds about the sale. As for him, until he wrote his memoir, which describes his and Luisa's tour around the old crumbling building in great detail, he had always insisted that he had been unable to enter the house on that occasion and had never entered it since: "If I do, I will stop being a writer. The key is inside," he once said.[34] But in the memoir he goes in.

He says he immediately decided to give up "The House" and take a different direction. This is surprising at first sight: one might have thought that a return to the house would only encourage him to start working again on the novel already inspired by it—rather than, as was in fact the case, expanding his focus to include the whole town in which it was situated. But the truth is that the house evoked in "The House" was not in fact the real house but a fictional construct intended to screen it. Now, at last, he was preparing to openly confront the edifice which had been haunting him for so many years and to rebuild the old town, which he still retained in his imagination, around it. Thus was Macondo born.

It is impossible not to think of Proust. Except that García Márquez finds that although Aracataca itself is in many ways dead, he, after all, is alive. And he has, miraculously, got his mother back: he has no memo-ries of ever having lived in the house with her but now at last they have visited it together; and this is the first time in his entire life that he has been on a journey alone with her.[35] Naturally he does not say it—he does not say any of this—but their meeting in the Mundo Bookshop the previous day re-enacted the story of the "first" meeting between them (the first one he remembered) when he was six or seven—because in that later scene too, like a character inspired by *Oedipus Rex*, the nar-rator, García Márquez himself, has her say, "I am your mother."

The visit not only triggered his memory and changed his attitude towards his own past; it also showed him *how* to write the new novel. Now he viewed his home town through the lens given to him by Faulkner and the other 1920s modernists, Joyce, Proust and Virginia Woolf. "The House" had really been conceived as a nineteenth-century novel, inspired by the kind of books which the Cartagena set admired, books such as Hawthorne's *The House of Seven Gables*; now he would write it as a narrative structured by an awareness of the mul-tiple dimensions of time itself. He was no longer buried in that frozen house with his grandfather. He had escaped it.

It was obvious that something big was happening to his understanding of the relation between literature and life when, a few weeks later, he wrote an article entitled "Problems of the Novel?," which casts scorn on most fiction being written in Colombia at the time and then states:

> There has not yet been written in Colombia a novel evidently and fortunately influenced by Joyce, Faulkner or Virginia Woolf. And I say "fortunately" because I don't think we Colombians can be an exception at this point to the play of influences. In her prologue to *Orlando* Virginia Woolf admits her influences. Faulkner himself could not deny those exerted upon him by Joyce. There is something—especially in the management of time—in common between Huxley and, again, Virginia Woolf. Franz Kafka and Proust are everywhere in the literature of the modern world. If we Colombians are to take the right path, we must position ourselves inevitably within this current. The lamentable truth is that it has not happened yet and there is not the slightest sign of it ever happening.[36]

García Márquez was undoubtedly on his way to becoming a new man; he was no longer exiled from his own life; he had recovered his childhood. And he had discovered—or perhaps better, uncovered—a new identity. He had reinvented himself. And all by suddenly perceiving, as in a lightning flash, how the avant-garde writers of the 1920s had learned to view the world from within their own artistic consciousness.

Few of his friends, either in Cartagena or Barranquilla, knew much about his origins. Now the "boy from Sucre" became the "boy from Aracataca" and he would never change his origin again. If there is good reason to believe that at this stage "The House" was in part a Sucre novel, now it would evolve towards being an Aracataca novel, albeit under an alias: Macondo. Before long, indeed, the earlier book would give way completely to the new one and García Márquez would be writing something much more directly autobiographical. Now the jokes he told his friends and colleagues had a different twist: for example, that he had gone back "home" to get his birth certificate and the Mayor had not had an official stamp to hand so had called for a large banana; when it was brought he had cut it in half and stamped the document with it.[37] García Márquez assured his friends that the story was true, only he couldn't prove it just now because he'd left the certificate in the "Skyscraper." They all roared with laughter but they half-believed him. Whether or not there was a certificate to prove it, the story-teller from Aracataca was born; in his next incarnation he would become the magician from Macondo. At last he knew who he was and who he wanted to be.

Soon after his return to Aracataca with Luisa Santiaga in February 1950 he had written a "Giraffe" entitled "Abelito Villa, Escalona and Co."[38] This piece, demonstrating that the journey with his mother reminded him of journeys he had already made and, equally significant, inspired journeys he intended to make in the future, briefly recalled the November 1949 expedition with Zapata Olivella, and celebrated the lives and adventures of the wandering troubadours of the Magdalena and Padilla regions. In particular it exalted the work of another young man who was to play a major role not only in his understanding of *vallenato* music but also in his direct participation in the culture of the Atlantic hinterland. The young man was Rafael Escalona, the *vallenato* composer, who, having already talked to Zapata Olivella about García Márquez, now, on reading the favourable review García Márquez had written of his music, set out to meet him.[39] Their first one-on-one encounter (they may actually have met the year before) was in Barranquilla's Café Roma on 22 March 1950, less than two weeks after the publication of the article about the 1949 trip and less than a month after the life-changing journey with Luisa Santiaga. To make an impression on the young troubadour, García Márquez arrived to meet him at the Café Roma, singing his composition "Hunger at School" ("El hambre del liceo"). There is a rare photograph from those days in which we can see García Márquez singing one of Escalona's songs to the man himself, while drumming on a counter, with a pursing of the lips that García Márquez has always used not only to sing but to smoke, and to pout—whether to women or to men with whom he is in one way or another infatuated.[40]

On 15 April 1950 Vinyes left his disciples and returned whence he had come. Before his departure a farewell dinner was arranged for him, a veritable last supper. In the photograph taken that evening Vinyes, euphoric, has his arm around a disconsolate Alfonso Fuenmayor; next to them, the only man without either a jacket or tie and wearing a brightly coloured tropical shirt, is the youngest person present, Gabriel García Márquez, "thin as a fishbone," as a waitress at the América Billiards Hall had recently said, eyes shining, delighted to be there, his expression both ingenuous and sardonic but above all bursting with energy and life.

Soon after this he was persuaded by Alfonso Fuenmayor to contribute to a new independent weekly magazine, produced tabloid-style at the *El Heraldo* workshop, called *Crónica (Chronicle)*, which was unveiled on 29 April 1950 and survived until June 1951.[41] García Márquez became the jack-of-all-trades of *Crónica*, as well as its director; some of his contributions were drawn, somewhat desperately, from real life. His story "The Woman Who Came at Six O'Clock" originated in a challenge from Fuenmayor that he could not write a detective story. García Márquez recalled an anecdote about Obregón's first efforts, in Catholic Barranquilla, to find a nude model. His friends set about the search for a willing prostitute and finally located a promising candidate; she asked Obregón to first write a letter for her to a sailor in Bristol, agreed to turn up at the School of Fine Arts the next day and then . . . disappeared.[42] "The Woman Who Came at Six O'Clock" is about a prostitute who appears to have just murdered a client and comes into a bar to establish an alibi. A debt to another of his new enthusiasms, Hemingway (perhaps "The Killers"), is evident.[43] It is a rare example of a story by García Márquez which is set directly and recognizably in the Barranquilla of his time.

"The Night of the Curlews" was another even more successful story, admired by connoisseurs such as Mutis and Zalamea Borda up in Bogotá. It had originated in one of the visits to Black Eufemia's brothel in Las Delicias, where the gang tended to turn up almost every night. Fuenmayor would later insist, as if the thought had never even occurred to him, that they certainly did not go there for the women, "those pathetic little girls who went to bed out of hunger," but rather to buy a bottle of rum for thirteen pesos and watch the Yankee sailors stagger around the floor amid the resident curlews, as if they had lost their human partners and were looking to dance with the red-feathered waders. One night García Márquez was dozing there and Fuenmayor shook him awake and said: "Careful the curlews don't peck out your eyes!" (It is believed in Colombia that the birds blind children because they see fish move in their eyes.) So García Márquez went straight back to the office to write the story of three friends in a brothel who are blinded by birds, just in order to fill a space in *Crónica*. The author himself would later say that it was the first literary piece he ever wrote which did not embarrass him half a century later.

He was hypnotized by the literary achievement of the European and American modernists of the 1920s and 1930s; but he was also fascinated by their fame and glory and the use some writers had made of this, notably Faulkner and, above all, Hemingway, in developing myths

about themselves and their writing. The 1949 Nobel Prize for Literature had been left vacant because, although Faulkner had won an overwhelming majority vote of the Swedish Academy, he had not achieved
unanimity. On 8 April García Márquez had already written an article,
"Nobel Prize Again," in which he predicted that Faulkner, whom he
always called "el maestro Faulkner," would never win the prize because
he was "too good a writer." When Faulkner was in fact awarded the
1949 prize retrospectively in November 1950, García Márquez
declared that it was long overdue because Faulkner was "the greatest
writer of the contemporary world and one of the greatest of all time,"
one who now would have to accept "the uncomfortable privilege of
becoming fashionable."[44] Much later he would sort out the great
dilemma—Faulkner or Hemingway?—by remarking that Faulkner
had nourished his literary soul whilst Hemingway had taught him the
writer's trade.[45]

After he became famous García Márquez found himself repeatedly
lured into discussing how much he had been "influenced" by Faulkner.
Beneath the question, invariably, was a more sinister question: whether
he had "plagiarized" Faulkner; in short, whether he lacked true originality. Perhaps, given the extraordinary parallels between their back-
grounds, the remarkable thing is that García Márquez was not more
influenced by Faulkner, especially since Faulkner was unquestionably
the favourite writer of the entire Barranquilla Group. The almost
equally decisive influence of Virginia Woolf on García Márquez is
much less frequently mentioned; James Joyce hardly at all. Since his
points of reference were many, and his own originality unmistakable, it
is little wonder that García Márquez grew weary of the attempts to
reduce him to the status of a Colombian Faulkner, despite his passing
enthusiasm for the Mississippian and the many things they had in common. We have almost no private documents written by García
Márquez in this period; not even the manuscripts of his stories and
novels have been preserved. But some time between the middle of
1950 and, say, October of that same year, García Márquez, possibly
under some non-literary influence—alcohol perhaps—wrote a two-
page letter to his friend Carlos Alemán in Bogotá. Miraculously, the
letter has survived and here is an excerpt:

idonthavejuanbsaddressimsendingyoualetterforhim
      aleman im writing in reply to the epistolary absurdity you
   sent me as im too busy i wont have time to put full stops or com-

mas semi colons and all the other pieces of punctuation in this letter i hardly have time to put the letters pity telepathy doesnt exist to reply by telepathic post which must be the best as its not subject to censorship as you know we are doingcronicaweekly which leaves us no time for expeditions in search of stupefying grasses so for the moment youll have to be content with ordinary crocodile prick until cronica goes bust and we can go back to our stamping ground at son of the night aurelianobuendia sends greetings likewise his daughter remedios semi whore who went out in the end with the singer salesman the son tobias became a policeman and they were killed so the only one left is the girl without a name who won't ever have one they all just called her the girl sitting all day in her rocking chair listening to the gramophone which like everything else in this world went wrong and now its a problem in the house because the only one in the town who knows about machinery is an italian shoemaker whos never in his life seen a cobbled gramophone he goes to the house and tries to hammermendrepair it in vain whilst all the water boys are talkingspillingwaterwhistling and pieces of the grammy end up in every house sayinggramophonecolonelaurelianodamaged that same afternoon people have to run togetdressedclosedoorsputtheirshoesoncombtheirhair to go to the colonel's house he for his part was not expecting visitors since the townsfolk hadn't been back to his house for fifteen years since when they refused to bury gregorios body for fear of the police and the colonel insulted prieststownfellowpartymembers withdrew from council and shut himself up in his house so that only fifteen years later when the gramophone wasdamagedbustbroke did people go back to the house and catch the colonel and his wife dona soledad completely unawares . . . the woman spends all night in a corner not talking to anyone and when dona soledad embarrassed gets to go over its dawn and the people leave its just stuff you know that as the son became a policeman when the police come with his funeral the colonels sitting at the door like always and when he sees the funeral coming he pulls the doors shut well stuff like that its as if it happened in mompos just so you can see how the great book is going that apart i can tell you that german alfonso figurita and i are passing our time talkingwritingthinkingdoingcronica and not like before drinkingwhoringsmokingcigarettesgrass cos life cant be like that if you dont like virginia you can go fuck yourself ramiro likes her and knows more about novels than you so go to fuck tell ramiro i owe him a letter but to write to me anyway in december ill ask for a vacation from cronica and to keep me a place in the apartment don ramon left and has written were all well tito brinqueit eduard puteit old fuenmayors turned out a great guy we all say hello and wish you merrychristmashappynewyear your affectionate friend gabito[46]

This letter is a revelation. As well as the evident influence of the rarely mentioned Joyce—also Virginia Woolf—and the vivid sense it gives of García Márquez's life in Barranquilla and his feelings of euphoria about it, it also shows us a young man still thinking like an impressionable teenager totally obsessed with his own creative process and immersed in his own stories but also, for those familiar with his development, a serious and committed writer riding the wave of a transition between one long-term project, "The House," and another, *Leaf Storm*, as well as writing several stories which would later appear in anthologies and writing his daily column. Colonel Aureliano Buendía is of course the best-known character ever created by García Márquez, and here he is. Nevertheless he is soon to be sidelined, his name a mere legendary mention in one book after another until his moment eventually comes in the mid-1960s; not quite yet, though. Clearly García Márquez has not at this point renounced "The House," despite what he would later assert in his memoir. He was still working on details which, elaborated and modified, would eventually form part of *One Hundred Years of Solitude*.

So perhaps the most interesting detail in the letter is the explanation of the Colonel's problems with the townsfolk and why he has closed down his house: namely, that for some unstated reason they would not let him bury his slave Gregorio and so he buried the slave himself beneath the almond tree in the patio.[47] Here, unmistakably, is one of the first seeds not only of *Leaf Storm*, a novel in which a colonel finds himself under siege because he has a duty to arrange the burial of a man hated by the town in which he lives, but also of *One Hundred Years of Solitude*, in which one of the central characters is tied to a tree in the patio and another dies beneath it.

The careful reader can also divine another influence at this time. García Márquez had included stories by the brilliant Argentine writer Jorge Luis Borges in several editions of *Crónica*. Precisely in August

1950, the month in which the reactionary President Laureano Gómez was invested, García Márquez's reading of the great exponent of "fantastic literature" seems to have borne fruit. Borges was remarkable for taking his influences from anywhere and everywhere and he was already pursuing the line in essays that the concept of "influences" was misleading because "all writers create their own precursors." Not only was this attitude highly liberating for a Latin American writer but Borges's lack of respect for the sources he did use was also extremely refreshing. He has sometimes been called the "Latin American Kafka" but nowhere in Kafka do we find his good-humoured irony. It is doubly appropriate, then, that at the time that García Márquez takes up many of Borges's ideas (though without acknowledging this new influence), he should choose to write a satirical story about a suicide which he entitles "Caricature of Kafka."[48] It can safely be said that at this point García Márquez dispatches Kafka (and his "influence" upon him) to the past and henceforth views Kafka's themes through the more whimsical lens of Borges. One might say that part of the trouble with "The House" was that it carried an excessive dose of Kafka; *One Hundred Years of Solitude*, when it came along, would be a distinctly Borgesian book.

Leaf Storm, the emerging novel, would be about different conceptions of honour, duty and shame. A colonel, one of the accepted aristocrats of the town of Macondo, has vowed to take responsibility for the burial of his friend the Belgian "doctor" (a character based, of course, on "Don Emilio" in the Aracataca of García Márquez's childhood); he intends to carry out his pledge, against the wishes of his wife and daughter, even though the Doctor betrayed his hospitality by sleeping with his servant and even though the townsfolk would like to see the Doctor "rot" because many years earlier he had refused to attend to the town's wounded following a political conflict. Now he has committed an even worse crime against the laws of God as Catholics interpret them—his suicide—and all the Colonel can hope to do is have the man buried in unconsecrated ground.

Despite this moralistic plot-line, a variation on the theme of Sophocles's *Antigone*, *Leaf Storm* is also, in a purely factual sense, the most autobiographical of all García Márquez's novels. The central characters are a holy trinity forming a three-way family romance based on Gabito, Luisa and Nicolás; but if the child, the mother and the grandfather were to be based upon these real people, such a choice required the suppression of other real people, notably Tranquilina (the grandmother in the novel has died and is replaced by a second wife), Gabito's brothers and sisters (the child is an only son), and, above all, Gabito's real father, Gabriel Eligio García. In his case the suppression is merely a displacement. There is indeed a character closely based on Gabriel Eligio and he is the child's real father in the novel; but his name is Martín—Gabriel Eligio's second surname, which would have been his first had he been legitimate, was Martínez—and his motives for the marriage are unscrupulous and self-serving. Moreover he abandons his wife after a brief time (*her* feelings about *him* were always apparently lukewarm), leaves Macondo, and the child never thinks about him in the entire novel. Obviously this allowed García Márquez to fantasize while he wrote that his mother never really loved Gabriel Eligio, and that it was Gabriel Eligio, the father, who became separated from her, not himself, Gabito, the son.[49]

The novel has a dual, Faulknerian timescale. The three characters spend half an hour, between 2.30 and 3 p.m. on 12 September 1928, sitting in the room where the Doctor has died while they wait for him to be placed in his coffin and carried out; they are in a state of high tension because they fear that the townsfolk, who hate the Doctor, may prevent the funeral from taking place. But during that half-hour they also think back over the entire life of their family—the Colonel's family, originally from the Guajira—in flashbacks viewed fragmentarily through the consciousness of each of them. It is a more complex version, though also a more static and mechanical one, of Faulkner's *As I Lay Dying*: the novel as a detective story, a labyrinth or a puzzle which the reader has to solve. Here is a classic example of a young writer dazzled by geniuses such as Faulkner, Woolf and, probably, Borges, and wanting to show it as much as conceal it.

What we have, then, is, simultaneously, a *return* and a *distancing*—clearly an extraordinarily powerful and defining experience with a fusion of the emotional and the intellectual, the past and the present. If the view of Colombian reality is not as yet a cruelly satirical one, that is because García Márquez does not wish to include his grandfather in the condemnation or to make his own past too bitter (or too deluded!) in retrospect; at this point, the Colonel is a contradictory but still mainly admirable figure, treated with only the lightest irony. Still, in making his return to his birthplace, García Márquez has realized that Macondo has already been devastated by a force which the inhabitants see as fate but which he, now, sees as history.

Many years later, in 1977, García Márquez would remark, "I have a great affection for *Leaf Storm*. And a great compassion for the guy who wrote it. I can see him clear as day: he's a boy of twenty-two, twenty-three, who thinks he's never going to write another thing in his life, this is his only chance, so he tries to put everything in, everything he remembers and everything he's learned about technique and literary craft in all the authors that he's read."[50] Work on *Leaf Storm* would continue, on and off, for several more years but the book was well and truly launched. And although this young man would never be complacent, with luck and much more hard work his literary future would undoubtedly be assured. He was not, however, a man about whom one could write the usual cliché—that he would never look back.

OF COURSE García Márquez still had a living to earn and he continued to produce his "Giraffes" for *El Heraldo* on almost a daily basis and to act as the dynamo for *Crónica*. Almost everything he wrote at the time, however trivial and however rushed, was touched in some degree by the grace of discovery and creation. Biographically, however, the most interesting article during this period is one which appeared on 16 December 1950, called "La Amiga." "Amiga" in Spanish can mean any female friend or it can mean "girlfriend." It was, in brief, a public reaction to the excitement of having met up with Mercedes Barcha again, in an article whose cool tone can scarcely contain the pleasure of the event. This "friend" is described as Mercedes was then and is today, "oriental in looks," with "slanting eyes," "high cheekbones," "dark skin" and a "cordially mocking" manner. Mercedes was in town because her family had fled their home some months before in the face of the *Violencia*, which had come to Sucre with a vengeance.

The courtship between Gabriel García Márquez and Mercedes Barcha is an enigma from start to finish.[51] Both of them have always joked about his insistence that he decided he would marry her when she was nine, her insistence that she was almost unaware of him until shortly before he left for Europe in 1955. The December 1950 article, which cannot of course be taken literally, nonetheless says that it is three years since its protagonists last met up. In fact 1947 was the year when García Márquez graduated from Zipaquirá, went home for the summer and then left for university in Bogotá; after that he went home as little as possible and Mercedes was in any case away from Sucre studying at a convent school in Medellín and only returned home for the end-of-year holidays. There are persistent stories that Gabito used to hang around Mompox before 1947, when she was studying there, and Ramiro de la Espriella recalls that he used to talk about her in Cartagena in 1949; but there seems to have been very little contact or communication between them in the six years that passed between their first acquaintance and their meeting at the end of what must already be counted the most decisive year in García Márquez's life.

Everything suggests that he had been anticipating her return from school to Barranquilla for Christmas for some time before they met. For one thing he finally left the "Skyscraper" and moved into a respectable boarding house run by the Avila sisters, whom he knew through connections with Sucre and who lived in the upper part of town just a few blocks from the Hotel Prado, near where his friend the poet Meira Delmar lived.[52] It also happened to be very close to the new pharmacy which Demetrio Barcha had established on the corner of 65th Street and 20 July Avenue. García Márquez had also changed his image, with a shorter haircut, a more neatly clipped moustache, a suit and tie, and some decent shoes to replace his tropical sandals. The reaction from his friends was merciless, some of them predicting that he would be unable to write a word as soon as he left the "Skyscraper." The move evidently coincided both with the realization that his new novel—a novel about him and his own life—was now a secure reality, and with the resolve to bump into Mercedes. He was, after all, in many ways a new man, with much more to offer a woman than in the past.

His timidity remained a problem however and the family still joke about it today. Ligia García Márquez recalls, "When Mercedes moved to Barranquilla Gabito spent hours talking to Demetrio Barcha in the pharmacy, which was right next door to their house. So people said to Mercedes again, 'Gabito's still got a crush on you,' and she'd reply, 'No, he's got a crush on my dad, it's him he talks to all the time. He doesn't even say good evening to me.' "[53] García Márquez himself has admitted that he spent ten years as a "street-corner man," hanging around waiting for a glimpse of the haughty and ironic Mercedes, suffering agonies of frustration and even the occasional humiliation from a girl who seems to have found it difficult, for a long time, to take him seriously and showed very little interest in him.[54] Barranquilla Group members later recalled driving round and round in Cepeda's jeep and García Márquez asking Cepeda to crawl slowly past the pharmacy, where Mercedes sometimes helped out during the vacations and after she left school, just to get a glimpse of her—oblivious to the jeers of his macho friends who had quite another attitude to women. Mercedes herself, who has only ever given two newspaper interviews (one of them to her sister-in-law, with the teasing title, "Gabito Waited for Me to Grow Up"), told me in 1991, "I only ever went out with Gabo in a group. But I did have a Palestinian aunt who always used to cover for us and was always trying to get us together; she was always starting sentences with the phrase, 'When you marry Gabito. . . .'"

That Christmas of 1950, somehow or other, Gabito finally persuaded Mercedes to give him a chance and took her dancing at the Prado several times. She was teasingly non-committal, without overtly rejecting the young man's advances, and he chose to believe that they had some kind of tacit agreement and that he was in with a chance. This was an entirely new situation.

A person who knows at least something about these early dates is Aida García Márquez, who was banished to Barranquilla by her parents, to keep her away from her own beloved suitor Rafael Pérez. She told me: "Mercedes was not my best friend but I was hers. We used to go out dancing together at the Prado, and I would dance with her father so Gabito could be with Mercedes."[55]

Thus García Márquez began 1951 in the most optimistic mood imaginable, little knowing that his carefully arranged and hard-earned new life was about to be cruelly demolished. On 23 January he heard from Mercedes again. A brief note informed him that his friend Cayetano Gentile had been murdered in Sucre. The two families were very close—Cayetano's mother Julieta was Nanchi's godmother—and García Márquez would later discover that several of his own brothers and sisters had been witnesses to what had happened; the only absentees from Sucre at the time were Aida, Gabriel Eligio, who was in Cartagena at a Conservative Party conference, and Gabito himself.

Cayetano Gentile had been killed by the brothers of Margarita Chica, the girl who had roomed with Mercedes in Mompox. During her wedding night Margarita had revealed to her husband that she was not a virgin and he had returned her to her family as damaged goods. One of the rumours in Mompox is that she had been raped by a policeman during the *Violencia* and was unable to tell the truth for fear of reprisals. So she said that her virginity had been taken by Cayetano Gentile, who was, indeed, a former boyfriend.[56] The truth will never be known. Her brothers set out immediately to restore the family's honour by killing the alleged offender in the main square of Sucre, in front of the whole town. This is the story that García Márquez would convert into his novel *Chronicle of a Death Foretold* thirty years later, in

1981. It was a savage murder and an act that would haunt García Márquez and his whole family for decades.

A week later, before he had had time to learn much about this horrific event, he received a message that, instead of returning to Sucre after his conference, Gabriel Eligio had arrived in Barranquilla. Gabito took the bus down to the centre and met his panic-stricken father at the Café Roma: he too had heard the news. He and Luisa Santiaga had already feared for the future of the family because of the growing political violence and this barbaric killing was the last straw. (Truth to tell, Gabriel Eligio had recently been having a hard time financially in Sucre since the moment when a real doctor moved into his part of town.) He had been in Cartagena with Gustavo, henceforth his right-hand man, and had already made inquiries among his Conservative friends and relatives in the city and was arranging to move the family there. He wanted Gabito to help them get installed and then move back to Cartagena himself to help out with the finances in a situation that was bound to be difficult, if not desperate. A further advantage, Gabriel Eligio said, was that Gabito could return to his law studies.[57]

Gabriel Eligio's fears were at first sight surprising. Sucre was essentially Conservative territory and he himself had got involved in local politics and should have been able to count on protection; it was the Liberals, like Demetrio Barcha, whom one would expect to flee—as indeed he had—whereas the García Márquez family seemed to be sitting pretty. Besides, the murder of Cayetano was not politically motivated. But at that time slanderous posters (*pasquines*) began to appear which were a coded symptom of the disintegration of society and were devoted not only to political matters, notably corruption, but, above all, to sexual accusations designed to ruin people's reputations. Vendettas proliferated. And of course Gabriel Eligio had sexual scandals of his own to worry about.

With a heavy heart Gabito reluctantly agreed to his father's demands; and Gabriel Eligio went back to Sucre to organize the exodus. Luisa was heartbroken. Ligia recalls, "Just as my mother wept when she arrived in Sucre, so she wept when she left."[58] The family had lived in Sucre for more than eleven years. Jaime, Hernando, Alfredo and Eligio Gabriel had all been born there; Tranquilina had died there. And Gabriel Eligio had, for once, for a time, achieved a certain prestige and authority in the small waterlocked town. He had even built his first house there. But the whole García Márquez family, like the Barchas shortly before them, like Gabito and Luis Enrique in 1948, had now become refugees from the *Violencia*.

For Gabito himself this was a disaster; we can only imagine the anguish with which he allowed himself to be dragged back into the bosom of a family with whom he had almost never lived for any significant period of time. He negotiated with the management of *El Heraldo* to continue to send his "Giraffes" from Cartagena. They generously agreed to advance him 600 pesos for six months of the column and seven—often politically compromising—editorials a week, making life a nightmare for him but easy for Fuenmayor.

The first year was absolutely chaotic. None of the children was ever again sent away to study and the younger ones didn't even start their education. After all his previous failures Gabriel Eligio must have known he would not make it in Cartagena as a pharmacist, though he briefly tried again. He also made a half-hearted effort to carry on his work as a doctor but Cartagena was not a promising arena for a quack, and before a year had passed he was off on his travels once more, roaming the Sucre region as a peripatetic doctor just as he had done fourteen years before when they moved to Barranquilla. Gabriel Eligio would never again be fully able to support his wife and children. It would be ten years before the family would even begin to be able to say that it was back on its feet—and even then only because most of the children had left home and Margot was taking most of the strain.

It seems likely that Gabito went back to Cartagena hoping not to have to stay too long, but feeling the need to show willing in getting the family installed in this expensive and not necessarily welcoming new environment. He crawled back to *El Universal* with his tail between his legs and was surprised and gratified to be received with open arms by Zabala, López Escauriaza and all his old colleagues— even more so when they offered him a monthly salary larger than he had been receiving in Barranquilla.[59]

What he did not do was return to his studies. Only when he went, reluctantly, to enrol did he realize that he had failed not two but three subjects at the end of 1949, which meant that instead of taking the fourth year he would have to repeat the whole of the third year.[60] He quickly dropped the idea but his father got wind of the decision and lost his temper with his evasive eldest son. Gustavo remembers Gabriel Eligio confronting Gabito about the matter, appropriately enough on the Promenade of the Martyrs just outside the old city. When he heard his son admit that he had decided to give up the law and concentrate on his writing, Gabriel Eligio uttered a phrase that has become legendary in the family: "You'll end up eating paper!" he bellowed.[61]

The arrival of that large, unruly, impoverished family into his urban world must have been desperately embarrassing, not to say humiliating, for a young man used to hiding his own poverty and his own complexes beneath a clown's uniform and a clown's performance. On his first night in the new house García Márquez remembers bumping into a sack containing his grandmother's bones which Luisa Santiaga had brought to re-bury in their new city of residence.[62] Ramiro de la Espriella's wry amusement at the family predicament was summed up in the name he coined to refer to Gabriel Eligio in those days: "the stud horse."[63] Nor were Gabriel Eligio's feelings about his son concealed from public gaze. On one occasion when Carlos Alemán met Gabriel Eligio and asked after Gabito, the father complained loudly that his son was never around when he was wanted: "Tell that peripatetic spermatozoa to come and see his mother," he roared.[64] And when de la Espriella, trying to defend Gabito against some other criticism, said that he was now considered "one of the best story writers in the country," his father exploded, "He's a story-teller, all right, he's been a liar since he was a small boy!"[65]

At the beginning of July, his debt having been paid, García Márquez ceased sending "Giraffes" to *El Heraldo* and no more were published until February 1952. Meanwhile, he went on with his own writing, in the midst of the family chaos, as best he could. An incident recalled by Gustavo gives the measure of his ambition: "Gabito doesn't remember but he . . . once said to me, 'Listen, help me with this,' and he fetched the original manuscript of *Leaf Storm* to go through it. We were halfway through reading it when he stood up and said: 'This is OK but I'm going to write something that will be read more than the *Quixote*.' "[66] In March García Márquez had had another of his stories published in Bogotá, "Nabo: The Black Man Who Made the Angels Wait."[67] This is the first story called something that sounds like a "García Márquez" title and has something of the manner of his later works.[68]

Around then an exiled Peruvian politician and adventurer called Julio César Villegas, the representative in Bogotá of Buenos Aires's influential Losada publishing house, which at that time could make the continental reputation of any Latin American writer, was travelling around the country, including the Costa, looking for promising material, and told García Márquez that if he completed his work in progress and submitted it to Losada it would be considered for publication in Buenos Aires as a representative of contemporary Colombian fiction. In a state of great excitement, García Márquez set about his manuscript with renewed vigour and enthusiasm. By mid-September the first version of *Leaf Storm* was more or less ready.

It was now that a young man arrived in Cartagena who was to become one of García Márquez's lifelong friends: the poet, traveller and business executive Alvaro Mutis—perhaps the only Colombian writer of the past half century in a position to be something like García Márquez's equal as an interlocutor.[69] García Márquez would later describe him as having "a heraldic nose and a Turk's eyebrows, an enormous body and tiny shoes like Buffalo Bill."[70] Partly brought up in Europe where his father died when he was nine, he was a relative of the famous Spanish-Colombian colonial botanist José Celestino Mutis. His first published poem "No. 204" ("El 204") had appeared in *El Espectador* shortly before García Márquez's first short story, and his second, "The Curses of Maqroll the Lookout" ("Las imprecaciones de Maqroll el Gaviero") appeared a couple of weeks later. Just as García Márquez had already invented his Aureliano Buendía, so Mutis had already invented Maqroll, a character similarly destined for worldwide celebrity. By then Mutis had worked for a time at the Colombian Insurance Company, had spent four years at the Bavaria Brewing Company as Head of Publicity, and then almost two years as a radio presenter; now he was Head of Publicity for LANSA, the same airline in which Luis Enrique had previously been employed—hence Mutis's fabled ability to fix flights at short notice. Mutis had just met García Márquez's old student friend Gonzalo Mallarino in Bogotá and Mutis, in a characteristic gesture, swept his new friend off to encounter the sea the very day he discovered that Mallarino had never seen it.[71]

At the weekend they looked for Gabito in *El Universal*, then went off to Bocagrande to have a drink on the terrace of their small hotel. As they sat and drank, a tropical storm gathered force around them, rolling in from the grey–white Caribbean. At its height, as coconuts exploded all around them, in staggered García Márquez from the chaos, painfully thin, pale, wild-eyed as always, his pencil moustache now widening to fountain pen size, and the inevitable trademark tropical shirt.[72] "What gives?" ("Qué es la vaina?") he exclaimed, as he would whenever he met Alvaro Mutis over the next fifty years.[73] So the three friends spent several hours discussing *la vaina*: life, love and literature, among other things. Two characters more different than Mutis and García Márquez could hardly be imagined and yet their friendship has lasted half a century. Their only true enthusiasm in common is Joseph Conrad and they disagreed about William Faulkner from the moment they met. Mutis told me in 1992, "He tried to act the *costeño* but after five minutes I realized he was an intensely serious type of guy. He was an old man in a young man's body." The visit was particularly timely, because Mutis, whose networking was always the astonishment of his friends, knew the Losada agent Julio César Villegas and urged García Márquez to get on with the job and send his manuscript off as soon as possible. García Márquez set to producing a fair copy of his chaotic typescript and a few weeks later Mutis returned to Cartagena, carried the finished version back with him to Bogotá and sent it airmail to Buenos Aires. This was a prophetic act; many years later the same Alvaro Mutis would personally carry a duplicate copy of *One Hundred Years of Solitude* to Buenos Aires for consideration by another great Argentine publishing house, Sudamericana.

In early December 1951 García Márquez turned up in the *El Heraldo* office in Barranquilla and in response to Alfonso Fuenmayor's enquiry as to the cause of his reappearance, said, "Maestro, I've had it up to here."[74] Now that the novel was completed he could no longer bear the strains of living with the family in Cartagena and relieving an ungrateful Gabriel Eligio of his responsibilities. Of course, the timing of his return probably had something to do with the fact that the end-of-year vacations had begun and Mercedes Barcha was back in Barranquilla after completing her fifth grade of high school in the tyrannical convent academy run by the Salesian nuns in Medellín, where the girls had to bathe in specially designed shifts ("so that none of us," she told me, "would ever see any part of another girl's body"). García Márquez went back to stay with the Avila sisters, despite the extra expense, and not to the "Skyscraper."

In early February he received a letter from Losada via the *El Heraldo* office. It was perhaps the greatest disappointment of his life. García Márquez had understood that *Leaf Storm*'s publication was a near sure thing and was shattered to learn that the editorial committee in Buenos Aires had rejected the book and, in a manner of speaking, had rejected him. Because the committee in Buenos Aires had sent a devastating letter from its chairman, Guillermo de Torre, one of Spain's leading literary critics in exile and, as it happened, brother-in-law to Jorge Luis Borges, whom García Márquez so much admired. The letter granted the novice writer some poetic talent but declared that he had no future as a novelist and suggested none too delicately that he look for some other profession. All García Márquez's friends, almost equally disconcerted, rallied round and helped him pull himself together—which was as well because he was in danger of falling sick with the shock and dismay. Alvaro Cepeda snorted, "Everyone knows Spaniards are stupid," and all of them backed their own judgement against De Torre's.[75]

For the rest of 1952 he continued to earn his living with *El Heraldo* and his "Giraffes" appeared throughout the year. They were never again quite so refreshingly novel and eager as in the first magical year.[76] Before long, though, Séptimus would be dead and García Márquez would write no more "Giraffes"—though neither he nor any member of the group has ever given an adequate explanation of how or why the relationship with *El Heraldo* came to an end. The truth is that, despite his bravado, the rejection of *Leaf Storm* had been a devastating, sickening blow. His confidence had been savagely dented and there seemed little point in continuing with the "Giraffes"; what had they done for him, where had all his hard work taken him? It was no doubt because he saw himself as a failure, publicly at least, that he had felt morally constrained to make one more gesture at studying to be a lawyer and saving the family. And once he saw, yet again, that it was not going to work, he was utterly lost.

IRONICALLY, IT WAS his erstwhile nemesis, the Losada agent Julio César Villegas, who offered him a desperate way out and he took it. Villegas had started his own bookselling business and turned up one day when García Márquez was in Barranquilla, took him to the Hotel Prado, plied him with whisky and sent him away with a promise of employment and a bookseller's briefcase. Gabriel García Márquez, self-styled contender to write "the next *Quixote*," was now a travelling salesman hawking encyclopedias and medical and scientific manuals around the small towns and villages of north-eastern Colombia. He must have reflected that he had turned into his father.

Fortunately García Márquez has always had a sense of humour and a Cervantine sense of irony. He could probably take it. Just about. The consolation, needless to say, was that he could now learn more about his family history by retracing the steps of his grandparents all those years before, as he travelled the dusty roads of the Valley of Upar, between the Sierra Nevada and the River Cesar. This was not the world of Guillermo de Torre; but it was his world. Appropriately enough, as he set off on his first trip he met up with his brother Luis Enrique in Santa Marta. Luis Enrique, who had married the previous

October, was already finding marriage a straitjacket that he would do almost anything to loosen. He had been involved in a series of real and fictitious jobs, first in Ciénaga and then Santa Marta; now he jumped at the chance of a jaunt with his brother. The two went to Ciénaga together and Gabito began his new job there, in one of the towns where his grandparents had briefly lived before moving to Aracataca. Luis Enrique then accompanied him on his first arc through Guacamayal, Sevilla, Aracataca, Fundación and Copey to Valledupar, La Paz and Manaure, targeting particularly doctors, lawyers, judges, notaries and mayors.

After Luis Enrique's departure back to Ciénaga, Gabito looked up Rafael Escalona, who accompanied him for a week through the towns of the Guajira—Urumita, Villanueva, El Molino, San Juan del Cesar, and possibly Fonseca. They picked up Zapata Olivella on the way and between them they organized a travelling *parranda*, a kind of *vallenato* jam session and contest involving several participants and huge quantities of liquor, a session which in this case included friends and relatives such as Luis Carmelo Correa from Aracataca and Poncho Cotes, a cousin of García Márquez and close friend of Rafael Escalona.[77] Forty-five years later Zapata told me, "We would go on celebratory outings. One night a car would arrive and you'd wake up the next morning with a hangover in the Guajira or the Sierra Nevada, that's what life was like then; we'd go out to someone's farm and eat a *sancocho*, or drive over the Sierra de Perijá to Manaure; but always we'd end up drinking with the best accordionists of the era, Emiliano Zuleta, Carlos Noriega, Lorenzo Morales."[78] Thus Escalona took his citified friend to meet the cowboy troubadours and the legendary characters of the region.

The historic centre of *vallenato* activity is now conventionally considered to be Valledupar itself, the capital city of El Cesar, situated in the Valley of Upar (*vallenato* means "born in the valley"). Once heard, traditional *vallenatos* are instantly recognizable: they have a driving, swinging beat brought about by the unusual instrumental combination of the European accordion, the African drum and the Indian *guacharaca* (scraper), led by the strong, assertive and defiantly masculine voice of the singer, usually the accordionist himself.[79] A song by Alonso Fernández Oñate sums up the *vallenato*'s prevailing ideology very succinctly:

> I'm true *vallenato* born
> Pure of heart and stock

Indian blood in my veins
Some black and Spanish on top
I have my *vallenato* pleasures
Women, music, my accordion
And all these things I love
Come out in the voice of my song.[80]

Not many Latin American writers have been in such close contact with what could be called a genuine popular culture as García Márquez was to be over the next fifty years. He would go so far as to say that his encounter with the *vallenato* genre and the musicians who created it really gave him the idea for the narrative form of *One Hundred Years of Solitude*.[81] The comparison is interesting, given that more events are narrated on every single page of that novel than in any other narrative one can think of. But García Márquez takes it further, establishing a parallel between the concreteness of the *vallenato* and the direct relation between his own novels and his own life: "There's not a line in any of my books which I can't connect to a real experience. There is always a reference to a concrete reality." This is why he has always asserted that far from being a "magical realist," he is just a "poor notary" who copies down what is placed on his desk.[82] Perhaps the only surprising aspect of all this is that García Márquez, usually admired for his sympathy with women, should have identified quite so fully with a movement that so assertively exalts maleness and masculine values.

It was with Escalona that García Márquez had another of the great mythic encounters of his life. They were drinking iced beer and rum in a cantina in La Paz when a young man strode in, dressed like a cowboy, with a wide hat, leather chaps, and a gun at his waist. Escalona, who knew him well, said: "Let me introduce you to Gabriel García Márquez." The man asked, as he shook his hand, "Would you have anything to do with Colonel Nicolás Márquez?" "I'm his grandson." "Then your grandfather killed my grandfather."[83] The young man's name was Lisandro Pacheco—though in the memoir García Márquez would say he was called José Prudencio Aguilar, like the character based on him in *One Hundred Years of Solitude*. Escalona, who always carried a pistol himself, moved quickly to say that García Márquez knew nothing about the matter and suggested that he and Lisandro should try some sharp-shooting, the purpose being to empty the gun. The three men spent three days and nights drinking and travelling in Pacheco's truck—used mainly for smuggling—around the region.

Pacheco introduced García Márquez to several of the Colonel's illegitimate children from the time of the war.

When his friends and travelling companions were otherwise engaged, the reluctant encyclopedia salesman would stay in small run-down hotels sizzling in the heat. One of the better ones was the Hotel Welcome in Valledupar. It was during this stay that he read Hemingway's *The Old Man and the Sea*, which appeared in the Spanish edition of *Life* magazine at the end of March, sent by his friends in Barranquilla. It was "like a stick of dynamite."[84] García Márquez's deprecating attitude to Hemingway the novelist was transformed.

As well as *The Old Man and the Sea* he vividly recalls having re-read Virginia Woolf's *Mrs. Dalloway* in some other hotel-cum-brothel during this journey, amidst clouds of mosquitoes and asphyxiating heat—probably not the kind of place Virginia Woolf herself would have much enjoyed. Although he had taken his nom de plume from her novel, he had not previously been so struck by it, and especially by a passage about the King of England passing by in a limousine which would later have a major influence on *The Autumn of the Patriarch*.[85]

When he got back to Barranquilla after this brief excursion García Márquez had actually come to the end of a very long journey through his own popular regional culture and, indeed, through his own past and his own prehistory.[86] He was now ready to inhabit "Macondo"—at the very moment, ironically enough, when Hemingway's example would shortly lure him away from the worlds of memory and myth. Nowadays the great writer "García Márquez" is associated intimately with that Latin American village which is also a state of mind: "Macondo." But "Macondo," as we know, is only half the García Márquez story, though it is the half which would give him his international identity and prestige. The real region around the literary town "Macondo" is the northern part of the old Department of Magdalena, from Santa Marta to the Guajira by way of Aracataca and Valledupar. It is the territory of his mother and his maternal grandparents, to which his father came as an unwanted interloper, one of the so-called "leaf-trash." The other half of the story is that father's own territory: the city of Cartagena and the towns of Sincé and Sucre, in the departments of Bolívar and Sucre, the territory of a man with vainglorious dreams of legitimacies past and future, and therefore a territory to be rejected both because of the region's colonial, repressive splendour and the humiliations still undergone by its less illustrious sons; a territory which would become condensed into the anonymous *pueblo*, unworthy of a literary name but equally representative of Latin America—the "real," historical Latin America, one is tempted to say.[87]

Now that his long journey was over, García Márquez could return briefly to Barranquilla and survey this entire conquered space—conquered, at last, by him—from its very centre, located at the apex of the entire backward-looking territory but not itself of that territory. Not only was Barranquilla a gateway, it was also a twentieth-century, modern town, with neither colonial pretensions nor guilts, where one could escape from the weight of the past and its ghostly generations and make oneself anew. By now it had almost done its job.

The whole period of drift was about to end at a time when political change was again looming, menacingly, in the background. García Márquez was on a bus back to Barranquilla on 13 June 1953 when he learned that General Rojas Pinilla, Commander-in-Chief of the armed forces, had taken over the government in a coup against the regime of Laureano Gómez. Gómez, sufficiently recovered from the illness that had forced him to hand over to his Vice-President even before the coup, was trying to return to power but the military had decided that his return was not in the national interest and that they would serve out the rest of his term, with Rojas Pinilla at their head. There was overwhelming national support for this coup; even the editors of some national newspapers serenaded the new leader. García Márquez remembers having a violent political argument with Ramiro de la Espriella in Villegas's bookshop—Villegas would shortly be thrown in prison for alleged fraud—the day after Rojas Pinilla moved against Gómez. García Márquez had even allowed himself to provoke his friend by saying, "I do, I feel identified with the government of my General Gustavo Rojas Pinilla."[88] His position was essentially that anything was better than Gómez's falangist regime whereas de la Espriella wanted outright revolution, feared that a military dictatorship might prove worse than a reactionary dictatorship and argued that the military could not be trusted. Both men had a point; this was a significant disagreement and a prophetic one. García Márquez would several times in the future argue that a progressive dictatorship was better than a fascistic government doing mischief under the cover of a false democracy.

Despite his reluctance to return to *El Heraldo*, García Márquez only managed to keep out of that frying pan by tumbling into a different fire. Alvaro Cepeda Samudio, who had been working in car sales, had long nurtured the desire to compete with *El Heraldo* and build a better newspaper which would dominate the Costa. Around October he was given a chance to run *El Nacional,* hoping to turn it into the kind of modern paper he had learned about in the USA. He hired his newly unemployed friend as his assistant. García Márquez later remembered it as one of his worst times. The two young men spent entire days and nights at the newspaper office, yet very few editions actually came out, and hardly any of them on time. Unfortunately there are no collections extant so it is impossible to judge their efforts. All we really know is that Cepeda directed the morning edition, which he sent to the interior, and García Márquez directed the evening edition, which sold in Barranquilla. They concluded that at least part of the problem was the old-timers on the payroll trying to sabotage an innovatory newspaper.[89] Unfortunately the truth appears to be that Cepeda proved incapable at that time of the discipline and subtlety required to manage such an operation. García Márquez recalls discreetly that "Alvaro left with a slam of the door."[90]

García Márquez himself still had a contract and carried on for a time, trying desperately to survive by using old material, but he was also provoked into writing a new story, "One Day After Saturday," another of the few early tales of his which he would later admit to actually liking. It is most interesting for the fact that, although still reminiscent of "The House," it was set in a place called "Macondo." Not only that: anyone who had been there could have worked out that "Macondo" was clearly based on Aracataca, with, somehow, a transparency of focus despite the air of mystery, and open skies instead of the grim darkness that seems to characterize both "The House" and "the town" *(el pueblo),* based on Sucre. Why, there was even a railway station! At the same time the story—really a short, highly condensed novella—was no longer confined within a house, like most of the earlier stories and published fragments, and was overtly political, focusing on the mayor and the local priest. Moreover Colonel Aureliano Buendía and José Arcadio Buendía were named, as was their relative Rebeca, "the embittered widow." There was also a poor boy from outside the town, treated with a quite new sympathy that was clearly tinged with social and political critique. At the same time the story displayed a whole range of what would later be García Márquez's favourite themes, beginning with the topic of plagues (in this case a plague of dead birds) and the concept of human solitude.[91]

Alvaro Mutis, who was now Head of Public Relations with Esso, returned to Barranquilla close to the end of the year and, seeing his friend's predicament, tried again to persuade him to move to Bogotá. He told him that he was "rusting away in the provinces."[92] Mutis had good reason to believe that García Márquez could get a job with *El Espectador*. Nothing in the *costeño* wanted to go and he flatly refused. Mutis said, "Well, I'll send you an open ticket and you can come when you're ready."[93] Finally García Márquez had second thoughts but realized that he couldn't go to Bogotá even if he wanted to, because he had no clothes. He scraped his last pesos together and bought a business suit, a couple of shirts and a tie. Then he took the air ticket out of his drawer and looked at it. Then he put it in the pocket of his new suit. He had tried his very hardest but there was no way a poor boy without a degree could earn a decent living on the Costa. Maybe one day he would be able to marry Mercedes, to whom he had now committed himself, at least in his own mind. His friends said, "Fine, but don't come back a *cachaco*." Then they took him down to celebrate his departure in one of their favourite down-market bars, The Third Man. And that was that.

8

Back to Bogotá: The Ace Reporter

1954–1955

GARCÍA MÁRQUEZ ARRIVED back in Bogotá in early January 1954. He came in by plane, despite an already pathological fear of flying that would only deepen over the years. Alvaro Mutis, whose life had long been full of planes, and automobiles and even ships, greeted him at the airport. The new arrival had a suitcase and two hand-carried packages, which he gave to his friend to stow in the boot of the car: the manuscripts of "The House" and *Leaf Storm*, both still unpublished. Mutis drove him straight to his office in the centre of the city; back into the cold and the rain, back into a world of tensions and alienations which he thought he had left behind for ever when he flew out of the city almost six years before.[1]

At this time the Esso headquarters in Bogotá was in the same building on Avenida Jiménez de Quesada as the new premises of *El Espectador*, which had moved from its previous site just a few blocks away. Mutis's office in public relations was four storeys above that of the editor of the newspaper, Guillermo Cano. Mutis was vague and ambiguous about how they should proceed during the early days of García Márquez's stay—even the prospect of a job with *El Espectador* was left in limbo—and García Márquez's already gloomy and anxious mood began to grow. He was never confident in new situations or with men and women he didn't know; people were rarely impressed by him on first appearance and he only gained confidence through intimacy and familiarity or by showing what he could do. However, Mutis, in whose personality the entrepreneur and the aesthete seemed to be combined in ways that few had seen or even imagined, was not a man to take no for an answer. He was a master salesman even when he was not sure of the quality of his product; when he had a commodity as valuable as this almost unknown writer he was usually irresistible. And Alvaro Mutis cared deeply about literature and was an unusually generous man.

Physically the two could hardly have been more different—Mutis tall, elegant, vulpine; García Márquez short, skinny, scruffy. García Márquez had been writing novels and stories since he was eighteen; in those days Mutis was exclusively a poet and would only start writing novels in his mid-sixties, after his retirement from a succession of jobs in the employ of U.S.-based international companies. Even now, when both are internationally famous novelists, the two Colombians are separated by the whole history of Latin American literature. And they have always stood at opposite poles of the political spectrum: Mutis, almost theatrically reactionary, a monarchist in a country which has been a republic for almost two hundred years, has always had, in his own words, "a complete lack of interest in all political phenomena later than the fall of Byzantium into the hands of the infidels," that is, later than 1453;[2] while García Márquez's post-1917 predilections would later become well known—though never a communist, he would be closer to that world-view in its broadest sense than to any other ideology in a long life of practical commitments. Theirs would be a long, close relationship but never a confessional one.

For the first couple of weeks García Márquez sat around not in *El Espectador* but in Mutis's office, smoking and shivering, as he always did in Bogotá, talking to Mutis's recently appointed "assistant"—none other than his old friend Gonzalo Mallarino, who had first introduced them that stormy night in Cartagena—or simply twiddling his thumbs. Sometimes, especially in Latin America and other parts of the so-called "Third World," where most people are completely powerless, you just have to wait for situations to evolve. (This is why so many of García Márquez's novels and stories are about waiting and hoping—it is the same verb in Spanish: *esperar*—for things that may never come and usually don't.) Then, near the end of January, *El Espectador* suddenly offered him a staff position and the incredible sum of 900 pesos a month. To earn that in Barranquilla he would have had to write three hundred "Giraffes"—ten a day! It would be the first time he had ever had any spare money and it meant he could help out the family in Cartagena, sending enough for both rent and utilities.

He had been living temporarily in Mutis's mother's house out in Usaquén. Now he moved into a "boarding house with no name" near the Parque Nacional, the home of a French woman who had once put up Eva Perón in her dancing days. He had his own suite of rooms, an undreamed-of luxury, though he would spend little time there. Occasionally in the months to come he would find the time and energy to smuggle some transient female into his apartment.[3] Mainly, however, he would spend the next year and a half between the newspaper, the boarding house, Mutis's office and Bogotá's gothic cinemas carrying out his duties as staff writer, cinema critic and, eventually, star reporter.

Surprisingly, perhaps, newspaper warfare in Bogotá was mainly about competition between the two great Liberal newspapers. *El Espectador* had been founded in 1887 by the Cano family of Medellín (it moved to Bogotá in 1915), and was thus older than its bitter rival, *El Tiempo*, founded in 1911 and bought by Eduardo Santos in 1913. The Santos family still owned and ran *El Tiempo* right up to 2007, when the Spanish publishing house Planeta took a majority stake. The director of *El Espectador* when García Márquez arrived that January was Guillermo Cano, the myopic, unassuming grandson of the founder; he had only recently taken over this position because, incredibly, he was still in his early twenties. He and García Márquez would be in touch for more than thirty years.

García Márquez already had two solid contacts among the leading writers: Eduardo Zalamea Borda, who had discovered him six years before, and his cousin Gonzalo González, "Gog," who had begun to work on the paper while a law student in 1946. It was Zalamea Borda who baptized him with the name by which the whole planet would later know him, "Gabo." A well-known photo from those days shows a new and wholly unfamiliar García Márquez, slim and elegant, with refined features, eyes at once questioning yet already knowing, with the merest whisper of a smile beneath his Latin moustache. Only the hands betray the permanent state of tension in which this man lives.

The news editor at *El Espectador* was José "Mono" ("Blond" but also "Monkey") Salgar, a demanding, no-nonsense manager whose slogan was "news, news, news." García Márquez would say that working for him was "the exploitation of man by monkey."[4] He had been employed by the paper since he was little more than a boy and had thus been educated both in the school of journalism and that of life; he was to become an institution in his own right. From the start he was unimpressed by García Márquez's reputation and deeply suspicious of his unmistakable literariness and incorrigible "lyricism."[5]

After a couple of weeks, however, García Márquez showed his worth with two articles on monarchical power and solitude, myth and reality: the first, highly amusing, was "Cleopatra," a piece which fervently prayed that a new statue reputedly of the Egyptian queen would not modify the romantic image men have had of her for two thousand years; the second, "The Queen Alone," was about Elizabeth the Queen Mother of England, recently widowed. It may be García Márquez's single most striking elaboration in that era of certain themes—especially the conjunction of power, fame and solitude—which would reach their culmination twenty years later in *The Autumn of the Patriarch*:

> The Queen Mother, who is now a grandmother, is truly alone for the first time in her life. And as she wanders, accompanied only by her solitude, along the immense corridors of Buckingham Palace, she must remember with nostalgia that happy age in which she never dreamed nor wished to dream of being a queen, and lived with her husband and their two daughters in a house overflowing with intimacy . . . Little did she know that a mysterious blow of fate would turn her children and the children of her children into kings and queens; and her into a queen alone. A desolate and inconsolable housewife, whose house would fade into the immense labyrinth of Buckingham Palace, its endless corridors and that limitless backyard which extends to the bounds of Africa.[6]

This article in particular convinced Zalamea Borda, who somewhat bizarrely had a soft spot for the young Queen Elizabeth II, that García Márquez was ready to move on to bigger things.[7] Guillermo Cano said that when García Márquez arrived he naturally had to adapt to the newspaper's cautious and somewhat anonymous house style; but after a while the other writers began to adjust to the newcomer's brilliant improvisations and then to imitate him.[8]

García Márquez remembers that he would be sitting at his desk writing a piece for the paper's "Day by Day" column and José Salgar or Guillermo Cano would tell him, across the noisy room, with just a thumb and forefinger, how much was needed to fill the space. Some of the magic had gone out of his journalism. Worse, Bogotá did not provide him with the vital stimulation he found everywhere on the coast. In late February, already bored to tears, he managed to persuade the management to let him try out as a film critic and publish his review on Saturdays. It must have been a wonderful relief to escape several times a week from the tensions of living under a dictatorship in "the gloomiest city in the world," and under an irksome and unnecessary apprenticeship in the newspaper office, and to take refuge in the fantasy world of the movies. He was in fact something of a pioneer, because no other journalist had written a regular movie column in any Colombian newspaper before this time; they confined themselves to providing plot summaries and naming the stars.

From the start his view of cinema was literary and humanistic, rather than specifically cinematographic.[9] In fact García Márquez's fast-evolving political ideology at the time must have sharpened his sense that he had a chance to "educate the people" and perhaps relieve them of the false consciousness that made them prefer the prepackaged Hollywood product to the more aesthetically crafted works from France and, especially, those "authentically" conceived and executed works from Italy which he particularly favoured. But in any case the film-goers of 1950s Bogotá were unlikely to appreciate avant-garde evaluations of the movies they went to see and García Márquez was from the beginning obsessed with the idea of viewing reality from the standpoint of "the people" whilst going on, of course, to modify it in progressive directions. Certainly his film reviews took up aesthetically and ideologically questionable "common-sense" positions; but one of the qualities of García Márquez, always, is that his version of "common sense" is invariably "good sense" and is almost never "non-sense."[10]

From the very beginning he was hostile to what he perceived to be the shallow commercial and profoundly ideological values of the Hollywood system—he considered Orson Welles and Charlie Chaplin exceptions—and he routinely defended European cinema, whose production and moral values he sought for the development of a national cinema in Colombia. This, with an added Latin American dimension, would become a permanent obsession down the years. He was surprisingly preoccupied with technical questions—script, dialogue, direction, photography, sound, music, cutting, acting—which perhaps gives insight into what he would later call the "carpentry" of his literary works: professional "tricks of the trade" that he has never been fully willing to share, at least not in terms of the novel.[11] He insisted that scripts should be economical, consistent and coherent; and that close-ups and long shots should receive the same attention. He was concerned from the beginning with the concept of the well-made story, an obsession which would remain with him for the rest of his career and would explain his continuing reverence for *The Thousand and One Nights, Dracula, The Count of Monte Cristo* and *Treasure Island*—all brilliantly narrated works of popular literature. This was what he looked for in the cinema too. Objective reality should predominate but the inner world, even the fantastic world, should not be neglected. He noted that the outstanding feature of Vittorio De Sica's *The Bicycle Thieves* was its "human authenticity" and its "lifelike method." These central ideas would dominate his perspective for the next few years, and were not far removed from the central tenets of both bourgeois and socialist realism which found classic fusion in Italian neo-realism. Avant-garde they were not. He showed little awareness of the theories of the nascent French New Wave to be found among Brazilian, Argentine or Cuban cinematographers at this time. Indeed, his selections for best films of the year on 31 December demonstrate unequivocally that for García Márquez in 1954 Italian neo-realism was *the* way of making movies. Certainly it is ironic to consider that De Sica, his favourite film-maker in this era, and Cesare Zavattini, the incomparable script-writer, would never have got involved in filming a script like the plot of *Leaf Storm*. Which is why, for the moment, García Márquez would not be writing any more novels like *Leaf Storm*.

The working week was intense. At its end he took part in the journalists' regular "cultural Fridays," a euphemism for heavy drinking across the avenue in the Hotel Continental, where the *El Espectador* and *El Tiempo* hacks would meet up and exchange drinks and insults; sometimes they drank until dawn.[12] He also participated in the Bogotá cine-club organized by another of the many energetic Catalan exiles the young writer would get to know over the years. His name was Luis Vicens; he had himself collaborated with the great critic Georges Sadoul on *L'Écran Français* and was now making a living in Colombia selling books as well as running the cine-club with two Colombians, the film critic Hernando Salcedo and the painter Enrique Grau. After the cine-club's sessions he would go on to the inevitable party at the house of Luis Vicens and his Colombian wife Nancy, not far from the newspaper office.[13]

Nevertheless this new, rather middle-class lifestyle in the world of the *bogotanos* could hardly replace the sheer fun and exhilaration, not to say interest, of life on the Costa. Early in his stay in Bogotá García Márquez wrote to Alfonso Fuenmayor:

> Your noble paternal concerns will be eased if I tell you that my situation here is still quite good, although the question now is to consolidate it. There is an excellent atmosphere in the newspaper and up to now I've been allowed the same privileges as the longest-term employees. However the sad part of the song is that I still don't feel at home in Bogotá, though if things go on as they are I'll have no option but to get used to it. As I don't lead an "intellectual" life here I'm lost as to developments in the novel, because "Ulysses" [Zalamea Borda], the only genius I see here, is always buried in great big indigestible novels in English. Recommend me some translations. I received a copy of *Sartoris* in Spanish but it fell to pieces and I returned it.[14]

His new-found prosperity did allow him to go back from time to time to Barranquilla, to visit his friends, to keep a watchful eye on Mercedes, to keep in touch with his roots—and of course see the sun; plus the bonus of simply getting out of Bogotá. Certainly the fact that he would appear in the credits for a film which Alvaro Cepeda would shortly direct, a short experimental movie entitled *The Blue Lobster*, suggests that his visits to the Costa were reasonably frequent.[15]

By now his old friends had a new hang-out and the Barranquilla Group would become synonymous with a less portentous crowd, "the piss-takers of the Cueva," as García Márquez would dub them five years later in his story "Big Mama's Funeral." Not long after he had left Barranquilla the gang had regrouped and moved the focus of their activities away from the old city centre to the Barrio Boston, not far from where Mercedes Barcha lived. Alfonso Fuenmayor's cousin Eduardo Vilá Fuenmayor, a reluctant dentist (Mercedes had been one of his patients), started up a bar which was at first called The To and Fro (El Vaivén), the name of the store it had once been, but which the group later baptized "The Cave" ("La Cueva"—like the dockside bar in Cartagena). This place would become immortalized, like some sacred temple, in García Márquez–related mythology, although the man himself would never be able to go there with much regularity. So rowdy was it, with so much heavy drinking and fighting, that Vilá would eventually put up a sign which said, "Here the customer is never right."

Back in Bogotá, García Márquez was witness to one of the new military regime's most notorious atrocities on 9 June 1954 as he returned in the late morning along Avenida Jiménez Quesada from a visit to his ex-boss Julio César Villegas, who was serving out his jail sentence in the Model Prison. He heard a sudden burst of machine-gun fire: government troops were firing on a student demonstration and caused heavy casualties, including several dead, before the horrified writer's eyes. It was the event that ended the uneasy truce between the new government and the Liberal press. García Márquez's radical political views had been quite unequivocal from the time of his early days in *El Universal*, only weeks after the *Bogotazo*; but this third experience of living in or close to Bogotá brought him to commit himself not only to a particular political ideology—socialism—but also, for a few years at least, to a particular way of viewing and interpreting reality and a particular way of expressing and communicating it technically. The result would be his political reportage, and the writing of the novels *No One Writes to the Colonel* and *In Evil Hour* and the stories of *Big Mama's Funeral*. He had been longing for several years now to be given the opportunity to be a reporter; but *El Universal* and *El Heraldo* lived off international cables and, given their resources and, more to the point, the prevailing regime of censorship, hardly went in for serious reporting. Their mission, in many ways, was to publish something, anything, that was not the usual Conservative propaganda. The owners of *El Espectador* were made of sterner stuff. And they now had at their disposal a young writer who was fascinated by the variety of people in his country, by the things they did and the things that happened to them; a man who loved stories, who whenever possible turned his own life into a story and would now seize the opportunity to turn the lives of others also into narratives which would grip the imagination.

In Colombia in those days the news was generally terrible. It was the height of the *Violencia*. Massacres of Liberals continued in rural areas, carried out by the oligarchy's barbaric paramilitary assassins known as *chulavitas* or *pájaros*, and Liberal guerrillas were fighting desperate rearguard actions in many parts of the country. Torture, rape and the sadistic desecration of corpses were commonplace. Rojas Pinilla had imposed press censorship on 6 March and hardened it after the killing of the students in Bogotá. Ex-President López Pumarejo proposed a bipartisan agreement for running the country on 25 March, an idea which would bear fruit three years later with the invention of the so-called National Front but was not greeted positively at this time.

All of this was in part the reflection in a peripheral country of the

Cold War frenzy of the era. McCarthyism was at its height in the United States; Eisenhower even outlawed the Communist Party in August 1954 and McCarthy was finally censured by the Senate only in December of that year. Meanwhile the Communist bloc was working on the Warsaw Pact, which would be signed in May 1955. In Barranquilla García Márquez had listened more sympathetically to the communist rantings of Jorge Rondón than most of his friends and colleagues. During his last period in Barranquilla, several months after the death of Stalin in Moscow and several weeks after the Rojas Pinilla coup in Colombia, García Márquez had been visited by a man ostensibly selling watches who was in fact a Communist enlisting members for the Party, particularly among journalists, in exchange for his timekeeping wares. Not long after García Márquez arrived in Bogotá, where he was working from the start with politically progressive colleagues, another watch salesman came to visit and before long García Márquez found himself in contact with Gilberto Vieira, Secretary General of the Colombian Communist Party, who was living clandestinely just a few blocks from the city centre.[16] It became clear to García Márquez that the Party had been watching him ever since he had worked with Cepeda on El Nacional and considered him promising material; but according to him it was agreed that his best use for the Party was in writing committed journalism which did not appear to compromise him in Party terms. The Party would seemingly continue to take this view of García Márquez's activities down the years and usually supported his positions if at all possible.

At the end of July Salgar suggested that García Márquez go to Antioquia to find out "what the fuck really happened" in the 12 July landslide. He found himself on a plane to Medellín where the hillside community out at La Media Luna, east of the city, had collapsed two weeks before with heavy loss of life. There were suspicions that the blame could be attributed to government corruption and jerry-building. García Márquez's brief was to reconstruct the truth on the spot. The intrepid reporter would later confess that he was so nervous about flying that Alvaro Mutis travelled with him to calm his nerves and installed him in the upmarket Hotel Nutibara. When he was left alone there he felt sick with nerves and totally intimidated by the physical challenge and the moral responsibility; he almost resigned from the newspaper on his first day in Medellín. After he had managed to calm himself he discovered that there was no one out by the Media Luna any more and so there was nothing to be added to the reports of journalists who had been there long before him. He hadn't the faintest idea what to do. A violent rainstorm postponed his agony. He again considered fleeing back to Bogotá; finally sheer desperation, and a chance conversation with a taxi driver, prodded him into action. He began to think, truly think, about the event he was investigating: what might have happened, where he should go, what he should do. Slowly but with accelerating excitement, he discovered the joy of being a reporter-detective, the creativity of discovering—and in a way inventing—the truth, the power of shaping and even changing reality for tens of thousands of people. He realized that the idea of people travelling out to deaths they could not anticipate was his "angle" and he had a taxi driver take him straight out to Las Estancias, the zone from which most people who had died in the catastrophe had travelled. He soon discovered evidence of official negligence, both short term and long term (it seemed the landslide had been incubating for sixty years!), but also revealed an unexpected and more dramatic aspect of the tragedy, one that most readers would have preferred not to know: that many deaths had been due to people from other parts of the city trying to help without official guidance or assistance and thereby triggering a second landslide. He interviewed numbers of survivors and witnesses, and also the authorities, including local politicians, firemen and priests.[17]

Then he started to write. Very likely it began as something out of Hemingway but by the time he finished it was pure García Márquez, with that inimitable presentation of life as a drama filled with the horrors and ironies of fate, the fate of human beings condemned to live in a world of unknown causes governed by time:

> Juan Ignacio Angel, the economics student standing on the ledge ran down below, preceded by a girl of about fourteen and a boy of ten. His companions, Carlos Gabriel Obregón and Fernando Calle, ran in the opposite direction. The first, half buried, died of asphyxia. The second, an asthmatic, stopped, gasping, and said, "I can't go on." He was never heard of again. "When I ran down with the girl and the boy," Juan Ignacio said, "I came to a big hollow. The three of us threw ourselves to the ground." The boy never got up again. The girl, who Angel was unable to identify among the corpses, got up for a moment but sank down again screaming in desperation when she saw the earth soaring above the hollow. An avalanche of mud crashed

over them. Angel tried to run again but his legs were paralysed.
The mud rose to his chest in a split second but he managed to
free his right arm. He stayed like that until the thunder-like
noises ceased and he felt in his legs, at the bottom of that dense
and impenetrable sea of mud, the hand of the girl who, at the
beginning, held on to him with desperate strength, then clawed
at him, and finally, in ever weaker contractions, relaxed her grip
on his ankle.[18]

The sub-headings were almost certainly chosen by García Márquez
himself: "The tragedy began sixty years ago"; "Medellín, victim of its
own solidarity"; and "Did an old gold mine precipitate the tragedy?"[19]
He had learned how to convert his own world-view into a set of
journalistic "angles." "Gabo," the best friend to his friends, had
only recently been born; now the great story-teller "Gabriel García
Márquez" had finally appeared on the scene. It was noteworthy that
although he was pleased to blame the authorities for their part in the
disaster, he was also concerned to tell the whole truth, including
the involuntary contribution of so many well-meaning rescuers to the
tragedy.

The next piece of pioneering reporting was a series on one of
Colombia's forgotten regions, the department of El Chocó, on the
Pacific side of the country. On 8 September 1954 the government
decided to carve up the Chocó, an undeveloped, forested department,
and distribute the pieces between the departments of Antioquia, Caldas and Valle. There were vehement protests and García Márquez was
sent down with a cameraman, Guillermo Sánchez, to report on the
conflict. The journey was so bad, in an aircraft so old, that he remembers it "raining inside the plane" and says that even the pilots were
terrified. The Chocó, a department mainly inhabited by Afro-
Colombians, reminded García Márquez at once of Aracataca and its
hinterland. For him the proposed dismemberment of the Chocó was
symptomatic of Bogotá's cold and heartless mentality, though other
commentators blamed the ambitious Antioquians. When he arrived he
discovered that the demonstrations he had gone to report on had
petered out—so he got a friend to organize some more! This ensured
the success of his mission. After a few days, as the news item began to
grow and other reporters flew in to cover it, the government cancelled
its plan to restructure the four departments.[20]

In late October it was announced that García Márquez's new role model Ernest Hemingway was to be awarded the Nobel Prize for Literature, just as Faulkner had been when he was in his Faulkner phase. García Márquez wrote a note under the "Day by Day" byline repeating comments he had made before about the Nobel Prize phenomenon, and this time downplaying the possible importance of an award which had already gone to so many "undeserving" writers and which, in the case of Hemingway, he speculated, must surely have been one of the less exciting occasions in a life "so full of exciting moments."[21]

The year 1955 would see the publication of García Márquez's most famous newspaper story. It was based on an immensely long interview, in fourteen sessions of four hours each, with a Colombian navy sailor called Luis Alejandro Velasco, the only survivor of eight crewmen who fell overboard from the destroyer *Caldas* when she rolled out of control in late February—supposedly during a storm—on the way back from refitting in Mobile, Alabama, to her home port of Cartagena. Velasco survived on a raft for ten days without anything to eat and very little to drink. He became a national hero, decorated by the President and fêted by the media, including the new television service. All this up to the moment when García Márquez decided to interview him . . . The interviews, which were Guillermo Cano's idea—García Márquez considered the story had gone cold—took place in a small café on Avenida Jiménez.[22] Velasco had an astonishing memory and was himself an excellent narrator. But García Márquez had developed a facility for asking revealing questions and then highlighting the essence of the answers or getting to the most human aspects of the story. Velasco began by stressing the heroic point of view: the battle with the waves, the problem of controlling the raft, the fight against the sharks, the struggle with his mind, until García Márquez interrupted: "Don't you realize that four days have passed and you still haven't had a pee or a shit!"[23] After each interview he would go back to the office in the late afternoon and write up the corresponding chapter until deep in the night. José Salgar would take them from him, sometimes uncorrected, and run them straight over to the printers. Guillermo Cano told García Márquez he would have liked it to run to fifty chapters. After the fourteen-part series had come to an end, *El Espectador* put out a special supplement on 28 April reprinting the entire story with what it claimed was "the biggest print run any Colombian newspaper has ever published!"

García Márquez, with his rigorous and exhaustive questioning, and his search for new angles, had inadvertently revealed that the boat had not pitched and rolled in a violent storm but had sunk because it was carrying illegal merchandise which was improperly secured; and that regulation safety procedures were grossly inadequate. The story put *El Espectador* in direct confrontation with the military government and undoubtedly made García Márquez still more of a *persona non grata*, a troublemaker considered an enemy of the regime. Those who routinely question his courage and commitment should certainly reflect on this period in his life. García Márquez must undoubtedly have been a marked man and, although he has characteristically played down the dangers of the time, it is easy to imagine his feelings whenever he had to walk home late at night through a grim, lugubrious city floating uneasily in the tension of a military dictatorship. It is something of a miracle that he survived unscathed.[24]

Many years later the story was re-published, after García Márquez became a world-famous writer. It was entitled *The Story of a Shipwrecked Sailor* (*Relato de un náufrago*, 1970). Astonishingly, it became one of his most successful books, selling 10 million copies in the next twenty-five years. García Márquez never directly challenged the reactionary government in 1954–5 but in report after report he took up a point of view which was implicitly subversive of official stories and thus challenged the ruling system more effectively than any of his more vocal leftist colleagues, guided always by rigorous investigation, reflection and communication of the realities of the country. All in all, it was a sustained and brilliant demonstration of the power of the story-teller's art and of the power and central importance of the imagination even in the representation of factual material.

Immediately after those implicitly committed and campaigning pieces, *Leaf Storm* finally appeared in Bogotá at the end of May under a little-known imprint owned by the publisher Lisman Baum and produced by Sipa Editions at five pesos a copy. García Márquez's friend the painter Cecilia Porras designed the cover, which depicted a little boy sitting on a chair with his legs dangling, waiting for something: the little boy that García Márquez had once been in the dreaming time before his grandfather died and which he had now transposed into his first published novel. The printers claimed to have produced 4,000 copies, few of which were ever sold.[25] Its publication made a strange counterpoint to his current status as a hard-hitting, high-profile journalist, for it belonged not only to an era but to a narrative mode that García Márquez had left behind: at once static and time-tormented, fatalistic and mythical.

Still, a book in print at last. Although it had by no means resolved or even assuaged his obsessions, it was a book based directly on his own childhood, something which had suddenly "dropped off" "The House" after he had made his fabulous return to Aracataca with Luisa Santiaga, now five years before. The title had been rapidly improvised in 1951 in order to be able to send the novel off to Buenos Aires; and some time in the months before publication García Márquez composed a sort of prologue or coda dated "1909," which made more sense of the title and gave the novel a perspective, both historical and mythological at one and the same time, clarifying its social meaning and adding a clearer sense of decadence, loss and nostalgia. All this is conveyed by a narrative voice similar to that of the Colonel's in the novel, a voice which laments the arrival of the "leaf-trash," the migrant workers—rather than lamenting the arrival of capitalism and imperialism—and then reluctantly accepts what has happened in the town as part of the "natural" state of affairs, the cycle of ups and downs inherent in life itself. Here we have a man in his mid to late twenties writing with the voice of a seventy-year-old but viewing him with just a trace of irony. The book was dedicated to Germán Vargas, and was well received by Colombian critics, though inevitably many of the reviews were by García Márquez's close friends and associates.

He was exhausted, tired of Bogotá and drained by the cumulative effort of researching his reports, the responsibility of meeting growing expectations, and the well-grounded fears that the government might take reprisals against him for his evidently antagonistic positions. Thus when the chance came to get away—and to Europe—he seized it with alacrity, despite many subsequent protestations to the contrary. As ever there is uncertainty about the reasons for his journey. Legend has it that he needed to get out of the country to avoid threats from the government; legend also has it that this explanation is itself one of many examples of García Márquez's alleged instinct for self-dramatization. But the political explanation cannot be simply discounted: he had made several trips down to the Costa simply to lie low after some of his most provocative stories; and several other *El Espectador* journalists had received threats or been beaten up by unknown assailants. The trip may well have been intended as a brief self-exile in the guise of a journalistic mission. Or as a jaunt to Europe in the guise of a politically motivated self-exile. Or it may have been intended simply as what the newspaper said it was: a brief foreign assignment beginning with the meeting of the "Big Four" powers—the USA, the USSR, the UK and France in Geneva.

He left his apartment in Bogotá and gave away most of his possessions. He had also saved a tidy sum of money in Bogotá and, despite the family's continuing straitened circumstances in Cartagena, took it with him.[26] Clearly he had agreed to go for a few months at least—in some stories he claims he had expected to be away as little as "four days"—but had it at the back of his mind that he might stay even longer.[27] On the other hand, even he cannot have imagined he would be away for two and a half years. The least charitable but most likely explanation for the different versions in this case is that he could not bring himself to confess either to his impoverished family or to his future wife that he was wilfully abandoning them for a significant period of time after having already spent eighteen months away in Bogotá. His sense of responsibility was strong but the lure of Europe and the unknown was even stronger.

On his last evening in Bogotá, 13 July, there was a riotous farewell party in Guillermo Cano's house which made García Márquez miss his early morning plane to Barranquilla, but he got another flight at midday. The family is said to have reluctantly agreed they could do without his subsidies for a time but of course they had no inkling of how long he would actually be away. He must have been utterly overwhelmed and exhausted but there was Mercedes, now twenty-two, to see—but what could he say to her?—and of course another round of festivities, with his local friends and ex-colleagues. Mercedes had been his "intended" for more than a decade in his own mind but now it was to be decided whether she would finally become his "fiancée"—that is to say, whether he would also become *her* "intended." It was actually ten years since he had asked her to marry him, back in Sucre. No one has ever asked the question about other loves in her life—she told me categorically there had never been any—or why García Márquez felt able to leave her loyalty—or rather, her fate—to chance. Perhaps he reconciled the implications of his own fear of rejection, and the fact that he had no material security to offer her, with the thought, like Florentino Ariza in *Love in the Time of Cholera*, that no matter how long it took to get his woman and no matter what she did in the meantime, *one day* they would be together and she would be his. This entire departure has been told in several different ways and is shrouded in mystery.

His eventual proposal to Mercedes, if such it was, may suggest not only an anguished fear of losing the woman he loved even though he was playing a long—a very long—game but also an unconscious fear of losing Colombia and thus a way of securing his future connection to the country. Mercedes was from his own region and background and guaranteed he would have someone at his side who would understand where he was "coming from" for the rest of his life. In short, she was not only a kind of platonic ideal on the Dantean model—not that he did not find her extremely attractive physically—but also a highly practical strategic choice: the perfect combination. He, though, unlike Dante, would actually marry his unattainable "lady of my mind," the woman he had chosen when she was nine years old.[28] It seems certain, then, that he proposed now precisely because he was intending to be away from her for a long time. Perhaps he felt better able to take the risk of rejection now that he was a celebrated journalist travelling to Europe on a glamorous mission; perhaps she was more inclined to accept for the very same reason. But the truth is that Mercedes hardly features in the memoir and the details of this extraordinary relationship have never been filled in by either of the two parties. Before he left Barranquilla for Bogotá in 1954, they had hardly spoken in any concrete way but he felt they had a sort of understanding.[29]

In fact, typically—perversely—the woman who will most feature as a romantic interest in the 2002 memoir is not Mercedes, the love of his life, but another woman, Martina Fonseca, his first love, the married woman with whom he had carried on that frenzied affair in Barranquilla when he was a stripling of fifteen—until she put an end to it. He mentions her several times during the Bogotá chapter.[30] Did she even exist? Apparently, because one day, towards the end of 1954, he hears her "radiant voice" on the phone and meets her, in the bar of the Hotel Continental, for the first time in twelve years. She is showing the first signs of "an undeserved old age" and asks him if he has missed her. "Only then did I tell her the truth: that I had never forgotten her but her goodbye had been so brutal that it changed my way of being." She behaved sportingly but he was resentful and somewhat spiteful; she had had twins but assured him they were not his. She said she had wanted to see how he was, so he asked, "And how am I?" She laughed and said, "That you'll never know." He ends the episode by stating—teasingly—that he had been longing to see Martina once she'd phoned yet also terrified that he might have spent the rest of his life with her, "the same desolate terror I felt many times after that day whenever the telephone rang."

This is an intriguing confessional episode and it is interesting to ask how revealing it is meant to be and why. Is it a confession about him and women? And also a justification of some unspoken attitude towards them? It seems odd that Martina should appear again, quite gratuitously, just before García Márquez finally commits himself to Mercedes. Does it confirm, in some coded fashion, in a culture where men could have no sexual relations with the women they intended to marry while having frequent relations with prostitutes and servants, or indeed other men's wives, that he had decided to separate his feelings between the unofficial Don Juan, open to "crazy loves," and the official husband in a stable—somehow "arranged"—marriage to a woman who would be a lifelong "virgin" (as far as other men were concerned) and a loyal, reliable wife, the object of "good love"?[31] If the anecdote about Martina Fonseca is true—or if it is invented but some other woman had this chastening effect on him at this or some other time—it would explain why he is so frequently concerned in his fiction and his essays to separate love from sex, why he would cling for so many years to the idea of his self-arranged marriage with someone significantly younger than himself, why he doesn't bother to express any feelings for Mercedes in the memoir (those feelings can and must be taken for granted, for ever), and possibly also why, when I asked her about this time in their lives in front of her good friend Nancy Vicens, Mercedes—who, García Márquez had already informed me, "never tells me she loves me"—assured me with grim meaningfulness (though not a trace of bitterness) that "Gabo is a very unusual person; *very* unusual."[32] It was clear to me that a request for clarification would be unwise.

Of course much of this is a game played out between two very strong, very ironic and very private people. Despite other versions down the years which speak of agreements being made before his departure,[33] García Márquez assures us in his memoir that he did not "see" his sweetheart before he left for Europe—unless it is really true that he saw her in the street through the window of a taxi and did not stop. And so, in the absence of a meeting with Mercedes, there was—inevitably—another violent farewell celebration in "The Cave" to add to the alcoholic overdose he had brought with him from Bogotá. The next day the group members able to get out of bed saw him off at the airport. His well-deserved hangover was the worst possible preparation for what turned out to be a thirty-six-hour journey across the Atlantic Ocean to the Old World. Still, he was more than ready for the experience: he was twenty-eight years of age, a successful journalist and a respected writer who had published his debut novel. It was an appropriate moment for such a journey. The splendours of European civilization awaited him but those who knew him best could be certain that he would view those splendours entirely from his own hard-earned perspective. Needless to say, his memoir makes no mention of either Ulysses or Penelope.

PART II

Abroad: Europe and Latin America

1955-1967

9

The Discovery of Europe: Rome

1955

THE AVIANCA AEROPLANE *The Colombian*, one of the Lockheed Super Constellations famously conceived by millionaire eccentric Howard Hughes, made a weekly journey to Europe stopping several times in the Caribbean, including Bermuda, and then the Azores, before flying on to Lisbon, Madrid and Paris. García Márquez would comment in his first despatch from the Old World that he had been surprised that such a spectacular flying machine could have been designed by Mr. Hughes, "who designs such terrible movies."[1] As for himself, and despite a monumental hangover, García Márquez was lucid enough to write a brief letter to Mercedes, which he posted in Montego Bay. It was a do-or-die effort to formalize their relationship. He says in the memoir that its motive was "remorse" for not letting her know he was leaving but maybe he had simply lacked the courage to ask her to write, with all its implications.

When the aircraft finally reached Paris it descended with warnings of possible undercarriage problems and the passengers had to prepare for the worst. But they landed safely. García Márquez had arrived in the Old World.[2] It was almost exactly ten years since the end of the Second World War in Europe. There was no time for sightseeing and early the next morning he took the train to Geneva and arrived in the afternoon, two days after leaving Barranquilla. The only thing he would bother to tell his readers about his brief stopover in Paris was that the French were far more interested in the Tour de France than in what was happening in Geneva; and when he got to Geneva on 17 July, he discovered that the Swiss too were more interested in the Tour de France than what was happening in Geneva. In fact, he remarked, the only people who seemed interested in what was happening in Geneva were the journalists who had been sent to cover it. With the exception, he intimated slyly, of Colombian journalist Gabriel García Márquez.[3]

He dived into the first hotel he found, changed his clothes and set about sending this first, anti-climactic story through All American Cable. After this he would have to content himself with registered airmail. There was a heatwave that summer in snowy Switzerland and he was disappointed by that and by the fact that, as he recalled years later, "the grass I saw through the train window was exactly like the grass I'd seen through the train window in Aracataca."[4] He spoke no foreign languages, and had no experience of finding his way around in foreign countries. He rushed off to look for the United Nations building with the providential help of a German pastor who spoke Spanish and then met up, to his immense relief, with members of the Latin American press corps including the haughty *cachaco* Germán Arciniegas, representing *El Tiempo*, all of them there to report on the negotiations between the representatives of the "Big Four" nations—Nikolai Bulganin of the Soviet Union, Anthony Eden of the United Kingdom, Dwight D. Eisenhower ("Ike") of the United States and Edgar Faure of France. All in all, there were two thousand journalists present from around the world.

The Big Four were the countries most actively engaged in the Cold War. They had each negotiated control of a part of the defeated city of Berlin; they were also the countries with a veto at the United Nations Security Council and the countries that possessed or were well on the way to possessing nuclear weapons. Understanding between them was crucial if the world was to survive the unfamiliar and terrifying new era lived out under the shadow of global nuclear catastrophe which had begun with the destruction of Hiroshima and Nagasaki in August 1945. Thus they began, for a time, to meet one another separately from umbrella organizations like the United Nations, NATO or the soon to be created Warsaw Pact. Later, following the Suez Crisis in 1956, France and the UK would lose much of their influence and the game would be concentrated on the relationship between the USA and the USSR. But at this time the meetings of the Big Four were considered to be the first chink of light in the post–Second World War period—with constant speculation about a possible "thaw in East–West relations"—and were greeted with loud fanfares and intense newspaper and television coverage in the West.

García Márquez's first cable must have disappointed the bosses who had financed his trip across the Atlantic and must have disconcerted the newspaper's readers. The article appeared under the title "Geneva Indifferent to the Conference." Surely this was not the way to sell a story. Later titles were equally anti-climactic in intention—and clearly the work of García Márquez himself—including "The Big Four in Technicolor," "My Nice Customer Ike," "The Four Happy Pals" and "The True Tower of Babel." Needless to say, the Big Four conferences—the one the previous January had been held in Berlin—engaged the interest of the world because the world was genuinely terrified of nuclear holocaust; but García Márquez, who understood better than most people what was at stake, given his political education over the previous eighteen months as a reporter in Bogotá, reduced this meeting to the status of a Hollywood event reported on by a social columnist. Eventually, many years later, he would often enough travel through the looking glass of high politics himself—probably he was already longing to do so—but he was never deceived by the fanfares or by any naive illusions about the mystificatory role of the international press in reporting on political affairs. Entertaining though his reports are about "Ike," Bulganin, Eden and Faure, not to mention their wives—all carefully polishing their images, like film stars, with the connivance of the world's newspapers—this was not García Márquez's favourite kind of journalism.

Sobered by the material and cultural difficulties of his enterprise, he set about finding his journalistic feet. Most of his articles would remain wilfully superficial and humorous—as if, since he could not cover the news seriously, he refused to take it seriously himself. He soon faced the fact that he was never, during his time in Europe, going to be able to carry out the direct investigation which had made him celebrated in Colombia nor, therefore, to achieve any spectacular scoops. But gradually he would learn how to make the best of his circumstances, how to make it seem as if his material was original, how to look for "the other side of the news,"[5] and, equally to the point, how to shape his stories to best impress the folks back home. He became much more aware, almost immediately, of the way in which, in the "advanced" countries, the news was concocted. So he went in for his own journalistic *cuisinerie*; if the Bogotá articles had already shown the power of the informed imagination to add not only the missing piece of information but also the literary dash to bring out its flavour as part of a professional expertise, long before the emergence of the "New Journalism" in the 1960s, now, when he needed it more than ever, this professional know-how would save him time and again. That is why from the start his pieces were as much about him, both implicitly and explicitly, as they were about the events he was meant to be reporting; and from the start he showed that the news was made not by the rich and famous themselves but by the journalists who followed them around and turned them into "stories."[6]

Inevitably he was more impressed than he let on—as well as more nervous and more intimidated. He may have become a feared reporter in Bogotá but that image belied what was still a timid and self-conscious personality. Despite the *costeño* "piss-taking," these first weeks in Europe made a profound impact on García Márquez, as his frequent references back to the experience in articles written a quarter of a century later—appropriately enough, in *El Espectador*—would demonstrate. Curiously, the one thing García Márquez did conspicuously lack when he arrived in Europe was a Latin American consciousness. He was more than content with his own *costeño*—rather than Colombian—culture; but he had not yet converted this cultural awareness into a fully Latin American "continental nationalism." What he would most discover in Geneva, Rome and Paris was not "Europe" but "Latin America."[7] But in him this remained tentative and he would have to go back to Latin America itself in order to discover what it was that he had discovered in Europe.

Before he left Geneva, perhaps to his surprise, certainly to his delight, he received a letter back from Mercedes. This undoubtedly changed his entire perspective—though paradoxically, despite his pleasure and relief, it probably made him even more determined to make the most of his European experience and his now temporary freedom than he already was. In tying him to her she gave him the confidence to go further away—and for longer.

After the excitement of Geneva while the Big Four circus was in town, García Márquez travelled on to Italy where he was scheduled to cover the 16th Exhibition of Cinematographic Art in Venice, better known as the Venice Film Festival, at the beginning of September. This was undoubtedly his idea rather than that of his bosses at *El Espectador*. He would later tell his friends that he had rushed off to Italy because the newspaper had cabled him with instructions to travel to Rome in case the Pope should die of hiccups.[8] Secretly, however, Italy had always been his personal number one destination. He had even been given a checklist of objectives by his friends in the cine-club of Bogotá. Above all, though, he was keen to travel to Rome in order to visit the famous film city of Cinecittà, where his great hero the script-writer Cesare Zavattini did most of his work. His other secret ambition was to get to Eastern Europe; he wanted to be able to compare the two sides of the Iron Curtain, East and West, two worlds concealed behind the rhetoric of the Big Four. He knew what he thought in theory about capitalism and socialism; now he wanted to see for himself, in practice.

He reached the Italian capital on 31 July. It too was blazing, like Geneva. A porter led him from the station to a nearby hotel in the Via Nazionale, as he recalled many years later with his usual dose of mythic value added: "It was a very old building reconstructed with diverse materials, and on each floor there was a different hotel. Its windows were so close to the ruins of the Colosseum that you could not only see the thousands of cats dozing in the heat on the terraces but you could smell the intense stench of fermented urine."⁹ As for "the eternal city" itself, the Colombian special correspondent sent only two dispatches at this time, one of them on Pope Pius XII's vacation in Castelgandolfo, where he attended the public audiences. The reports were written with just enough respect to placate his Catholic readers and just enough ironic insinuation to amuse the less reverent customers of a newspaper which was, after all, to the Liberal left of centre. García Márquez hinted almost imperceptibly that the Pope should not be trying to join the world of Hollywood celebrity, into which politicians were now being lured, by passing on agency information about his height and shoe size: this venerable figure was, after all—his readers were invited to reflect—only a man!

Given his plans to travel to places in Eastern Europe from which it would not be possible to send reports, García Márquez realized that he had to produce something substantial to earn his "vacation" in advance. He wrote nothing about the political situation in Italy, then still making its transition from pre-war fascism to post-war Christian Democracy and from being a predominantly rural society to a pre-dominantly urban one. Instead, his first big story was a series on the so-called "Wilma Montesi scandal," which he worked on for the whole of August, calling it, somewhat hyperbolically, "the scandal of the century." Montesi was the twenty-one-year-old daughter of a Roman carpenter; her murder two years before had been covered up for reasons that were still not clear at the time of writing but evidently involved upper-class decadence, police corruption and political manipulation. (It is thought the case helped to inspire Federico Fellini's break-through movie *La dolce vita* in 1959.) García Márquez visited the quar-

ter and the house where Montesi had lived, the beach forty-two kilometres away where her body had appeared, and a couple of the bars
where locals might have some information to give. As for the rest, he
used other sources with great efficiency, carried out his own research
wherever possible and wrote one of his most effective pieces of
reportage.[10] In announcing the series *El Espectador* stated: "For a
month now, visiting the places in which the drama took place, Gabriel
García Márquez has found out the most minute details of the death of
Wilma Montesi and the trial which has followed."[11]

He realized immediately that beyond the matter of the details of
the case, the detective mystery as such, there was something about the
time, the place and the story that foreshadowed the future: what a cultural critic would later call "the intersections of cinema, paparazzo
photography, tabloids, femininity, and politics."[12] His own endeavour
would be to discover whether there was any necessary connection, as
its Italian exponents themselves believed, between the neo-realist
mode in film and the advance of a socialist aesthetic. Long before the
influential analyses of French critic André Bazin, García Márquez
clearly intuited that the Italian films of the era were a kind of "recon-
stituted reportage" with a "natural adherence to actuality" which made
Italian national cinema a "form of radical humanism."[13] His film
reviews in Bogotá had intimated as much. He may also have reflected
that, through a correction of the mystification Hollywood had
achieved, Italian post-war cinema and journalism were producing a
new, more critical approach to celebrity—this knowledge would be an
invaluable protection for him when he too became famous—but also,
more ominously, that in the second half of the twentieth century even
those who were not famous had begun to imagine themselves as
though constantly in front of a camera, permanently in danger of being
exposed, misrepresented or even betrayed. Few people at that stage of
the critical game had reached the conclusion that there was no essential reality or truth to communicate in the first place. This would be
left to the theorists of postmodernity, though García Márquez would
be there too when they arrived.

Once the Montesi reports were safely despatched, for publication
between 17 and 30 September, he set off for Venice to take part in the
sixteenth annual film festival there. Winter had come early to Venice
and with it the Eastern Europeans, for the first time since the war. García Márquez spent several days soaking up the atmosphere of a great
European film competition and watching movies day and night, with

occasional excursions around Venice, where he noted the eccentricities of the Italians and the abyss between the rich and the poor—the Italian poor, who "always lose but they lose in a joyful and different fashion."[14] It was what he already thought about Latin Americans and he would devote much of his career to making Latin Americans more aware of it and more content with what they were. Years later he would add that Italians have "no other aim than to live" because they "discovered a long time ago that there is only one life and that certainty has made them allergic to cruelty."[15]

As in his Geneva reports, he made the best of his situation by sending stories not only on the movies themselves but on more superficial matters such as which stars did and did not turn up; among those who did he expressed disappointment at the fading attractions of Hedy Lamarr, who had once set Venice alight with her nude romp in *Ecstasy*; scorn for the sexual hypocrisy of Sophia Loren's supposedly reluctant appearances in a different swimsuit every day on the beach; and scepticism at Anouk Aimée's self-presentation as a star who did not behave like a star. Prophetically, although Carl Theodor Dreyer's *The Word (Ordet)* deservedly won first prize, the director for whom García Márquez expressed the most enthusiasm was a young Italian who was showing *Amici per la pelle* (1955), Francesco Rosi, "a tousle-haired boy of twenty-nine with a footballer's face, who stood and acknowledged, also like a footballer, the greatest ovation ever given in the palace of cinema."[16]

Now García Márquez took a train in Trieste and arrived in Vienna on 21 September 1955, two months after the departure of the last occupying troops and two months before the Viennese Opera reopened. Pretending that his journey had ended in Vienna and that he had remained there "in October," he wrote merely three articles on the city which were published on 13, 20 and 27 November.[17] It would be four years before he considered it prudent to publish any reports on the rest of his journey.

Like many other people in those days, García Márquez found it impossible to separate Vienna from Carol Reed's film *The Third Man* (whose script had been written by Graham Greene), and he assiduously visited the movie's already mythical locations. It was in Vienna too that he later claimed to have met "Frau Roberta," later renamed "Frau Frida," a fellow Colombian and clairvoyant who earned her living in the Austrian capital by "renting herself out to dream."[18] When the unlikely oracle told him, after an evening on the Danube beneath a full moon, that she had recently dreamed about him, and that he should leave Vienna at once, the superstitious boy from Aracataca took the next train out.[19] He did not mention to his readers that the train in question had taken him beyond the Iron Curtain.

So García Márquez travelled on from Austria to Czechoslovakia and Poland. He had managed to fix himself up with an invitation to the International Film Congress in Warsaw while he was at the Venice Film Festival. However, no reports by García Márquez on those two countries would be published for four years so we cannot be certain either of the exact timing, which he does not remember, or of his initial impressions; by that time those impressions had been updated and merged with the stories of brief returns to the two countries in the summer of 1957 when he travelled to Moscow and Hungary, a cursory account of which he would publish in November 1957. The reports on the first 1957 journey would finally appear in *Cromos*, Bogotá, in August 1959, by which time he would be working for the Cuban Revolution and was less concerned to hide his tracks. He would never acknowledge the journey he made alone in 1955, however: even when he finally published articles on Czechoslovakia and Poland he inserted them into the subsequent Eastern European trip he had made, in the company of others, in 1957.[20]

In view of all these suppressions and manipulations it is difficult either to establish a clear itinerary or to speculate about the development of García Márquez's political consciousness. What we can certainly infer is that right from the start he saw a paradox: Prague was a majestic, relaxed city, with every appearance of being like any of the Western European capitals, yet the inhabitants seemed to lack all interest in politics; Poland, still pre-Gomulka, was far more underdeveloped, with the scars of the Nazi holocaust still everywhere apparent, yet the Poles were much more politically active, surprisingly enthusiastic readers, and somehow managing to reconcile Communism with Catholicism in a way no other Communist country was even attempting. Four years later García Márquez would reflect that the Poles were the most anti-Russian of all the socialist "democracies." On the other hand he would also use a number of pejorative adjectives, such as "hysterical," "complicated" and "difficult," and would say that the Poles had "an almost feminine over-sensitivity," which meant it was "difficult to know what they want."[21] He disliked Cracow for what he perceived as its inherent conservatism and regressive Catholicism. However, his description of a visit to Auschwitz, though brief, is stunning. For once the usually flippant commentator confesses to having been on the point of weeping and gives a heart-rendingly sober account of his tour:

> There is a gallery of enormous glass cases full to the roof with human hair. A gallery full of shoes, clothing, handkerchiefs with initials sewn by hand, the suitcases the prisoners carried in to that hallucinatory hotel still bearing the labels from hotels for tourists. There is a case full of children's shoes with worn metal heels: little white boots to wear to school and the boot extensions of those who before going to die in the concentration camps had taken the trouble to survive infantile paralysis. There is an immense room crammed with prosthetic devices, thousands of pairs of glasses, false teeth, glass eyes, wooden legs, woollen gloves for missing hands, all the gadgets invented by human ingenuity to put humankind to rights. I separated myself from the group moving silently across the gallery. I was gnawing on a suppressed fury because I wanted to cry.[22]

In contrast the narration of the absurdities of Communist bureaucracy at border crossings is hilarious.

At the end of October he was back in Rome, and sent his three articles on Vienna, four more on the Pope and another three on the rivalry between Sophia Loren and Gina Lollobrigida, back to Colombia; interestingly, he remarked that, beyond the question of the battle of their "vital statistics," Lollobrigida, clearly less talented than Loren, had a far more positive image; he predicted, however, that Loren would eventually triumph when she realized that "Sophia Loren, in the respectable role of Sophia Loren, is unique and invulnerable."[23] He moved into a boarding house in Parioli with a Colombian tenor, Rafael Ribero Silva, who had been in Rome for six years. Like García Márquez, Ribero Silva was from a poor background and was the same age. He was another man who had worked his way up through determination and sacrifices, staying in and practising his singing, as García Márquez noted, when others were out on the town.[24]

For several weeks Ribero Silva acted as his informal translator and guide and in the late afternoon the two would borrow a motor scooter and tour the city. Their favourite treat was to watch the prostitutes in Villa Borghese plying their trade as night began to fall. Inspired by this innocent hobby Ribero Silva gave García Márquez one of his sweetest memories of the Italian capital: "After lunch, while Rome slept, we would go on a borrowed Vespa to see the little whores dressed in blue organdy, pink poplin or green linen, and sometimes we would meet one who would invite us to an ice cream. One afternoon I didn't go. I fell asleep after lunch and was awoken by some very timid taps on the door. I opened it, half asleep, and in the darkness of the pasageway I saw an image out of a delirium. It was a naked girl, very beautiful, freshly bathed and perfumed, with her whole body covered in talc. '*Buona sera*,' she said in a very soft voice, 'the *tenore* sent me.' "[25]

García Márquez had made his first tentative contact with Cinecittà, the great studio complex to the south-east of Rome, just after his arrival. It was the largest such dream factory anywhere in the world, and he was interested in studying film-making there at the Centro Sperimentale (Experimental Film Centre). At that time there had been no classes functioning but now he was able to meet active Italians and Latin Americans, like the Argentinian Fernando Birri, an exile who had fled the Peronist regime and who would be an important friend and collaborator in the future, as would other Latin American film-makers who studied in Rome during that period, such as the Cubans Tomás Gutiérrez Alea and Julio García Espinosa. Birri welcomed the young man with the new beret and the over-sized duffel coat, took him back to his apartment at the Piazza di Spagna, and for drinks at the Café di Spagna, and a long and fruitful relationship began.

García Márquez now enrolled on a course on cinema direction in the Experimental Film Centre. His main interest, not surprisingly, was in script-writing, which is why De Sica's script man Cesare Zavattini was a particular idol, a man, he would enthuse, who breathed an "unprecedented humanity" into the cinema of his era.[26] Looking back on those days, he would comment: "Today you can't imagine what the emergence of neo-realism at the beginning of the 1950s meant for our generation. It was inventing the cinema anew. We'd been seeing films from the war or films by Marcel Carné and other French directors which were setting the artistic trend. Then suddenly neo-realism arrived from Italy, with movies made out of reject celluloid with actors it was said had never seen a camera in their lives . . . Everything seemed to have been done in the street; it was impossible to tell how the scenes were put together, how the rhythm and the tone were maintained. For us it was a miracle."[27] He must have been surprised and disappointed to find that Italian neo-realism was less admired in Italy than elsewhere, in part because it showed aspects of the country that post-war Italy was trying to shrug off. Appropriately enough, he says that it was *Miracle in Milan* (1952), which he saw again with Fernando Birri in 1955, and on which De Sica, Zavattini and Fellini all worked, which made him feel that cinema could change the world, because both he and Birri felt that reality itself had changed when they emerged from the movie-house. In fact, Cinecittà, which was right then at its zenith, was about to provide the backdrop for the work of Fellini, a film-maker who would depart from the neo-realist aesthetic then dominating the scene and develop towards a sort of "magical realism" not dissimilar to the style for which García Márquez himself would later be admired.[28]

It turned out that at the Film Centre script-writing was just a minor section of the course in film direction. Perhaps predictably, García Márquez was bored almost immediately, with the exception of Dottoressa Rosado's classes on montage, which, she insisted, was "the grammar of cinema." The truth is that García Márquez was never much taken with any type of formal education and if it was not actually compulsory he would drift away; now he drifted away from Cinecittà (though in later years he would say that he spent several—even nine—months there). Yet when his friend Guillermo Angulo turned up some time later in search of García Márquez, Dottoressa Rosado remembered the latter, a generally lazy student, as one of her best.[29] Many people would be surprised to discover, in later years, that García Márquez had a firm understanding of the technical aspects of movie-making which, despite his reluctance, he had learned at Cinecittà.

As he would so often remark in the future, García Márquez still liked the cinema but would come to wonder whether the cinema liked him. He never did become disillusioned with Zavattini, however, and had a very personal view of his particular genius: "I am a child of Zavattini, who was a 'machine for inventing plots.' They just bubbled out of him. Zavattini made us understand that feelings are more important than intellectual principles."[30] This conviction would enable García Márquez to resist the attacks he would have to face from the literary and cinematographic "socialist realists" in the years to come, not least in Cuba. And this alone had made his brief stay in Italy, and his brief acquaintance with Cinecittà, worthwhile.

When a Latin American in Europe is bored and doesn't know what to do he gets on a train to Paris. That was not what García Márquez had intended but that is what he did as the last days of 1955 approached. Ironically, in attempting to move to another field, the cinema, he had merely found his way back to literature—not to mention his overriding obsession, Colombia. He was thinking about a novel, a neo-realist one, of course, inspired, cinematographically, in Rome but destined to be written in literary Paris. His train pulled in after midnight one rainy evening not long before Christmas. He took a taxi. His first image was of a prostitute standing on a street corner near the station beneath an orange umbrella.[31] The taxi was supposed to take him to the Hotel Excelsior, recommended to him by the poet Jorge Gaitán Durán, but he ended up at an Alliance Française hostel on Boulevard Raspail. He would stay in Paris for almost exactly two years.

10

Hungry in Paris: *La Bohème*

1956–1957

W HO CAN SAY what Gabriel García Márquez was looking
for as he made his way to the French capital in December
1955? Anyone who knew him would have guessed that
Italy would always be more congenial to the Colombian *costeño*—both
socially and culturally—than the cooler, more confident, more colonial, more critical—more Cartesian—country to the north. His attitude to Europe in general, from the start, was that it had little to teach
him that he had not already learned in books or on newsreels; it was
almost as if he had come to see it rot—the smell of boiled cabbage, one
might say, rather than the fragrance of the tropical guava that would
always be so dear to his heart and his senses. Yet here he was, after all,
in Paris.[1]

From the Alliance Française hostel he moved on to a cheap hotel
favoured by Latin American travellers: the Hôtel de Flandre at 16 Rue
Cujas, in the Latin Quarter, run by a Monsieur and Madame Lacroix.
Directly opposite was the more opulent Grand Hôtel Saint-Michel,
another Latin American favourite.[2] One of its long-term residents was
the influential Afro-Cuban poet and Communist Party member
Nicolás Guillén, one of a large number of Latin American writers in
exile during that age of dictators—Odría in Peru (1948–56), Somoza in
Nicaragua (1936–56), Castillo Armas in Guatemala (1954–7), Trujillo
in the Dominican Republic (1930–61), Batista in Cuba (1952–8), Pérez
Jiménez in Venezuela (1952–8), and even Rojas Pinilla in Colombia
(1953–7). The entire zone is dominated culturally by the nearby Sor-

bonne, though the ominous bulk of the Panthéon is the most imposing piece of architecture in the vicinity.

Almost immediately García Márquez contacted Plinio Apuleyo Mendoza, whom he had known briefly in Bogotá before the April 1948 uprising. Mendoza junior, that serious and rather pretentious young man whose view of the world had been shattered by his father's political defeat and exile in the months after the assassination of Gaitán, leaned towards radical socialism and was well on his way to becoming a fellow traveller of the international communist movement. He had read about the publication of García Márquez's *Leaf Storm* in the Bogotá press and had "assumed from his photograph and the title that he must be a bad novelist."[3] On Christmas Eve 1955 he was in the Bar La Chope Parisienne in the Latin Quarter with two Colombian friends when a duffel-coated García Márquez came in from the wintry afternoon. The newcomer struck Mendoza and his friends as arrogant and self-satisfied during their first conversation about literature, life and journalism, as if the eighteen months he had recently spent in Bogotá had turned him into a typical *cachaco*. He claimed to be totally unimpressed with Europe. In fact he appeared interested only in himself. He had already published one novel and only became animated when he began to talk about the development of the second one.

As it happened, in Plinio Mendoza García Márquez had just met his future best friend, though by no means the most constant. Because he would come to know García Márquez better than almost anyone else, and was also less constrained than other people by conventional considerations of discretion and taste, he would become, ironically, one of the more reliable witnesses to García Márquez's life and development. Despite his negative first impression, Mendoza invited the new arrival to a dinner party on Christmas Day, hosted by a Colombian architect from Antioquia, Hernán Vieco, and his blue-eyed American wife at their apartment in Rue Guénégaud, by the Seine. There the assembled Colombian émigrés and exiles ate roast pork and endive salad with large quantities of red Bordeaux and García Márquez picked up a guitar and sang *vallenatos* composed by his friend Escalona. This improved the first impressions the Colombians had of him but the hostess still complained to Plinio that the new arrival was "a horrible guy" who not only seemed self-important but stubbed out his cigarettes on the sole of his shoe.[4] Three days later the two men met again, after the first snowfall of the winter, and García Márquez, child of the tropics, danced along the Boulevard Saint-Michel and over the Place du Luxembourg. Mendoza's reserve melted like the snowflakes glistening on García Márquez's duffel coat.

They spent much of January and February 1956 together, before Mendoza returned to Caracas, where most of his family were now living. In those first weeks the two new friends would spend time at Mendoza's favourite haunts around the Sorbonne, the Café Capoulade on Rue Soufflot, or L'Acropole, a cheap and cheerful Greek restaurant at the bottom of the Rue de l'École de Médecine. If some acquaintances have described García Márquez at this time, perhaps uncharitably, as unprepossessing, Plinio Mendoza was equally or more so. Moreover few Colombians, when they hear his name—he is known all over Colombia as simply "Plinio," just as García Márquez is known as "Gabo"—react with indifference. Many consider him devious, a supposedly typical product of the highlands of his native Boyacá; but no one denies that he is a brilliant journalist and polemicist. Unpredictable he is, and sentimental; but he is also funny, self-mocking (genuinely self-mocking, quite a rare thing), enthusiastic and generous.

At the end of the first week of January the two friends sat in a café in the Rue des Écoles reading *Le Monde*, only to discover that Rojas Pinilla had finally brought about the closure of *El Espectador* through a cynical combination of censorship and direct intimidation. (*El Tiempo* had already been closed for five months.) Mendoza recalls that García Márquez played down the significance of the event: " 'It's not serious,' he said, just like the bullfighters do after they've been gored. But it was."[5] The newspaper had already been fined 600,000 pesos earlier in the month; now it closed down entirely. García Márquez's cheques stopped coming and by the beginning of February he could no longer pay for his room in the Hôtel de Flandre. Madame Lacroix, a charitable soul, allowed him to fall behind with his rent. According to one of García Márquez's versions she would gradually move him higher and higher in the building until eventually he ended up in an unheated attic on the seventh floor and she pretended to forget about him.[6] There his friends would find him writing wearing gloves, a *ruana* and a woolly cap.

García Márquez was already living on a shoestring before they heard the bad news about *El Espectador* and Mendoza was struck by how few possessions he had brought with him from Colombia. Mendoza introduced him to Nicolás Guillén and another communist activist, the wealthy Venezuelan novelist and journalist Miguel Otero Silva, who, with his father, had founded the influential Caracas newspaper *El Nacional* in 1943. They met by chance in a bar in the Rue Cujas in the days before Mendoza left for Venezuela, and Otero Silva invited them to eat in the well-known brasserie Au Pied de Cochon by the market of Les Halles. Years later, when they became friends, Otero Silva would not remember the pale and painfully thin young Colombian who listened so earnestly to the communist diagnosis of the situation in France and Latin America while he bolted down a providential free meal.[7] Otero Silva and Guillén had just heard about Khrushchev's stunning denunciation of Stalin and the cult of personality on 25 February near the end of the 20th Congress of the Communist Party of the Soviet Union; they were deeply troubled by the newly declared policy of co-existence, which they considered defeatist, and speculated anxiously about the future of the international communist movement.[8]

Guillén would be the protagonist of one of Garcia Márquez's favourite anecdotes about the Paris period: "It was when Perón ruled Argentina, Odría Peru and Rojas Pinilla in my country, the time of Somoza, Batista, Trujillo, Pérez Jiménez, Stroessner; in fact, Latin America was paved with dictators. Nicolás Guillén used to get up at five in the morning as he read the newspapers over a cup of coffee; then he'd open the window and shout so he could be heard in both hotels, which were full of Latin Americans, just as if he was in a patio in Camagüey. One day he opened his window and said, 'The man has fallen!,' and everyone—Argentinians, Paraguayans, Dominicans, Peruvians—thought it was their man. I heard him too and thought, 'Shit, Rojas Pinilla's gone!' Later he told me it was Perón."[9]

On 15 February 1956, a new newspaper, *El Independiente*, had been launched as a direct replacement for *El Espectador*, six weeks after the closure of its predecessor. It was edited for two months by Liberal ex-President Alberto Lleras Camargo, who was also the former Secretary of the Organization of American States. García Márquez, after a very difficult and anxious few weeks, breathed a sigh of relief; and when Plinio Mendoza left for Caracas at the end of the month he was satisfied that his new friend was back on his feet and secure. García Márquez's first article in almost three months appeared in the new paper on 18 March. He sent a seventeen-part report—almost a hundred pages when eventually reprinted and included in a book—on the trial of those accused in the recent espionage scandal in which French government secrets were passed to the Communists during the last months of French rule in Vietnam. Thus on 12 March 1956 *El Independiente* announced on its first page, "Special envoy of *The Independent* travels to the most sensational trial of the century." (Little wonder García Márquez would later get a reputation for hyperbole.) Ironically enough, despite the effort invested in the series, the closure of *El Inde-pendiente* on 15 April would mean that García Márquez never got to relate the climax of the trial, which left his readers frustrated at the end of what was not, in any case, the most interesting of his efforts at reporting, nor the best narrated. Once again, however, although he did not know it, García Márquez had found himself connected, at a distance, with someone who would loom large in his later life. The star of the judicial proceedings was the ex-Minister of the Interior and then Minister of Justice, François Mitterrand: "a fair-haired young man, dressed in a light blue suit, who gave the session a faint touch of the movie-house."[10] Mitterrand himself was under suspicion in the case because of his well-known opposition to the colonial war in Vietnam. For now, though, Mitterrand and the rest of the courtroom cast were in the way of García Márquez's new novel.

He could hear the chime of the Sorbonne's clock from his attic. As he sat writing Mercedes Barcha, the fiancée he hardly knew, watched him from a picture frame above the bedside table. Plinio Mendoza recalls that when he first went up to his friend's room, "I moved to the wall to look at his fiancée's photograph, fixed there; a pretty girl with long straight hair. 'It's the sacred crocodile,' he said."[11] After García Márquez arrived in Europe Mercedes had begun to send him letters at least twice and frequently three times a week. He wrote back equally assiduously.[12] His letters to her were usually sent via his parents: his brother Jaime, then fifteen, remembers taking them to Mercedes in Barranquilla from time to time.

The new novel was inspired by the small remote river town where he and Mercedes had first met, though there was to be nothing romantic about the book. Eventually it would be entitled *In Evil Hour (La mala hora)*. Though he could not know it, this ill-fated novel would not be published until 1962. It was not a book about the time in which the García Márquez and Barcha Pardo families had lived in that small community together but instead was set a few years later, in a period contemporary with its composition, and would focus on the local repercussions of the *Violencia*. This was because the *Violencia* was dominating the thoughts of all Colombians, at home and abroad—he himself was once more an indirect victim of it—and his recent journalism, before leaving Bogotá, had brought his anti-government postures into sharp focus.

The town in García Márquez's novel is based almost cinemato-graphically on Sucre. Indeed, the topographical details are so exact that the reader could almost draw a map of a place where all attention is focused on the river, the boardwalk, the main square and the houses which surround it. Sucre would be home to several brief, disturbing novels down the years: *In Evil Hour, No One Writes to the Colonel* and *Chronicle of a Death Foretold*. All would be direct expressions of its violent destiny.

It would be many years before anyone would even begin to focus on the identity of this small river town; indeed, most readers have continued to try to reconcile it vainly with the quite different descriptions and atmosphere of Macondo-Aracataca. In future years, in interviews, García Márquez himself would never refer to Sucre by name, just as he almost never mentioned his father; the two facts are surely inseparable. On one occasion he would comment, "It is a village in which there is no magic. That's why my writing about it is always a journalistic sort of literature."[13] Yet the real Sucre, on which, so to speak, he makes his stand for critical realism—against his father and against Colombian Conservatism—and which inspires him to invent long-suffering characters reminiscent of those in De Sica's *Umberto D.* or *Bicycle Thieves*— that real Sucre was not so very different, socially, from Aracataca; indeed, as his brothers and sisters almost unanimously attest, it is in some ways a much more exotic and romantic place. Magic, as always, is in the eye of the beholder. The difference is that when Gabito had lived in Sucre he was not experiencing it as a child between infancy and the age of ten, as he had experienced Aracataca; nor was he living with his beloved grandfather the Colonel, and in any case he never lived there fully because he was sent away to school—and although being sent away to school was a privilege, he had undoubtedly construed it at the time as yet another expulsion from the family. Besides, he had lived in Aracataca in the wake of a thrilling economic boom; the Sucre period saw the start of the *Violencia*.

When *Leaf Storm* was published just before he left Bogotá for Europe, García Márquez's communist friends had commented that although the book was—of course—excellent, there was too much myth and poetry in it for their taste. García Márquez would confess both to Mario Vargas Llosa and to Plinio Mendoza—who at the time agreed with the communist critique—that he had developed a guilt complex because *Leaf Storm* was a novel that didn't "condemn or expose anything."[14] In other words, the book did not conform to communist conceptions of a socially committed literature which would denounce capitalist repression and envisage a better socialist future. Indeed, for most communists the novel form itself was a bourgeois vehicle: the cinema was the twentieth century's only truly popular medium.

Although *In Evil Hour* is a political work intended as an "exposé," García Márquez is still a subtle narrator and still uses an oblique approach to political and ideological critique: for example, he doesn't even specify that the regime carrying out the repressive acts he describes is a Conservative government—though this would of course be obvious to any Colombian reader. And despite the fact that tens of thousands of people were being murdered every year by the police, the army and the paramilitary militias during the period in question, many of them in the most savage and sadistic fashion imaginable, there are only two deaths in this novel: one a civilian "honour crime" which anticipates the central incident in the later *Chronicle of a Death Foretold*, and the other a more predictably political crime carried out by the government—though at first sight more as a result of incompetence than design. In fact the novel's intention is to demonstrate, without saying so overtly, that the entire structure of power depicted in the book must inevitably and repeatedly produce such repressive actions: to put it crudely, the Mayor has to kill some of his opponents if he is to survive.

This surprisingly dispassionate understanding of the nature of power takes the novelist far beyond the desire to moralize or engage in facile propaganda; naturally he deplores the Conservative mentality but he never plays to the gallery. In his autobiography García Márquez would state that the figure of the Mayor had been inspired by the policeman husband of his black lover "Nigromanta"; but he had previously given another explanation, recalled by Germán Vargas: "The Mayor in *In Evil Hour* has a basis in fact. He was from a town near Sucre. García Márquez has said he was a relative of his wife Mercedes. And that he was a real criminal. He wanted to kill Mercedes's father and so he always carried a gun. Sometimes, to annoy her, García Márquez reminds her that this guy was from her family."[15]

Despite his best efforts the novel stubbornly refused to take off and he began to lose his grip on it. Sunk in Colombia at its most depressing, indeed flailing about somewhat aimlessly in that disenchanted world he was re-creating, García Márquez was seeing less and less of Paris as winter turned to spring; but occasionally he would go out into the world. France too, in the dog-days of the Fourth Republic, was in a depressed condition. Pierre Mendès-France, the utopian President of the Council of State who had famously tried to get the French to drink milk instead of wine, had recently been forced from power; Edgar Faure had replaced him, but not for much longer. France had been defeated in Vietnam and was struggling in Algeria. Yet, though no one was aware of it at the time, Paris was in one of its most evocative moments, the last before European Community modernity began inexorably to change it in the 1960s from smoky blue to space age silver. García Márquez would mainly eat in cheap student restaurants such as the Capoulade and the Acropole; and whereas most other Latin Americans would feel the need to wander into the Sorbonne or the Louvre for the occasional piece of intellectual elevation, and to view other people like themselves in those gilded Parisian mirrors, he as usual would spend his days in the university of the streets.

Then, out of the blue, or the grey, came a sudden change in his life. On an evening in March he met a young woman by the purest chance when he was out with a Portuguese journalist who was also covering the French spy trial for a Brazilian newspaper. She was a twenty-six-year-old actress from Spain known as Tachia. She was about to give a poetry recital. Almost forty years later, she would recall that Gabriel, as she would always call him, refused to go to the recital: "'A poetry recital,' he sneered, 'what a bore!' I assumed he hated poetry. He waited in the Café Le Mabillon down on the Boulevard Saint-Germain-des-Prés, near the church, and we joined him there after the recital.[16] He was as thin as a finger, he looked just like an Algerian, curly hair and a moustache, and I've never liked men with moustaches. I don't like crude macho men either; and I'd always had the Spanish racial and cultural prejudice that Latin American men were inferior."[17]

Tachia had been born María Concepción Quintana in January 1929 in Eibar, Guipúzcoa, in the Spanish Basque country. She was one of three daughters born to a Catholic family who supported the Franco regime after the civil war. Her father, a lover of poetry, had read to her constantly when she was a child, little knowing how this would determine her future. In 1952 she met the already famous Spanish poet Blas de Otero in Bilbao, where she was working as a nanny, one of the few opportunities for women to work independently in Franco's Spain. Otero, thirteen years her senior, renamed her by loosely reorganizing the name Conchita: "Tachia." He also seduced her. Soon after that she ran away to Madrid—although in those days you had to be twenty-five to leave home without parental permission—to study theatre and become an actress, and there she began a passionate but ill-starred affair with this man who was a great poet but profoundly unstable and an inveterate womanizer. The name Tachia appears in some of his best-known poems. Otero put her through hell with his manic unpredictability. To get away from him—though it would be many years before she got away from him entirely—she fled from Spain: "I went to Paris late in 1952 as a sort of au pair for six months; the city just dazzled me. Then on 1 August 1953 I went back there for good. I had none of the necessary skills, I attended theatre courses to try and find an entrée."

Tachia was adventurous, magnetic, curious, open to every experience. She was the kind of woman considered especially attractive in the post-war existentialist period and—though her own great love was the theatre—in the New Wave movies about to be made in late 1950s Paris: a slim, dark left-banker, usually dressed in black, with a close-cropped *gamin* haircut of the kind Jean Seberg would shortly make famous, and with energy to burn. Sentimentally, though, at just that moment she was at a loose end. As a foreigner her chances of making it in the French theatre had to be considered little more than *zéro* but she had no intention of returning to Spain. Nor of seeking long-term emotional attachments. She had been through an *amour fou* in her own country and nothing since had captured her emotions or her imagination in the same way. Now here she was telling her life story to this unprepossessing Colombian.

"I'd say I disliked Gabriel on sight: he seemed despotic, arrogant, yet also timid: a really unattractive combination. I liked the James Mason types—Blas looked quite like him—the British gentleman types, not the pretty boy Latin lover types like Tyrone Power. Also I'd always preferred older men and Gabriel was more or less my own age. He immediately started boasting about his job, he seemed to consider himself a journalist, not a writer. The friend left the bar at ten and we stayed on, talking, and then started to walk around the streets of Paris. Gabriel said terrible things about the French . . . Though the French got their own back on him later because they proved too rational for his magical realism."

Tachia discovered that when you started to talk to this sarcastic Colombian, there was another side to him. Something in the voice, the confidential smile, the way he told a story. García Márquez and the forthright young Spanish woman began a relationship that very quickly became intimate. And perhaps archetypal. The most famous

Latin American novel early in the following decade would be Argentinian Julio Cortázar's *Hopscotch (Rayuela)*, published in 1963. It would be about a Latin American expatriate wandering about Paris in the 1950s, surrounded by a group of bohemian friends, artists and intellectuals, mainly focused on the Quartier Latin. The feckless protagonist, Oliveira, no longer young, would have no job, nor any interest in finding one; he would be finding himself and finding the world; and his inspiration, his melancholy muse, would be a beautiful young woman, a sort of hippy *avant la lettre* known as "La Maga," "the Sorceress." Cortázar never really lived this romance; but García Márquez did. Walking and talking, one thing led to another: "Gradually I came to like Gabriel, despite my initial reservations, and the relationship developed. We started to go steady after a few weeks, April some time, I suppose. At the beginning Gabriel had enough money to buy a girl a drink or a cup of chocolate or pay for the cinema. Then his newspaper was closed and he was left with nothing."

Yes. Three weeks after García Márquez met Tachia *El Independiente* was closed in Bogotá: this time, although he could not know it, for almost a year. It was a disastrous background to a new relationship. Instead of making up his back pay, the management eventually sent him a one-way ticket to Colombia. When the ticket arrived García Márquez gulped, took a deep breath, and cashed it in. Was this a desire to know Europe better; a desire to complete his new novel; or was he in love? He had already been working for three months on *In Evil Hour* and he intended to go on with it. So for many reasons he was nowhere near ready to leave Paris. In Bogotá he had found little time for his own writing and now he had the bit between his teeth again. It was his own decision. But it would be hard. And then there was Tachia.

I myself first met Tachia Quintana in Paris in March 1993. We walked around the same city streets that she and García Márquez had walked in the mid-1950s. Six months later, in García Márquez's house in Mexico City, I took a deep breath and asked him, "What about Tachia?" At that time her name was known to only a few people, and the outlines of their story to even fewer; I guess he must have been hoping it would pass me by. He breathed in equally deeply, like someone watching a coffin slowly open, and said, "Well, it happened." I said, "Can we talk about it?" He said, "No." It was on that occasion that he would first tell me, with the expression on his face of an undertaker determinedly closing a coffin lid back down, that "everyone has three lives: a public life, a private life and a secret life." Naturally the public life was there for all to see, I just had to do the work; I would be given occasional access and insight into the private life and was evidently expected to work out the rest; as for the secret life, "No, never." If it was anywhere, he intimated, it was in his books. I could start with them. "And anyway, don't worry. I will be whatever you say I am." On the matter of Tachia Quintana, then, as she was perceived from the standpoint of García Márquez, both in 1956 and after, we will have to examine the books. Tachia herself, though, was happy enough to tell her side of the story.

> When I met Gabriel I was just about to move to a tiny room in the Rue d'Assas. I can't remember where I was before, you'd never believe how many hotels and apartments I lived in in Paris. I even shared a room with Violeta Parra. The new place was near Montparnasse, between Les Invalides and Saint-Germain-des-Prés close to the brasseries of La Coupole, La Closerie des Lilas, Le Dôme and Le Select, and only yards from the Luxembourg Garden and the theatres, cinemas and jazz-bars of Montparnasse. We went to his room in the Hôtel de Flandre sometimes but mainly we slept in the Rue d'Assas. It was a former *hôtel particulier* which had been converted. I was in the old kitchen, it was minute, like a maid's room, a *chambre de bonne*, with a little patio garden right outside. It was just a bed and orange boxes; imagine, twelve people used to sit on that bed. The owner was a strict Catholic but she mainly closed her eyes and basically let us get on with it. The best thing was the little garden out in the open air. How often he used to wait for me, sitting out there! Often with his head in his hands. He drove me crazy but I was very fond of him.

Soon after he met Tachia, the Colombian found that the book he had begun and on which he had made significant though always painful progress was slowly slipping away from him. Many years later he would become one of the most technically assured "professional" writers in the world, a man who always knew exactly what he wanted to write and then invariably accomplished it. But at this time in his life each work seemed to break off into another one; composition was an agonizing experience; and conception never seemed to lead to the expected process of development. So it was now. One of the secondary characters began to grow, to become autonomous and, eventually, to demand his own separate literary environment. In this case it was an old colonel, at once diffident and obdurate, a refugee from Macondo and from the smell of overripe bananas, a man waiting, fifty years after the event, for the pension due him because of his service in the War of a Thousand Days. The original novel, now set aside, was a cool, cruel work requiring nerve and detachment, but its author was finding himself quite unexpectedly in a moment both of passion and great privation, living out his own version of *La bohème*.

Just as nostalgia brought about by the journey with his mother was the instrument which had given birth to *Leaf Storm*, a not dissimilar emotion, poignancy (nostalgia about the impossibility of living in the present), was the lever which separated what would become *No One Writes to the Colonel* (*El coronel no tiene quien le escriba*: literally, "The Colonel has no one to write to him") from what would eventually become *In Evil Hour*, the novel endlessly delayed and postponed. And once again a woman was the inspiration: in a desperate, haunting way the novel about the colonel would be a projection of the drama García Márquez was starting to live out, right there and then, with Tachia. They were involved in a surprising, exciting, passionate, totally unexpected affair; but quite soon they ran short of money. From the very beginning the relationship was conditioned by poverty and then, soon enough, threatened by tragedy. So the first novel, still a work in progress, was tied up, not for the last time, with an old striped necktie, and pushed to the back of the rickety wardrobe in the Hôtel de Flandre; and the intense, obsessive, desperate story of a starving colonel and his hapless, long-suffering wife took hold some time in May or early June of 1956.

García Márquez's debts at the hotel mounted alarmingly, yet, tellingly perhaps, he held on to the room even though he couldn't pay for it. Or said he couldn't. After a few weeks he and Tachia were finding it difficult even to eat. Of course he had been through this before, in Bogotá, in Cartagena, in Barranquilla. It was almost as if he had to go hungry in order to justify clinging to his vocation. His family could not complain that he was not pursuing his law degree, because he was starving; Tachia should not complain that he was not working to support her, because there were no lengths of suffering to which he himself was not prepared to go while he was writing his book. Granted, his French was still rudimentary and jobs were not easy to come by; but the truth is that he was not really looking. When the air fare was gone, he collected empty bottles and old newspapers and received centimes in return at local stores. At times, he says, he "borrowed" a bone from a butcher so that Tachia could use it to make a stew.[18] One day he had to beg a fare in the metro—missing the last five centimes again—and was humiliated by the reaction of the Frenchman who gave him the money. He sent messages to his friends in Colombia appealing for financial help, then found himself waiting hopefully for good news, week after week, like his grandfather waiting for his pension all those years before, and like the colonel in his new novel. Perhaps the irony sustained him.

In a way the relationship with Tachia never really had a chance. He had lost his job just three weeks after they met. And a couple of months later another disaster struck: "I realized I was pregnant one evening when we were walking along the Champs Elysées. I was feeling strange and I just knew it. After I got pregnant I was still out looking after children and cleaning floors, vomiting as I did so, and when I got back he'd have done nothing and then I'd have to start cooking. He said I was very bossy, he called me 'the General.' Meanwhile he was writing his articles and *The Colonel*—it was about us of course: our situation, our relationship. I read the novel as it was written, loved it. But we fought all the time for nine months, all the time. It was hard, exhausting, we were destroying one another. Were we just sparring? No, really fighting."

"But," remembers Tachia, "he was also very affectionate; he was tenderness itself. We told each other everything. Men are very innocent and so I taught him things, things about women, I gave him a lot of material for his novels. I have the impression that Gabriel had had very few women; certainly at that time he had never lived with one. Although we fought a lot we also had good times. We used to talk about the baby and what he would be like, and come up with names for him. And Gabriel told me endless stories, fascinating ones about his childhood, his family, Barranquilla, Cepeda, and so on. It was wonderful, I loved that. Gabriel also used to sing a lot, especially *vallenatos* by Escalona—like the 'House in the Sky' ['La casa en el aire']. He sang *cumbias* too, like 'My Pretty Girl' ['Mi chiquita linda']; he had a beautiful voice. And of course, although we fought all day every day we never had any problem understanding one another at night.

"Gabriel would often sing at the endless parties at Hernán Vieco's place at Rue Guénégaud. Vieco was very seductive, blue eyes, large eyebrows, very attractive. He was the only one with a house, money and a car—the MG sports car he so adored. Gabriel used to sing there and play the guitar; he danced divinely too. We also had French friends who lived in the Rue Chérubini, over the river. It was there we got to know all Brassens's songs. It was Gabriel who took me to the Communist Party's Fête de l'Humanité for the first time, him and Luis Villar Borda, I think. In that way I was still a very traditional woman: I just sat there without saying anything while the men talked about politics. I had no political knowledge or ideas at all in those days, though my instincts were progressive. Whereas Gabriel seemed to me an admirably focused and principled person, at least politically. I formed the impression that as far as political morality was concerned, he was a man of integrity, serious, honourable. I thought of him as something hardly any different from a communist. I remember once saying, as if I knew what I was talking about, 'I suppose there are good and bad communists.' Gabriel gave me a look and replied, rather severely, 'No, ma'am, there are communists and non-communists.'

"I must admit that over the pregnancy he was totally fair. It's one thing that could be said for him. We had an open discussion and he asked me what I wanted. I think he would have been happy enough to have the baby. *Il s'assouvit*, as they say here: he put up with whatever I wanted. I was the one who didn't want it. He knew how serious I was about children and so he knew I would expect him to marry me. He was both good about it and weak. He simply let me do whatever I decided. I don't think he was as horrified as I was. Probably from his Latin American standpoint it wasn't so unusual or shocking; he may even have been proud, for all I know.

"It was absolutely my decision, not his. Of course by then, despite or perhaps because of my family background, I had broken with God. By the time we'd been through all this I was four and a half months pregnant; and desperate. It was a terrible, terrible time. Then I had the haemorrhage. He was absolutely horrified, he nearly fainted—Gabriel, when he sees blood, well, you know . . . I spent eight days in the Maternité Port Royal, very close to where I lived. Gabriel was always the first of the fathers to arrive in the hospital at visiting time in the evening.

"After the miscarriage we both knew it was over. I kept threatening to leave. And finally I did, I just left, first to Vieco's house, to convalesce, and then to Madrid. I was very upset, worn out. I was always on top in the relationship but the pregnancy undermined me. I left Paris from Gare d'Austerlitz in December 1956. Gabriel organized a whole group of friends to take me to the station. I had recovered from the operation but I was very fragile inside. We were late, of course, the luggage had to be thrown on to the train, I had to rush aboard and there wasn't even time to say goodbye to everyone. I had eight suitcases. Gabriel always says it was sixteen. I was distraught as the train pulled out, weeping into my hands against the window. Then as the train started to move I stared out at Gabriel, and Gabriel with that soulful look on his face, started walking to keep up and then fell away. Really he let me down in 1956. He just couldn't cope. Of course I could never have married him. I never had the slightest regret about it. He was too unreliable. And I couldn't bring children into the world with such a father. Because nothing is more important, is it? Yet in a way I was completely wrong because he turned out to be an excellent father."

Tachia was a woman who was brave, lucky, determined, adventurous, foolish or intelligent enough to lead a completely independent life long before this became a woman's "right." Although her story is that of subordinating her needs to García Márquez, it is difficult to imagine it was not her choice. With one important relationship behind her—one in which she had also found herself "sacrificed" to a literary vocation—it is hard to think she would have put up with anything ultimately unacceptable to her. Probably their relationship was a strong attachment that began to sour and to demand too much once she was pregnant—she had either to marry or put an end to it. And this was not her first serious relationship—though it was the first time either of the couple had ever lived with anyone.

García Márquez was probably unhappy about the abortion attempts; children are not considered a problem on the Costa and he was from a family where the women—Tranquilina, his grandmother; Luisa, his own mother—took in numerous children directly related to them; and so he was probably very troubled by the child's death. It would have been hard on Mercedes if he had had a baby by another woman but Latin Americans are more accustomed to such things and less judgemental than Europeans. As for him returning to marry Mercedes soon after, he may have thought: so what? She was really only a child before. What would anyone have expected of a twenty-eight-year-old Latin American man but that he would have an affair in Paris? His friends would have been disappointed with anything less. If Tachia had had the baby he might still have left her. In Mercedes he seems very deliberately to have chosen a woman from his own milieu, someone who would understand exactly where he was from and what made him tick.

Tachia had left. But he had his novel. That novel, uniquely for García Márquez, is set during the very time he wrote it, the later months of 1956, framed by the Suez crisis in Europe. The details of the plot had been established long before Tachia left for Madrid. It is October: a colonel, whose name the reader will never know, and who used to live in Macondo, is a man of seventy-five rotting away in a small, asphyxiating river town lost in the forests of Colombia. The Colonel has been waiting fifty-six years for his pension from the War of a Thousand Days and has no other means of support. It is fifteen years since he received even a letter from the state pension department but still he goes to the post office every day in hope of information. Thus he spends his life waiting for news that never comes. He and his wife had a son, Agustín, a tailor, who was murdered by the authorities at the beginning of the year for distributing clandestine political propaganda.[19] When Agustín, who used to look after the old couple, was killed, he left behind his champion fighting cock, which is worth a significant sum of money. The Colonel endures innumerable humiliations in order not to have to sell the bird, which for him and his son's friends (named Alfonso, Alvaro and Germán) becomes a symbol of dignity and resistance, as well as a reminder of Agustín himself. The Colonel's wife, who is more practical, and also ailing and in need of medical treatment, disagrees with him and repeatedly urges him to sell the rooster. At the end of the novel the Colonel is still obdurately resisting.

García Márquez has said that the novel had a multiple inspiration: firstly—given that he always has a visual image as a point of departure for his works—there was the memory of a man he saw in the Barranquilla fish market years before, waiting for a boat "with a kind of silent anxiety."[20] Secondly, more personally, there was the memory of his grandfather waiting for his own Thousand Day War pension although, physically, the model was Rafael Escalona's father, also a colonel but a slimmer man, as befits the starving protagonist García Márquez imagined for the book.[21] Thirdly, obviously, there was the political situation in Colombia during the *Violencia*. Fourthly, in terms of artistic inspiration, there was De Sica's *Umberto D.*, scripted by Zavattini, about another man, with another cherished creature (his dog), who lives out a silent *via crucis* in post-war Rome, amidst the general indifference of his contemporaries. But what García Márquez has never acknowledged is that *No One Writes to the Colonel* was based—fifthly and most directly of all—on the drama that he and Tachia were living through at the time, with the Suez crisis as a political backdrop both in their lives and in the novel.[22]

In both cases the woman puts up with what she interprets as the selfishness or weakness of the man she lives with, a man who has convinced himself that he has a historical mission, one which is more important than she is. In each case she babies him (in the novel the old couple have already lost their son; in the real world Tachia would eventually grow tired of babying Gabriel when she lost her own baby . . .) and she carries out all the indispensable material and maternal functions of the household. She does all the practical work while he keeps labouring away vainly on a hopeless utopian enterprise, horribly constipated, with the fighting cock as the symbol of his courage, independence and eventual triumph. She is convinced everything will turn out badly; he is indomitably optimistic. Nine months have passed between the death of the Colonel's son and the events of the novel proper; when the wife says to the Colonel, "We are the orphans of our son," it could be the epitaph to the affair between García Márquez and Tachia. The cock (the novel, the writer's personal dignity) is a symbol of an individual's identification with collective values. And guilt, and grief—the miscarriage, the death of the son— can only be assuaged by going on, almost as a memorial. García Márquez's personal motto might always have been: "the only way out is through."

No One Writes to the Colonel is one of those prose works which, in spite of its undeniable "realism," functions like a poem. It is impossible to separate its central themes of waiting and hoping, weather phenomena and bodily functions (not least excreting or, in the unfortunate Colonel's case, not excreting), politics and poverty, life and death, solitude and solidarity, fate and destiny. Although García Márquez has always said that dialogue is not his forte, the world-weary humour communicated by his characters, modulated in a fractionally different way to distinguish each of them from the others, is one of the defining features of his mature works. That unmistakable humour, as characteristic as that of Cervantes, reaches its definitive expression in this wonderful little novel, just as the Colonel himself, however briefly depicted, becomes one of the unforgettable personages of twentieth-century fiction. The last paragraph, one of the most perfect in all literature, seems to concentrate and then release virtually all of the themes and images marshalled by the work as a whole. The exhausted old man has managed to fall asleep but his exasperated wife, almost beside herself, shakes him violently and wakes him up. She wants to know what they will live on now that he has finally decided not to sell the fighting cock but to prepare it instead for combat:

"What will we eat?"

The Colonel had taken seventy-five years—the seventy-five years of his life, minute by minute—to arrive at that instant. He felt pure, explicit, invincible, at the moment he replied: "Shit."[23]

The reader too feels a sense of release; and finds no little aesthetic pleasure in the implicit contrast between the perfectly synthesized ending and a sense of liberation and relief: a raising of consciousness, resistance, rebellion. Dignity, always so important to García Márquez, has been restored.

Years later, *No One Writes to the Colonel* became a universally acknowledged masterpiece of short fiction, like Hemingway's *The Old Man and the Sea*, almost perfect in its self-contained intensity, its carefully punctuated plot and its brilliantly prepared conclusion. The writer himself would say that *No One Writes to the Colonel* had the "conciseness, terseness and directness I learned from journalism."[24]

Yet the end of the novel was not the end of the story. There is always another way of telling a tale. Twenty years later, García Márquez would write a strange and disturbing short narrative, "The Trail of Your Blood in the Snow." It might be called *No One Writes to the Colonel* revised and corrected. If the first work would turn out to be his version of the affair at the time, an unmistakable self-justification, the later work is equally clearly a self-criticism and a belated vindication of Tachia. Had he changed his mind or was he trying to mollify his ex-lover many years down the line? In the later story a young Colombian couple travel to Madrid on their honeymoon and then drive to Paris. As they leave the Spanish capital the young woman, Nena Daconte, receives a bunch of red roses and pricks her finger, which then bleeds all the way to Paris. At one point she says, "Imagine, a trail of blood in the snow all the way from Madrid to Paris. Wouldn't that make a good song." The author must have remembered, naturally, that after losing so much of her own blood, Tachia had travelled in the opposite direction, all the way from Paris back to Madrid, in the middle of winter. Is all this an exorcism? In the story, when the young couple arrive in Paris, Nena, who knows France well, and is two months pregnant, checks herself into the very hospital—a "huge, gloomy hospital" just off Avenue Denfert-Rochereau—where Tachia's haemorrhage was treated in 1956, where she too might have died, and where her unborn child did indeed die. Nena's untutored husband, Billy Sánchez de Avila, who has never left Colombia before this trip to Europe, and who dances in the Parisian snow just as García Márquez himself had done the first time he saw it, proves completely incapable of coping with the crisis, in a cold, hostile Paris, and Nena dies in the hospital without him ever seeing her again.[25]

Tachia was gone. At Christmas García Márquez was back in the Hôtel de Flandre full time, at the end of what he would later call "that sad autumn of 1956,"[26] blamed by most of his friends for Tachia's problems and her dramatic departure. But he was in the final stages of his novel, he had found a way to justify what had happened, at least to himself (he considered it a point of honour not to talk with other men about his personal relationships) and nothing would stand in his way. The survival of the cock at the end of the novel is also the survival of the novel itself despite a nagging woman; and, in the end, its completion took place just a few weeks after Tachia departed for Madrid. He would date it "January 1957." No baby was born but the novel was. Tachia said he was "lucky" to finish it under the circumstances of those months. It is difficult to agree that luck had anything to do with it.

Now there was no Tachia to buy food, haggle over prices and cook cheap meals. García Márquez was scraping the barrel just like the old Colonel scrapes his coffee pot on the first page of the novel. He would tell his friend José Font Castro that he once spent a week in his frozen attic hiding from the hotel administrators without eating, and drinking only from the tap in the washbasin. His brother Gustavo recalls, "I remember a confidence Gabito passed to me when we were drinking in Barranquilla: 'Everyone's my friend since *One Hundred Years of Solitude* but no one knows what it cost me to get there. No one knows how I was reduced to eating garbage in Paris,' he told me. 'Once I was at a party in the house of some friends who helped me out a bit. After the party the lady of the house asked me to put the garbage out in the street for her. I was so hungry that I salvaged what I could from the garbage and ate it there and then.' "[27]

In other respects he was at a loose end too. Some friends were alienated by what they took to be his abandonment of Tachia and treated him less benevolently and less generously as a result. He got a job singing in L'Escale, the Latin American nightclub where he had spent evenings with Tachia and where she herself had found occasional work before. Mostly he was not doing *vallenatos* but Mexican *rancheras* in duet with the Venezuelan painter and sculptor Jesús Rafael Soto, one of the pioneers of kinetic art. He earned a dollar a night (equivalent to about eight dollars in 2008). He mooched around. He tried to get back to *In Evil Hour* but it had lost its hold on him after the months he had spent in the company of the old Colonel. The Barranquilla friends at "The Cave" had formed a "Society of Friends to Help Gabito" ("Sociedad de Amigos para Ayudar a Gabito," or SAAG); together they bought a 100-dollar note, and met in the Rondón Bookshop to work out how best to send it to their friend. Jorge Rondón, using his Communist Party experience, explained how he had learned to send clandestine messages inside postcards. This the friends did and simultaneously sent a letter explaining the trick. Of course, the card arrived before the letter, and the indignant García Márquez, who was hoping for more than best wishes, snorted: "Bastards!" and threw the card in the waste paper bin. That same afternoon the explanatory letter arrived and he was fortunate to be able to retrieve the postcard after rummaging through the hotel's dustbin.[28]

Then he had no way of changing the money. The photographer Guillermo Angulo—in Rome at the time, looking for García Márquez!—recalls: "Someone told him about a friend called 'La Puppa' who had just got in from Rome after getting paid her salary and should have a lot of money on her. So he went to see her—he was bundled up as usual, since it was wintertime—and 'La Puppa' opened the door and a current of warm air from a well-heated room greeted him. 'La Puppa' was naked. She was not pretty, but she had a great body and she would take her clothes off without any provocation. So 'La Puppa' sat down—according to Gabo, what bothered him most was that she carried on as if she were fully dressed—and crossed her legs and started to talk about Colombia and the Colombians she knew. He started to tell her his problem, and she nodded and went across the room to where she had a little money chest. He realized that what she wanted was to have sex, but what he wanted was to eat. So he went off to eat and pigged out so much that he was sick for a week with indigestion."[29] No doubt this second-hand anecdote has gained a good deal in the telling. It was "La Puppa" who would take a copy of *No One Writes to the Colonel* back to Rome for Angulo to read. Despite Angulo's uncharacteristic discretion, it seems that she and García Márquez had a brief fling after Tachia returned to Madrid. Good for the battered ego, no doubt.

The fact remains, though, that García Márquez lived in Paris for eighteen months with only a cashed-in air ticket, sporadic charity from friends and some scant savings of his own to survive on; and no means of getting back to Colombia. By now however he spoke French, knew Paris well and had an assortment of friends and acquaintances, including one or two French people, Latin Americans from several different countries and a number of Arabs. Indeed García Márquez himself was frequently mistaken for an Arab—it was the era not only of Suez but of the Algerian conflict—and more than once he was taken in by the police as part of their regular security sweeps:

> One night, as I was leaving a cinema, a police patrol set about me in the street, spat in my face and punched me as they bundled me into an armoured wagon. It was full of silent Algerians, also picked up and beaten and spat on in local cafés. They too, like the police who arrested me, thought I was Algerian. So we spent the night together, crammed like sardines in a cell in the nearest police station, whilst the police, in shirt sleeves, talked about their kids and ate wedges of bread dipped in wine. To piss them off the Algerians and I stayed awake all night singing songs by Brassens against the abuses and stupidity of the forces of law and order.[30]

He made a new friend inside overnight, Ahmed Tebbal, a doctor who gave him an Algerian viewpoint on the conflict and even involved him in a few subversive activities on behalf of the Algerian cause.[31] Economically, however, things just got worse and worse. One grim night he saw a man crossing the Pont Saint-Michel:

> I didn't have a full appreciation of my situation until one night when I found myself by the Luxembourg Garden without having eaten a chestnut all day and without a place to sleep . . . As I crossed the Saint-Michel bridge I felt I was not alone in the mist, because I could clearly hear the steps of someone approaching in the opposite direction. I saw his outline appear in the mist, on the same sidewalk and moving at the same speed as me, and I clearly saw his tartan jacket with its red and black squares, and in the instant we passed one another halfway across the bridge I saw his untidy hair, his Turk's moustache, that sad expression that told of daily hungers and sleepless nights, and I saw his eyes were filled with tears. My blood froze because that man looked like me, on my way back.[32]

Later, talking of those days, he would declare: "I too know what it is to wait for the mail and be hungry and beg: that's how I finished *No One Writes to the Colonel* in Paris. He is a bit me, the same."[33]

It was around this time that Hernán Vieco, whose financial status was quite different, and who had taken Tachia in after the miscarriage, resolved most of García Márquez's problems by lending him the 120,000 francs he needed to pay Madame Lacroix at the Hôtel de Flandre. On the way back from a party one night, drunk but by no means incapable, Vieco told García Márquez they needed a heart to heart. He asked him how much his hotel account had now risen to. García Márquez refused to discuss the matter. One of the reasons people often helped him in his youth was because they could always see that no matter how bad his circumstances he never felt especially sorry for himself and he never asked for help. Eventually, after a scene of inebriated theatricality, Vieco flourished a fountain pen, wrote out a cheque on the roof of a parked car and stuffed it in his friend's coat pocket. It was for the equivalent of 300 dollars, a substantial sum at the time. García Márquez was overwhelmed both with gratitude and with humiliation.[34] When he took the money to Madame Lacroix her response was to stammer, red with embarrassment in her turn—this was, after all, Paris, home of bohemianism and of struggling artists—"No, no, monsieur, that's too much, why don't you pay me part now and part later."

He had survived the winter. He was not the father of a baby. He had not been trapped by a European Circe. Mercedes was still waiting for him in Colombia. One bright day early in 1957 he caught sight of his idol Ernest Hemingway walking with his wife Mary Welsh down the Boulevard Saint-Michel in the direction of the Jardin du Luxembourg; he was wearing old jeans, a lumberjack's shirt and a baseball cap. García Márquez, too timid to approach him, too excited not to do something, called from the other side of the road: "Maestro!" The great writer, whose novel about an old man, the sea and a big fish had partly inspired the younger man's recently completed novel about an old man, a government pension and a fighting cock, raised his hand and shouted back, "in a slightly puerile voice": "Adios, amigo!"[35]

11

Beyond the Iron Curtain: Eastern Europe During the Cold War

1957

I N EARLY MAY 1957 Plinio Mendoza returned to Paris with his sister Soledad to find his friend thinner, wirier and more stoical. "His pullover had holes at the elbows, the soles of his shoes let in water as he walked the streets and the cheekbones in his ferocious Arab's face protruded starkly."[1] But he was impressed by his friend's progress with the French language and how well he knew his way around the city and its problems. On 11 May they were together drinking at the famous café, Les Deux Magots, when they heard that Rojas Pinilla had been overthrown and had gone into exile, just ten days after he had been condemned by the Colombian Catholic Church. A five-man military junta had taken over and neither of the two friends was optimistic about what might follow.

Both García Márquez and Mendoza had leftist affiliations and illusions and were keen to visit Eastern Europe, especially in view of conflicting reports during the previous year which had begun with Khrushchev's denunciation of Stalin and ended with the furore over the Soviet invasion of Hungary. They decided to begin with Leipzig, where Luis Villar Borda had been living in exile for a year on a student grant. Mendoza, who had been in work, bought a second-hand Renault 4 for the summer and on 18 June drove the vivacious Soledad

and the downbeat García Márquez off along the great German auto-
bahns at 65 mph, taking in Heidelberg and Frankfurt.[2] From Frankfurt
they drove in to East Germany. García Márquez's first article about
this other Germany—once again he would have to wait a long time to
see it published—declared that the Iron Curtain was actually a red and
white roadblock made of wood. The three friends were shocked by
conditions at the border and by the scruffy uniforms and general ignorance of the border guards, who, perhaps unsurprisingly, did not find it
easy to write down the name of García Márquez's birthplace. Soledad
Mendoza then drove them off by night towards Weimar. At breakfast
they stopped at a state restaurant and were again dismayed by what
they saw. Mendoza remembers that before they went in García
Márquez, stretching and yawning as he got out of the car, said to him,
"Listen, Maestro, we've got to find out about all this." "About what?"
"About socialism." García Márquez recalled that venturing into that
unattractive eatery was like "crashing headlong into a reality for which
I was not prepared."[3] Around a hundred Germans sat there eating
breakfasts of ham and eggs fit for kings and queens, though they themselves, defeated and embittered, looked like humiliated beggars. Later
that night the three Colombians arrived in Weimar, from where they
visited the nearby Buchenwald concentration camp early the next
morning. García Márquez, much later, noted that he never did manage
to reconcile the reality of the death camps with the character of
the Germans, "as hospitable as the Spaniards and as generous as the
Soviets."[4]

The three friends drove on to Leipzig. Leipzig reminded García
Márquez of the southern districts of Bogotá, which was not the highest
of recommendations. Everything in Leipzig was shabby and depressing and he reflected, "We, in our blue jeans and shirt-sleeves, still covered in dust from the highway, were the only sign of popular
democracy."[5] At this point he was not clear whether to blame socialism
itself or the Russian occupation.

García Márquez would state in the article he wrote about it that he
and "Franco" (Plinio Mendoza) had "forgotten" that Leipzig was the
site of the Marx-Lenin University, where they were able to meet
"South American students" and discuss the situation more concretely.[6]
This was in fact the very reason they had chosen the city: it was the
home of Villar Borda, whom García Márquez disguised in his report
as a Chilean communist called "Sergio," thirty-two years of age, exiled from his country two years before and studying political economy.

Villar Borda was indeed living in exile—from Colombia, of course—having been closely involved with the Communist Youth in Bogotá, and had managed to obtain a grant to study in the East German city.[7] He had visited García Márquez at Tachia's room on Rue d'Assas when he had returned to Paris to renew his visa and "actually existing socialism" was one of their principal topics of conversation. "Gabo and I," Villar Borda told me in 1998, "thought much the same about the communist system and wanted much the same thing: a humanitarian and democratic socialism." García Márquez would spend a great deal of his life surrounded by fellow travellers, communists and—more often—ex-communists. Among the latter there would be regretful ex-communists, who stayed on the left, and resentful ex-communists, many of whom moved sharply to the right. García Márquez would reluctantly conclude that democratic socialism was preferable, at least in pragmatic terms, to communism.[8]

Villar Borda took the friends out to a state cabaret which had all the appearance of a brothel, with taximeters on the doors of the toilets, much heavy drinking and couples involved in low-level sexual activity. García Márquez wrote: "It wasn't a brothel. Because prostitution is prohibited and severely punished in the socialist countries. It was a State establishment. But from the social point of view it was something worse than a brothel."[9] He and Mendoza decided they should do their chasing of women in the streets. The Latin American students whom they met, even the committed communists, insisted that the system imposed on East Germany was not socialism; Hitler had exterminated all the real communists and the local leaders were bureaucratic lackeys imposing a so-called revolution "brought from the Soviet Union in a trunk" without consulting the people. García Márquez commented: "I believe that at bottom there is an absolute loss of human sensitivity. Concern for the masses makes the individual invisible. And this, which is valid with respect to the Germans, is also valid with respect to the Russian soldiers. In Weimar people objected to the railway station being guarded by a Russian soldier with a machine gun. But no one cared about the poor soldier." García Márquez and Mendoza asked Villar Borda to put them out of their misery by finding some dialectical explanation for the state of East Germany. Villar Borda, a committed socialist all his life, began a spiel and then paused and said, "It's a heap of shit."

All in all, García Márquez's reaction to East Germany was almost entirely negative. He had mixed emotions during his time in West

Berlin, where the Americans were demolishing and rebuilding with even greater enthusiasm than usual in an effort to make the Soviet bloc look bad:

> My first contact with that gigantic capitalist operation within the domain of socialism left me with a feeling of emptiness . . . Out of that rowdy surgical operation something is beginning to emerge which is the exact opposite of Europe. A shining, antiseptic city where things have the unfortunate effect of seeming too new . . . West Berlin is an enormous capitalist propaganda agency.[10]

Ironically, the propaganda worked very effectively on him and on his descriptions of East Berlin, which carry with them a grim disenchantment: "By night, instead of the advertising slogans that flood West Berlin with colour, only the red star shines on the eastern side. The merit of that sombre city is that it does correspond to the economic reality of the country. Except for Stalin Avenue."[11] Stalin Avenue, built on a monumental scale, was unfortunately also built with monumental vulgarity. García Márquez predicted that in "fifty or a hundred years," when one or other of the regimes had prevailed, Berlin would again be one vast city, "a monstrous commercial fair built out of the free samples offered by both systems."[12] Given the political tension and the competition between East and West, he concluded that Berlin was a panicky, unpredictable and indecipherable human space where nothing was what it seemed, where everything was manipulated, everyone was involved in daily deceptions and no one had a clear conscience.

After a few days in Berlin the friends went back to Paris, as fast as they could. Soledad Mendoza went on to Spain, and the two men wondered what to do next.[13] Perhaps their impressions were too hasty; perhaps things were better in other countries. Within a few weeks friends in Leipzig and Berlin scheduled to travel to the 6th World Youth Congress in Moscow suggested that García Márquez and Mendoza should go too. Earlier, in Rome, García Márquez had tried to obtain a visa for Moscow but was refused four times because he had no official sponsorship. But in Paris, by an extraordinary stroke of good fortune, he now connected again with his talisman, Manuel Zapata Olivella. Zapata was accompanying his sister Delia, an expert in and practitioner of Colombian folklore, who was taking a troupe of mainly black Colombians from Palenque and Mapalé to the Moscow Festival.[14] García Márquez was a reasonably convincing singer, guitarist and drummer, and he and Mendoza signed up, then travelled to Berlin to meet the rest of the party. There they would be joined by other Colombians bound for the festival, including Hernán Vieco and Luis Villar Borda.

Until the very last minute García Márquez was unsure whether he would be able to go. He sent a melodramatic letter to Madrid to inform Tachia, with whom he was perhaps surprisingly back in contact, that Soledad Mendoza would be flying there in a few days and announcing that he himself would be leaving either for Moscow "before midnight today" or for London, where he would continue working on his unfinished novel *(In Evil Hour)* prior to returning to Colombia. He would be meeting Soledad in the Café Mabillon later that day. (The reference to the Mabillon, where they had first talked, was no doubt intended, like most of the apparently insouciant letter, to wound his ex-lover.) As for *No One Writes to the Colonel*, which was their book: "I've lost interest in it, now that the character is up and walking on his own. He can speak now and eats dirt." In fact he could afford to lose interest in it because the book was finished. He said that he saw Tachia's youngest sister Paz quite often and made a suggestive remark about his relationship with all three Quintana sisters. Finally, after saying that he was delighted to be leaving "this sad and lonely city," he lectured her with evident (or feigned) bitterness: "All I hope is that you will realize that life is hard and it always, always, always will be. One day maybe you'll stop inventing theories about love and realize that when a man seduces you, you have to do something to seduce him in return, instead of demanding every day that he love you more. Marxism has a name for this but I don't remember it just now."[15]

Berlin to Prague involved a nightmare train journey lasting thirty hours in which García Márquez, Mendoza and the latter's Colombian friend Pablo Solano had to sleep standing outside a toilet with their heads resting on each other's shoulders. They then had twenty-four hours in Prague to recover and García Márquez was able to rapidly update his impressions from two years before. The next stretch was easier, to Bratislava, then through Chop, situated where Slovakia, Hungary and the Ukraine all meet; then towards Kiev and on to Moscow.[16] He was staggered at the sheer size of the vast Tolstoyan country: on the second day in the Soviet Union they had still not passed through the Ukraine.[17] All along the route ordinary Ukrainians and Russians threw flowers at the train and offered gifts whenever it stopped. Most had hardly seen foreigners in the previous half century.

García Márquez talked to Spaniards, evacuated as children during the civil war, who had tried to return to Spain, given the difficulties in the USSR, but were now on their way back to Moscow. One of them "could not understand how anyone could live under the Franco regime; he did understand, on the other hand, how people could live under Stalin." García Márquez was disappointed to note, however, that Radio Moscow was the only channel on the train's wireless system. After almost three days of travel they reached Moscow in the morning, around 10 July, just a week after the fall of Molotov following his defeat by Khrushchev.[18] García Márquez's first and lasting impression of Moscow was that it was "the largest village in the world" and now 92,000 visitors, almost 50,000 of them foreign, had arrived there for the festival. Many of them were Latin Americans, some already famous like Pablo Neruda, but others younger men who would later have a big impact on their countries, such as Carlos Fonseca, eventual leader of the Nicaraguan Sandinistas, or, indeed, Gabriel García Márquez. The organization of the festival functioned like clockwork and García Márquez wondered, as so many had before and after him, how the Soviet regime could put on such an event or, three months later, send a Sputnik into orbit, yet fail so spectacularly to give its people a reasonable standard of living or produce moderately attractive clothes and other consumer goods.[19]

García Márquez, Mendoza and their new companions dropped out of the Youth Festival almost immediately and spent two weeks exploring Moscow and Stalingrad. There is a picture of a group of friends in Red Square in which, as so often, the wafer-thin García Márquez, kneeling in front of the others, stands out from even a dim 1950s black and white photograph as the one brimming with vitality and barely containing a desire to jump up and get on with the action the second he hears the shutter click. He confessed in his article about that time that in two weeks, with no knowledge of Russian, "I couldn't come to any definitive conclusions."[20] Moscow was all dressed up and on its best behaviour and García Márquez commented, "I didn't want to know a Soviet Union with its hair done up to receive a visitor. Countries are like women, you need to know them when they've just got up." So he tried provoking his hosts ("Was Stalin a criminal?"), eventually resorting to asking whether there were no dogs in Moscow because they'd all been eaten, and was told that this was a "capitalist press slander."[21] The most illuminating conversation was with an old woman who was the only person in Moscow who dared to talk to him about Stalin, even though Stalin had supposedly been discredited by Khrushchev in February 1956. She said that she was not anti-communist in principle but that Stalin's regime had been monstrous and that he was "the most bloodthirsty, sinister and ambitious figure in the entire history of Russia"—in short, she told García Márquez things in 1957 which would take many years to emerge into the full light of day. He concluded, "There was no reason to think that woman was mad except for the lamentable fact that she seemed it."[22] In other words, he already suspected it was all true but had no evidence and no wish to believe it.

García Márquez made several attempts to see the tombs of Stalin and Lenin and finally gained admittance on the ninth day. He said that the Soviets had banned Kafka as a "pernicious metaphysician" but that he could have been "Stalin's best biographer." Most people in the USSR had never laid eyes on their leader. Although not a leaf on any tree had been able to move without his permission, some people doubted his very existence. Thus only Kafka's books had prepared García Márquez for the almost incredible bureaucracy of the Soviet system, including obtaining permission to visit Stalin's tomb. When he finally got in he was astonished that there was no smell; he was disappointed by Lenin, "a wax dummy"; and surprised to find Stalin himself "submerged in a sleep without remorse." Stalin indeed resembled his own propaganda:

> He has a human expression, alive, a smirk that doesn't seem to be a mere muscular contraction but the reflection of an emotion. There is a slight sneer in that expression. Apart from his double chin, it doesn't correspond to the person. He doesn't look like a fool. He's a man of calm intelligence, a good friend, with a definite sense of humour . . . Nothing impressed me as much as the delicacy of his hands, with their thin transparent nails. They are the hands of a woman.[23]

Later Plinio Mendoza would say he believed that in that very moment the first spark of *The Autumn of the Patriarch* was ignited.[24] This subtle presentation of Stalin's embalmed corpse was, in a sense, an implicit explanation of how Stalin had managed to deceive the world as to his real methods and motives—through the image of "Uncle Joe."[25]

Unlike most foreign visitors García Márquez felt that the money wasted on the Moscow metro would have been better spent on improving the lives of the people. He was disappointed to find that free love was now just a doubtful memory in a surprisingly prudish country. He noted with disapproval that the avant-garde film director Eisenstein was almost unknown in his own country, but he approved of the attempt by Hungarian philosopher Gyorgy Lukács to overhaul Marxist aesthetics, the gradual rehabilitation of Dostoyevsky and the tolerance of jazz (though not rock'n'roll).[26] He was surprised to note that there was no sign of any hatred whatever of the United States—a sharp contrast with Latin America—and was particularly struck by the fact that the USSR was constantly having to invent things already existing in the West. He tried hard to understand why things were as they were but evidently sympathized with the reaction of a young student who, when upbraided by a visiting French communist, retorted, "You only have one life." He thought the director of the collective farm he visited was like "a socialized feudal lord." He stayed on after most of the other delegates to try to understand the extraordinary complexity of the Soviet experience—"a complexity that cannot be reduced to the simplistic formulas of either capitalist or communist propaganda."[27] Because of this extended stay he was alone when he crossed the border and a Soviet interpreter who looked like the actor Charles Laughton said to him: "We thought all the delegates had gone by. But if you like we'll fetch the children out to throw flowers again, all right?"[28]

On the whole García Márquez's view of the Soviet Union was sympathetic and favourable, reminiscent now, all these years later, of the way he would respond to Cuba and its difficulties in the 1970s. But he made no attempt to hide the negatives he had been able to detect. On the return journey he and Plinio Mendoza, still with Pablo Solano, visited Stalingrad (now Volgograd), and sailed down the Volga to the entrance of the great Volga–Don ship canal, where there was a gigantic statue of Stalin presiding complacently over one of the country's great achievements. García Márquez left Plinio Mendoza in Kiev and travelled on to Hungary. Mendoza, who was later stranded for over a week in Brest-Litovsk because Solano came down with pneumonia, travelled back through Poland. He was utterly disillusioned by everything he had seen—"we lost our innocence," he would say later—and gradually came to believe that communist regimes were all cursed by the same regressive genetic code (though he would try once more to believe—in Cuba—in 1959); but García Márquez, who had no bourgeois past to mourn, and no bourgeois tastes to cultivate, was still eager for more experience. He had managed to get himself included in a group of eighteen foreign writers and observers, including two reporters—himself and Belgian Maurice Mayer—invited on to Budapest.

This was less than a year after the Soviet invasion of October 1956. János Kádár had replaced Imre Nagy as leader when the Soviet forces quelled the Hungarian uprising in November 1956. At this time, the summer of 1957, Hungary had been closed for ten months and, according to García Márquez, his was the first delegation of foreigners allowed back into the country. The visit was for two weeks and the authorities arranged an itinerary giving no time for free access to the city or the Hungarian people: "they did all they could to stop us forming any concrete impression of the situation."[29] On the fifth day García Márquez escaped his escort after lunch and set out into the city alone. He had been sceptical about Western reports relating to the suppression of the 1956 uprising but the state of the city buildings and the information he was given by Hungarians he met convinced him that the number of Hungarian casualties—estimated at 5,000 dead and 20,000 wounded—might have been even higher than he had read in the Western press. On succeeding evenings he talked to ordinary Hungarians, including several prostitutes, housewives and students, whose alienation and cynicism shocked him. His audacious behaviour and that of his companion Maurice Mayer produced an unexpected outcome: the authorities decided that the foreigners had to be taken more seriously and thus they were introduced to Kádár himself and taken off on one of his speaking tours, to Ujpest, eighty miles from Budapest. The strategy worked—not the last time that García Márquez would be intoxicated by direct access to the powerful. He stated that Kádár was obviously just the kind of ordinary working man who "goes to the zoo on a Sunday to throw peanuts to the elephants"; he was a modest individual who had found himself in power, clearly had no monstrous appetites and had to choose between supporting the nationalist ultra-right or giving his backing to the Soviet occupation of the country in order to save it for the communism he fervently believed in.[30]

García Márquez was clearly pleased to be given arguments that made him feel better about the depressing picture he had seen in the streets of Hungary. He analysed the contradictions of the communist regime and the way the workers were denied the fruits of their labour in order to build the communist state, and said, tellingly, that looting could have been avoided the previous year: "It was a question of pent-up appetites that a healthy communist party could have channelled in other directions."³¹ Now, he concluded, Kádár needed to be helped out of the hole he was in but the West was only interested in making things worse. And things were indeed getting worse: the government was being forced to bring in a system of surveillance whose overall effect was "simply monstrous":

> Kádár doesn't know what to do. From the moment he made his precipitate call for Soviet troops, irremediably committed with a hot potato in his hands, he had to renounce his convictions in order to move forward. But circumstances are pushing him backwards. He got caught up in the campaign against Nagy whom he accused of having sold out to the West because it's the only way he can justify his own *coup d'état*. Since he can't raise the salaries, since there are no consumer goods, since the economy is destroyed, since his collaborators are untried or incompetent, since the people will not forgive him for calling in the Russians, since he can't perform miracles, but since he can't let go of the potato either and slip out by a side entrance, he has to put people in prison and maintain against his own principles a regime of terror which is worse than the one before, which he himself had fought.³²

Despite the effort to make excuses for Kádár, García Márquez was deeply shocked and discouraged. In early September, on his return to Paris from Budapest, he phoned Plinio Mendoza just before Mendoza returned to Caracas. Despite his ongoing efforts to write positive reports on his experiences in Hungary, he exclaimed: "Everything we've seen up to now is nothing compared to Hungary."³³ Of course the journey remained, for the time being, a secret. As late as mid-December he would inform his mother back in Cartagena that "a Venezuelan magazine funded a long journey" but he did not say where the journey had taken him.³⁴

García Márquez had returned to Paris from his long journey with no money and nowhere to stay. "After fifty-one hours on the train all I had in my pockets was a telephone token. As I didn't want to lose it and it was too early, I waited until nine in the morning to call a friend. 'Wait there,' he said, and took me to a *chambre de bonne* he was renting in Neuilly and lent it to me. There I sat down again to write *In Evil Hour*."³⁵ First, though, in late September and October 1957, in that maid's room in Paris, García Márquez wrote up his impressions of the recent journey, seamlessly weaving in the experience of Poland and

Czechoslovakia back in 1955. The result was a long series of articles which would eventually appear as "90 Days Behind the Iron Curtain (De viaje por los países socialistas)" in 1959, though he published his experiences of the USSR and Hungary immediately in *Momento* (Caracas) through Plinio Mendoza.[36] They make up a remarkable testimony of a moment in history and a strikingly judicious and prescient critique, by a well-disposed observer, of the weaknesses of the Soviet system.[37] He sent them back to his mentor Eduardo Zalamea Borda, "Ulysses," for publication in *El Independiente*, where he was now assistant editor. Who knows with what emotions the old leftist editor picked them up and salted them away in his filing cabinet, where García Márquez would find them two years later and finally manage to get them published in the weekly magazine *Cromos*.[38]

Meanwhile, Tachia had spent nine months in Spain: "After the affair with Gabriel I spent three years totally disoriented: scarred, embittered, all my relationships had gone wrong, I had no man." She had gone straight to Madrid in December, before Christmas, and was hired immediately. She worked for the theatre group of Maritza Caballero, a rich Venezuelan, starting, ironically enough, with *Antigone*, the play so closely connected to García Márquez's first novel, *Leaf Storm*: she played Ismene, Antigone's sister.

Then she went back to Paris: "My boss Maritza Caballero drove me all the way in her Mercedes, which was a glamorous experience." One day she saw him—"sooner than I wanted to"—in the window of what is now the Café Luxembourg on Boulevard Saint-Michel. She went in, they talked and decided they should "finish things properly." They went to a cheap hotel nearby and spent the night together. "It was difficult, anguished, but better. That was not long before he left Paris. After that final parting in 1957 Gabriel and I didn't meet again till 1968."[39]

García Márquez's time in Paris was almost at an end. De Gaulle had returned to power in June, supposedly to save the Fourth Republic from losing Algeria. Instead he had announced the inauguration of the Fifth Republic and would eventually save the French from themselves by giving Algeria away.

In early November, a couple of weeks after the announcement that Albert Camus had won the Nobel Prize for Literature, García Márquez moved to London,[40] where he intended to hold out as long as possible, as he had in Paris, on the basis of articles hopefully published in *El Independiente* and the Venezuelan magazine *Momento*, of which Plinio Mendoza was now the editor. Mendoza would only publish two of these articles, "I Visited Hungary" ("Yo visité Hungría") and "I Was in Russia" ("Yo estuve en Rusia"), in late November. García Márquez had always wanted to study English and the journey through Eastern Europe had emphasized more starkly its growing importance because no one there spoke Spanish. As it happened he had been showing an interest in British affairs—the monarchy and the politicians (Eden, Bevan, Macmillan)—ever since his arrival in Europe, even if his professed interest was only in Britain's stereotypical decadence. Although Franco's Spain was off ideological limits (and perhaps he even feared he might be picked up there, given the close links between Spain and Colombia, and the possibility that he was on the Rojas Pinilla government's anti-communist blacklist), he had spent the best part of a year with a Spanish woman; and clearly a visit to Europe's other old colonial country was a logical part of his grand design. Indeed, it is striking how much of Europe East and West he managed to see, given the difficulty of the times and his dire financial straits. But the attempt to live in London on the flimsiest of shoestrings without knowing the language and without the Latin American contacts always available in Paris was certainly a valiant endeavour.

He lasted almost six weeks in a small hotel room in South Kensington, writing not *In Evil Hour* but yet more stories that had peeled off from it and would later become much loved by readers when they appeared as part of the collection *Big Mama's Funeral and Other Stories*. Like his novella about the colonel and his pension, and unlike *In Evil Hour*, these would be stories not about the cold-hearted authorities who run the small towns in which they take place but about the poor people doing what they can in the face of adversity, as he liked to think that he had done during his dark year in Paris, stories with a human face and positive values. Zavattini-type stories. Despite his best intentions, he gave himself very little opportunity to learn the local language, though on Saturdays and Sundays he would listen to the orators at Speakers' Corner in Hyde Park. His article "A Saturday in London," in which he sums up, almost folklorically, his experiences in the British capital, may be "the best piece of journalism he wrote in Europe."[41] It was composed while he was still in London and published both by *El Nacional* of Caracas and by *Momento* in January 1958. In it he remarks:

When I arrived in London I thought the English talked to themselves in the street. Later I realized they were saying sorry.

On Saturdays, when the whole city piles into Piccadilly Circus, it is impossible to move without bumping into someone. Then there is a vast buzzing, a uniform street chorus: "Sorry." Because of the fog the only thing I knew about the English was the sound of their voices. I would hear them excusing themselves in the midday penumbra, navigating on their instruments like the planes do through the dark cotton wool of the fog. Finally this last Saturday—in the light of the sun—I saw them for the first time. They were all eating as they walked the streets.[42]

His main complaint, however, he would later tell Mario Vargas Llosa, by then living in London himself, was the absence of black tobacco; he spent much of his money buying imported Gauloises. Yet he would also say that London had held a strange attraction for him: "You are lucky to be in a city which, for mysterious reasons, is the best to write in, apart from being, for my taste, the best in the world. I went there on a tourist basis, and something obliged me to shut myself away in a room where one could literally levitate in the tobacco smoke and in one month I wrote nearly all the stories of *Big Mama*. I wasted the visit but I gained a book."[43]

On 3 December he sent a letter to his mother in Cartagena via Mercedes in Barranquilla. In it he mentioned writing to Aunt Dilia in Bogotá, presumably to send his condolences for the recent death of her husband Juan de Dios, Luisa Santiaga's only sibling. At that time García Márquez's plans were still fluid, though he said he thought he would soon be home: "I've been in London a fortnight and preparing myself for the return to Colombia. In the next few weeks I'm thinking of making a quick trip back to Paris and then to Barcelona and Madrid—since Spain is the only European country I don't know—so I calculate I'll be in Colombia for Christmas or New Year at the latest. I'm still not tired of travelling round the world but Mercedes has been waiting for too long. It's not fair to make her wait any longer, although—if I'm not mistaken—she may have just a bit of patience left. But it wouldn't be right, because if there's one thing I've learned in Europe it's that not all women are as solid and serious as she is."[44] He said he had no money and no job, though *El Espectador* had made promising noises. He asked his mother to get two copies of his birth certificate, commenting, "Believe it or not, I haven't got married in Europe."

Less than two weeks later, on 16 December, he received an unexpected telegram from Caracas. Plinio Mendoza's boss was offering him a plane ticket to the Venezuelan capital to work on *Momento* with him and Mendoza. It was an offer too good to refuse, given the obvious lack of options in London, a city where, as he later told me, "it was impossible for a foreigner to live without a minimum of money."[45] Still, he phoned Mendoza to say that a madman had called from Caracas complaining about his—the madman's—misfortunes and offering him a job. Mendoza confirmed that Carlos Ramírez MacGregor was indeed crazy but the job was real. García Márquez flew out of London just before Christmas, not to Colombia, as he had only recently promised, but to Venezuela.

Forty years later, he said to me: "You know, when I lost the job in Europe early in 1956, I let everything go again, just like in Barranquilla. I could easily have picked something up, with some other paper, but I just drifted, for two years. Until of course I stopped and got back to my things. But for most of that time I just attended to my emotions, my inner world, I had experiences and I built a personal world. Most Latin Americans get culture when they're in Europe but I didn't do any of that."[46]

12

Venezuela and Colombia: The Birth of Big Mama

1958-1959

ARCÍA MÁRQUEZ FLEW in to Venezuela's Maiquetía Airport
on 23 December 1957, a week after receiving the telegram
from Caracas. He was full of excitement and anticipation. He
had travelled via Lisbon, where it was snowing, then flew far away
from Europe and landed in Paramaribo, Surinam, where it was asphyxiatingly hot and reeking of guavas, the smell of his childhood.[1] He was
wearing blue jeans and a brown nylon shirt he had bought in a sale on
Boulevard Saint-Michel, which he washed every night, and he was carrying the rest of his possessions in a single cardboard suitcase mainly
filled by the manuscripts of *No One Writes to the Colonel*, the new stories
he had started in London, and the still unnamed *In Evil Hour*. Mendoza remembers picking his friend up at about five in the afternoon,
with his sister Soledad for company, giving him a brief tour of central
Caracas and then taking him to the smart suburb of San Bernardino
and lodging him in a *pensión* whose owners were Italian immigrants.

It was his first visit to a Latin American country other than Colombia. Caracas was a conurbation of perhaps a million and a half people.
On the ride into town in Mendoza's white open-topped MG sports car,
García Márquez asked him and Soledad where the city was. Caracas
was by then a sprawling, disorganized, motor-dominated urban rib-
bon, shining white against the green foothills and mauve summit
of Mount Avila. It was like a North American city in the tropics.

Venezuela, not for the first time, was in the grip of a ruthless military dictatorship. Indeed, the native land of the great Liberator Simón Bolívar had almost no tradition or experience of parliamentary democracy. The portly General Marcos Pérez Jiménez had been absolute ruler for six long years but he had presided over an industrial boom based on the petroleum industry which had unleashed a frenzy of building and highway construction such as no other Latin American country had yet experienced.[2]

The owner of *Momento*, Carlos Ramírez MacGregor, dubbed "the madman" ("el loco") by his employees, was thin, bald and, so Mendoza said, given to fits of hysteria; he wore crumpled white tropical suits and spent most of his life behind the dark glasses which were then at the height of their popularity in a Latin America dominated by military dictatorships. He did not even return García Márquez's greeting the first morning. Perhaps, like Guillermo Cano before him at *El Espectador*, he could not reconcile the garish, skeletal figure before him with the picture Mendoza had painted of an outstanding writer and journalist who had enhanced his already substantial reputation during two and a half years in Europe.

García Márquez was undaunted. He would later describe his time in Caracas as a period when he was "happy and undocumented" (the eventual title of the anthology of the articles he wrote there), though he did not feel immediately at home. After Europe's grey restraint he found Venezuelans somewhat overbearing. But for all the excesses in terms of decibels and glad-handing, the atmosphere in Caracas was reminiscent of the life of tropical gaiety and informality that he had loved in Barranquilla, with one extraordinary advantage: Caracas was actually the capital city of this unfamiliar Caribbean country.

García Márquez and Mendoza, excited to be together again, celebrated both Christmas and New Year in the house of another of Plinio's sisters, Elvira. Gabo, who had spent much of the last year quite alone, and his brief time in London completely isolated, was delighted to have an audience—if occasionally a reluctant one—for his endless ideas for stories, a stream which had increased dramatically ever since he encountered Cinecittà and the movie scripts of Zavattini. Mendoza had not previously lived in close proximity to a García Márquez with a fixed abode and a steady job and was soon astonished to discover that a friend who worked with such intensity in the newspaper office nevertheless managed to sustain another, completely separate life: "Everywhere I witnessed his secret work as a novelist, the way he always contrived to get on with his books. And I even shared in that strange schizophrenia of the novelist who manages, day by day, to live with his characters, as if they were creatures with a life of their own. Before writing each chapter, he would narrate it to me."[3]

The most important and unforgettable moment of García Márquez's entire stay in Venezuela occurred at the end of the very first week. On 15 December, only days before he flew from London to Caracas, Pérez Jiménez had been confirmed in power by a popular plebiscite which had been scandalously rigged. On the afternoon of 1 January 1958, after preparing the end-of-year special number and taking part in rowdy New Year celebrations the previous night, García Márquez, Mendoza and Mendoza's sisters planned to go to the beach, but as everyone gathered their towels and swimsuits García Márquez had one of the premonitions so common in his family and in his fiction, not to mention his own always unpredictable life. He told Plinio, "Shit, I have the feeling something's about to happen." He added darkly they should all look out for themselves. A few minutes later they were at the window watching bombers sweeping over the rooftops of the city and listening to the sound of machine-gun fire. Just then Soledad Mendoza, who had been delayed, arrived at the building and shouted the news up from the street: the air base in the city of Maracay had rebelled and was bombing the presidential palace of Miraflores. Everyone rushed up to the roof to watch the spectacle.[4]

The rebellion was put down but Caracas was thrown into turmoil. Three electric weeks of anxiety, conspiracy and repression followed. From 10 January, after years of terror and intimidation, crowds of demonstrators began to defy the police in protests across the capital city. One afternoon the two Colombians were out of the building when the National Security Police raided the *Momento* office, arrested all the staff present at the time, and took them to headquarters. The director was away in New York and Mendoza and García Márquez spent all day driving around the crisis-torn city in the white MG until curfew time, thereby avoiding arrest and gathering material. On 22 January the entire Venezuelan press stopped work as the prelude to a general strike called by a "Patriotic Junta" of democratic party leaders organizing from New York. That night tension reached its maximum. The two friends stayed up in the Mendozas' apartment listening to the radio. At three in the morning they heard the engine of a plane climbing over the roofs of the city, and saw the lights of Pérez Jiménez's aircraft taking him away into exile to Santo Domingo. The streets filled with joyful people celebrating the news and klaxons were still sounding at dawn.[5]

Just three days after Pérez Jiménez's departure, García Márquez and Mendoza were waiting in the ante-room of the city's Blanco Palace with a crowd of other journalists anxious to see what the military had decided during the night about the status of the newly declared governing junta. Suddenly the door opened and one of the soldiers inside, evidently on the losing side of the argument, backed out of the room with his machine gun at the ready, leaving muddy footprints on the floor as he retreated from the palace and into exile. García Márquez would later say: "It was in that instant, in the instant in which the soldier left the room where they were discussing how the new government would be formed, when I had the first intuition of power, the mystery of power."[6] A few days later he and Mendoza had a long conversation with the major-domo of the presidential palace of Miraflores, a man who had worked for fifty years for all of the presidents of Venezuela since the first days of the archetypal strongman and patriarch, Juan Vicente Gómez, who had run the country from 1908 to 1935, and had a blood-curdling reputation; yet the major-domo talked about him with particular reverence and unmistakable nostalgia. Until that time García Márquez had nurtured the usual democratic knee-jerk attitudes to dictators. But this encounter set him thinking. Why were large sections of the people attracted to these figures? Days later he told Mendoza that he was becoming drawn to the idea of writing a great novel about a dictator, exclaiming, "Haven't you noticed, there still isn't one?"[7] Gómez would eventually be a central model, perhaps *the* central model, for *The Autumn of the Patriarch*.

Soon after these thought-provoking encounters García Márquez would read Thornton Wilder's novel, *The Ides of March*, a re-creation of the last days of Julius Caesar. Reminded of his own recent vision of Stalin's embalmed body in Moscow, he began to collect the details which would eventually make a dictator of his own come to life, fleshing out the obsessions with power and authority, impotence and solitude which had been haunting his imagination since childhood. Mendoza recalls that his tireless friend spent a lot of time in those days reading about Latin America's seemingly interminable list of tyrants, and would regale him, as they lunched in a local restaurant, with picturesque and preferably hyperbolic details about their lives, gradually developing a profile of boys without fathers, men with an unhealthy dependence on their mothers and an immense lust for taking possession of the earth.[8] (Gómez had the reputation of running Venezuela as if it were a large cattle ranch.) The elements of a new novel were fast falling into place, yet once again it would take many exasperating years before the project came to full fruition.

Still, in the present at least, García Márquez was in his element. He responded to the euphoria and the opportunities of the new environment as if he himself were a Venezuelan citizen and began to develop a more explicit rhetoric of human rights, justice and democracy. Many readers have judged his articles for *Momento* as among the best of his entire career. Where in Europe the first-person perspective had given credibility and immediacy to his reporting, he now progressed to a sense of almost impersonal detachment which only enhanced the clarity and even the underlying passion of his presentation.[9]

A bare two weeks after the fall of Pérez Jiménez, García Márquez wrote a well-researched political article entitled "The clergy's participation in the struggle,"[10] which explained the role of the Venezuelan Church as a whole and the courage of certain priests in particular, not least the Archbishop of Caracas himself, in contributing to the downfall of the dictator at a time when many democratic politicians had all but given up. He was well aware of the Church's continuing influence in Latin American politics and referred several times in the article to its "social doctrine." This was not only pragmatic but prescient because in October of that year John XXIII would become the new Pope at a time when the first portents of what would soon be known as "liberation theology" were in evidence in Latin America. His own friend from university days in Bogotá, Camilo Torres, would become the best-known priest in all the Latin American continent to be involved in guerrilla struggle based on the tenets of the new religious creed.

One day in March he was sitting drinking with Plinio Mendoza, José Font Castro and other friends in Caracas's Gran Café when he looked at his watch and said, "Fuck it, I'm going to miss my plane." Plinio asked him where he was going and García Márquez said, "To get married." Font Castro recalls, "It surprised the lot of us because hardly anyone knew he even had a girlfriend."[11] It was more than twelve years since García Márquez had first asked Mercedes Barcha to marry him and more than sixteen years, according to him, since he had first decided she would be his wife. Now he had just turned thirty-one and she was twenty-five. They hardly knew one another, except through letters. Plinio Mendoza, on the other hand, did know about García

Márquez's affair with Tachia Quintana—who had even asked him by letter if she would be able to find work in Venezuela—and his sister Soledad had met the Spanish actress and struck up a firm friendship with her; indeed, she had asked García Márquez, shortly after his arrival in Caracas, how he could have given up such a woman. Mercedes would be moving into a world, her new husband's world, about which she herself knew almost nothing—much less, indeed, than most of the people who would surround her. It would be years before she could feel completely confident in her position as the woman in the life of this apparently outgoing but also highly private and even secretive man.

The family in Colombia had not seen Gabito for almost three years and even before that they had hardly seen him more than once or twice since the end of 1951, when he returned to Barranquilla after briefly living with them in Cartagena. In fact things had gone rather badly in Cartagena for the García Márquez family until quite recently and even now they remained difficult. However, the Colonel's old house in Aracataca had finally been sold on 2 August 1957.[12] The income from the rent had fallen to a trickle as the building slowly deteriorated and eventually the García Márquez family decided to sell it for 7,000 pesos to a poor peasant couple who had just won the regional lottery. It was this money that helped to complete a new house which Gabriel Eligio was now building in Pie de la Popa, Cartagena.

Luisa had been zealous about ensuring that Gabito got the best education possible—perhaps she had promised this to her father before he died—but gradually she had become worn down by her life as a mother of eleven and her initial concern for the education of the older girls seems to have been motivated more by a desire to keep them out of the clutches of the "local yokels" in Sucre than to help them towards an independent future. One result was that Aida, who had taught primary classes at a Salesian convent school in Cartagena after graduating from Santa Marta, had rather suddenly decided to become a nun and had left for Medellín a couple of years before Gabito returned in 1958. Gabriel Eligio and Luisa Santiaga had both opposed Aida's decision at the time—just as they had disapproved of her relationship with Rafael Pérez, the boy who wanted to marry her in Sucre—but on this occasion to no avail. At any rate, the family was soon to pay a heavy price for Gabriel Eligio's laissez-faire approach to education as Cuqui (Alfredo), now a teenager, began to go astray and fall victim to drugs, a problem which would eventually shorten his life.

Meanwhile Rita, the youngest sister, had become involved in a drama which risked turning into *Romeo and Juliet*. "The only lover I ever had was my husband, Alfonso Torres. I returned to Cartagena from Sincé in November 1953 and I met him in December at his sister's, a neighbour of ours. That's where the tragedy began because no one except Gustavo liked him."[13] She was fourteen when she met Alfonso. The family violently opposed the relationship. It didn't help that Alfonso, though dashingly handsome, was decidedly dark-skinned. Rita and Alfonso met clandestinely for four years, against all odds; once she became so upset at the situation that she cut off all her hair in protest at the attitude of her parents, who would not even have the young man in the house. They never wanted any of their daughters to marry. (Like Aida, Margot had had her own Rafael in Sucre, Rafael Bueno; by the time she decided to defy her parents he had got another girl pregnant and Margot turned her back on love for ever.) It was now that Rita's eldest brother Gabito, some of whose stories she had studied at school (she particularly remembers *The Story of a Shipwrecked Sailor*), would come to her rescue.

García Márquez had taken a four-day leave from the magazine and flew to Barranquilla, where he stayed in the old Alhambra Hotel on 72 Street and Carrera 47. He arrived with an empty suitcase. "Clothes are very expensive in Caracas," he said.[14] Mercedes would later insist that he "just turned up" at her house but presumably he had contacted her some time before and this is just part of the long-term comic routine they have always put on when anyone asks them about their courtship and marriage. She told me that she would always vividly remember lying on her bed above the pharmacy and a sister shouting, "Gabito's arrived."[15] But she still wouldn't say whether she was excited or just surprised. That night Luis Enrique flew in from Ciénaga and he, Gabito, Fuenmayor and Vargas went on a kind of stag night pilgrimage to "The Cave."

The couple were married on 21 March 1958 at eleven in the morning in the Perpetuo Socorro church on Avenida 20 de Julio after an engagement of just under three years.[16] Almost all the "Cave" gang were in attendance. Alfonso Fuenmayor would recall that Gabito seemed dazed by the solemnity of the moment, thinner than ever in his dark grey suit, with his once-in-a-blue-moon tie carefully knotted. The bride arrived terrifyingly late in a startling full-length electric blue dress and veil. The reception was held in her father's pharmacy down the road.[17]

Two days later the newly-weds travelled to Cartagena to visit Mercedes's new in-laws. It must have been strange for Luisa to see her eldest son turn up married after so long away. Alfonso took the opportunity to arrange a meeting with his girlfriend's eldest brother in the Miramar ice-cream parlour. The next morning, as Rita was leaving for school, Luisa said to her, "Gabito talked to Alfonso yesterday and today he's going to talk to your father, so your situation will be decided today." Rita later heard that her brother had said to his father, "It's time for you to start selling the merchandise." Alfonso was at last allowed into the house. Demonstrating his seriousness, he said he was prepared to wait another year until Rita had finished high school; demonstrating his lack of seriousness, Gabriel Eligio said he didn't approve of long engagements and the couple should marry at once. The deed was done within three months, so Rita never did graduate from school. Instead she would have five children and then work in the local civil service to support her family for twenty-five years; and Alfonso Torres would gradually become the man of the García Márquez family in Cartagena.[18]

The youngest of the García Márquez children, Yiyo, recalled Gabito's lightning visit forty years later: "He had just got married and had come to Cartagena with Mercedes for their honeymoon, or to say goodbye. Or both things, I don't know. But I remember them perfectly: both sitting on the sofa in the lounge, in that big house in Pie de la Popa where I spent my adolescence, talking non-stop, and smoking. They smoked a lot: there in the lounge, in the kitchen, at the table and even in bed, where they each had their own ashtray and three packs of cigarettes. He was thin and so was she. Him, nervous, with his pencil moustache. Her, with her incredible resemblance to Sophia Loren."[19]

Too soon for friends and family, the newly-weds flew off to Caracas, via Maracaibo. The little girl who, as a childhood friend later told me, had leaned against a wall in the afternoon sunlight in a patio in Sucre, saying, "Oh, I want to go round the world, live in big cities, move from one hotel to the other," was on her way. There had been no reason to think such dreams would ever come true in a life like hers. As they sat talking on the plane Gabo told Mercedes some of his own dreams: that he would publish a novel called *The House*; that he would write another novel about a dictator; and that at the age of forty he would write the masterpiece of his life. She would later reflect: "Gabo was born with his eyes open . . . He has always got what he wanted. Even our marriage. When I was thirteen he said to his father, 'I know who I'm going to marry.' At that time we were just acquaintances."[20] Now she was married to this man she hardly knew.

This was a new García Márquez, transformed by the reality of marriage and new responsibilities, openly planning the future. It was not only that the new husband, naturally, was trying to impress his new bride; he was also initiating a new era, a new project; and even his beloved literature, his very own thing, would have to be part of the new equation. Instead of living just anyhow, literally from hand to mouth, everything would have to be planned and structured—including writing.

In Caracas the entire Mendoza family turned up at the airport, including the now ageing ex-Minister of Defence, Don Plinio Mendoza Neira, who had gradually come to recognize that his political aspirations in Colombia had evaporated with the passage of time. The Conservatives in Colombia had won the historic battle that had just been lost—apparently for good—in Venezuela.

Mercedes was overwhelmed by this noisy, outgoing, perhaps over-confident and even overbearing new family. The middle sister, Soledad, was no doubt comparing her implicitly, and probably negatively, with the cosmopolitan Tachia. Two decades later the youngest sister, Consuelo, would unwittingly reveal, in an article for a posh Bogotá magazine, just why Mercedes felt so uncomfortable. Recalling her arrival all those years before, Consuelo would write: "She is a woman with the classic build of the women of the Coast: slim but wide-boned, dark-skinned, taller rather than shorter, slanting eyes, a full-lipped smile, serious and mocking at one and the same time. When Mercedes Barcha travelled abroad for the first time and arrived in Caracas, she seemed a timid, quite ordinary person, with narrow skirts, somewhat larger than was the fashion, and short hair, with a permanent wave that did her no favours."[21] In short: of possibly African origins, unfashionable and undistinguished. Unsurprisingly Mercedes would later tell me that she had spent "too much time" with the Mendozas in Caracas, time which was "not to my taste, far from enjoyable—to be honest, I wanted out of the Mendoza family." But at the start she had to eat with them almost every day. García Márquez had organized a small apartment in Edificio Roraima, San Bernardino, with almost no furniture or household goods.[22] It would be the newly married couple's story for years. And according to Mario Vargas Llosa, chortling at the idea more than thirty years later as he related the story to me, Plinio Mendoza was never out of the García Barcha household even during the honeymoon period.[23] Mendoza's own memoir *The Ice and the Flame* implicitly confirms the story. One might imagine that this would ensure discretion but Plinio has told the world about Mercedes's first disastrous efforts at cooking—Mercedes herself admits she could not even cook an egg and that Gabo had to teach her how to do it[24]—and the fact that she never said a word after her arrival in Caracas: "Three days after I met Mercedes I told my sisters, 'Gabo's married to a mute.' "[25]

Mercedes says she had no problem communicating with her husband, however. When I asked her in 1991 what she thought had clinched their relationship, she said: "It's a question of the effect of skin on skin, don't you think? Without that, there's nothing."[26] But that was just the start; soon she would get right under his skin but in a way quite different from all those years of frustration before he really knew her; she would become indispensable to a man who thought of himself as absolutely self-reliant, a man who had not been able to count on anyone since his grandfather died when he was ten years old. She would bring coolness and method to his life. Gradually, as her confidence grew—or, rather, as she found a way to give her inner confidence outward expression—she began to impose her now legendary sense of order on García Márquez's much-cultivated chaos. She sorted out his articles and press clippings; his documents, stories, the typescripts of "The House" and *No One Writes to the Colonel*.

In fact before the wedding García Márquez had been working feverishly on his literary activities despite the intense period of political and journalistic activity since his arrival in Caracas. He wrote "Tuesday Siesta," his fourth Macondo story, almost at one sitting, after Mendoza suggested that his friend enter a short story competition organized by the newspaper *El Nacional* and funded by Miguel Otero Silva. García Márquez's story, written, according to Plinio, during Easter week 1958 (if his friend was telling him the truth; again, there may already have been a first version which Plinio had not seen), was based on an event he had remembered since he was a child, when he heard the shout, "Here comes the mother of that thief," and saw a poor woman go by the Colonel's house in Aracataca.[27] The short story narrates the experience of just such a woman and her daughter arriving in Macondo by train and obliged to walk through the streets under the hostile gaze of the townsfolk in order to visit the cemetery where her son is buried, having been shot dead while attempting a robbery. Although one of the few stories set in Aracataca-Macondo, its style operates strictly within the neo-realist aesthetic characteristic of this period of García Márquez's life. He has often said that he considers it his best story and also, intriguingly, "the most intimate"—presumably because the memory from his childhood became fused, magically, with that of his own return, with his mother, walking through the midday heat of Aracataca in 1950.[28] For all its merits, it was not awarded the prize.

In terms of inspiration, of course, this and the other Macondo-Aracataca stories draw on the author's memories, many of them nostalgic, from his "prodigious" childhood, whereas the stories set in "the town" (Sucre) exorcise the memories of his painful adolescence. But whether set in Macondo or in "the town," these stories focus not on the cold-hearted authorities who run the two communities—though the priests of Macondo are never as cold-hearted as the priest we find in "the town," and the same goes for the other authorities (Macondo doesn't even seem to have a mayor)—but on the ordinary people, in close-up, and in warm colour, trying with great difficulty to live their lives with as much courage, decency, dignity and honour as their always adverse circumstances will allow. If this sounds sentimental and unlikely to be "realistic," well, it is the genius of this writer that he manages to convince the most sceptical readers of his view of the matter.

As fate would have it, García Márquez would be able to spend the second half of May and all of June on his stories. Because once again, as in 1948 and 1956, an unwelcome ill wind would bring good luck as far as literature was concerned. United States Republican Vice-President Richard Nixon arrived in Venezuela on a catastrophic goodwill visit on 13 May, less than four months after the fall of Pérez Jiménez, whom his boss President Eisenhower had recently decorated as a friend of the United States. Nixon's car was besieged on the way from the airport, stoned, and spat on, and he could easily have lost his life. The event received worldwide coverage and was taken as a historic sign of how low relations between the United States and Latin America had sunk. Heart-searching about this humiliating rebuff would have a lot to do with the founding of the Alliance for Progress three years later. Like other newspaper owners Ramírez MacGregor decided to write an exceptional editorial lamenting Nixon's reception and effectively apologizing for the incident. Mendoza found himself involved in a bitter argument about the incident, shrieked at the proprietor "Eat shit!," resigned on the spot and walked out. On the way down the stairs he met García Márquez, arriving late at the office. He explained what had happened and García Márquez turned around and went back down the stairs with him. They were out of a job.[29]

The two unemployed journalists went back to San Bernardino, picked up Mercedes, and went for a drink and a meal, half post-mortem, half celebration, in El Rincón de Baviera, a local restaurant. Mercedes, who would prove to have both a phlegmatic disposition and a black sense of humour, roared with laughter as they told her how and why they had been sacked. The spare time allowed García Márquez both to extend his honeymoon and to go on with his short stories. So the newly-weds were able to spend more time together.[30]

She had brought her huge collection of letters from Gabo to Caracas with her. There were 650 sheets. After a few weeks he asked her to destroy them because, according to her recollection, "someone might get hold of them." His own version was that whenever they had a disagreement about something she would say, "You can't say that because in your letter from Paris you said you'd never do such a thing." When she proved reluctant—given their characters, this must have been a cagey and difficult discussion—he offered to buy them from her and they eventually settled on the symbolic sum of 100 bolívares, after which she destroyed them all.[31] The incident is interesting—if it is true (and even if it is not, come to that). First and foremost, it suggests that he was implicitly guaranteeing to remain married to her for the rest of her life; there would never be a "Gabito" period for her to look back on because there would never be a distance between them which might make sense of a nostalgic moment looking through old correspondence. Secondly, perhaps, the letters were for him, secretly, a memorial to a time when he had indeed forsaken her, during the affair with Tachia and the fling with "La Puppa"; no doubt his conscience demanded that the evidence be destroyed (possibly because he was not ruling out making contact again with Tachia, whom he had met two years to the day before he married Mercedes). Finally, however unlikely it may seem at first sight, it could also suggest that the young man who had boasted on the plane of his future exploits really was expecting to be famous and had the instinct from the start that he should destroy all his lifetime's evidence in advance and construct his own image for future students, critics and biographers, ready-made. Whatever the truth, the gesture fits in any case with a profound instinct in García Márquez not to hold on to the past, nor to collect souvenirs or mementoes—even of his novels.

Plinio Mendoza got himself rehired by *Elite*, the top news magazine in the country. There García Márquez would meet one of his most important Venezuelan contacts for the future, Simón Alberto Consalvi, who would later be Foreign Minister of the republic. Mendoza managed to find García Márquez himself another job in the same organization through Miguel Angel Capriles, owner of the Capriles group, one of Latin America's most powerful newspaper corporations. Thus on 2 7 June García Márquez became editor in chief of the most frivolous of the Capriles magazines, *Venezuela Gráfica*, popularly known as "*Venezuela Pornográfica*" because of the large number of scantily dressed "vedettes" for which it was renowned.[32] He had just written an important article on the execution of Hungarian ex-President Nagy for *Elite* (28 June 1958) but he wrote little for his new magazine.

The good news from Colombia was the unexpected publication of *No One Writes to the Colonel* in Bogotá in the June edition of *Mito*, a literary review which had previously published a García Márquez story called "Monologue of Isabel Watching It Rain in Macondo" just after he left for Europe in 1955. He had given Germán Vargas a copy of the novel and Vargas had passed it on, "without my knowledge," so García Márquez would say, to the editor Gaitán Durán.[33] The publication of *No One Writes to the Colonel* in a literary magazine meant that once again a novel of his had appeared almost clandestinely and would be read by no more than a few hundred people. Better than nothing, he must have thought in those days when best-sellerdom was quite outside his expectations.

Once again, however, another sort of politics was about to intervene to make a radical change in his destiny. Ever since Nicolás Guillén had told him in Paris in early 1956 that a young lawyer called Castro, the leader of the 26 July movement, was the only hope for Cuba, García Márquez had been following the man's exploits, including his preparations in Mexico, the epic though almost disastrous voyage to Cuba in the motor cruiser *Granma* and the guerrilla war in Cuba's Sierra Maestra. Castro had quickly become the object of another of García Márquez's intuitions. Venezuela was feeling its way anxiously towards a new democratic order through a process which García Márquez would never forget but Venezuela was not his country and things had become less absorbing for him as time went on; in any case his ability to participate through his writing—reporting, editorials—had again been taken away from him. But Cuba, since Castro's political struggle had unmistakable continental implications, not to say ambitions, might indeed become García Márquez's country.

He had interviewed Castro's sister Emma in Caracas in "My Brother Fidel" ("Mi hermano Fidel"), a report published in *Momento* on 18 April 1958, and he had followed events in Cuba with mounting excitement throughout the year. Although Castro had not yet declared his movement a socialist one, García Márquez had found himself able, for the very first time in his now long career as a journalist, to demonstrate an unrestrained enthusiasm for a politician and an evident optimism about his revolutionary crusade. He mentioned that Castro's favourite food, which he cooked expertly himself, was spaghetti, and then noted: "In the Sierra Maestra Fidel is still doing spaghetti. 'He's a good man, a simple man,' says his sister. 'He's a good conversationalist but, above all, a good listener.' She says he can listen for hours, with the same interest, to any kind of conversation. That concern for the problems of his fellow men, added to an unbreakable will, seems to be the essence of his personality."[34] Forty-five years later García Márquez would be saying almost exactly the same thing—not to mention eating spaghetti cooked by Castro in Castro's own kitchen—and little wonder: Fidel Castro was one of the few things in which he was ever able to believe. And the discovery, now, that Castro had been involved in the *Bogotazo* gave an extra twist of biographical coincidence to García Márquez's interest in the young Cuban's epic adventure. Indeed, after his favourable interview with Emma Castro, members of Castro's 26 July movement in Caracas would begin to feed García Márquez information which he in turn would feed into the magazines he worked for.

On New Year's Eve 1958, García Márquez and Mercedes had been at a New Year party hosted by one of the Capriles family. When they got back to their building at three in the morning the elevator was out of service. Because they had both had a lot to drink they sat down to rest on each landing as they climbed the stairs to the sixth floor. When they finally opened the door to their apartment they heard pandemonium breaking out across the city, people cheering, car horns sounding, church bells ringing and factory sirens wailing. Another revolution in Venezuela? They had no radio in the apartment and had to run back down the six flights of stairs to find out what was going on. The concierge, a Portuguese woman, told them that it was not Venezuela: Batista had fallen in Cuba![35] Later that day, 1 January 1959, Fidel Castro led his guerrilla army into Havana and opened a new era in Latin American history. And for the very first time since the discovery, the whole planet would be touched directly by political events in Latin America. Perhaps the continent's time of solitude and failure was at an end, García Márquez may have speculated. Later that day he and Plinio Mendoza would celebrate the news together over a large number of cold beers on the balcony of the Mendoza family apartment in Bello Monte, as cars drove around the Caracas freeway system with their klaxons blaring and Cuban flags waving out of the windows. Over the next two weeks the two friends would follow every last detail through press cables in their respective offices.

On 18 January 1959 García Márquez was tidying his desk in the *Venezuela Gráfica* office prior to leaving for home when a Cuban revolutionary arrived and said a plane was waiting at Maiquetía Airport to take interested journalists to the island to observe the public trial of Batista criminals, called "Operation Truth" ("Operación Verdad"). Was he interested? The decision had to be made on the spot because the plane was leaving later that evening and there was no time even to go home. Mercedes in any case had returned to Barranquilla for a brief vacation with her family. García Márquez called Plinio Mendoza—"Put two shirts in a suitcase and get down to the airport: Fidel's invited us to Cuba!"—and the two of them set off that same night, García Márquez in the clothes he stood in and without a passport, in a twin-engined plane captured from Batista's army which gave off "an unbearable smell of rancid urine."[36] As they climbed aboard, with press and television cameras recording the entire event, García Márquez was horrified to see that the man at the controls was a well-known radio presenter, a Cuban exile whom no one knew as a pilot. Then he heard him complaining to the airline company that the plane was overloaded, with people and luggage piled high in the aisle. García Márquez asked the pilot in a quavering voice if he thought they could make it and the pilot told him to put his trust in the Virgin. The plane took off in a tropical storm and had to make an emergency stopover in Camagüey in the middle of the night.

They arrived in Havana on the morning of the 19th, three days after Fidel Castro became premier, and were plunged at once into the excitement, confusion and drama of the new revolution. Everywhere there were red flags, bearded guerrillas with rifles on their shoulders mingling with dreamy-eyed peasants wearing straw hats, and an unforgettable euphoria. One of the first things the two friends noticed was pilots from Batista's air force who were letting their beards grow to show that they were now revolutionaries. In no time at all García

Márquez found himself in the national palace, where, he recalls, there was absolute chaos—revolutionaries, counter-revolutionaries and foreign journalists all intermingled. Mendoza would remember that as they filed in to the press room he saw Camilo Cienfuegos and Che Guevara talking and he clearly heard Cienfuegos saying, "We ought to shoot all those sons of bitches."[37] Minutes later García Márquez was interviewing the legendary Spanish General Alberto Bayo when he heard the sound of a helicopter overhead as Castro flew in to explain "Operation Truth" to a crowd of a million people gathered along the Avenida de las Misiones in front of the building.[38] García Márquez interrupted his interview as Castro entered the vast room and was only three people away from him when the new leader prepared to speak. As he started, García Márquez felt a pistol in his back; the presidential guard had mistaken him for an infiltrator. Fortunately he was able to explain himself.

The next day the two Colombians went to Sports City (Ciudad Deportiva) to witness the trial of the Batista supporters accused of war crimes, and they stayed there all day and all night. The purpose of "Operation Truth" was to show the world that the revolution was trying and executing only war criminals, not all "Batista supporters," as sections of the press in the United States were already alleging. García Márquez and Mendoza attended the trial of Colonel Jesús Sosa Blanco, one of the most notorious members of Batista's armed forces, charged with murdering unarmed peasants. There was a kind of boxing ring in the stadium, illuminated by floodlights, in which the accused stood in handcuffs. The two Colombians found themselves in the front row, as the crowd, eating improvised meals and drinking beer, bayed for blood and Sosa Blanco, with a mixture of contempt, cynicism and terror, tried to defend himself. When Sosa was finally found guilty, Plinio Mendoza found himself handing the microphone to the condemned man so he could respond to the verdict; but Sosa refused all comment. García Márquez later said that this event changed his idea of *The Autumn of the Patriarch*, which he now conceived as the trial of a recently overthrown dictator, to be narrated through monologues around a corpse. Both he and Mendoza declined to accompany other journalists to see the condemned man in his cell that evening. The next morning the wife and twelve-year-old twin daughters of Sosa Blanco went to the hotel to plead with the foreign journalists to sign a petition asking for clemency, which all of them did. The mother had given the daughters drugs the previous evening to keep them awake, "so they'll remember this night for the rest of their lives."[39] García Márquez seems to have signed more out of sympathy for the family and lifelong opposition to the death penalty than out of a concern for the justice of the proceedings. The trial had indeed been a "circus," as Sosa Blanco protested, but hardly a Roman one. His guilt was not in doubt, and many years later both García Márquez and Mendoza would say that they believed, despite the irregularities, that the sentence was a just one.[40]

Three days later the two friends flew back to Caracas. Plinio Mendoza, already exasperated by what he saw as growing xenophobia in Venezuela, decided to return to Bogotá. He left at the end of February and began to work freelance for magazines such as *Cromos* and *La Calle* while he waited for news from Cuba. The utopian euphoria had convinced Mendoza, always more impressionable and impulsive than his older friend, that he should work in some way for the new revolution which both men saw as a phenomenon of continental dimensions and importance. García Márquez himself had already made it plain to contacts in Cuba that he too might be prepared to work for the new regime. If they could find him something useful to do.

The U.S. press was talking ever more grimly of a "bloodbath" in Havana, with wholesale executions of any and all "Batista supporters" who could be rounded up, whereas the new revolutionary government continued to insist that it was simply trying and executing proven war criminals. García Márquez and Mendoza were persuaded of the justice of the Cuban cause, and convinced of the iniquity of the reactions of the United States's government and media. An Argentinian journalist, Jorge Ricardo Masetti, interviewed during the events at Sports City, had declared that the U.S. coverage of events in Cuba "demonstrates yet again the need for a Latin American press agency to defend the interests of the Latin American people."[41] This concern to present the news from a Latin American perspective was already an obsession of García Márquez's. Eventually, the new government invited Masetti himself to set up the kind of press agency he had recommended, in Havana; it was to be called Latin Press (Prensa Latina, or, familiarly, Prela). As soon as the creation of this indispensable revolutionary vehicle was agreed, Masetti would start looking for workers and contributors from every country in the continent, and opening offices in all the major Latin American capitals.

· · ·

IN APRIL, shortly after Castro had made an eleven-day visit to Washington and New York in which he had been snubbed by the U.S. government, a Mexican called Armando Suárez arrived in Bogotá, the worse for drink, with a suitcase full of banknotes. After talking to Guillermo Angulo, now back in Bogotá, he proposed that Plinio Mendoza and García Márquez should open the new Prensa Latina office planned for the city. Mendoza accepted at once and said that his friend García Márquez, who was still in Venezuela, a brilliant journalist and an ardent supporter of the revolution, was only waiting for the word. "Send for him right now!" was the immediate response.[42] The revolution was being made up as it went along. García Márquez would later say, "It was all word of mouth, no cheques and no receipts; that was the Revolution in those days."[43] Days later the Royal Bank of Canada notified Mendoza that 10,000 dollars had arrived in his name. He cabled García Márquez and told him to catch the next plane.

When push came to shove García Márquez's desire to work for Cuba overcame his reluctance to return to Bogotá. Venezuela's political advance, for all its problems and hesitations, had profoundly impressed him. But Cuba was going a step—several steps—further. García Márquez and Mercedes arrived in Bogotá in early May, still not knowing exactly what for, according to Mendoza's version, and Gabo celebrated the news as Mendoza drove them from the airport: "Cuba! Brilliant!"[44] It was his first opportunity in twelve years as a journalist to do exactly the kind of work he wanted, with no censorship and no compromises—or so he thought. The new Prensa Latina office was on 7th Carrera—Séptima: just that must have felt like revolution!—between 17th and 18th streets, opposite the Café Tampa, and in fact quite close to the boarding house in which he had stayed on first arrival in Bogotá fifteen years before, on his way to Zipaquirá.[45] Bogotá was no longer just the impregnable stronghold of the *cachacos* in García Márquez's eyes: now it was the city where Fidel Castro had learned important revolutionary lessons back in April 1948 and where he and Plinio were going to spread the revolution. He started work at once. There was much to learn and much to improvise. Before long the office on 7th Carrera became a meeting place for the Colombian left. Its staffers, who included Mercedes's brother Eduardo, were in at the very beginning of the most turbulent, passionate and—ultimately—tragic period in Latin America's twentieth-century history. At that time progressives around the world were watching events in Cuba with the most intense and often fervent attention; and young Latin Americans began to apply the "lessons of Cuba" to their own countries and to set up guerrilla movements all over the continent. Mendoza and García Márquez themselves would organize frequent pro-Cuban rallies in the streets around the office.

Despite this activity, Colombia, as so often, was proving the exception to the continental rule. Events there were less promising to the progressive eye than in either Cuba or Venezuela. When Rojas Pinilla had begun to totter in March 1957, after the Colombian Church condemned his regime, there had been a civic movement led by Liberal leader Alberto Lleras Camargo which called for a general strike. The dictator had resigned on 10 May in favour of a five-man junta under General Gabriel París Gordillo which felt constrained to promise a return to democracy. On 20 July, at the beach resort of Sitges on Spain's eastern Mediterranean coast, Lleras and the exiled Conservative leader Laureano Gómez had planned an arrangement, to be called the "National Front," by which the Conservative and Liberal parties would alternate as a two-headed governing entity for the foreseeable future in order to prevent both political chaos—code for a swing to the left—and the danger of a return to military rule. The junta had announced a plebiscite in October and the country had approved the plan on 1 December 1957. After a bizarre primary-type poll which decided who were the most popular of the Liberal and Conservative candidates, Lleras stood unopposed in the 1958 elections and soon after García Márquez and Mercedes Barcha returned to Venezuela following their marriage in March, the Liberal leader had been hailed as the next "democratic" President of Colombia as of August 1958.

García Márquez had summed up Colombia's recent history in no uncertain terms in an article which was published in Caracas on the day he was married:

"After eight years, nine months and eleven days without elections, the Colombian people went back to the polls to re-elect a congress which had been dissolved on 9 November 1949, by order of Mariano Ospina Pérez, a Conservative president who had previously been just a discreet millionaire. That act of force initiated, at 3.35 one Saturday, a period of three successive dictatorships which have cost the country 200,000 dead and the worst social and economic imbalance in its history. This implacable armed persecution of the Liberals has disfigured our national electoral reality."[46]

To complete his damning assessment, García Márquez sneered that Lleras Camargo—who he felt was ultimately to blame for allowing the Liberal Party to lose power in 1946—had emerged as the candidate because he was a virtual Conservative who had predictably recruited the Liberal candidates from among the same set of "oligarchs" who had stood for the party twenty years before. A new party, the Liberal Revolutionary Movement (Movimiento Revolucionario Liberal, MRL), founded on 13 February 1959 by Alfonso López Michelsen, would cause a temporary stir in the 1960s but finally made little impact on the struggle between the two political dinosaurs.

As usual, quite apart from the frustrations of Colombian politics in general, García Márquez was by no means pleased to be back in dreary Bogotá. But he now had a wife to share his reactions and his *costeño* resistance to the perfidious ways of the *bogotanos*. Mercedes was several months pregnant, had short hair and often wore trousers, which shocked the Bogotá neighbours, especially in the case of a pregnant woman, as did her husband's gaudy shirts and weakness for Cuban heels.[47] Plinio Mendoza, still a bachelor, turned up at the apartment most days and took Mercedes to the cinema when Gabo was busy. He and his friend had bought identical dark blue raincoats and looked, so their friends teased, "like two boys dressed by the same mother."[48]

In the second half of the year came the publication of the articles García Márquez had written in 1957 about the visit to the Eastern Bloc. They appeared in *Cromos*, under the general title "90 Days Behind the Iron Curtain," between 27 July and 28 September 1959. It was perhaps significant that he did not repeat the Hungarian article, presumably because Kádár had executed Nagy after García Márquez had given Kádár such a good press. So he had written a separate article on the subject—though even that piece did not remind his readers of his familiarity with Kádár, and it was noticeable that he blamed Khrushchev rather than the Hungarian: "Even those of us who as a matter of principle believed in the decisive role Khrushchev was playing in the history of socialism must recognize that the Soviet prime minister is beginning to look suspiciously like Stalin."[49] Interestingly, what García Márquez most emphasises is that the execution of Nagy was "an act of political stupidity," not the last time he would take up such a pragmatic position in the face of authoritarian policies he might have been expected to condemn on principle. It should perhaps not surprise us that the man who wrote it, who at this time clearly believes that there are "right" and "wrong" men for particular situations, and who quite cold-bloodedly puts politics before morality, should eventually support an "irreplaceable" leader like Fidel Castro through thick and thin. Ironically enough, the series on Eastern Europe was more relevant in 1959 than it had been when he wrote it in Paris before his departure for London two years before, because Latin America was moving sharply to the left and debates about communism, socialism, capitalism and democracy would be argued over—and killed for—during the next twenty-five years.

Mercedes gave birth to their first child, Rodrigo García Barcha, on 24 August. The unfortunate infant was born a *cachaco* but he had the christening of a child destined for great things. The godfather, predictably enough, was Plinio Mendoza, and the godmother was Susana Linares, the wife of Germán Vargas, who was now living in Bogotá; but the baby was baptized by Father Camilo Torres, the turbulent priest whom García Márquez had known as a fellow law student at the National University back in 1947. Torres had left the university late in 1947 and his unfortunate girlfriend had retired to a convent. He had become a priest in 1955 and then studied sociology at the Catholic University of Louvain, coinciding in Europe with his three old university friends, García Márquez, Plinio Mendoza and Luis Villar Borda. On his return to Colombia he had taught sociology back in the National University where they had all first come together. By the time they met up again in 1959 Father Torres was active among the marginal communities of Bogotá and finding himself increasingly alienated from the traditional Church hierarchy.[50] García Márquez would no doubt have wanted Torres as the officiating priest at the christening for sentimental reasons—but he was also the only priest that he and Mercedes knew. At first Torres rejected Plinio Mendoza as godfather, not only because he was an unbeliever but for his proven irreverence. As the child was christened, Torres intoned, "Whoever believes that the Holy Spirit is descending over this child should now kneel." All four members of the congregation remained standing.[51]

Whenever the two *compadres* got in from the office, almost always late at night, after Rodrigo was born, they would try to wake the baby up to play with him; when Mercedes protested, as she always did, García Márquez would say, "All right, all right, but don't nag our *compadre*."[52] Camilo Torres remained a frequent visitor to the García Barcha household. Six years later Father Torres, still a blessed innocent, would join the National Liberation Army (Ejército de Liberación Nacional—ELN) guerrillas and would die in his first combat. He

remains the most famous revolutionary priest in the history of twentieth-century Latin America.

1959, the year of the Cuban Revolution, was almost at a close. Long
before it ended García Márquez had finished writing what must be
counted, without a doubt, the most important short story he ever
wrote. Really, the extraordinary creation that is "Big Mama's Funeral"
should never have been placed in the same anthology as the other stories started in London and completed in Venezuela, which were a continuation of his neo-realist works, companions both in style and
ideology to *No One Writes to the Colonel*. Far from being a continuation,
or even the culmination of that literary mode and of that ideological
era, "Big Mama's Funeral" was something quite new: it is one of the
key texts of García Márquez's entire literary and political trajectory,
the one which unites his two literary modes—"realist" and "magical"—for the very first time, and which paves the way for the whole of
the mature work over the next half century, in particular for those two
definitive masterpieces, *One Hundred Years of Solitude* and *The Autumn
of the Patriarch*. Indeed, such is the scale of this story, especially its ending, and such its fusion of different elements within García Márquez's
personal mythology and poetics, that he himself would have to spend
years trying to separate its most important strands in order to conceive
the endings of those two monumental works waiting for him down the
years.

The fact is that the return to Colombia, politically speaking, had
been a violent, if not unexpected, culture shock for García Márquez.
No One Writes to the Colonel had been written in Europe where, despite
everything, he could still have some sentimental feelings about home
and about some of the people there. The other stories of the forthcoming collection were also started in Europe and then completed in
his early months in Venezuela; they exude affection for ordinary
Colombians similar to his unmistakable affection for the unnamed
colonel. "Big Mama's Funeral," however, was the product of his return
to Colombia itself, not only after more than three years away but also,
unmistakably, after Europe, after Venezuela, after Cuba. To read it for
the first time is to feel the weight of all those different experiences
bearing down one after another on his perception of the country; it is
to feel all the writer's accumulated frustration, and scorn, and anger at
a country which endlessly consumed its own children and seemed as
though it would never, ever change.

So the first thing to say about "Big Mama's Funeral" is that almost nothing happens in it, it is a great song and dance about nothing. Or almost nothing. It tells the story—indeed, a narrator very like Gabriel García Márquez himself tells the story—of the life and death (much more of the death than the life) of an old Colombian matriarch known as "Big Mama" whose funeral is attended by all the politicians and dignitaries of Colombia and even by distinguished visitors from abroad, such as His Holiness the Pope. The story shows but does not say that Big Mama's entire life has been spent in the middle of absolutely nowhere, that her wealth is based on a shameless relationship of ruthless exploitation with the labouring peasant masses, and that she herself is ugly, vulgar and in every way ludicrous. Yet no one in her unnamed but unmistakable nation seems to notice these obvious facts. In other words, García Márquez is creating an allegory which shows the real moral status of the still feudal semi-"oligarchy" first identified by Gaitán and the hypocrisy of a *cachaco*-dominated ruling class that pretends that Colombia's is the best of all possible worlds and that the only ones letting the side down are the poor misbegotten people that these superior beings themselves oppress. What we have, in García Márquez's view, is a colonial land-tenure system overseen by a nineteenth-century political system. When, oh when, would Colombia's twentieth century come! Thus his story begins as the representation of a world inside out and upside down:

> This is, for all the world's unbelievers, the true account of Big Mama, absolute sovereign of the Kingdom of Macondo, who lived for ninety-two years, and died in the odour of sanctity one Tuesday last September, and whose funeral was attended by the Pope.[53]

And fifteen pages later it ends:

> Now the Supreme Pontiff could ascend to Heaven in body and soul, his mission on earth fulfilled, and the President of the Republic could sit down and govern according to his good judgement, and the queens of all things that have ever been or ever will be could marry and be happy and conceive and give birth to many sons, and the common people could set up their tents where they damn well pleased in the limitless domains of Big Mama, because the only one who could oppose them and had sufficient power to do so had begun to rot beneath a lead

plinth. The only thing left then was for someone to lean a stool against the doorway to tell this story, lesson and example for future generations, so that not one of the world's disbelievers would be left who did not know the story of Big Mama, because tomorrow, Wednesday, the garbage men will come and will sweep up the garbage from her funeral, for ever and for ever.[54]

One thinks of the tone and rhetoric of Karl Marx himself.[55] But this narrator's voice and point of view steer just shy of outright sarcasm and rest content with an almost Swiftian or Voltairian irony so forceful that he is able to state the very opposite of what he believes to be the case, certain that the reader will stay with him.

Obviously "Big Mama's Funeral" is García Márquez's furious reaction to the national situation and his own sense of let-down on his return, after four long years away from the country. The big difference now is that his voice is that of a writer of authority, a writer whose scorn and contempt has been well earned, based as it is on experience of the wider world.[56] The narrator paints a Colombia incapable of change but from a perspective (the USSR? Venezuela? Cuba?) which knows that change is possible, something the narrator of *Leaf Storm* did not yet know. Such a story could only have been composed in 1959, when García Márquez underwent what Marx would have termed the "dialectical" experience of contrasting the Colombian National Front with the Cuban Revolution—thereby giving his already looming magical realism a savage, satirical, carnivalesque, political edge. This story is, indeed, a unique moment both of distillation and of balance. One of the things it is saying is: "I can no longer write stories like those in this collection. My 'realist' phase is over." But now he too was about to become the victim of a grand historical irony.

As fate would have it, although he himself had reached the end of his realist, or neo-realist phase, he was now in enthusiastic contact with Cuba; and paradoxically, the Cuban regime, which was opening up the imagination of so many Latin American writers and intellectuals, would nonetheless shortly be arguing for the kind of socialist realist writing that García Márquez had just now become incapable of producing. He would need the reassuring spectacle of other Latin American writers publishing novels based on myth and magic, before he could conceive an entire novel of his own which ignored—indeed, implicitly rejected—the tenets of socialist realism. And there would also be strictly biographical factors at work over the next few years.

Another—yet another—change of location, and the need to support a wife and children, would be enormously influential in the coming period: he would be distracted from his vocation in a way he never had been before because he no longer had the sinister luxury of being able to starve while he responded to the call of inspiration whenever and wherever it came to him. Thus, for a long time, "Big Mama" would seem to be merely the end of an era (or even, for a time, the end of his career as a writer); it was only much later that it could be seen as an indispensable and historic point of reference, the beginning of his mature period.

In fact, then, in terms of literature, by the middle of 1960 García Márquez was at a loose end. He was even thinking of going back to Barranquilla to work on cinema with Alvaro Cepeda, if the job with the Cuban Revolution did not work out.[57] On one of his visits to Barranquilla the Medellín cinema delegate Alberto Aguirre and García Márquez sat waiting in the Hotel del Prado for Cepeda, who was supposed to be coming with a proposal for a national cinematographic organization but failed to arrive. Over lunch García Márquez mentioned in passing that Mercedes had phoned from Bogotá to tell him they needed to pay 600 pesos to prevent their services from being disconnected. Aguirre was a lawyer and editor, who had admired *No One Writes to the Colonel* when it was published by *Mito* two years before. At the end of the meal he offered to re-publish the novel. García Márquez said: "You're mad, you know my books don't sell in Colombia. Remember what happened with the first edition of *Leaf Storm*." Aguirre set out to persuade him, however, and offered him 800 pesos, 200 in advance. García Márquez thought about the electricity bill and agreed on the spot. In a letter a year later, he would complain that he was "the only person who makes verbal contracts when he's hung over, sprawling in a bamboo rocking chair, in the afternoon heat of the tropics."[58] What he said to Aguirre was right, though. When the book came out in 1961 only 800 of the first 2,000 copies would be sold. If he had waited for success in Colombia he might have waited for ever.

13

The Cuban Revolution
and the USA

1959~1961

IN SEPTEMBER 1960 the Argentinian Jorge Ricardo Masetti, the
founder of Prensa Latina, arrived in Bogotá on his way to Brazil.
Masetti, who had film star looks and a dashing manner to rival his
friend and compatriot Ernesto Che Guevara, was already involved in a
desperate struggle against Communist Party sectarianism, a subject he
had discussed frequently in Havana with Plinio Mendoza. During his
brief two-day visit to Bogotá Masetti visited García Márquez at his
home and told both him and Mendoza that he could no longer afford
to have two trustworthy people in Colombia. Which of them, he
asked, was willing to leave for another posting? Despite being unmarried, Mendoza, who had already been to Cuba seven times that year as
well as to San Francisco for a meeting of the Inter-American Press
Association (SIP), said he wanted to stay in Colombia, so García
Márquez, who had hit it off with Masetti from the very beginning,
agreed to go.[1] The idea was for him to spend a few months on and off
in Havana to orientate himself about Prensa Latina's latest methods, to
help in training new journalists, and then be sent on some specific
assignment. He set off almost at once, via Barranquilla, where he left
Mercedes and Rodrigo for another holiday with her family.

He travelled to Havana at least four times in the next three months,
staying for an entire month on one occasion. Havana was a city under
siege, struggling to make its revolutionary progress amidst constant

fears of counter-revolution and the daily possibility of the seemingly inevitable U.S. invasion. Castro had nationalized numerous enterprises earlier in the year and in August he had finally expropriated all U.S. property on the island in revenge for U.S. "economic aggression." A month earlier Khrushchev had backed Cuba's historic claim to the U.S. enclave of Guantánamo as relations began to harden. On 3 September the Soviet leader demanded that the United Nations be removed from New York to a more neutral location; by the 29th he would be thumping the desk with his shoe in the same United Nations and ostentatiously embracing Fidel Castro. This, undoubtedly, was war, or at least the prelude to it.

The Prensa Latina office was just two blocks from the Malecón, the avenue that winds along Havana's Caribbean seafront. The roads outside were barricaded with sandbags and roadblocks and there were revolutionary soldiers on guard at all times. When he was in Havana García Márquez shared a small apartment on the twentieth floor of the Retiro Médico Building with a Brazilian journalist, Aroldo Wall. They had two bedrooms, a lounge and a terrace overlooking the sea. They would eat in the Cibeles restaurant at the base of the building or in other restaurants close by. For the three months he spent on and off in Havana these were almost the only places García Márquez saw.[2] Yet again he found himself in at the early stages of a project which required that everyone, including him, should strive to the very limits of their capacity. There was no timetable of any kind; everyone worked whenever it was necessary and there was some new crisis every day. Sometimes he would slip off to the cinema in the evening and when he got back to the office late at night Masetti would still be there; often García Márquez would then work with him until five in the morning; and then Masetti would be calling him again at nine.

Before long the office was heavily infiltrated by orthodox Communists, led by the influential and experienced Aníbal Escalante, who were apparently plotting to take over the revolution from within; on one occasion Masetti and García Márquez actually caught them organizing a secret meeting late at night.[3] The hard-liners (known as *mamertos* in Colombia), "dogmatic" and "sectarian," who had a long history in Cuba of collaborating, sometimes "opportunistically," with "reformist" "bourgeois" parties and governments, were suspicious of anyone who was not a Party member. They kept information to themselves, attempted to channel the new revolution's policies within Moscow-style perspectives using Moscow-style rhetoric and doctrines, and sabotaged initiatives led by others even when they suited the purposes of the new government. Watching this as closely as he now did, García Márquez would learn bitter lessons which would mark all his political attitudes and activities in the future. Already he was asking himself the same question that was being asked by almost everyone on the island and that they would still be asking almost half a century later: what was Fidel thinking?

His closest relationships were with Masetti and another Argentinian writer and journalist, Rodolfo Walsh, who was there with his wife, Poupée Blanchard, and in charge of the so-called Special Services. In 1957 Walsh had written one of Latin America's classic documentary narratives, *Operation Massacre (Operación Masacre)*, about a military conspiracy in Argentina, in a style not dissimilar to García Márquez's *Story of a Shipwrecked Sailor*. The high point of García Márquez's time in Cuba came when Walsh deciphered the CIA's coded messages about the preparations for what would be known as the Bay of Pigs invasion (or as Playa Girón to the Cubans). Masetti followed the work of each national agency every day and had noticed garbled paragraphs from Tropical Cable on the teleprinter. Tropical Cable was the Guatemalan affiliate of All American Cable and Masetti began to smell a rat. Walsh, aided by a manual of cryptology, managed to decipher the entire document after several days and nights without sleep. It was a coded message from Guatemala to Washington about the plans for invading Cuba in April 1961. When the code was cracked García Márquez was called in to join in the celebrations. Masetti wanted Walsh to visit the counter-revolutionary training grounds at Retalhuleu in Guatemala disguised as a Protestant Bible-selling pastor, but the Cuban authorities had other, less romantic intelligence strategies in mind and Walsh was kept in Havana.[4]

Between visits to Cuba García Márquez would return to Bogotá and his family. His last trip to the island was in December 1960 on a Pan-American flight from Barranquilla via Camagüey. In Camagüey he was waiting for his connection to Havana but the weather was bad and the flight was delayed. Suddenly, as he stood around waiting for news, there was a commotion in the airport lounge: Fidel Castro had arrived with his companion Celia Sánchez. The Comandante was hungry and asked for a chicken dish at the airport cafeteria. When told there was no chicken Castro said he had been out touring chicken farms for three days and why couldn't the revolution deliver chicken to the airport, especially as the gringos were always saying that the

Cubans were starving to death and here was the airport proving their point. No one intervened when García Márquez approached Celia Sánchez and explained who he was and what he was doing in Cuba. Castro came back, greeted García Márquez and then remonstrated with him too about the problems in Cuba relating to chickens and eggs. Castro and Sánchez were waiting for a DC-3 to take them back to Havana; in the meantime chicken was finally found and Castro disappeared to the restaurant. Then he reappeared and was told the airport in Havana was closed due to the continuing bad weather. Castro retorted, "I have to be there at five. We go." García Márquez, hoping as usual that his own flight would be long delayed, was unsure whether the Cuban leader was insane or simply reckless. When he arrived in Havana hours later in a Cubana Viscount he was relieved to see Castro's plane parked on the runway. He has been worrying about the Cuban leader's welfare ever since.

Just before Christmas Masetti dropped by one day and said, "We're going to Lima, the office there has problems." They stopped off for a day in Mexico City and García Márquez was dazzled by his first sight of the majestic Aztec capital, little imagining that he would spend much of his future life there. Alvaro Mutis had recently been released from Lecumberri Prison after fourteen months serving a sentence for embezzlement in Colombia, where he had been excessively generous to friends with the budget his employers at Esso had given him for his work in public relations. García Márquez paid him a visit and was given the usual warm welcome, with Mutis proving just as hospitable when he had to stump up himself.

Then García Márquez and Masetti flew on towards Lima via Guatemala City in a 707 jet, the first time García Márquez had had this near supersonic experience. Given Masetti and Walsh's discovery of Guatemala's involvement in the preparations of the Cuban exiles, Masetti was excited at stopping off, albeit briefly, in the Mayan country's capital city. In the airport, on an impulse, Masetti argued for travelling to the insurgents' training camp which Walsh had identified at Retalhuleu and causing some mischief. García Márquez said it would be foolhardy and Masetti sneered, "You're just a timid little liberal, aren't you!" So instead of that adventure they played a prank on the local dictator Miguel Ydígoras Fuentes. The information about the rebel training camp had not been published internationally but Masetti, somewhat irresponsibly, decided to give Ydígoras a fright. In the airport was a large photograph of a Guatemalan national park in front of a volcano. The two men had their photograph taken in front of the picture and then enclosed the photograph in an envelope with a message which said, "We've travelled your entire country and we've discovered what you are doing to assist in the invasion of Cuba." They gave details of locations and numbers of troops. After they had mailed the letter the airport was closed due to bad weather. García Márquez said to Masetti, "Do you realize we're going to have to sleep in this airport tonight and tomorrow that bastard Ydígoras is going to receive our letter and cut our balls off!" Fortunately the airport reopened in time and they flew on out.[5]

García Márquez never made it to Lima on that trip. When they stopped over in Panama Masetti heard him trying to call Mercedes. He asked where she was and when García Márquez said "Barranquilla" Masetti told him to go on home to his wife and baby because it was immediately before Christmas. So García Márquez changed his ticket and flew to Barranquilla, though not before being briefly detained by the Panamanian police.

Even in the few months García Márquez had been in Havana, relations had worsened in Prensa Latina between Masetti's people and the Communist Party sectarians who wanted to bring the revolution in line with the Soviet Union's Euro-centred conception of world revolution. He and Mendoza watched in anguish as the time-servers and bureaucrats, reciters of Moscow mantras, began to harass, supplant and eventually persecute the romantic, open-hearted, long-haired revolutionary vagabonds with whom Masetti and García Márquez identified. These men and women, and the Cuban people for whom they had fought, had established a style, prompted by Castro and Guevara, in which everything was improvised, spontaneous and informal: hence, just for a start, the two supreme leaders were called "Fidel" and "Che," and there was also "Raúl," and "Camilo." But Masetti had already told García Márquez and Mendoza that a Communist Party spy was watching their every move in Colombia following the visit of a Cuban agent to the Bogotá office. Masetti reproached Mendoza for sending him letters of complaint which could be read by his enemies and forwarded to his superiors: one of them had ended up in the hands of Che Guevara himself.[6] In each fibre of the new Cuba, in each office, in each factory, the struggle was under way for the heart and soul of the revolution. Plinio Mendoza believes that the old-style communists won the first round—hence Masetti's difficulties (and, eventually, those of Guevara)—but that Castro would win the second when he put Escalante on trial and began to give the communists a taste of their own medicine.[7] The struggle, far too complex for facile interpretation, has continued ever since.

Back in Havana again in the new year, Masetti, under increasing pressure, decided to send García Márquez to Montreal, to open the new office there. That quickly fell through but there was an opening in New York. Even better! García Márquez went back to Bogotá to tidy up his affairs at the Colombian office; he cancelled his apartment rental, left his dining-room suite and other furniture to Mendoza, and kept his plans quiet, staying clandestinely with his old friend from Cartagena, Franco Múnera, who by then was also living in Bogotá.[8] Then he flew down to Barranquilla to pick up Mercedes and Rodrigo, who had stayed on there with her family. He left all his books with his sister Rita in Cartagena in a huge wooden box. Eligio, the family book-worm, would speculate about "Gabito's box" for many years.[9]

The young family travelled to New York in early January 1961. The United States had broken off relations with Cuba on 3 January, so this was not an ideal time to be embarking on such an adventure but it shows once again García Márquez's extraordinary knack of arriving in the right place at around the time that everything is just beginning to happen there. On 20 January John F. Kennedy was installed as the youngest ever President of the United States. Though compromised by the policy of the outgoing administration towards Cuba, he would probably have supported an invasion of Cuba in any case. The New York Prensa Latina office, in a skyscraper near the Rockefeller Center, was short-staffed so they were happy to have García Márquez aboard.[10] It was a moment of maximum paranoia and the new arrival was not impressed by his prospects. "I had never known a better place to be murdered in," he would write later. "It was a sordid, solitary office in an old building by the Rockefeller Center, with a room full of teleprinters and an editorial office with just one window which looked out on a courtyard way down below, always gloomy and smelling of frozen soot, from which rose day and night the sound of rats fighting for scraps in the garbage bins."[11] Years later he would tell American novelist William Kennedy that New York at that time was "like no place else. It was putrefying, but also was in the process of rebirth, like the jungle. It fascinated me."[12]

By now there were a hundred thousand Cuban refugees in Miami and thousands more were arriving every month. Many of them came on to New York. The United States was planning on using many of these refugees in its invasion and was sending them to the clandestine camps in Guatemala for training. Although the coming invasion of Cuba was a state secret, almost everyone in Miami knew about it. As García Márquez would later say, "there never was a war more foretold."[13] In New York pro- and anti-revolutionary Latin Americans would take care to go to different bars, restaurants and cinemas. It was dangerous to stray into enemy territory and full-pitched battles were frequent; the police were usually careful not to arrive until it was all over. García Márquez was equally careful to avoid the confrontations.

The family spent only five months in New York but García Márquez would later remember it as one of the most stressful periods of his life. They lived in the Webster Hotel near Fifth Avenue, in the very heart of Manhattan. The Prensa Latina workers were under constant pressure from Cuban refugees and anti-Castro hysteria. Telephone abuse from counter-revolutionary *gusanos* ("worms," the term the revolution used) was a daily occurrence, to which García Márquez and his colleagues would routinely reply: "Tell that to your mother, you bastard." They made sure that they had improvised home-made weapons with them at all times. One day Mercedes had a call threatening her and Rodrigo, with the caller saying that he knew where they lived and at what time of the day she took the child for a walk—usually to nearby Central Park. Mercedes had a friend in Jamaica, at the other end of the city; she said nothing about the call to her husband but went to stay with the friend for a while, saying she was bored being stuck in the hotel all day. It was probably appropriate that García Márquez was again revising *In Evil Hour*, his most sinister book, at the time.

After Mercedes left the hotel he spent most of his time in the office, sleeping there at night on a couch under conditions of increasing tension. On 13 March he attended a historic press conference in Washington at which John F. Kennedy announced that he was setting up the Alliance for Progress.[14] This presaged a brief period in which the United States began to talk the language of human rights, democracy and cooperation after many decades supporting Latin American dictators, a policy to which the USA would soon, however, return—in 1964, in Brazil—and would ratchet up with a vengeance in the 1970s. García Márquez acknowledged that Kennedy's speech was "worthy of an Old Testament prophet" but dubbed the Alliance "an emergency patch to keep out the new winds of the Cuban Revolution."[15]

Once again, most of the internal tension in the New York office, as García Márquez saw it, was between old-style hard-line Cuban communists and the new breed of Latin American leftists recruited by Masetti. "And in the New York office I was seen as Masetti's man."[16] Things rapidly became intolerable and García Márquez began to consider his position. Eventually he decided that he wanted out. One evening at midnight, alone in the office, he received a direct threat from a Caribbean voice which declared, "Get ready, arsehole, your time is up. We're coming for you now." García Márquez left a message on the teleprinter saying, "If I don't turn this off before I leave, it's because I've been killed." A message from Havana replied, "OK, *compañero*, we'll send flowers." Then, in his panic, when he left the building at one o'clock he forgot to turn the machine off.[17] He stole home to the hotel in terror, past the vast grey mass of St. Patrick's Cathedral beneath the falling rain, afraid of his own footsteps, and slept in the clothes he was wearing.

Before long the impulsive Masetti had been trapped into resigning by increasing pressure from the communists. On 7 April García Márquez sent a letter to Plinio Mendoza informing him of Masetti's resignation and saying that he had decided to follow suit: he had given in his notice for the end of April and told Mendoza he was thinking of going to Mexico. But after the Bay of Pigs invasion on 17 April, one day after Castro's declaration that the revolution, as many had suspected, was now a socialist one, Castro himself asked Masetti to continue in his post and to take part in the live television interviews of the counter-revolutionary prisoners. Masetti agreed and García Márquez too decided to hold on until the post-invasion crisis was over.[18] In fact he has since claimed that what he really wanted to do in those days was return from New York to Cuba.

On the day after the great Cuban victory at the Bay of Pigs, in which Castro had personally directed the defence of the island and the arrest of the invaders, Plinio Mendoza had found that, mysteriously, and for the first time, the telecom office in Bogotá refused to carry his dispatches and immediately suspected that the USA had pressured the Colombian authorities into cutting off the service to Cuba. He phoned García Márquez in New York and García Márquez said, "Hold on, there's a public telex out in Fifth Avenue, right by the office." Thus the two friends proudly outwitted the CIA on the day of the legendary defeat of the counter-revolutionary invaders, claimed by the Cubans as the "first victory against imperialism on Latin American territory." But soon afterwards García Márquez went home to his hotel and wrote Masetti a letter by hand—something he almost never did (he even dated the letter)—outlining his grievances, his opposition to Moscow-style sectarianism and his fears for the future of the revolution if the orthodox communist line prevailed. He left the letter in the hotel room awaiting what he knew was the inevitable moment of his resignation. It was as well that he stayed on until the battle of the Bay of Pigs, for had he got out just before it he would surely have been branded for ever as the rat who left the sinking ship.[19] Little did he know that Masetti too would soon be leaving Prensa Latina for good and that he would later return to Argentina and die in a hopeless revolutionary campaign in 1964.

It was almost the end of García Márquez's time in New York. Plinio Mendoza flew to Havana to discuss the situation with Masetti and was lunching with him and his wife Conchita Dumois when the news came that "they," the *mamertos*, the hard-liners, had finally taken over the Prensa Latina office under a new director, the Spaniard Fernando Revueltas. When Mendoza arrived in New York again on a Pan-American flight in late May, on his way home from Havana, he was met, after a CIA interrogation, by Mercedes and Rodrigo. Mercedes smiled, in that imperturbable way of hers, and said, "So the *mamertos* have taken over Prela, *compadre*?" "Yes, *comadre*, they have." When he told her that he had handed in his resignation to the new head of Prensa Latina, with a copy to President Dorticós, she told him that Gabo's own letter was already written and merely awaiting his arrival.[20]

García Márquez has never said much about these problems since the 1960s—even in his subsequent conversations with Antonio Núñez Jiménez, himself an orthodox communist, he merely said, without entering into details, that he felt the communist hard-liners were "anti-revolutionaries"[21]—despite the fact that the events of 1961 would cast a shadow over more than ten long years of his life. The reason, evidently, is that he has continued to view the Cuban Revolution as an endless struggle between the "schematic" *mamertos*, supposedly represented in those days by Castro's brother Raúl, and the more intuitive revolutionary romantics supposedly represented by Fidel himself. Twenty-five years later Mendoza would say that his own experiences in Cuba, following on from the journey to Eastern Europe in 1957, were decisive in distancing him from socialism by convincing him that all socialist regimes eventually became bureaucratic and tyrannical, and that this was inevitable. And he would insist that in the early 1960s García Márquez was as alienated by all that happened as he, Mendoza, was and that in those days they saw things in exactly the same way.[22]

Mendoza stayed on in New York for a few days awaiting the news about his friend's back pay and tickets. He and Mercedes strolled around Central Park by day with Rodrigo, as García Márquez wound up his affairs at the office. Then García Márquez and Mendoza wandered together around Fifth Avenue, Times Square and Greenwich Village, discussing what had happened, the future of Cuba and their own uncertain plans. Stranded between two different ideologies, and two different worlds, a hard time was about to begin for both of them. García Márquez wrote to Alvaro Cepeda on 23 May:

Now, after a bloody awful crisis that went on a month and only finally came to a head this week, the decent young men of Prensa Latina have fucked off, with very high-flown resignation letters. Despite all the shit we could see looming ahead I never thought that events would become so overwhelming and I thought I would still have a few more months in New York. However, my last hope of staying here evaporated for good this evening and I'm going to Mexico on 1 June, by road, with the aim of crossing the deep disordered South. I don't know exactly what I'm going to do but I'm trying to salvage some dollars from Colombia which I hope will allow me to live for a time in Mexico while I look for work. Who knows what the fuck as, because as for journalism I've thrown in the towel. Maybe as an intellectual.[23]

Just after Mendoza left New York Masetti called García Márquez and said that the situation was improving again. He had talked to President Dorticós and had been told that he was still in Fidel Castro's good books after all. He asked García Márquez to delay his journey to Mexico but by this time the Colombian had made his plans and was only waiting for his pay-off, which the Prensa Latina authorities were in no hurry to concede. He was trying to persuade them to give him some kind of severance pay plus tickets to Mexico for him and the family. So he reluctantly refused Masetti's entreaties. As he explained in a letter to Mendoza:

I know Masetti: this personal help he asks for at the start will turn, whatever we try to do, into some huge and complex undertaking which I'll be caught up in until the comrades see the guava is ripe and decide to eat it, just as they did with Prensa

Latina. Moreover: if Masetti were still entrapped and in danger, as you told me he was, I'd have done anything to overturn my plans and help him. But I have the impression that the President has found a way of making things OK for him and he is no longer in such urgent need of help.[24]

Later he said, "I have become a stranger in an office I'm supposed to be managing down to the most minute details. Fortunately all this will be over in 48 hours."[25] He feared that Prensa Latina would not pay the family's return passages and said he only had 200 dollars to his name.

In effect, the García Márquez family had no way of flying back to Colombia and so they were heading for Mexico by road. In Mexico they would try to enlist help to return home (though Mendoza himself believes that an extended stay in Mexico had long been one of García Márquez's keenest aspirations; it may be that many of the misunderstandings about his movements and motivation down the years have come from the fact that he was always reluctant to admit that he did not wish to return to Colombia and the extended family). Not surprisingly the New York management said he had resigned, not been sacked—clearly he was considered a deserter, if not actually a *gusano*—and that they were not authorized to give him tickets to Mexico. Later the communists would tell friends who asked about him in Havana, "García Márquez went over to the counter-revolution."[26] In mid-June, resigned to getting nothing out of Prensa Latina and the revolution, the García Barcha family took a Greyhound bus for New Orleans, where Mendoza would be sending a further 150 dollars from Bogotá.

The fourteen-day journey, with an eighteen-month-old child, was arduous, to say the least, involving frequent stops and, as the couple would later report, endless "cardboard hamburgers," "sawdust hot dogs" and plastic buckets of Coca-Cola. In the end they began to eat Rodrigo's processed baby food, especially the stewed fruit. They saw Maryland, Virginia, the two Carolinas, Georgia, Alabama and Mississippi. For García Márquez himself it had the advantage of taking him through Faulkner country, a long-standing dream. Like all foreign visitors in those days, the young couple were shocked by the stark examples of racial discrimination throughout the American South, particularly in Georgia and Alabama, before the civil rights reforms later in the decade. In Montgomery they missed a night's sleep because no one would rent "dirty Mexicans" a room. By the time they reached New Orleans they were desperate for "proper food" and used some of

Mendoza's 150 dollars, sent to the Colombian consulate, for a square meal in Le Vieux Carré, a high-class French-style restaurant. They were disappointed, however, to see a large peach atop each steak as their dinners arrived at the table.[27] In 1983 García Márquez would remember their great adventure:

> At the end of that heroic journey we had confronted once more the relation between truth and fiction: the immaculate parthenons amidst the cotton fields, the farmers taking their siesta beneath the eaves of the roadside inns, the black people's huts surviving in wretchedness, the white heirs to Uncle Gavin Stevens walking to Sunday prayers with their languid women dressed in muslin; the terrible world of Yoknapatawpha County had passed in front of our eyes from the window of a bus, and it was as true and as human as in the novels of the old master.[28]

He would tell Mendoza in his first letter after the trip, "We arrived safe and sound after a very interesting journey which proved on the one hand that Faulkner and the rest have told the truth about their environment and on the other that Rodrigo is a perfectly portable young man who can adapt to any emergency."[29]

Finally, after two long and unforgettable weeks they reached the border at Laredo. There, on the world's most contrast-filled frontier, they found a dirty, sordid town where, nevertheless, they felt that life was suddenly real again. The first cheap restaurant provided a delicious meal. Mercedes decided that in a country like Mexico where, she had discovered, they knew the secret of cooking rice as well as many other things, she might be able to live. They took a train and arrived in Mexico City in late June 1961. There they would find a vast but still manageable city where the boulevards were lined with flowers and where—in those days—the immensely distant sky was usually a transparent, glorious blue and you could still see the volcanoes.

14

Escape to Mexico

1961–1964

O N MONDAY 26 JUNE 1961 the train bringing the García
Barcha family to Mexico City pulled slowly into Buenavista
Station. "We arrived one mauve-coloured evening, with our
last twenty dollars and nothing in our future," García Márquez would
recall.[1] There on the platform to meet them was Alvaro Mutis, welcoming them to Mexico with that wide, wolfish smile just as he had
welcomed Gabo to Bogotá in 1954. Mutis took the exhausted family to
the Hotel Apartamentos Bonampak on Calle Mérida. It was just outside the newly fashionable "Pink Zone" and only a few blocks from the
very heart of the city at the place where its two great throbbing arteries, the Paseo de la Reforma and Avenida Insurgentes, were bisected
beneath the gaze of the Aztec warrior Cuauhtémoc. Mercedes was
already suffering from the stomach complaint that, whether the rice is
cooked well or not, greets most first-time travellers to the Mexican
capital, where early days are often difficult for this and many other reasons. García Márquez would recall that they had only four friends in
the city at that moment: Mutis himself, the Colombian sculptor
Rodrigo Arenas Betancourt, the Mexican writer Juan García Ponce,
whom he had met in New York, and the Catalan film-maker and bookseller Luis Vicens, who had been keeping his mail for him.[2]

In Mexico's one-party system—ruled by the ambiguously named
Revolutionary Institutional Party (PRI)—the government's rhetoric
was far more radical than its political practices. The PRI had emerged
in the years following the 1910–17 Mexican Revolution, the world's

first social revolution of the twentieth century and a continuing example to Latin American progressives until Castro's triumphant entry into Havana in 1959; but forty years of power had slowed revolutionary progress to a virtual standstill. García Márquez had to learn very fast about this complex new country, where, more than anywhere else in Latin America, things are never quite what they seem.

A week later—though García Márquez has always said it was the day after he arrived—he was woken up first thing in the morning by García Ponce. "Listen to this," bellowed the Mexican, who had once made an uproarious visit to Barranquilla and had quickly learned how to speak like a *costeño*, "that bastard Hemingway has blown his head off with a shotgun."[3] So the first thing García Márquez wrote, shortly after his arrival in Mexico, was a long article in homage to the late American writer. This essay, "A Man Has Died a Natural Death," was published on 9 July by the influential intellectual Fernando Benítez in *México en la Cultura*, the literary supplement of one of Mexico's leading newspapers, *Novedades*. García Márquez, clearly moved by the death of the man he had seen on that Paris boulevard years before, predicted that "time will show that Hemingway, as a minor writer, will eat up many a great writer through his knowledge of men's motives and the secrets of his trade . . ."[4]

He also said that this death seemed to mark "a new era."[5] Little did he know that it would be his own leanest era so far in terms of literary creation, with the end of one mode of writing not leading quickly or automatically to the beginning of another. How could he or anyone else have thought, moreover, that, with one exception, this first article would also be the last serious and significant piece that he, a born journalist, would write for thirteen years?

Alvaro Mutis had arrived in Mexico in its last years as "the most transparent region"; now its crystalline sky was just beginning to be smeared with the grey streaks of late-twentieth-century pollution. Really Mexico was not Mutis's kind of country at all. But his ability to charm his way into high society had proved essential to his own extraordinary rehabilitation after his release from Lecumberri Prison and was now invaluable in easing the García Barchas into a society as resistant and as difficult to penetrate as a prickly pear. With Mutis's help, the newly arrived couple found an apartment on Renán Street near the city centre; not for the first time they slept on a mattress on the floor. They had a table and two chairs: the table served both for eating and working. So it had been in Caracas, at the start; then in

Bogotá; in New York Mercedes had had to live in one room in a hotel, with a small child; now they were without money again and back to basics. García Márquez wrote to Plinio Mendoza, "Here we are, for the third time in our three years of marriage, installed in an empty apartment. In accordance with our traditions, lots of light, lots of glass, lots of plans but almost nowhere to sit."[6]

For the first two months very little went right. Despite the efforts of Mutis and Vicens, García Márquez could not find work and he and Mercedes spent endless hours queuing at the Ministry of the Interior in Bucareli Street to regularize their residence papers. García Márquez was not entirely sure what work he wanted—the film industry seems to have been his preferred destination. He started to become anxious and depressed. Prensa Latina appeared determined not to give him the back pay they owed him. He went on waiting; he joked in a letter to Plinio Mendoza that if things continued as they were the logical thing would be to write *No One Writes to the Colonel*—except that it was already written.[7] Mendoza received the news that Mercedes was now expecting "Alejandra"—García Márquez insisted that it was a girl and had already decided on the name—the following April.[8] However, the child would not in fact be "the daughter I dreamed of having all my life and never had,"[9] because it would be a boy and it would also be the last.

Mutis saw that his friend's nerves were starting to jangle and took him on a jaunt down to the Caribbean in late August, to the seaport of Veracruz on the Gulf of Mexico. Until then García Márquez hadn't really absorbed the fact that Mexico, a desert country and a high plains country, was also, in effect, a Caribbean country. The pretext was the planned publication by the University of Veracruz at Xalapa of *Big Mama's Funeral and Other Stories*. It was the advance of 1,000 pesos for this book that had allowed García Márquez to put down the month's deposit on the apartment and start to buy "the third fridge of our marriage" on instalments.[10] He had no money, no job and a wife and child to support; politically he had lost touch with the first development in Latin American politics that had ever inspired him whilst hundreds of others climbed on the revolutionary bandwagon. Literarily, he had also lost his way: the story "Big Mama's Funeral" was written from a post-Cuban perspective but he had parted company with its inspiration, Cuba, however reluctantly, and now he was coming to terms with a new, very different and immensely complex and powerful cultural world which might take years to assimilate. In Mexico one had to learn to fit in.

One day Mutis climbed the seven flights of stairs, carried two books into the apartment without saying hello, slapped them down on the table, and roared: "Stop fucking about and read that *vaina*, so you'll learn how to write!" Whether all García Márquez's friends really swore all the time during these years we will never know—but in his anecdotes they do. The two slim books were a novel entitled *Pedro Páramo*, which had been published in 1955, and a collection of stories entitled *The Burning Plain (El llano en llamas)*, published in 1953. The writer was the Mexican Juan Rulfo. García Márquez read *Pedro Páramo* twice the first day, and *The Burning Plain* the next day. He claims that he had never been so impressed by anything since he had first read Kafka; that he learned *Pedro Páramo*, literally, by heart; and that he read nothing else for the rest of the year because everything else seemed so inferior.[11]

It is interesting to note that García Márquez apparently knew nothing about one of the greatest Latin American novelists of the century. He had reached 1961, thirty-four years of age, knowing really rather little about either the Latin American continent or its literature. By now the extremely new wave in Latin American fiction which would be known as the "Boom" had started—yet at this late date he knew none of the writers who would shortly be his peers, colleagues, friends and rivals, nor indeed many of the works of their essential precursors: the Brazilian Mário de Andrade, the Cuban Alejo Carpentier, the Guatemalan Miguel Angel Asturias, the Mexican Rulfo, or the Peruvian José María Arguedas. He was only really familiar with the Argentinian Borges, in many respects the least "Latin American" of them all, though already one of the most influential. In that sense his time in Europe had not Latin-Americanized him as decisively as it had so many writers of the 1920s: in truth, almost all his friends in Paris had been Colombians. One might say that he saw other Latin Americans as distant cousins rather than as brothers. (A very Colombian perspective: the country, full of talented people, has almost never pulled its cultural weight in the continent.) That decisive process of Latin Americanization was left to Mexico to complete; fortunately for him, there could have been no better teacher. It was Mexico which had initiated most of the processes of Latin America's twentieth-century "quest for identity" in the 1920s, which had received an extraordinary injection of highly educated Spanish refugees in the 1940s, and was now on the threshold of another great cultural moment.

García Márquez tried new angles. He told Plinio Mendoza that during an early visit to the state of Michoacán he had seen the Indians making straw angels which they dressed in their own local fashion and this had given him the idea for a story that he began now but would only finally complete in 1968, entitled "A Very Old Man with Enormous Wings."[12] He said at the time that it was part of "my old project of writing a book of fantastic stories." This one was quickly discarded for another, entitled "The Sea of Lost Time" ("El mar del tiempo perdido"), also written during those first desperate months in Mexico. He did not say so but these and other stories seem to have emerged from a nostalgia for the good old days, remembered or imagined, in and around Barranquilla, days that he himself had mainly missed, a world obliquely conveyed by Cepeda's dream-like movie *The Blue Lobster*. "The Sea of Lost Time" is an important development, although initially an isolated one. It has caused chaos and confusion among the literary critics because it seems to give many different messages all at once. The story is a continuation, though in a much lower key and with no declamatory interventions by the narrator, of the mode he had initiated in "Big Mama's Funeral." It was what in Latin America and eventually elsewhere would be known as "magical realism," a technique already developed by Asturias, Carpentier and Rulfo, in which the story, or part of the story, is narrated through the world-view of the characters themselves without any indication from the author that this world-view is quaint, folkloric or superstitious. The world is as the characters believe it to be.

Or almost. Because in "The Sea of Lost Time" there is, in fact, a character who knows more than the others. The post-Cuban García Márquez, who had confined himself to national issues in "Big Mama's Funeral," now—for the first time—introduces the question of economic imperialism through the character of Mr. Herbert, a "gringo" who comes as a kind of secular evangelist to the small, semi-abandoned town. In the days before he appears the villagers know something transcendent is afoot because there is a smell of roses everywhere in the usually salty and fish-filled air. Then the newcomer arrives and makes an announcement:

> "I'm the richest man in the world," he said. "I've got so much money I haven't got room to keep it any more. And besides, since my heart's so big that there's no room for it in my chest, I have decided to travel the world over solving the problems of mankind."[13]

Needless to say Mr. Herbert solves no problems; he completes the impoverishment of the town, enriches himself still further, and goes on his way. But before he does so he paints pretty pictures in the minds of the inhabitants—like a Hollywood movie-maker—and leaves them with dissatisfactions they never had before and longings they can hardly even express. Well, a personage with just this name—Mr. Herbert, exactly the same character to all intents and purposes—will later bring the banana company to Macondo in *One Hundred Years of Solitude*, and to similar effect. Whereas "Big Mama's Funeral" had settled García Márquez's accounts with Colombia and attributed the country's problems to a bankrupt political system, a reactionary ruling class, and a medieval national Church, "The Sea of Lost Time" at last introduces the great Latin American staple, U.S. imperialism—just as Castro had begun by attacking Batista and the Cuban ruling class and then moved on to confront the United States imperialists who had backed and funded them.

It is perhaps surprising that someone as close to the Communist Party as García Márquez had been for several years now should have waited so long to apply this diagnosis—imperialism—to his country's ills. It has to be concluded that between the actually existing socialism that he had witnessed in Eastern Europe in 1955 and 1957, and the United States, whose culture had fed so many of his "Giraffes" and whose writers had done so much to make him what he was, the choice for him was not easy—whereas most Latin American writers from the previous generation would not have hesitated simply to launch attacks on the hated gringos. On the other hand, García Márquez had not yet separated himself entirely from the perspectives of communist orthodoxy and therefore did not yet clearly see the USSR itself as an imperialist power with the Stalinist adaptation and deformation of Marxist ideology as its principal weapon. Contrary to the jibes of some of his later detractors, this was not a man who ever rushed to judgement or simplified complex problems (despite the provocative impression he would sometimes enjoy giving in the bourgeois press): he always took his time to think matters through in the most laborious fashion and never took the easy way out where intellectual reflection was concerned. The diaphanous readability of his most characteristic works would always be hard earned.

For the longer term, this short story has another aspect. It is a pointer to the future, away from Macondo-Aracataca and El Pueblo-Sucre, that is, away from Colombia and towards not only Latin America but literary universality. "Big Mama's Funeral" had finally fused the two small towns and in a sense had ironized both of them, preparing them for liquidation as the writer searched for a way to paint on a larger canvas. *One Hundred Years of Solitude* would still be set in Macondo but it would be obvious to the informed reader from the first page that this was an allegory of Latin America as a whole: Macondo had made the leap from national to continental symbol.

He still did not yet see clearly that the way to greatness for a Latin American novelist at this time in history was also, fortuitously, through Latin America itself, through a continental vision. He was still a Colombian. Writers in other countries with, ironically, a much less developed political consciousness than his, were nevertheless already making the leap that he was not yet prepared to make: the Argentinian Julio Cortázar, the Peruvian Mario Vargas Llosa and, above all, the Mexican Carlos Fuentes, were writers who were becoming conscious of being Latin Americans and were right then composing Joycean, "Ulyssean" books precisely about their own change of consciousness, their own reconquest of the continent, just as that earlier writer from a colonized country, James Joyce himself, had written about his own conquest of Europe forty years before (remember Stephen Dedalus's ambition to "forge . . . the uncreated conscience of my race"). Now García Márquez had to redefine his obsessions—his grandfather, his mother, his father, Colombia—and place them within a Latin American perspective. Other Latin American writers—Asturias, Carpentier, Arturo Uslar Pietri—had become Latin Americans in their early twenties; it took García Márquez until he was thirty-eight, and it might never have happened at all without the Boom and, in particular, without the Boom's great creator and propagandist, the Mexican Carlos Fuentes. Fortunately for García Márquez he would soon be meeting Fuentes, and the meeting would be decisive in his life.

Again what we see is the extraordinary, perhaps unparalleled restraint of a writer who, long before he was famous, always knew how to wait, sometimes in the face of great pressure or great temptation, until a book was right. It merely added to the anguish that this solitary story, "The Sea of Lost Time," was narrated from the anti-imperialist perspective which Cuba had given him yet he was not in touch with Cuba—on the contrary, it seemed to have spurned him. So in Mexico, blind as he was—without a political soul, as Mao Zedong might have said, now that he'd lost Cuba—he began to wonder, not for the first time, whether he should give up writing literature for good and move, as soon as he could, to writing film scripts. He had a family now and he could not in conscience sacrifice Mercedes, Rodrigo and the unborn child to his still largely unfulfilled literary vocation: if he had failed to make the big breakthrough when he was single, why should they suffer while he tried again and again to succeed? Film work, which he had always longed to do in any case, must have seemed, increasingly, like the most logical aspiration for a man in his situation and it was in that direction that he turned his endeavours. After all, it was still a form of writing.

Mexico was the country with the largest film industry in the Spanish-speaking world.[14] But at the beginning nothing materialized in the movies either. Then one evening when he got home after a fruitless search for work—and García Márquez was never very good at asking for anything—Mercedes told him she'd run out of money for food and had not been able to give Rodrigo his usual drink of milk before bedtime. García Márquez sat his two-year-old son down, explained the position and swore to him that this would never happen again. The child "understood," went to sleep without complaining, and did not wake up in the night. The next morning, sufficiently desperate to ask for another favour, García Márquez called Mutis, who seems to have judged that his friend might finally face up to being a beggar rather than a chooser. He used his own business contacts to arrange a couple of interviews. The first was with Gustavo Alatriste, an entrepreneur who had spent the previous years diversifying miraculously from the manufacture of furniture to several other industries including cinema and journalism.

Alatriste arranged to meet him in the bar of the Hotel Presidente on 26 September 1961, exactly three months after his arrival in Mexico. García Márquez would recall that the sole of one of his shoes was hanging and so he turned up early for the interview and waited for Alatriste to leave before he himself padded away.[15] Alatriste had produced some of Luis Buñuel's best films and was married at the time to Silvia Pinal, Mexico's most glamorous actress and leading lady in three of Buñuel's movies.[16] Obviously García Márquez was hoping that he would get immediate access to the film world through Alatriste. But Alatriste had recently bought several popular publications including *The Family (La Familia)*, a women's-interest magazine, and *Stories for Everyone (Sucesos para Todos)*, a very Mexican crime and scandal sheet. Editing these magazines was what Alatriste decided to offer the disenchanted supplicant, though he was doubtful even about that. Mutis had made the mistake of showing Alatriste some of García Márquez's previous journalism as part of his recommendation and Alatriste was doubtful: "This guy's too good," he growled. But Mutis assured him that his friend could turn his hand to anything. After some hesitation García Márquez took the job—the two jobs—and went home and asked Rodrigo what he would like most in the world. "A ball." His father went out and bought the biggest one he could find.

So García Márquez bade farewell for the moment to his dreams about the movies and took on both of Alatriste's magazines, on the extraordinary condition that his name should not appear anywhere on the staff lists and that he would not have to sign any pieces. He was in charge of *The Family* and *Stories for Everyone*—The Home Front and The Street, he must have thought. This was not only a humiliating retreat back into journalism, but the lowest level of journalism possible. He worked in the office down on Avenida Insurgentes Sur without a typewriter, and directed affairs there as if with gloves and tongs. It was almost too much for him to bear. The last time he had been forced to sacrifice his vocation in quite this way was during the crisis after his parents moved from Sucre to Cartagena in 1951; and even then he had found time to go on writing *Leaf Storm* in the cracks between his commitments. But now there was a wife and child and they had to eat even if he was used to doing without food. He gritted his teeth and prepared to say goodbye not only to the cinema but to literature too.

Another of the house magazines, called *S.nob*, had successfully lived up to its name by selling almost no copies up to that point but was now able to survive parasitically on the backs of García Márquez's populist mouthpieces. *S.nob* was run in those days by two avant-garde writers, Salvador Elizondo and Juan García Ponce, and García Márquez complained bitterly that they were literary aristocrats exploiting his labour—little knowing that one day his still-unborn son would marry Elizondo's still-unborn daughter.[17] From time to time, adding insult to injury, Alatriste would forget to pay his long-suffering employee. Once he fell three months behind and García Márquez had to pursue him everywhere. In the end he pursued him to a Turkish bath and a perspiring Alatriste had to give him the cheque in the midst of the rising steam. When García Márquez got it outside he saw that the writing had run and he had to scurry back in and pursue Alatriste all over again into the changing room.[18] He was beginning to resemble Cantinflas, the Mexican comedian.

Within weeks, despite his distaste for the work, he had improved the layout, the style and the mix of both the magazines. In amongst the recipes and knitting patterns of *La Familia*, which had a huge conti-

nental readership, and the blood-curdling stories and gruesome pictures of *Sucesos*, he infiltrated great novels in condensed form, biographical serials, detective stories, general interest features on other
cultures and any other quality padding he could think of. He had done
it all before both for *Crónica* in Barranquilla and for *Venezuela Gráfica*
in Caracas. Much of it was achieved by ransacking other magazines
from other countries, using scissors and paste and egged on by a dash
of desperation, a large dose of boredom, and a smidgen of cynicism.[19]
By the early months of 1962 *Sucesos* had increased its circulation by
around a thousand copies each issue and still rising. By April a cooler
García Márquez was able to report to Plinio Mendoza that he had "an
office with carpets and two secretaries, a home almost, and with a garden, and a boss who is either a rare genius or stark raving mad, I'm still
not sure. I'm not yet a magnate but although I've moved to within
three blocks of the office I'm thinking of buying a Mercedes Benz in
July. It would not be surprising if I moved from here to Miami to
organize the counter-revolution . . . We're expecting Alejandra within
ten days and Mercedes is in that interminable period in which women
become unbearable not only as wives but also as spectacles. Nevertheless she is preparing her revenge: she's going to buy loads of dresses
and shoes and other things when she goes back down to her normal
size."[20]

Guillermo Angulo had suggested in September 1961 that García
Márquez should put his unpublished manuscript, *In Evil Hour*, in for
the Esso-sponsored 1961 Colombian Literary Prize, which would be
awarded retrospectively in 1962.[21] Alvaro Mutis also put pressure on
him. It was said that Esso had received 173 submissions and none
looked promising; hence the suggestion that García Márquez should
send in a last-minute entry. The man himself would recall that he
undid the necktie, looked again at his much-travelled typescript, and
gave it one last, rigorous revision.[22] Unloved by its author, *In Evil Hour*
has never been a favourite with critics either. The plot is somewhat
over-fussy; the characters a little undeveloped. Yet it has a lucid, cinematographic quality and a cool hands-off technique that cannot fail to
impress themselves on the reader, even if the sombre subject matter is
unrelieved by humour or local colour.

The decision was made on Esso's behalf by the Colombian Academy, and García Márquez's manuscript was adjudged the winner. He
had been asked to provide a title and he set aside "This Shitty Town"
and came up with *In Evil Hour*. It transpired however that the Presi-

dent of the Colombian Academy was a priest, Father Félix Restrepo, who, as guardian both of the Spanish language and of the morals of his flock, had been troubled by the inclusion of words such as "contraceptive" and "masturbation." Father Restrepo asked the Colombian ambassador in Mexico, Carlos Arango Vélez, to take a letter to García Márquez and to have a discreet and delicate conversation with him in the course of which he should be asked to cut those two offending words. García Márquez decided, Solomon-like (though with the 3,000 dollars prize money already safely in his custody), to allow the ambassador to cut one. He chose "masturbation."

As fate would have it, the jury's favourable decision was made on the day that the second García Barcha child, Gonzalo, was born, 16 April 1962. García Márquez would later tell Plinio Mendoza that the baby was delivered "in six minutes" and "our only worry was that he might be born in the car on the way to the clinic." After winning the prize he was temporarily, relatively, rich. He used part of the money to pay for Mercedes's stay in the clinic.[23] But since he felt the money was "stolen"—he would later say, perhaps hypocritically, that entering the novel for the prize was the worst decision he had ever taken in his life—he then decided, superstitiously, not to spend it on routine housekeeping and instead purchased a car, a white Opel 62 saloon with red upholstery, to transport his family about the vast metropolis. He told Plinio Mendoza: "It's the most extraordinary toy I've had in all my life. I get up in the middle of the night to see if it's still there."[24]

But none of this was enough. He had won a literary prize but he was no longer a writer. He went on fretting. He found himself still yearning for work in the cinema. Despite his high hopes, and his strategy of seducing Alatriste through his devotion to duty, nothing came.[25] Indeed, the more money he made for Alatriste by overhauling and improving the two downmarket magazines, the less Alatriste was likely to allow him to move.

He was no longer sure whether he would be able to write even under the right conditions. Since he had been married he had only written a few short stories and even the despised *In Evil Hour* seemed a long book to him. The truth is that his mind was filled with nonsense at work, family matters at home, and movie talk with his friends. It is ironic to think that he had embarked, without conviction, on the next book after *One Hundred Years of Solitude*—*Eréndira and Other Stories*—but could not get to the novel he had been waiting to write, in one sense, for the whole of his life. So after a few months he went back to it; in other words, back to "The House," in his spare time. But "The House" was inhabited only by ghosts and again he got nowhere. So back he went to another idea that he felt deep down was a winner, a novel entitled *The Autumn of the Patriarch*.[26] *One Hundred Years of Solitude* did not even exist as a title, but this other, once aborted novel even had its eventual name. By the time the stories of *Big Mama's Funeral* were published in April 1962, the month he won the prize for *In Evil Hour*, and soon after he received the first copies of *No One Writes to the Colonel*, he had put together three hundred pages of *The Autumn of the Patriarch* and he still felt that he was on the wrong track. In the end he abandoned it again; later he would say that only the names of the characters survived.[27] Perhaps that dictator novel—partly about himself, in the present—could never have been written before the problem of "The House"—about his family, in the past—was dealt with. Desperate, discouraged, distraught, he put the manuscript away again and, for the first time, contemplated a future without literature.

But that was intolerable. He became more and more frustrated with his work on the two mediocre magazines and now complained to his *compadre* Plinio Mendoza: "For the time being I'm swallowing tranquilizers spread on my bread like butter and I still can't sleep more than four hours. I think my only hope is to get myself completely rewired . . . As you can imagine, I'm not writing anything. It's two months since I opened the typewriter. I don't know where to start, I'm troubled by the idea that in the end I won't write anything and I won't get rich either. Nothing more to say, *compadre*, I'm fucked, victim of a good situation."[28]

Politically, the question of his own relationship with Cuba was grating on him. As far as he was concerned, the matter was still pending; as far as the Cubans were concerned, it was closed. Despite the problems he had experienced in New York, García Márquez still felt that his difficulties were with the sectarians, not the Cuban regime itself. Perhaps he felt deep down that he should have hung on longer. His admiration for Castro can only have been growing as he watched the young Cuban leader and the steely Guevara defying the power of the United States and the serried ranks of bourgeois liberal Latin American countries. In April 1962, as Castro confronted both the entire capitalist world and the dogmatists in the Cuban Communist Party, García Márquez, who would always love to boast of having inside information, wrote to Plinio Mendoza: "I know the whole story about Fidel's 'purge' of Aníbal Escalante and I was sure that Masetti would be quickly rehabilitated. Fidel said such tough things to the comrades—'Don't think you won this Revolution in a raffle'—that for a while I was afraid the crisis would be a grave one. It's incredible how Cuba is racing through phases that take ten or twenty years in other countries. I have the impression the comrades bowed their heads to Fidel but I do not rule out the possibility—and I know exactly what I'm saying—that they might kill him any day now. For the moment, though, I'm delighted for Masetti and all of us and, of course, for our beautiful little Cuba which is proving to be an incredible education for everyone."[29]

The letter is illuminating: here is García Márquez, two years after his separation from Prensa Latina and his disillusionment with sectarian attempts to take control of it, continuing to invest his political faith and dreams for the future in Cuba and his confidence in its leader, for whom his admiration is unlimited. Here we see how two different approaches to Castro coincide: first, a way of talking that suggests that, like so many socialists at the time, García Márquez feels he knows "Fidel" personally, almost as a friend or elder brother, in the way that we know someone well but still from the outside; second, more unusually, the novelist's sense that he has an inside vision of the Cuban leader, as if Castro is a character in one of his books, acting and talking more or less in fulfilment of García Márquez's wishes. For now, though, Cuba was closed to him; so were the movies; and so, it seemed, was the one thing under his own control: his literature. He was beginning to lose hope.

NINETEEN SIXTY-TWO DRAGGED ON. The Cuban missile crisis came and went and the world, shaken and stirred, survived it. But still there was no light at the end of García Márquez's endless tunnel. Then: Hallelujah! In April 1963 he finally escaped from *The Family* and *Stories for Everyone* and became, as he wrote jubilantly to Plinio Mendoza, a "professional writer."[30] He meant script-writer but it was a telling paraphrase. After discussing his predicament with Mercedes, he had taken a chance on a desperate piece of private enterprise by writing a screenplay, on his own initiative, in five days, over the Easter holiday. The script was for a film to be called *El Charro (The Cowboy)*, and García Márquez had the great Mexican actor Pedro Armendáriz in mind to play the protagonist. When Alatriste heard about the project he wanted to take it over with the idea of that most Mexican of film-makers, Emilio "The Indian" Fernández, directing the film. When he discovered that García Márquez had already promised the script to the young director José Luis González de León in exchange for complete control of the screenplay and when he became convinced that García Márquez would not break his word with the other director, Alatriste suddenly changed his previous tune and told García Márquez that he would pay him the same salary as he had paid him for editing the magazines to stay at home for a year and write two more film scripts of his choice.[31] García Márquez was delighted that his gamble had paid off.

Unfortunately the unpredictable Alatriste ran out of money over the summer and asked García Márquez to release him from their deal whilst promising to continue to provide him with visa cover. Having succeeded once in provoking competition among film producers, García Márquez contacted another of Alvaro Mutis's friends: Manuel Barbachano, the producer, who was only too happy to take him on as long as it was on a freelance basis. One of Barbachano's obsessions was the work of Juan Rulfo and he planned to carry the story "The Golden Cock" ("El gallo de oro") to the screen. It is the tale of a poor man who saves a dying fighting cock and discovers he has found a champion; he aspires both to great wealth and to the local belle, the mistress of a rich man, and eventually all concerned lose everything they have fought for. In several respects it was the world of *No One Writes to the Colonel* and Mutis had recommended his excited friend as the very man for the job. No better opportunity could have come García Márquez's way. The director, Roberto Gavaldón, was one of the best-known, and politically best-placed of the country's film-makers—while the director of photography, Gabriel Figueroa, was probably the most brilliant cameraman in all of Latin America. García Márquez would finally meet the tortured alcoholic author of the story, Juan Rulfo, at a wedding in late November 1963—on the day Lee Harvey Oswald died shortly after being accused of assassinating President John F. Kennedy—and they became as friendly as Rulfo's condition and García Márquez's state of anxiety and depression would allow.

Barbachano was not offering García Márquez the same security as Alatriste and the bills still had to be paid, so García Márquez called the Walter Thompson advertising agency in September and was taken on immediately. Though far from what he was ideally looking for, advertising suited his temperament better and left him with far more freedom than the treadmill of running magazines. At least in this new situation he was in a better position to do what he had always done: attend to his day job efficiently and responsibly while still retaining the energy and somehow finding the time to work on what really interested him.[32] He was destined to spend late 1963, all of 1964 and much of 1965 working simultaneously in freelance movie work and in advertising agencies—first Walter Thompson, and then Stanton, Pritchard and Wood, which was part of another global giant, McCann Erickson. Walter Thompson and McCann Erickson were among the top three advertising agencies in the world and so for a time García Márquez found himself working for the standard-bearers of U.S. monopoly capitalism, Madison Avenue branch, not something he has ever been keen to highlight. Mutis had preceded him in this as in other things, having worked at Stanton early in his stay in Mexico, from the moment it was established.

Much later, the experience gained during this somewhat bizarre interlude prepared García Márquez, ironically enough, to negotiate his own future celebrity—to understand fame, to think about self-presentation, to produce a personal brand-image and then to manage it. Still more ironic, this early training in advertising and public relations would allow him to live out his political contradictions in public without hostile U.S. commentators ever seriously laying a finger on him in the decades to come. He had the knack, and whenever García Márquez was inspired his manager, a reformed alcoholic, would raise his right hand and punch the air like a prize fighter. He also had help at home: Mercedes was always coming up with memorable phrases about products—"You can't live without a Kleenex" was one of them—and he turned several of her off-the-cuff remarks into profitable slogans.[33]

García Márquez now became fully installed in the Mexican cultural milieu at one of its most influential and effervescent moments; the Zona Rosa, Mexico's answer to Swinging London's Carnaby Street and King's Road, would really get going in 1964. Era, the recently funded left-wing publishing house, had just brought out the second edition of *No One Writes to the Colonel* in September 1963, to García Márquez's delight—though still with a print run of only 1,000 copies. He began to live quite a social whirl among the black leather jackets and dark glasses of the city's fashionable writers, painters, movie actors, singers and journalists. The couple were now prosperous and well dressed. Rodrigo and Gonzalo would go to private English schools, first the Colegio Williams kindergarten, then the Queen Elizabeth School in San Angel.[34] The family owned a car and started looking around for a house with more space.

Within a few months of starting as a freelance movie writer García

Márquez had produced the script for Rulfo's "The Golden Cock."[35]
Barbachano considered it excellent, with just one reservation—he said
it was written in Colombian, not Mexican. It was at this moment that
García Márquez's luck improved still more, indeed decisively. Carlos
Fuentes, the country's leading young writer, eighteen months García
Márquez's junior, returned to Mexico late in 1963 after a longish stay
in Europe.[36] He and the Colombian had a plethora of friends in com-
mon. Whoever introduced them, it helped when they first met that
Fuentes knew who García Márquez was and already admired his work.
As the Mexican would recall, "I'd first heard about Gabriel through
Alvaro Mutis, who in the late 1950s gave me a copy of *Leaf Storm*.
'This is the best thing that's come out,' he said, wisely failing to specify
either time or place."[37] As a result of this recommendation Fuentes had
published "Big Mama's Funeral" and the "Monologue of Isabel
Watching It Rain in Macondo" in the *Revista Mexicana de Literatura*.
He had even written an enthusiastic review of *No One Writes to the
Colonel* in *La Cultura en México (¡Siempre!)* in January 1963.

Still, Fuentes was enough to worsen anyone's inferiority complex.
He had enjoyed a privileged upbringing, which he had made the most
of. He spoke both English and French superbly, in the virile but modulated tones of the classic Mexican tenor. He was handsome, dashing
and dynamic, glamorous in every way. In 1957 he had married the
leading actress Rita Macedo; later he would have a dramatic affair with
the ill-fated Hollywood star Jean Seberg when she was filming *Macho
Callahan* up in Durango. And in 1958 he had published what can fairly
be considered the work which announced the imminent Boom of the
Latin American novel, *Where the Air Is Clear (La región más transpa-
rente)*. Like García Márquez, Fuentes had travelled to Cuba immediately after the revolution but was always politically independent: he
would eventually manage the unlikely feat of being banned from communist Cuba, fascist Spain and the liberal United States. In 1962 he
had published two more outstanding books, the gothic novella *Aura*
and *The Death of Artemio Cruz (La muerte de Artemio Cruz)*, one of the
great Mexican novels of the century and perhaps the greatest of all
novels about the Mexican Revolution—a work which he completed in
Havana, where he had viewed his own country's fading revolutionary
process from the perspective of Cuba's new one. At thirty-five, then,
Carlos Fuentes was without question the leading young writer in Mexico and a rising international star.

With so many shared interests and a vocation in common, the two men soon developed a close and mutually profitable relationship. Of course García Márquez had infinitely more to gain. Fuentes was not only several years ahead of him in terms of career development, he was a Mexican in his own country and he had developed over the previous decade a quite extraordinary network of contacts with many of the leading intellectuals in the world—the worlds—in which García Márquez aspired to move. Fuentes could take him to places that almost no other writer in Latin America could reach; and his intellectual generosity was unrivalled. Above all, Fuentes's Latin American consciousness was much more developed than that of García Márquez and he was able to tutor and groom the still raw and uncertain Colombian for a role in a vast Latin American literary drama that Fuentes, more than any other man alive, could foresee and for which, more than any other man alive, he would be personally responsible.

García Márquez and Fuentes began to work together on the script of "The Golden Cock" with Roberto Gavaldón. García Márquez would later claim that he and Fuentes spent five long months arguing with the director about the script and got nowhere. The movie was eventually filmed between 17 June and 24 July 1964 at the famous Churubusco studios and on location in Querétaro, with star actors Ignacio López Tarso and Lucha Villa as the leads. When the ninety-minute production eventually opened on 18 December 1964 it would be a commercial and critical flop. Rulfo's writing is ritualistic and implicitly mythic but it is always spare and suggestive, never overt, and nothing could have been more difficult to adapt to the big screen.

Although both men would persist with the genre, particularly García Márquez—he said it was "a safety valve to liberate my ghosts"—neither of them would ever be entirely at home in film work.[38] It is not difficult to see why they persisted, however: there was no money to be made in literature in those days, or so it seemed, and the movies were a way to appeal directly to the consciousness of the great Latin American public. Moreover, in the 1960s, in a relatively repressive society like Mexico's, the cinema, with its new approach to sexuality and nudity, and its use of beautiful actresses and young, outgoing, avant-garde directors, gave rare and privileged access both to glamour and to the cultural future. Unfortunately the 1960s also encouraged much effervescent but vacuous nonsense, not least in Mexico. To be up to date, fashionable and "where it was at," or better, to be "in," became essential in those days and even García Márquez and Fuentes found themselves seduced by the cultural market and its public relations machine.

In July he confessed to Plinio Mendoza that his admiration for

Alejo Carpentier's recent novel *Explosion in a Cathedral* was beginning to make him think—following Fuentes, no doubt—about the relation between the tropics and the literary baroque. He drew Plinio's attention to the success in Europe the year before of translations of *Explosion in a Cathedral*, Fuentes's *The Death of Artemio Cruz*, Julio Cortázar's *Hopscotch*, and Mario Vargas Llosa's *The Time of the Hero*, a list which included the first three novels of what was not yet known as the "Boom."[39] Little did he dream that the fourth and most famous novel of all would be written by him.

Gabo and Mercedes were now offered the opportunity of moving straight into a new house that was ideal for their purposes.[40] It was, he told Plinio, "a great house, with a garden, a study, a guest room, telephone and all the comforts of bourgeois life, in a very quiet and traditional sector full of illustrious oligarchs." This was something of an exaggeration: it was true that the house was close to such a sector but they were separated from it by a major roadway. Still, agreeable, quiet and comfortable it undoubtedly was. And he, at long last, had his own study, a "cave full of papers." The house was sparsely furnished but roomier than anywhere the family had lived before, and although largely empty of possessions it would always be full of music, especially Bartók and the Beatles.[41]

Yet in the midst of all the social whirl, behind the fake bonhomie and despite his new-found security and respectability, García Márquez was increasingly unhappy. Pictures of him from this period are painful to look at: he exudes tension and stress. Some said they saw him close to fist fights at parties. He was writing nothing that he cared about, except, on and off, *The Autumn of the Patriarch*, which he felt was going nowhere. He was a petty-bourgeois script-writer and ad man. Successful authors such as Julio Cortázar and Mario Vargas Llosa, who had no revolutionary antecedents, were being courted by the Cuban Revolution while he was out in the cold. When the influential Uruguayan literary critic Emir Rodríguez Monegal, who would play a fundamental role in publicizing not only Fuentes and García Márquez but all the other writers of the rapidly swelling Boom, had visited Mexico in January 1964 to teach at the Colegio de México, he had found García Márquez in a disturbing mental condition: "a tortured soul, an inhabitant of the most exquisite hell: that of literary sterility. To try to speak to him about his earlier work, to praise (for example) *No One Writes to the Colonel*, was like torturing him with one of the most subtle machines of the Inquisition."[42]

He soldiered on. In late 1964 he rewrote his first original screenplay, *El charro*, originally to have been filmed by José Luis González de León. Now it was directed by the twenty-two-year-old Arturo Ripstein and retitled *Tiempo de morir (Time to Die)*.[43] Its origin, like so many of García Márquez's works, lay in one image, a memory, a lived incident in the past. He had once gone back to an apartment of his in Colombia to find the doorman, an ex-hit-man, knitting a sweater.[44] In the screenplay a man who has spent eighteen years in prison for a murder he was provoked into committing returns to his home village, despite the fact that the sons of the dead man have sworn to kill him. He too knits sweaters. The younger son has a change of heart but the other repeatedly provokes the older man—history repeating itself—until finally, ironically, the protagonist shoots the older son and the younger son then shoots the protagonist dead without resistance on the other's part. Obviously this was a rewrite of his grandfather's experience in Barrancas, when he too was provoked by a younger man—though of course Nicolás Márquez eventually shot his adversary and spent only one year in jail, not eighteen.

The movie was eventually filmed at Churubusco and in Pátzcuaro between 7 June and 10 July 1965, only weeks after García Márquez had completed the script. It would star Jorge Martínez de Hoyos, Marga López and Enrique Rocha; the dialogue would be adapted by Carlos Fuentes, the camera work was by the great Alex Phillips, and the titles were produced by García Márquez's friend Vicente Rojo. It was ninety minutes long and premiered on 11 August 1966 at the Cine Variedades in Mexico City. Yet again a movie involving García Márquez was generally considered a failure, though the young director's raw cinematographic talent was evident to all. García Márquez and Ripstein would each blame the other. García Márquez's contribution was typical of his cinematographic virtues and vices: the plot was almost worthy of Sophocles in its perfection; the dialogue was far too sententious for a movie. García Márquez had seen with disillusioning clarity that for him at least writing movie scripts was less satisfying than writing literary stories, even if almost no one reads them: first of all, writing for films was completely different from writing for a reading public; second, you inevitably lost your independence, your political and moral integrity, and even your identity; because finally, producers and directors inevitably saw you as merely a means to an end, a commodity.[45]

Nevertheless what was, in many respects, García Márquez's most historic moment in the movies had come almost at the start of this ultimately disillusioning new era, when many of Mexico's best-known celebrities, mostly friends of his, took part in the filming of his story "There Are No Thieves in This Town" in late October 1964. It was the tale of a layabout in a small town who decides to make some money by selling the ivory billiard balls in the local pool hall, only to bring disaster upon himself, his long-suffering wife and their recently born child.[46] Filming took place in Mexico City and in Cuautla. García Márquez himself, who would also work on the montage, played the ticket collector outside the village cinema and, always self-conscious in such situations, gave a particularly uneasy performance. Luis Buñuel played the priest, Juan Rulfo, Abel Quezada and Carlos Monsiváis were dominoes players, Luis Vicens was the owner of the pool hall, José Luis Cuevas and Emilio García Riera were billiards players, María Luisa Mendoza was a cabaret singer, and the painter Leonora Carrington played a churchgoer dressed in mourning. The leads were Julián Pastor, Rocío Sagaón and Graciela Enríquez. Decidedly one of the better films of the era, *There Are No Thieves in This Town* was ninety minutes long and premiered on 9 September 1965.

Despite these and other developments, the movies had started to lose their charm for García Márquez at just the moment that he found himself fully installed in the industry and finally earning good money. Was that the point? He could see that he could go on working in the Mexican cinema with tolerable success for as far into the future as he wanted. Yet he was also becoming aware that this was not where his talent lay, that the satisfactions of script-writing were limited, and in any case the script-writer was never in full control of his own destiny. He was beginning to feel trapped again. Besides, the world of Latin American literature was changing rapidly and becoming, ironically, much more glamorous than the movies. And just around then, as the movies palled, he began to perceive that the movies were part of the trouble he had had with literature. It was not so much that he was writing literary scripts for a quite different medium, though undoubtedly he was; the real problem was that the movies had taken over his conception of the novel, years before, and he needed to go back to his own literary roots. Looking back several years later, he reflected: "I always thought that the cinema, through its tremendous visual power, was the perfect means of expression. All my books before *One Hundred Years of Solitude* are hampered by that uncertainty. There is an immoderate desire for the visualization of character and scene, a millimetric account of the time of dialogue and action and an obsession with indicating point of view and frame. While actually working in cinema, however, I came to realize not only what could be done but also what couldn't be done; I saw that the predominance of the image over other narrative elements was certainly an advantage but also a limitation and this was for me a startling discovery because only then did I become aware of the fact that the possibilities of the novel itself are unlimited."[47]

In 1965 a grand symposium of intellectuals was held at the site of the Mayan archaeological ruins of Chichén Itzá. Carlos Fuentes, José Luis Cuevas and William Styron were among the participants in what was a real jamboree with its much-advertised intellectual dimension somewhat sidelined by high jinks of every kind. Of course no one at that time would have thought of inviting García Márquez, still unknown internationally, nor would García Márquez have thought of exposing himself to such an occasion. However, when the participants set off for their various destinations via Mexico City Fuentes organized a huge and now legendary party at his house, at which García Márquez was a guest and met the Chilean novelist José Donoso, who admired *No One Writes to the Colonel* and would remember García Márquez as "a gloomy, melancholy person tormented by his writer's block, a blockage as legendary as those of Ernesto Sábato and the eternal block of Juan Rulfo . . . and William Styron."[48]

Following the party came two visits which were to prove decisive in García Márquez's return to literature and the revolutionizing of his life. While Ripstein was shooting *Tiempo de morir* in Pátzcuaro, Michoacán, in June, García Márquez was visited by Luis Harss, a young Chilean-American who had met him briefly in the United Nations building in New York in 1961 and who was now preparing a book of critical interviews of leading Latin American novelists of the last two generations in response to the sensational phenomenon that would later be called the Boom.[49] He had originally planned nine interviews. Most of the other writers included were fairly obvious, though still shrewdly chosen: Miguel Angel Asturias, Jorge Luis Borges, Alejo Carpentier, João Guimarães Rosa, Juan Carlos Onetti and Juan Rulfo, from the previous generation; and Julio Cortázar, Mario Vargas Llosa and Carlos Fuentes from the writers of the Boom. García Márquez, however, was the brilliant exception. The recommendation, inevitably, came from Fuentes.[50]

The visit by Harss and his inclusion in this top ten list must have been an exhilarating shot in the arm for García Márquez. The interview remains today one of the most extraordinary insights into a man who, at that time, in his first serious major interview, had not yet developed the brash celebrity persona of later years, though he did begin by calling Colombian literature "a casualty list." It was the first time García Márquez had been subjected to public interrogation and its effect on his own self-scrutiny and self-analysis is likely to have been dramatic. Harss described him thus:

> He is stocky, but light on his feet, with a bristling mustache, a cauliflower nose, and many fillings in his teeth. He wears an open sports shirt, faded blue jeans, and a bulky jacket flung over his shoulders . . . A strenuous life that might have wrecked another man has provided García Márquez with the rich hoard of personal experiences that form the hard core of his work. For years he has been living in Mexico. He would go home if he could—he says he would drop everything if he were needed there—but at the moment he and Colombia have nothing to offer each other. For one thing, his politics are unwelcome there, and he has strong feelings on the subject. Meantime—if life abroad can be an ordeal, it also has its compensations—he is like a jeweler polishing his gems. With a handful of books behind him, each born of the labor of love, like a pearl in an oyster, he has begun to make a solid reputation for himself.[51]

Later in the interview, however, García Márquez would try to undermine Harss's view of him as constant and tenacious: "I have firm political ideas. But my literary ideas change according to my digestion." And Harss noted that he also seemed somehow to carry drama with him:

> Angel Gabriel, tightening his belt, comes out of a dark bend in the corridor with lights in his eyes. He lets himself into the room stealthily, a bit on edge, wondering what is going to happen to him, but at the same time, it seems, rubbing his hands with anticipation . . . He has a way of startling himself with his own thoughts. Now—the night is fragrant and full of surprises—he lies back on a bed, like a psychoanalytic patient, stubbing out cigarettes. He talks fast, snatching thoughts as they cross his mind, winding and unwinding them like paper streamers, following them in one end and out the other, only to lose them before he can pin them down. A casual tone with a deep undertow suggests he is making a strategy of negligence. He has

a way of eavesdropping on himself, as if he were trying to over-
hear bits of a conversation in the next room. What matters is
what is left unsaid.[52]

Was García Márquez already like this or was he becoming this as he
spoke, urged on by the drama in which he felt he was taking part? Who
knows. Harss would entitle his interview "Gabriel García Márquez, or
the Lost Chord."

Just a few weeks later, following this first public camera flash, came
a crucial business visit. Since 1962 the Barcelona literary agent Carmen Balcells had been acting for García Márquez in a largely hypothetical sense as the negotiator of his translations; whereas he, up to
now, had been having a hard time getting the novels published even in
their original language. Balcells arrived in Mexico on Monday 5 July
after a visit to New York, where she had negotiated a contract with
Roger Klein of Harper and Row to publish García Márquez's four
extant works in English translation for 1,000 dollars.[53] She was an
ambitious international literary agent and he was a promising young
writer aching for success. She introduced herself to her new author,
explained the contract and waited for his reaction: "The contract is a
piece of shit," was his reply. The ebullient Balcells, rotund of face and
body, and her husband Luis Palomares, had already been disconcerted
by the Colombian's curious but characteristic mixture of diffidence,
indifference and arrogance, and must have been astounded that a
writer almost no one had heard of could have such a high opinion of
his own worth. This was not a good start: "I found him most unlike-
able, petulant. But he was right about the contract."[54] Fortunately
García Márquez and Mercedes soon rallied and put on three days of
guided tours and parties, culminating on 7 July 1965 in the signing of a
second, spoof contract in which, like a colonel in one of his stories, and
in the presence of Luis Vicens, he authorized Balcells to represent him
in all languages and on all sides of the Atlantic for 150 years. Now his
own short story was weaving its magic: he had found his own Big
Mama in real life, and for the long term. She at once negotiated with
Era for new editions of *No One Writes to the Colonel* and *In Evil Hour*,
and would soon negotiate Italian translations with Feltrinelli. She
probably thought he should be grateful for his luck. Little did she
know how lucky she was going to be.

After these unexpected visits from afar and their accompanying
good news, García Márquez decided to take the family for a brief vaca-

tion in Acapulco the following weekend, having been away filming in Pátzcuaro for so long. The road down to Acapulco is one of the most tortuous and testing in a country of terrifying twists and turns, and García Márquez, who has always enjoyed driving, was delighting in the piloting of his little white Opel through the ever-changing panorama of the Mexican road. He has often said that driving is a skill at once so automatic and yet so demanding of concentration that it allows him to displace the surplus concentration to a consideration of his novels.[55] He had not been driving long that day when, "from nowhere," the first sentence of a novel floated down into his brain. Behind it, invisible but palpable, was the entire novel, there as if dictated—downloaded— from above. It was as powerful, as irresistible as a magic spell. The secret formula of the sentence was in the point of view and, above all, in the tone: "Many years later, as he faced the firing squad . . ." García Márquez, as if in a trance, pulled over at the roadside, turned the Opel around, and drove back in the direction of Mexico City. And then . . .

It seems a pity to intervene in the story at this point but the biographer feels constrained to point out that there have been many versions of this story (as of so many others) and that the one just related cannot be true—or at least, cannot be as miraculous as most of its narrators have suggested. The different versions vary as to whether it was the first line that García Márquez heard or whether it was just the image of a grandfather taking a boy to discover ice (or, indeed, to discover something else).[56] Whatever the truth, something mysterious, not to say magical, had certainly happened.

The classic version, just interrupted, has García Márquez turning the car round the very moment he hears the line in his head and peremptorily cancelling the family vacation, driving back to Mexico City and beginning the novel as soon as he gets home. Other versions have him repeating the line to himself and reflecting on its implications as he drives, then making extensive notes when he gets to Acapulco, then starting the novel proper as soon as he gets back to the capital city.[57] This is certainly the most convincing of the different alternatives; but in all the versions the vacation is truncated and the boys and the long-suffering Mercedes, little knowing how long-suffering she would now be called upon to be, had to swallow their disappointment and wait for another holiday—an occasion which would be a long time coming.

15

Melquíades the Magician: *One Hundred Years of Solitude*

1965~1966

Y EARS LATER GARCÍA MÁRQUEZ would say that after he got home he sat down at his typewriter the next day, just as he did every day, except "this time I did not get up for another eighteen months."[1] In fact the writing would take not much longer than a year, July 1965 to July or August 1966, including several interruptions, yet he would always say it was eighteen months; perhaps because it had really taken him eighteen years. He told Plinio Mendoza that his biggest problem had been: "Getting started, I remember quite distinctly the day that with enormous difficulty I finished the first sentence and I asked myself, terrified, what the hell came next. In fact, until the galleon was discovered in the middle of the jungle I didn't really think the book would get anywhere. But from that point on the whole thing became a kind of frenzy, and very enjoyable as well."[2]

In other words, only when he got about ten pages in and wrote the episode in which the first José Arcadio Buendía comes aross a Spanish galleon in the tropical forest did he realize that the magic was not going to end this time and that he really could begin to relax. This was evidently in the very first week, while he still had vacation time away from the office. All the burdens of the previous five years began to fall away. He expected to write eight hundred typed pages which he would eventually reduce to about four hundred; not a bad guess, as it turned out. In those four hundred pages he would tell the story of four generations of the Buendía family, the first of whom arrives at a place called Macondo some time in the nineteenth century and begins to experience a hundred years of Colombian history with a mixture of perplexity, obduracy, obsessiveness and black humour. The family moves from a posture of childlike innocence through all the stages of man and woman to eventual decadence and the last of them is swept away by a "biblical hurricane" on the last page of the novel. Critics have speculated endlessly on the meaning of this conclusion ever since the book first appeared. The six central characters, who begin the novel and dominate its first half, are José Arcadio Buendía, the excitable founder of the village of Macondo; his wife Ursula, the backbone of not only her family but also the entire novel; their sons José Arcadio and Aureliano—the latter, Colonel Aureliano Buendía, generally considered the principal character of the book; their daughter Amaranta, tormented as a child and embittered as a woman; and the gypsy Melquíades, who brings news of the outside world from time to time and eventually stays on in Macondo. The history of Colombia is dramatized through two principal events: the War of a Thousand Days, and the massacre of the banana workers in Ciénaga in 1928. These were of course the two main historical references which had been the context of García Márquez's own childhood.

The book he had always wanted to write was a family saga set in Aracataca but renamed Macondo. And this book he was now writing was indeed a family saga set in Aracataca, renamed Macondo. But the family was no longer only Colonel Nicolás Márquez's family, still suffused with nostalgia and longings for epic validation as in *Leaf Storm*, though now also treated with lofty irony; but also Gabriel Eligio García's family, treated parodically and satirically, with a comic turn which oscillated between the affectionate and the cruel. And the book was written not by the twenty-year-old man who had started "The House" but, in a curious way, by the small boy whose experience that twenty-year-old had recalled with such nostalgia, and that small boy was walking hand in hand not with Colonel Márquez but with the family man of nearly forty that García Márquez himself now was, a writer who had read all the world's literature and had lived through the most decisive of the ages of man.

What had happened to Gabriel García Márquez? Why was he now able, after so long, to write this book? He had realized, in a lightning flash of inspiration, that instead of a book about his childhood he should write a book about his memories of his childhood. Instead of a book about reality, it should be a book about the representation of reality. Instead of a book about Aracataca and its people, it should be a book narrated through the world-view of those people. Instead of trying yet again to resurrect Aracataca he should say farewell to Aracataca by narrating it not only through the world-view of its people but by putting into the novel everything that had happened to him, everything he knew about the world, everything that he was and that he embodied as a late-twentieth-century Latin American; in other words, instead of isolating the house and Aracataca from the world he should take the entire world to Aracataca. And above all, emotionally, instead of trying to raise the ghost of Nicolás Márquez he himself should somehow become Nicolás Márquez.

What he felt was relief coursing through him on multiple levels from a hundred different directions, all the efforts and all the anguish and all the failures and frustrations of his life relieved; liberation and self-recognition and self-affirmation all embodied in this extraordinary creation which he knew—he *knew*—could be a unique, possibly immortal work even as he started to write and then, as he worked on it with growing excitement, began to take on the grandiosity of a myth in its own right. So of course it felt magical, miraculous, euphoric, even to him, as he wrote it; and then, later, to his readers. It was, indeed, an experience of the magic of literary creation raised to the highest degree of intensity. Moreover, the writing was also radically therapeutic: instead of obsessively, neurotically, diligently trying to re-create the events of his life exactly as he remembered them he now rearranged all that he had been told or personally experienced in the way he wanted to, so that the book took on the shape its author needed. And so the book really was magical, miraculous, euphoric: it was curing him of many ills.

Now a man who usually wrote one paragraph a day was writing several pages every day. A man who turned his books inside out and upside down looking first for the sequence and then for the structure was now writing the chapters one after another like God himself ordaining the shape and rotation of the Earth. A man who had always suffered every twist and turn, every small technical and psychological decision in each of his books, was playing with his life: fusing his grandfather with his father with himself, Tranquilina with Luisa Santiaga with Mercedes, weaving Luis Enrique and Margot in and out of several characters, turning his paternal grandmother into Pilar Ternera, smuggling Tachia in through the character of Amaranta

Ursula, and fusing the history of his entire family with the history of Latin America, uniting his Latin American literary ingredients—Borges, Asturias, Carpentier, Rulfo—with the Bible, Rabelais, the chronicles of the Spanish conquest and the European novels of chivalry, Defoe, Woolf, Faulkner, Hemingway. No wonder he felt like an alchemist; no wonder he fused Nostradamus and Borges—and himself, García Márquez—into the figure of the great Writer-Creator Melquíades, another genius who locked himself away in a small room to encapsulate the entire cosmos in that enchanted space, at once transhistorical and intemporal, known as literature. What he now did, in short, was not only to mix everything in but above all (and this is why he succeeded, according to many, in writing something like the Latin American equivalent of *Don Quixote*) to confront and combine the two principal, contradictory characteristics of that little-known but extraordinary and life-enhancing continent: over the dark story of conquest and violence, tragedy and failure, he laid the other side of the continent, the carnival spirit, the music and the art of the Latin American people, that ability to honour life even in its darkest corners and to find pleasure in ordinary things, a pleasure which for so many Latin Americans is not just a consolation for oppression and failure but a premonition of that better world which to them is always so close and which they celebrate not only through their revolutions but also through the festive victories of daily life. Later, of course, García Márquez would deny all such transcendent intentions: "I was never conscious of any of it," he would tell Elena Poniatowska in 1973, "I am a man who tells stories, anecdotes."[3]

By the end of the first week in September he had made huge strides. He soon discovered that he needed total commitment and a complete suspension of his other activities. Trying to write the book and work on in the advertising agency gave him excruciating headaches. He decided to give up both paid employment and his regular social life. This was an extraordinary gamble for a family man.

The book was set in Aracataca, in Macondo, but Macondo was now a metaphor for the whole of Latin America. He knew Latin America all right; but he had also visited the Old World and he had personally witnessed the difference between the old liberal democracies of the capitalist world and the new socialist countries including the USSR. And he had also lived for a time in the iconic city of the USSR's historic rival, the country that was defining the future of the planet and had already, for more than half a century, circumscribed and controlled

Latin America's own destiny: the United States. This man knew a lot about the world. All this he knew before we even start to recall what he had learned about literature.

So Macondo, the living image of a small town anywhere in Colombia or Latin America (or, indeed, as readers in Africa and Asia would later attest, anywhere in the Third World), would become a symbol of any small community at the mercy of historical forces not only beyond its control but even beyond its ken.

The story, as it now emerged, was the saga of a family which migrated from the Guajira to a place very like Aracataca some time in the nineteenth century. The father figure, José Arcadio Buendía, had killed his best friend out of honour and machismo, and was forced to leave because he was haunted by his friend's ghost. José Arcadio founded a new village named Macondo where he and his resilient wife Ursula built a house and became the unofficial leaders of the new community. They had three children, Arcadio, Aureliano and Amaranta, and over time took in a number of others. One of the household servants, Pilar Ternera, had relationships with several male members of the family down the years, contributing to the family's terror that eventually there would be an incestuous coupling which would produce a child with a pig's tail and bring about the end of the family line. Gypsies visited frequently, including an especially shrewd and talented fellow named Melquíades, who eventually stayed in Macondo and moved into the family house. But there was also a negative arrival: the central government in Bogotá (unnamed in the novel), which sent political and military representatives to control the innocent little community; this original sin led to a series of civil wars in which Aureliano, once grown up, became an enthusiastic and indeed fanatical participant on the side of the Liberal Party until eventually he became known throughout the country as the legendary warrior Colonel Aureliano Buendía. Later, even more sinister outsiders would appear: the North Americans who would arrive with their Fruit Company to transform the town's economy and culture until the locals rebelled by going on strike, at which point the gringos prodded the central government into action and three thousand striking workers and members of their families were massacred beside the railway station in Macondo. After this dark episode Macondo went into decline, a decline signalled by Ursula herself—the heart and soul of the novel—finally dying, whereupon the less vigorous younger generation, who live more as victims of history than as creators of myth, find themselves returning to some sort of primordial darkness and sinfulness. Eventually the last member of the family, as was predicted, engendered a child with a pig's tail after a wild affair with his youthful aunt, and both he and the whole of Macondo were swept away, as was also predicted (by Melquíades), in an apocalyptic hurricane wind.

The novel would also be modernist in the sense that García Márquez would write a book which would condense all books, macrocosm contained within a microcosm: it begins and ends in biblical style and contains some of the universal myths of anthropology, the characteristic mythemes of Western culture and the peculiar negative thrust of Latin America's own specific experience of grandiose aspiration and humiliating failure, right down to the multifarious continental theories of the best-known Latin American thinkers. Yet almost everything in the book would be the result of García Márquez's own lived experience. Anyone familiar with the outlines of his life can find half a dozen or more items on every page which correspond directly to García Márquez's biography—the writer himself has claimed that every single incident and every single detail corresponds to a lived experience. ("I am just a mediocre notary.")

Most wondrous of all was the form, which somehow managed to contain all these multifarious elements, a remarkable combination of high art with the ways of oral communication. Yet while it is true that the novel has assimilated large quantities of Colombia's own popular experience it is not entirely easy to agree with those who see the book as a storehouse of folk wisdom. What García Márquez has achieved, and the achievement is no less extraordinary, is the magical *appearance* of a world of folk wisdom—because, after all, what characterizes the inhabitants of this novel is how little wisdom they actually possess and how ill equipped they are to confront the world it is their destiny and misfortune to inhabit. Theirs is a world where folk wisdom is no longer relevant or valid. The form could not be further from the form of those typical modernist works which are, nevertheless, the point of reference of this novel—written as if it were a "timeless classic" yet informed by every discovery made by the novel in the first sixty years of the twentieth century. It is as if James Joyce set out to write a novel using the story-telling tone and narrative techniques of García Márquez's Aunt Francisca.[4]

There it is, then. A man who writes about village, nation and the world using the discoveries of the great Western myths (Greece, Rome, the Bible, the imported *Arabian Nights*), the great Western classics (Rabelais, Cervantes, Joyce) and the greatest precursors from his own continent (Borges, Asturias, Carpentier, Rulfo) to produce a work—a mirror—in which his own continent at last recognizes itself, and thus founds a tradition. If it was Borges who designed the viewfinder (like a belated brother Lumière), it is García Márquez who provides the first truly great collective portrait. So Latin Americans would not only recognize themselves but would now be recognized everywhere, universally. This was the meaning of the book Luisa Santiaga Márquez Iguarán de García's son was writing in his tiny smoke-filled room at his crude, diminutive writing desk in the midst of a vast and chaotic Third World city. His excitement was more than justified and its nervous, euphoric intensity is embedded in the pages of the book.

García Márquez's run of luck was by no means over; indeed, in a sense it would never end. After Luis Harss left Mexico at the end of June he had travelled on through various Latin American capitals and eventually arrived in Buenos Aires, where his book of interviews was to be edited by the prestigious publishing house Sudamericana. Harss's contact at Sudamericana was Francisco "Paco" Porrúa, who would later confess, "I had never heard of García Márquez until Harss mentioned him to me. And there he was, alongside Borges, Rulfo . . . and other greats. So the first thing that came into my head was, 'Who is he?'" He wrote to García Márquez enquiring about his books. Months later a deal would be struck.[5]

Early in September García Márquez had taken time off from his writing one afternoon to attend a talk by Carlos Fuentes about his new novel *A Change of Skin* (*Cambio de piel*) at the Instituto de Bellas Artes. At the end Fuentes had mentioned several of his friends, among them the Colombian, "to whom I am linked as much by our Sunday rituals as by my admiration for the ancient wisdom of this bard from Aracataca." Perhaps symbolically Fuentes asserted on this occasion that earning fame and fortune was a legitimate part of a writer's aspirations: "I do not think it is a writer's obligation to swell the ranks of the needy."[6] Afterwards Alvaro Mutis and his wife Carmen had invited Fuentes and Rita Macedo, Jomí García Ascot and María Luisa Elío, Fernando del Paso, Fernando Benítez and Elena Garro, as well as García Márquez and Mercedes, among others, to a paella in the Mutises' apartment in Río Amoy.[7] García Márquez had begun to relate anecdotes from his new novel on the way out from the talk, in the street, in the car and had continued in Mutis's apartment. Everyone had heard more than enough already and only María Luisa Elío continued to pay attention. In the tiny, crowded apartment María Luisa made him go on all evening telling her stories, most notably the one about the priest who takes chocolate in order to levitate. There and then—for listening with such rapt attention—he promised to dedicate the new novel to her. He had the skills of Scheherezade, she the beauty.

Latin American critics and journalists have been obsessed with this period ever since the publication of the novel in 1967. García Márquez's own brother Eligio devoted an entire book to the genesis and creation of the novel thirty years after it was published. Every single detail has been given cabbalistic, not to say fetishistic, significance. Yet the room where the writer worked could not have been less magical, though many people, years later, would want to call it "Melquíades's Room." The "Cave of the Mafia," as García Márquez himself dubbed it, was ten feet by eight feet with its own small bathroom adjoining and a door and a window on to a yard. There was a couch, an electric heater, some shelves and a very small, absolutely rudimentary table with an Olivetti typewriter on it. It was now that García Márquez took to wearing blue worker's overalls in order to write—he who had been getting quite conventional lately (even wearing ties). He had already made the revolutionary decision to move from night-time to day-time work. Now, instead of writing at the ad agency after a day's work or at the offices of the film studios, he worked in the mornings until the boys came home from school. Instead of the family demands crippling his creative faculties and cramping his style, they had now forced the change which would transform García Márquez's whole approach to work and self-discipline. Mercedes, previously a wife, mother and housekeeper, now became receptionist, secretary and business manager as well.[8] Little did she know it would be for ever. The new novel would benefit directly and dramatically from these changes.

García Márquez would drive his sons off to school in the morning, sit at his desk by 8.30 a.m. and work through until 2.30 p.m. when the boys got home. They would remember their father as a man who spent most of his time incarcerated in a small room, lost in blue cigarette smoke, a man who hardly noticed them, appeared only at meal times and answered their questions in a vague and distracted manner. They little suspected that he was inscribing this too into his all-consuming novel—José Arcadio Buendía's belated discovery of his own children, after his experimental obsessions, in chapter 1.

García Márquez would later recall, "From the first moment, long before it was published, the book exerted a magic power on everyone who in some way came into contact with it: friends, secretaries, etc., even people like the butcher or our landlord, who were waiting for me to finish so I would pay them."[9] He told Elena Poniatowska, "We owed the landlord eight months' rent. When we only owed three months, Mercedes called the owner and said, 'Look, we're not going to pay you these three months, nor the next six.' First she'd asked me, 'When do you think you'll finish?' and I said in about five more months. So to be sure she added an extra month and then the owner said to her, 'If you give me your word, all right, I'll wait until September.' And in September we went and paid him . . ."[10]

One of the many people waiting for García Márquez to finish was the long-suffering "Pera" (Esperanza) Araiza, a typist who worked for Barbachano and who also typed Fuentes's novels. Every few days García Márquez would take Pera another chunk of the novel, typed by him but heavily corrected by hand, and she would produce a clean fair copy. Since his own spelling was never better than shaky, he relied on Pera to clean up his literary act; but he nearly lost her and the start of the novel on the very first day when she was almost run over by a bus and the papers flew all over the wet streets of an autumnal Mexico City. Only much later did she confess that she invited her friends round each weekend to read the latest chapter.

Everything we know about this time suggests that García Márquez was indeed touched by magic. He was, at last, the magician he had always wanted to be. He was pumped up, high on literary narcotics. He was Aureliano Babilonia. He was Melquíades. Glory awaited him. The book was a grand mythological enterprise punctuated by rituals. Every evening, after his session with his notes, friends would come round. It was nearly always Alvaro Mutis and Carmen, Jomí García Ascot and María Luisa, supportive friends who for a whole year would turn into privileged witnesses and would watch the construction of one of the great edifices of Western literature. As the novel went on and he realized its scale, so his confidence and self-importance grew. By day he would sit in his smoky dungeon making it all up and in the afternoon he would consult the reference books and see how much of it could be true. Jomí and María Luisa could hardly wait for successive episodes. María Luisa particularly had grasped that she was witness to something of transcendental importance and was his most intimate confidante. He would later say that although she was admittedly entranced by his book, he in return was repeatedly stunned by her own insight

Colonel Nicolás
R. Márquez
(1864–1937),
GGM's maternal
grandfather,
c. 1914.

Tranquilina
Iguarán Cotes
de Márquez
(1863–1947),
GGM's maternal
grandmother.

Colonel Nicolás R. Márquez (*top left*) on a tropical day out, in style, in the 1920s.

Luisa Santiaga Márquez Iguarán
(1905–2002), GGM's mother,
before her marriage.

Gabriel Eligio García
(1901–1984), GGM's
father, and Luisa
Santiaga on their
wedding day, Santa
Marta, 11 June 1926.

Part of the Colonel's old house in Aracataca before any reconstruction work took place.

Elvira Carrillo ("Aunt Pa"), one of the aunts who looked after GGM and his sister Margot during their childhood in Aracataca.

GGM on his first birthday. This is the picture GGM chose for the cover of his 2002 autobiography.

(*Left to right*) Aida GM, Luis Enrique GM, Gabito, cousin Eduardo Márquez Caballero, Margot GM and baby Ligia GM, in Aracataca, 1936. The photograph was taken by the GM children's father, Gabriel Eligio.

The Liceo Nacional in Zipaquirá, where GGM studied between 1943 and 1946.

Gabito at the Colegio San José, Barranquilla, 1941.

The GM brothers, Luis Enrique and Gabito (*right*), with cousins and friends, Magangué, *c.* 1945.

Argemira García (1887–1950), paternal grandmother of GGM (*right*), in Sincé with her daughter Ena, who died in 1944 aged twenty-four, allegedly as a result of witchcraft.

GGM, the budding poet, Zipaquirá, mid-1940s.

Berenice Martínez, GGM's girlfriend in Zipaquirá, mid-1940s.

Mercedes Barcha at school in Medellín in the 1940s.

Steamship *David Arango*, on which GGM travelled to Bogotá from the Costa in the 1940s.

Fidel Castro (*left*) and other student leaders during the *Bogotazo*, April 1948.

Barranquilla, April 1950: farewell party for Ramón Vinyes. Drinkers include Germán Vargas (*top, third left*), Orlando Rivera ("Figurita") (*top right*), "Bob" Prieto (*seated first left*), GGM and Alfonso Fuenmayor (*centre*), next to Ramón Vinyes (*second from right*).

Barranquilla, 1950: (*from left*) GGM, Alvaro Cepeda, Alfredo Delgado, Rafael Escalona and Alfonso Fuenmayor in the *El Heraldo* office.

GGM, journalist at *El Espectador*, Bogotá, 1954.

GGM in the Hôtel de Flandre,
Paris, 1957.

Tachia Quintana, Paris.

GGM and friends (Luis Villar Borda, *standing left*), Red Square, Moscow, summer 1957.

The Soviet invasion of Hungary: Russian tanks on a
Budapest street in 1956. This was the moment when
socialists worldwide concluded that the USSR's problems
were not caused only by Stalin.

Caracas, 13
May 1958:
demonstrators
attack U.S.
Vice-President
Richard Nixon's
limousine. A
historic wake-up
call for U.S. Latin
America policy.

GGM working for Prensa Latina, Bogotá, 1959.

Mercedes Barcha in Barranquilla before her marriage to GGM.

Cuba, December 1958: Che Guevara and comrades relax after battle before marching into Havana.

GGM and Plinio Mendoza in Prensa Latina, Bogotá, 1959.

GGM and Mercedes on Séptima, Bogotá, 1960s.

Havana, January 1961: Cuban militia prepare for the expected U.S. invasion, at the time GGM arrives in New York to work for the revolution.

Havana, 21 April 1961: U.S.-backed invaders are taken to prison following defeat at Playa Girón (Bay of Pigs), at the time GGM is planning to leave Prensa Latina and travel to Mexico.

Mexico, 1964: GGM (in glasses, looking distinctly alienated) with Luis Buñuel (*front, second left*), Luis Alcoriza (*front, first left*), and (*top left to right*) Armando Bartra, unknown, unknown (probably Cesare Zavattini), Arturo Ripstein, Alberto Isaac and Claudio Isaac.

GGM in Aracataca, 1966, with accordionist: this improvised event was the seed of the later *vallenato* festivals in Valledupar.

Camilo Torres: university friend of GGM, baptized his first son Rodrigo, became Latin America's best-known revolutionary priest and died in action in 1966.

Valledupar, Colombia, 1967: (*left to right*) Clemente Quintero, Alvaro Cepeda, Roberto Pavajeau, GGM, Hernando Molina and Rafael Escalona.

Wizard or dunce? GGM in Barcelona, crowned by the famous cabbalistic cover of
One Hundred Years of Solitude, 1969.

Mercedes, Gabo, Gonzalo and Rodrigo, Barcelona, late 1960s.

into the worlds of magic and esoteric wisdom and that many of her perceptions eventually ended up in the book. He would call her at any time of the day to read the latest episode.[11]

A few months later García Márquez was invited by the cultural section of the Mexican Foreign Office to give a lecture and, where he would normally have refused, he in fact agreed, though specifying that he would like to give a literary reading rather than a talk. Always self-critical and concerned with the quality of his work, he had become anxious that he was now lost in a world of his own with Alvaro and María Luisa and that their enthusiasm for his ideas might have hypnotized him:

> I sat down to read on the illuminated stage; the stalls with "my" audience completely in the dark. I started to read, I can't remember which chapter, but I went on reading and at a given moment there was such silence in the hall and I was in such a state of tension that I panicked. I stopped reading and tried to peer through the darkness and after a few seconds I could see the faces of those in the front row and on the contrary, I could see they had their eyes open wide, like this, and so I was able to go on calmly with the reading. Really people were hanging on my words; not a fly buzzed. When I finished and stepped down from the stage, the first person to embrace me was Mercedes, with an expression on her face—I think it was the first time since I married her that I realized she loved me, because she looked at me with such an expression on her face! . . . She'd been managing on virtually nothing for a year so that I could write and the day of that reading the expression on her face gave me the certainty that the book was heading in the right direction.[12]

Mercedes went on fighting her own campaign to keep the family finances afloat. By early 1966 the money set aside from previous earnings had gone but although her husband's writer's block was a thing of the past, the book just got bigger and bigger and seemed set to go on right through the year. Finally García Márquez drove the white Opel to a car pound in Tacubaya and came back with another large sum.[13] Now their friends had to drive them around. He even considered letting the telephone go, not only to save the money but to avoid his greatest distraction: talking endlessly to his friends on the phone. When the money for the car ran out Mercedes began to pawn everything: television, fridge, radio, jewellery. Her three last "military positions" were her hairdryer, the liquidizer for the boys' meals and Gabo's electric fire. She bought her meat from Don Felipe, the butcher, on ever more elastic credit; she persuaded Luis Coudurier, the landlord, to wait even longer for the rent. And their friends brought regular supplies of every description. They kept the record player, though. García Márquez could not at this stage in his life compose a novel while music was playing; but he could not live without music either and his beloved Bartók, Debussy's *Preludes* and the Beatles' *Hard Day's Night* were in the background of most of what he did in those times.

His worst day in the entire writing was the death of Colonel Aureliano Buendía (chapter 13). Like many writers he experienced the loss of his principal character as a personal bereavement, perhaps even as a homicide. The narration of the death is invested with some of García Márquez's own most poignant childhood memories and, though the critics have not realized it, the novelist had put more of himself into this apparently unsympathetic character than into any other in his fiction before that time. Aureliano, although the second child, is "the first human being to be born in Macondo"; he is born in March, like García Márquez; born, moreover, with his eyes open, eyes which gaze around that house the moment he emerges from the womb, as little Gabito's were said to have done. From early childhood he is clairvoyant, just as Gabito is reputed to be in his family. He falls in love with a little girl (and marries her before she reaches puberty); but after her death he is "incapable of love" and acts only out of "sinful pride." Though capable of great empathy and even kindness as a young man (and though a writer of love poetry—which later embarrasses him), Aureliano is solitary, egocentric and ruthless; nothing can stand in the way of his personal ambition. In Aureliano Buendía, then, García Márquez fuses selected memories of Colonel Márquez (the war, the workshop, the little gold fish) with a self-portrait which amounts to a self-critique; a self-critique which amounts to a perception that he has now achieved his lifelong ambition but that the quest to do so has been calculating, all-consuming and ultimately narcissistic and egotistical. The vocation for writing (for becoming Melquíades), which he would later stress so strongly in *Living to Tell the Tale*, in fact screens another more elemental and perhaps less palatable instinct, the will to triumph and the desire for fame, glory and riches (Colonel Aureliano Buendía). *The Autumn of the Patriarch* would take this self-critique to even more surprising lengths.

At two in the morning, after the deed was done, he went up to the bedroom, where Mercedes was fast asleep, lay down and wept for two hours.[14] It requires little biographical insight to suppose that in killing off his central character he was brought to confront not only his own mortality and the end of this novel but also the end of a uniquely euphoric experience—indeed, the end of an entire era of his life and of a person he had been, and the end of a particular inexpressible relationship with the most important person in his life, his grandfather (now lost for ever because literature could not resurrect him). Now, irony of ironies, García Márquez was back, in the midst of his triumphs, to being the man envisaged by his first stories, a man doomed to multiple, successive deaths as he left behind each moment of his life and each object and person that he had loved. Except his wife and children.

Although he has always given the impression that he stayed in his smoke-filled room until the book was completed, the opportunity of travelling to Colombia at someone else's expense arose and, after much consideration, he decided to take the opportunity. He had persuaded the Ripsteins to enter *Tiempo de morir* in the Cartagena Film Festival and travelled by cruise liner from Veracruz to Cartagena, arriving on 1 March 1966 (two weeks after the death in combat of his friend Camilo Torres, now a guerrilla). The film won first prize at the festival, despite García Márquez's own doubts about the job Ripstein had done. He had much to celebrate on 6 March: the triumph of his movie, the prospects for his novel, and his thirty-ninth birthday back home with the family in Cartagena. He made a brief visit to Bogotá and then flew in to Barranquilla, where Plinio Mendoza was now living. Mendoza received a phone call at work.

"Gabo, great to hear your voice, where are you?"

"Sitting in your house, asshole, having a whisky."[15]

He told Mendoza and Alvaro Cepeda about his novel: "It's nothing like the others, *compadres*. This time I've finally let my hair down. Either I'm going to make my big hit or fall flat on my face." During the visit he walked round the old haunts in Barranquilla with Alfonso Fuenmayor, reliving old times and reminding himself of places and faces. To complete the whirlwind tour, he returned to Aracataca for the first time in a decade.[16] This time he travelled not with his mother but with Alvaro Cepeda, in a jeep driven by Cepeda himself. They were conveniently accompanied on their quest for time past by the Barranquilla correspondent of *El Tiempo*, who wrote a detailed report: suddenly García Márquez was being converted into a folk hero by the media—prior to his further metamorphosis into a superstar.[17]

He had intended to stay several weeks but embarked for Mexico

after a few days, arriving towards the end of March. Alfonso Fuenmayor protested at his departure, and García Márquez explained that
the night before he left he had suddenly seen the end of his novel so
clearly that he could dictate it word for word to a typist. He locked
himself away in that room again, and set about assimilating what had
just happened to him. The ending that had occurred to him—which
speaks perhaps to a sense of how much he had moved on and how
much his Colombian friends had not—was one of the greatest conclusions to a novel in all of literature.

One Hundred Years of Solitude was a book that had a publisher almost
from the moment it was started. It had a daily audience of enthusiasts
on whom its author could count. And the euphoric writer was hardly in
need of encouragement: he was a man possessed. Possessed of creative
powers of literature pulsing through him and possessed of the certainty
that the work's success was in the stars, preordained. James Joyce's
Ulysses is the closest example of a mythic book which the cognoscenti
knew was coming and which they knew was destined for greatness; but
Joyce had no publisher and could never expect to be a best-selling
author. Yet so confident was the normally hyper-cautious García
Márquez that, far from succumbing to the superstitions that usually
restrained him, during his visit to Bogotá in March he had given his old
colleagues in El Espectador the first chapter, which they published on 1
May. Carlos Fuentes, by now back in Paris, received the first three
chapters in June 1966 and was dazzled.[18] He passed them to his friend
Julio Cortázar. The reaction was the same. Then Fuentes passed chapter 2 to Emir Rodríguez Monegal to publicize it in the first edition of a
new literary magazine, Mundo Nuevo, in Paris in August 1966.

In an interview with the editor, Fuentes announced that he had just
received the first seventy-five pages of García Márquez's "work in
progress" (the reference to Joyce was unmistakable) and considered it
without the slightest doubt an absolute masterpiece which immediately consigned all previous Latin American regional classics to a dusty
past.

Then Fuentes sent an article to La Cultura en México (¡Siempre!)
announcing to his compatriots also, on 29 June, that One Hundred Years
of Solitude was coming and was a great novel (García Márquez probably
hadn't even finished it): "I have just read eighty magisterial pages: the
first eighty pages of One Hundred Years of Solitude, the novel Gabriel
García Márquez is working on."[19] People could hardly express their
astonishment. There were no precedents for what was happening.

In view of the climate of expectation, it was as well that García Márquez was able to finish the novel. He told Plinio Mendoza: "The book arrived at its natural end in a rush, at eleven in the morning. Mercedes was out and I couldn't find anyone on the telephone to tell the news. I remember my confusion as if it were yesterday: I didn't know what to do with myself and tried to make something up to survive until three o'clock in the afternoon!"[20] Later that day a blue cat came into the house and the writer thought, "Hmmm, maybe this book is going to sell." Minutes later the two boys came in with brushes and blue paint all over their hands and clothes.

His first act was to send a copy off to Germán Vargas in Bogotá, prior to sending the manuscript to Sudamericana. García Márquez asked Vargas if he thought it was all right to have made references to himself and his friends in Barranquilla. First Vargas, then Fuenmayor, replied that they were honoured to be friends of the last of the Buendías. Then Vargas, in that slow way of his, digested the book and wrote an article entitled "A Book That Will Make a Noise," which he published in April 1967 in *Encuentro Liberal*, the weekly he himself edited in Bogotá; Vargas's own essay itself made a noise and was the first Colombian prediction of the novel's future status.[21] Plinio Mendoza also received a copy in Barranquilla and, cancelling work for the day, read it from start to finish. He told his new wife Marvel Moreno, an ex–beauty queen and future novelist, "He's done it. Gabo's made the big hit he wanted." Plinio passed it on to Alvaro Cepeda. Alvaro read it, took the cigar out of his mouth, and shouted, "No shit, Gabo's pulled off a helluva novel."[22]

The way García Márquez has always told it, his return to the world was almost as dramatic and confusing as that of Rip Van Winkle.[23] It was the year of Swinging London. Indira Gandhi was now running the largest democracy on earth and Fidel Castro, in whose company García Márquez would meet that same Indian leader many years later, was busy organizing the first Tricontinental Conference of Asian, African and Latin American States to be held in Havana in August 1967. A right-wing actor called Ronald Reagan was running for Governor of California. China was in uproar and Mao would proclaim the Cultural Revolution a few days after García Márquez sent the first tranche of his precious package to Buenos Aires. In fact García Márquez himself had to leave the magical world of Macondo in a hurry and begin to make some money. He felt unable to take even a week off to celebrate. He was afraid that it might take him years to pay off the debts he had accumulated. He would say later that he had written 1,300 pages of which he had finally sent 490 to Porrúa; that he had smoked 30,000 cigarettes and owed 120,000 pesos. Understandably, he still felt insecure. Soon after he had finished it he attended a party at his English friend James Papworth's house. Papworth enquired about the book and García Márquez replied, "I've either got a novel or just a kilo of paper, I'm still not sure which."[24] He went straight back to working on film scripts. Then, in his first article for five years, dated July 1966 and still not written for consumption in Mexico, García Márquez wrote a self-referential meditation for *El Espectador* entitled "Misfortunes of a Writer of Books":

> Writing books is a suicidal profession. No other demands as much time, as much work, as much dedication, by comparison with its immediate benefits. I don't think many readers finishing a book ask themselves how many hours of anguish and domestic calamities those two hundred pages have cost the author or how much he received for his work . . . After this grim assessment of misfortunes, it is elementary to ask why we writers write. The reply, inevitably, is as melodramatic as it is sincere. One is a writer, simply, as one is a Jew or a Black. Success is encouraging, the favour of one's readers is stimulating, but these are mere additional gains because a good writer will go on writing anyway, even though his shoes need mending and even if his books don't sell.[25]

The new García Márquez, the first sight of whom could be glimpsed in the interviews he gave when he arrived in Cartagena the previous March, has been born. He has started to say almost the exact opposite of what he means. He writes about his misfortunes because his misfortunes are almost over. The man who never complained, never made a fuss in even the most straitened circumstances, is intending to make a fuss henceforth about everything—not least about the cupidity of publishers and booksellers, a topic that will become an obsession. Here he is, the García Márquez who will endlessly fascinate the public and permanently irritate the critics, particularly those who will be convinced that he does not deserve his success and that they, who are far more sophisticated, far less vulgar and far more important literarily speaking, should have his glittering prizes. This new personage—a true man of the sixties, apparently—is provocative, opinionated, demagogic, hypocritical, wilfully uncouth and yet impossible to pin down; but the people will love him for all this because he seems to be one of them, making it big and getting away with it thanks to his wit, which is their wit, their view of the world.

Around the same time, soon after completing the novel, García Márquez wrote a long letter to Plinio Mendoza. It begins with a striking statement of his feelings at the time and then moves on to an explanation of his newly finished masterpiece and what it means to him:

> After so many years of working like an animal I feel overwhelmed by tiredness, without clear prospects, except in the only thing that I like but which doesn't feed me: the novel. My decision, which speaks to an overwhelming impulse, is to arrange things any way I have to in order to go on writing my stuff. Believe me, dramatic or not, I don't know what's going to happen.
>
> What you've said about the first chapter of *One Hundred Years of Solitude* has made me very happy. That's why I published it. When I got back from Colombia and read what I'd already written I suddenly had the demoralizing feeling that I was embarked on an adventure that could as easily be catastrophic as successful. So to find out how it would be viewed by other eyes I sent that chapter to Guillermo Cano and here I brought together the most demanding, expert and candid people and I read them another one. The result was great, above all because the chapter I read was the riskiest: Remedios the Beauty's ascent to heaven, in body and soul . . .
>
> I'm trying to answer, without any modesty, your question as to how I write my things. In reality *One Hundred Years of Solitude* was the first novel I tried to write, when I was seventeen, entitled "The House," which I gave up after a while because it was too much for me. Since then I've never stopped thinking about it, trying to see it mentally, to find the most effective way of narrating it, and I can tell you that the first paragraph hasn't a comma more or less than the first paragraph written twenty years ago. My conclusion from all of this is that when you have a topic that pursues you it starts growing in your head for a long time and the day it explodes you have to sit down at the typewriter or run the risk of murdering your wife . . .[26]

The letter makes it clear that in writing all this he is partly preparing himself to defend his views—and his novel—in public and that he is expecting a parallel high-profile career in journalism. He also says he now has three different projects for novels which are "pushing" him.

In early August, two weeks after writing that letter, García Márquez accompanied Mercedes to the post office to mail the finished manuscript to Buenos Aires. They were like two survivors of a catastrophe. The package contained 490 typed pages. The counter official said: "Eighty-two pesos." García Márquez watched as Mercedes searched in her purse for the money. They only had fifty and could only send about half of the book: García Márquez made the man behind the counter take sheets off like slices of bacon until the fifty pesos were enough. They went home, pawned the heater, hairdryer and liquidizer, went back to the post office and sent the second tranche. As they came out of the post office Mercedes stopped and turned to her husband: "Hey, Gabo, all we need now is for the book to be no good."[27]

16

Fame at Last

1966~1967

GARCÍA MÁRQUEZ HIMSELF was less anxious about the book's eventual success than whether the two packages would even arrive in Buenos Aires. Alvaro Mutis had been working as the Latin American representative of 20th Century Fox for a year and was shortly off to Argentina; García Márquez asked him to take another copy to Paco Porrúa in the Sudamericana office in Buenos Aires. Mutis phoned Porrúa on arrival and said he had the manuscript. Porrúa said: "Forget it. I've already read it, and it's absolutely brilliant."[1] If Porrúa thought the book was "absolutely brilliant," it was likely to be a sensation.

Back in Mexico City García Márquez had all his daily notes and his family trees written in forty school notebooks. He and Mercedes claim to have torn them up and burned them as soon as they heard the manuscript had arrived safely in Argentina. They were mainly about structural and procedural questions, he has said. His friends, much more aware of academic and historical considerations, were appalled and said he should not have destroyed them but rather saved them for posterity (or even, as things turned out, to make a handy profit out of them).[2] But García Márquez has always defended himself by explaining his sense of embarrassment ("pudor"), which means that he would no more want people to sift over his literary scraps than his household scraps or bits of gossip about his family intimacies. "It's like being caught in your underwear."[3] Of course there is also something about the artist—or the magician—wanting to protect the tricks of the trade.

Unfortunately for biographers he has the same attitude to revealing the most innocent details about his own life. He has always wanted to control the version of his life that would be told—or tell several versions so that no one version can ever be told—as if to cover over for ever the feelings of loss, betrayal, abandonment and inferiority that came to him from his childhood.

He was already being talked about as the fourth member of that small band of brothers who were leading the Latin American narrative vanguard to international attention through the so-called literary Boom. These four writers—Cortázar, Fuentes, Vargas Llosa and, from this moment, García Márquez—would receive unparalleled publicity in the years to come but at that particular time the movement had not entirely gelled and no one writer had emerged as what might be called the brand leader of this extraordinary range of new products. But his peers already knew; metaphorically, they had already bowed their heads: Gabriel García Márquez was it. Nothing would ever be the same again in Latin America after the publication of *One Hundred Years of Solitude*. The first people to realize this were the Argentinians.

Argentina, in terms of high culture, was the leading nation in Latin America. Buenos Aires, its glamorous cosmopolitan capital, where García Márquez's novel was soon to be published, was something like a fusion of Paris and London in the New World. Literary culture there was intense and sometimes pretentious but the quality of debate was always high and its influence on the rest of Latin America undeniable, particularly after the Spanish Civil War when the mother country ceased to have significant intellectual or literary impact on the great continent to the south. When García Márquez read Kafka in Bogotá in 1947, and so many other writers in Barranquilla between 1950 and 1953, it was invariably in Argentinian editions that he did so. Losada had turned down his first novel fifteen years before; now his early dream was about to come true and that early wrong was about to be righted: he was about to be published in Buenos Aires.

Down in the Argentinian capital the publishers at Sudamericana were making no secret of the fact that they thought they had a Latin American prodigy—and possibly a critical sensation—on their hands. As it happened, the name García Márquez had already received a modest amount of publicity in Buenos Aires over the preceding months. Around the middle of 1966 the Jorge Alvarez Editorial published *The Ten Commandments (Los diez mandamientos)*, an anthology of Latin American short stories which included "There Are No Thieves in This

Town." This book, which was an early attempt to cash in on the grow-ing Boom, was a best-seller throughout the second half of 1966.[4] The publishers had invited each writer to give a literary self-portrait. Gar-cía Márquez's was emblematic of his new approach to self-advertising once he became convinced that he was about to become a literary suc-cess:

My name, Señor, is Gabriel García Márquez. I'm sorry: I don't like the name either because it is a string of commonplaces I've never been able to connect to myself. I was born in Aracataca, Colombia, forty years ago and I'm still not sorry. My sign is Pisces and my wife Mercedes. Those are the two most impor-tant things that have happened in my life because thanks to them, at least until now, I've been able to survive by writing.

I am a writer through timidity. My true vocation is that of magician, but I get so flustered trying to do tricks that I've had to take refuge in the solitude of literature. Both activities, in any case, lead to the only thing that has interested me since I was a child: that my friends should love me more.

In my case, being a writer is an exceptional achievement because I am very bad at writing. I have had to subject myself to an atrocious discipline in order to finish half a page after eight hours of work; I fight physically with every word and it is almost always the word that wins, but I am so stubborn that I have man-aged to publish four books in twenty years. The fifth, which I am writing now, is going slower than the others, because between my debtors and my headaches I have very little free time.

I never talk about literature because I don't know what it is and besides I'm convinced the world would be just the same without it. On the other hand, I'm convinced it would be com-pletely different without the police. I therefore think I'd have been much more useful to humanity if instead of being a writer I'd been a terrorist.[5]

Here, patently, was a writer expecting to be famous. Once more he had mainly said the opposite of the truth in a way calculated to make himself not only more visible but also more lovable. The image is of the ordinary guy with—implicitly, sheepishly—the extraordinary gift. The contrast between the surface timidity and self-deprecation and the underlying confidence and desire for attention is notable, and would irritate future adversaries beyond measure. Readers of the statement would also have divined that this ordinary guy was politically progressive too, though with a great sense of humour about politics and everything else. He was a man of his age, a man of the moment. Who, reading this, would not look out for his books?

Argentina's most influential weekly magazine at the time was *Primera Plana*. Its editor was Porrúa's friend the writer Tomás Eloy Martínez, who would later become a good friend of García Márquez himself. *Primera Plana* was a major opinion former and sold 60,000 copies a week. Its proprietors were always looking for the next big cultural sensation and in December 1966, primed by Paco Porrúa, they decided to send Ernesto Schóo, their star reporter and a member of the editorial board, to interview García Márquez in Mexico. Given the cost of air fares in those days this was quite an investment for any magazine but *Primera Plana* trusted Porrúa and knew what they were about. The Argentinian journalist effectively lived with the García Barcha family in Mexico for an entire week. When the magazine eventually published his piece six months later it put García Márquez on the cover, not in his own unglamorous street but in the picturesque cobbled lanes of old San Angel. The photos were taken by Schóo himself and showed García Márquez clowning about in typical sixties style wearing his familiar black and red checked jacket. This was not the way Argentinian writers dressed, it was more Jack Kerouac; soon it would just be García Márquez; then "Gabo." So instead of the gloomy writer described by Luis Harss in that influential book published only a few weeks before Schóo's interview, Schóo's pictures would show a happy, indeed euphoric, novelist essentially at home in the world.[6]

In April Mario Vargas Llosa, who had recently published his scintillating second novel *The Green House*, rode one of his own hobby horses into battle by announcing that García Márquez's forthcoming book was, not Latin America's "Bible," as Carlos Fuentes had asserted, but Latin America's great "novel of chivalry." Vargas Llosa must have been stunned by the sudden appearance of this unexpected rival from Colombia but, like Fuentes, he opted, appropriately enough, for the chivalrous approach. His groundbreaking article, "Amadís in America," appeared in *Primera Plana* in April and declared that *One Hundred Years of Solitude* was at one and the same time a family saga and an adventure story: "A sharply focused prose, an infallible technical wizardry and a diabolical imagination are the weapons which have made this narrative deed possible, the secret of this exceptional book."[7]

The Argentinians decided to give García Márquez the full treatment. He was invited to visit Buenos Aires in June, both to publicize the novel and as the member of a jury of the *Primera Plana*/Sudamericana fiction prize. In the interim both Sudamericana and *Primera Plana* redoubled their efforts to publicize the novel. *One Hundred Years of Solitude* was finally printed on 30 May 1967. It was 352 pages long and cost 650 pesos, about U.S.$2. The initial idea had been to produce the standard print run of 3,000 copies, high by Latin American standards but fairly normal in Argentina. But the overwhelming enthusiasm of Fuentes, Vargas Llosa and Cortázar, plus Porrúa's own intuition, made them take a chance. So they moved to 5,000; but demand from booksellers for pre-publication copies put it up to 8,000 two weeks before printing. They expected these to sell in six months if things went well. After a week the book had sold 1,800 copies and was third in the list of best-sellers, an unheard-of achievement for a Latin American novel by a virtually unknown writer. By the end of the second week it had tripled that number in Buenos Aires alone and was out in first place, with the initial print run of 8,000 now looking totally inadequate.

Ironically enough, *Primera Plana* itself, after all the staff's efforts, was a little slow out of the blocks. The intention had been to publish Schóo's six-month-old report with García Márquez's picture on the front page of the edition for the week 13 to 19 June but the Six Day War in the Middle East broke out on the 5th at 3.10 a.m. Buenos Aires time and García Márquez's moment was postponed until the 29th. Inside the magazine a note introducing the issue said that this was not just an extraordinary event but that it (the book but also, implicitly, this issue of *Primera Plana*) was the baptismal font from which the new Latin American novel would emerge. Schóo's essay was entitled "The Journeys of Sinbad," implicitly comparing García Márquez's work from the outset with the *One Thousand and One Nights* which had indeed been so important in the fashioning of his imagination. Magic was in the air. Between the book being printed and going on sale the Beatles' *Sergeant Pepper*, also destined for mythical status, appeared in record shops all over the world.

García Márquez had tried to placate his friend Vicente Rojo, sore at the Colombian not selling the book to his friends at Era in Mexico, by inviting him to design the cover. Rojo worked hard to communicate the chaotic, multiple, popular flavour of the novel. He put the E of SOLEDAD backwards, leading in due course to the most recondite and esoteric theories of literary critics and to a letter from a bookseller in Guayaquil protesting the receipt of defective copies which he had had to correct by hand so as not to annoy his customers.[8] Rojo's cover would eventually appear on more than a million copies of the book, and become a Latin American cultural icon; but it did not appear in the first printing because it failed to arrive in time. So for the first edition a house designer, Iris Pagano, drew up a blueish galleon floating in a blueish jungle against a grey background, with three orange flowers blooming beneath the ship. This is the cover which collectors would later seek for their transactions, not the much more sophisticated cover designed by one of Mexico's leading artists. The second, third and fourth editions in June, September and December each carried Rojo's design and were produced in print runs of 20,000 copies, a phenomenon without precedent in the history of Latin American publishing.

In early June García Márquez was interviewed in Mexico by *Visión*, the Latin American equivalent of *Time*, and the only magazine sold all over the continent (though published, significantly enough, from Washington). García Márquez told his interviewers that he was planning to take his family for two years to "a beach resort near Barcelona."[9] He repeated the now familiar story that he had started *One Hundred Years of Solitude* when he was "seventeen" but that the "package" was too big for him to manage. But he also said something surprising: "When I finish writing a book it no longer interests me. As Hemingway said: 'Every finished book is like a dead lion.' The problem then is how to hunt an elephant." García Márquez tired of *One Hundred Years of Solitude*: could he be serious! The statement was published in other magazines and newspapers all over Latin America and was typical of a new journalistic phenomenon: the *boutade à la* García Márquez.[10] It was a multiple contradiction in terms: consciously nonchalant, and irritating to his critics for that and other reasons; as knowingly hypocritical as a wink of the eye, with a kind of my-way arrogance passing for modesty; all wrapped up in a popular witticism allowing its author to escape from aggression with the effortless elegance of a Chaplinesque pirouette—and yet, underneath, and paradoxically, it would always contain some undeniable kernel of truth.

García Márquez and Mercedes set off for Argentina on 19 June to begin to meet their destiny. He had confessed to Plinio Mendoza that he was "as frightened as a cockroach" and looking for "a bed big enough for me to hide under."[11] They flew first to Colombia and left their two sons with their maternal grandmother on the way. The boys, both effectively Mexicans, would not return to their home country for many years. On the plane to Buenos Aires their parents discussed their options for the future and Mercedes must have reflected on the promises Gabo had made about his future objectives when they took their first flight together almost ten years before. He had indeed now written "the novel of his life" at the age of forty. On 20 June they landed at Ezeiza Airport in Buenos Aires at three in the morning, three weeks after the publication of the novel. Despite their clandestine arrival, Paco Porrúa recalls that the whole city seemed to be in party mode, having "succumbed immediately to the novel's seductive charm."[12] He and Martínez were there to greet the unsuspecting couple, whose life had changed more even than they knew. Far from exhausted by the journey, García Márquez asked to see the pampas and to eat an Argentine grilled steak.[13] As a compromise they took him to a restaurant on Montevideo Street. As they tried to accustom themselves to this man from the tropics, with his psychedelic lumberjack's overcoat, his tight Italian trousers, his Cuban boots, his black-capped teeth and his curious mixture of sententiousness and nonchalance, they persuaded themselves that this indeed was what the author of *One Hundred Years of Solitude* had to look like. As for his wife, she was a wonderful apparition who looked like an Amerindian version of Queen Nefertiti.[14]

García Márquez was dazzled by Buenos Aires—his first experience, he would say, of a Latin American metropolis that didn't look "unfinished." One morning he saw a woman with a copy of the novel stuffed in her shopping bag, between the tomatoes and lettuces, as he breakfasted in a café on a street corner. His book, already "popular" in both senses of the word, was being received "not like a novel but like life."[15] That same night he and Mercedes went to an event in the theatre of the Instituto Di Tella, the motor for Argentinian cultural life in that era. Tomás Eloy Martínez has recorded the moment when García Márquez became, for ever, a character in a story he had written in advance, like his character Melquíades, without knowing it: "Mercedes and Gabo moved towards the stage, disconcerted by so many early furs and shimmering feathers. The auditorium was in shadow but for some reason a spotlight followed them. They were about to sit down when someone shouted 'Bravo!' and broke into applause. A woman echoed the shout. 'For your novel!' she said. The entire theatre stood up. At that precise moment I saw fame come down from the sky, wrapped in a dazzling flapping of sheets, like Remedios the Beautiful, and bathe García Márquez in one of those winds of light that are immune to the ravages of time."[16]

Martínez says that García Márquez wove his magic all over Buenos

Aires. He was just about to leave a party one evening by the banks of the Río de la Plata when he noticed "a young woman who was almost levitating with happiness. García Márquez said, 'That young woman is really sad but doesn't know how to realize it. Wait a moment, I'm going to help her to cry.' He whispered a few secret words in the young woman's ear. Huge uncontrollable tears sprang from her eyes. 'How could you tell she was sad?' I asked him later. 'What did you say to make her cry?' 'I told her not to feel so alone.' 'She felt alone?' 'Of course. Have you ever known a woman who didn't feel alone?'" Martínez continues, "I met him again, furtively, the night before his departure. They had told him that in a glade in the Palermo woods, couples would hide in dark fiery caves where they could kiss one another freely. 'It's a place they call El Tiradero, Fuck Corner,' he ventured. 'Villa Cariño, Love's Abode,' I translated. 'Mercedes and I are desperate,' he said. 'Every time we try to kiss one another someone interrupts.'"[17]

García Márquez could not possibly know just how famous he was going to be but he must have had some inkling. Back in Mexico City, he and Mercedes began to make plans and wind up their affairs. They were resolved to exercise their new-found freedom. Faced by the sudden, totally new perspective of celebrity and possibly even financial security, García Márquez had decided that he would leave Mexico and move to Spain. And he was in a hurry.

The novel was published in Mexico City, on 2 July, six years after the family had arrived in the country.[18] María Luisa Elío, to whom it had been dedicated, recalls: "We went crazy. He brought me a copy, then we went from bookstore to bookstore buying books for my friends and making him write dedications. Gabo told me, 'You're heading for financial ruin.' I was buying all the copies I could afford. We went to Gabo's house and drank toasts with Mercedes. The following day, well, we didn't have any money back then, neither do we have any nowadays, but we manage . . . You probably remember there's a passage in *One Hundred Years of Solitude* . . . where it rained yellow daisies. Well, that day I bought a large basket, the largest I could find, and I filled it with yellow daisies. I had on a gold bracelet, so I took it off and put it in the basket, then looked for a little gold fish and a bottle of whisky. I put it all in the basket and we went to their house."[19] This tendency to turn the world of reality into the magical world of *One Hundred Years of Solitude* would gather pace like a snowball and would before too long make the author himself utterly weary of the constructions placed on his extraordinary novel. He would eventually himself wish to move on from the sixties but he would find himself endlessly dragged back there.

On 1 August he left for Caracas to attend the 13th International Congress of Ibero-American Literature organized by the University of Pittsburgh, which was to coincide with the presentation of the newly created Rómulo Gallegos prize to Mario Vargas Llosa for his 1966 novel *The Green House*. Their planes from London and Mexico landed almost simultaneously at Maiquetía and they met, symbolically enough, in the airport: both men would be taking many flights in the years to come.[20] There had already been correspondence. Now they became room-mates. It was to be a profound but ultimately turbulent literary friendship. García Márquez felt overwhelmed. He had not written a script for this eventuality. He was a late arrival at the banquet of the Boom—although nine years younger, Mario Vargas Llosa, who had lived in Europe since 1959, already knew most of the other writers both in Paris and Barcelona; he was handsome, debonair, critically sophisticated (he had been working towards a PhD), yet he knew how to wow the literary masses. In the face of this unmistakable star quality García Márquez, the new sensation, suddenly felt nervy, intimidated, defensive. At one party he had his Venezuelan friends put up a sign saying "Forbidden to speak of *One Hundred Years of Solitude*." Nevertheless he also acted up for the press: he told them, straight-faced, that Mercedes wrote his books but made him sign them because they were so bad. And, asked whether the local sacred cow, ex-President Rómulo Gallegos, was a great novelist, he replied: "In his novel *Canaima* there's a description of a chicken that's really quite good."[21] Now García Márquez would begin to meet everybody who was anybody; now that there was a García Márquez, there could really be a Boom; now, there could be anything. This man was magic. His book was magic—his name was magic: "Gabo" was a Warhol-era dream and not just for fifteen minutes.

Emir Rodríguez Monegal told García Márquez that two days before flying to Caracas he had been in the Coupole in Paris with Fuentes and Pablo Neruda; Fuentes was giving Neruda a rave review of *One Hundred Years of Solitude*, predicting that it would be as important for Latin America as Cervantes's *Don Quixote* had been for Spain.[22]

The Gabo–Mario show moved on to Bogotá on 12 August. *One Hundred Years of Solitude* had still not begun to circulate there and there had been little feedback from Buenos Aires. Neither *El Espectador* nor

El Tiempo published anything about the novel in the early weeks. It was almost as if Colombians were deliberately withholding their interest; as if they were waiting until it was impossible to ignore this astonishing phenomenon in their midst. The truth is that he would never be as much appreciated in his home country as in other parts of Latin America.[23] Plinio Mendoza had travelled up to Bogotá with Cepeda: "I remember that just before *One Hundred Years of Solitude* was published in Colombia García Márquez came to Bogotá with Mario Vargas Llosa. Mario had just won the Rómulo Gallegos prize in Caracas with *The Green House*. As happens with all the personalities who turn up there, 'le tout Bogotá' rushed out to celebrate him. There were all those people fluttering, bubbling around him, always attending to the etiquette of success, still unaware of the bomb García Márquez had made, still valuing the home writer in quite modest terms; and leaving him discreetly in the background."[24]

Vargas Llosa left for Lima on 15 August but the show went on again when García Márquez joined him there for a week of literary events at the start of September. The friendship was symbolically cemented when García Márquez acted as godfather to Mario and Patricia Vargas Llosa's second son, named Gonzalo Gabriel.

He was back in Cartagena by the end of September and took the opportunity to visit Valledupar with Alvaro Cepeda and Rafael Escalona. A young woman called Consuelo Araujonoguera had organised a small *vallenato* festival similar to the improvised event García Márquez and Cepeda had arranged in Aracataca the previous year; the event would acquire permanent status the following year. After it was over García Márquez began to finalize arrangements for the departure. It was good to see the Colombian families before leaving but despite all the water that had flowed under their respective bridges, the relationship between García Márquez and his father seemed beyond repair. Eligio would recall, "In October 1967 Gabito was in Cartagena with Mercedes and the two boys. I can still feel how embarrassed I was to see Gabito sitting there on a bed, totally intimidated by my father, who was lying in the hammock. It was as if my father inspired some indescribable fear, almost a terror, which was a false impression (the family profession!); later, talking it over with Jaime and Gabito, we came to the conclusion that Gabito just didn't know how to behave in front of him."[25] No truer word was ever said. But the reason was no longer fear, one can be sure. One can also be sure that the father was still not giving the son due credit for his achievements, even though it now looked as if, far from eating paper, Gabito could perhaps start eating banknotes; and one can be equally sure that the son, that "peripatetic spermatozoa," would not have welcomed the belated credit anyway. He still saw Gabriel Eligio as his stepfather.

No doubt politics remained among the difficulties between them. In September Governor Ronald Reagan of California had urged the escalation of the American war in Vietnam and divisions were growing all across the Western world. Presumably García Márquez and his father discussed the death of Che Guevara, whom Gabito had briefly met in Havana, which was announced to the world by the Bolivian High Command on 10 October. This painful news was perhaps compounded shortly afterwards by the announcement that another father figure always rejected by García Márquez, Guatemalan writer Miguel Angel Asturias, had been awarded the Nobel Prize for Literature, the first Latin American novelist ever to be so honoured. (A poet, the Chilean Gabriela Mistral, had won in 1945.) This was obviously interpreted all over the world as a symbolic acknowledgement of the ongoing Boom of the Latin American novel. Asturias and García Márquez, the two greatest "magical realists" who seemed to have so much in common, would soon come to cordially detest one another. Asturias, belatedly crowned, would fear the young pretender, and García Márquez, newly acclaimed, would seem bent on parricide.[26]

There is undoubtedly a sense that he fled to Europe to give himself freedom from day-to-day pressure and room to manoeuvre and regroup. Journalists were asking him his opinion about everything under the sun, but above all about politics. It would be a mistake, however, to think that his intention was to escape from political commitment altogether. He was lucid enough to realize that he could only be influential if he was writing successful novels; thus the first thing was to ensure himself the time and space to write the next one—not least because the next one, like *One Hundred Years of Solitude*, had already been a long time coming. Of course García Márquez was now able to act more overtly and to take symbolic stands that would have interested nobody just a few short months before. In November, just before his departure, and in the face of pressure from students to make some public commitment to social and political change, he told *El Espectador* that producers of culture were "persecuted" in Colombia by its reactionary ruling class.[27] Another interview that appeared after his departure was with Alfonso Monsalve for *Enfoque Nacional*, which included the statement "The revolutionary duty of a writer is to write well."[28] It would be reprinted in *El Tiempo* in mid-January. It came several years after Fidel Castro's first (and last) words on the topic, which were somewhat different. Castro's famous speech, "Words to the Intellectuals," had declared that literary form should be free but literary content rather less so: "Inside the Revolution, everything; outside the Revolution, nothing." Castro had also declared that the most revolutionary writer would be one who renounced his writing for the revolution.

García Márquez, troubled by his relations with the press (and through them, with his new reading public), would find himself working harder than even he had expected in these early years to give himself that room to manoeuvre politically and aesthetically that he was seeking; if he was to find himself in some difficult moral and ideological corners, he was determined that they would be of his own making or, at the least, that he would manage them on his own terms. He told Monsalve that serious "professional" writers put their vocation before all things and should never accept any kind of "subsidy" or "grant." He said he felt a profound responsibility towards his readers and that *The Autumn of the Patriarch* had been almost ready for publication when *One Hundred Years of Solitude* was published but now he felt he would have to completely rewrite it—not in order for it to be like the great best-seller but precisely to be different from it. Here already he introduces a disconcerting idea: that the success of *One Hundred Years of Solitude* is in part due to certain "technical devices" (he will later call them "tricks") which he could use as trademarks but he would rather move on and write something completely different. "I do not wish to parody myself." Monsalve presents his compatriot as someone who at first looks and sounds more like a Mexican than a Colombian until he relaxes, "finds the thread of his ideas" and becomes once again "the typical Colombian *costeño*, talkative, candid, straightforward in his concepts and putting into each of his expressions a wit syncretized in his dual Black and Spanish ancestry beneath the stupefying sun of the tropics." Clearly this man, presented here with an evidently sympathetic intention, was still perceived very much as an alien in the capital of his own country, as he had been, once upon a time, in his own family.

So it would always be. García Márquez could hardly wait to leave.

PART III

Man of the World:
Celebrity and Politics

1967–2005

17

Barcelona and the
Latin American Boom:
Between Literature and Politics

1967-1970

THE GARCÍA BARCHA FAMILY arrived in Spain on 4 November 1967.[1] After almost a week in Madrid they travelled to Barcelona. They intended a quite brief stay but, as in Mexico, they would remain almost six years.[2] Once again it would be impossible for García Márquez to work as a journalist because the press was ruthlessly censored and he was a figure of international renown. But this would turn out to be a blessing: the separation from journalism and politics in Mexico City had coincided with one big book, *One Hundred Years of Solitude*, and in Barcelona it would coincide with an almost equally large one, *The Autumn of the Patriarch*.

To many the journey to Barcelona seemed a curious venture for a left-leaning Latin American, and García Márquez had always claimed to have avoided visiting Spain out of hatred for the Franco dictatorship.[3] Mexico was the most hostile of all Hispanic countries to the Spanish regime and it was certainly an irony that García Márquez would travel from there to live in a country from which so many of his Catalan friends in both Mexico and Colombia were exiled. But although he would usually deny it, the spectacle of the old Spanish dictator near the end of his life and power was inevitably a stimulus to the writing of the book he had long since planned on an even more geriatric Latin American tyrant, a literary one whose power would seem eternal to his helpless and long-suffering subjects.

In fact there was much else to be said for the decision. His literary agent, Carmen Balcells, was in Barcelona and was already on her way to becoming one of the most influential agents not only in Spain but in the whole of Europe. With the Seix Barral publishing house and many others already in existence or springing up, Barcelona was, despite Franco, at the very centre of the 1960s publishing boom in Latin American fiction. Behind it was a renascent if necessarily muted Catalan nationalism and an economic upturn which, despite everything, the policies of the Franco dictatorship had recently begun to foment. The raw material fuelling the publishing boom was of course the creative "Boom" of the Latin American novel itself of which García Márquez was already the brightest star.

He arrived in Barcelona at the very moment the Boom's importance was becoming clear. The unparalleled albeit temporary openness of horizons which characterized the 1960s created an aesthetic moment of extraordinary fertility. This openness, this choice between alternatives, is clearly visible in both the subject matter and the structures of the canonical Latin American texts of the era. All are about the historical formation of Latin America, the contribution of both history and myth to contemporary Latin American identity, and, implicitly, about its possible futures, both good and bad.

Looking back, the intense historical moment that was the Boom ran from 1963, when Julio Cortázar's *Hopscotch (Rayuela)* appeared, to 1967, when García Márquez's *One Hundred Years of Solitude*—the Boom novel par excellence—was published. Everyone agreed that *Hopscotch* was something like "Latin America's *Ulysses*"—appropriately enough, because the Boom is best understood as the crystallization and culmination of Latin America's twentieth-century modernist movement. But *One Hundred Years of Solitude* changed the entire perspective, making it clear at once that something much more far-reaching had occurred for which a quite different time-frame was required—because, as almost everyone again agreed, *One Hundred Years of Solitude* was "Latin America's *Don Quixote*."

García Márquez became the focus of attention, almost the icon of the burgeoning literary movement; it would begin to seem as if he alone attracted as much media coverage as all the other writers put together. No one said it in so many words but clearly here was some kind of Exotic Phenomenon, some Noble Savage, some Caliban of

Letters metamorphosed magically into a new image of the writer for this contradictory era of pop culture and post-colonial revolution. The Spanish press, culturally and politically underdeveloped after thirty years of Francoism, was completely unprepared for the novelties and complexities of the Latin American new wave and García Márquez was subjected to dozens of thoughtless and embarrassing interviews. Few journalists were interested in the fact that this man from nowhere, who seemed to have appeared, like his book, out of thin air, through some form of spontaneous Third World combustion, was actually a deadly serious, inconceivably industrious, ferociously determined writer who had worked unceasingly for two decades to get where he was and would be prepared to work equally tenaciously to stay there—whatever he might say, in throwaway remarks, to gullible journalists. This was a writer who would use his literary celebrity to become a great public figure and on a scale unimagined by any of his predecessors except perhaps Hugo, Dickens, Twain or Hemingway.

Yet he would be consistently underestimated. Over nearly four decades, his critics would fail to see what was there before their very eyes: that he was cleverer than they were, that he was manipulating them at will, that the public loved him more than they loved the critics and would forgive him almost anything, not only because they loved his books but because they felt that he was one of them. Just as they had loved the Beatles in part because instead of being managed by the media (like Elvis or Marilyn) they knew how to play the journalists at their own game: taking them deadly seriously by appearing not to take them seriously at all. He was, it seemed, an ordinary guy—not pretentious, pompous or pedantic. He was just a man like his readers but one who made genuine literature accessible and easy.

His arrival in Barcelona started a trend. Before long José Donoso and Mario Vargas Llosa would also arrive. García Márquez was soon acquainted with such leading Spanish writers and intellectuals as the critic José María Castellet, Juan and Luis Goytisolo and Juan Marsé.[4] At this time underground opposition to the Franco dictatorship was growing all across Spain, led and mainly organized by the Communist Party through figures such as Santiago Carrillo, Jorge Semprún and Fernando Claudín, but paralleled by the Socialist Party (PSOE) and young clandestine militants such as Felipe González.[5] Historically Catalonia has been not only the home of the bourgeois businessmen who famously stoked the engine that pulled Spain's otherwise empty carriages in the nineteenth century but also a land of anarchists and

socialists, painters and architects, the stage of Gaudí, Albéniz, Granados, Buñuel, Dalí, Miró and, by adoption, Picasso. Second only to
Paris as a cultural laboratory or greenhouse for "Latin" culture,
Barcelona had been an avant-garde city between the great *Renascenza*
of the 1880s and 1890s and the fall of the Spanish Republic in 1939.
Now, in the 1960s, with its language officially suppressed, Spain's most
industrious and productive province was beginning to assert itself once
more; however, in the 1960s politics had to masquerade as culture and
Catalan bourgeois nationalism, denied normal expression, took on a
radical left-wing persona through a heterogeneous group of mainly
middle-class writers and architects, film-makers and professors,
painters and media celebrities, philosophers and models known as the
gauche divine (divine left).

One of García Márquez's first contacts was Rosa Regás, today one
of Spain's leading women writers and cultural impresarios but in those
days a tall, beautiful young woman who looked like the Vanessa Redgrave of Antonioni's *Blow-Up* and was one of the "muses" of the divine
left. Her brother Oriol, who was big in public relations (like so many
of the people García Márquez knew in his Mexican and Spanish years),
was also the owner of Bocaccio, the "in" bar up on Calle Muntaner
where the beautiful and dangerous young people of the avant-garde
used to meet. The mini-skirted Rosa was a married woman in her mid-
thirties with children, but she led a life of sixties freedom that scandalized the traditionalist majority and was a standard-bearer for every
new cultural fashion. At this time she was organizing public relations
in Carlos Barral's office, though by the end of the decade she would be
running her own imprint, La Gaia Ciencia. She had read *One Hundred
Years of Solitude* and was "blown away": "I was madly in love with that
book; indeed, I still travel with it now as I do with Proust and I always
find something new in it. It's like *Don Quixote*; I have no doubt it will
last. But in those days it seemed to speak to me directly, it was my
world. We all loved it; it was like a children's craze, we all passed it
around."[6]

Rosa Regás immediately invited Gabo and Mercedes to a party in
their honour at her house, where she introduced them to some of the
influential members of Barcelona's avant-garde society. It was there
they met a couple, Luis and Leticia Feduchi, who were to be their closest Spanish friends over the next thirty years. Part of the attraction was
that the Feduchis were not from Catalonia. As in Mexico, the García
Barchas would interact above all with the émigré crowd. Luis Feduchi

was a psychiatrist born in Madrid and Leticia was from Málaga and had recently studied literature at the University of Barcelona.[7] He and Leticia gave "the Gabos," as they were beginning to be called, a lift home after the party, stopped the car, talked for a long time, and arranged to meet again. Their three daughters, the *"infantas,"* as García Márquez would call them, were much the same age as Rodrigo and Gonzalo, and the five children too would also become lifelong friends, like favourite cousins.[8]

A young Brazilian woman, Beatriz de Moura, was another early acquaintance, another "muse" of the divine left and another person who, like Rosa Regás, would be running her own publishing house, Tusquets (her then husband's family name), in 1969, at the age of thirty. If this was salon society, the new hostesses were astonishingly young. Beatriz had arrived in Spain because, as the daughter of a diplomat, she had broken with her conservative family over politics and made her way through her talent and, no doubt, her youthful glamour. (If Rosa was like the Vanessa Redgrave of Antonioni's *Blow-Up*, Beatriz resembled the Jeanne Moreau of Truffaut's *Jules et Jim*.)

However, García Márquez, it turned out, was in Barcelona to work, and he and Mercedes soon began to limit their socializing. They moved from one apartment to another, all in the pleasant but unfashionable Gracia and Sarriá areas north of the Diagonal, before finally renting a quite small apartment in a new block on Calle Caponata, still in Sarriá. Guests were struck by the sobriety of its decor—essentially the Mexican conception of white walls with furniture of colours that varied from room to room—which would characterize all their residences from this time forward. Here they would stay, in a pleasant area surprisingly reminiscent of the unpretentious and sensible, almost suburban zone where they had lived in Mexico, until the end of their stay in the Catalan capital.

They decided to send Rodrigo and Gonzalo to the local British School, the Colegio Kensington. The headmaster, Mr. Paul Giles, was a Yorkshireman who had studied law at Cambridge and had something in common with the García Barchas: before opening his school in Barcelona, he had lived in Mexico. As for his pupils' famous parent, García Márquez had a tendency to the sarcastic which Giles, quintessentially English, did not appreciate: "I didn't pay him much attention, he wasn't that well known in those days. He was pleasant enough but also rather aggressive. I assumed he had a chip on his shoulder against the English. But why be disagreeable about other people's cultures? I mean, why pour beer in someone else's Beaujolais? . . . Do you think García Márquez is as good as they say? What, as good as Cervantes? Good Lord, who says that? Him, I should think."[9]

The two biggest editorial contacts available in Barcelona were the formidable Carmen Balcells and Carlos Barral, one of the founders of the Seix Barral publishing house. García Márquez's relationship with Barral was already doomed: although Barral did more to promote the Boom than any other single individual, he was also the man, so it was said, who back in 1966 had "missed," or "lost" (it is the same word in Spanish) *One Hundred Years of Solitude*, which, if true, would be the single biggest misjudgement in the history of Spanish publishing. By contrast Balcells is, without a doubt, García Márquez's most important contact in Barcelona and the most important woman in his life after Luisa Santiaga and Mercedes. She had started out negotiating contracts for Barral at the beginning of the 1960s and then struck out on her own. "When I started out I knew nothing. There was snobbery everywhere, and beautiful girls; I felt like a peasant woman by comparison. Of course, in the end I made it; my first customers were Mario Vargas Llosa and Luis Goytisolo; but it was Gabo who really pulled my chestnuts out of the fire."[10]

With Mercedes to run the home (he told interviewers, "she gives me pocket money for sweets, like she does with the boys")[11] and Carmen to run his business and other affairs, which she did first with alacrity and then with devotion, García Márquez was in a position to administer his fame and write his next book. He would not be long in realizing that the world was now at his feet. His telephone vice would now reach unimagined heights: he could be in daily contact with whoever he wanted in any of his strategic places—Colombia, Mexico, Cuba, Venezuela, Spain and France—or indeed anywhere else in the world, at a moment's notice. In terms of business, however, he would need to chase no possibilities, launch no initiatives, seek no advantages: from now on the world would be coming to him, through Carmen. This would take some adjusting to but he would get there.

Part of the process of adjustment lay in explaining—not least to himself—the relation between the already mythical *One Hundred Years of Solitude*, the "dead lion," and his current project, *The Autumn of the Patriarch*. He would have been immortal thanks to *One Hundred Years of Solitude* even had he written no other book but he was not interested in talking about it: he wanted to concentrate on the new one. So he began to tell journalists that he was bored with *One Hundred Years of*

Solitude—as much as anything he was bored by their stupid questions—and even, horror of horrors, that the book was "superficial" and that its success was largely due to a series of writer's "tricks."[12] In short, he seemed to be saying, he was not really a magician, just a talented conjuror.

In one way of course he was obviously right: *One Hundred Years of Solitude* is indeed full of "tricks"; not only the sleight of hand readers love so much in the *Thousand and One Nights* (which foreshadowed Melquíades and his associated themes and strategies) but the modernist techniques, arduously acquired, which had allowed the author to distance himself from the preoccupations of "The House" and hence to dissolve all his lifelong obsessions—both biographical and literary—into thin air.[13] But behind this, no doubt, there is some further dimension of disappointment and even resentment. Now it was as if the book had robbed him of that house and that past. He could never go back again. He had not necessarily wanted to know that.[14]

Another reason for him to react against *One Hundred Years of Solitude* was the question of celebrity with all its attendant pressures, responsibilities and expectations.[15] He was ambivalent about this, even hypocritical at times, but there can be no doubt that, from the start, he—a large part of him—sincerely deplored and lamented it. Like so many others before him, he had wanted the glory but he was reluctant to pay the price. Thus the novel had released him from a tormented past but condemned him to a complicated future. So among other things the story of the rest of his life would be that of a man who had deserved the fame he now enjoyed and then had to learn how to live with it, to meet both the expectations and the responsibilities, and to triumph again (this time over fame and success themselves) and keep on triumphing with each new book.[16]

Viewed in this way, *One Hundred Years of Solitude* is evidently the axis of García Márquez's life: the end of Macondo (his previously unassimilated world) and the beginning of "Macondo" (its successful representation, now achieved and behind him); the end of his obscurity and virtual anonymity, the beginning of his "power" (as *The Autumn of the Patriarch* would put it); the end of his modernist period and the beginning of his postmodernist period. Even more grandiosely, the novel is also the axis of Latin America's twentieth-century literature, the continent's only undisputable world-historical and world-canonical novel. And more grandiose still, but nonetheless true, it is part of a worldwide phenomenon which marks the ending of all "modernity" with the post-colonial arrival of the Third World and its literatures on the global stage (hence the parallel importance of Cuba and Castro): the end of the period, we could say, that began with Rabelais (saying farewell to the Middle Ages by satirizing its world-view) and was confirmed by Cervantes; and whose end was announced by *Ulysses* and, it may be asserted, confirmed by *One Hundred Years of Solitude*.[17] No one would have found it easy to adjust to the idea—even the possibility—of that degree of historical significance.

IN APRIL AND May 1968 the family made their first foray outside Spain, taking in Paris and Italy, where Giangiacomo Feltrinelli was publishing the first translation of *One Hundred Years of Solitude* into a foreign language. Feltrinelli's book launches were usually "happenings," media spectacles which exalted the celebrity status of literary figures. But although Feltrinelli presented him as "the new Quixote," García Márquez was true to his word and refused to have anything to do with the launch of the book or with its publicity. He felt strongly that publishers exploited writers and that they should at least handle their own end of the business: "Editors don't help me write my books so why should I help them sell them."[18]

This European tour was completed while the almost revolutionary events of May 1968 took place in Paris. García Márquez has barely ever mentioned this huge historic phenomenon, whereas Carlos Fuentes and Mario Vargas Llosa hastened to Paris to take part and Fuentes wrote a well-known eyewitness report and analysis of the failed insurrection, *Paris: The May Revolution*.[19] Of course, although he was undoubtedly disappointed by the outcome, García Márquez had little faith in the ability of the French bourgeoisie, even its student youth, to transform a country and a culture about which he had fundamental reservations; and in any case he still had his eyes firmly fixed on Latin America. Nevertheless he decided to return to Paris over the summer, at the end of which he communicated his feelings to Plinio Mendoza:

> Paris came out of me as if it were a splinter I had stuck in my foot . . . The last threads that linked me to the French just broke. That precision, that fabulous ability to split a hair in four, is something that has simply aged and the French don't realize it . . . We arrived there when the paving stones were still broken

after the battles in May and those battles were already petrified in the minds of the French: the taxi drivers, the baker, the grocer, made wearisome analyses of the events, drowned us in a bucket of rationalizations, and left us with the impression that all that had happened was a collision of words. It was infuriating . . .

My fate is that of a bullfighter and I don't know how to cope with it. In order to go over the translation of *One Hundred Years of Solitude* I had to take refuge in Tachia's apartment; she is now a well-set up lady, with a marvellous husband who speaks seven languages without an accent, and on first meeting she established a very good friendship with Mercedes based principally on complicity against me.[20]

It was true: García Márquez had met Tachia again. She had been living for some years with Charles Rosoff, a French engineer born in 1914 whose parents had left Russia after the failed 1905 uprising. His father had gone back in 1917 to join the revolution and then left again in 1924, disillusioned after the death of Lenin. Before meeting Rosoff Tachia had some transient relationships but no new love, though Blas de Otero had sought her out again in Paris and attempted to rekindle their tempestuous affair. Ironically it was through Blas, in 1960, that she had met the man she was to marry. But now, in 1968, García Márquez was back in her life. "We all met up at our apartment in Paris; I was very nervous. We all behaved terribly well and talked brightly but it was actually a very tense occasion, very strange, very difficult. But we all managed to act 'as if nothing had ever happened' and carried it off."

García Márquez was still in Paris when the Soviet army invaded Czechoslovakia on 21 August to crush the socialist reform movement or "Prague Spring" led by Alexander Dubček, the recently elected First Secretary of the Czech Communist Party. Czechoslovakia was a far more serious matter for García Márquez than the events in Paris because it seemed to demonstrate that Soviet communism was incapable of evolution. He told Plinio Mendoza: "My world collapsed but now I think maybe it's better like this: to demonstrate, without nuances, that we stand between two imperialisms, equally cruel and voracious, is in a certain sense a liberation for one's conscience . . . A group of French writers sent Fidel a letter published in *L'Observateur*, saying his support for the Soviet invasion was 'the Cuban Revolution's first serious error.' They wanted us to sign it but our reply was very clear: it's our dirty washing and we'll do it at home. But the truth is I don't think it will be washed very easily."[21]

Politically, 1968 was proving the most turbulent year in living memory. In January Colombia had re-established diplomatic relations with the USSR for the first time in twenty years and Pope Paul VI had visited the country in August on the first ever papal visit to Latin America. ("Big Mama's Funeral" had predicted such a visit.) Martin Luther King had been assassinated in Memphis in April and Bobby Kennedy was assassinated in Los Angeles in June; Andy Warhol was shot in New York the same month; the Chicago police had run riot at the Democratic Party convention in August and Richard Nixon would be elected President in November. And of course the French students had rioted in Paris in May, largely unaided by the workers; the USSR had carried out its invasion of Czechoslovakia, supported by Cuba; and in early October the Mexican army would kill hundreds of unarmed demonstrators at Tlatelolco, in Mexico City, just before the first Olympic Games ever held in the Third World. All this while García Márquez himself spent most of his time closeted away in Barcelona with his paper "patriarch," though living under a real dictatorship.[22]

As for Spain, indeed, García Márquez took so little interest in the nation's politics that many people in Barcelona thought he was "apolitical." During his period in the city there would be two major "sit-ins" which crystallized opposition to the Franco regime, participated in by many of his friends, including Vargas Llosa, and virtually every major member of the Divine Left; but not by García Márquez. Thirty years later Beatriz de Moura told me: "In those days Gabo was completely apolitical. Underlined: *apolitical*. You never heard him talk about politics and it was impossible to know what his opinions were. It was considered de rigueur to be politically committed in those days. And Gabo never was."[23]

Novelist Juan Marsé was left with quite a different recollection of the "apolitical" García Márquez. In the late summer of 1968 Marsé was one of the foreign jury members invited to award literary prizes for the Fourth Competition of the National Union of Writers and Artists of Cuba (UNEAC). When it became clear to the authorities that the poetry prize was going to the allegedly counter-revolutionary poet Heberto Padilla and the theatre prize to the homosexual playwright Antón Arrufat, a crisis broke and the juries were effectively sequestered in Cuba for several weeks. This was the beginning of a conflict about freedom of expression which—three years on—would eventually

The Soviet invasion of Czechoslovakia, August 1968: the last straw for many former supporters of the USSR.

GGM, Barcelona, late 1960s.

GGM and Pablo Neruda in the garden of Neruda's Normandy home, c. 1972.

Boom couples: (*left to right*) Mario Vargas Llosa, his wife Patricia, Mercedes, José Donoso, his wife María Pilar Serrano and GGM, Barcelona, early 1970s.

GGM writing *The Autumn of the Patriarch*, Barcelona, 1970s (taken by his son Rodrigo).

GGM with Carlos Fuentes, Mexico City, 1971.

GGM and Mercedes, 1970s.

Cartagena, 1971: GGM visits his parents Gabriel Eligio and Luisa Santiaga with his son Gonzalo and Mexican journalist Guillermo Ochoa.

Writers of the Boom: (*left to right*) Mario Vargas Llosa, Carlos Fuentes, GGM and José Donoso. Only Julio Cortázar is missing.

Julio Cortázar, Miguel Angel Asturias and GGM, West Germany, 1970.

Paris, 1973: the wedding of Charles Rosoff (*left*) and Tachia Quintana (*right*). GGM, the best man, looks on.

Santiago de Chile, 11 September 1973: President Salvador Allende defends the Moneda Palace against rebel forces. Just behind him is Dr. Danilo Bartulín, who, unlike Allende, survived, and became a good friend of GGM's in Havana.

Santiago de Chile, 11 September 1973: General Pinochet and his henchmen.

Cuban troops in Angola, February 1976.

"Fidel is a king": Castro, President of Cuba, 1980s.

General Omar Torrijos, President of Panama, 1970s.

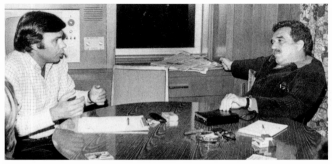

GGM interviews Felipe González in Bogotá, 1977.

Bogotá, 1977: GGM with Consuelo Araujonoguera ("La Cacica") and Guillermo Cano, editor of *El Espectador*. He would be killed by Pablo Escobar's hitmen in 1986 and she would be murdered, allegedly by FARC guerrillas, in 2001.

GGM with Carmen Balcells and Manuel Zapata Olivella, El Dorado Airport, Bogotá, 1977.

Mexico City, 1981: GGM buried by press attention following his self-exile from Colombia.

Mexico City, October 1982: Alvaro Mutis chauffeurs GGM and Mercedes around to protect them from media attention.

Stockholm, December 1982: (*left to right*) Jaime Castro, Germán Vargas, GGM, Charles Rosoff (*behind*), Alfonso Fuenmayor, Plinio Mendoza, Eligio García (*behind*) and Hernán Vieco.

Stockholm, December 1982. GGM celebrates his prize in a *costeño* "*sombrero vueltiao*."

Stockholm, December 1982: GGM in the chalk circle; King Carl XVI Gustav applauds.

Cartagena, 1993: Luisa Santiaga and her children. (*Top row, left to right*) Jaime, Alfredo (Cuqui), Ligia, GGM, Gustavo, Hernando (Nanchi), Eligio (Yiyo), Luis Enrique; (*bottom row, left to right*) Germaine (Emy), Margot, Luisa Santiaga, Rita, Aida.

GGM and Fidel Castro, by the Caribbean, 1983.

Havana, 1988: GGM and Robert Redford.

Bogotá, mid-1980s: GGM and Mercedes with President Betancur and his wife Rosa Helena Alvarez.

Bogotá's Palacio de Justicia in flames, 6 November 1985 (during Betancur's presidency), after the army stormed the building to dislodge M-19 guerrillas.

The world changes: celebrations at the fall of the Berlin Wall, November 1989.

Bogotá, 1992: GGM salutes his admirers in the Jorge Eliécer Gaitán Theatre.

GGM and Mercedes, La Santamaría bullring, Bogotá, 1993.

GGM, 1999.

Barcelona, *c.* 2005: Carmen Balcells ("La Mamá Grande") in her office, with photo of Gabo triumphant behind.

Havana, 2007: Gabo visits his ailing friend Fidel before travelling to Cartagena for his eightieth birthday celebrations.

Cartagena, March 2007: GGM and Bill Clinton.

Cartagena, March 2007: GGM and King Juan Carlos I of Spain.

Cartagena, 26 March 2007: GGM waves to admirers during the celebrations for his eightieth birthday.

change Cuba's international image for ever, especially in Europe and the USA, and cause an irremediable rupture between many writers and what at this time was still seen as a reasonably liberal socialist revolution. The juries finally insisted on their verdicts and the authorities had to content themselves with printing a "health warning" in the two books when they were published. So after his six weeks stranded in Cuba while Fidel Castro waited in vain for the juries to change their mind, Marsé arrived back in Barcelona in late October and narrated his experiences to a group of friends at a party, among them García Márquez. Marsé told me, "The jury gave the prize to Padilla because his book was the best. UNEAC said it wasn't and of course the message had come down from above. It was true that Padilla turned out to be a provocateur and a really twisted guy, a nutcase. But even if I'd known that I wouldn't have changed my mind. His was the best book and that was that. Anyway I got back to Barcelona and Carmen held a party for me, so I told my story. I can see Gabo now, with a red kerchief round his neck, pacing up and down while I'm explaining what happened. He was furious with me, really angry. He said that I was an idiot, that I didn't understand anything about literature and even less about politics. Politics always came first. It didn't matter if they hanged all us writers. Padilla was a bastard who worked for the CIA and we should never have given the prize to him. It was an extraordinary display. He didn't actually abuse me but he made it clear that we inhabited totally different intellectual and moral universes. After that we remained friends but I have the feeling that nothing was ever quite the same again, especially for him."[24]

What Marsé did not know was that García Márquez, who intuited how serious this problem might eventually become, had supported a direct behind-the-scenes approach to Castro over the Padilla problem. In mid-September he had prolonged another visit to Paris to see Julio Cortázar, with whom he had been corresponding but whom he had never managed to meet. Cortázar had just separated from his first wife, Aurora Bernárdez, and wrote a gloomy letter to Paco Porrúa in Buenos Aires. The only bright spot, he said, was his meeting with García Márquez: "I want you to know that I met Gabriel, who stayed two extra days to meet me; I found both him and Mercedes marvellous; friendship springs up like a fountain when life puts you in touch with people like them."[25] The two men had discussed the Cuban situation— appropriately enough because they were the two who would subsequently support the revolution through thick and thin and, in doing so, distance themselves from most of their contemporaries and certainly from the most famous of them: Vargas Llosa, Donoso, Cabrera Infante, Goytisolo and even Fuentes. García Márquez claims that it was he who suggested a private approach by sending a joint letter to Fidel, though Cortázar seemed to believe it was his initiative. In essence the idea seems to have been to appeal privately to Fidel not to punish Padilla in return—implicitly—for their silence. No reply ever came but Padilla, who had been removed from his work at Casa de las Américas, was reinstated. In 1971 the whole affair would blow up once more; but people such as Vargas Llosa, Juan Goytisolo and Plinio Mendoza had already turned away from Cuba in 1968 and nothing would ever be the same again.

On 8 December García Márquez travelled on an extraordinary expedition to Prague for a week with his new friend Julio Cortázar, Cortázar's new partner the Lithuanian writer and translator Ugné Karvelis, who worked at the top Parisian publisher Gallimard, and Carlos Fuentes. They were keen to find out what was really happening in the newly occupied Czech capital and wanted to talk to novelist Milan Kundera about the crisis.[26] According to Carlos Fuentes, "Kundera asked us to meet him in a sauna by the river bank to tell us what had happened in Prague. Apparently it was one of the few places without ears in the walls . . . A large hole opened in the ice invited us to ease our discomfort and reactivate our circulation. Milan Kundera pushed us gently towards the irremediable. As purple as certain orchids, the man from Barranquilla, and I, the man from Veracruz, immersed ourselves in that water so alien to our tropical essence."[27]

Despite these adventures, the dominant image of García Márquez during this period is that of the solitary hero, tied to his vocation as to a ball and chain yet bereft of inspiration, wandering the dead-end corridors and empty halls of his mansion (forget that he lived in a small apartment) like some Citizen Kane of narrative fiction; or perhaps like Papa Hemingway only with literary bullets that were blanks instead of live ones. He was actually far from house-bound during the writing of *The Autumn of the Patriarch* as he had been during the writing of *One Hundred Years of Solitude*. Still, his anguish was undoubtedly real, despite the often ludicrous spectacle of his private torment being splashed repeatedly over the pages of newspapers all across Latin America.

After a while he began to visit Carmen Balcells's office between five and seven in the evening several days a week, ostensibly to leave the latest section of *The Autumn of the Patriarch* for safe keeping—Carmen Balcells's archive started receiving substantial sections of the novel as early as 1 April 1969 and was still receiving them as late as August 1974, with strict instructions "Not to be read"—but also to use her telephone on an unlimited basis for his commercial deals and confidential assignations. This kept business out of the home and perhaps saved Mercedes knowing about things that might have upset her, not least the large amounts of his new wealth that García Márquez would choose to give away over the coming years and, as time went on, the political and other affairs in which he became increasingly involved. In addition Balcells began to act as a kind of sister, a sister he could tell almost anything, a person who would come to love him dearly and who would make any sacrifice on his behalf. "After he had been in Barcelona for a while," she told me, "he would come in and say, 'Get ready, I've a job for Superman.' That was me. And that's who I've been ever since for him."[28] (She was later not averse to a joke, though. Years later he asked her during a telephone conversation, "Do you love me, Carmen?" She replied, "I can't answer that. You are 36.2 per cent of our income.")

Meanwhile the boys were growing up. García Márquez would later remark that the relationship between parents and children, unchanging for centuries, was radically transformed in the sixties: those parents who adjusted remained young for ever, those who did not were even older than middle-aged people had been before. Rodrigo, today a successful film-maker in Hollywood, told me, "What I most remember is that although we had a very social life it was really just the four of us, always. Just the four of us in the world. We were a wheel with four spokes, never five. So much so that when my brother had a baby a few years ago I was traumatized, I simply couldn't believe that now there was a fifth spoke. And that's after me living away from home for many years."[29]

He added: "The two of us were breast-fed with a number of essential values. There were things you just had to know. One was the great importance of friendship. There was a huge emphasis on the sheer fascination of other people and their lives. It was my father's drug. You had to know about their lives and all their business and you had to share in other people's experiences and share your own with them. At the same time we were brought up to be completely unprejudiced, except in a couple of significant respects. Firstly, Latin American people were the best people in the world. They were not necessarily the cleverest, they might not have built a lot, but they were the very best people in the world, the most human and the most generous. On the other hand, if anything went wrong you always had to know that it was the government's fault, it was always to blame for everything. And if it wasn't the government, it was the United States. I've since discovered that my father loves the United States and has a lot of admiration for its achievements and a lot of affection for some Americans but when we were growing up the United States was to blame for almost everything bad in the world. Looking back, it was a very humanistic, politically correct upbringing. Although I was christened by Camilo Torres we never had any kind of religious education. Religion was bad, politicians were bad, the police and the army were bad.[30]

"There were other essentials too. If there was one word we kept hearing it was 'seriousness.' For example, my parents were very strict about manners. You had to hold doors open for ladies and you couldn't talk with your mouth full. So there was this great belief in seriousness, in manners, in punctuality. And you had to get good grades, you couldn't possibly not get good grades. But you also had to fool around, you had to know how to fool around and when to fool around; it was almost as if fooling around was part of 'seriousness.' And if we went over the top and fooled around too much, then we would be punished. Only two things in the world were really worthy of respect: service—being a doctor or a teacher or something like that—and, above all, creating works of art. But it was always embedded in our brains that fame was of no importance at all, he always said it wasn't 'serious.' You could be immensely famous and still not a great writer; indeed, fame might even be suspicious. For example, he said, his friends Alvaro Mutis and Tito Monterroso were very great writers but no one had ever heard of them. On the other hand, we boys quite liked it when Dad started to be recognized in the street."[31]

It was around this time that García Márquez gave up smoking. He had been an addict since the age of eighteen and at the time he set them aside he was often smoking eighty cigarettes a day of black tobacco. Only two years before he had said that he would rather die than give up smoking.[32] The conversion took place one evening over dinner with his psychiatrist friend Luis Feduchi, who explained how he himself had given up a month before and why. García Márquez would not reveal the full details of this conversation for more than three decades but he stubbed out the cigarette he was smoking over dinner and never smoked another; though he was outraged two weeks later when Luis Feduchi started smoking a pipe.[33]

In January 1970 *One Hundred Years of Solitude* was named Best Foreign Novel of 1969 in France, recipient of a prize first instituted in 1948; but García Márquez flatly refused to attend the ceremony. Months afterwards he would tell an interviewer that "the book doesn't feel right in French" and hadn't sold very well despite positive reviews—perhaps because, unfortunately, "the spirit of Descartes has defeated that of Rabelais" in France.[34]

Ironically, the situation was totally different with regard to the United States. No novel in recent history had received more unqualified praise than García Márquez now began to receive there. John Leonard, in the *New York Times Book Review*, declared:

> You emerge from this marvelous novel as if from a dream, the mind on fire. A dark, ageless figure at the hearth, part historian, part haruspex, in a voice by turns angelic and maniacal, first lulls to sleep your grip on a manageable reality, then locks you into legend and myth . . . With a single bound, Gabriel García Márquez leaps onto the stage with Günter Grass and Vladimir Nabokov, his appetite as enormous as his imagination, his fatalism greater than either. Dazzling.[35]

London followed on 16 April. In June *The Times*, the then establishment pillar and in some respects the most conservative newspaper in the world, which had only recently permitted photographs, dedicated an entire broadsheet page to the first chapter of *One Hundred Years of Solitude*, accompanied by "psychedelic" illustrations that might have been stolen from the Beatles' cartoon movie *Yellow Submarine*. In December the *New York Times* named *One Hundred Years of Solitude* one of the twelve books of the year: it was the only fiction title among them. Gregory Rabassa's inspired English version of *One Hundred Years of Solitude* was widely considered the best foreign translation of the year.

As for the other "Boom" writers, Mario Vargas Llosa finally made his long-heralded move to Spain that summer. He had completed his monumental novel *Conversation in the Cathedral* the previous year and now left his teaching position at the University of London and moved to Barcelona. His friends would call Mario "the cadet," not only because of the topic—a military academy—of his best-seller *The Time of the Hero* (1962) but because Mario himself was always neat, tidy, well organized and, in theory at least, aiming to do the right thing. Yet controversy often surrounded him: by now this brilliant but ostensibly conventional young man was married to his first cousin Patricia, having put behind him the scandalous adolescent marriage to his aunt which would later become the subject of his novel *Aunt Julia and the Scriptwriter*. Meanwhile, another of his projects, a biographically oriented study of García Márquez's narrative fiction, was surely one of the most generous and remarkable acts of homage in literature from one great writer to another. It was to be entitled *García Márquez: The Story of a Deicide (García Márquez: historia de un deicidio)*, and it remains arguably, thirty years later, the single best book ever written on García Márquez and still a fundamental reference source today—even if, as many critics have said, it turned the Colombian into a writer with many of the attributes and the obsessions of Mario himself.

Another writer now in residence was the hypochondriac Chilean José Donoso, whom García Márquez had first met in Carlos Fuentes's house in 1965. Donoso was the "fifth member of the Boom" (about equivalent to being the "fifth Beatle"), writer of the remarkable *The Obscene Bird of Night* (1970). Donoso later authored two important chronicles of the era, his *Personal History of the "Boom"* (1972) and his novel, *The Garden Next Door* (1981), which casts a satirical—and envious—eye on the relationship between Carmen Balcells (Núria Monclús) and her "favourite" writer, García Márquez (Marcelo Chiriboga).[36]

And Plinio Mendoza and his wife Marvel Moreno had decided to move across the Atlantic, first to Paris and then to Mallorca.[37] Living in the most stringent austerity, Mendoza would soon become a frequent visitor to Barcelona, thanks to García Márquez's largesse, but he found things difficult: "I would stay in his house. But in that apartment on Caponata Street, roomy and quiet, that lady with airs and pearl necklaces, Celebrity, was also staying."[38]

It was at this time that García Márquez met Pablo Neruda and his wife Matilde. Neruda was Latin America's greatest poet, an old-style communist who was also an old-style bon vivant whose approach to life even the sybaritic Alvaro Mutis must have envied and admired. Yet another Latin American writer terrified of flying, Neruda was on his way back by boat from a trip to Europe to be present at the elections which would bring socialist candidate Salvador Allende to power. One of the victorious Allende's first decisions would be to make Neruda Chile's ambassador to Paris in 1971. When Neruda's ship stopped in Barcelona in the summer of 1970, meeting García Márquez was one of his principal objectives.[39] Afterwards García Márquez wrote to Mendoza, "It's a shame you didn't see Neruda. The bastard caused a hell of an uproar during the lunch, to the point where Matilde had to send him to hell. We pushed him out of a window and brought him here for a siesta and before they went back to the boat we had a fantastic time."[40] This was the occasion on which Neruda, who had still not quite completed his all-important siesta, dedicated a book to Mercedes. García Márquez recalls, "Mercedes said she was going to ask Pablo for his signature. 'Don't be such a creep!' I said and went to hide in the bathroom . . . He wrote, 'To Mercedes, in her bed.' He looked at it and said, 'This sounds a bit suspicious,' so he added, 'To Mercedes and Gabo, in their bed.' Then he thought, 'The truth is it's even worse now.' So he added, 'Fraternally, Pablo.' Then, roaring with laughter, he said, 'Now it's worse than ever but there's nothing to be done about it.' "[41]

The next few months saw the high-water mark of the Boom. This brief moment began when Carlos Fuentes's play *The One-Eyed Man Is King* was premiered in Avignon in August and he invited all his Boom companions to attend. An expedition was organized from Barcelona. Mario Vargas Llosa and Patricia, who had only just moved to the Catalan capital, José Donoso and Pilar, and Gabo and Mercedes, with their two sons, all took the train from Barcelona to Avignon for the premiere. Spanish novelist Juan Goytisolo, another honorary member of the Boom, travelled down from Paris. Avignon was only forty miles from the village of Saignon, Julio Cortázar's country home in the Vaucluse, and Fuentes chartered a bus to take the group, and many hangers-on, to see Cortázar and Ugné Karvelis on 15 August. For his part Cortázar organized a huge lunch at a local restaurant and then the entire party descended on his house and spent a long afternoon and evening there.

For many reasons, but above all because this was the first and only time when the entire Boom clan ever got together, the occasion has since taken on a legendary character. Unfortunately, behind the joviality there lurked a couple of problems, one of which had been growing ever since the first Padilla Affair in Cuba in 1968 and had deepened with Castro's support of the Soviet invasion of Czechoslovakia. Now both problems were about to reach a crisis point and the already significant latent divisions between the six friends would shortly become unbridgeable. But not quite yet. The first problem was Cuba's repression of writers and intellectuals; the second, related to it, was Juan Goytisolo's project for a new magazine, to be located in Paris and to be entitled *Libre*, "Free," a name which by now several of the friends gathered together were convinced would itself be considered a provocation in Havana and proof that the architects of the Boom were, as the Cubans already suspected, a bunch of "petty-bourgeois" liberals.

A week after the party Cortázar would write: "It was at once very nice and very strange; something outside of time, unrepeatable of course, and with some deeper meaning that escapes me."[42] It was the last moment when the utopian longings enshrined in the Boom could still be partly sustained as a collective enterprise; and it was ironical that this first great gathering had taken the form of a pilgrimage to Cortázar's solitary dwelling, he who had always avoided crowds and false bonhomie but who now was not only a member of a mafia welded together by frequent male bonding on a monumental scale but was also gravitating towards the vast collectivist projects of the socialist dream.

On 4 September Salvador Allende was elected as President of Chile on a minority vote and would be inaugurated on 3 November, promising the Chilean people "socialism within liberty." But even before he was installed, a CIA-inspired attack fatally wounded General René Schneider, the Commander-in-Chief of the Chilean army, on 22 October. García Márquez had recently met Chilean writer Jorge Edwards, later the biographer of Neruda, whose role in Cuba as Chilean ambassador would have much to do with the ultimate outcome of the Padilla Affair.

A week before Christmas Cortázar and his wife Ugné drove from Paris to Barcelona, via Saignon. After their arrival all the writers and their wives went off to a Catalan speciality restaurant, La Font des Ocellets (The Bird Bath) in the old quarter. The system there was for the customers to write their orders on a printed form but everyone was so busy talking that after an extended period of time the form was still blank and the waiter complained to the owner. He emerged from the kitchen, scowling, and with heavy Catalan sarcasm uttered the immortal words: "Don't any of you know how to write?" There was a silence, part embarrassment, part indignation and part amusement. After a moment Mercedes spoke up, "Yes, I know how to write," and she proceeded to read out the menu and organize the order. Her coolness under fire was legendary. Once an anxious Pilar Serrano rang to tell her that Donoso, an inveterate hypochondriac, was convinced he had leukemia. Mercedes replied, "Don't worry, Gabito's just had cancer in his head and now he's doing fine."[43]

Christmas Eve was spent in the small apartment of the Vargas

Llosas so that the Peruvian couple could pack their young children off to bed. Cortázar, who had already been throwing snowballs at all and sundry, now engaged Vargas Llosa in a frenetic competition with the electric racing cars the boys had received for Christmas. Then, after Christmas, Luis Goytisolo and his wife María Antonia organized a party to which both Spaniards and Latin Americans were invited. Donoso, who retained his almost English sense of restraint and decorum, recalled in 1971: "For me, the Boom as an entity came to an end—if it ever was an entity outside one's imagination and if, in fact, it has ended—in 1970 at the home of Luis Goytisolo in Barcelona with a party presided over by María Antonia who, while weighed down by outrageous, expensive jewelry and in multi-colored knickers and black boots, danced, bringing to mind a Leon Bakst model for *Scheherezade* or *Petrouchka*. Wearing his brand-new beard in shades of red, Cortázar danced something very lively with Ugné. In front of the guests who encircled them, the Vargas Llosas danced a Peruvian waltz and, later, the García Márquezes entered the same circle, which awarded them a round of applause, to dance a tropical *merengue*. Meanwhile, our literary agent, Carmen Balcells, lay back on the plump cushions of a couch, licking her chops and stirring the ingredients of this delicious stew, feeding, with the help of Fernando Tola, Jorge Herralde, and Sergio Pitol, the fantastic, hungry fish that in their lighted aquariums decorated the walls of the room. Carmen Balcells seemed to have in her hands the strings that made us all dance like marionettes, and she studied us: perhaps with admiration, perhaps with hunger, perhaps with a mixture of the two, just as she studied the dancing fish in their aquariums. More than anything else that evening, the founding of the magazine *Libre* was talked about."[44]

After Cortázar and Ugné returned to Paris through the late-December blizzards the festivities gradually wound down. García Márquez and Mercedes have always liked to organize New Year parties rather than Christmas ones and it was in their house that the small group of remaining Boomers—the Vargas Llosas and the Donosos—welcomed in the year 1971. Little did they know that this was the last time they would be celebrating or indeed fraternally discussing anything together. The Boom was about to implode.

18

The Solitary Author Slowly Writes:
The Autumn of the Patriarch
and the Wider World

1971~1975

B Y 1971, after more than three years in Barcelona and with his book still not completed, García Márquez had decided on a break from the stresses of writing and set off for nine months in Latin America. He felt he needed to refamiliarize himself with his world. His own preference was Barranquilla but the previous March he had told Alfonso Fuenmayor that he was not sure the family would let him return there: "The boys are chronically homesick for Mexico and only now have I realized that they lived there long enough for that to be the Macondo they'll drag around the world for the rest of their lives. The only rotten patriot in this house is me, but I carry less weight all the time."[1] Somehow, though, he had convinced his reluctant family to stay a few months in Barranquilla before revisiting Mexico.

So in mid-January the García Barcha family arrived in Colombia. García Márquez smiled briefly as he left the plane in Barranquilla and gave a double thumbs-up sign to those waiting to greet him. Photographs show him in full Caribbean dress—Mexican guayabera shirt, leather moccasins and no socks—looking full of cares. With all the inactivity and extra carbohydrates in Barcelona he had filled out; his hair had filled out too and was now in a semi-Afro style characteristic of the era and he sported an equally characteristic Zapata moustache. Mercedes was behind dark glasses apparently pretending to be somewhere else, but the two boys, who hardly knew the country, looked bold and excited.[2] The local press and radio were out in force and the taxi drivers shouted from a distance that they would take Gabito to Macondo for just thirty pesos, for old times' sake. García Márquez, who before leaving Barcelona had announced, at first sight rather ungraciously, that he was going home "for a detox,"[3] had by now thought of a more positive way of explaining his visit and coined one of his defining phrases when he said that he had followed his nose back to the Caribbean after the "smell of the guava."[4]

The family travelled down to the home of Alvaro and Tita Cepeda, who by now lived in a magnificent white mansion between the city centre and the Prado area, although—ominously—Cepeda himself was in New York for medical tests. The García Barchas would be staying with Tita until they could find a suitable house or apartment. Journalist Juan Gossaín was allowed in on the first round of beers and listened to the conversation. García Márquez explained, as if in confidence, why he had made this prodigal return. All his life he had wanted to be a world-famous writer and had endured years of misery as a reporter in order to become one. Now that he really was a full-time "professional" author he wished he was a reporter again, a searcher after information, and so his life had come full circle: "I've always wanted to be what I no longer am."[5]

Some weeks later a Mexican journalist, Guillermo Ochoa, pursued García Márquez to the beach at Cartagena, where he, Mercedes and the boys were relaxing underneath a coconut palm during a visit to his parents. Ochoa's first article would concentrate on Luisa Santiaga and helped inaugurate her legend. To celebrate the return of her eldest son she had lovingly fattened a turkey:

"But I discovered I couldn't kill it," she told us. And then, with that stern gentleness that typifies Ursula Iguarán, the character of *One Hundred Years of Solitude* that she inspired, she added: "I'd become fond of him." The turkey is still alive and well and Gabito, on his return, had to be content with the seafood soup he has eaten every day since he got back to the city. That's how Luisa Márquez de García is. She's a woman who has never combed her hair at night. "If I did, it would delay the sailors," she explains. "What is the greatest satisfaction of your life?"

we asked her. And she, without hesitation, replied: "Having a daughter who's a nun."[6]

The house Gabito and Mercedes rented in Barranquilla was almost on the outskirts of the city at that time. For Gonzalo it was a thrilling environment and he retains pleasant memories of the whole experience. Although their parents had fixed up a school in advance, the boys mainly remember an exotic period during which large snakes got into the house and they hunted for iguanas to relieve them of their eggs. But although it was exciting to be back in the tropics and to be enveloped in the lives of two large extended families in Cartagena and Arjona, and a whole network of new friends in Barranquilla, they were also acutely aware that they were Mexico City boys: "The truth is that Rodrigo and I are both urban people; we have almost no experience of the rural world. Whereas our parents are both rural people, and above all tropical people. I can hardly recognize them when I see them in Cartagena or Havana. They are both relatively uptight everywhere else."[7]

In the first week of April García Márquez and Mercedes set off for Caracas alone. He was concerned to recharge his Caribbean batteries to bring his new book alive but it was also in a real sense a symbolic journey, a return to the place they first lived together and then a journey around the Caribbean, as well as the beginning of a pattern in which, increasingly, the boys would be left behind while their parents travelled the world in response to the lures and obligations of García Márquez's ever-increasing fame.

But while he was sailing around the Caribbean on this second honeymoon he was also thinking about a problem that had just recurred in the largest of its islands, a problem which would make this cruise the last relatively uncomplicated moment in his political existence. On 20 March the Cuban government had arrested Heberto Padilla,[8] the writer whose poems had caused such a storm of controversy on and off the island in the summer of 1968 and had led to García Márquez's angry confrontation with Juan Marsé in Barcelona. Now the Cuban poet was accused of subversive activities connected to the CIA. On 5 April, still in prison, Padilla signed a long—and obviously insincere—statement of self-criticism.

Although so many writers lived in Barcelona, Paris was still in many respects the political capital of Latin America. On 9 April a group of writers based in Europe organized a protest letter addressed to Fidel Castro, first published in *Le Monde* in Paris, in which they said that although they supported the "principles" of the revolution they could not accept the "Stalinist" persecution of writers and intellectuals. The list of names included, among many others, Jean-Paul Sartre and Simone de Beauvoir, Juan Goytisolo and Mario Vargas Llosa (the true instigators of the protest), Julio Cortázar and Plinio Apuleyo Mendoza (organizers, with Goytisolo, of the forthcoming magazine *Libre*) and . . . Gabriel García Márquez.[9]

In fact García Márquez had not signed the letter: Plinio Mendoza had assumed he would support the protest and had signed for him. García Márquez had his name withdrawn but the damage to his relationship with Cuba was done, followed by lasting difficulties with all the friends who remained signed up: the worst of all outcomes. It was to be, without doubt, the single most important crisis in Latin American literary politics in the twentieth century, one which divided both Latin American and European intellectuals for decades to come. Writers and intellectuals had no choice but to commit and take sides in this cultural equivalent of a civil war. Nothing would ever be the same again, not least the relationship between García Márquez and Vargas Llosa, which would eventually prove to be the noisiest and most violent of all the casualties of this political drama. It was the more ironic because just at that very moment Seix Barral were preparing publication of Vargas Llosa's *García Márquez, the Story of a Deicide*, which would appear in December of 1971, as their famous relationship, slowly but surely, began to cool. Vargas Llosa would not allow a second edition of the book for thirty-five years.[10]

As Castro's reactions became increasingly furious and defiant García Márquez, whom friends and family members remember as distraught during this period, nevertheless managed the coolest and most measured public response in a carefully stage-managed "interview" with Barranquilla journalist Julio Roca. He conceded that Padilla's self-criticism did not seem authentic and acknowledged that this had done damage to the image of the revolution; but he also insisted that he had never signed the first letter, claimed that Fidel Castro had been malevolently misquoted, declared his continuing support for the Cuban regime and, in a characteristic move, stated that if there were Stalinist elements in Cuba Fidel Castro would be the first to say so and to start to root them out, as he had done a decade before in 1961.[11]

Subtle though García Márquez's response was, its attempt to be solomonic and to please all sides failed to satisfy anyone. On 10 June the Colombian press demanded that he "define himself publicly on the Cuban issue" and the next day, still dodging and weaving but less so, he announced: "I am a communist who has not yet found a place to sit." Most of his friends and colleagues preferred the Chilean route to socialism; García Márquez, even at the beginning, did not. Of his behaviour Juan Goytisolo would later say, with undisguised bitterness, "With his consummate skill in wriggling out of tight corners, Gabo would carefully distance himself from his friends' critical position while avoiding confrontation with them: the new García Márquez, scintillating strategist of his own enormous talent, victim of fame, devotee of the great and good in this world, and promoter at the planetary level of real or would-be 'advanced' causes, was about to be born."[12]

García Márquez went through a very particular agony of anxiety and indecision because, just before the Padilla crisis broke, he had accepted an invitation from Columbia University in New York to be presented with an honorary doctorate at the beginning of June. The timing could hardly have been more disastrous. He knew only too well that Pablo Neruda, a well-known communist, and Carlos Fuentes, a supporter of Cuba from the beginning, had both been excommunicated by the Revolution in 1966 for making visits to New York. And here was he, already seen by many as a rat who had left the apparently sinking ship around the time of the Bay of Pigs invasion in 1961, accepting an honour from New York's premier university, an honour which, to Cuban eyes, was obviously an attempt to "recuperate" him (in the language of the era) for U.S. interests.[13]

Eventually his official line was that he was accepting the award "on behalf of Colombia," that everyone in Latin America knew that he was against the regime prevailing in the USA, as indeed was Columbia University itself, and that he had consulted "the taxi drivers of Barranquilla"—champions of common sense, he declared—in order to make up his mind.[14] Nevertheless, if his future relationship with the United States—him criticizing but the Americans still welcoming him—was now established, to his evident relief, he was back in the doghouse as far as Cuba was concerned. For the next two years, despite his statement assuring the world that he had not signed the first letter, he again had no contact whatever with the revolutionary island.

Yet once again García Márquez was about to be lucky. If Cuba was closed to him for the time being, another controversy was about to blow up which would show, again, that on the political barometer García Márquez still had good readings almost everywhere but Cuba and Colombia. Whether coincidentally or not we do not know, a few weeks later a Spanish journalist called Ramón Chao pushed a microphone under the nose of 1967 Nobel Prize winner Miguel Angel Asturias and asked him what he thought of the allegations that the author of *One Hundred Years of Solitude* had plagiarized a novel by Balzac, *The Quest of the Absolute*. Asturias paused for a moment and then said he thought there might be something to the accusation. Chao published his scoop in the Madrid weekly *Triunfo* and *Le Monde* reprinted it in Paris on 19 June.[15]

In October 1967 Asturias had become only the second Latin American, and the first novelist from the continent, to win the Nobel Prize. But he had been heavily criticized in recent years for taking a politically controversial ambassadorship in Paris. He was about to discover that "Gabriel García Márquez," not "Miguel Angel Asturias," was now the name of Latin American literature. The truth was that García Márquez had been provoking Asturias for years, despite the older writer's generous comments on the younger man's work and achievement. Early in 1968 García Márquez had vowed that with his new book about a Latin American political patriarch, he would "teach" the author of *The President*, Asturias's signature work, "how to write a real dictator novel."[16]

It seems possible that García Márquez's attitude to Asturias was conditioned in part by the fact that Asturias had won the Nobel Prize, the accolade that he, García Márquez, had wanted to be the first Latin American novelist to win, and in part because Asturias was obviously the Latin American precursor not only of magical realism (of which *One Hundred Years of Solitude* is frequently considered the paradigm) but also, through *The President*, of the dictator novel (of which *The Autumn of the Patriarch* was, similarly, intended to be the defining version). Asturias made a large and easy target because of his own vulnerability over the ambassadorship and because he was never the most lucid or coherent of debaters; and by now he was old and sick. Taking him on was like shooting an elephant from a safe distance. In fact, Asturias's decision in the late 1940s, 1950s and 1960s to act as a kind of literary fellow traveller to world communism, supporting the movement of history in general but without having to tie himself down in detail, was a model for precisely what García Márquez himself would attempt to do; and, to some extent echoing Asturias's relations with Guatemala's Marxist President Jacobo Arbenz, García Márquez would shortly befriend the most charismatic of all Latin American Communist revolutionaries, Fidel Castro.

García Márquez did not yet know that he had once again been banished from the Cuban political Eldorado and played brilliantly to the leftist gallery. He had not directly caused Asturias's difficulties but he had helped provoke them and Asturias fell into an ambush—an elephant trap, one might say. The question then arises whether García Márquez had not also been setting a series of psychological traps for Mario Vargas Llosa, his only serious rival among his contemporaries, traps which would cause another even more violent confrontation a few years down the road. And whether the final version of *The Autumn of the Patriarch*, a self-critical work about a man who cannot tolerate competition from those close to him, whether in public or private life, is not in some measure an expiation for these sins.

On 9 July the García Barcha family left Soledad Airport in Barranquilla for Mexico. They had spent less than six months back in Colombia. García Márquez arrived in the Mexican capital on 11 July complaining that he had seen no girls during the stopover in Florida because the "Executive Authority" was with him, a joke that Mercedes must have found increasingly tedious down the years. He spent his first day escorted around the city by journalists and photographers from *Excelsior*, to whom he declared that this was the city he knew best in the world and that he felt as if he had never left. The journalists watched him eating tacos, changing money and cracking jokes ("I'm a very serious guy on the inside but not on the outside"). Young Rodrigo said he would rather be a baseball player or a mechanic than a student. "You can be what you want," said his indulgent father. Still accompanied by the photographers, he visited Carlos Fuentes and his actress wife Rita Macedo—dressed in black leather hot pants—at their house in San Angel. Fuentes shouted "Plagiarist, plagiarist!" as García Márquez's car arrived.[17] That evening Fuentes held one of his famous parties, attended by a familiar array of Mexico's progressive intellectuals and artists.

García Márquez was a different person in Mexico now, the person he would remain for the rest of his life: a favourite foreign son and honorary Mexican. Mexicans would never forget that it was in their capital city, not Paris or London, that *One Hundred Years of Solitude* had been written. It was one of the ways of papering over the bad memories of the Tlatelolco massacre in 1968 with good publicity and García Márquez lent himself to it. On 21 August he went to see President Luis Echeverría, who had been Minister of the Interior at the time of Tlatelolco, at the presidential residence of Los Pinos, where they talked, so García Márquez claimed, about "writing and liberation."[18] He would never publicly criticize either Echeverría or ex-President

Díaz Ordaz for the events of 1968, just as he would never criticize Fidel Castro over any of Cuba's controversies. Cuba and Mexico were both involved in a complex diplomatic struggle with the United States and, to a lesser extent, with each other. The Mexicans were forced to cooperate with U.S. anti-communist efforts but would insist on retaining a diplomatic corridor to Cuba until the end of the PRI period at the close of the twentieth century. Castro and García Márquez would both be grateful to them for holding out.

In late September the family flew back to Barcelona from Mexico City via New York, London and Paris. García Márquez now got back to work. It was more than four years since a new book of his had appeared and he was keen to reduce the pressure. During the period since late 1967, although *The Autumn of the Patriarch* was undoubtedly his major project, he had also settled down to composing his first short stories for several years, and he added to the new ones—which included "A Very Old Man with Enormous Wings"—the earlier "The Sea of Dead Time" from 1961.[19] They would all be published together as *Innocent Eréndira and Other Stories* in 1972. *Innocent Eréndira* itself had a long history—in one sense going back to the mythical world of his grandparents in the deserts of the Guajira. The direct source, however, was from a real life story which had already inspired a brief episode in *One Hundred Years of Solitude* about a young prostitute who is forced to sleep with hundreds of men per day. The finished story had been conceived as a film script before it became a long short story, and had been published in that form by the Mexican magazine *¡Siempre!* as early as November 1970.[20] Because all the stories had been started before—in some cases long before—García Márquez was able to use them to "warm up his arm" for the return to his unfinished novel.

The stories of *Innocent Eréndira* are not at all what one would have expected from a writer who had returned to the Caribbean to re-experience the "smell of guava." True, they are at first sight more primitive, elemental and magical (sea, sky, desert and the frontier) than the stories of *Big Mama*, but in a rather painterly and "literary" way, as if the fantastic element of the earliest stories were somehow being applied to a concrete geographical scenario; as if Macondo and the "Pueblo" were real, whereas the Guajira (which García Márquez had never even seen) is a realm of magic and myth (Bogotá and its surrounding highlands being always, by contrast, a bogeyland of shadows and menace). Ironically enough, these stories—on which the critics are divided—are reminiscent of the most cloying tales of García Márquez's magical realist predecessor, Miguel Angel Asturias, for example in *The Mirror of Lida Sal*.[21]

Now, for the first time, García Márquez set about *The Autumn of the Patriarch* with the certainty that he would be completing it. There were no more excuses, he had had his sabbatical and there was nowhere to escape to, even in his mind. By now the first number of the Boom-based magazine *Libre* had appeared in Paris, a year after Cortázar's party in the south of France, at which it had originally been discussed, and less than six months after the Padilla Affair. It was no doubt being minutely scrutinized in Cuba as García Márquez gave an interview to Plinio Mendoza, the magazine's editor, for *Libre* no. 3, in Franco's Spain.

In October the traditional left—and Salvador Allende's beleaguered Popular Unity government in Chile—received a boost when Pablo Neruda, Allende's ambassador in Paris, was announced as the winner of the Nobel Prize for 1971. Neruda, whom journalists described as looking frail and ill, was asked if he would recommend any other Latin American for the prize and said that his first thought was García Márquez, "author of one of the best novels in the Spanish language."[22] Just before the official announcement of the award was made Neruda called García Márquez and invited him and Mercedes to go to Paris for dinner the next evening. García Márquez naturally said that it was impossible to get there at such short notice given his fear of flying but Neruda used his well-known tactic of sounding as if he was about to cry and the Colombian couple felt obliged to make the trip. By the time they got there the news was out and they dined in Neruda's house with the Mexican muralist David Alfaro Siqueiros (who was suspected of having assassinated Trotsky, and certainly had once attempted it), the Chilean painter Roberto Matta, Jorge Edwards, recently expelled from Cuba, the French intellectual Régis Debray, back in Paris after his release from prison in Bolivia and a subsequent period in which he was closely involved with the Allende regime in Chile, and the great photographer Henri Cartier-Bresson—a politically challenging dinner party if ever there was one.

In December Vargas Llosa's *García Márquez: History of a Deicide* was published in Barcelona by Barral. The two writers, whom friends from that era describe as "almost brothers," had more in common than a first impression might suggest: both had experienced an especially painful version of the childhood "family romance." Both would always have problems with fathers known belatedly (until he was ten years of age Vargas Llosa thought his father was dead), men who would attack their characters and question their literary vocations. Both had been much indulged, bookish boys brought up in the house of their maternal grandparents for the first, defining years of their lives. Both would leave the comfort and security of their early home for the alienating rigours of a boarding-school regime and an early acquaintance with prostitution and other low-life experiences. Both worked as journalists at a precocious age and then travelled to Paris, eventually even staying in the same hotel, though at different times. Both were great friends of their friends and both, when they met, were fervent supporters of the Cuban Revolution, though the older man, García Márquez, had already been through many difficult moments with the Cuban process—while Vargas Llosa's worst difficulties lay ahead of him. Despite their closeness at the time, García Márquez would always insist that he had never even read Mario's book about him, "because if someone showed me all the secret mechanisms of my work, the sources, what it is that makes me write, if someone told me all that, I think it would paralyse me, don't you see?"[23]

Vargas Llosa and García Márquez had first come together on the occasion of the Rómulo Gallegos prize awarded to the young Peruvian in 1967. Now in 1972 García Márquez himself became the second recipient of the prize and his reaction underlined the vast gulf opening up between them in this extraordinary friendship: whereas Vargas Llosa had refused to donate his prize to the causes supported by the Cuban Revolution, García Márquez had decided to give his money to a dissident Venezuelan party, Movimiento al Socialismo (Movement Towards Socialism) or MAS, led by an ex-communist friend of his, Teodoro Petkoff. Like Petkoff, García Márquez had convinced himself that Soviet communism was no longer a genuine revolutionary force, nor was it concerned to address the real needs and interests of Latin America. Carmen Balcells, who travelled to Caracas with García Márquez, told me: "It was an interminable journey, though we were in first class, drinking all the way, and Gabo, who already knew he was going to give all the money to MAS, and to Petkoff, spent the entire time worrying in the most minute detail about what Mario was going to say. It was all he could think about."[24]

The Venezuelans were shocked to see a man with an Afro hairstyle, an open-necked Hawaiian-style tropical shirt, grey trousers, white shoes and no socks saunter on to the rostrum in Caracas's Teatro París to receive the prize. Recalling that Vargas Llosa had refused to donate the prize to the armed struggle in Latin America, people all over the continent were wondering what García Márquez would do with his cash. When asked this question immediately after the ceremony he declared that he was tired of being poor and would be buying "another yacht" from a contact in Caracas, or from Carlos Barral back in Barcelona. This became one of his most famous *boutades*.[25] Mercedes had not flown in with him—she would arrive later with the Feduchis— but also witnessing the performance were his son, twelve-year-old Rodrigo, and his two near namesakes, his father Gabriel Eligio and his youngest brother Eligio Gabriel, who had recently married a girl from the Colombian Llanos, Myriam Garzón. Gabito had invited them to Caracas for their honeymoon, to coincide with his acceptance of the Gallegos prize. Gabriel Eligio had invited himself along and the trio visited the places where Gabito and Mercedes had spent their own honeymoon fourteen years earlier and stayed in the same hotel together. Myriam remembers: "Eligio's father was put in a separate wing of the hotel and protested bitterly to the management: 'How can you do this to me, he's my son.' Next morning he called us at 6 a.m.: 'What time are we going down to breakfast?' "[26]

Gabriel Eligio was predictably unimpressed by his son's comportment on this vast and prestigious stage. Little did he know what was to follow. The next morning Gabo took his cheque for $22,750, his son Rodrigo, his brother Eligio, who had arranged with *El Tiempo* to write a series of reports on the award of Latin America's most important literary prize to his elder brother, one or two other privileged journalists, a photographer and a large bag to a Caracas bank where he changed the cheque into cash. Then he took the bag, the money and his escort to the headquarters of the Movement Towards Socialism and handed the money over to the party's leader Teodoro Petkoff, his "friend for many years."[27] MAS, he explained, was a new, youthful movement of the kind Latin America needed, with no remaining ties to the communist movement and no fixed schemes or dogmas.

A storm of criticism blew in from everywhere, near and far, not excluding García Márquez's own family. MAS was only a tiny organization but the fallout was enormous. Most of the left considered him a "deviationist" and the right branded him a "subversive." Even though it eventually transpired that the money was specifically intended for MAS's political magazine and not for guerrilla warfare, by late August even Moscow would be calling him a "reactionary" and his own father could be found informing the press in Caracas that his eldest son was "very sly—he was the same as a child, always making up stories."[28] García Márquez must have been more troubled when he got back to Europe by the criticism of Pablo Neruda, whose views—despite the Chilean's long-time membership of the Communist Party—were similar in many ways to those of García Márquez himself. The next time they met Neruda told him that he could understand his action but any benefit done to the interests of MAS was far outweighed by the divisions this kind of gesture caused within the international socialist movement.[29] It was probably then that García Márquez began his policy—already applied to Cuba—of never openly criticizing socialist groups, not excluding Moscow-line communist parties, because of the comfort it gave to their enemies.[30]

After he had sorted out his own affairs he flew to New York in the middle of August to visit his old friend Alvaro Cepeda, who was being treated for cancer in the Memorial Hospital. García Márquez was already terrified of hospitals and of death and the experience only confirmed his sense of the great city's staggering inhumanity. When he got back to Barcelona a week later he sent Cepeda's wife a letter:

Tita,
    I couldn't phone you. Besides, I had nothing to say: the maestro was so keen to reassure me that he made me believe that he had never been ill and instead devoted himself to looking after me. I found him very pale and almost worn out but I soon realized that it was because of the radiation because after a week of rest, in which we did nothing other than talk and eat, he had recovered quite a lot. I was alarmed that he had almost completely lost his voice but he convinced me that that too was down to the radiation. Indeed, with a decongestant jelly, whose prescription I read, he started to get his voice back within a few days. It wasn't possible for me to talk to the doctor. However I talked to other doctors, friends of mine, and they agreed that certain kinds of lymphoma have been curable for six years now! . . .
    Big hug, Gabo

Yet again he felt frustrated at interrupting *The Autumn of the Patriarch* and yet again he felt reluctant to get back to it. Soon afterwards, Plinio Mendoza was with him in Barcelona when Alejandro Obregón called to tell him that all hope had gone and Cepeda was dying. After a day of anguish García Márquez bought a plane ticket. Mendoza recalls, "But he didn't go. He couldn't. His guts or his knees refused to take him: at the door to his house, with a suitcase in his hand, and the taxi approaching down the street, he had something like vertigo and instead of heading for the airport he shut himself in his room, pulled the curtains and lay down. Mercedes told me about it in the kitchen, by a washing machine that was moaning and sighing as if it were human. 'Gabito's been crying.' I was surprised. Gabo crying? Gabo shut in his room? I have never seen a tear on his Arab face—and as they say in my homeland, only God knows what he's been through in his time."[31]

On 12 October 1972, Columbus Day, Alvaro Cepeda died in New York. Wayward as he was in almost every respect, Cepeda was the only member of the Barranquilla Group who never went away from Barranquilla for long, despite his yearnings for the USA. (Alfonso, Germán and Alvaro had all appeared in *No One Writes to the Colonel* and they all reappeared in *One Hundred Years of Solitude*, which had predicted that Alvaro would pass on first, followed by Germán, then Alfonso.) The body was flown back to Colombia two days later and Obregón and Julio Mario Santo Domingo held a vigil over the coffin until the morning of the 15th when a huge crowd of mourners escorted the hearse to Barranquilla's Garden of Rest.[32] A few weeks later García Márquez sent Alfonso Fuenmayor a letter reflecting on Cepeda's death: "Well, Maestro, this is a fucking awful thing to have to say: I'm turned to shit, in a wretched state of dismay and demoralization and for the first time in my life I can't find a way out. I say this to you because I think it will help me to say it to you and because perhaps my saying it will help you too. Gabito."[33]

The following year, when Neruda died, García Márquez would tell journalists in Bogotá: "The death of my great friend Alvaro Cepeda last year hit me so hard that I realized I can't cope with the disappearance of my friends. 'Hell,' I thought, 'if I don't face up to this business it's me that'll die one of these days the next time I get this kind of news.'"[34] It was true that given his growing celebrity García Márquez had put in quite an effort to see his stricken friend and certainly his grief was real. But it was also true that he had been moving away from Cepeda and all the Barranquilla Group and the 1971 visit to the city had only emphasized this. More than most men García Márquez, who felt nostalgia with great intensity, had also learned early in his life how to fight it. Now the death of Cepeda drew a definitive line under the Barranquilla experience.

It was a gloomy autumn following his friend's demise. On 7 November came the ominous news that Richard Nixon had been re-elected President of the United States. In that same month ex-President Juan Perón made his at first euphoric but ultimately disastrous return to Buenos Aires after seventeen years away and Salvador Allende had to refashion his Popular Unity government to put an end to a wave of strikes in Chile, while Pablo Neruda's cancer forced him to resign his ambassadorship to Paris. García Márquez was there to see the old Communist poet set off on his last return to South America. They would never meet again.

García Márquez went on with *The Autumn of the Patriarch* in a state of depression but also with a curiously renewed vigour. Alvaro Cepeda's death had made him more aware than ever that life was short and perhaps he realized that he did not want to be in Europe while events in Latin America were passing him by. In Spain everything was paralysed while the country waited for General Franco to expire. The regime was clearly on its last legs—on 8 June Franco appointed Admiral Luis Carrero Blanco President, after ruling alone for thirty-four years—but its end was a long time coming, almost as long as the passing of García Márquez's own "Patriarch" in the novel he had nearly completed. In May 1973 he began to tell newspapermen that *The Autumn of the Patriarch* was finished. However, he was going to let it sit for a year or more, "to see whether I still like it."[35] Behind the blasé appearance—apparently this writer didn't really care whether his books were published or not and certainly did not respond to pressure either from publishers or readers—there was evidently still the same insecurity about the novel, which he had been working on intensively since his return from Barranquilla and Mexico late in 1971.

It is typical of García Márquez's prescience that his first book after *One Hundred Years of Solitude* should be a novel which not only confronted the pitfalls of fame and power before they had even fully engulfed him but also anticipated and in that sense cauterized middle and old age long before he had reached them. However, it is impossible to talk of *The Autumn of the Patriarch* in simplistic terms. No other work by García Márquez even begins to approach its complexity—best illustrated perhaps by the contrast between the seductive beauty of the book's poetic imagery and the ugliness of its subject matter.[36] There is, indeed, a curious historical paradox relating to the conception of this work. The novels which had created the sense of a Latin American Boom in the 1960s—*The Time of the Hero, The Death of Artemio Cruz* and *Hopscotch*—were mainly updated versions of the great European and American modernist novels of the 1920s and 1930s—works such as *Ulysses, In Search of Lost Time, Manhattan Transfer, Mrs. Dalloway* or *Absalom, Absalom!* Yet the book which crystallized and consecrated that Latin American Boom, *One Hundred Years of Solitude*, seemed infinitely less labyrinthine and modernist than the others. At a time when the term "postmodernist" had not yet been invented, critics like Emir Rodríguez Monegal talked of the curious "anachronism" of García Márquez's novel—because it was apparently transparent, easy to read, and accessible even to people who only had a modest literary education.[37] For his follow-up, however, García Márquez felt challenged to write something more like a typical Boom novel: this is why the Joycean and Woolfian features of *The Autumn of the Patriarch* are immediately obvious to the experienced readers for whom the book was evidently intended. This was at the very moment when most other writers, stung by García Márquez's success, were turning away from the characteristic Boom mode and writing much more transparent "postmodern" works of the kind *One Hundred Years of Solitude* was supposed to represent.

The new novel went through many versions. It is the story of an uneducated Latin American soldier from an unnamed, composite nation who seizes power despite having little political experience and contrives to rule as dictator of his tropical country for two centuries. Among the tyrants García Márquez drew on for his horrifying portrait were the Venezuelans Juan Vicente Gómez (in power 1908–35) and Marcos Pérez Jiménez (1952–8), Porfirio Díaz of Mexico (1884–1911), Manuel Estrada Cabrera of Guatemala (1898–1920), the Somozas of Nicaragua (Anastasio, Luis and Anastasio Jr., 1936–79) and Rafael Trujillo (1930–61) of the Dominican Republic. Spain and Franco, García Márquez still insisted, had, if anything, got in his way. He still, to this day, knew very little about Franco, because such a cold and ascetic European figure was of little use or interest to him.

Known to the reader only as "the Patriarch," the book's monstrous protagonist is as solitary as he is powerful and as sentimental as he is barbaric. Though apparently insensitive almost to the point of stupidity, he has an extraordinary instinct for power and an intuitive insight into other men's motives—though women, not excluding his beloved mother, remain a mystery to him. García Márquez had realized, he told interviewers, that this dictator was what Colonel Aureliano Buendía would have turned into if he had won his war—in other words, if Colombian history had been different and the Liberals rather than the Conservatives had triumphed over the course of the nineteenth century.[38] For his protagonist to maintain his mythical force he had decided that he should have no name: just "the Patriarch" (known also to his staff as "the General"). Rather shockingly, García Márquez explained that he had written a relatively sympathetic portrait because "all dictators, from Creon onwards, are victims." The unfortunate truth, he insisted, was that Latin American history was not as people would wish: most dictators were from the popular classes and were never overthrown by the people they oppressed. It was not that myth had triumphed over history but rather that history itself always becomes mythologized. It was an essential purpose of literature, he declared, to show this process. But he was not prepared to give any further enlightenment: "The political aspect of the book is a good deal more complex than it seems and I'm not prepared to explain it."[39]

What is unmistakable is that this new novel altered and deepened García Márquez's approach to the twin problematics of power and love—his two central themes—with their associated motifs of memory, nostalgia, solitude and death. Power and love, the love of power, the power of love, are central aspects of human experience, with a particularly strong momentum in Latin American history, society and literature.

The book is set in a fictitious Caribbean nation, which seems to have Colombia—or, more particularly, Bogotá—as its neighbour, so that we can think of it as either something like Venezuela or as the Colombian Costa itself. In that sense this nameless state is similar to the fictitious countries invented by Joseph Conrad in *Nostromo* (1904) or by Spain's Ramón María del Valle-Inclán in *Tirano Banderas* (1926). The portrait of its crude and violent Latin American dictator is focused in particular on his "autumn," that is, the later years of his regime.

The book unfolds in an impossible historical time which stretches over some two hundred years, probably from the late eighteenth century until the 1960s.[40] Most of it is narrated through flashbacks and follows the general contours of Latin American history until the sea is expropriated by the gringos at the "twilight" of the Patriarch's autumn, followed by his death and the consequent end of his regime (winter and dissolution). The protagonist lives in a world where the military, the Church and the gringos are incessantly jockeying for power. "The people" themselves are virtually passive; there is no dialectical progress in the novel because there is no history, no real passage of time, no true social or political participation or interaction. Yet the relationship between the dictator and the people is perhaps the central focus of the novel. One might say that García Márquez's intended gesture is that the novel should be handed over from the patriarch to the people in its closing lines, whose euphoria—clearly a memory of the fall of Pérez Jiménez in Venezuela in 1958—seems to be intended literally, not ironically.

In more individual terms, the Patriarch's closest relationship on earth is to his mother, Bendición Alvarado. His wife is the ex-nun Leticia Nazareno, whom he kidnaps and possibly murders; the lover he pursues but never wins is the beauty queen Manuela Sánchez, and his only successful erotic relationship is, bizarrely, with a twelve-year-old schoolgirl when he is already senile. On the male side he has a double, or public face, Patricio Aragonés; just one good friend, Rodrigo de Aguilar; and later an evil genius, the glamorous Security Minister José Ignacio Sáenz de la Barra, similar to the advisers of the military juntas in Chile and Argentina in the 1970s, at the time the novel was being completed. This structure of relationships conforms to the classic pattern of Western myth.[41]

But this is wisdom after the event. The reader's overwhelming experience is one of uncertainty and confusion. The whole point of view, structure and even chronology of the novel are determined by the uncertainty of a succession of narrators who are never sure of anything. One might say that the endless dilemma as to whether the dictator does or does not control "all of his power," which is perhaps the most reiterated and the most confusing aspect of the novel—magnified enormously by the fact that it is considered above all from his point of view (at once stupid and unreflective, hypocritical and self-serving)—is governed by a three-way oscillation between the classical enlightenment view of human consciousness as that of a rational unified subject; a more Marxist perception of class domination and imperialism (these two perceptions, combined, would be a modernist view); and the Foucauldian view that power is everywhere, epistemic, always to be resisted but impossible to defeat and beyond even the most "powerful" subject's ability to control (this of course would be a postmodernist view and is in fact dominant in the novel). In this work's absolutely ruthless cynicism about human beings, power and effect we find ourselves forced to consider that power is there to be used and that "someone has to do this," because García Márquez's view of history is very close to that bleak vision which Machiavelli first theorized and Shakespeare repeatedly exemplified. He would go straight off after completing the book to seek a relationship with Fidel Castro, a socialist liberator who was, as it turned out, the Latin American politician with the potential to become the most durable and the most loved of all the continent's authoritarian figures.

The novel's sentences are immensely long: there are only twenty-nine in chapter 1, twenty-three in chapter 2, eighteen in chapter 3, sixteen in chapter 4, thirteen in chapter 5 and just one in chapter 6, making a total, apparently, of one hundred. The early chapters begin with three or four paragraphs on the first page, like an orchestra tuning up, and then they grow longer and longer. There are constant switches of narrative person from first ("I," "we") to second ("General sir," "Mother of mine," etc.) to third ("he," "they"), although the latter is nearly always inside another voice. García Márquez himself as third-person narrator is almost absolutely absent, yet no novel is more dominated by his characteristic literary voice. Each chapter begins with his usual obsession, the matter of burial, though the reader cannot be sure whether the body found is that of the tyrant—or indeed, if it is, whether he is really dead. Thus the "we"—we the people who found the corpse—are conjuring up a world in retrospect through a few short sentences on the first page of each chapter with variable details about the discovery of the body, after which the narrative plunges into the labyrinth or whirlpool of flashbacks into the life of "him," "the General," which dissolves gradually into an autobiographical "I," the Man of Power. The labyrinth, as in all modernist works, is both topic (life) and technique (the way through it).

Manifestly *The Autumn of the Patriarch* is a novel written obsessively, by a solitary writer, about an obsessive, solitary dictator. Yet according to the author the critics, many of whom tended to feel outraged that he had given a moderately sympathetic portrait of this horrific personality, were slow to see what the book was really about. So in Mexico City in December 1975, almost two years after completing it and several months after its publication, a frustrated García Márquez, who declared that his reviewers, without exception, had read the book "superficially," supplied a totally unexpected explanation of its meaning. It was, he asserted, a kind of autobiography: "It's almost a personal confession, a totally autobiographical book, almost a book of memoirs. What's happened, of course, is that they are encoded memoirs; but if instead of seeing a dictator you see a very famous writer who is terribly uncomfortable with his fame, well, with that clue you can read the book and make it work."[42]

This is at first sight an astonishing assertion. García Márquez was a man trying to impress his readers with a follow-up to a popular classic, a man under pressure who might have been expected to ingratiate himself with the public; whereas *The Autumn of the Patriarch* was an ugly portrait of a profoundly ugly persona. This dictator, although in some ways treated indulgently, is one of the most repugnant characters ever created. Was García Márquez merely trying to scandalize the international bourgeoisie with sensational declarations to the press or had he, in truth, written one of the most shockingly self-critical works of world literature, a fictional parallel with Rousseau's *Confessions*, for example? Are the author's relationships with men, women and the world as a whole in some way comparable with those of his hideous yet pathetic creation? And if García Márquez thinks so, is he merely using himself as an example of a world fuller of vile bodies and dangerous liaisons than we have ever dreamed or is this an exclusively personal and thus uniquely devastating self-analysis? Given the cruel aridity of the self-portrait, it seems not impossible that the sojourn in the grotesque sterility of late *franquista* Spain very quickly turned into a self-imposed penance of self-analysis for the person he had always been as he looked now towards the future. Writing *The Autumn of the Patriarch* perhaps involved trying to deserve his fame morally as well as trying to show he deserved it literarily (despite the fact, ironically, that many readers saw the manifestly ambitious result as a proof of overweening arrogance and complacency).

The Patriarch's "first death" might easily be a metaphor for 1967, the year of *One Hundred Years of Solitude*, when the "real" García Márquez disappeared for ever beneath the weight of celebrity and mythology: he may be describing his gradual farewell to anonymity, normality and privacy, a process through which a crisis of failure in the 1960s turned, with almost comic irony, into a crisis of fame and success in the 1970s. And this may also have represented, in his own consciousness, a farewell to youth (he had just turned forty when *One Hundred Years of Solitude* was published). Moreover it is not entirely surprising that García Márquez, a man always predisposed to reflections on old age, should bring forward his own mid-life crisis and begin his own "autumn" earlier than anyone else, so that the mid-life crisis in Barcelona was mingled in his case with the crisis of fame that surrounded it. Perhaps after assimilating all these lessons in the writing of this literally nightmarish work, he would put his fame and influence at the service of good causes by becoming, like the Patriarch in his prime, "master of all his power," only consciously so and with benevolent intent.

Perhaps the result of his sudden celebrity had indeed been another splitting of a personality that García Márquez had desperately been trying to unify ever since he was an adolescent, a struggle whose first traces are clearly visible in the early stories and which, it might be speculated, the writing of *One Hundred Years of Solitude* had triumphantly completed. But perhaps he had resolved one problem of doubling only to find that now he had to confront another: the divorce between what he would later call his secret and private personas, on the one hand, and his public persona on the other. Perhaps that was why the novel raises the possibility that the corpse the people discover at the start of each chapter may not even be the Patriarch. Now that he too was famous, García Márquez, like the tyrant, was constantly confronted, in the media, by his own representation, "his perfect double, the humiliation of seeing himself in such a state of equality, God damn it, this man is me." As for the tyrant's doppelgänger, his official double or public image, Patricio Aragonés, "he had become resigned to live forever a destiny that was not his." Well, García Márquez felt that he was both men: "the real one" and "the double." At first the Patriarch had found it difficult to adjust to the new names the people or the media, or, later, state propaganda, chose to call him (like García Márquez's many brand names: "Gabo," the "Master of Macondo," "Melquíades the Magician," etc.). But however disconcerted he was by this double or indeed multiple existence, he was never as confused as those around him.

Thus the matter of autobiography (especially his own predicament as a uniquely famous writer) took García Márquez over as he wrote a book that seemed to be about a man who was his polar opposite, and so the Patriarch slowly became him, just as Aureliano Buendía had become him in *One Hundred Years of Solitude*, only now he was truly plumbing the darkest depths of the human condition, reflected deep in his own soul. The Patriarch, *c'est moi*: fame, glamour, influence and power, on the one hand; solitude, lust, ambition and cruelty on the other. Needless to say, it is a great autobiographical irony that the writer had in fact set out to write this book about power and celebrity in the late 1950s, many years before he himself actually experienced those phenomena. At all events, by the time he began the final assault on the topic, he too was famous and powerful, he too was solitary, he too was "him," the "other," the desired object. The literary monster he had created but was determined to satirize and expose (but whom he had possibly always envied and desired in others) was a figure of the phenomenon he himself had become.

In an interview with Juan Gossaín in 1971 García Márquez had linked the themes of love and power. Insisting that all his characters were in some way autobiographical, he had declared: "You know, old friend, the appetite for power is the result of an incapacity for love."[43] This statement could begin to trace a hidden connection between all of García Márquez's novels, a thread to help his readers out of the intricate moral and psychological labyrinth created by his oeuvre. Perhaps at first, as his sense of his own potential gradually increased, he began to fantasize that he could have it all: he could gain power and be loved for it. Then came the crisis of fame in the late 1960s and early 1970s, when García Márquez, a man of great self-control, great linguistic potency, and great psychological penetration (with above all a remarkable power of private persuasion, an extraordinary capacity for intimacy, for non-public activity) suddenly found himself at the mercy of other, often less talented beings—critics, journalists, agents, publishers, hangers-on—within the public domain. He, who had enjoyed the power of the reporter, was now himself at the mercy of reporters. He had become an image and a commodity which he could not himself entirely control. No wonder Carmen Balcells became so important to him: she became his "agent" in many more ways than simply arranging his contracts with publishers. She helped him, undoubtedly, to realize the possibility of becoming, as much as any human being can, the "master of all his power."

So maybe then, like the dictator, he decided to take control of his public self, to become another self (which would only be partially himself, but now he would get to choose his image); instead of protesting about his predicament as he had for the past eight years, he would *assume* his famous self, *use* his fame, go past all his rivals, become a man of power and influence based not only on his public success achieved through the solitary act of writing but on his private, behind-the-scenes brilliance and power of seduction.

Because the dictator, however crude he may seem in García Márquez's intimate portrayal, was a political genius, for a very simple reason: "he saw the others just as they were while the others were never able to glimpse his hidden thoughts."[44] Although "hermetic to himself," the Patriarch was "crystal clear in his ability to see the reality and future of others."[45] His patience was immense and he would always win in the end, as when finally—in the case of his unreadable and apparently indispensable adviser Sáenz de la Barra—"he discovered the imperceptible crack he had been seeking for so many years in that obsidian wall of fascination."[46] Is this a picture of García Márquez himself, always wanting to "win"—against all-comers, friends and family, wife and lovers, professional rivals (Asturias, Vargas Llosa), the world? And would Fidel Castro become the only man—his very own Patriarch, his grandfather figure—against whom he could not, would not dare, would not even wish, to win?

The lesson—it might be called a postmodern one—finally learned by the reader of this novel, through his or her reluctant co-existence with the Patriarch, is that life is undoubtedly impossible to understand but there are certain moral "truths," notwithstanding all our illusions and all our contemporary relativities.[47] They relate not only to charity and compassion but to power, responsibility, solidarity, commitment and, finally, love. Perhaps it was the complex inter-relation between these human questions which was the lesson that García Márquez himself learned in becoming famous and which he would not have learned unless he had become famous—which, indeed, for the most part, perhaps only the famous and powerful *can* learn—even though most powerful figures who experience the process of learning go on, like the Patriarch himself, to become even more despicable as their power and influence increases. It raises the radical possibility that the García Márquez who began to give interviews about politics and morality between, say, 1972 and 1975 was a new García Márquez who had learned what the old, still relatively naive and "innocent" García Márquez was truly like and had resolved to be better and to do better now that fame had shown him the truth.

As for love, when readers these days think about García Márquez and love they are inclined to smile and think of the apparently ingenuous romantic Florentino Ariza from *Love in the Time of Cholera* and of the wise and knowing face of García Márquez himself reproduced on the covers of millions of novels. Yet his treatment of love and sex, both in *The Autumn of the Patriarch* and elsewhere, is curiously brutal and disenchanted. The Patriarch's attitude to women is coarse and unimaginative in the extreme, with two exceptions: the beauty queen Manuela Sánchez, the unattainable woman he idealizes from afar but never gets to know, and at the other extreme the twelve-year-old schoolgirl Lolita figure whom he seduces when he is already senile. Still, the only woman he has ever truly loved appears to be his mother. So is the whole relationship with Luisa Santiaga a key to this novel? And does Manuela Sánchez represent an illusory quest for mere external glamour? And does Leticia Nazareno stand for the destiny of all wives (Mercedes is one of Leticia's other names)? And is all of it somehow the other, dark side of his suppression of his father, given that in this novel there are not even any grandfathers? Because the Patriarch regards himself as self-generated:

> . . . he considered no one the son of anyone but his mother, and only her. That certainty seemed valid even for him, as he knew that he was a man without a father like the most illustrious despots of history, that the only relative known to him and perhaps the only one he had was his mother of my heart Bendición Alvarado to whom the school texts attributed the miracle of having conceived him without recourse to any male and of having received in a dream the hermetical keys to his messianic destiny, and whom he proclaimed matriarch of the land by decree.[48]

The truth, it appears, both prosaic and profound, is that men want a wife to be their long-term lover but when they get one they find they wanted a mother all along whilst continuing to want other, idealized lovers. During the Patriarch's early times with Leticia Nazareno she would sit him down each day to learn to read and write; then they would spend every afternoon naked under her mosquito net, and she would wash him and dress him like a baby. Thus one half of a man is moved to suppress and rape women, considered by definition "younger" and inferior to him, and to wrest them away from other men; the other half wants to be treated like a child or baby by those same women, considered anterior or superior to him—because, once again, equality and democratic interaction are considered unrealistic or even (because unexciting) undesirable. In this book as in others García Márquez hardly ever uses the word "sex," which causes permanent ambiguity about the meaning of love and the relation between sex and love. Evidently the only certainty that most of us can have about love is that our mother loves us, whatever our faults or crimes. Yet as we know, even this certainty was not given to García Márquez himself in the early years of his life.

By the end of *his* life the Patriarch can hardly remember anything at all, "conversing with spectres whose voices he couldn't even decipher,"[49] amidst all the signs of advanced old age, still vainly wanting sex, since love is forever denied him, and so his staff bring him women from abroad, but to no avail, because best of all he still likes jumping on working-class women, which always makes him start to sing again ("bright January moon . . .").[50] Finally, at the very end of the novel, he remembers what his whole life has been dedicated to forgetting, "a remote childhood which for the first time was his own image shivering on the icy barrens and the image of his mother Bendición Alvarado who stole the innards of a ram away from the garbage-heap buzzards for lunch."[51] Childhood, as *Memories of My Melancholy Whores* will also remind us, does not necessarily excuse but it may explain.

GARCÍA MÁRQUEZ WOULD CONTINUE to tinker with the novel during the latter part of 1973 and well into 1974.[52] But the book was essentially finished and he was able to start planning the future. He had been a solitary writer locked away in solitary conflict with a solitary protagonist, yet simultaneously conducting an interminable conversation with the world about his solitude and about that most collective of matters: politics. It had been a bizarre spectacle for newspaper readers, to say the least, and García Márquez only just managed to carry off the endeavour without making an international fool of himself; but carry it off he did and the experience made him a far tougher literary and political animal, and gave him a thicker skin with which to confront almost any challenge of the many which his talent and his fame would have in store for him.

In the early spring of 1973 he and Mercedes had travelled up from Barcelona to be at Tachia's wedding in Paris. She and Charles were finally married on 31 March—by then their son Juan was eight—and went to live opposite the hospital where she had miscarried in 1956; later they would move to the Rue du Bac. She would recall, "Gabriel was best man at my wedding and my sister Irene was matron of honour. Gabriel is also the godfather of my son Juan. I'd have liked Blas at the wedding too, it would have been wonderful—but he was so unreliable and unpredictable."[53] There is no reason whatever to think that García Márquez had any regrets about the separation from Tachia, other than the manner of it; but for a man who would be writing insistently about love, she would remain a productive point of reference, a symbol of paths not taken, of relationships outside of marriage, indeed of alternatives to monogamy itself.

Later that year, at the very time he was in the final stages of *The Autumn of the Patriarch*, García Márquez received another major international honour, the Neustadt Prize, awarded in association with the magazine *Books Abroad* of the University of Oklahoma. This was a surprising and indeed commendable decision for an American institution to take only six months after the scandal surrounding his donation of the Gallegos Prize to MAS.[54] After perfunctorily performing his duty in Oklahoma in return for the ceremonial eagle feather and cheque, García Márquez flew to Los Angeles and San Francisco for a brief family holiday and then on to Mexico City, where the family were to spend the summer. So excited were they all to be back in Mexico together, among their old friends, in Rodrigo and Gonzalo's true nation home, that they bought a ramshackle country house on the outskirts of Cuernavaca, that beautiful resort town given notoriety by Malcolm Lowry's *Under the Volcano*.[55] It was a bargain, with 1,100 square metres of garden, near the house of their old friends Vicente and Albita Rojo, in the direction of Las Quintas, with views of the sierra. This time, unlike his near-purchase of a country house outside Barcelona, García Márquez went ahead with the deal. When he registered the property at the notary public, all the employees from adjoining offices came out to have their copies of *One Hundred Years of Solitude* signed. García Márquez exulted, "I'm a capitalist, I own a property!" He was forty-eight.

On 9 September he left Mexico, after a stay of more than two months. Mercedes flew to Barcelona, where the boys were returning reluctantly to school. García Márquez was on his way to Colombia on business. But he told the Mexican press that he was so pleased by his reception in Mexico that he would be going on to Barcelona to pack his things and get back to Mexico as quickly as possible.[56] He also declared that Latin America was very short of great leaders. The only true leaders in the continent were Castro and Allende, the rest were "mere presidents of the republic." Two days later, on the first of the doom-laden September the elevenths, one of those two leaders was dead and Latin America would never be the same again.

19

Chile and Cuba: García Márquez Opts for the Revolution

1973-1979

ON 11 SEPTEMBER 1973, like millions of other political progressives across the world, García Márquez, sitting in front of a television in Colombia, watched in horror as Chilean air force bombers attacked the government palace in Santiago. Within a few hours it was confirmed that the democratically elected President Salvador Allende was dead, whether murdered or having committed suicide no one knew. A military junta took power and began to round up what would become more than thirty thousand alleged left-wing activists over the coming weeks, many of whom would never emerge from custody alive. Pablo Neruda lay dying of cancer in his house at Isla Negra on Chile's Pacific coast. Allende's death and the destruction of his political dreams as Chile fell into the hands of a fascist regime made up the content of Neruda's last days on earth before he succumbed to the illness which had beset him for several years.[1]

Allende's Popular Unity government had been watched by political commentators and activists around the world as an experiment to see whether a socialist society could be achieved through democratic means. Allende had nationalized copper, steel, coal, most private banks and other key sectors of the economy, yet, despite constant propaganda and subversion from the right, his government had increased its share of the vote to 44 per cent in the mid-term elections in March

1973. This only prompted the right into redoubling its efforts to undermine the regime. The CIA had been working against Allende even before his election: the United States, beleaguered in its Vietnamese quagmire and already obsessed with Cuba, was desperate that there should be no further anti-capitalist regimes in the Western hemisphere. The savage destruction of the Chilean experiment, before the eyes of the entire world, would have something of the effect on leftists that the defeat of the Republicans in the Spanish Civil War had exerted almost forty years before.

At eight o'clock that evening García Márquez wrote a telegram to the members of the new Chilean junta: "Bogotá, September 11, 1973. Generals Augusto Pinochet, Gustavo Leigh, César Méndez Danyau and Admiral José Toribio Merino, Members of the Military Junta: You are the material authors of the death of President Allende and the Chilean people will never allow themselves to be governed by a gang of criminals in the pay of North American imperialism. Gabriel García Márquez."[2] At the time he wrote this message Allende's fate was still unknown but García Márquez later said that he knew Allende well enough to be sure he would never leave the palace alive; and the military must have known it too. Although some said that sending this telegram was a gesture more appropriate to a university student than a great writer, it turned out to be the first political action carried out by a new García Márquez, one who was already looking for a new role but whose politics had now been brutally focused and radically hardened by the violent end to Allende's historic experiment. He later told an interviewer, "The Chilean coup was a catastrophe for me."

The Padilla Affair had turned out, predictably, to be the great dividing of the waters in Latin American Cold War history, and not just for intellectuals, artists and writers. García Márquez, despite the criticisms of his friends—ranging from "opportunism" to "naivety"—had remained the most politically consistent of the major Latin American authors. The Soviet Union was not the socialism he wanted but from the Latin American standpoint he considered it essential as a bulwark against U.S. hegemony and imperialism. This was not, in his eyes, "fellow travelling" but a rational appraisal of reality. Cuba, though also problematical, was more progressive than the USSR and had to be supported by all serious anti-imperialist Latin Americans, who should nonetheless do what they could to moderate any repressive, undemocratic or dictatorial aspects of the regime.[3] He chose what seemed to him to be the path of peace and justice for the peoples of the world: international socialism, broadly defined.[4]

He had undoubtedly wanted the Chilean experiment to succeed but had never believed that it would be allowed to do so. In answer to a question from a New York journalist in 1971, he had said:

My ambition is for all Latin America to become socialist, but nowadays people are seduced by the idea of peaceful and constitutional socialism. This seems all very well for electoral purposes, but I believe it to be completely utopian. Chile is heading toward violent and dramatic events. If the Popular Front goes ahead—with intelligence and great tact, with reasonably firm and swift steps—a moment will come when they will encounter a wall of serious opposition. The United States is not interfering at present, but it won't always stand by with folded arms. It won't really accept that Chile is a socialist country. It won't allow that, and don't let's be under any illusions on that point. It's not that I see [violence] as a solution, but I think that a moment will come when that wall of opposition can only be surmounted by violence. Unfortunately, I believe that to be inevitable. I think what is happening in Chile is very good as reform, but not as revolution.[5]

Few observers had seen the future as clearly as this. García Márquez realized that he was now living at a critical juncture in world history. Over the next few years, despite his deep-rooted political pessimism, he would make a series of statements about political commitment which were perhaps best summed up in a 1978 interview: "The sense of solidarity, which is the same as what Catholics call the Communion of Saints, has a very straightforward meaning for me. It means that in every one of our acts each one of us is responsible for the whole of humanity. When a person discovers this it's because his political consciousness has reached its highest level. Modesty apart, that is my case. For me there is no act in my life which is not a political act."[6]

He looked for a way to take action. He was more convinced than ever that the Cuban road was the only feasible route to Latin America's political and economic independence—that is, its dignity. But he was distanced, yet again, from Cuba. In the circumstances he decided that the route back lay, in the first instance, through Colombia. He had been involved in discussions for some time with young Colombian intellectuals, particularly Enrique Santos Calderón of the *El Tiempo* dynasty,[7] whom he had recently got to know, Daniel Samper whom he had known for a decade, and later Antonio Caballero, the son of the liberal upper-class novelist Eduardo Caballero Calderón, with a view to creating a new form of journalism in Colombia—specifically by founding a left-wing magazine.[8] García Márquez had come to the conclusion that the only way for his deeply conservative country to reform itself was by what he would jokingly call the "seduction" and "perversion" of the younger generation from the old ruling families.[9] Other key participants were the nation's best-known chronicler of the *Violencia*, the internationally respected sociologist Orlando Fals Borda, and a left-wing entrepreneur called José Vicente Kataraín, who would later become García Márquez's publisher in Colombia. The new magazine would be called *Alternativa*, its point of departure was "the increasing monopoly of information suffered by Colombian society at the hands of the same interests which control the national economy and national politics," and its purpose was to show "the other Colombia that never appears in the pages of the big press nor on the screens of a television service more closely subordinated each day to official control."[10] The first number would appear in February 1974. The magazine would last six turbulent years and García Márquez, who would spend relatively little time in Colombia despite his best intentions, would nevertheless be a regular contributor and would make himself permanently available for consultations and advice. He and the other leading participants invested large amounts of their own money in this inherently risky business. In the meantime he announced that he would be moving back to Latin America and, more sensationally, that he would be writing no more novels: from now on, and until the military junta led by General Pinochet in Chile fell from power, he was "on strike" as far as literature was concerned and would be devoting himself full time to politics.

In December, as if to underline his new resolutions, García Márquez accepted an invitation to become a member of the prestigious Second Russell Tribunal investigating and judging international war crimes. More significant perhaps than it might seem at first sight, this invitation was the first clear sign that he was going to achieve international acceptance in places and at levels unknown to most other Latin American writers and that despite his controversial commitment to Cuba he was going to have a relatively free hand to participate in political activity wherever and whenever he chose.

The first number of *Alternativa* in February 1974 sold 10,000 copies in twenty-four hours. The police in Bogotá confiscated several hundred copies but this would be the only case of direct censorship in the magazine's history (though there would be "indirect censorship" through bomb attacks, court interventions, economic blockades and a sabotage of distribution, all of which would eventually bring about its demise). Later it would have persistent financial problems but the response in the early months was extraordinary. Before long it was selling 40,000 copies, an unheard-of figure for a left-wing publication in Colombia. The first number had a slogan about consciousness raising—"To Dare to Think Is to Begin to Fight"—and an editorial, "A Letter to the Reader," which stated that the new magazine's aim was to "fight the distortion of national reality in the bourgeois press" and to "counter disinformation" (a theme which had been famously exemplified by the aftermath of the banana massacre in *One Hundred Years of Solitude*).

The magazine, which appeared twice a month, included the first of two articles by García Márquez under the headline "Chile, the Coup and the Gringos."[11] It was his first incursion into openly political journalism since he had become famous and it achieved worldwide distribution (published in the USA and UK in March) and immediate classic status. García Márquez lamented what he construed as Salvador Allende's misguided end:

> He would have been sixty-four years old next July. His greatest virtue was following through, but fate could only grant him that rare and tragic greatness of dying in armed defence of the anachronistic booby of bourgeois law, defending a Supreme Court of Justice which had repudiated him but would legitimize his murderers, defending a miserable Congress which had declared him illegitimate but which was to bend complacently before the will of the usurpers, defending the freedom of opposition parties which had sold their souls to fascism, defending the whole moth-eaten paraphernalia of a shitty system which he had proposed abolishing, but without a shot being fired. The drama took place in Chile, to the greater woe of the Chileans, but it will pass into history as something that has happened to us all, children of this age, and it will remain in our lives for ever.[12]

It was the same tone of contempt with which García Márquez had been speaking about the Colombian parliamentary system since the mid-1950s, best exemplified in "Big Mama's Funeral." As for Salvador Allende, he had become a García Márquez character, one more martyr in the ghastly pantheon of Latin America's failed heroes; many others were to follow and many optimistic but fearful politicians would become friends of García Márquez in the coming years in a perhaps desperate or superstitious effort to avoid such a destiny.

Just as García Márquez almost fled from Mexico once *One Hundred Years of Solitude* had been published and he had managed to pay off his debts, he now prepared to leave Barcelona after the completion of *The Autumn of the Patriarch* and the preparation of his *Collected Stories*.[13] He had always had a half-hearted, somewhat distracted and occasionally patronizing attitude to Spain and now his mind was on other matters and other places. The next year would involve a gradual adjustment of both his place of residence and his attention from Europe to Latin America and from literature to politics. Meanwhile Mario Vargas Llosa, who had arrived in Barcelona after him, was leaving before him. On 12 June 1974 Carmen Balcells hosted a farewell party for Vargas Llosa, who was going back to Peru.[14] Most of the Latin American writers in residence during that period were there, including José Donoso and Jorge Edwards, as well as the Catalans José María Castellet, Carlos Barral, Juan Marsé, Juan and Luis Goytisolo, Manuel Vázquez Montalbán, and many others. This, surely, with Vargas Llosa leaving and García Márquez preparing his own departure, was the ceremony which marked the end of the Boom in all its European splendour.[15] Vargas Llosa set sail for Lima with his wife and family, leaving their many friends in Barcelona bereft, though Carmen Balcells would continued to provide a point of focus.

At the end of the summer García Márquez and Mercedes themselves took an extraordinary decision. They left the boys in Barcelona, in the tender care of their friends the Feduchis, Carmen Balcells, and the woman who cooked and cleaned the house, to travel, somewhat surprisingly, to London. García Márquez had decided it was time at last to attend to what he considered the only great failure of his life—his inability to learn English. He and Mercedes had suggested to Rodrigo and Gonzalo that they might consider two years in London. The boys flatly refused but were astonished, and resentful, when their parents announced that they at least would be going and left the two teenagers behind.[16] The couple stayed for a time in the Kensington Hilton, a hotel they knew well, and enrolled in an intensive course in the Callan School of English on Oxford Street, which guaranteed excellent results in a quarter of the normal time with its "infallible" methods.

Learning English—which did not go well—was not García

Márquez's only preoccupation. It was in London, curiously, that the first steps were taken to reintegrate him into the Cuban Revolution. Since the 1971 Padilla Affair he had been even more ostracized than before but in London he contacted Lisandro Otero, a writer whose confrontation with Heberto Padilla had led indirectly to the first phase of the affair in 1968. Otero knew Régis Debray and Debray agreed to act as an intermediary between García Márquez and Cuban Foreign Minister Carlos Rafael Rodríguez. He told Rodríguez that the revolution was making a big mistake in leaving a figure of García Márquez's significance in "political limbo." Rodríguez agreed and the Cuban ambassador to London invited García Márquez to lunch and informed him: "Carlos Rafael wants me to tell you that it's time for you to go back to Cuba."[17]

Early in his stay in London García Márquez had been discovered in his hotel by several Latin American journalists from the pro-U.S. weekly *Visión*. He sidestepped most of their questions but gave an interesting insight into his impression of London:

London is the most interesting city in the world: the vast and melancholy metropolis of the last colonial empire in liquidation. Twenty years ago, when I came here for the first time, it was still possible to find, amidst the fog, those Englishmen with bowler hats and striped trousers who looked so much like Bogotanos of the time. Now they've taken refuge in their mansions in the suburbs, alone in their sad gardens, with their last dogs, their last dahlias, defeated by the irresistible pressure of the human tide coming in from the lost empire. Oxford Street looks like a street in Panama, Curaçao, or Vera Cruz, with intrepid Hindus sitting at the doors of their shops full of silks and ivory, with splendid black women dressed in bright colours selling avocadoes and conjurors who make the ball disappear from beneath the cup before the eyes of the public. Instead of fog there's a hot sun which smells of guavas and sleeping crocodiles. You go in for a beer in a bar, like a cantina in La Guaira, and a bomb goes off under your seat. You hear Spanish, Portuguese, Japanese, and Greek being spoken all around you. Of all the people I've met in London, the only one who spoke impeccable English in an Oxford accent was the Swedish finance minister. So don't be surprised at finding me here: at Piccadilly Circus I feel as if I'm in the Portal of the Sweets in Cartagena.[18]

Few observers had foreseen London's future identity as "world city" quite so early and with such clarity. Asked if any regime in Latin America would ever have unarmed police like the British ones, García Márquez retorted that there already was one: Cuba. And the big news in Latin America, he went on, was the consolidation of the Cuban Revolution—hostile observers at the time believed such "consolidation" was in fact "Stalinization"—without which none of the current progressive developments in the continent would have been possible— nor, he added, the literary Boom itself. Finally, he reiterated that he would not be writing any more fiction until the Chilean resistance had overthrown the Chilean dictatorship, whose members were paid by the Pentagon. There was a clear sense in this hostile interview that García Márquez was burning boats and raising the flag of his socialist commitment. Why? Because he was sure that he was on his way back to Cuba.

When he was not attending his English lessons in London, he tinkered with the definitive version of *The Autumn of the Patriarch* and played with different ideas for radical film scripts. He and Mercedes were visited by his youngest brother Eligio and his wife Myriam, who had moved to Paris in September, and Eligio and his famous brother Gabito became closer despite the twenty-year gap between them. Eligio and Myriam would spend Christmas 1974 in Barcelona with Gabito, Mercedes and their two sons.

In September 1974 political problems had arisen within the *Alternativa* editorial board and Orlando Fals Borda's faction left the magazine. Enrique Santos Calderón later told me, "We intended to be pluralist but people divided very quickly into different groups. Gabo suffered acutely with all the troubles, he finds internal tensions between his friends very difficult to deal with. Each furtive return he made caused him anguish but they also politicized him, woke him up to the reality of armed struggle and made him an idol of the left."[19] In December García Márquez interviewed CIA renegade Philip Agee, whose revelations about the organization's activities in Latin America would shortly be causing a sensation worldwide.[20] By now no one was refusing a meeting with García Márquez. In the 1974 elections in Colombia, after the formal ending of the National Front pact, Liberal Alfonso López Michelsen had come to power with 63.8 per cent of votes cast, though over 50 per cent of the electorate failed to vote. Despite his doubts about López Michelsen's politics, García Márquez was happy to have him as president, given their distant kinship through the Cotes family link in Padilla, his own prior relationship when he took López Michelsen's law course at the university in Bogotá and the possibilities of working with a man who was certainly not a reactionary.[21]

The Autumn of the Patriarch was published at last, in March 1975, in Barcelona. The Latin American press had been full of rumours that the novel's publication was imminent right up to the day that it—the most eagerly awaited book in Latin American history—hit the bookshops. It was launched by his Spanish publisher, Plaza y Janés, with a print run of a staggering 500,000 copies in hardback. In June Plaza y Janés would publish his *Collected Stories* and García Márquez would have settled his accounts, for the time being, with his literary readers. Despite, or perhaps more accurately because of, the high expectations, the reviews were disconcertingly mixed and many of them were downright hostile.[22] Some critics liked the book for its extraordinary poetry and ironic rhetoric which both exalt and parody Latin America's darkest fantasies at one and the same time; others disliked it for a whole battery of reasons ranging from its alleged vulgarities to its incessant hyperboles, from its lack of punctuation to its apparently problematical political stance. These divergences were particularly marked at the time the book was published but the radical disagreement has continued down the years.

Nevertheless it was *The Autumn of the Patriarch* that finally confirmed García Márquez as a professional author, the book that showed he could write another big novel after *One Hundred Years of Solitude*. Even those who disliked it did not attempt to deny that it had been written, manifestly, by a great writer. Although *One Hundred Years of Solitude* evidently proclaims a vast and unmistakable continental dimension, it is still a recognizably Colombian book. *The Autumn of the Patriarch*, on the contrary, is a Latin American book, written with that symbolic readership in mind, with almost no significant Colombian dimension, not least because Colombia never had the sort of patriarch it portrays: formally, it was a "democratic" nation through most of the twentieth century.

In a sense it is *The Autumn of the Patriarch* and not *One Hundred Years of Solitude* which stands as the decisive oeuvre of García Márquez's career as a writer, because, contrary to first impressions, it encapsulates all his other works. Whether or not it is considered his "best" novel, as García Márquez himself has frequently asserted, it is not difficult to see why he thinks it his most "important" one, especially if we add to its compendiousness two further considerations already mentioned: the insistence that the portrait of the Patriarch is a portrait of himself and the fact that he wrote the book to "prove himself" as an author after the stupefying success of *One Hundred Years of Solitude*. It might be said, then, that while *One Hundred Years of Solitude* is undoubtedly the axis of his *life* (and the most important book as far as the wider world, and perhaps posterity, are concerned), *The Autumn of the Patriarch* is the pivot of his *work*: after this, ironically enough, the all-consuming nature of his literary obsession with power would be at an end—at the very moment that power became the central theme of his life. When he had declared that he would not write another novel until Pinochet fell, it was for two very good reasons: firstly, and above all, he was determined to make contact with Latin America's own living patriarch, Fidel Castro; but secondly, for the time being, he had nothing really important left to write—because, it can now be seen, the first half of his career as a writer did not end with the ecstasy of *One Hundred Years of Solitude* but with the agony of *The Autumn of the Patriarch*. As far as literature was concerned, he was not at all sure where to go next. So he concentrated on Castro.

That spring he was in London again with Lisandro Otero, who recalled: "García Márquez and I were dining with Matta in the House of Brahimi, the Algerian ambassador, when a servant came to the table with an urgent message for Gabo. He went to the phone. It was Carmen Balcells, who had just arrived from Barcelona with the first copies of *The Autumn of the Patriarch*. As soon as we finished dinner we went to her hotel. She gave Gabo the five copies that had come off the press that very afternoon. He immediately took a pen and dedicated them to Fidel and Raúl Castro, Carlos Rafael Rodríguez, Raúl Roa and me. I felt that with that gesture he was trying to declare his commitment, in the most unequivocal fashion, to the Cuban Revolution."[23]

Assuming his overtures to Castro were successful, his new strategy would require a complex and subtle self-presentation. He would support both socialism and liberal democracy at one and the same time, through his very own but secret "popular front." At the beginning of June 1975 he flew into Lisbon on Russell Tribunal business—the business of human rights and democracy. But the Portuguese Revolution had broken out in April 1974—a revolution in Europe: perhaps everything was possible!—and it had been carried through in the first instance by soldiers. Its implications for Africa—and Cuba—would be far-reaching, as they would be for García Márquez himself. He met

Prime Minister Vasco Gonçalves and the poet José Gomes Ferreira, among others, and would soon publish three major articles in *Alternativa* on the course of events in Portugal after the revolution.[24] His support for the Portuguese Revolution, for the Peruvian military revolution then in full swing, and the heavily militarized Cuban regime, showed a surprising openness to martial involvements. He said in Lisbon that the Peruvians expropriating newspapers was no different from the expropriation of oil, which he also supported; he personally did not believe in bourgeois freedom of the press, which was "in the last analysis, freedom only for the bourgeoisie."[25] This infuriated Mario Vargas Llosa, by then back in Peru.

García Márquez headed for the Caribbean by way of Mexico City. On his arrival in the Mexican capital he prayed to the Lord that he would never be awarded the Nobel Prize and although, as it later turned out, the Lord was not listening, *Excelsior* conveniently was and the possibility of García Márquez attaining such future glory was planted in many thousands of minds.[26] As for wealth, on 17 June *Excelsior* reported that between them *One Hundred Years of Solitude* and *The Autumn of the Patriarch* had made García Márquez a very rich man.[27] Evidently he could afford his self-imposed literary vacation and he could afford to take risks with his popularity in pursuit of his political vocation.

Back in the Caribbean he went in search of answers to the questions that now obsessed him. Cuba's government was run by revolutionary guerrillas who had turned themselves, and indeed the whole of the Cuban people, into soldiers. Allende had been overthrown by a reactionary military. Now, in Portugal, Europe's longest-lived dictatorship had also been overturned by the army. Were revolutionary soldiers—arise General Simón Bolívar!—the answer to Latin America's problems? He travelled to Central America to find out. There he interviewed a tempestuous, swashbuckling figure second only to Fidel Castro in his attractiveness to García Márquez, General Omar Torrijos, the populist dictator of Panama since 1968, another of those characters who argued that dictatorship for and of but not by the people was sometimes necessary given the neo-colonial condition of contemporary Latin America.[28] García Márquez and Torrijos would become bosom buddies, almost blood brothers. (It was Torrijos who, after sitting down and reading *The Autumn of the Patriarch*, would look up at García Márquez and say, "It's true, it's us, that's what we're like.") Torrijos, a quite different personality to Castro (whose "popular" performances were strictly—some would say cynically—choreographed), had begun a historic campaign to recover the Panama Canal for Panama and he explained to García Márquez his negotiations with the USA for a new Canal Treaty and the conditions he would and would not accept. As García Márquez himself pointed out, it was to say the least inconvenient for the USA to have a military rebel appear in the country where the U.S.-run School of the Americas, "in which the soldiers of the continent learn to combat the insurgency of their peoples," was located. Torrijos told his new friend that he was prepared to go to "the ultimate consequences" to get the canal back and to eradicate colonialism from his country.

García Márquez was particularly interested in Panama. Not only was it once a part of Colombia, before U.S. imperialism encouraged its secession; it was also the country where his own grandfather, Nicolás Márquez, had travelled as a young man and had pursued one of his most important love affairs. Torrijos was a man who could easily have been born in Barranquilla—indeed, in many respects he was reminiscent, even in looks and manner, of García Márquez's dead friend Alvaro Cepeda. Quite quickly the two men would come to build a friendship based on a deep emotional attraction which evidently turned over time into a kind of love affair. And García Márquez was not alone: even the ice-cool English writer Graham Greene developed a close and affectionate relationship with the Panamanian leader and eventually wrote a surprisingly unguarded book about the process of "getting to know the general."

BUT COMPARED TO Fidel Castro, already by then one of the great political personalities of the twentieth century, even Torrijos was a minor figure. It is easy to imagine how fascinating the thought of getting to know Castro must have been for a man as obsessed from an early age with the theme of power as García Márquez. In *The Autumn of the Patriarch* some parallels are unmistakable. The novel, which appeared three months before García Márquez's first visit to Cuba in fourteen years, described a dictator obsessed with rural activities, especially cattle breeding, yet who had "smooth maiden hands with the ring of power." Both details point to Fidel. Some references may be coincidental, others are unmistakable: "he built the largest baseball stadium in the Caribbean and imparted to our team the motto of victory and death."

Similarly the Patriarch arbitrarily changes dates and times and even suppresses Sundays, just as Fidel Castro himself would eventually abolish Christmas and then, years later, resurrect it. And just like Fidel, García Márquez's dictator, during his early years of messianic power, turns up unexpectedly all over the country and personally inspects public works or sets them in motion, and this gives him an enduring popularity so that the people would not blame him for their misfortunes: "every time they learned of a new act of barbarism they would sigh inside, if only the general knew." Eventually, after the Americans take the sea away—which could be interpreted as the almost fifty-year "blockade," heroically resisted by the Cuban people—the Patriarch reflects, "I had to bear the weight of this punishment alone . . . no one knows better . . . that it's better to be left without the sea than to allow a landing of marines." The brutal irony is that the portrait has increasingly fitted Castro more than twenty-five years after the novel was written; he too, with the embargo, had the "sea" taken away from him, and he too presided over a regime which decayed before the eyes of the world while he himself appeared imperturbable. Though only the most fanatical of his enemies have considered him a "monster."

In 1975, however, Castro was beginning one of his most successful periods. The regime was coming through the "Stalinist" moment that had included the Padilla Affair and was soon to launch its historic and audacious military campaign in Africa. In 1975 fourteen Latin American countries would restore diplomatic relations with the island regime, including, on 6 March, García Márquez's forty-eighth birthday, Colombia, which had broken with Cuba under Alberto Lleras in 1961. The decision—taken by López Michelsen—must have seemed an extraordinary augury to García Márquez, who had already made his own secret decision to re-establish relations with the Cuban Revolution, and had arrived in Bogotá only four days before.

In July the moment finally came and he travelled to Cuba with Rodrigo. Back at last. The revolutionary authorities gave them all the facilities necessary to travel the length and breadth of the island, going where they pleased and talking to whoever they wished. Rodrigo would take over two thousand photographs. García Márquez recalled, "My idea was to write about how the Cubans broke the blockade inside their own homes. Not the work of the Government or the State but how the people themselves solved the problem of cooking, washing and sewing their clothes, in short, all those daily problems."[29] In September he published three memorable dispatches, under the general heading "From One End of Cuba to the Other," which brilliantly combined large compliments with small criticisms in such a way as to demonstrate to the authorities that here was a big-league revolutionary player with an unprecedentedly safe pair of hands.[30]

Over the summer the entire family regrouped in Mexico. García Márquez and Mercedes had found a house down in the south of the city, in Calle Fuego ("Fire Street"), in the Pedregal del Angel zone, just beyond the National University. This modest house is still their main residence more than thirty years later. There were some family bridges to be rebuilt, which is perhaps why García Márquez had taken Rodrigo with him to Cuba, when he must have been a distraction. Of the return to Mexico Rodrigo would tell me, "The fact is that Mexico is the country we've always gone back to, not Colombia. It's as if my parents became Mexicans in that period between 1961 and 1965."[31]

The return to Mexico would allow the boys to confirm and rebuild their long-term identity. Neither of them felt either Colombian or Spanish but their relationship with Mexico had also been severely interrupted. Rodrigo would be determined to establish his own independence and get on without the García Márquez name; eventually he would leave the country. Gonzalo, as the younger son, would be less hypersensitive on this score but he too would try to find his own way without too much reliance on his father's celebrity, though this would be especially difficult in Mexico. Once again the boys were sent to English schools in order to complete their secondary education.

In Bogotá, meanwhile, a bomb exploded in the offices of *Alternativa* in November 1975, attributed to some form of vigilante unit—"at exactly the time," Enrique Santos Calderón would tell me, "when we were denouncing problems of corruption at the very top of the army."[32] Undaunted, though admittedly safe in Mexico, García Márquez released a statement in which he said that the bomb was obviously the work of the Colombian army and must have come from the very top. Clearly, he said, López Michelsen's refusal to close the magazine had spurred the military into vigilante action. Evidently his recent enthusiasm for soldiers did not extend to the Colombian variety. Even more provocatively, he specifically named the Minister of Defence, General Camacho Leyva, as personally implicated in these repressive policies. The Colombian military would not forget this. Nor would they forget their suspicion that the organizers of *Alternativa* sympathised with, perhaps even colluded with, the guerrillas of M-19, the middle-class rebels of choice and the group who had symbolically stolen Simón Bolívar's sword in 1974.

Still, the wider world was changing fast, apparently for the better. General Franco, whose regime had executed five Basque militants on 27 September, despite worldwide protests (Olof Palme of Sweden said the Spanish government were "bloody murderers"), had a major heart attack on 21 October and Prince Juan Carlos took over as Head of State. On 20 November Franco finally died, to the general delight of left-wingers all around the planet. Juan Carlos was declared King on the 22nd and three days later announced a general amnesty. Spain was about to embark on a transition to democracy which would change it dramatically. On 10 November Angola had become independent of Portugal, amidst violent conflict: the Marxist forces of the governing MPLA, already assisted by Russian advisers, were ranged against the U.S.-backed UNITA of Jonas Savimbi. On 11 November Cuba announced the decision to send thousands of troops to Angola, where they would remain for thirteen years. This would be García Márquez's chance to show what a great journalist could do for the revolution.

But not everyone was impressed by García Márquez's attention-grabbing behaviour. On 12 February 1976, now a resident of Mexico City, he turned up at the premiere of a film version of *Survivors of the Andes*. As he arrived, Mario Vargas Llosa, in town for the event—he had written the screenplay—was standing in the foyer. Gabo opened his arms and exclaimed, "Brother!" Without a word Mario, an accomplished amateur boxer, floored him with one mighty blow to the face. With García Márquez semi-conscious on the ground, having struck his head as he fell, Mario then shouted, depending on the source: "That's for what you said to Patricia." Or: "That's for what you did to Patricia." This was to become the most famous punch in the history of Latin America, still the subject of avid speculation to this day. There were many eyewitnesses and there are many versions not only of what actually happened but why.[33]

It is said that the Vargas Llosa marriage went through a difficult moment in the mid-1970s and that García Márquez took it upon himself to console Mario's apparently distraught and resentful spouse. Some say that he did this by advising her to initiate divorce proceedings; others that the comfort he offered was more straightforward. Evidently Mario concluded that García Márquez had put his concern for Patricia before their friendship. Only García Márquez and Patricia Llosa know what did or did not happen.[34] And only Patricia Llosa knows what she told her husband when they were reunited. In other words, only she knows the entire story.[35] As for Mercedes, she would never forgive Vargas Llosa. And she would never forget what she considered a cowardly and dishonourable act, whatever the provocation might have been.

The ingredients of politics, sex and personal rivalry make up a potent cocktail, in whatever proportions they are shaken together. Behind Vargas Llosa's evident sense of betrayal may have lurked an anxiety that the small unprepossessing Colombian was proving too much for him. Mario's own extraordinary and well-deserved literary success and matinée-idol good looks were not in themselves enough; so perhaps his only remaining weapon was the big punch. And he probably only managed that with the benefit of surprise: one imagines a forewarned García Márquez running around him, like Charlie Chaplin, and kicking him repeatedly up the rear. No matter how well Mario himself wrote, no matter how much publicity he received, it was García Márquez whom the newspapers and the public most wanted to hear about; and however justified Mario felt in his rejection of Castro and Cuba, García Márquez seemed to have emerged scot-free from the fallout after the Padilla Affair and had become the unchallenged literary champion of the Latin American left. It must have been intensely frustrating.[36] The two men would never meet again.

In March and April García Márquez was back in Cuba. He had already had worldwide acclaim with his articles on the Chilean coup and he must have felt that his was a talent that Fidel Castro would be foolish to ignore. So he set out to make the Cuban leader an offer he could not refuse. He proposed to Carlos Rafael Rodríguez that he should write the epic story of the Cuban expedition to Africa, the first time a Third World country had ever interposed itself in a conflict involving the two superpowers from the First and Second worlds. Given Cuba's history of slavery and colonialism, the African liberation movements of the era were of particular interest to Cuba and no less a figure than Nelson Mandela would later judge that Cuba had made a significant and perhaps decisive contribution to the overthrow of apartheid in South Africa.

Cuba's Foreign Secretary passed García Márquez's idea on to Fidel Castro and the Colombian spent a month waiting in Havana's Hotel Nacional for the Comandante's call.[37] One afternoon at three o'clock Castro turned up in a jeep and took over the driving so that García Márquez, who was with Gonzalo, could sit next to him. They set off into the country and Fidel talked for two hours about food. "I asked him," García Márquez would recall, "'So how come you know so much about food?' 'Chico, when you have the responsibility to feed an entire people, you'll find out about food!'" Like so many others before and since, García Márquez was stunned by Castro's astonishing love of facts and phenomenal mastery of detail. He might have anticipated this from listening to the great leader's unscripted eight-hour speeches but he was not prepared for Castro's personal charm and courtesy, which could light up not only a tête-à-tête like this one but a room of twenty or thirty people.

At the end of the expedition Fidel said, "Invite Mercedes across and then talk to Raúl." Mercedes arrived the next day but then they waited another entire month for Raúl Castro's call. Raúl was the head of the armed forces and it was he who personally briefed García Márquez: "In a room where all the advisors were, with the maps, he began to uncover the military and state secrets, in a way that surprised even me. The specialists brought in coded cables, deciphered them and explained everything to me, the secret maps, the operations, the instructions, everything, minute by minute. We were at it from ten in the morning to ten at night. They gave me a list of key people with instructions to talk freely to me. I took all that material off to Mexico and wrote a complete description of 'Operation Carlota,' as it was called."[38]

When García Márquez had completed the article he sent it to Fidel "so he'd be the first to read it." Three months later nothing had happened and García Márquez returned to Cuba for discussions. After consultation with Carlos Rafael Rodríguez he revised what he had written and "clarified important questions and added details that were missing." The article was syndicated all over the world and the Castro brothers were delighted. García Márquez had won his revolutionary spurs; or, as Mario Vargas Llosa would later put it, had become Fidel Castro's "lackey."

Not only had he pleased Fidel but later García Márquez received the International Press Organization's world journalism prize for his chronicles on Cuba and Angola. It may be assumed they were unaware that he had had three distinguished collaborators. For a while to come García Márquez, understandably intoxicated by his personal friendship with the most important figure in recent Latin American history, would tell journalists that he was unwilling to talk about Fidel because he was afraid of seeming to be a sycophant—and then he would rave on anyway. These statements enraged Cuban exiles in Miami and elsewhere.

García Márquez continued his research and self-education as an informed defender of the Cuban Revolution. He had probably already abandoned his book on daily life under the blockade, though he continued to use it as cover for a time. He had realized from the beginning that the question of human rights and political prisoners would be a crucial issue that his enemies would fling at him. But once the Americans under Nixon and Kissinger had taken the gloves off in their treatment of Latin American progressive movements and were training military regimes in "security methods," including assassination, torture and disinformation, and now that he had thrown in his lot with Castro's Cuba, he needed to document himself on the prisons issue—even if documenting himself meant doing whatever he had to do to persuade himself that the situation was acceptable and supportable in all the circumstances. (He was learning a lot about prison regimes in his work for the Russell Tribunal.) At the same time, ironically, the USA itself now had a new leader and the puritan President Jimmy Carter was preaching human rights and seemed sincere about the matter. So Nixon had taught García Márquez that U.S. governments would never really change but Carter taught him that public relations, diplomacy and propaganda were also now a vital part of the ideological struggle on the international stage. García Márquez was convinced that the external opposition actually wanted Cuba to have political prisoners so that they could continue their attacks and he thus believed, perhaps naively, that the country should reduce the number of such prisoners to as close to zero as possible. This would be a large part of his endeavour in the coming years. And it would shift his focus from militancy with *Alternativa* and a defence of Cuba's African intervention to international diplomacy and, over time, as things got more difficult, a rearguard defence of Cuba's sovereign integrity *tout court*.

Late in 1976 he arranged to talk to long-term counter-revolutionary prisoners at the prison of Batanabó. From that list, at random, he chose the case of Reinol González. González was an opposition leader who had worked through the Christian trades union movement, a committed Catholic, and, effectively, a Christian Democrat.[39] He had been arrested in 1961, accused of plotting to kill Fidel Castro with a bazooka near Rancho Boyeros Airport and of setting fire to the El Encanto shopping centre in Havana and killing an administrator called Fe del Valle. González himself would later admit that these charges were true. After García Márquez's conversation with González at Batanabó, his wife Teresita Alvarez contacted the writer in Mexico City and asked for his help in securing her husband's release. García

Márquez was moved by her entreaties and saw the possibility of a win-win manoeuvre. He resolved to talk to Castro but saw him four or five times without daring to broach the matter.

Eventually Castro took him and Mercedes out for a ride in his jeep. On the way back, García Márquez recalled, "We were in a bit of a hurry and I had six points noted down on a card that I wanted to bring up with him. Fidel laughed at my precision with each point and said, 'This yes, this no, we'll do that, we'll do the other.' When he'd answered the sixth point we were going through the tunnel to Havana and he asked me, 'And what's number seven?' There was no number seven on the card and I don't know if the devil whispered in my ear but, put like that, I thought, 'This could be the right moment.' I said, 'Point number seven is here but it's really awkward!' 'OK, but tell me what it is.' Like someone throwing himself overboard in a parachute, I said, 'You know, it would give great satisfaction to a family if I could take Reinol González, liberated, to Mexico to spend Christmas with his wife and kids.' I hadn't looked behind me but Fidel, without looking at me, looked at Mercedes and said, 'And why is Mercedes looking like that?' And I, without looking back, without seeing what expression Mercedes had on her face, answered: 'Because she's probably thinking that if I take Reinol González and he ends up playing some dirty trick on the Revolution, you're going to think I messed up.' Then Fidel answered not to me but to Mercedes: 'Look, Mercedes, Gabriel and I will do what we think is right and if after that the other guy turns out to be a louse, that's another problem!'" Back in their hotel room the always judicious Mercedes rebuked her husband for his impertinence but García Márquez was exultant. Months went by, however, and Castro said that he had not yet been able to persuade his colleagues on the Council of State. Complex issues were involved and García Márquez and González would have to be patient.[40]

Meanwhile, August 1977 saw García Márquez's first significant connection with a European socialist who would be a crucial contact, and friend, over the coming years: Felipe González, the leader of the Spanish Socialist Party, PSOE. González had been elected Deputy for Madrid in Spain's first elections for forty-one years on 15 June, an election in which Adolfo Suárez became Prime Minister for the ruling right-of-centre UDC party. The legendary Communist militant La Pasionaria had returned to Spain for those elections, for the first time since the Civil War. At the end of August, González, a lawyer, was in Bogotá and gave an interview to Antonio Caballero (editor), Enrique

Santos Calderón (director), and García Márquez ("editorial adviser") of the *Alternativa* staff. The article was entitled "Felipe González: a Serious Socialist."[41] PSOE's policy in Latin America was to support all popularly based regimes in more or less democratic countries and to support liberation movements in non-democratic countries: "We are united by the objective of liquidating regimes which slow the democratic rhythm." The article did not include González's views on Cuba, a question which would eventually cause trouble between him and García Márquez years later.[42]

It is possible that this interview started a lot of bells ringing in García Márquez's head. Before long he would be closely engaged, despite his own scepticism about their beliefs and activities, with numbers of members of the moderate and democratic Socialist International, from his good friend Carlos Andrés Pérez, the President of Venezuela, whose parents had Colombian connections, through France's François Mitterrand, to Felipe González himself. Both Mitterrand and González had closely followed Allende's progress and demise—but surely Europe was different? In December García Márquez would have an intense conversation in Paris with Régis Debray, another one-time revolutionary contemplating the democratic road (which he would eventually take, inside François Mitterrand's government). By this time Debray himself was already a member of the French Socialist Party and García Márquez quizzed him as to whether he was still a "real socialist" and what he thought of the progress of revolution in Latin America.[43] It is more than likely that from this moment García Márquez was on his way out of *Alternativa* and looking for another role. And it would be a dual role: one approach in Latin America and another in Europe. Once again García Márquez was searching for room to manoeuvre.

In early June he had published another article about his friend Omar Torrijos, unashamedly referencing one of his own works in the title: "General Torrijos Does Have Someone to Write to Him."[44] This could stand of course for a question about García Márquez then and in the future. Was he writing about men of power, to men of power, or for them? As in Cuba, he began by addressing the Panamanian human rights question, presenting himself as an honest broker between reality and the reader (just as eventually he would attempt to mediate between Castro and Torrijos, on the one hand, and González and Mitterrand on the other). Thus he made a show of finding out the situation of alleged political prisoners in Panama—Torrijos has been accused over time of being involved in torture—and offered to mediate between the Torrijos regime and Panamanian exiles in Mexico. Then in August another major article by García Márquez appeared about the Panamanian *caudillo*, his negotiations with the USA, and the threats upon his life.[45] García Márquez characterized Torrijos as "a cross between a mule and a tiger," a formidable adversary and a brilliant negotiator, intensely human and popular with the ordinary people.[46]

The new Panama Canal Treaty was signed at last on 7 September 1977 in Panama City. The Panamanian delegation included two additional members, Graham Greene and Gabriel García Márquez, both travelling on Panamanian passports—as many of the world's criminals were accustomed to doing—and thoroughly enjoying the experience, like two overgrown schoolboys.[47] They particularly enjoyed their close physical proximity to the dastardly Pinochet. In October Panamanians approved the new treaty by plebiscite, though the USA continued to make amendments and then finally ratified the revised version on 18 April 1978.

In 1977 the García Barcha family finally began to make its adjustment to the inevitabilities of separation as the boys grew up and began to go their own way in life. Of course in a sense Gabo and Mercedes had left their sons in 1974–5 before the two boys could leave them, but at that time there was still a family home—though a temporary one—in Barcelona to which everyone would naturally return. Now the boys were on their way to leaving home. In particular Rodrigo was on his way to cookery school in Paris and Gonzalo was thinking of following him there to study music.

García Márquez had been waiting all this time for news of his initiative over Reinol González. At last, in December 1977, matters began to move.[48] At a reception in Havana for Jamaica's Prime Minister Michael Manley, Fidel Castro approached García Márquez and said, "Well, you can take Reinol." Three days later García Márquez and a stunned Reinol González arrived in Madrid, to be joined almost immediately by his wife Teresita. In early January 1978, García Márquez, Mercedes and Rodrigo would meet up with González and his family in Barcelona, where they would hear in detail about his harrowing experiences in Cuban prisons. After that, on 15 January, the González family would fly to Miami. Later, González would vindicate García Márquez's strategy and Castro's agreement to it by playing a key role in negotiations when the revolution started the dialogue with the exile community abroad after Castro decided that it was time to reduce tensions with the families of the three thousand imprisoned counter-revolutionaries.

For years García Márquez would play down his part in helping to persuade the Cuban leadership to make this crucial gesture of releasing the great majority of these prisoners. He had shown the Castro brothers that he was not only full of good intentions but also a sincere supporter of the revolution, less liberal and more socialist than he appeared and, above all, as they had intuited, a safe pair of hands. Gradually the relationship with Fidel moved beyond the purely instrumental and political, both men flattered by the other's attention, to something like a friendship. (García Márquez would always insist to the press that he and Castro mainly talked about literature.) Castro, a confirmed workaholic, had a circumscribed and utterly secret private life and a limited social life. For many years it was believed that his only long-term relationship with a woman was that with his revolutionary comrade Celia Sánchez, who would die in 1980, and that following her death he had occasional dalliances with other women which sometimes produced illegitimate children. Only recently has it become clear that by the end of the 1960s he had begun a long-term relationship, effectively a marriage, with Dalia Soto del Valle, with whom he had five sons, a relationship that continues to this day. But Dalia was never given any official role and the image of Castro's apparent solitude has been constantly underlined by the fact that she has not been a part of that limited social life.

Equally Castro has not been known, since the death of Che Guevara, to have many significant male friends, beyond his eternally loyal brother Raúl and men like Antonio Núñez Jiménez, Manuel Piñeiro and Armando Hart. So that the friendship with García Márquez was highly unusual and totally unexpected. How surprising, on reflection, is perhaps another matter. García Márquez was the most famous writer the Spanish-speaking world had produced since Cervantes and, by an extraordinary piece of luck, was a socialist and a supporter of Cuba. Moreover he was almost the same age as Fidel, both men were from the Caribbean, and both had become anti-imperialists partly as a reaction to the proximity of the U.S. monopoly producer of bananas, the United Fruit Company. Anecdotally, both men had been in Bogotá in April 1948 during the *Bogotazo* and some conspiracy theorists even believe that they began to subvert Latin America together from that time. Although a great writer, García Márquez was in no sense an aesthete or an intellectual snob and his lifestyle allowed him to keep Castro in contact with the wider world despite his virtual confinement within the borders of his tiny island in the sun. Castro himself told me that their shared Caribbean heritage and a shared Latin Americanist vocation were crucial foundations on which to build a friendship. "Besides," he added, "we are both country people and we are both seasiders . . . We both believe in social justice, in the dignity of man. What characterizes Gabriel is his love of others, his solidarity with others, which is a characteristic of every revolutionary. You cannot be a revolutionary without admiring and believing in other people."[49]

Generally things were going well for Cuba now, with a new revolutionary enthusiasm injected by the African adventure. But a quite new era was dawning. On 6 August Pope Paul VI died; John Paul I was appointed and died a month later, leading to the appointment of Karol Wojtyla, John Paul II, who, allied tacitly with Ronald Reagan and Margaret Thatcher, both elected within eighteen months of his appointment, would turn the terms of political trade against Cuba for the next twenty-five years (not to mention hastening the demise of the Soviet Union). Worse, from the Cuban standpoint, only two days after the death of Pope Paul VI in August 1978 the Shah of Iran imposed martial law in his country, an act which would accelerate his overthrow and in turn bring about the fall of President Jimmy Carter and the election of right-winger Ronald Reagan.

The left performed as badly as ever in the Colombian elections in 1978 and the Liberal candidate Julio César Turbay Ayala was elected President and began his term on 7 August. *Alternativa* had been aggressive towards Turbay, a right-wing Liberal, from the beginning, with both cartoons and texts emphasizing how fat he was, with his trademark bow tie and nothing behind his glasses.[50] Hoping to undermine his candidacy and provoke the Liberals into finding a more moderate contender, the magazine had constantly questioned his motivation and his electability. García Márquez and *Alternativa*, both separately and together, would attack his presidency with unusual violence during the next four years, only to find that Turbay, or at least the forces that he represented, were more than capable of hitting back in even more violent and indeed unexpected ways.

Meanwhile, Central America continued its convulsive revolutionary process with Jimmy Carter apparently unable, like Pontius Pilate, to decide whether to referee the contest or join one of the teams. In Nicaragua the Sandinista (FSLN) rebels had been intensifying pressure on the Somoza dictatorship throughout the year. Sandinista leaders quite often met in García Márquez's house in Mexico City and he sometimes saw Tomás Borge, a co-founder of the Sandinista movement, in Cuba. García Márquez helped to negotiate the agreement to unify the three opposing groups into a common Sandinista Front and would later even claim that it was he who dubbed the young revolutionaries *los muchachos* ("the kids").[51] On 22 August 1978 a group of Sandinista commandos led by Edén Pastora took the National Palace in Managua, kidnapped twenty-five House representatives, held them for two days and then flew four of them to Panama with sixty political prisoners freed in exchange for releasing the other hostages. Pastora, "Commander Zero," had conceived this plan eight years before.[52] García Márquez called Torrijos immediately and said he would like to publicize this extraordinary revolutionary success. Torrijos offered to keep the guerrillas incommunicado until García Márquez arrived. He set off at once and spent three days in a barracks talking to the exhausted leaders of the spectacular assault—Edén Pastora, Dora María Téllez and Hugo Torres—for a report which he would publish in early September.[53] By the end of that month the USA was urging Somoza to resign. García Márquez said later that this report was exactly what he had in mind when he gave up literature for political journalism: "Edén Pastora and Hugo Torres fell asleep worn out by fatigue. I went on working with Dora María, an extraordinary woman, until eight in the morning. Then I went to write up the report in my hotel. When they woke up they corrected it, specifying particularly the right terms for weapons, group structures, etc. That next night I couldn't sleep, I was so excited, like when I did my first job as a reporter, at the age of twenty."[54] Later in the year García Márquez would tell *Alternativa* that he had been involved in numerous high-level discussions about the Nicaraguan crisis.

In September, in the midst of his father's feverish political activism, Rodrigo, disillusioned with cookery school, left for Harvard, where he would major in history. It seems a surprising destination for a member of this revolutionary family and perhaps it was this apparent contradiction which prompted García Márquez to assure *El Tiempo* in October that "my family is more important to me than my books."

Once Turbay arrived on the scene in Colombia things began to change for the worse. A month after his inauguration in August he had proved his reactionary credentials by bringing in a security statute which would be roundly criticized by Amnesty International. During these months García Márquez had been involved in organizing, with a number of friends on the left, a human rights movement called "Habeas." Jimmy Carter's human rights policy, while undoubtedly sincere, was also an effective means of deflecting attention away from the many organizations which were protesting and contesting the wave of right-wing dictatorships in Latin America—in Chile, Argentina, Uruguay, Brazil, Guatemala and Nicaragua. Carter of course argued that the governments of Cuba and Panama were also dictatorships and that the Sandinistas wished to build the same kind of regime. García Márquez fronted the new organization, which was headquartered in the relatively secure environment of Mexico City and inaugurated at a big metropolitan hotel on 20 December 1978.[55] (Whether promises were made to the Mexican authorities that Mexico itself would not be fingered is not clear.) At that meeting García Márquez was able to declare that Cuba no longer had political prisoners. He was careful not to claim any credit for this.

Habeas was formed as a human rights institute for Latin America specifically to defend political prisoners, the cause which had first brought Enrique Santos Calderón and García Márquez together in the autumn of 1974.[56] García Márquez was instrumental in the constitution of the new organization and undertook to finance it to the tune of $100,000 out of his royalties for the next two years. His friend Danilo Bartulín, formerly Salvador Allende's personal doctor, who had been with him in his last hours in the Moneda Palace, was to be the executive secretary and there would be representatives in every Latin American country, including Ernesto Cardenal, Nicaragua's revolutionary priest, and many others of similar stature and similarly progressive credentials. Most of them had a history of anti-Americanism and none of them were likely to want to turn the problems of habeas corpus in the direction of Cuba—and given the horror of what was going on in Chile, Argentina and Uruguay, neither was anyone else. García Márquez sarcastically declared that *Alternativa* intended to "help President James Carter carry out his human rights policy." He suggested that the American leader should begin in Puerto Rico, where revolutionary patriots such as Lolita Lebrón had been in prison for twenty-five years for crimes far less serious than those which the Cuban government was currently pardoning.[57]

In January 1979 García Márquez had an audience with the new Pope, John Paul II, asking him for support for Habeas. He saw the pontiff in the Vatican library for fifteen minutes.[58] He did not say so at the time but it was obvious that García Márquez found his brief encounter frustrating: he would later remark that the Pope was incapable of thinking about the rest of the world—even the "disappeared" of Latin America—without relating it to his "obsession" with Eastern Europe. Then on Monday 29 February he had an audience with the King and Queen of Spain, accompanied by Jesús Aguirre, Duke of Alba, the national Director of Music. They met in the Zarzuela Palace and their discussion about human rights in Latin America lasted over an hour. García Márquez was becoming a figure whom not only important leftist figures like Régis Debray and Philip Agee would have to see but also members of the international establishment. Asked how he'd got on with monarchs as compared with the politicians he was used to, García Márquez replied, "Well, the truth is they are very natural people to whom you can talk about anything. As for protocol, the King made things easy for me . . . They are well informed about Latin America and we had a number of memories of people and landscapes in common. They talked about our continent with real affection throughout." *El País* took it as an extremely positive sign that the young constitutional monarch should be talking to such an important international figure, one whose last novel had been a critique of absolutist power.[59]

On 19 July 1979 the Sandinistas took power in Nicaragua. This news had been anxiously awaited all year, particularly since the USA broke off relations with the Somoza regime on 8 February. Somoza had declared a state of siege on 6 June and had finally faced reality and fled the country on 19 July. This was the first piece of really good news for the Latin American left in a long time, in a year in which things seemed at last to be looking up: Maurice Bishop's pro-Cuban New Jewel movement had ousted the Prime Minister of Grenada on 13 March and on 27 October the island would become independent from Britain; the Panama Canal Treaty was due to become effective on 1 October; and Central America would continue on the revolutionary road with a military coup, deposing President Carlos Romero of El Salvador on 15 October. Four weeks before the Sandinistas took power García Márquez had carried out a telephone interview from Mexico City to Costa Rica with friend and fellow writer Sergio Ramírez, who had just been proclaimed one of five leaders of the new Provisional Government of Nicaragua in exile.[60] The two men had discussed the make-up and functions of the new government, the military situation, Colombia's policy of not breaking off relations with Somoza and the possible U.S. reaction. When García Márquez asked what a writer was

doing mixed up in politics, Ramírez had replied, "Look, during a patriotic war, a war of liberation, against an occupation force like Somoza's,
everyone leaves their jobs, including the poet, and picks up a rifle; I
consider myself on the battlefield."[61]

García Márquez would always take an interest in the Nicaraguan
revolution and would give it considerable support but he never showed
the enthusiasm for it that he had shown for Cuba. For one thing he
never had the same familiarity with Nicaragua as he had with Castro,
nor at that time did he have the intimate relationship with any one
member of the leading group which he enjoyed with Fidel. For
another thing he always had a certain inevitable scepticism, as he had
also shown towards the Chilean experiment: unless a country took the
same ruthless military and political measures adopted by the Cubans,
there was little chance that the USA would tolerate any kind of left-
leaning regime. Moreover his doubts were underlined by Cuba's own
response. The Cubans helped Nicaragua but within a continental perspective on continuing revolution; and they too now had to be far
more sensitive to the USA, which had been forced to accept a Soviet
veto over invading Cuba itself but would never accept anything
remotely like a "second Cuba."

After a summer in which the family travelled the world, taking in
Japan, Vietnam, Hong Kong, India and Moscow, Rodrigo went back to
Harvard and Gabo, Mercedes and Gonzalo moved on to Paris, where
Gonzalo would begin his musical studies, concentrating on the flute,
and his father would spend a month on Unesco business. He had been
invited to serve on the MacBride Commission inquiring into the First
World's monopoly of information through the international press
agencies. He was interviewed by his friend Ramón Chao and Ignacio
Ramonet for an article which, prompted by his work with the commission, was provocatively entitled "The Information War Has Begun."[62]
The two journalists said that García Márquez was in Paris "almost on
an incognito basis, almost clandestinely."

García Márquez explained that the commission had been set up by
Unesco Director-General Amahdou-Mahtar M'Bow following discussions in 1976. From the start it involved major compromises, since the
Russians of course wanted a completely statist press and the Americans
a completely private one. The official languages were English, French
and Russian and the report would be sent to the General Conference
of Unesco in Belgrade in late October 1980.[63] García Márquez would
later say that he had never been so bored nor, as a "solitary hunter of

words," felt so useless, but equally he had never learned so much—above all, that information flows from the strong to the weak and is a crucial means of domination of the poor by the rich.[64] The work of MacBride would be opposed by both the USA and the UK and would eventually lead to both countries withdrawing from Unesco in the mid-1980s.

Curiously enough, it was precisely now—coinciding with the Soviet Union's disastrous invasion of Afghanistan—that García Márquez began to alter his public pronouncements and his public persona. An early example was his statement at a meeting in Mexico City on 25 January 1980 that Latin America was a helpless victim, a mere bystander in the face of the conflict between the USA and the USSR.[65] Perhaps for all his big talk with Chao and Ramonet, García Márquez was not as confident about either the future of the planet in general or of Latin America in particular as he had said—and certainly not that the future of the world would be socialist. Reflecting on Ronald Reagan's election, he would muse in public that since Reagan was not as tough as he pretended, he would prove his gunslinger reputation in Latin America, "that immense, solitary backyard for which nobody apart from us is prepared to sacrifice their happiness."[66] This proved a very accurate prophecy.

But in any case he was hankering for a return to literature. There were insistent hints now from interviewers that García Márquez was wearying of his reckless promise about Pinochet made almost six years before. *Excelsior* on 12 November reported that he was writing a series of stories about Latin Americans in Paris and that he would publish them twenty-four hours after the fall of Pinochet. This was something of a disappointment to those who had construed him as saying that he would cease not just publishing but all literary activity as such until the Chilean dictator's demise. Here he was apparently writing works which, as soon as his "literary strike" was over, would be queuing up for publication like jetliners circling above one of the world's big cities waiting to land.

He was still not admitting an even larger truth: that he was embarked on a new novel. Earlier in the year he had continued to declare that he had "run out of themes," that he "didn't have another novel" in him.[67] In fact his next novel, apparently apolitical, would signal a significant shift. Neither his readers nor García Márquez himself would realize that he was in fact looking for love. A vast return to the personal was under way everywhere in the world and García Márquez himself, contrary to first impressions, would be a part of that process.

Alternativa had been a remarkable endeavour but it had encountered increasing financial difficulties, especially once government pressure began to deter advertisers after Turbay came to power. By the end of 1979 these problems had grown critical. The organizers of the magazine continued to subsidize it out of their own resources but when it finally closed, on 27 March 1980, Santos Calderón and Samper sloped back to *El Tiempo* and those who were not connected to the Bogotá establishment began to look for other means of support; while García Márquez was free to reconsider his political and literary options and plan the next stage of his career.

20

Return to Literature:
Chronicle of a Death Foretold and the Nobel Prize

1980~1982

NOW COMFORTABLY INSTALLED in the Sofitel Hotel in Paris, García Márquez divided his time between his creative writing in the morning, and the business of Unesco's controversial MacBride Commission in the afternoon. MacBride's task, in line with "third-worldist" ideologies of the time, was to consider the possibility of a new "world information order" which would loosen the grip of Western agencies on the content and presentation of international news.[1] Much as he approved of it, this collaboration would in fact mark the end of the era of public militancy for García Márquez. There would be no further Russells or MacBrides, no more *Alternativa* or *Militant Journalism* (an anthology of his political essays published in Bogotá in the 1970s); even Habeas was an activist endeavour which he would soon relinquish. He had taken the decision to cease his more strident political activism and turn to diplomacy and mediation behind the scenes. And since Pinochet was not apparently likely to be overthrown any time soon, he had resolved to abjure and go back to creative fiction, which was in any case the best form of public relations he could devise. In September 1981, apparently unabashed, García Márquez would declare that he was "more dangerous as a writer than as a politician."[2]

Although he was now one of the most famous authors in the world, he had really only published two novels, *One Hundred Years of Solitude* and *The Autumn of the Patriarch*, in the almost twenty years since *In Evil Hour* appeared. He needed more if he was to be considered one of the great writers of his era. As for politics, although he would never abandon either Latin America or his core political values, he had decided to concentrate on Cuba above all as his principal object of attention, his political heart's desire, and also of course on Colombia, to the extent that it was possible to imagine positive outcomes for that unhappy country. Cuba, whatever its political and economic short-comings, was at least, for García Márquez, a moral triumph. And Fidel was a Latin American who was not a failure, not defeated, but the bearer of an entire continent's sense of hope and, above all, dignity. García Márquez decided to stop banging his head against the adobe wall of Latin American history. He would stick to the positive.

As he distanced himself imperceptibly from direct confrontation of the problems of Latin America, other than Cuba and Colombia, he began to spend time in two places he had previously disliked: Paris and Cartagena. It was during this period that he would buy apartments in both places: on Rue Stanislas in Montparnasse, and in Bocagrande, Cartagena, overlooking the tourist beach and his beloved Caribbean. When in September 1980 he broke his literary strike, the vehicle, "The Trail of Your Blood in the Snow," would reflect this new existen-tial reality exactly: the story would begin in Cartagena and end in Paris (as well as re-encoding his own Parisian past with Tachia).[3] It was typi-cal of his intuition, his timing, or his luck that during this period his two friends François Mitterrand and Jack Lang would be elected to government in France, as President and Culture Minister respectively, and a third, Régis Debray, would become a prominent though contro-versial government adviser; while Cartagena, thanks to improved air services and a gradual change of *cachaco* mentality, would become a weekend playground for the wealthy power-brokers of Bogotá.

It turned out to be a moment of exhilarating rejuvenation for a man now in his fifties who could certainly claim that he had given revolu-tionary activism his best shot. Rodrigo had begun the exodus to Paris with his brief experience of mastering Gallic haute cuisine and García Márquez set about looking for music classes for younger son Gonzalo now that Rodrigo was studying at Harvard. Eligio had also been living in Paris for several years, though he had recently moved to nearby London. At the same time young Colombian journalists such as the ex-*Alternativa* comrades Enrique Santos Calderón and Antonio Caballero, and *El Espectador*'s María Jimena Duzán, were in Paris, and Plinio Mendoza was working in the Colombian embassy. García Márquez's high-level contacts were invaluable to them all.[4] Although she spent less time in Paris than Gabo, Mercedes mothered all the young Colombians, acted as their occasional matchmaker and dried their tears when their *amours* turned sour. García Márquez himself engaged in interminable late-night discussions which showed his friends that his tactics might have changed but not his underlying beliefs.[5]

Gonzalo, who had his own studio apartment, soon lost interest in the flute, much to his father's disappointment. Now nineteen, he took up graphic arts in 1981 and met his future wife Pía Elizondo, the daughter of Mexican avant-garde writer Salvador Elizondo, one of the former editors of *S.nob*. Tachia acted as a kind of aunt to Gonzalo when his parents were out of town. She was still living on the Boulevard de l'Observatoire, opposite the gloomy hospital of their evil hour. When "The Trail of Your Blood in the Snow" appeared in *El Espectador* on 6 September 1980 the picture on the cover of *Magazín Dominical* was of a rose dripping spots of blood.

Only a few weeks after the publication of this encrypted story a rare article about Mercedes appeared, written by Plinio's sister Consuelo Mendoza de Riaño. It alluded openly to Gabo's Parisian *amour* in the 1950s, mentioned that he "may have loved her a lot" and insinuated that Mercedes was naive about this and many other things. Whether or not Mercedes had understood the meaning of the recently published short story, this entirely uncoded follow-up must have been a nasty surprise for her. It ended however with a defiant counter-attack from the interviewee. Consuelo Mendoza recorded: "She is not bothered by the writer's female admirers. She says: 'You know, Gabito is an eternal admirer of women, you can see it in his books. He has female friends everywhere whom he loves a great deal. Though most of them are not writers. After all, women writers are sometimes a pain, don't you think.'"[6]

On 19 March 1980, on a visit to Cuba, García Márquez had announced that he had completed—"last week"—a novel that almost no one knew he was even writing, entitled *Chronicle of a Death Foretold*. It was, he said, "a sort of false novel and a false reportage." Later he would claim that it was "not that far from the U.S."'s 'new journalism.'" He repeated a favourite image, that writing stories was like mixing concrete whereas writing a novel was like laying bricks. Then he added a new one: "The novel is like a marriage: you can keep fixing it day after day, whereas a story is like a love affair: if it doesn't work, it can't be fixed."[7]

Not everyone found the new García Márquez as lovable as he evidently intended. When he tried to explain away the problem of the Cuban asylum seekers who had recently flooded into the Peruvian embassy in Havana, Cuban dissident writer Reinaldo Arenas, as if to show that García Márquez was not fooling *him*, wrote an article whose title was an untranslatable pun to which we may nonetheless essay an equivalent: "Gabriel García Márquez: Is he an Ass or an Asshole?" Referring specifically to García Márquez's alleged criticism of the Vietnamese boat people and the Cuban asylum seekers, Arenas declared:

> That a writer like Señor García Márquez, who has lived and written in the West, where his work has had an immense impact and reception which has guaranteed him a lifestyle and intellectual prestige, that such a writer, protected by the freedom and opportunities that such a world affords him, should use them to produce apologies for totalitarian communism, which turns intellectuals into policemen and policemen into criminals, is simply outrageous . . . It's time for all intellectuals in the free world (no others exist) to take a position against this kind of unscrupulous propagandist for communism who, taking refuge in the guarantees and facilities which liberty provides, sets out to undermine it.[8]

In an interview with Alan Riding of the *New York Times* in May, García Márquez, who had "visited Havana this month in the midst of Cuba's refugee problem with the United States," explained to Riding that he had founded Habeas to "take on special cases requiring contact with both the left and the Establishment, occasionally helping obtain the release of victims of guerrilla kidnappings."[9] This sounded very much like someone who wanted it both ways and the possibilities of being seduced by "the Establishment," whoever they might be, were obvious. As for his long-awaited book on Cuba, "Every door was opened to me, but now I realize that the book is so critical that it could be used against Cuba, so I refuse to publish it. Though the Cubans want me to go ahead." Riding noted, "Despite his frequent trips to

Havana, he says he could not settle there: 'I could not live in Cuba because I haven't been through the process. It would be very difficult to arrive now and adapt myself to the conditions. I'd miss too many things. I couldn't live with the lack of information. I am a voracious reader of newspapers and magazines from around the world.' But he also feels unable to live in Colombia. 'I have no private life there,' he said. 'Everything concerns me. I get involved in everything. If the President laughs, I have to give an opinion on his laugh. If he doesn't laugh, I have to comment on why he didn't laugh.' Mr. García Márquez," Riding noted, "has therefore lived in Mexico City almost continuously since 1961."

As usual, the new book, eventually entitled *Chronicle of a Death Foretold*, was really an old project: a novel based on the horrifying murder of his close friend Cayetano Gentile in Sucre thirty years before. Significantly enough, it was a work inspired by the political violence of the early 1950s, with a theme that would not have been out of place in *In Evil Hour*, and yet the writer, who had just devoted seven years to politics, would set the novel backwards in time, in a less explosively political period of Colombia's history; and he would blame its events not so much on capitalism, nor even mainly on a remote but ruthless Conservative government, as he had in *In Evil Hour*, but upon an apparently much older and deeper social system, heavily influenced by the Catholic Church and obsessed less, in the first instance, with ideological and political differences than with moral and social ones. This was a huge shift in his literary outlook, though one that has barely been noticed by his readers and critics.

On his wedding day in January 1951, out in the real world, a young man called Miguel Palencia had received a note in the small town of Sucre saying that his new bride Margarita Chica Salas was not a virgin and he had returned her to her family in disgrace. On the 22nd her brothers Víctor Manuel and José Joaquín Chica Salas murdered her ex-boyfriend Cayetano Gentile Chimento in the main square, in front of the whole town, for allegedly having seduced, deflowered and abandoned Margarita.[10] The killing was particularly gruesome: Gentile was almost cut to pieces.[11] Gentile's mother was a good friend (and *comadre*) of Luisa Santiaga Márquez and Cayetano was a good friend of Gabito, his brother Luis Enrique and his eldest sister Margot. Luis Enrique had spent the previous day with Cayetano and Margot had been with him minutes before he was killed; eleven-year-old Jaime had watched him die. Since that very day Gabito had always wanted to write the inside story of this terrible death but because those involved were all people he and his family knew intimately, his mother asked him not to do so while the parents of the principal protagonists were still alive. (The murder was of course the reason why the García Márquez family fled from Sucre in February 1951.) By 1980, when Gabito began to write the novel, those who would have been most affronted had passed away and he was in a position to shuffle the facts of the case and the personalities of the people he knew with the same ruthlessness he had applied to his own character in *The Autumn of the Patriarch*.[12]

García Márquez had conceived the final shape of the new book on his way home from the family's round-the-world journey in 1979. In the airport at Algiers the sight of an Arab prince carrying a falcon had suddenly opened his eyes to a new way of presenting the conflict between Cayetano Gentile and the Chica brothers. Gentile, of Italian immigrant stock, would become Santiago Nasar, an Arab, and in that way closer to Mercedes Barcha's family heritage. Margarita Chica, Mercedes's friend, would become Angela Vicario. Miguel Palencia would become Bayardo San Román. Víctor Manuel and José Joaquín Chica Salas would become the twin brothers Pedro and Pablo Vicario. Most of the book's other details are the same as in real life; or similar. Some of the relationships are modified, particularly in terms of class, and naturally García Márquez rewrites the whole dramatic affair with the novelist's magical insight.

Whereas the modernist *Leaf Storm*, García Márquez's most autobiographical novel, omits all direct self-referentiality, the postmodern *Chronicle of a Death Foretold* makes its autobiographical dimension explicit: its narrator is Gabriel García Márquez, who is not named but we know it is he because he has a wife called Mercedes (and seems to expect us to know who she is), a mother called Luisa Santiaga, brothers called Luis Enrique and Jaime, a sister called Margot, another, unnamed, who is a nun, and even, for the first time, a father, who is also unnamed. Here García Márquez toys with his readers and with reality, since these details relating to his family and his own life are largely but not entirely true: for example, Luisa Santiaga, Luis Enrique, Margot and Jaime were indeed in Sucre on the day of the murder but Gabito, Gabriel Eligio, Aida and Mercedes were not; and Aunt Wenefrida had been lying in the cemetery in Aracataca for many years but appears alive at the very end of the book. The family members appear not only with their own names but with their own characters and manner of speaking. The narrator mentions that he proposed to Mercedes when she was just a little girl, as indeed he did, but he also includes the local prostitute, María Alejandrina Cervantes, whom he gives the name of a woman he actually knew in the Sucre area, and he spends much of the novel in bed with her. As for the town, which is unnamed, it has a river just like Sucre's; and the family house is located along the river bank away from the main square, in a mango grove, just like the García Márquez family's real house in Sucre—though Sucre never had big steamboats, as the town in the novel does, nor were there ever any cars there; and Cartagena could certainly not be seen in the distance. But in most other respects the town is almost identical to the original.

The novel is conceived quite consciously as a literary tour de force. The author is now, patently, another man, another writer, a quite different persona. Here indeed he is like a bullfighter who is going to kill his bull in an unforgettable fashion, at once dramatic and aesthetic. The result is as populist, compulsive and irresistible, as, say, Ravel's *Bolero*. And equally as self-parodic: which is its saving grace. Because, implicitly mocking the concept of suspense, the writer announces the death of his character in the first line of the first chapter, announces it several times more in the following chapters, and then finally, perhaps uniquely, has the protagonist himself, holding his own intestines like a bunch of roses, declare it on the final page: "They killed me, Miss Wenefrida." Whereupon the poor wretch collapses, and the novel ends. Thus when García Márquez refers in his title to "a death foretold" he is referring both to the nature of the story he is telling and the way he himself has chosen to tell it. All of this, with its ironies and ambivalences, is packed into a brief work whose extraordinary complexity is skilfully concealed from its readers, whom the experienced author pilots through with apparently effortless aplomb.

When Bayardo San Román returns Angela Vicario to her family on the wedding night after discovering she is not a virgin she eventually says that her seducer was Santiago Nasar. After her brothers carry out their murder of Nasar in revenge, they take refuge in the church and tell the priest: "We killed him in full knowledge but we are innocent." The twins' lawyer argues that the murder was in legitimate defence of honour. Yet although they are unrepentant it seems they did everything possible to warn Nasar or be stopped by others and they waited for him where they were unlikely to see him and where everyone else could see them. The narrator comments: "There was never a death more announced." For the rest of the town there is only one true victim, the deceived bridegroom Bayardo San Román, who remains a mystery and says nothing to the narrator twenty-three years later when they meet again. Incredibly, from the moment he rejects Angela, who had been reluctant to marry him, she falls in love and becomes obsessed with him. Finally, when they are both old, he turns up with two thousand unopened letters and the laconic greeting: "Well, here I am."

The honour, shame and machismo syndrome is the central social thematic of the novel, as of so many Spanish works from the seventeenth-century "Golden Age" down to Lorca's twentieth-century dramas. (This choice of theme is in itself an obvious conservative turn by the author.) A possible conclusion from García Márquez: men deserve the violence they do to one another because of what they do to women.

The story of Colonel Márquez and Medardo must have been in García Márquez's mind once more throughout the writing of this book. To what extent are we responsible for our actions, in control of our destiny? Irony functions at every level: the ultimate absurdity is that Santiago Nasar may not have done the deed for which he is killed and anyway the brothers do not really want to kill him. It is the combination of fate and human fallibility, and above all the confusion of the two, which brings about the death.

Chronicle of a Death Foretold is perhaps García Márquez's most influential title, used in a thousand newspaper headlines and references in magazines. The reason of course is that it implies that whatever is announced can be prevented and that human agency can predetermine the world (though the novel, ironically enough, seems to give the opposite message). On the whole García Márquez's earlier work tended to imply that more things were subject to human agency than Latin American popular consciousness tended to believe; on the whole the later work tends to question more sceptically what is and is not subject to human agency and tends to show that most things are not. Paradoxically the earlier work appears more pessimistic but is in fact infused with the implicit optimism of a socialist perspective; it is intended to change hearts and minds. The later work is much jauntier but is underpinned by a world-view not too far from despair.

AT THE END of his extended period of political propaganda and activism between 1973 and 1979, and in preparation for the future that he intuited, he now embraced a role he had hitherto rejected: he became a celebrity. Immediately after the completion of *Chronicle of a Death Foretold*, anticipating his return to Colombia, he negotiated with his friends in the press in order to embark upon a quite different kind of journalism. His new articles were a return to the kind of thing he had written in the 1940s and 1950s in Cartagena and Barranquilla, closer to literature than to journalism.[13] They were, as well as political and cultural commentaries, a kind of serialized memoir, a weekly letter to his friends, a circular to his fans, an ongoing public diary.[14] But this was not the diary of a columnist who needed a nom de plume to give himself an identity; this was very much the diary of a Somebody.

He syndicated the articles most prominently to *El Espectador* in Bogotá and *El País* in Spain, as well as other newspapers in Latin America and Europe. The most striking thing about them from the beginning was the extraordinary change of position. Though many of them were on current political themes, gone was the urgent leftist tone. The man writing these articles was a Great Man, like some nine-teenth-century novelist who had already received universal acclaim and confirmation. He was still friendly—indeed it was evidently a priv-ilege to have such an important man being so friendly (both things were in the voice)—but it was no longer the unique matiness with which young "Séptimus" had written his "Giraffes" or the comrade-liness of the recent *Alternativa* journalist. This change of position and tone was one of his most effective publicity wheezes, undertaken with consummate sleight of hand. Manifestly this calm, measured voice, which knew everything but demanded nothing, would not be causing trouble if its owner returned to Bogotá where the articles were being published each Sunday.

The articles began to appear in September 1980 and would con-tinue virtually without interruption until March 1984, an astonishing total of 173 weekly articles during one of the busiest periods of the writer's entire life.[15] In retrospect, however, perhaps the most astonish-ing thing of all is that the first four articles were all about the Nobel Prize.[16] They revealed between the lines that García Márquez had not only done a great deal of research but was also very familiar with Stockholm and, most striking of all, had met the key academician Artur Lundkvist and been to his home. He had researched the compo-sition of the Nobel Committee, the method of selection and the proce-dures of the ritual of bestowal. He comments in the first article that the Swedish Academy is like death, it always does the unexpected. Not in his case!

From the start he gave his readers the impression that they were being allowed into "The Lives of the Rich and Famous," with their "Champagne Lifestyles and Caviar Dreams."[17] Not only did García Márquez constantly narrate his own current life and lifestyle and the important people he knew but he reminisced about his own past, as if that past were self-evidently of interest to his readers all round the world. It was almost as if twenty-five years had somehow passed between the last *Alternativa* article in 1979 and the first *El Espectador* article in September 1980, the kind of thing that might have happened—"The Secret Miracle"—to one of Jorge Luis Borges's characters. At the same time, in a lofty kind of way, he managed to carry on an unceasing campaign against the Reagan government's neo-imperialist campaign in Central America and the Caribbean without alienating mainstream liberal international opinion. This was a remarkable achievement and would involve replacing the emphasis on revolutionary friends and contacts such as MAS's Petkoff and M-19's *costeño* guerrilla leader Jaime Bateman with references to respectable democratic politicians such as González, Mitterrand, Carlos Andrés Pérez and Alfonso López Michelsen.

His readers discovered that, like many of them, this great man was terrified of flying, and he was able to confide that other great men such as Buñuel, Picasso and even the much-travelled Carlos Fuentes were similarly afflicted. Yet despite his terror, he seemed to be travelling constantly and he described each of his glamorous journeys for his avid fans: where he went, who he went to see, what they were like, their foibles (because, it was clear, we all have our little foibles). He was also superstitious and, he appeared to assume, much the more lovable for that. He even had doubts and insecurities: in December 1980 he reflected in Paris on the murder of John Lennon and the nostalgia associated for several generations with the music of the Beatles, lamenting: "This afternoon, thinking about all that as I gaze through a gloomy window at the falling snow, with more than fifty years upon my shoulders and still not knowing very well who I am, nor what the hell I'm doing here, I have the impression that the world was the same from the moment of my birth until the moment the Beatles started to play."[18] He stressed that Lennon had above all been associated with love. He himself—his readers might perhaps have reflected—had been more closely identified with power, solitude and the absence of love; but that was about to change.

The article on John Lennon was a coded message. Paris, Europe, was not the answer. He needed, as he broadcast in a whole series of interviews at this time, to return to Colombia, where his latest novel, once again, had been set. He had been promising to return for years. But the country had already begun to lurch back into chaos by the time *Alternativa* closed in early 1980: a new surge in violence, a new wave of drug-trafficking and a new kind of guerrilla group wedded to spectacular operations.

It was against this background that García Márquez and Mercedes returned to Turbay's repressive and reactionary Colombia in February 1981. Gabito organized a grand family reunion in Cartagena where the star turn was Aunt Elvira, "Aunt Pa," whose prodigious memory astonished all those present.[19] After this he began to work in the apartment he had recently bought for his favourite sister Margot in Bocagrande. Colombian poet-critic Juan Gustavo Cobo Borda visited him there not long after García Márquez's arrival and was allowed to take away the manuscript of *Chronicle*, which he read in two hours on the nineteenth floor of a nearby hotel.[20] Cobo Borda reported that the writer was working each day at Margot's, then would walk down the four flights of stairs to the ground floor, drive to visit his mother in Manga and listen to "the unintelligible jokes of his father."

On 20 March, in Bogotá, García Márquez attended a Légion d'Honneur gala organized by the French embassy and then saw Cobo Borda again for what they agreed to call "the meeting between the slimy *cachaco* and the vulgar *costeño*." Cobo Borda said he had never seen his interviewee looking so happy in Colombia. This contentment was short-lived: the two men spoke on the day the President would announce the breaking off of relations with Cuba. And there was more: García Márquez had begun to receive information that the government was trying to link him to the M-19 guerrilla movement, which in turn was being linked to Cuba, and there were even rumours that he might be assassinated. He later told Mexican reporters that he had heard four different versions of a story that the Colombian military was planning to kill him.[21] On 25 March, surrounded by friends who had gathered to protect him, he asked for asylum in the Mexican embassy and slept there overnight.[22] At ten past seven the next evening he flew north under the protection of the Mexican ambassador to Colombia, María Antonia Sánchez-Gavito, to be greeted by another large group of friends and an even larger number of journalists at the Mexico City airport. The Mexican government immediately gave him a personal bodyguard.

During the flight he had had a long conversation with the Colombian journalist Margarita Vidal, who later wrote an in-depth account of the drama.[23] As they flew over the Caribbean García Márquez assured her that neither Castro nor Torrijos was supplying arms to the Colombian guerrillas: Castro had reached an agreement with López Michelsen not to assist them militarily and he had kept to it. He, García Márquez, would return to Colombia when, as he expected, López Michelsen became President again. He said he was totally opposed to terrorism: revolution was the only long-term solution, whatever the cost in blood, but he didn't see how it could be achieved. Colombia had always been a country with a low consciousness, ripe for populism but not for revolution. Colombians no longer had any belief in anything, politics had never got them anywhere, and now the attitude was each for himself, threatening complete social dissolution: "A country without an organized left, with a left incapable of convincing anyone, that spends its life dividing itself into pieces, can't do anything."

All of this was an extraordinary backdrop for the publication of a novel entitled *Chronicle of a Death Foretold*. One imagines Colombian officers sitting in their barracks a few days earlier and having a hearty chuckle about the unpleasant and ironic surprise they had in store for the conceited *costeño* lefty. In the event the bird had flown and the celebration of his homecoming gift to Colombia—his new novel—would take place in Bogotá without him.

Readers discovered that *Chronicle of a Death Foretold* narrated a story that could hardly have been more dramatic. Yet it was also one of those novels that have their own dramatic story after they are published. First, the sales were astronomical when the book was released—simultaneously—in Spain (Bruguera), Colombia (Oveja Negra), Argentina (Sudamericana) and Mexico (Diana). On 23 January 1981 *Excelsior* had reported that more than a million copies were being produced for the Hispanic world—250,000 paperbacks in each of the four countries and 50,000 hardbacks in Spain. Oveja Negra was reported as having completed this work in April, the longest single printing of any Latin American novel in history. On 26 April *Excelsior* said 140,000 dollars was being spent on advertising in Mexico alone and the book was being translated into thirty-one languages. It was being sold by newspaper sellers and chewing-gum vendors on streets all over Latin America.

Oveja Negra boss José Vicente Kataraín was interviewed soon after publication.[24] It turned out that there were not one but two million copies of the book: a million printed in Colombia and another million in Spain and Argentina—though Kataraín would always be unreliable about numbers, as befitted the name of his company, "Black Sheep." And whereas the previous biggest number of copies of a Colombian first edition had been 10,000, García Márquez's new book was printing more than for any other first edition of any literary work ever published in the world. Two million copies had meant buying 200 tons of paper, ten tons of cardboard and 1,600 kilos of ink. Forty-five Boeing 727s had been needed to transport the copies out of Colombia alone. As if to help all this along, García Márquez declared on 29 April that *Chronicle of a Death Foretold* was "my best work." On 12 May however some Colombian critics claimed that the book was "a swindle," little more than a long short story which added nothing to the writer's earlier achievements.[25] But *Chronicle* went straight to the top of the sales lists in Spain, where the book was compared, inevitably, to Lope de Vega's *Fuenteovejuna*, and remained there until 4 November. It was the best-selling book in Spain in 1981. And Gabo the great novelist was back with a bang.

On 7 May a Bogotá lawyer, Enrique Alvarez, sued García Márquez for half a million dollars for slandering the brothers portrayed in the novel since they had both been found "innocent" of the crime, whereas the book showed them as murderers. Thinking of the unfortunate and possibly even innocent Cayetano Gentile who had indeed been murdered—if not according to law—by the brothers thirty years before, this would seem to have been adding insult to injury with a vengeance.[26] Some of the other "central characters" of the book, people who were portrayed in it or thought they were, plus other family members, gathered in Colombia—some having flown from distant parts of the world—to discuss their grievances. They would all be disappointed: they would never get a cut of García Márquez's astronomical profits because the courts in Colombia, where most of the professional classes have always had a solid literary education, would make subtle literary distinctions between historical truth and narrative fiction, and authorial freedom would be resoundingly upheld.

Chronicle of a Death Foretold has been one of García Márquez's most successful novels with the reading public and even with the critics—once read, never forgotten. Yet it is perhaps the most pessimistic of all his works. Clearly this shift must bear some relation to the frustrations of his political activity between 1974 and 1980, and to the condition of Colombia at the end of that period.

On 21 May García Márquez was in Paris for François Mitterrand's inauguration, together with Carlos Fuentes, Julio Cortázar and Salvador Allende's widow Hortensia. It was the first of many presidential inaugurations staged by personal friends of his in the coming years, though none would be more imposing, more theatrical or indeed poetic than the extraordinary spectacle put on by this most self-aware—and historically aware—of politicians. How far García Márquez had come since the days when he was not far above the Parisian *clochards*![27] The next month would find him in Havana, staying in a suite in the Hotel Riviera which the authorities kept permanently reserved for him. His relationship with Fidel had settled into a pattern. They began to have an annual vacation together at Castro's residence at Cayo Largo where, sometimes alone, sometimes with other guests, they would sail on his fast launch or his cruiser *Acuaramas*. Mercedes particularly enjoyed these occasions because Fidel had a special way with women, always attentive and with an old-style gallantry that was both pleasurable and flattering.

By now Gabo and Fidel were sufficiently relaxed together for the Colombian to play the role of reluctant younger brother, the non-athletic and sulky one who was constantly complaining about chores and hunger and others among life's unfortunate imperatives, a pantomime which always made Castro laugh. Of course the weaknesses of his fellow men did not always amuse the Comandante but in the case of García Márquez there were reasons to make an exception. He not only acted the younger brother and was generally deferential but he knew when to joke and play court jester and how far to go. Fidel was not necessarily a respecter of writers in general—nor of their freedoms—but he always acknowledged when someone was the best at what they did.

Someone who respected García Márquez even more than Castro and treated him as an older, wiser but equally irreverent brother was Panama's General Torrijos. Felipe González later told me that his enduring memory of Torrijos and García Márquez was the two of them drinking a bottle of whisky together in one of Torrijos's houses. After much carousing and "piss-taking," a tropical downpour began. The two men ran down from the balcony where they were drinking and rolled on the lawn below in the pouring rain, kicking their legs in the air and roaring with laughter like two small boys who just loved being together.[28] García Márquez visited Torrijos in late July with Venezuela's Carlos Andrés Pérez and Alfonso López Michelsen, who García Márquez was hoping would win the next year's elections; they spent the weekend on the beautiful island of Contadora. García

Márquez stayed on with his military friend for a few days and then went back to Mexico, at a moment when the entire planet, even Latin America, was gawping at the televised wedding of Prince Charles and Lady Diana Spencer in London. However on 31 July came one of the worst blows García Márquez had ever suffered personally, and the worst politically since the death of Salvador Allende in 1973, when it was reported that Torrijos had been killed in an air accident in the mountains of Panama. García Márquez had decided only at the last moment not to accompany him on the flight.

There was much speculation in the press as to whether Torrijos had been murdered and also, in the next four days, as to whether García Márquez would attend the funeral, and much surprise and disappointment when he did not. His explanation immediately entered the canon of classic García Márquez justifications: "I do not bury my friends."[29] It was an extraordinary statement to come from the author of *Leaf Storm* and *No One Writes to the Colonel*, both of which involved burials and were based on the assumption that ensuring the dignified disposal of a corpse was a key moral duty—perhaps the minimum requirement of our always uncertain humanity—as in *Antigone*.

García Márquez did not bury his friends but he continued to praise them: his obituary article, "Torrijos," appeared in *El Espectador* on 9 August while he was at the Galician Fair in Coruña.[30] Some thought his behaviour callous and ambivalent. Yet Torrijos's death had hit him hard. Mercedes would later remark, "He and Torrijos were great friends, he really loved him. He was very upset at his death: so much so, that he fell ill from the effect of it. He misses him so much he hasn't been back to Panama."[31] Later he himself would reflect, "I think Torrijos travelled too much by plane, sometimes without a real reason: he travelled compulsively. He gave fate as many opportunities as he gave his enemies. But there is a high-level rumour that one of his aides left a walkie-talkie on a table shortly before leaving on the official flight. They say that when the escort went back to pick up the machine they'd changed it for another with explosives." Being García Márquez, he added: "If it's not a true story it's attractive in a literary way."[32]

It was election year in Colombia and López Michelsen, backed by García Márquez, was the Liberal opponent of Belisario Betancur, the Conservative candidate. García Márquez warned on 12 March that López Michelsen was the best hope for democracy in the country.[33] Two days later in his column he revealed that he himself was on the hit-list of MAS, a right-wing death squad (not to be confused with

Petkoff's political party in Venezuela). Also on the list was María Jimena Duzán, who had travelled to interview M-19 guerrillas two weeks before. García Márquez accused the military and the government of collusion with MAS and said that he had always hoped to die "at the hands of a jealous husband" and certainly not through the actions of "the clumsiest government in the history of Colombia."[34]

Despite his support for López Michelsen, a majority of the 55 per cent of the electorate that voted did not agree and Conservative Belisario Betancur won with 48.8 per cent of the vote to López's 41.0 per cent, with the dissident Liberal Luis Carlos Galán effectively winning the election for the Conservatives by taking 10.9 per cent. Outgoing President Turbay lifted the state of siege which had been in effect on and off for thirty-four years in the land of Macondo. Betancur's own son Diego campaigned against his father on behalf of a Maoist workers' revolutionary party. On his accession Betancur immediately declared an amnesty for the guerrilla movements and began the first serious peace negotiations with them in modern times.

García Márquez's first intervention in democratic politics had not gone well and there now followed another Latin American calamity to disappoint him. At the start of that month the Argentinian army occupied the Falkland Islands in the South Atlantic and the British sent a task force to recover them. The phenomenon of a fascist military junta, but nevertheless a Latin American regime, confronting a European nation would test García Márquez's new-found democratic rhetoric to the limits over the coming twelve months, when, like Fidel Castro, he would find himself preferring Latin American dictators to European colonialists. His first comment, an article entitled "With the Malvinas or Without Them," appeared on 11 April.[35] Over the coming weeks, as it became clear that the Argentinian forces were heading for humiliation, the mood of dismay in the continent would increase.

Indeed, all the political news in Latin America since the Sandinista victory in 1979 seemed to be going from bad to even worse. Then there were the problems of the Communist regime in Poland, where the trade union movement led by Solidarity was questioning the government's legitimacy. Everything everywhere seemed to be heading in the wrong direction, from García Márquez's perspective. Meanwhile García Márquez was flying backwards and forwards across the Atlantic—and telling his readers about it—including a trip by Concorde "among the impassive businessmen and the radiant high-class whores";[36] he had also flown to "Bangkok the horrendous" after hiring a Rolls-Royce in Hong Kong ("none of my friends has one"), convincing himself once again that, "as always," even in the world capital of sex tourism, "American hotels are the best places to make love, with their pure air and clean sheets."[37] But he seemed to have run out of literary topics. Now that socialism was on the wane, now that the solitude and power he had always written about appeared to be destined to prevail across the entire planet, he felt the need to find another subject, something to feed his own optimism and inspire others to follow suit. What could it be? Of course: love! Gabo would become the Charlie Chaplin of the literary world: he would make them smile and he would make them fall in love.

The first public sign of this move was an article entitled "Peggy, give me a kiss," inspired by a message scrawled on a wall in the Mexico street where he lived.[38] García Márquez said that he was touched by this naive appeal in a world where the news was always bad, especially the news from Colombia. But he suspected that love was making a welcome comeback. (Just four months earlier he had confided to his readers that he "never dares to write" unless there is a yellow rose on his desk—placed there, of course, by his loving spouse.)[39] Not that he was against sex—he informed the entire world right there and then that he had lost his virginity at the precocious age of thirteen—but "sex is better with all the rest, which is complete love." Novels about love were once more the ones selling best, he declared, and even the old Latin American *boleros* were back in fashion.

Perhaps it was not entirely coincidental, then, that, after many refusals, he had consented to a long-awaited interview with *Playboy* magazine in—naturally—Paris, the world capital of love. The magazine had sent Claudia Dreifus, who would later become one of the world's most successful interviewers, and this would be one of the best-researched and most comprehensive conversations with the writer.[40] He explained his political positions for *Playboy's* American readers, insisting that he and Fidel "talked more about culture than politics": theirs was really just a friendship! Then he moved on to matters of love and sex. He said that none of us ever knows another person completely and he and Mercedes were no exception; he still had no idea how old she was. He explained that most of his relationships with prostitutes when he was a young man were simply a matter of finding company and escaping solitude.

> I have fond memories of prostitutes and I write about them for
> sentimental reasons . . . Brothels cost money, and so they are

places for older men. Sexual initiation actually starts with servants at home. And with cousins. And with aunts. But the prostitutes were friends to me when I was a young man . . . With prostitutes—including some I did not go to bed with—I always had some good friendships. I could sleep with them because it was horrible to sleep alone. Or I could not. I have always said, as a joke, that I married not to eat lunch alone. Of course, Mercedes says that I'm a son of a bitch.

He said that he envied his sons living in an age of equality between men and women: *Chronicle* showed how things were when he was a young man. He finally described himself as a man who desperately needed love: "I am the shyest man in the world. I am also the kindest. On this I accept no argument or debate . . . My greatest weakness? Umm. It's my heart. In the emotional-sentimental sense. If I were a woman, I would always say yes. I need to be loved a great deal. My great problem is to be loved more, and that is why I write." *Playboy*: "You make it sound like being a nymphomaniac." García Márquez: "Well, yes—but a nymphomaniac of the heart . . . If I had not become a writer, I'd want to have been a piano player in a bar. That way, I could have made a contribution to making lovers feel even more loving toward each other. If I can achieve that much as a writer—to have people love one another more because of my books—I think that's the meaning I've wanted for my life." Of course now he would try to do that for people through his love stories and for countries through his mediations.

Just before this celebrity interview—which would not appear in print for almost a year—one of the best-known books about García Márquez had been published, one which would go on selling large numbers of copies down the years. *The Fragrance of Guava* was a favour to Plinio Mendoza, who had again fallen on hard times. It was an apparently frank but carefully calculated conversation—expertly staged—which surveyed the whole of García Márquez's life and work and gave his opinions on everything from, again, politics to women.[41] It is difficult not to imagine that the sometimes startling insinuations about sexual flirtations and possible extramarital affairs were not in some way the opening up of a new market for a writer for whom the literary expression of love seemed always previously to have been associated with violence and tragedy.

So García Márquez confirmed his decision to go back to writing and now would never forsake it again, as long as he was capable of practising it. Until quite recently it had been a vocation, a compulsion, an ambition, sometimes a torment. Now he started to truly enjoy it. Years before, during his literary "strike," he had told an interviewer somewhat wistfully that he was coming to realize that he was never as happy as when he was writing.[42] Now at last he had an idea for a new book: a book about love and reconciliation. As spring arrived in Europe he began to make notes.

That summer he and Mercedes travelled around the Old Continent with Colombian friends Alvaro Castaño, who owned Bogotá's leading classical music radio station, HJCK, and his wife Gloria Valencia, Colombia's best-known television presenter. They took in Paris, Amsterdam, Greece and Rome. Then Gabo and Mercedes returned to Mexico. By now he had fixed on the specifics of the new novel; it would be created around, of all things, the love affair between his parents, about which he had so long been in denial.

In late August García Márquez and Mercedes vacationed once more with Fidel Castro on the Cuban coastland. Rodrigo had just graduated from Harvard and accompanied them on the visit. He was now considering a career in the cinema. Their great friends the Feduchis and Carmen Balcells also spent time with them and the Comandante. Fidel not only honoured them with a cruise on his yacht *Acuaramas* but also gave them a dinner invitation to his apartment on 11th Street, where few foreigners had eaten since the death of Celia Sánchez. Castro is an enthusiastic chef and cooking is one of his favourite topics of conversation, especially at that time as he was engaged in a campaign to produce a Cuban Camembert and a Cuban Roquefort. The next night everyone ate at Antonio Núñez Jiménez's house and on this occasion conversation turned from cooking to money.[43] Castro was considering making a visit to Colombia and said that "Gabriel," as he has always insisted on calling him, should accompany him, "unless you're afraid of being accused of being a Cuban agent."

"It's a bit late for that," replied García Márquez.

"When I hear people saying Castro pays García Márquez," said Mercedes, "I say it's about time we saw some of the money."

"That would be bad, if you sent me the bill," said Castro. "But I have an unbeatable argument. 'Señores, we can't pay García Márquez because he is too expensive.' Not long ago, so as not to come out with the boast that we can't be bought, I said to some Yankees: 'It's not that we won't sell ourselves, you understand, the fact is that the USA hasn't got enough money to buy us.' More modest, right? And it's the same with García Márquez. We can't make him our agent. You know why? We haven't got enough money to buy him, he's too expensive."

Rodrigo, silent until then, said: "When I arrived at a North American university, they asked me how my father reconciled his political ideas with his money and his lifestyle. I answered as best I could but there's no satisfactory answer to the question."

"Look, you just say to them, 'That's a problem for my mother, not my father,'" said Castro. "You should say, 'Look, my father hasn't got a sou, my mother's the one who spends the money.'"

"And she only gives me money for gasoline," said García Márquez without a shadow of a smile.

Castro replied, "I'm working out a policy here for when they talk to you about your bank accounts. You must tell them that the socialist formula is from each according to his ability and to each according to his work and as Gabriel is a socialist—he's not yet a communist—he gives according to his ability and he receives according to his work. Besides, the communist formula isn't applied anywhere."

Rodrigo warmed to the topic: "Once, out of nowhere, a boy turned to me and said, 'Your father's a communist.' I asked him, 'What does that mean, that he has a party card, he lives in a communist country?'"

Castro replied, "You should tell him, 'My father is a communist only when he travels to Cuba and they pay him nothing; he gives according to his ability, they've printed about a million of his books, and he receives according to his needs.'"

"They pay me nothing. They never pay me a centavo in royalties here," said Gabo.

During this visit García Márquez and Castro also talked about the implications of Betancur's election in Colombia, which, at first sight, was a considerable setback for both García Márquez and the Cuban Revolution. Betancur had been inaugurated on 7 August. Although a Conservative and an ex-editor of the reactionary newspaper *El Siglo*, his reputation had always been that of a "civilized" politician who was not sectarian and he was an amateur poet who counted many other poets among his personal friends. García Márquez had begun flirting with the new regime in press interviews soon after the election, in addition to repeating how "homesick" he was feeling.

Despite refusing to attend Betancur's inauguration García Márquez spoke well of the new President to Castro, declaring that he was "a good friend of mine." He was the son of a muleteer; they had known one another since 1954 when "Gabo" was at *El Espectador* and "Belisario" at *El Colombiano*. They had always been in contact since then. García Márquez explained to Castro, "In Colombia you are either Conservative or Liberal from birth, it doesn't matter what you think." Betancur, he said, was not a true ideological Conservative, and his government was full of independent people. "He's a great rhetorical speaker, he gets through to people, really gets through to them. And," and here came the payoff, "he asks my advice all the time."[44]

THE NOBEL SEASON was approaching once more and, as in previous years, García Márquez's name was being mentioned again, only this time even more insistently. All the more surprising, then, that he chose, less than a month before the award was announced, to launch a withering attack on Israeli leader Menachem Begin—and, by direct implication, the Nobel Foundation which had awarded him the Nobel Peace Prize in 1978. In early June Begin had ordered the invasion of neighbouring Lebanon and his military commander General Ariel Sharon had neglected to protect Palestinian refugees from attack, thereby enabling the massacres in the Sabra and Chatila camps in Beirut on 18 September. García Márquez suggested that Sharon and Begin should be awarded a Nobel Death Prize.[45]

But there is every sign he had been working on his own candidacy, too. When his friend Alfonso Fuenmayor asked him later in the year whether he had been to Stockholm before, he replied with a grin: "Yes, I was here three years ago when I came to fix myself up with the Nobel Prize."[46] Naturally this could just be one of his *boutades* but the truth is that he had made several visits to Stockholm in the 1970s and had gone out of his way to make contact with Artur Lundkvist, the left-wing Swedish academician and distinguished writer who had already had a strong influence on the prize going to Latin Americans Miguel Angel Asturias and Pablo Neruda. And García Márquez had vacationed in Cuba with the Swedish ambassador in the summer of 1981.

If he was looking for omens he couldn't have had a better one than the return to power of Olof Palme's Social Democrats in the Swedish elections of 19 September 1982. Palme had been a friend of García Márquez for years and had always emphasized his personal debt to Lundkvist's literary works for opening his eyes to the wider world. Meanwhile brother Eligio, the family's literary expert, was always absolutely certain that Gabito was going to win the prize in 1982 and was sure that Gabito himself thought so too. Alvaro Mutis had said his friend's behaviour was "suspicious" at the time. And on Saturday 16 October, when Eligio talked to him by phone and mentioned the prize, Gabito, roaring with laughter, said he was sure that if someone was going to win it, the Swedish ambassador would have talked to that person a month beforehand . . .[47]

On Wednesday 20 October the Mexican newspapers were announcing that García Márquez's new novel was to be about love. As he and Mercedes sat down for lunch in the early afternoon, a friend called from Stockholm to say that all indications suggested that the prize really was in the bag but that he must keep it to himself or the academicians might change their minds. After he hung up Gabo and Mercedes looked at one another in stupefaction, unable to say a word. Finally she said, "My God, what are we in for now!" They got straight up from the table and fled to Alvaro Mutis's house for comfort, only returning to their own home in the early hours to wait for confirmation of this accolade which he at least had wanted but which was also a life sentence for them both.

Neither of them slept. At 5.59 the next morning, Mexico City time, Pierre Shori, Vice Foreign Minister of Sweden, called the house in Mexico City and confirmed the news. García Márquez put down the telephone, turned to Mercedes and said: "I'm fucked."[48] They had no time to discuss it or to prepare themselves for the inevitable onslaught before the phone began to ring. The first caller, just two minutes later, was President Betancur, from Bogotá. Betancur had heard the news from François Mitterrand who had heard it from Olof Palme, but the official version said Betancur had heard it from an RCN journalist at 7.03 a.m. Bogotá time.[49] García Márquez and Mercedes got dressed as they fielded the first calls and picked at the improvised breakfast brought up by their maid Nati when she heard them moving about upstairs.

With the exception of the writing of *One Hundred Years of Solitude*, nothing in the great García Márquez mythology has been discussed as much as the announcement of the Nobel Prize, the ensuing pandemonium, and García Márquez's journey to Stockholm to receive it. If an American or an English man or woman wins the honour, it barely makes the news. (What do writers matter; and who do the Swedes think they are, anyway . . .) But this was not only an award to a man from Colombia, a country quite unused to international congratulations; it was—it transpired—an award to a man admired and adored throughout a vast, isolated continent, a man who millions in that continent considered their own representative and, indeed, their champion. Congratulations rained down on the house in Mexico City from around the world by telephone and telegram: Betancur, first, but also Mitterrand, Cortázar, Borges, Gregory Rabassa, Juan Carlos Onetti, the Colombian Senate. Castro could not get through so sent a telegram the next day: "Justice has been done at last. Jubilation here since yesterday. Impossible to get through by phone. I congratulate both you and Mercedes with all my heart." Graham Greene also sent a telegram, "Warmest congratulations. Pity we couldn't celebrate it with Omar." Norman Mailer too: "Couldn't have gone to a better man." Above all, though, it was an opportunity for Latin America to say at last what it felt about García Márquez—Colombia, Cuba and Mexico all claimed him as their own—and a vast amount of eulogistic copy was logged with newspapers there and all over the world. It was as if *One Hundred Years of Solitude* had just been published and a billion people had read it simultaneously, five seconds after its appearance, in some strange and magical time, and wanted to celebrate together.

Within minutes the house in Mexico City was under siege from the media, and the police set up roadblocks at either end of Calle Fuego. The first journalists invited him out into the street for a glass of champagne—with photos, of course—and the neighbours came out to applaud. When Alejandro Obregón turned up that morning to stay with his old friend and saw the chaos he thought to himself, "Shit! Gabo's died!" (Obregón was in Mexico to restore a painting he had given García Márquez, a self-portrait one of whose eyes had been shot out by the painter himself in a drunken fit.)[50] Dozens of journalists thronged through the García Márquez house, fetishistically describing every last detail outside and in—they particularly noticed the yellow roses and guavas on every table—and each clamouring for an "exclusive" interview with the man of the moment.

García Márquez had not spoken to his mother for three weeks because her phone was down and an enterprising Bogotá journalist used the wonders of technology to link them up for a public conversation. So Luisa Santiaga told the whole of Colombia that she thought the best thing about the news was that "Maybe now I'll get my phone fixed." Which she very soon did. She also said that she'd always hoped Gabito would never win the prize because she was sure he would die soon afterwards. Her son, well used to these eccentricities, said that he would be taking yellow roses to Stockholm in order to protect himself.

García Márquez eventually organized an improvised press conference for the more than a hundred journalists by then swarming over his house. He announced that he would not wear evening dress at the ceremony in Stockholm but a *guayabera* shirt or even a *liquiliqui*—the white linen tunic and trousers worn by Latin American peasants in Hollywood movies—in honour of his grandfather. This topic became an obsession in *cachaco* Colombia, right up to the moment of the ceremony, emblematic of the fear that García Márquez would cause some international scandal or behave with unbearable vulgarity and let the country down. He also announced that he would use the prize money to found a newspaper to be called *El Otro* (The Other), in Bogotá: in his opinion half of the prize had been awarded in recognition of his journalism. He would also build his dream house in Cartagena.

At one in the afternoon, García Márquez and Mercedes left the journalists to it and fled the Calle Fuego, took a room in the Hotel Chapultepec Presidente and began to ring their closest friends. They spent the afternoon in seclusion with just eight people while their house was still in uproar. Alvaro Mutis was designated as the García Barcha family chauffeur for the duration of the media furore.

Washington, meanwhile, confirmed on that same day that despite his new status García Márquez would still not be given a visa to visit the United States, from which he had been banned ever since working for Cuba in 1961. (On 7 November he would write in his column in *El Espectador* that he would rather "the door be closed than half open"—which was quite untrue because he was still profoundly irked by the prohibition—so on 1 December he would make another of his rash threats, vowing to ban the publication of his books in the United States since, if they were still refusing him a visa, why should they allow his books to enter?)[51] This happened also to be the day the dissident poet Armando Valladares was released from prison in Cuba, largely thanks to García Márquez's mediation between Castro and Mitterrand. Valladares, supposedly paralysed, according to his supporters, was accompanied by Mitterrand's adviser Régis Debray, and astonished everyone by rising from his wheelchair and walking on arrival at the airport in Paris.

All around the world García Márquez's friends celebrated. Plinio Mendoza wept in Paris. He was not the only one. By contrast the publisher José Vicente Kataraín, already on his way to Mexico, learned the news in the airport on arrival and began to dance; the girl at the news stand asked if he'd won the lottery. Indeed he had. Down in Cartagena, as the family celebrated, Gabriel Eligio said, to anyone who would listen, "I always knew it." No one reminded him of the prediction that Gabito would "eat paper." Luisa Santiaga said her father the Colonel must be celebrating somewhere; he had always predicted great things for Gabito. Most of the reports would present the family as eccentric inhabitants of their own little Macondo: Luisa Santiaga was Úrsula and Gabriel Eligio was José Arcadio, though as usual he wondered aloud whether he might not be Melquíades. But little by little, despite his pride and undoubted euphoria, Gabriel Eligio began to misbehave: Gabito had got the prize through Mitterrand's influence, he said ("those things count, you know"); Gabito was just one of the many writers in his family; he couldn't think why this one got quite so much attention.

The Governor of the Department of Magdalena decided to declare 22 October a regional holiday and proposed that Colonel Márquez's old house in Aracataca should become a national monument. In Bogotá the Communist Party organized street demonstrations pleading with García Márquez to return to the country as a spokesman for the oppressed, to save Colombia. A reporter asked a prostitute in the street if she'd heard the news and she said a client had just told her about it in bed; this was thought to be the best homage García Márquez could receive. In Barranquilla the taxi drivers on the Paseo Bolívar heard the news on their radios and all sounded their horns in unison: after all, Gabito was one of them.

Newspapers began to call García Márquez "the new Cervantes," echoing an idea which Pablo Neruda had been one of the first to suggest when he read *One Hundred Years of Solitude* in 1967.[52] This comparison would be made many times down the years from this moment on. *Newsweek*, which also had García Márquez on the cover, called him "a spellbinding storyteller."[53] Perhaps Salman Rushdie, writing from London, best summed up the opinion that prevailed both then and thereafter. His piece was entitled "Márquez the Magician": "He is one of the Nobel judges' most popular choices for years, one of the few true magicians in contemporary literature, an artist with the rare quality of producing work of the highest order that reaches and bewitches a mass audience. Márquez's masterpiece, *One Hundred Years of Solitude*, is, I believe, one of the two or three most important and most completely achieved works of fiction to be published anywhere since the war."[54]

Meanwhile, just a week after the announcement of the prize, one of his good friends, Felipe González, leader of the Spanish Socialist Party, was elected Prime Minister of his country, yet another cause for celebration and political euphoria. Last year Mitterrand; now González. Was the prize somehow a sign that everything was beginning to change? García Márquez told *Gente* of Buenos Aires, "I can die happy because now I am immortal." Perhaps he was joking.

On 1 December Miguel de la Madrid was inaugurated as the President of Mexico for the next six years. He and García Márquez would never be close but García Márquez attended the ceremony. That same day Felipe González was inaugurated as Prime Minister of the new Spanish government in Madrid. In the first days of December, after visiting Cuba, García Márquez flew on to Madrid to salute González— and be saluted. He let it be known that he had talked to Castro for eleven hours in Havana and that the Reagan government had refused him an unconditional visa to touch down in New York. Meanwhile, in Paris, Mercedes met up with Gonzalo. But not Rodrigo. The only disappointing note for García Márquez was that his elder son, filming in the north of Mexico, was too busy working to travel to Stockholm, the undoubted high point of his distinguished father's career. The two had met up in Zacatecas the previous month and no one knows what transpired. Neither man has ever been prepared to say more about the matter.

At seven in the evening on Monday 6 December a government-chartered Avianca jumbo jet took off on a twenty-two-hour journey from Bogotá to Stockholm, carrying the official delegation led by Minister of Education Jaime Arias Ramírez, together with García Márquez's twelve closest friends chosen by Guillermo Angulo— García Márquez had pleaded with his old friend Angulo to save him from this invidious task—plus their spouses, a large number of people invited by Oveja Negra, and seventy musicians from various ethnic groups organized by the Minister of Culture with the advice and assistance of an anthropologist, Gloria Triana.

When García Márquez's guests finally arrived in Stockholm the temperature had just fallen to freezing point. Hundreds of Europe-based Colombians and other Latin Americans were waiting at the airport. As the night wore on the temperature would fall to minus ten degrees but the Swedes told them they were lucky it wasn't colder and that it hadn't snowed.[55] Groups of friends and family from Spain and Paris had arrived earlier in the afternoon: Carmen Balcells and Magdalena Oliver from Barcelona, together with the Feduchis and journalist Ramón Chao; Mercedes and Gonzalo, Tachia and Charles, and Plinio Mendoza, from Paris, together with Régis Debray and Mitterrand's wife Danielle, though without Culture Minister Jack Lang, another friend, who had to cancel at the last moment. The Colombian ambassador was also there, plus the Cuban ambassador and the Mexican chargé d'affaires, all waiting in the Arctic cold.[56]

Tachia appointed herself official photographer to García Márquez and his friends and she even managed to get herself a press pass. As her old flame advanced from the plane to the waiting room she thrust herself forward and took the first photo of the conquering hero, and then she photographed the wildly enthusiastic Colombians trying to touch García Márquez through the airport's steel barriers in the Northern darkness. Gabo and Mercedes went on to the Grand Hotel, where an opulent suite of three rooms awaited them and where they would spend the next few nights.[57] Exhausted, jet-lagged, over-excited and overwhelmed, García Márquez fell asleep. Then, "I suddenly woke up in bed, and I remembered that they always give the same room in the same hotel to the Nobel winner. And I thought, 'Rudyard Kipling has slept in this bed, Thomas Mann, Neruda, Asturias, Faulkner.' It terrified me, and finally I went out to sleep on the sofa."[58]

The next morning García Márquez had breakfast in the hotel with a huge group of friends representing his entire past, including Carmen Balcells and Kataraín. Such a group of people had never been brought together before. Some didn't even know one another, some probably didn't like one another. Plinio Mendoza said that García Márquez had behaved at the airport like a visiting bullfighter saluting his fans and that he got dressed every day in his suite, again like a bullfighter, with all his friends around him. On one occasion he took Alfonso Fuenmayor from "the suite of the happy few" into the solitary bedroom and showed him his speech: "Take a look at that, Maestro, and tell me what you think." Fuenmayor read the piece with admiration and said at last he understood García Márquez's political position. His friend replied, "What you've just read is One Hundred Years of Solitude, no more, no less."[59]

As the hour approached, Mendoza recalls, "In the middle of the lounge I saw Gabo and Mercedes, placid, untroubled, talking, completely oblivious to the coronation ceremony advancing upon them, as if they were still, thirty years ago, in Sucre or Magangué, in the house of Aunt Petra or Aunt Juana some Saturday evening."[60] The literature prize winner's speech was to be given at 5 p.m. in the theatre of the

Swedish Academy of Literature situated in the Stock Exchange, with 200 specially invited guests and a total audience of 400, followed at 6.30 by a dinner in honour of all the prize winners in the house of the Academy Secretary.

At 5 p.m. García Márquez, wearing his trademark hound's-tooth jacket, dark trousers, a white shirt and a red polka-dot tie, was introduced by the lanky Lars Gyllensten, Permanent Secretary of the Academy and himself a well-known novelist, who had written the communiqué announcing the award of the prize. Gyllensten, who was speaking in Swedish, could barely be heard because the Colombian radio commentators present at the ceremony sounded as if they were doing a football match and García Márquez had to make a "turn it down" gesture with his fingers before he started his own speech, entitled "The Solitude of Latin America." It was delivered by its author in an aggressive, defiant, almost incantatory style. Combining a deconstructed magical realism with politics, the speech was an undisguised attack on the inability or unwillingness of Europeans to understand Latin America's historical problems and their reluctance to give the continent the time to mature and develop that Europe itself had required. It restated his lifelong objection to "Europeans" (including North Americans), whether capitalists or communists, imposing their "schemes" on Latin America's living realities. García Márquez claimed that the prize had been awarded in part for his political activism and not only his literature. He finished at 5.35 and received an ovation for several minutes.[61]

On the evening of Thursday the 9th García Márquez and Mercedes travelled out to the Prime Minister's residence at Harpsund for a private dinner with Palme and eleven other special guests, including Danielle Mitterrand, Régis Debray, Pierre Schori, Günter Grass, Turkish poet-politician Bülent Ecevit, and Artur Lundkvist. The Swedish Foreign Office said this invitation was a special distinction, rarely given before. García Márquez had been introduced to Palme by François Mitterrand in his Rue de Bièvre home years before. Now, although he was absolutely exhausted, he found himself talking for another two hours about the situation in Central America in a conversation which would be influential in proposing a peace process to be brokered by the six presidents of the isthmus, what would later be known as the Contadora Process.[62]

All of this was but a series of hors d'oeuvres to the main course on 10 December, the day of the "Nobel Festival": in the morning the rehearsal in the Konserthus, in the afternoon the great event, the presentation of the Nobel Prizes by the King of Sweden at four o'clock before an audience of 1,700 people. That day Mercedes, "the wife of the Nobel," appeared in Colombia on the cover of *Carrusel*, an *El Tiempo* supplement. The article inside was by her sister-in-law, Beatriz López de Barcha, entitled "Gabito Waited for Me to Grow Up."[63] One can imagine Mercedes's sister-in-law having said to her, "OK, you want to wipe out that piece by Consuelo Mendoza last year, why not let me do a really favourable interview, with flattering pictures?" Mercedes: "OK, but just this once."

Soon after lunch the man of the hour got dressed. He had been talking about his *liquiliqui* since the day he heard the news. Sometimes he declared that it was to honour his grandfather the Colonel, sometimes, less modestly, that it was to honour his own most famous creation, Colonel Aureliano Buendía. *El Espectador* carried a letter the day after the ceremony from Don Aristides Gómez Avilés in Montería, Colombia, who remembered Colonel Márquez well and said he would never have been seen dead in a *liquiliqui*: he was far too posh for that and would never have been caught out in the street without a jacket on, still less at a Nobel Prize ceremony.[64] In these discussions a man who really had worn a *liquiliqui* in his youth, Gabriel Eligio García, never got a mention.

Suite 208, Grand Hotel Stockholm, 10 December 1982, 3 p.m. Before travelling from Paris Tachia had bought García Márquez the Damart thermal underwear which appears in a famous photograph of the great writer standing in his intimate apparel, surrounded by his male friends in the dinner jackets which they had all rented for 200 krona apiece. Mercedes handed them yellow roses, one by one, to ward off *la pava*, as bad luck is called in the Spanish Caribbean, and helped fix them to lapels: "Now then, *compadre*, let me see. . . ." Then she organized the photographs.[65] Then out came the *liquiliqui* which, Ana María Cano in *El Espectador* cattily observed three days later, meant that García Márquez arrived at the ceremony looking "as wrinkled as an accordion."[66]

All this was later. Now, dressed defiantly in his *liquiliqui*—the closest thing when all is said and done to a recognizably Latin American lower-class uniform—with, oh horror, black boots, García Márquez prepared himself for the moment of truth. If the *liquiliqui* was wrinkled, no doubt those of Nicaragua's Augusto Sandino and Cuba's José Martí and other heroes of Latin American resistance had been wrinkled, not to mention that of Aureliano Buendía. He covered himself with an overcoat against the Nordic elements. Plinio Mendoza recalls the moment: "We all crowded tightly together and went down the steps to accompany Gabo for the most memorable moment of his life."[67] Then Mendoza switches to the eternal present: "The streets are covered in snow, photographers everywhere. By Gabo's side, I see his face tighten for a moment. I can feel, with the antennae of my Pisces ascendant, the sudden tension. The flowers, the flashes, the figures in black, the red carpet: perhaps from the remote deserts where they lie buried his Guajiro ancestors are talking to him. Perhaps they're telling him that the pomp and ceremony of glory is the same as the pomp and ceremony of death. Something like that is going on because as he pushes on through the magnesium glow and the figures in formal dress I hear him mutter in a low voice in which there is a note of sudden, alarmed, pained astonishment: 'Shit, this is like turning up at my own funeral!' "[68]

Into the grand ballroom of the Konserthus, designed to evoke a Greek temple, they stride. One thousand seven hundred people including three hundred Colombians. A gasp when García Márquez appears in his all-white outfit: he looks as if he is still in his thermal underwear! To the right of the stage, which is covered in yellow flowers, sitting in blue and gold armchairs, are the royal family: King Carl Gustav the Sixteenth, Queen Silvia, the beautiful half-Brazilian who spent her childhood in São Paulo, Princess Lilian and Prince Bertil, who all just arrived as the national anthem was played. Beside them is a podium from which Permanent Secretary Gyllensten will speak. The laureates are all to the left, on red seats: Swedes Sune Bergstrom, Bengt Samuelsson and Briton John Vane for medicine, American Kenneth Wilson for physics, South African Aron Klug for chemistry and American George Stigler for economics. Behind are two further rows of seats in which the academicians, the Swedish cabinet and other notables are seated. García Márquez alone in his *liquiliqui* surrounded by dress suits, stoles, furs, pearl necklaces. Between him and the King the huge N for Nobel inscribed in the circle—painted or chalked?—that awaits him.

He was visibly nervous when Professor Gyllensten of the Swedish Academy started to speak. When it came to García Márquez's moment, last but one, Gyllensten spoke in Swedish, then turned to the Colombian *costeño*, who stood, with glittering eyes, looking for all the world like the hapless little boy in the Colegio San José de Barranquilla, and switched to French, summarizing what he had said and inviting the Colombian to approach the King to receive the prize. García Márquez, who had chosen Bartok's *Intermezzo* as his accompanying piece of music, left his yellow rose on his seat as he moved to receive the award, exposed for a moment to unimaginable misfortune without that totemic flower as he walked across the immense stage with his fists clenched and the trumpets sounding, then stopped inside the painted circle to await the King. Now, as he shook hands with the medal-bedecked monarch he looked like Chaplin's tramp ingratiating himself with some toff. After receiving the medal and parchment, he bowed stiffly to the King, then to the guests of honour and then the audience, whereupon he received what was generally agreed to have been the longest standing ovation in the history of those august ceremonies: several minutes.[69]

The ceremony finished at 5.45 p.m. and as García Márquez filed out with the other winners he raised his hands above his head like a champion boxer, a gesture he would henceforth be making many times in his life to come. Those fortunate enough to be invited had forty-five minutes to get themselves across to the vast blue hall of the Stadhus (Stockholm Town Hall) for the grand Swedish Academy banquet. The menu had been prepared by Johnny Johanssen, Sweden's top chef, and was a "typically Swedish" affair. Reindeer fillets, trout and sorbet, with banana and almonds. Champagne, sherry and port.[70] García Márquez, defiantly, lit a Havana cigar. The highlight of the proceedings—as everyone would agree—was the arrival of the seventy Colombian musicians. García Márquez's friend Nereo López had been following their adventures and misadventures in Stockholm with his camera.[71] He had watched Gloria Triana anxiously chaperoning all the women: "They're all virgins and I've promised their mothers." On arrival in the Town Hall, which was draped in monarchical tapestries, one of the group from Riosucio had knelt and prayed, thinking he was in a church. López wondered how the Swedes felt when they saw "that heterogeneous group from Macondo coming down the stairs, that amalgam of Indian, Black, Carib and Spanish which makes up the mix of Colombian identity." Up to then, according to him, the great ice cream known as the *Nobel Flambé* had been the main attraction at these ceremonies. Now life itself was flooding in. The entire performance, led by Totó la Momposina and Leonor la Negra Grande de Colombia, was a triumph and the applause encouraged them to go on for thirty minutes instead of fifteen.[72]

Each laureate read a three-minute speech followed by a toast. García Márquez went first with a piece entitled "In Praise of Poetry," which claimed that poetry was "the most definite proof of the existence of man."[73] What no one knew at the time was that he had more than just a little help from his friend Alvaro Mutis, as anyone, reading the speech and then thinking about it, might have deduced. Two of the other laureates asked him to sign copies of *One Hundred Years of Solitude*. After the toasts everyone filed up to the first floor to the "Great Gold Room" for dancing. This started with a waltz followed by sundry North European dances, then, unexpectedly, "Bésame mucho," "Perfidia" and other *boleros*, followed by foxtrots and rumbas.

Late that evening, after everyone got back to the hotel, there was a phone call from Rodrigo, up in the northern desert of Mexico. The new laureate was with twenty of his friends, still drinking champagne. Everything went quiet and García Márquez, with shining eyes, went over to the phone. Later he would proudly tell journalists that his sons had "the flavour of their mother and their father's business sense."[74]

By then, thousands of miles away in the small Caribbean town of Aracataca, Colombia, where of course it was still light, an even more vibrant and enthusiastic celebration was under way. There had been a Te Deum in the church where Gabito was baptized at nine in the morning, followed by a pilgrimage to the house where he had been born. A campaign was proposed to make Aracataca a historic tourist town on the model of Proust's Illiers-Combray. Then the Governing Council of the Magdalena Department assembled in the House of Culture, chaired by the energetic Governor Sara Valencia Abdala, herself an Aracataca native.[75] García Márquez's sister Rita recalled: "The day the prize was presented there was a celebration in Aracataca organized by the Magdalena government. The Governor hired a train to take all the guests; it picked up all the family on the way, cousins, uncles, aunts and nephews, and so we all arrived in Aracataca, where there were more cousins, more uncles and aunts, more family. A lot of people. It was a wonderful day, there were fireworks, a mass, a side of beef roasted in the open air and drinks for the whole town. Our cousin Carlos Martínez Simahan, the Minister of Mines, was there. That day they inaugurated the Telecom building which our brother Jaime had built. Though the best thing of all was when they released the yellow butterflies."[76]

Back in Stockholm the man of the hour was beginning to relax. He had felt responsible for communicating a positive image of Latin

America to the world, knowing that in Colombia, above all, his enemies could hardly wait for him to make a mistake because their view of what might be a "good image" of the country was entirely different from what he was trying to do. He would later say: "No one ever suspected how unhappy I was during those three days, attending to the minutest detail so that everything would turn out well. I could not afford any mistakes because the smallest error, however insignificant, would have been catastrophic in those circumstances."[77] (Later, when they were both back in Mexico City, the new laureate would say to Alvaro Mutis: "Tell me about that Stockholm business, I can't remember a thing. I just see the photographers' flashes and see myself enduring the journalists' questions, always the same questions. Tell me what you remember.")[78]

Yet so stunningly successful was he that even *El Tiempo*, with which his relationship would never be easy, gave him an almost unqualified thumbs up in an editorial. It congratulated García Márquez, acknowledging that his life had been hard and he had earned every last ounce of his glory. It ended: "After the euphoria involved in the Nobel ceremony, the country must return to reality, face up to its problems and go back to its routine. But there is something that will not be the same as before: the conviction that our potentialities are still an unexplored richness and that we have barely begun to emerge on the world stage. And there to prove it is García Márquez, so that we will never forget this invaluable lesson."[79]

21

The Frenzy of Renown
and the Fragrance of Guava:
Love in the Time of Cholera

1982~1985

THE NEXT MORNING, the morning after, Gabo and Mercedes flew to Barcelona, accompanied by Carmen Balcells. There they checked into the Princesa Sofía Hotel to sleep it all off until the New Year. They did, however, make another visit to the new Spanish Prime Minister. García Márquez would dutifully record in his weekly column—not interrupted for anyone or anything—that he had visited the Moncloa Palace twice in the last two weeks to chat to the youthful "Felipe," who had looked "more like a university student" than a president, and to his wife Carmen, accompanied by Mercedes and Gonzalo.[1] It was clear that the new Nobel Prize winner was going to be less discreet and more bumptious than ever. In his next article he remarked, "I consider myself, and I take pride in it, the human being most allergic to formality . . . and I still can't get used to the idea that my friends become presidents nor have I yet overcome my susceptibility to being impressed by government palaces." The international jet-setter was convinced that Felipe, who understood Latin America "better than any other non-Latin American," was going to have "a decisive influence on Latin American–European relations." Whether Felipe himself saw things the same way we cannot know but clearly García Márquez was hoping to bounce him into supporting his long-term strategy for Cuba, the Caribbean and Latin America, and had no compunction in letting the world know about it.

Nevertheless at their informal exchange with the press, the first thing González mentioned was "the status of Cuba within the region and the need for a security agreement for all," not necessarily what García Márquez had in mind. García Márquez declared that love would solve all the world's problems and said he wanted to get back to his latest novel on that very subject: he'd really rather have won the prize next year so that he could have finished the book.[2]

On 29 December the new laureate left for Havana, having declared that he still wanted to found his own newspaper to enjoy "the old dignity of bearing news," which perhaps sounded uneasily like the instinct of the go-between, which in Spanish has a less agreeable word, *correveidile*: "run-see-and-tell-him." The Madrid–Havana axis would be a crucial concern of García Márquez's over the coming years, though even he would not be able to reconcile the differences between Castro and González.

Two oft-repeated general truths about the Nobel Prize for Literature are that it is usually given to writers who have completed their creative cycle and no longer have any worthwhile works left inside them; and that, even in the case of younger writers, the prize is a distraction which robs them of time, concentration and ambition. The first was clearly not true of García Márquez: he was one of the youngest of all Nobel Prize winners as well as one of the best-known and most popular. The second was predicted by those who resented his success, or were jealous of it, but the fact is that García Márquez had already experienced celebrity on a scale that even Nobel Prize winners rarely encounter. Not only was he not the kind of man to rest on his laurels but he had already been through this kind of experience in the years after *One Hundred Years of Solitude* was published: it had been like winning a first Nobel Prize. Alternatively, then, one might expect him to be newly galvanized: to write more, travel more, find new things to do. And so it turned out. He was more than ready for his new status. And yet . . .

And yet . . . he had already decided in 1980 on a new way of life appropriate to his new position of authority and respectability. He was already a friend of presidents: to the not very respectable relation with Fidel, the pirate captain, he had added López Portillo of Mexico, Carlos Andrés Pérez of Venezuela, López Michelsen and Betancur of Colombia, Mitterrand of France and lastly González of Spain. He had now increased his own vast celebrity by acquiring a kind of roving presidential status. (Fidel Castro would say, "Yes, of course García Márquez is like a head of state. The only question is, which state?") He told journalists he was taking a sabbatical, but clearly he was also hoping to use his new influence to mediate more effectively with his new presidential allies. One might say that his openly political period lasted from about 1959 to 1979, and most intensively from 1971 to 1979. Thereafter followed a more "diplomatic" period. The question was whether he would merely be concealing his real politics during this diplomatic period whilst remaining a well-meaning fellow traveller, as in the period 1950–79, or whether he would gradually adjust his political position behind the cover of his mediations, clandestine negotiations and cultural enterprises.

As he flew back across the Atlantic in all his glory, even García Márquez, who planned so very much in his life, whether consciously or unconsciously, must have felt the weight of celebrity and awesome responsibility settling on his shoulders. He had got what he wanted but sometimes, as Marilyn Monroe had famously sung, after you get what you want you don't want it. For some time now he had been forced to adjust to levels of adulation that, unless one has witnessed them, are almost unimaginable for a serious writer: nothing less than the "frenzy of renown."[3] Now he would have to turn his entire life into a carefully organized spectacle.

People who had known him most of his life would say that he became much more cautious after winning the prize. Some of his friends were grateful that he continued to attend to them at all, others resented a process of perceived neglect. Many people said his vanity increased exponentially, others that it was extraordinary how normal he managed to remain; his cousin Gog said he had always been like a "new-born Nobel Prize winner."[4] Carmen Balcells, who was able to view literary celebrity more coolly than most, said that the extent of his success and fame was "unrepeatable."[5] ("When you have an author like Gabriel García Márquez you can set up a political party, institute a religion or organize a revolution.") García Márquez himself would later say that he tried everything possible to "stay the same" but that no one viewed him as the same after the journey to Stockholm. Fame, he would say, was "like having the lights on all the time." People tell you what they think you want to hear; the prize requires dignity, you can no longer just tell people to "fuck off." You are required always to be amusing and intelligent. If you start talking at a party, even with old friends, everyone else stops speaking and listens to you. Ironically, "as you're surrounded by more and more people, you feel smaller and smaller and smaller."[6] Before long he would take up tennis because it became completely impossible to exercise by taking walks in the street. In every restaurant waiters would go rushing off to the nearest bookstore for copies of his books to be signed. Airports have always been the worst places of all because there he can find no escape. He is always put first on every plane but even then the flight attendants themselves all want books or flight magazines or napkins signed. Yet this is an essentially shy, timid and in many ways anxious man.[7] "My main job now is to be me. That's really tough. You can't imagine how that weighs you down. But I asked for it."[8] There is every reason to believe that he would find the coming years much more difficult than he affected and yet he would no longer feel able to complain in the way he had done during the writing of *The Autumn of the Patriarch*.

García Márquez and Mercedes flew in to Havana at five in the morning of 30 December 1982 for an extended stay and were installed in Protocol House number six which, not many years later, would become their Cuban home. Castro had recently been to Brezhnev's funeral in Moscow, where he and Indira Gandhi had discussed inviting García Márquez to the meeting of Non-Aligned Nations to be held in Delhi in March 1983. (Gandhi had mentioned that she had been reading *One Hundred Years of Solitude* when the Nobel award was announced.) While in Moscow Fidel had bought García Márquez a large supply of his favourite caviar. García Márquez, for his part, was carrying messages from Felipe González and Olof Palme, together with *bacalao* from the Feduchis and cognac from Carmen Balcells.

Graham Greene passed through Havana that week with his Panamanian friend Chuchú Martínez, one of Torrijos's closest collaborators, and on 16 January García Márquez wrote about the English novelist in an article entitled "Graham Greene's Twenty Hours in Havana." He and Greene had not seen one another since 1977. García Márquez revealed that Greene and Martínez had arrived in the greatest secrecy and that Greene had been given a top politician's protocol house for the day and loaned a government Mercedes Benz. Greene and Castro had discussed the former's famous experiment with Russian roulette at the age of nineteen. The column ended: "When we took our leave of one another, I was disturbed by the certainty that that encounter, sooner or later, would be remembered in the memoirs of one of us, and maybe all of us."[9] It was becoming dangerous to talk to

García Márquez—you would be in the international press within forty-eight hours—and some were asking whether it was maintaining the dignity of Nobel Prize winners to be interviewing other celebrities and acting the role of newspaperman.

The article on Graham Greene was simply too much for Cuban exile Guillermo Cabrera Infante, who responded with a withering piece entitled "Notable Men in Havana":

> I know that there are South American (and Spanish) readers (and writers) who read the weekly García Márquez column to laugh out loud, and consider his statements with superior disdain as when observing the chattering of a churl or the flourishes of a *métèque* . . . Is this the ultimate peak of the ridiculous or merely a corny copy? For readers in the know, García Márquez's article in *El País* every week is the sure promise of a *frisson nouveau*. But not for me. I take the novelist very seriously. This writing is the proof. Although there may be some who counter my opinion by fabricating exclusive excuses: man, it's hardly worth it, don't bother, nobody pays any attention. But I do. I believe, with Goldoni, that with the servant one can beat the master.[10]

The Latin American right, and the Cuban exiles in particular, understandably embittered by the award of the prize, were beginning to panic about García Márquez. Perhaps they had thought that because the Nobel committee knew that he was a "red," as near a communist as made no difference from their point of view, somehow he would never be given the prize. Or perhaps, now that his prestige had reached the very limits, there was nothing to lose and everything to gain by openly attacking him. Or perhaps they simply couldn't bear his success, his unconcealed delight and unmistakable popularity. Certainly, as soon as he had given up militant journalism, García Márquez himself had been advertising his personal relationship with Fidel for over a year. And now, if it had not been clear before, it was evident that Fidel needed García Márquez more than García Márquez needed him. At any rate, what is certainly clear is that although the prize gave García Márquez access to even higher strata of political and diplomatic influence in Latin America, it also unleashed an unparalleled level of right-wing hostility which has never ceased in the two decades since (though it has done him surprisingly little damage); whereas in the rest of the world, even in the neo-liberal West, the Nobel certificate of respectability has protected the Colombian writer against all but the most violent—or most determined—of critics.

In case Mexico was feeling left out by his cosying up to Betancur, Mitterrand, González and Castro, he wrote a warm and affectionate piece about the importance of Mexico in his life entitled "Return to Mexico," which appeared on 23 January.[11] His affection did not restrain him from calling it a "luciferine city" only exceeded in ugliness by Bangkok. He now had a nap hand of five influential politicians representing all of the countries which had been most important to him in his life except Venezuela (Colombia, Cuba, France, Spain and Mexico) and which, not entirely coincidentally, were crucial to him if he was to carry out the international political role of which he dreamed. It would be fascinating to see how long he could hold these five cards, whether he could improve his hand and whether he would be able to replace cards successfully used and discarded by other cards of the same suit.

On 30 January, with all those presidential cards in his grasp, García Márquez published an article on Ronald Reagan entitled "Yes, the Wolf Really Is Coming."[12] The article traced his own experience of U.S. imperialism back to the Bay of Pigs. Thinly veiled anti-Americanism was an impulse which would more or less unite his five countries at a moment when the decadence and growing impotence of the Soviet Union was beginning to be taken for granted. It was only unfortunate that at such a favourable time for García Márquez personally, the international situation was so unfavourable to his political "interests." Although the foreign secretaries of what would come to be known as the Contadora countries (Colombia, Mexico, Panama and Venezuela) had recently met, he was convinced that U.S. destabilization efforts would bear fruit during the year. He was right, of course.

Belisario Betancur had announced at the beginning of his presidency that Colombia would seek to join the Organization of Non-Aligned Nations of which, at that time, Fidel Castro was President.[13] In early March 1983 the Cuban delegation set off for Delhi. Aboard were Castro, García Márquez, Núñez, Carlos Rafael Rodríguez, Jesús Montané, Maurice Bishop, the leader of the Grenadan New Jewel movement, who would be dead in six months and his island occupied by the United States, and the sinister Désiré Delano Bouterse, Chairman of the Suriname Military Council. Though Castro put a brave face on it, his entire presidency had been vitiated by the fallout from the Soviet invasion of Afghanistan and he was now relieved to be handing over to someone less closely identified with the USSR. After the official ceremonies, the Cubans all went off to the official venue, the Ashok Hotel, but García Márquez had booked himself a special suite in the Sheraton so that he could welcome all the old friends he was expecting to meet. The next morning Núñez found him in chaos, with his clothes all over the room, trying to find the appropriate outfit for the opening reception. Mercedes usually made these decisions. He said to Núñez: "If all men only knew how good marriage is, we'd run out of women and that would be a disaster."[14] He and Mercedes would be celebrating their twenty-fifth wedding anniversary on 21 March.

Finally, on 11 April García Márquez made the latest of his "returns"—to Colombia, where he had not set foot since the news of the Nobel award almost six months before. There was much speculation in the press about the visit. One thing they did not speak about was the question of García Márquez's personal security but Betancur insisted that he should have a team of bodyguards in Colombia organized and paid for by the government. A few days after his arrival García Márquez published an article in his column entitled "Return to the Guava."[15] Needless to say, readers in Bogotá would be well aware that "guava" was a code word that signified that he was not so much returning to "Colombia" as to his beloved "Costa." Although it was difficult to know where García Márquez was located from reading his articles now (they would become much less of a diary and much more a loosely serialized narrative of memoirs and eccentricities), the truth is that he would spend much of this "sabbatical" year in Bogotá, believing no doubt that the prize had finally given him more purchase on the oligarchy and now they would just have to be impressed by him, or at least respectful. Many remained sceptical, however, and some sections of the press began to attack him almost immediately.[16]

He flew down to the old colonial city of Cartagena at the end of May. Cartagena would soon become his principal destination in Colombia and the setting for most of his future books. Since the installation of the new convention centre down by the harbour in 1982 it was possible for important international meetings to take place in the historic city. Now it was celebrating the 450th anniversary of its foundation and the Cartagena Film Festival was also in full swing. The principal foreign visitor invited to the celebrations was none other than the Andalusian Felipe González, and García Márquez strolled through the carnival crowds with the Spanish leader, wearing his now signature *liquiliqui* and occasionally dancing with some privileged admirer.[17] García Márquez revelled in the "magic" and "chaos" of his family's home town. Like Betancur, González, who was on his way to talks in the United States, was strongly committed to active encouragement of the Contadora process to bring peace to Central America and while in Cartagena held discussions with the foreign ministers of the four countries guaranteeing the talks.[18]

In late July García Márquez was in Caracas as part of an official Colombian delegation to celebrate the bicentenary of Bolívar's birth. He had not been to Venezuela for five years. Here he and Mercedes met up again with now exiled Argentinian writer-journalist Tomás Eloy Martínez, with whom he was hoping to set up the new daily newspaper *El Otro*. They discussed the project in a truckers' café by one of the Caracas freeways, where his face, now far too famous, might go unnoticed. Martínez would recall:

> We met at about three in the morning. Mercedes, who had eaten that evening flanked by the President of Venezuela and King Juan Carlos of Spain, was wearing a magnificent long dress to which the sleepy truckers paid no attention. A lame waiter brought us some beers. The conversation suddenly turned to the past . . . but Mercedes took us back to reality. "This place is awful," she said. "Couldn't you find anywhere better?" "Blame your husband's fame," I said. "In any other bar in Caracas we'd have been constantly interrupted." "We should've gone to Fuck Corner, like in Buenos Aires that first time," García Márquez said. "Love Lane," I corrected him. "I'm afraid it's not there any more." Mercedes gave a sly wink: "Did you imagine then that Gabo would be this famous?" "Of course. I saw the moment when fame came down to him from the sky. It was that night in Buenos Aires, in the theatre. When fame starts like that, you know it will never end." "You're wrong," said García Márquez. "It started long before." "What, in Paris, when you finished *The Colonel*? Here, in Caracas, when you saw Pérez Jiménez's white plane leave and Perón's black one? Or was it before," I said sarcastically, "in Rome, when Sophia Loren walked by and smiled at you?" "Long before," he explained, in all seriousness. Outside, beyond the mountains, the dawn was coming. "I was already famous when I graduated from the *bachillerato* in Zipaquirá, or even before, when my grandparents took me from Aracataca to Barranquilla. I was always famous, from the time I was born. It's just that I was the only one who knew it."[19]

In October, persisting in another of his sporadic attempts to spend an extended period in Bogotá, García Márquez was brooding about the Nobel Prize for Literature being awarded to the "boring" Englishman William Golding and the Nobel Peace Prize to Polish freedom fighter Lech Walesa, leader of Solidarity, when some really bad news came in: Maurice Bishop was overthrown and executed in Grenada on 19 October.[20] Five days later the United States invaded the island, vindicating all García Márquez's fears about U.S. policy in the Caribbean. UN condemnation on 28 October had no effect whatever, nor did toughgal Margaret Thatcher bring herself to protest at the occupation of one of the British Queen's Commonwealth domains. On 23 October García Márquez's column included an obituary of the murdered President with reminiscences from the Non-Aligned Conference in New Delhi. In the coming weeks Betancur would mediate between Cuba and the United States over the return of Cuban prisoners taken on the island. He was in constant touch with García Márquez, as the latter would tell the nation in an interview in early November.[21]

Although he gave it his best shot, he was just not happy in Bogotá. The press speculated each and every week whether García Márquez was finding it difficult to adjust to Colombia; but Colombia was not the problem, the problem was Bogotá. The novelist Laura Restrepo told me about an incident that summer, when García Márquez, who only a few months before had helped Bogotá journalist Felipe López get privileged access to Fidel Castro, now volunteered to give some coaching to the journalists at *Semana*, which López, the son of Alfonso López Michelsen, directed. They got on to the topic of headlines. At one point, all enthusiastic, García Márquez asked what headline those present would put if, as he left the magazine's offices, he was shot in the street. "*Costeño* Killed," Felipe López said, quick as a flash and with only the shadow of a smile.[22] In Bogotá the Nobel Prize was no protection against homicidal put-downs from the oligarchy and its representatives.

Near the end of the year García Márquez took time off to fulfil a promise and make the last and most definitive of all his returns: to Aracataca. It was sixteen years since his last visit and the journey effectively finished off his "sabbatical." A week later he wrote a curious account of the day with the title "Return to the Seed," an unspoken reference to a famous story by Alejo Carpentier.[23] He admitted that he had been surprised to receive such a warm welcome (a symptom of guilt?—he was always being criticized for not having "saved" Aracataca from underdevelopment). He said he had remembered absolutely everything, overwhelmed by so many faces from the past, faces like his own face used to be when the circus came. But then he remarked that he himself had never mythologized Aracataca or been nostalgic about it (as everyone else had, he appeared to imply).[24] Too much had been made of the Aracataca–Macondo connection; now he'd been back the two places seemed less like each other than ever. "It is difficult to imagine anywhere more forgotten, more abandoned, more distant from the paths of God. How can one not feel one's soul torn by a feeling of rebellion?"

As usual, at the end of this dull sabbatical year, he slipped off to greet the new one in Havana. This time he invited Régis Debray to come and spend time in the Hotel Riviera with him and their old friend Max Marambio, former head of Allende's personal bodyguard and now an important fixer for Cuba's trading organizations. Debray found the same old García Márquez, "divided as usual between affection (for the old complicit fellow-Latin) and sarcasm (for the too French Frenchman, arrogant and circumspect), whilst overwhelming me with movies, Veuve Cliquot and songs by Brassens, whose words he knew by heart."[25]

NINETEEN EIGHTY-FOUR would be a better year for García Márquez and another very bad one for Colombia. Once the New Year festivities were over he shrugged off even the continuing diplomatic demands from Cuba and began to make a series of transitions: from his "sabbatical" to his real business, writing fiction; from his weekly column to the major novel he had begun the summer before the Nobel was announced, the "book about love"; and from residence in Bogotá, which was always bad for him, to Cartagena and the Costa.

The return to Aracataca had been predictably paradoxical. On the one hand, it was a return to the place he had transposed into his best-loved fictions under the name of Macondo, the place that had directly inspired his first novel, *Leaf Storm*, and *One Hundred Years of Solitude*. Yet the return had simply confirmed his own cancellation of that experience: he had effectively negated his relationship with Aracataca just as he had, in so many ways, negated *One Hundred Years of Solitude* itself.

Now he was going to rewrite his life—rewrite the rewrite—and fill in some missing gaps. No doubt it felt unseemly for a Nobel Prize winner still to be haunted by childhood traumas and the especially confusing oedipal twist that he had suffered when he was displaced from father to grandfather. Up to now he had simply omitted certain structural facts and papered over the problem while making some psychically satisfying and literarily dramatic adjustments. Now his twice illegitimate father was to be written back in to the story. Gabriel Eligio himself had returned to Aracataca a year before at the time of the Nobel celebrations and, as so often, had made himself the star of the show. (If there was one thing his son had inherited from him, it was his vitality.) But he had also been sincerely ecstatic at the news of Gabito's success and had basked publicly for the first time in the reflected glory.

The day García Márquez heard he had won the Nobel Prize he had declared to the press that he would like to build his dream house in Cartagena. This was exactly the kind of thing that did not go down well in traditionalist Cartagena—where the point has always been precisely to preserve the houses already there—and many people had very mixed, not to say negative, feelings about his return.[26] He himself had decided to shake off the Bogotá blues and refresh his image. Or perhaps he really just felt better back in the Caribbean. Or perhaps it was the effect of dedicating himself full-time to love. At any rate, friends and journalists found a new García Márquez in his now characteristic Caribbean all-white outfit, five kilos lighter, with his hair tidied, his nails manicured, smelling of expensive cologne, sauntering around the streets of old Cartagena, the beach at Bocagrande, the avenues of Manga—all of this when he was not roaring around in his new red Mustang.[27]

He would get up at 6 a.m. and read the papers, sit preparing himself for writing from nine until about eleven, then slowly take off (like the balloon he would invent both in this book and in the movie *Letters from the Park*). The great thing, he said, was that he had "got Colombia back." Mercedes would go to the beach at midday and wait there with friends until he turned up. Then they would lunch on shrimp or lobster and take a siesta. In the late afternoon he would talk to his parents and each evening he would walk the city or talk to friends and then "put it all in the novel the next day."[28]

Although he was living in a building dubbed "The Typewriter" because of its shape, García Márquez was beginning another revolutionary transition, this time a technical one.[29] Perhaps fortunately, he had already written the first sections of what would be *Love in the Time of Cholera*, his next novel, which gave him a kind of literary bridge across the whole Nobel experience. Now he decided to turn to writing with a computer and asked a typist to transfer the existing manuscript. This made it possible for a man who obsessively threw away every sheet of paper on which there was a typing error to move rather more quickly and may have helped him to pre-empt the kind of writer's block that has afflicted so many Nobel Prize winners over the years. Critics will argue about a possible change of style brought about by the new technology and whether it was for better or worse.

Yet the biggest shift in García Márquez's life, his psychic life at least, was in the relationship with his father. For the better part of sixty years they had barely talked. Now the son became reconciled with his father at least enough to drive over the bridge to Manga most afternoons and talk to him and Luisa Santiaga—nearly always separately—about their youth and their courtship. Of course the ostensible motivation was the overriding one of a new book that had to be written but there is every reason to think that García Márquez was finally ready for this transition and that the book allowed him to conceal and protect his pride whilst easing the guilt he no doubt had about this man, his father. Just three years earlier he had written about a character in *Chronicle of a Death Foretold* who comes to a sudden realization about her mother: "In that smile, for the first time since her birth, Angela Vicario saw her as she really was: a poor woman devoted to the cult of her defects."[30] Doubtless when all his own challenges were behind him, García Márquez was able to come to a similarly dispassionate though perhaps less cruel assessment of Gabriel Eligio.

It cannot have been easy. Gabriel Eligio was the man who had taken his mother away from him and then returned, years later, to take him away from his beloved grandfather, the—as Gabito saw it—infinitely superior Colonel. Gabriel Eligio, though by no means an abusive father, always seemed to threaten violence to maintain his often inconsistent and arbitrary authority; he kept his long-suffering wife locked inside the home on a strict, patriarchal basis, yet went away as and when he chose and betrayed her sexually—even scandalously—on numerous occasions; and although, taken overall, his ability to keep a large family fed, clothed and for the most part well educated was an extraordinary achievement, from the standpoint of his eldest son the unpredictability, the crazy schemes, the changes of plan, the silly jokes that everyone had to celebrate, the stubborn political conservatism, the sometimes painful abyss between the man's actual achievements and his assessment of himself—all of these things, on top of the basic oedipal resentments, were very difficult to bear.

In such relationships almost everything conspires to harden things and worsen them. Perhaps García Márquez's most quoted and best-loved statement around Latin America was that no matter how successful he became, he would never forget that he was nothing more than one of the sixteen children of the telegraphist of Aracataca. When Gabriel Eligio first heard this he burst into a furious diatribe. He had only been a telegraphist for a brief time, he was now a professional doctor and a poet and a novelist to boot.[31] He felt slighted at the fact that everyone knew how much the famous Colonel had influenced his son and how much he had inspired the most unforgettable characters in his books, whereas he, Gabriel Eligio, never got mentioned and seemed to have been deliberately excluded when he was not, as now, insulted.

By late August 1984 García Márquez had written three chapters—over two hundred pages—out of a planned six and the novel was taking shape. He was talking to his parents purportedly to get a general sense of the era and was discussing their own courtship in the middle of these rather vague discussions merely as a sort of case study. Or so he said. He told *El País* that the book could be summarized in one sentence: "It's the story of a man and woman who fall desperately in love but can't get married at the age of twenty because they are too young and can't get married at the age of eighty, after all the twists and turns of life, because they are too old." He said it was risky work because it was using all the devices of mass popular culture: all the vulgarities of melodrama, soap opera and *bolero*. The novel, influenced equally by the French nineteenth-century tradition, began at a funeral and would end on a boat. And would have a happy ending.[32] This was presumably why he had decided to set the novel way back in time: perhaps even García Márquez felt he could not carry off a love story with a happy ending set in the late twentieth century and be taken seriously.

Eventually, with the book half completed, he left Cartagena at the end of the summer and left a copy of the manuscript with Margot. The instructions were to keep it until he arrived safely in Mexico and then destroy it. "So I sat down with an empty biscuit tin on my lap and tore it up sheet by sheet, after which I burned the lot."[33] Then, after he made a reluctant business trip to Europe that autumn, came a shock. On 13 December 1984, not long after his eighty-third birthday, Gabriel Eligio García died unexpectedly in the Hospital Bocagrande, Cartagena, after a ten-day illness. Yiyo (Eligio Gabriel), usually thought of as the most nervous member of the family, recalled: "When my father died, everything turned upside down. I arrived the same day and the house was in chaos, no one was capable of taking a decision. I remember it was five in the afternoon and neither Jaime nor Gabito had showed up. I had to take charge of the family and extricate them from the swamp and get things moving. The next day we met to decide how to organize things. It was hell. No one agreed with anyone else."[34]

For once Gabito did attend a burial. He managed to arrive on the day of the funeral, after a ten-hour journey involving numerous changes of plane, as the coffin was about to be carried from the Salón Parroquial de Manga after the funeral service. (Gustavo would arrive from Venezuela too late for the service.) Gabito arrived with the Governor of the Department of Bolívar, Arturo Matson Figueroa, and both helped carry the coffin. The Governor wore a black suit and tie; Gabito a hound's-tooth jacket, an open-necked black shirt and black trousers. Jaime recalls that "the funeral was a disaster. All of us men turned to jelly, we became a bunch of cry-babies totally useless for the practicalities of the moment. Fortunately the women were there to organize everything."[35] (Turning to jelly did not deter the male siblings from making a ritual visit to a brothel for old times' sake—drinks only—and a bit of old-fashioned bonding.)

Suddenly, so soon after renewing his relationship with his father, García Márquez had lost him for ever. He had in fact been getting closer to all his family again for some time but naturally the death of Gabriel Eligio created an entirely new situation. Yiyo recalled, "A few days after my father died, my mother, like a good Guajira, said to Gabito: 'Now you're the head of the family.' He span round: 'And what have I ever done to you, why would you want to put me in such a fix?' The trouble is that as well as being many, my brothers and sisters are uncontrollable."[36] The world-famous writer was now the head of a very large and very extended family. He had already helped his brothers and sisters in innumerable ways—jobs, medical bills, school fees, mortgages—but now he was financially responsible for his mother as well. It was more than appropriate that this should happen when his own gradual "return" to Colombia was apparently under way and when he was writing a novel based on the events which had led to the creation of the García Márquez nuclear family.

The death of his father and the anguished widowhood of his mother obliged García Márquez to think not only about love and sex but also, once more, and even more, about old age and death. Though he has always said that the writing of *Love in the Time of Cholera* was a joyful time, things were less easy for him than he affected. He was already finding it hard to adjust to his post-Nobel responsibilities.

Experiencing the death of Gabriel Eligio and seeing his mother suffering so much was a traumatic process which of course the novelist assimilated by writing it into his novel, especially the early and late sections. His inveterate habit of destroying his manuscripts and all trace of their evolution has deprived us of what would no doubt have been a fascinating process of life being folded into art as it unfolded in reality. Of course the computer has in any case not only changed the entire process of literary composition but has also made it far more difficult to follow its phases of development.

He had always intended the novel to be a reflection not only on love but also on old age, though love had come to the fore since the Nobel award. In the late summer of 1982 he had published an article on "the youthful old age of Luis Buñuel" which showed not only that he was pondering these matters deeply—including the question of whether it was decent for old people to fall in love and have sex—but also that he had read Simone de Beauvoir's classic *The Coming of Age*.[37] In February 1985, back in Mexico City, he now told Marlise Simons that his first image of the novel, having read about two old people being murdered by a boatman, was precisely of two old people fleeing in a boat.[38] Before, he said, he used to write about old people because his grandparents were the people he best understood; now he was anticipating his own old age. There was a line from Yasunari Kawabata's *The House of the Sleeping Beauties* which haunted him: "Old people have death and young people have love, and death comes only once and love many times."[39] It is a line which gives insight into all his late works.

When he met the Colombian journalist María Elvira Samper in Mexico City for another of his updating interviews in the spring of 1985 (*Semana* claimed it was "exactly two years since he had last talked to the press in a big way"), he told her that he was not himself feeling old, merely detecting signs of age and facing up to reality. He found that inspiration came more often when one was older except now you realized it was not inspiration, it was when you were in the groove and writing, for a time, was "like floating." These days "I know the last sentence of the book before I sit down to write it. When I sit down I have the book in my head, as if I'd read it, because I've been thinking about it for years." He felt very "rootless" because he now felt exactly the same wherever he was in the world and he was experiencing "orphanhood and anguish" as a result. Then an extraordinary statement: "All my fantasies have been achieved, one after another. I mean, I've known for many years that everything would happen as it has. Naturally I've done my bit and I have had to harden myself." He considered himself "very tough," though like Che Guevara he believed you had to retain your "tender" side. All men are soft but the "inclemency" of women saves and protects them. He still loved women; they made him feel "safe" and "looked after." By now, he went on, he found himself bored talking to almost anyone who was not his friend; he could hardly bring himself to listen. "I am the most bad-tempered and violent man I know. That's why I am also the most controlled."[40]

He also talked about love and sex, of course. Though the latter, as noted, is a word that scarcely appears in García Márquez's novels. He uses the same word, *amor*, love, for both things and this promiscuous use of it creates a curiously undifferentiated atmosphere which explains much of the peculiar flavour, and possibly the allure, of his writing about this topic.

When the new novel, the last word on love, appeared it was dedicated "To Mercedes, of course." But when the French translation appeared, it would be dedicated to Tachia . . .

LOVE IN THE TIME OF CHOLERA is set in a Caribbean city immediately recognizable as Cartagena de Indias, between the 1870s and the early 1930s. It is about love and sex, marriage and freedom, youth and old age. It is based on a sexual triangle: the lordly upper-class doctor Juvenal Urbino, the painfully unglamorous shipping clerk Florentino Ariza, and the beautiful parvenue Fermina Daza. Juvenal has elements of Nicolás Márquez about him, though he is based above all on a distinguished local physician, Henrique de la Vega, who was in fact the García Márquez family doctor (who attended to Gabriel Eligio at the time of his death and then died himself less than five months later); Florentino, the main character, has elements of both Gabriel Eligio and Gabito himself, a most curious and fascinating fusion; and Fermina is an astonishing mixture of Mercedes (above all), the ghost of Tachia, and the external details of Luisa Santiaga at the time of her youth and courtship. The book is organized in six parts, with the first and last parts devoted to old age as the structural frame, parts two and three devoted to youth, and parts four and five devoted to middle age. The six-part structure is divided neatly into two halves of three chapters, and this is emblematic of a novel of twos and threes, of a triangle always threatening to collapse into a pair. All in all, the novel implicitly stages the four great reconciliations that García Márquez himself had effected as he approached old age: with France, above all Paris (where both Juvenal and Fermina are especially happy); with Tachia, whom he had loved there in the 1950s; with Cartagena, the reactionary colonial city; and, perhaps above all, with his father, for whom acceptance by Cartagena had always been an aspiration.

The action begins on a Pentecost Sunday in the early 1930s, soon after the Liberal Party has returned to power after almost half a century. Juvenal Urbino, now in his eighties, is killed when he falls from a ladder as he tries to retrieve the family parrot on the very same day that he has buried an old friend and discovered a shocking truth about him. At Urbino's funeral an old flame of his wife Fermina, Florentino Ariza, tries to rekindle the affair that took place between them when they were still adolescents, over half a century before. The rest of the novel involves a series of carefully embedded flashbacks which tell, first, the story of that original love affair, then Juvenal's intervention, Fermina's marriage to Juvenal and journey to Paris with him, and Juvenal's rise to eminence as Cartagena's leading authority on health issues, most notably the scourge of cholera. In parallel we follow the illegitimate and partly black Florentino's less conventional trajectory: he decides that he too must become a respected citizen and gradually rises through the ranks of his uncle's shipping company; but at the same time, because he has decided to wait for Fermina as long as it takes—until after the death of her husband, if necessary—he embarks upon a long chain of relationships with different women, above all prostitutes and widows, not to mention a fourteen-year-old niece, América Vicuña, who commits suicide when he forsakes her for the newly widowed Fermina near the end of the novel. In contrast Juvenal has only one fling, with a stunning black Jamaican patient, and this almost costs him his marriage.

By the end of chapter 3, the halfway point, the novel has shown how Fermina Daza, a lower-middle-class Colombian, has rejected the true Colombian Florentino Ariza in favour of the upper-class "Frenchified" Juvenal Urbino. So much so that she has, like Juvenal, come to know Europe, whereas Florentino Ariza has never left Cartagena nor has any wish to do so. Juvenal Urbino represents the Cartagena upper class for whom, in a sense, García Márquez was writing as he composed the book. Thus by halfway the novel has shown a decisive defeat by Europe and by modernity of the backward Creole or Mestizo world of illegitimate, lower-class Colombia. Then the second half of the novel reverses all these directions as Florentino improves his position and finally gets the "girl."

Though Juvenal Urbino is partly Henrique de la Vega, partly the Colonel and partly Gabriel Eligio—a "physician"—he is mainly everything about the upper classes that García Márquez envies, admires, resents and despises: the Bogotá and Cartagena ruling elites, much mixed in the last twenty-five years, the Bogotá elite that García Márquez believed rejected him and the Cartagena elite that rejected both him and his father. It is nevertheless notable that this novel is not in any primary sense about conflict or competition between men but about relationships between different men and women.

The epigraph is from a song by the blind *vallenato* troubadour Leandro Díaz: "The words I am about to express: they now have their own crowned goddess." This composite reference, which somehow conjures up ancient Greece, the imperial Spanish monarchy and the lower-class Colombia of beauty pageants, brilliantly encapsulates the cultural conflicts at issue in the novel. Its title, at first sight one of his least felicitous, has become much loved and admired: it speaks of both love and of time: love, as so often in García Márquez, as an irresistible sickness or disease; and time, as both mere duration and history but also as the worst disease of all, the one that gnaws away at everything. And yet the novel will stop at a moment where time has been, however temporarily, defeated.

Among the multiple reconciliations effected by this now dazzlingly successful writer approaching late middle age there is also a reconciliation, however parodic and postmodern, with the bourgeois novel itself, and even, however ironically and critically, with the Colombian bourgeois ruling class. This is not exactly Stendhal, Flaubert or Balzac (more Dumas or Larbaud, though of course parodied).[41] But this novel "knows" about all of them and all of that and is playing another game entirely. It flirts from its first line with aromas that take us back into the past and remind us, "inevitably," of unrequited love. Many of the elements are those of cheap romance or even soap opera and Latin American popular music, as the author had intimated; yet these are counterpointed with the conventionalities and *taedium vitae* involved in bourgeois marriage and the keeping up of appearances. García Márquez was taking huge risks here with his artistic reputation. The novel as a whole becomes a curious mixture of the bland and the banal with the ruthlessly realistic and the profound. It dares to explore the most familiar clichés involved in letters to agony columns and the desperate truisms usually proffered in reply: You never really know any-one. You can't really judge people. Some people can change their behaviour and, to that extent, their personalities; others can remain the same for ever despite the passage of time. You never ever know what is going to happen in life. You only understand life when it's too late—and even then you would probably change your view if you lived even longer. It is very difficult to moralize about love and sex. It is very difficult to separate love from sex. It is very difficult to separate love from habit, gratitude or self-interest. You can love more than one person at the same time. There are many kinds of love and you can love people in many different ways. It is impossible to know which is better, single life or marriage, bohemia or convention; similarly, it is impossible to know whether security is better than adventure or vice versa; but everything has to be paid for. On the other hand, there is only one life and no second chance. You are never too old. And yet, and yet: and yet one life is no better than another. All these themes are signalled in the first part and then intermingled and played out in the rest of the novel.

In *One Hundred Years of Solitude* readers discovered that Melquía-des's room functions as the space of literature itself and that Mel-quíades has written the story we are reading a century in advance. At the end of *Love in the Time of Cholera* Florentino Ariza writes Fermina Daza a long letter which is a similar *mise en abyme* device: it is not ostensibly a love letter but "an extensive meditation on life based on his ideas about, and experience of, relations between men and women," received by her as "a meditation on life, love, old age, and death." The scope of this ambition, combined with the work's remarkable accessi-bility, means that in some ways this is the sequel to *One Hundred Years of Solitude* that *The Autumn of the Patriarch* never quite became.

García Márquez ended his book with the phrase "for ever" and sent it off to Alfonso Fuenmayor in Barranquilla for him and Germán Var-gas to read. Carmen Balcells received her copy in London and report-edly spent two days weeping over the manuscript. García Márquez needed to have a business meeting with her and decided to take in New York on the way to Europe. His old friend Guillermo Angulo was at that time Colombian consul in the Big Apple and the photographer Hernán Díaz was also there. García Márquez was not only full of the excitement of having completed the novel, one which was such a new departure for him, but was also going through all the excitement and anguish of computer users in the early days. Did you have back-up, were the diskettes reliable, could you keep them safe, whether from physical damage or from theft? He was very aware that he was one of the world's first well-known writers—perhaps *the* first—to complete a major work using a computer. Accompanied by Mercedes and Gonzalo, plus their niece Alexandra Barcha, he flew to New York with the diskettes containing the novel around his neck, for all the world like a Melquíades who had found the philosopher's stone and could not bear to let it go.[42]

García Márquez took his younger son into Scribner's, one of New York's best-known bookshops, which he had walked past every day in 1961 on his way to work. Hernán Díaz was shocked to discover that Scribner's apparently had no novels by his illustrious friend but it transpired that they were all in the "classics" section. Much signing and dedication ensued when the staff discovered who the diminutive figure in the hound's-tooth jacket actually was. Out in the street passers-by approached him as he enjoyed a totemic New York hot dog under the photographer's gaze. Then, as amazed as if he were discovering ice, he went to a specialist store and printed off the first six copies of his book in a matter of minutes.[43]

Thus in that autumn of 1985, still wearing the three diskettes around his neck, García Márquez flew to Barcelona to deliver them personally to Carmen Balcells. He stayed at the Princess Sofía Hotel. In the event his room was broken into, just as he had feared, and he was indeed robbed but he told the press he did not think the thieves were after the manuscript of *Love in the Time of Cholera*.

He was still out of Colombia as one of the defining political moments in its twentieth-century history took place. Tension with M-19 had been growing, and on 3 July it had renounced Betancur's cease-fire and the country lurched towards disaster. (Many guerrillas suspected that Betancur, far from seeking a lasting peace process, was luring them into a historic trap.) On 9 August García Márquez himself had said the Minister of Defence, Miguel Vega Uribe, should resign over allegations of torture. On 28 August Iván Marino Ospina, the new leader of M-19 after the recent death of García Márquez's friend Jaime Bateman, had been killed by police. Finally, on 6 November, M-19 guerrillas took over the Palace of Justice, the Supreme Court building in Bogotá, initiating a series of events which would horrify spectators from all over the world as they watched the drama unfold on television. The President's hapless brother Jaime, recently kidnapped, was on the scene again. The Colombian army went in with tanks and heavy artillery and ended a twenty-seven-hour siege, as the whole world watched in stupefaction. Up to one hundred people were killed including Alfonso Reyes Echandía, the President of the Supreme Court. Judge Humberto Murcia was hit in the leg as he tried to escape, whereupon he threw the—wooden—leg away and escaped from the burning courtyard. The leaders of the guerrilla attack, notably Andrés Almarales, were killed in the battle, among many others. It was strongly rumoured that the army rather than Betancur was in charge of events—the controversy still rages today—and Betancur told me later that he considered it "an act of friendship" that García Márquez remained silent.[44] Only a week later another disaster rocked Colombia as the eruption of volcano Nevado del Ruiz buried the town of Armero and killed at least twenty-five thousand people.

The Palace of Justice tragedy was the last straw for García Márquez. He had bought a new apartment and transferred a significant quantity of clothes and other possessions to Bogotá but he did not move in. At the very moment when the event took place he was considering flying back to Bogotá but went to Paris instead. There he thought things over, cancelled his plans for returning to Colombia and went back to Mexico City, where the recent earthquake had left the city physically shattered but morally invigorated. By then, he was already planning his new project—a novel on Bolívar—and had had his first meeting with historian Gustavo Vargas in September 1985.

It was now, on 5 December, after this succession of disasters for Colombia, that *Love in the Time of Cholera* was launched. It astonished readers and critics around the world because it represented a new García Márquez, a writer who had somehow metamorphosed himself into a sort of nineteenth-century novelist for modern times, a man no longer writing about power but about love and the power of love. It would be his most popular work, his best-loved novel. Published almost twenty years after *One Hundred Years of Solitude*, *Love in the Time of Cholera* was only the second of his books to give the critics and general readers almost unalloyed pleasure. Its success encouraged García Márquez to go on writing about human relationships and the private realm, as one of his main preoccupations, and to make this the centre of his renewed activity in the movie business.[45] It associated his name not only with love, affection, smiles, flowers, music, food, friends and family, and the like, but also with nostalgia and a look back at the old ways of the past, at the roads and rivers of a bygone era: the fragrance of guava and the aromas of memory. These popular virtues would also allow him to blend in the darker currents he always had in mind under cover of this spell-binding writing.

Even *El Tiempo* was disarmed: the paper predicted on 1 December,

before the book was actually published, that it would "bring love to a
choleric country." A few—very few—critics were quite negative about
the work. But overall its reception was triumphant and a characteristic
response was an extraordinary eulogy from one of the most sceptical
of all great novelists, Thomas Pynchon, when the book appeared in
English. Pynchon said that García Márquez had incredible nerve to
write about love in these times but he "delivers and triumphantly":

> And—oh boy—does he write well. He writes with impassioned
> control, out of a maniacal serenity . . . There is nothing I have
> read quite like this astonishing final chapter, symphonic, sure in
> its dynamics and tempo, moving like a riverboat too, its author
> and pilot, with a lifetime's experience steering us unerringly
> among hazards of skepticism and mercy, on this river we all
> know, without whose navigation there is no love and against
> whose flow the effort to return is never worth a less honorable
> name than remembrance—at the very best it results in works
> that can even return our worn souls to us, among which most
> certainly belongs *Love in the Time of Cholera*, this shining and
> heartbreaking novel.[46]

Fifteen years later García Márquez said to me: "I've been looking at
Love in the Time of Cholera lately and, truly, I was surprised. My guts are
in there, I don't know how I managed to do it, to write about all that.
Actually, I felt proud of it. Anyway, I went through . . . I've been
through some very black times in my life."

"What, before *One Hundred Years of Solitude?*"

"No, in the years after the Nobel. I often thought I was going to
die; there was something there, in the background, something black,
something under the surface of things."[47]

22

Against Official History: García Márquez's Bolívar (The General in His Labyrinth)

1986–1989

J UST AS HE had proved, with the publication of *The Autumn of the Patriarch* in 1975, that *One Hundred Years of Solitude* was no fluke and that world literature should expect him to be around for the long haul, so now García Márquez had proved with *Love in the Time of Cholera* that he was not one of those writers whose career was going to be ended by the pressure of the award of the Nobel Prize. His move towards the theme of love in his writing was paralleled by a new emphasis upon peace, democracy and co-existence in his political activity. It was clear that in Central America and the Caribbean the Reagan government was not prepared to tolerate the triumph of any revolutionary regime; the Cubans, who had inspired or encouraged most of the revolutionary movements, were more cautious than before because they were heavily extended by their commitment to the liberation of southern Africa and could not afford further pressure from the United States in the Caribbean; moreover, developments in the Soviet Union seemed to suggest that it would not be safe to rely on the USSR's commitment to world revolution for much longer. At the same time Reagan had run into difficulties over his prosecution of the war against the Nicaraguan Revolution and even he might prove susceptible to talk of peace. (In mid-1986 the World Court at The Hague would find that the U.S. administration had broken international law by aiding the Contra rebels in Nicaragua; later in the year the Irangate scandal would break out in the USA itself and shake the entire Reagan government.)

Even in Colombia there had been a peace process since Betancur came to power in 1982, though by now most observers had despaired of his ability to pursue it successfully and García Márquez himself was speaking with increasing pessimism of the way the country was going. At the end of July 1986 he would warn that Colombia was "on the edge of a holocaust" and that the terrible events at the Palace of Justice late in 1985 had been the inevitable result of the noxious combination of reckless guerrillas, repressive government forces and generalized delinquency and violence.[1] Neutral observers might have been more impressed had this statement been made before the last week of Betancur's period in office, particularly since Amnesty International had been severely criticizing Betancur over human rights abuses by the military; in effect, then, the warning was for the incoming Liberal government of Virgilio Barco and not for García Márquez's Conservative friend Betancur.

Thus García Márquez himself now began to adopt a social democratic and merely anti-colonial discourse to go with his message of peace and love to a degree which must have disconcerted old friends and delighted his enemies, who would never be satisfied until both he and Fidel were toppled from their steeds. Among other things Vargas Llosa called him, yet again, a "lackey of Fidel Castro" and a "political opportunist."[2] The latter was a curious epithet to give a man who was causing himself huge amounts of political difficulty by his support for Cuba and who was also, moreover, prepared to spend large sums of money in support of his political commitments, as he had shown with *Alternativa* in Colombia in the 1970s and as he was about to demonstrate once more, on an even bigger scale, in Cuba.

In January 1983, at Cayo Piedras, during their first meeting after García Márquez's Nobel Prize adventure, Gabo and Fidel had begun to dream of a Latin American film school located in Havana; Fidel, who knew a thing or two about propaganda, and was no doubt impressed by García Márquez's worldwide prestige and influence after the award of the Nobel Prize, had become increasingly—and perhaps belatedly—aware of the ideological impact of culture. Now, as he discussed the cinema with García Márquez, he began to wonder whether the power of movies was not greater even than that of books and to question whether recent Latin American cinema had been as effective as the great films of the 1960s and early 1970s which had been inspired, all over the continent including Cuba itself, by the triumph of his revolution. As they sat together by the Caribbean in earnest discussion, Fidel, inevitably, had his own belligerent way of conceiving the matter: "We've really got to make that cinema take off . . . I, who have spent twenty years of struggle, think those films are like a battery of cannon firing inside and outside. How rich our cinema is in that way! Of course books influence people a lot but to read a book you need ten hours, twelve hours, two days; to see a documentary you only need forty-five minutes."[3] Whether Castro had been influenced by the unexpected impact of a Hollywood actor in the American White House can only be surmised, but he and García Márquez began to talk about the possibility of a Latin American film foundation to be located in Havana as a means of increasing continental production, improving standards, fomenting Latin American unity and, of course, propagating revolutionary values.

As soon as he had finished *Love in the Time of Cholera*, García Márquez began to work on the new project. From 1974 to 1979 he had concentrated on political journalism but from around 1980 into the 1990s the obsession with cinema had returned, and the articles he had written between 1980 and 1984 were often intimately connected to the cinema in general and to his own specific projects in particular. His most ambitious venture into film would be, precisely, the Foundation for New Latin American Cinema in Havana, combined with a new International School for Cinema and Television to be situated at San Antonio de los Baños outside the city.[4] Here, more than ever, he would put his capitalist money where his revolutionary mouth was. His maxim might have been: where politics is no longer feasible, turn to culture. The film foundation would help to unify the production and study of film in the continent and the school would teach the theory and practice of film-making not only to young Latin Americans but also to students from other parts of the world.

By 1986 plans for the two new institutions were well advanced and García Márquez was liaising closely with radical film-makers about future developments. But he had begun the year by working not on a movie but on a book about the making of a movie. His friend Miguel Littín, the exiled Chilean film-maker, had made a clandestine return to Chile in May and June 1985 and had escaped undetected with 100,000 feet of film about Pinochet's Chile.[5] García Márquez, who obviously felt that he had been symbolically defeated by Pinochet when he returned to publishing fiction before the dictator's downfall, saw a possibility of revenge and met Littín in Madrid early in 1986 to explore the options. There he conducted an eighteen-hour interview over the course of a week, then returned to Mexico and condensed a 600-page narrative into 150 pages. He noted: "I preferred to keep Littín's story in the first person, to preserve its personal—and sometimes confidential—tone, without any dramatic additions or historical pretentiousness on my part. The manner of the final text is, of course, my own, since a writer's voice is not interchangeable . . . All the same, I have tried to keep the Chilean idioms of the original and, in all cases, to respect the narrator's way of thinking, which does not always coincide with mine." The book, *Miguel Littín. Clandestine in Chile*, appeared in May 1986.[6] Oveja Negra published 250,000 copies and it must have been a particular satisfaction to García Márquez in November when 15,000 of them were burned in the Chilean port of Valparaíso. Silence would have been a much more effective reaction on the part of the Pinochet government, which, although no one knew it, was by then in its final years.

Despite this brief excursion into political provocation, so committed was García Márquez to his new mission as bringer of peace that he was prevailed upon to make a speech that summer on 6 August in Ixtapa, Mexico, at the Second Conference of the "Group of Six" countries whose political aim was the prevention of a nuclear holocaust. The "Six" (Argentina, Greece, India, Mexico, Sweden, Tanzania), on the forty-first anniversary of the destruction of Hiroshima, urged the suspension of all nuclear tests.[7] The conference was launched with García Márquez's speech "The Cataclysm of Damocles," in which he warned that although all the world's problems could now be solved, money was being spent instead on armaments—and completely irrationally because, as he put it, "only the cockroaches would be left after a nuclear holocaust."[8] It was in a sense a speech about the future of the planet to be read in tandem with his Nobel speech about the destiny of Latin America.

That autumn, as García Márquez worked on preparations for the new film foundation, Rodrigo enrolled in the American Film Institute in Los Angeles—a striking contrast with his father's activities in revolutionary Havana. He would be there four years. Meanwhile Gonzalo had moved back to Mexico with his girlfriend Pía Elizondo and worked on a project of his own, the establishment of a high-class publishing house called El Equilibrista (The Tightrope Walker), with Diego García Elío, the son of Jomí García Ascot and María Luisa Elío.[9] One of their first projects would be the publication of "The Trail of Your Blood in the Snow" in October in a de luxe edition.

García Márquez himself was interested in encouraging new independent movies by Latin American directors but other film-makers were more interested in adapting his novels to the cinema. In 1979 a film called *Maria My Dearest (María de mi corazón)* had been made by Mexican director Jaime Hermosillo based on a García Márquez script. In the early 1980s Brazilian director Ruy Guerra had filmed *Eréndira*, the story, almost unmodified from García Márquez's novella, about the adolescent girl in the Colombian Guajira forced to become a high-intensity prostitute—serving dozens of men per day—in order to compensate her heartless grandmother for accidentally burning down her house. Eventually Eréndira so values her freedom that she forsakes and flees even Ulysses, the young man who loves her and has helped her to kill and escape from the cruel grandmother—an interesting feminist rewriting of European-style fairy stories about Cinderellas, witches and handsome princes. In July 1984 it was announced that Jorge Alí Triana's remake of *Time to Die (Tiempo de morir)*, produced almost twenty years after Ripstein's first effort, would be shown on Colombian TV on 7 August. This time it had been made in Colombia, not Mexico, and in colour, not black and white. Once again Nicolás Márquez's killing of Medardo was silently vindicated and as before the clockwork precision of García Márquez's sub-Sophoclean plot was compelling, though once again his penchant for sententious epigrams in place of realistic dialogue was an unfortunate distraction. In December 1985 *Excelsior* had announced that preliminary work was beginning on the filming of *Chronicle of a Death Foretold*. Francesco Rosi was in Mompox with Alain and Anthony Delon. (Alain would later drop out.)[10] Irene Papas, Ornella Muti and Rupert Everett would also star. When *Le Monde*'s Michel Brandeau wrote about the movie in September 1986, he represented the effort of getting it filmed—in the tourist towns of Cartagena and Mompox—as almost as epic as the storyline itself.[11]

On 4 December 1986 the foundation was inaugurated during the 8th Havana Film Festival, with a speech by García Márquez, the President of the foundation, a widely disseminated interview with Fidel—not previously known as a great film-goer—and a few words from Gregory Peck, who was visiting the city. In his speech García Márquez said that between 1952 and 1955 Julio García Espinosa, Fernando Birri, Tomás Gutiérrez Alea and himself were all at the Centro Sperimentale di Cinematografia in Rome. The Italian neo-realism that had inspired them all in those days was "like our cinema has to be, the cinema with least resources but the most human that has ever been made."[12] Best wishes arrived from Ingmar Bergman, Francesco Rosi, Agnès Varda, Peter Brook, and Akira Kurosawa. On 15 December the International School for Cinema and Television (EICTV) was launched in its turn, with García Márquez's old friend Fernando Birri as its new director. Just over a week later it was reported that the foundation would film seven screenplays written by García Márquez himself, which was perhaps a world record for quick results from insider trading. His closest associates during the next few years would be Alquimia Peña, the Cuban director of the film foundation, and Eliseo Alberto Diego, known to everyone as "Lichi," the son of one of Cuba's greatest poets, Eliseo Diego. Lichi would work with the new President not only in his teaching seminars—or "workshops," as García Márquez insisted they be called—but also in the production and elaboration of a whole raft of film scripts. García Márquez would throw himself body and soul into these enterprises and his energy, enthusiasm and steadfastness would astonish both his collaborators and the many visitors to the new institutions over the coming years.

In the middle of all these celebrations shattering news arrived from Colombia to cast a pall over the new enterprise: Guillermo Cano, the Director of *El Espectador*, was murdered on 17 December as he left his office in Bogotá. The war between the Medellín drug baron Pablo Escobar and the Colombian justice system was now reaching its climactic phase. Escobar was already the seventh richest man on the planet and his "plata o plomo" (bribe or bullet) strategy of attempting to suborn or liquidate everyone in his way had added a second layer of corruption and inefficiency to Colombia's age-old system of manipulation and violence. His political ambitions had already been frustrated and *El Espectador*, which had valiantly opposed him, also supported the extradition of suspected drug-traffickers to the United States. Now Cano had paid the price of his courage. The Minister of Justice, the President of the Supreme Court and the head of the national police force had all been assassinated already but the murder of such a respected journalist had an especially devastating effect on national morale. *El Espectador* journalist María Jimena Duzán told me: "I saw García Márquez again in Cuba in December 1986, around the time of the launching of the film foundation. After a few days he came looking for me; eventually he reached me by phone. 'They've killed Guillermo Cano,' he said. 'It's just happened. That's why I don't want to go back to Colombia. They're killing my friends. No one knows who's killing who.' I went to his house, totally distraught. Gabo greeted me by saying that Guillermo Cano was the only friend who had ever really defended him. Castro arrived and I was weeping. Gabo explained what had happened and Fidel talked a lot. Gabo told me again he wouldn't go back, he was full of bitterness. I said to him, 'You know, you've really got to speak out about things in Colombia,' but he wouldn't. I concluded that he'd really freaked out after his episode with Turbay in 1981."[13] García Márquez made no public statement about the murder and sent no message to Cano's widow, Ana María Busquets.

Despite the cruel news from Colombia, García Márquez set about his new duties in Havana with gusto. He stayed on in Cuba for several months, working at many tasks at the same time, deciding everything, taking part in everything. News items appeared regularly in papers all over Latin America and Spain about Gabriel García Márquez's film-related activities and possible adaptations of his books.[14] This was more like it! Cinema was not like literature, its creators sentenced to solitude. Cinema was convivial, collective, proactive, youthful; cinema was sexy and cinema was fun. And García Márquez loved every minute of it; he was surrounded by attractive young women and energetic and ambitious but deferential young men, and he was in his element. Though it was costly. He would wryly remark that he had gone on with his expensive hobby despite Mercedes's disapproval: "When we were poor we spent all our money on the cinema. Now that we have money, I'm still spending it on the cinema. And I'm giving it a huge amount of my time."[15] Some say García Márquez gave the school $500,000 of his own money that year, as well as most of his invaluable time. It was now that he began to charge European or American interviewers $20,000 or $30,000 a session in order to raise money for the film foundation; astonishing numbers of them coughed up.

He came to specialize in story-telling and script-writing at the new school—he gave a regular course on how to write a story, then how to turn the story into a film script. Visitors and teachers over the next few years would include Francis Ford Coppola, Gillo Pontecorvo, Fernando Solanas and Robert Redford.[16] The relationship with Redford was particularly important to García Márquez: he would repay his debt to the handsome American radical by himself travelling to Utah to give a course at Redford's Sundance film school and festival in August 1989.[17] Generally he would say that his policy was to sell his works very dear to non-Latin American producers and very cheaply or for free to Latin Americans. Some books, especially *One Hundred Years of Solitude*, he would never allow to be adapted, a position which had brought him into conflict with Anthony Quinn a few years before. (It was said that Quinn had offered García Márquez a million dollars for the rights; Quinn said García Márquez had agreed, then reneged on the deal, which the Colombian always denied.)[18] Others, such as *Love in the Time of Cholera*, he would consider selling—but at that time he said he would only give it to a Latin American director. Finally, in 2007 he would at last allow another Hollywood film-maker, in this case the Englishman Mike Newell, to make the film in Cartagena with Javier Bardem as lead.[19] At that time gossips would report that Mercedes had finally lost patience with her husband's relentless philanthropy and wanted to put some money aside for their heirs. It was, after all, "her" book.

Given the move from power to love in his literary activity, it was logical that love should take pride of place in his movie projects. What the Cubans really thought of this development we shall probably never know but for the next few years the new film foundation would be awash with news of García Márquez's cinematographic explorations, through a series of different directors, of the theme of love in human relationships. The principal vehicle for this was a series of six films planned as a set to be collectively called *Difficult Loves (Amores difíciles)*, a title previously used by Italo Calvino in a little-known collection of short stories. (When the films appeared on the Public Broadcasting System in the United States they were called *Dangerous Loves*.) All of them were darker than their publicity might have suggested and all, in one way or another, would explore the relationship between love and death.[20]

Six years later, in 1996, García Márquez would make a fully Sopho-clean film, *Oedipus the Mayor* (as against *Oedipus the King*), again with Jorge Alí Triana (and again with a script by García Márquez and an ex-student of the Havana film school, Stella Malagón), about a small-town mayor confronting not only all the atrocities and terrors of late twentieth-century Colombia—drug-traffickers, paramilitaries, guer-rillas, the national army—but also the age-old tragedy of Oedipus killing his father and sleeping with his mother, in this case the still tem-pestuous Spanish actress Angela Molina. Many critics panned the movie mercilessly but it had important virtues and might more fairly and appropriately be considered a heroic failure: it conveyed the complexity and some of the horror of the Colombian predicament and Triana managed to prevent the mythical motifs from undermining the political narrative. He had wanted to film *No One Writes to the Colonel* as well, and would probably have made a good job of it; in the event, surprisingly, García Márquez gave that project to Arturo Ripstein, with whom he had always had a difficult relationship (it was said that Ripstein had been angered by Triana remaking *Time to Die*), and in 1999 the novel finally came to the big screen: a film which, despite Ripstein's huge international reputation, and a cast including international stars Federico Luján, Marisa Paredes and Salma Hayek, must be counted one of the least convincing versions of a work by García Márquez ever filmed.[21]

This mixed experience confirmed what García Márquez had said so often: that his relationship with the cinema was like some kind of unhappy marriage. He and the cinema couldn't get along, yet they couldn't do without one another. Perhaps, more cruelly, one might say that his love was unrequited (a one-way mirror, to quote the title of one of his Mexican television films): he could not live without the cinema but the cinema could in fact get along quite happily without him. Yet the truth is that he has often been blamed for the final versions of his movies when as the writer of the original text he is not ultimately responsible for the finished product. Mel Gussow wrote in the *New York Times* that García Márquez needed a film-maker of his own stature and that it would probably require a director with Buñuel's idiosyncratic genius to do him justice.[22] (This might explain why Hermosillo, a small chip off the Buñuelian block, was more successful than most.) García Márquez's son Rodrigo told me that his father is "hopeless" with dialogue, even in his novels; yet the structure of *A Time to Die* is an undoubted masterpiece and the conception of the movies—dialogue apart—is invariably compelling. What a pity, then, that Fellini never had a go and that Akira Kurosawa, who was extremely excited in these years about the possibility of filming *The Autumn of the Patriarch*, never managed to get his project off the ground.

Despite all his success and his exciting activities in Cuba, these were exceptionally difficult years for García Márquez. Even he had to recognize that perhaps he had taken on too much and spread his talent and his energy too thin. He found himself assailed by his enemies on the right and involved in numerous polemics and controversies for which he had little appetite at this time, not to mention a number of scandals or near-scandals laced with malicious gossip which were not entirely becoming to a man nearing sixty years of age. In March 1988 he celebrated both his sixtieth birthday and his and Mercedes's thirtieth wedding anniversary (21 April) in Mexico City and Cuernavaca. Belisario Betancur and thirty other friends from all over the world were in attendance. Much fun was had in the Colombian press as to whether it was García Márquez's sixtieth or sixty-first birthday—it was his sixty-first, of course—including headlines like "García Márquez sixty again," and he would not be able to continue with the farce of this deception for much longer—though most writers, truth to tell, including the blurb writers at his publishers, would continue to use a 1928 birth date until the publication of *Living to Tell the Tale* in 2002, and some even beyond that.

It was this month also that he published his much reprinted, definitive—humorous and affectionate—portrait of Fidel Castro, "Plying the Word," in which he stressed Castro's verbal rather than military attributes. He referred to his friend's "iron discipline" and "terrible power of seduction." He said it was "impossible to conceive of anyone more addicted to the habit of conversation" and that when Castro was weary of talking "he rests by talking"; he was also a "voracious reader." He revealed that Fidel was "one of the rare Cubans who neither sings nor dances" and admitted, "I do not think anyone in this world could be a worse loser." But the Cuban leader was also "a man of austere ways and insatiable illusions, with an old-fashioned formal education, of cautious words and delicate manners . . . I think he is one of the greatest idealists of our time and this, perhaps, may be his greatest virtue, although it has also been his greatest danger." Yet when García Márquez asked him once what he would most like to do, the great leader had replied: "Hang around on some street corner."[23]

Now came a temporary turn to the theatre. In January 1988 it was announced that the Argentinian actress Graciela Dufau would be starring in an adaptation of a brief work by García Márquez entitled *Diatribe of Love Against a Seated Man*.[24] García Márquez would say that the play was a *cantaleta*, a repetitive, nagging rant, a word that implies that the nagger—usually a woman, of course—gets no answer from the object of her attentions, nor does she expect one. (Throughout his adult life García Márquez had always said that there was no point arguing with women.) This theme, this form, had obsessed García Márquez for many years and indeed one of his early ideas for *The*

Autumn of the Patriarch was a *cantaleta* against the dictator by one of the main women in his life.[25]

The premiere in the Cervantes Theatre in Buenos Aires had to be delayed from 17 to 20 August 1988. In the end García Márquez, too anxious—"as nervous as a debutante," in his own words—to cope with the stress of confronting a live performance of his work, remained in Havana and sent Mercedes, Carmen Balcells and her twenty-four-year-old photographer son Miguel to face the critics of Buenos Aires, the most demanding and most terrifying in Latin America. The whole of Buenos Aires's "political and cultural world" was in attendance, including several government ministers. The notable absences were President Alfonsín and the distinguished playwright himself. Sadly, the return to a great theatre in Buenos Aires did not repeat the previous experience of 1967. The play received no more than polite applause and there was no standing ovation. Reviews from the Buenos Aires drama critics were mixed but the majority were negative. A typical reaction came from Osvaldo Quiroga of the heavyweight *La Nación*: "It is difficult to recognize the author of *One Hundred Years of Solitude* in this long monologue by a woman tired of being happy without love . . . It shows his complete ignorance of dramatic language. It cannot be denied that *Diatribe* is a superficial, repetitive and tedious melodrama."[26]

The play, a one-act monologue, is set, like *Love in the Time of Cholera*, in an unnamed city which is unmistakably Cartagena de Indias. Graciela's first words, subtly changed since first quoted by García Márquez, are: "Nothing is more like hell on earth than a happy marriage!" Novels have narrative irony built in but a play relies on dramatic irony, which needs a different kind of creative intuition, one for which he appears to have little feel. Worse than this, though, worse even than the lack of dramatic action, the play's most damaging flaw appears to be a deficit of serious reflection and analysis. Like *Love in the Time of Cholera* in part, *Diatribe of Love Against a Seated Man* deals with marital conflict (as indeed had *No One Writes to the Colonel*, over thirty years before);[27] and the central proposition—that traditional marriage doesn't work for most women—is obviously an important one, albeit one that this sixty-year-old author was by now perhaps insufficiently modern to explore in a radical or even meaningful way. Sadly, *Diatribe of Love Against a Seated Man* is a one-dimensional work which, unlike *Love in the Time of Cholera*, adds little or nothing to the world canon of great works about love. García Márquez had said not long before that he had never wanted to be a movie director because "I don't like to lose."[28] The theatre was an even riskier venture. Here for once he had lost. He would never try again.

AFTER THE TRIUMPHANT publication of *Love in the Time of Cholera*, despite a nagging, anguished sense of fragility which kept appearing in the midst of his apparent immortality, García Márquez had begun to act as if there were no limit to his energies or his ability to work at a high level over a whole range of different activities. Yet there were unmistakable signs of fraying. *Clandestine in Chile* bore obvious traces of haste; *Diatribe of Love Against a Seated Man* was an experiment in a medium in which he was out of his depth; and working on six film scripts simultaneously was perhaps too much for any man, added to all of which he had already started his next major book, nothing less than a novel on Latin America's most important heroic figure of all time, Simón Bolívar.

García Márquez had been intensely committed to the politics and administration of the new film foundation and film school but he had devoted much less time in recent months to international politics and his conspiracies and mediations. Although matters in Central America were grim, Cuba had seemed to be in one of its most comfortable and confident moments. But things were beginning to change there too. García Márquez was about to find that his brief sabbatical from politics and diplomacy would soon be over as dark clouds began to gather over both Cuba and Colombia, clouds which would not lift again for the rest of the century.

In July 1987 he was the guest of honour at the Moscow Film Festival. On the 11th he was received by Mikhail Gorbachev at the Kremlin and urged the radical reformist Soviet leader to travel to Latin America. At this time Gorbachev was the most talked-about politician on the planet. They discussed, so an official communiqué said, "the restructuring being carried out in the USSR, its international implications, the role of intellectuals and the transcendence of humanist values in the world today."[29] Gorbachev said that in reading García Márquez's books you could see there were no schemes, they were inspired by a love of humanity. García Márquez said that *glasnost* and *perestroika* were great words implying vast historical change—maybe! Some people—no doubt he was thinking of Fidel Castro—were sceptical, he said. Was he sceptical himself? That he was in two minds about the outcome was shown by later comments in which he revealed that he had told Gorbachev he was anxious that some politicians—presumably Reagan, Thatcher, Pope John Paul II—might wish to take advantage of his good faith and so there were dangers ahead. He said it was obvious to him that Gorbachev was sincere and declared that for him, García Márquez, the meeting had been the most important event of his recent life.[30] For once he may not have been exaggerating.

Towards the end of the following year he finally came into intimate proximity with power in Mexico, the country in which he had lived for more than twenty years in total. In December 1988 Carlos Salinas de Gortari became President and García Márquez moved quickly to secure his relationship with the new leader. They would work closely together on international politics during the coming years. From Mexico he travelled to Caracas to attend Venezuelan Carlos Andrés Pérez's second inauguration—in fulfilment of a promise he had made at a time when only he, García Márquez, thought that the mercurial populist might ever make a comeback.

He had been working on the Bolívar novel almost since the moment that he completed *Love in the Time of Cholera*. Though all his novels had been based on an understanding of Latin American and world history, and although he had read widely about dictators and dictatorship in order to write *The Autumn of the Patriarch*, he had never had to consider the methods of investigating and writing history as such. Now, because his central character was a historical actor, and one of the best-known ones at that, he felt that every event in his novel had to be verified historically and every thought, statement or foible of Bolívar's in the book had to be appropriately researched and contextualized. This would involve not only personally reading dozens of books about Bolívar and his era and thousands of Bolívar's letters but also consulting a whole range of authorities, including several of the leading experts on the life and times of the great Liberator.[31]

In creating his Patriarch in the 1970s, García Márquez had been free to choose whichever facet of whichever dictator he liked at any given moment in order to fashion a creative synthesis which would make sense within his overall design. With Bolívar, although every historian discovers, or invents, a different persona, the basic material was inevitably much more established and intractable, and he soon learned that for the historian each interpretative assertion has to be based on more than one, and in most cases many, pieces of evidence, the result being that what appears in the eventual work is merely the tip of a vast iceberg.[32] Somehow he had to process that vast archive of information and yet maintain his own creative faculty so that Bolívar would somehow arise refreshed from the research rather than lie buried under a mountain of desiccated facts.

Of course, although the Liberator had written or dictated ten thousand letters and there were innumerable memoirs written about him both by his own collaborators and others who came across him during his life, there were whole swathes of time when little was known about what he was involved in, and the question of his private life—especially his love life—remained relatively open. Moreover the sequence that most interested García Márquez, for both personal and literary reasons—Bolívar's last journey down the Magdalena River—had been virtually untouched by either letters or memoirs, leaving the novelist free to invent his own stories within the limits of historical verisimilitude.

The novel would be dedicated to Alvaro Mutis, whose idea it was and who had even written a brief fragment of a first version, "The Last Face," when he was in prison in Mexico at the end of the 1950s. Eventually García Márquez got him to concede that he was never going to finish the project and seized it for himself. The title, *The General in His Labyrinth*, was established almost from the beginning of García Márquez's research on the book.

Simón Bolívar was born in Caracas, Venezuela, in 1783, a member of the Creole aristocracy. At that time the whole of the continent of what we now call Latin America remained in the hands of Spain and Portugal, as it had for almost three centuries, while England and France each controlled a few islands in the Caribbean. Slavery existed in every Latin American country, as it did also in the recently independent United States of America. By the time Bolívar died in 1830 almost the whole of Latin America had become independent of external powers and slavery had been officially condemned and in some cases abolished. All of this owed more to Bolívar than to any other single individual.

Bolívar's father, a landowner, died when he was two and a half; his mother died when he was not yet nine years of age. When he was twelve he rebelled against the uncle who had taken him in and moved to the house of his tutor Simón Rodríguez; after travelling in Europe he married, at the age of nineteen, a young woman who died less than eight months later. At that moment he seems to have decided that it was his destiny to be alone in the world. (He would never marry again, though he would be linked with dozens of women, the best-known of whom was his doughty Ecuadorean mistress, Manuelita Sáenz, herself by now a not inconsiderable legend, who saved his life on more than one occasion.) On returning to Europe he was present at the coronation of Napoleon in Paris in December 1804; he was inspired by Napoleon's achievements as liberator of Europe but repelled by his decision to make himself a monarch. On returning to Latin America, having vowed to give his life to the liberation of the colonies held by Spain, he began a military career which eventually saw him achieve supreme prestige throughout the continent and the honourable title of Liberator. All other leaders, even great generals such as San Martín, Sucre, Santander, Urdaneta and Páez, were consigned willy-nilly, one after another, to Bolívar's shadow.

Beyond the matter of battles won and lost, when one considers the statistics of Bolívar's marches up and down the continent, across the Andes and along the mighty rivers of that still untamed geography, the facts and figures of his twenty-year campaign are stupefying; yet he was never seriously wounded in battle. His first mission along the Magdalena River in Colombia was at the age of twenty-nine; at the age of thirty he was proclaimed Liberator of Venezuela; at thirty-eight he was elected President of Colombia, which then included present-day Venezuela and Ecuador. During this period he wrote some of the key documents of Latin American identity, most notably his *Jamaica Letter* of 1815, in which he argued that all Latin American regions had more similarities than differences and that the continent's mixed-race identity should be accepted and embraced.

Yet once the Spaniards were vanquished local leaders began to assert their local and regional interests and the fragmentation of the now liberated republics began; anarchy, dictatorship and disillusionment appeared like tragic spectres on the horizon; and Bolívar's overriding dream, the unity of Latin America, began to fade. He became a nuisance, the voice of an impractical idealism; others might never have been able to achieve the almost impossible feats which Bolívar had undertaken but they now considered themselves far more realistic than he in the post-emancipation situation. The prime example was Colombia's Francisco de Paula Santander, Bolívar's nemesis and, in García Márquez's eyes, the paradigmatic *cachaco*. The novel begins at the moment when Bolívar has realized that there is no future for him in Colombia, despite all his achievements and continuing prestige, and begins the retreat from Bogotá, which is in effect the retreat from his own grandiose vision. At forty-six years of age, ailing and disillusioned, the great Liberator sets off down the Magdalena River on his way towards exile, though García Márquez suggests that Bolívar never finally gave up hope and was still intending to organize another expeditionary campaign of liberation, should that prove possible.

The novel is in eight chapters, and falls, once more, into two halves. The first half, chapters 1 to 4, narrates the journey down that great river that García Márquez himself would travel, over a century later, on his way to school.[33] In Bolívar's case, this last journey took place between 8 and 23 May 1830. The second half, chapters 5 to 8, narrates Bolívar's last six months of life, 24 May to 17 December 1830, six months spent by the sea on that Costa which would later be the scene of García Márquez's childhood and much of his youth. One of Spain's best-loved poems, Jorge Manrique's *Verses on the Death of My Father*, composed at the end of the medieval period, is known above all for the line, "Our lives are the rivers that flow down into the sea which is death." And for one further verse which states that death is the "trap," the "ambush," into which we fall. Or, as García Márquez might say, following Bolívar himself, the "labyrinth" into which we fall. Although García Márquez does not mention Manrique, his novel follows exactly the same logic as Manrique's great poem.

The subject of the title, "the General," signifies power but the concept of "the labyrinth" suggests before the work even begins that not even the powerful can control fate and destiny. Of course such impotence may also imply exculpation of, even sympathy for, the powerful, which the infant García Márquez may have felt when Colonel Nicolás Márquez was the only "powerful"—protective, influential, respectable—person he knew. Is his entire oeuvre in some way reflecting upon the impossibility of holding on to that old man, the anguish of having as a "father" someone so old and vulnerable that the most important lesson you learn as a small child is that your only security, your beloved grandfather, must "soon" die? Such a lesson teaches that all power is desirable, essential, yet frail, false, transient, illusory. García Márquez is almost alone in contemporary world literature in his obsession with, indeed his sympathy with, men of power. And although he has always been a socialist this permanent note of aristocratic identification, however much moderated by irony (or even moral condemnation), may explain why his books have an apparently inexplicable power of their own: tragedy, it goes without saying, is greater, wider and deeper when protagonists are aggrandised by power, by isolation, by solitude and, not least, by their influence on the lives of millions of people and history itself.

By the time he wrote *The General in His Labyrinth* García Márquez had long been closely acquainted with Fidel Castro, undoubtedly a leading candidate for the number two position—after Bolívar—in the list of Latin America's great men. Simply in terms of political longevity—almost half a century in power—Fidel Castro's record is difficult to deny. And Fidel, García Márquez once told me, is "a king." García Márquez himself, in contrast, has always insisted that he has neither the talent, the vocation nor the desire—still less the ability— to endure such solitude. The solitude of the serious writer is enormous, he has always averred; but the solitude of the political Great Leader is of quite another order. Nevertheless here, in this novel, although Bolívar's character is, undoubtedly, based factually on that of the Liberator, many of his foibles and vulnerabilities are a combination of Bolívar's, Castro's and García Márquez's own.

The central subject, then, is power, not tyranny. In other words, García Márquez's books are sometimes seen from the side of the powerful, sometimes from the side of the powerless, but they are not primarily intended to inspire hatred against tyrants or the "ruling class"—unlike hundreds of protest novels written within the main current of Latin American literary narrative. His constant themes, constantly interwoven, are the irony of history (especially power turning to impotence, life turning to death), fate, destiny, chance, luck, foreboding, presentiment, coincidence, synchronicity, dreams, ideals, ambitions, nostalgias, longings, the body, will and the enigma of the human subject. His titles frequently refer to power (Colonel, Patriarch, General, Big Mama), power which is usually challenged in some way ("no one writes," "solitude," "autumn," "funeral," "labyrinth," "death foretold," "kidnapping"), and to the different forms of representation of reality as related to the different ways of conceiving and organizing time into history or narrative ("no one writes," "one hundred years," "time of," "chronicle of," "news of," "memoir of"). His works almost always include the theme of waiting, which is, of course, merely the other side of power, the experience of the impotent. All the way through this novel, for example, Bolívar is announcing his departure, first from Bogotá, then from Colombia, but really of course he is leaving power, while pretending to himself that he is not leaving anything, least of all this life, though nothing can delay that inevitable departure. So waiting is again a huge theme; but delaying (which the powerful—Castro, for example—can do, and love to do) is a bigger theme here (Bolívar delaying his departure from Colombia, from power and glory, delaying accepting reality, death . . .).

Some of the impetus for the book must have come from García Márquez's work on his Nobel Prize speech in which, like others before him, he felt it incumbent upon himself to speak as a representative not of one country but of a whole continent. Much of what he said on that occasion was tacitly "Bolivarian" and many of the ideas turn up again in the novel; indeed, the Nobel speech provides indispensable background to a reading and interpretation of the work. This is all the more ironic since García Márquez, as we have seen, was very slow to come to an awareness of "Latin America," even during his stay in Europe. Only after visiting both the centre of capitalism and the centre of communism did he come to see that, despite his moral and theoretical attraction to socialism, neither system was the answer for Latin America because in practice both systems functioned primarily in the interests of the countries that advocated them. Latin America had to look after itself; and thus had to unify. Bolívar in the novel has trenchant views about the different European nationalities, favouring the British, of course, given the assistance Great Britain gave at that time to the South American liberation movements; the French come out badly; and the United States, in Bolívar's own words, is "omnipotent and terrible, and its tale of liberty will end in a plague of miseries for us all."

Such are the themes involved in the book and the central problems which structure it. But no matter how much research García Márquez had put into it, no matter how coherent its ideological design and the literary architecture which supported it, the novel would have failed absolutely if the central character had not come alive. And he does. García Márquez takes on the most famous and familiar of all Latin Americans and gives his own version, with breathtaking audacity and astonishing naturalness. Though this is certainly not his greatest work it may well be his greatest achievement because the magnitude of the challenge is there for all to see. Any reader familiar with biographies of Bolívar, on finishing this book, is likely to conclude that García Márquez's version of the man, achieved in well under three hundred pages and containing the whole of the life within the journey completed in the last six months of it, will henceforth be inseparable from whatever image of Bolívar is carried down to posterity.

Bolívar is alive, though already mortally ill, from the very first page, where he lies naked—buried, one might say—in his morning bath. His nakedness shocked many readers—as it would shock them to find him vomiting, farting, copulating and cursing, or cheating at cards, or showing a petulant, childish side to his character far removed from the hagiographic vision so common in Latin American speeches and ceremonial. Yet the portrait is also of a man transfused by a touching gallantry: cast down, certainly, by his misfortunes, his rejections and his approaching death, yet never finally defeated even in the darkest and most hopeless of times. Bolívar becomes a García Márquez character in this novel, it cannot be denied; but part of this writer's greatness is that the "Latin American character" is precisely what he has captured and rendered eternal, long before he turned to Bolívar, and the great Liberator is here revealed as the template for countless Latin Americans suffering, striving and sometimes succumbing in the arduous kingdom of this world. For all his own vanities and occasional arrogance, García Márquez, subjected to stresses that it is given to few other writers even to imagine, has himself, in turn, reacted to this aesthetic and historical challenge with a grace and a gallantry that few other writers are able to attain. Hence the moving impact the book makes upon most of its readers.

The novel's publication was flagged up weeks before it eventually appeared. García Márquez has always boasted that he never attends the launch of any of his books and often suggests that he personally finds it demeaning to have to peddle as a commercial product something which for him is, in its original impulse, an aesthetic creation quite indifferent to whatever exchange value it may eventually have in the capitalist book market. But the truth is that even *One Hundred Years of Solitude* was publicized long before it appeared. And with each new book the hype increased. All this was why, years later, some people would begin to call him "García Marketing."

On 19 February, the first reaction to the novel, read in typescript, was a letter from no less a reader than the ex-President of Colombia, Alfonso López Michelsen, whose response, "I devoured your latest book," published in *El Tiempo*, was used to advertise the book before it even came out.[34] López declared that García Márquez had shown an astonishing versatility: supposedly a magical realist, he had now written a naturalist work that Zola might have penned had he had the talent. López had been unable to put the book down: he said that although Bolívar's story was known to everyone in Latin America, the reader was sucked in as if by a detective story. García Márquez's original new thesis that Bolívar was still hoping to make a political comeback even on his deathbed was credible because "that's the story with all of us who have gone out of power." Later it would be revealed that ex-President Betancur had also read the book (he was less fulsome because of course its "liberal" interpretation was less acceptable to him, a Conservative, than to López),[35] and the current Liberal President, Virgilio Barco, had stayed up into the night to finish it.[36] Even Fidel Castro, that great admirer of Cuba's own would-be liberator, José Martí, had read the novel and had been heard to declare that it gave a "pagan image" of Bolívar.[37] No one was entirely sure what this meant, or whether it was good or bad.

There were innumerable reviews in newspapers and magazines all over the Spanish-speaking world. This was not only a new novel by the greatest literary name in the language but a portrait of the most important figure in the entire history of Latin America, whose persona and image were dear to millions, not least to the guardians of the Bolivarian flame, whether serious historians, ideologists or demagogues. Most of the reviews were extremely positive but, unusually for García Márquez but not surprisingly, there were also some determined attempts at demolition. A significant minority of critics argued that García Márquez's overweening sense of his own glory had got in the way of his presentation of Bolívar—a presentation allegedly full of linguistic effects conceived as spectacle, like self-congratulatory fireworks, instead of the appropriate communication of Bolívar's own possible subjectivity, plus a series of stock phrases and episodic structures whose true function was to draw attention to the García Márquez brand, with the novel as a mausoleum to the writer himself rather than to its protagonist.[38]

Predictably, perhaps, the most negative reaction came from García Márquez's old *bête noire*, *El Tiempo*, which, in an editorial no less, found the work anti-Colombian:

> But the book has a political background. During the course of its 284 pages the author cannot conceal his philosophy, especially in the ideological field. He gives vent to an unrepressed hatred for Santander and a cordial antipathy for Bogotá and its classic product the *cachacos*, whilst pointing out the General's personal characteristics, attributing to his Caribbean origin the greater part of the impulse that carried him to glory. With great subtlety and skill he emphasizes Bolívar's dictatorial personality and mulatto blood, as well as his earthy disposition, to create an impalpable comparison with Fidel Castro.[39]

This disturbing diatribe shows how offensive García Márquez's appropriation of Bolívar seemed to the guardians of Colombia's national identity: he had pressed every single button and the editorialist had evidently lost his cool. García Márquez, no doubt feeling the satisfaction of the warrior who has smoked his enemy out into the open, responded in kind: "I've said before that *El Tiempo* is a demented newspaper protected by a quite unusual impunity . . . It says whatever it wants against whoever it likes, without measuring the consequences or thinking about the political, social or personal damage it might do. Very few people dare to answer it back for fear of its immense power." "We need to discover ourselves," García Márquez concluded, "we don't want Columbus to remain as our discoverer." This was inevitably followed by a response from *El Tiempo* itself entitled "The Nobel's Tantrum," on 5 April; it declared that "García Márquez only accepts praise" and called him the "Baron of Macondo."[40]

It was clear that something was happening both to García Márquez himself and to his reputation. His relationships with the great and the good were continuing to grow—political leaders such as Castro, Salinas and Pérez clearly thought they needed him more than he needed them—but the rest of the world was beginning to notice and in some quarters there was less indulgence than before. Moreover García Márquez himself seemed suddenly to be under increased stress—over his relationship with Castro and Cuba, unsubstantiated newspaper insinuations of sexual dalliances, waning middle age, the fear that his popularity was declining and that his political influence might follow—and was more inclined to overreact to attacks or to criticism. He seemed, for the first time, to be ever so slightly losing his touch. Colombian articles would say, and did say, that his fame and influence had definitively gone to his head and he was simply reacting from a loftier height of vanity, narcissism and hypersensitivity.

But of course things were more complex than this. The truth was that the Cold War game, which García Márquez played better than anyone, was almost over, even if few observers were predicting that the end would come as soon as November 1989. The climate had changed immeasurably and García Márquez's manoeuvres were less confident and relaxed, and intuited as such by journalists who, even if they could not see the future in a crystal ball as clearly as he could, also responded inevitably to the changing atmosphere.

García Márquez had written the most talked-about book ever published on Bolívar—the most important politician in the history of Latin America—and had become embroiled himself, as he must have anticipated, in a whole series of political debates in different places and at different levels. His former friend Mario Vargas Llosa, meanwhile, was involved even more directly in matters political. Indeed he was running as a candidate to become the President of Peru on a neo-liberal ticket. He and García Márquez had diverged radically about Peruvian affairs in the late 1960s when García Márquez, like most Latin American leftists, conditionally supported the progressive military regime of General Juan Velasco, whereas Vargas Llosa was against him; indeed, dislike for the military was something which character-ized Vargas Llosa at all times, whereas García Márquez, always the realist, though personally non-violent, knew that no country, state or regime could survive without an army and thus the military always had to be given some form of respect. At the end of March García Márquez could be found wishing his former friend well, though with reserva-tions: "In Latin America it is inevitable that a person who has a certain public audience ends up in politics. But no one had gone as far as Mario Vargas Llosa. I hope he is not being dragged along by circum-stances but believes that he really can resolve the situation in Peru. Even with so many ideological differences, one can only wish, if he gets elected, that the presidency goes well for him, in the interests of Peru."[41] He added that when one is famous, "one should not be naive, so that no one can use you." In the event, to the disappointment of most literary spectators, Vargas Llosa was defeated by the almost unknown populist Alberto Fujimori, who went on to become one of Latin America's most notorious end-of-century rulers.

In March Spain confirmed what an irate García Márquez had been predicting for months, when it adopted European Community regula-tions which meant that Latin Americans would no longer be given automatic visas for entry to the Peninsula. In a fit of pique and mono-mania reminiscent of his Pinochet fiasco, he announced: "I will never go back to Spain."[42] Needless to say, he would have to change his tune, but he was genuinely affronted. Spaniards didn't have visas when they arrived in Latin America in 1492, he snorted. Why, even Franco had allowed Latin Americans to become Spanish citizens. He told the press he had warned Felipe González that when Spain entered the European Union, "you'll turn your backs on Latin America." Now they had.[43] The truth was that his relationship with González, though a close one, was continually troubled by two irremediable irritants. González had made the long march from clandestine subversion of the Franco regime to membership not only of the European Community but even of NATO, and so the interests of Spain were no longer "complementary" to those of Latin America, as the Spaniards were claiming, but antagonistic: Spain was now, really for the first time in its modern history, part of "the West," as González himself would announce quite soon when Spain sent forces to the Gulf War against Iraq in 1991. Secondly, there was nothing González would have liked to do more than satisfy García Márquez's constant demands for him to ease Cuba back into the international community of nations; but González found Castro's dictatorial practices unacceptable—as well as inconvenient—in the world in which he now moved and was constantly irritated by what he perceived as Castro's incorrigible stubbornness and inability to adjust to the way the world was moving. (Castro, needless to say, was increasingly convinced that González was a traitor to international socialism.)

Meanwhile Cuba was going through its own dramas. At the end of 1988 a so-called "Committee of One Hundred" had sent a letter to Castro condemning his country's policies on human rights and demanding the release of all political prisoners: "On January 1, 1989 you will have been in power for thirty years without having, up to now, held elections to determine if the Cuban people wish you to continue as President of the Republic, President of the Council of Ministers, President of the Council of State and Commander-in-Chief of the Armed Forces. Following the recent example of Chile, where after fifteen years of dictatorship, the people were able to express their view freely on the country's political future, we request by this letter a plebiscite so that Cubans by free and secret ballot could assert simply with a yes or a no their agreement or disagreement with your staying in power."[44]

This had appeared nine months after García Márquez had published his pen-portrait of Fidel Castro, lovable conversationalist and good friend to his friends. It was signed in Paris by a wide array of celebrities and intellectuals, though in essence the *Libre* group (Juan Goytisolo, Plinio Mendoza and Mario Vargas Llosa) were again at the centre of the action, and again with their mainly French allies. It was their first big push since the Padilla Affair, given added impetus now that communism was tottering in Europe. The American names are not especially impressive, apart from Susan Sontag, nor were the Latin American ones (no Carlos Fuentes, Augusto Roa Bastos, etc.), but this was nevertheless a powerful challenge.

It was in fact the single most serious verbal attack on Castro and Cuba since 1971 and was, indeed, the more telling because it was not

based on a single event or a single problem but on Cuba's entire political system. And it was signed by a very large number of influential
intellectuals who could not by any stretch of the imagination be called
"right-wing." Reagan and Thatcher's virulent anti-communism,
backed by the Pope and immeasurably bolstered by Gorbachev's effective surrender, was rapidly changing the international climate and
would in due course change the world. Fidel's Cuba would be one of
the most serious casualties. And 1989 would be the year of the apoca-
lypse. It was almost unbelievable that whilst all these clouds were gathering, García Márquez was sitting, much of the time in Havana,
writing a novel about the last days of another Latin American hero—
the only one who could rival Castro—also considered by some historians to have turned into a dictator late in his career.

Disillusioning events in Cuba must have strengthened García
Márquez's desire to return to Colombia. At a time when Mario Vargas
Llosa was beginning his quixotic campaign for the presidency of Peru,
the Cuban government was arresting (on 9 June) and trying General
Arnaldo Ochoa, its greatest military hero of the African campaign, that
adventure whose coverage had allowed García Márquez to get so close
to Fidel, Raúl and the revolution. Also on trial were two good friends
of García Márquez, Colonel Tony la Guardia, a kind of Cuban James
Bond, and his twin brother Patricio. García Márquez was in Cuba at
the time teaching at the film school. The defendants were found guilty
of smuggling narcotics and thereby betraying the Cuban Revolution
and Ochoa, Tony la Guardia and two others were sentenced to be executed on 13 July 1989. Patricio la Guardia was sentenced to thirty
years in prison.

Quite near the end of *The General in His Labyrinth* Bolívar, lost in
the rain and sick of waiting and not knowing why, touches rock bottom
and cries in his sleep. The next day he flees one of his worst memories,
the execution of General Manuel Piar in Angostura thirteen years
before. Piar, a mulatto from Curaçao, had consistently resisted the
authority of whites, including Bolívar himself, on behalf of blacks and
mestizos. Bolívar condemned him to death for insubordination, ignoring the advice of even his closest friends. Then, struggling with tears,
he was unable to watch the execution. The narrator comments: "It was
the most savage use of power in his life, but the most opportune as
well, for with it he consolidated his authority, unified his command,
and cleared the road to his glory."[45] All those years later, Bolívar looks
at his valet José Palacios and says, "I would do it again." (Which is what

Colonel Márquez was reputed to have said after he killed Medardo Pacheco in Barrancas.) There was no need whatever for García Márquez to place this example of an act of utter ruthlessness carried out for reasons of state at the end of his penultimate chapter, where it becomes, irremediably, the last major drama, the last narrative action of the novel (albeit thirteen years before the end of Bolívar's life and therefore shown in flashback). But he did. And so again, García Márquez's extraordinary ability to anticipate major events is quite blood-chilling. Fidel Castro must have read this episode a matter of weeks before participating in the judgement on Ochoa's fate. Did he remember it as he made his decision?[46]

One of García Márquez's close friends had now executed another of his close friends. (Naturally Castro declared that the decision was not in his hands.) The executions caused García Márquez much heartache and severe political embarrassment. Tony la Guardia's family appealed to him personally on more than one occasion. He gave his word that he would intercede with Fidel; if he did, it was without success.

He left Cuba before the executions and on the day they were carried out he was to be found with his friend Alvaro Castaño in Paris, where he met Jessye Norman and French Culture Minister Jack Lang, who was making final preparations for the bicentenary of another revolution which had ended up devouring its children. The following day García Márquez attended the celebration banquet for the 200th anniversary of the storming of the Bastille. He had feared he might have to sit next to Margaret Thatcher ("eyes of Caligula, lips of Marilyn Monroe," according to their host François Mitterrand) but was fortunate enough to sit next to the glamorous Benazir Bhutto of Pakistan, while Thatcher herself, who had declared that the French Revolution "foreshadowed the language of communism," appeared, as one British newspaper put it, like a "ghost at the feast."[47] The following day García Márquez arrived in Madrid and said he had seen Fidel Castro "last week," adding, lamely, that he had told Fidel he was "not only against the death penalty but against death itself." He said that the execution of four soldiers of the revolution was "a very painful thing, a drama we have all suffered." He said he had "very good information" that the dead men had been tried by a military tribunal and executed for treason, not drug-trafficking. And "treason is punishable by death all over the world."[48]

A return to Colombia was part of his ambitious new strategy—was he resigned or, as the French say, retreating the better to leap forward?—but Colombia was now entering a new nightmare period perhaps unparalleled in all its previous experience. On 18 August 1989, Luis Carlos Galán, now the official Liberal candidate and perhaps the most charismatic Colombian politician since Gaitán, met the same fate as his predecessor when he was assassinated at a political rally on the outskirts of Bogotá by hit men acting for Pablo Escobar. Even Colombia, so used to horror, reacted with stupefaction and widespread despair.[49] Once again, García Márquez sent no message to the widow Gloria Pachón, who had been the first journalist to interview him on his return to Colombia in 1966, but he declared the following day that the country "should support President Barco." He then appealed publicly to the drug-traffickers "not to turn Colombia into an abominable country where not even they, their children or their grandchildren will be able to live."[50]

Politically, this had been an extraordinary year. And yet the biggest event of all was about to take place: the fall, on 9 November, of the Berlin Wall. It was possible, as Margaret Thatcher had intimated, and as García Márquez himself had also divined, that two hundred years of Western history had come to an end. Now the demise of the USSR and of communism itself could not be far behind. In December García Márquez, who, for sure, was not passing on the real content of his conversations with Castro, confided to the world that "Fidel fears that the USSR will become infected by capitalism; and that the Third World will be abandoned."[51] He said that the USSR was still desperately needed as a counterweight to the USA and that if it withdrew its financial support from Cuba—for this was the great spectre confronting the revolution—it would be "like a second blockade." He acknowledged that Cuba needed profound changes, some of which had been well under way long before *perestroika*. But Cuba's enemies were continuing to oppose its reinsertion into "its natural world"—Latin America—because people would see it as a triumph for Fidel Castro. It was fortunate, García Márquez must have thought, that Felipe González and his PSOE government had been re-elected in Spain on 29 October, one of the few pieces of good news in an otherwise dismaying panorama.

From García Márquez's perspective, one entire plank of progressive thinking and political action in the world was on the way to disappearance. What would follow was an unprecedented period of economic and social change; but whereas in the past great moments of change, however disorienting, were accompanied by explanatory political and social ideologies, now everything was driven by economic change itself and the associated ideology of globalization. And simultaneously it might seem as if all meaning was being sucked out of existence by technological and biological advances. Hence the desperate return to fundamentalist religion, born out of anxiety, fear or even despair. Some of this he thought but very little would he say. Whatever happened out in the material world, García Márquez would set about finding another way to be optimistic. It was how he had responded to all but the darkest moments; now he saw it as his duty to the planet.

23

Back to Macondo?
News of a Historic Catastrophe

1990–1996

INETEEN EIGHTY-NINE had been the most terrible year in Colombia's recent history. In March Ernesto Samper, a future president, had received multiple bullet wounds in an assassination attempt at the El Dorado Airport and barely survived. In May paramilitaries attempted to blow up Miguel Maza Márquez, head of the DAS or secret police, who also miraculously survived. In August a leading presidential candidate, Luis Carlos Galán of the Liberal Party, was assassinated in full public view. In September the offices of *El Espectador* were devastated by another attack and the Hilton Hotel in Cartagena was bombed. The life of Galán's replacement, César Gaviria, a party technocrat, had been threatened by the drug-traffickers as soon as he was nominated.[1] In one attempt to kill him, in November, a civilian plane belonging to the national airline Avianca was bombed, with 107 dead, though Gaviria was not on board. In December another huge bomb was detonated in front of the DAS building in Bogotá, killing dozens of passers-by. And there were many other such episodes. All of this was new. Certainly there were no more people dying now than at the height of the *Violencia* in the 1950s but the vast majority of those had been anonymous deaths in the rural areas; indeed, the complaint that many had previously made about the Colombian political system was that almost anyone could be murdered except the candidates of the two traditional parties—unless (as was the case with both Gaitán and

Galán) those candidates were rocking the consensual boat in which each party sailed alternately to comfortable prearranged victories in smooth political waters.

The difference, of course, was drugs. The traditional political parties were no longer entirely in control because a significant proportion of the national resources was no longer theirs to distribute in whatever ways would maintain the "stability" of their status quo. Other interests were now at stake. So now there were new targets. On 3 November *Excelsior* reported García Márquez as saying that the so-called "war against drugs" (the increasingly popular U.S. phrase) was "doomed to failure" as currently conceived.[2] He began to urge the need for renewed talks between government, guerrillas and drug-traffickers. Otherwise, he said, Colombia would end up as a victim of the United States's own imperialist designs for the rest of the continent by fighting a proxy war on its behalf.

Just six weeks later everyone could see, who wished to do so, that once again García Márquez had shown that he knew his American hemisphere. In late December the United States under President George H. W. Bush, emboldened rather than relieved by the fall of the Berlin Wall, invaded Panama, killing hundreds of innocent civilians, and kidnapped a sitting Latin American president—their own creation, Antonio Noriega—for the first time in history. Sure he was a dictator, and a gangster, and a drug-runner, a real son-of-a-bitch (all of these were pretexts for the invasion); but he had been their son-of-a-bitch until just a few months before. Thus the USA returned to the policy of foreign invasions in precisely the year in which the Soviets acknowledged that their own great invasion, of Afghanistan, had been a mistake. García Márquez condemned the Panamanian intervention in Cuba's *Granma* (21 December), despite his detestation of Noriega, but *Granma* was not a publication the U.S. authorities were known to take much notice of. Much new writing was on the wall, for sure; much old writing also.

In 1990 Colombia went on as it had in 1989. A group of "Notables," leading public figures, apparently with support from President Barco, published an open letter proposing "less rigorous" punishment of drug-traffickers if they would bring the campaign of violence to an end. Leading elements of the Medellín cartel offered to halt the carnage and surrender cocaine-refining facilities in exchange for government guarantees. Not all the drug-traffickers went along with this proposal, however, and it soon broke down. A second presidential candidate, Bernardo Jaramillo, of the Unión Patriótica (ex-Colombian Revolutionary Armed Forces, or FARC), was assassinated by the Medellín cartel in late March. (The FARC is the oldest guerrilla organization, whose founders originated from the left of the Liberal Party during the later phases of the *Violencia* and then founded the FARC as the armed wing of the Communist Party in the 1960s; it is also the guerrilla organisation with the deepest roots in the peasantry, in a country reputed to have, at the start of the twenty-first century, the largest number of displaced peasants in the world. When it attempted to take the electoral road in the 1980s, the FARC lost some 2,500 candidates and officials murdered by paramilitary death squads, often in league with government forces. Not surprisingly it returned to full-scale guerrilla war.) The Interior Minister, Carlos Lemos Simmonds, was accused by opponents of provoking Jaramillo's murder and resigned. Then in late April a third presidential candidate, Carlos Pizarro, of another former guerrilla movement, M-19, was assassinated on an internal flight by a hit man who had been paid—so Pizarro's brother alleged—by police or army-backed death squads. Meanwhile Pablo Escobar, the leading drug-trafficker, offered a bounty of 4,000 dollars for each policeman killed. Bombs exploded all over the country, killing hundreds of people. When the presidential elections were held, César Gaviria, Galán's former chief of staff, won with 47.4 per cent of the vote. Only 45 per cent of the 14 million electorate went to the polls. A further offer by the drug-traffickers to suspend the violence was rejected by the new government. Gaviria's programme included continuing a policy of firm repression of the drug cartels, and constitutional reform.

It was at this moment that García Márquez decided to make another effort to instal himself in Colombia. It has to be wondered whether he would have considered doing so at such a sombre time nationally if Cuba had not been so politically embarrassing to him. When he found his feet again and began to consolidate his new political strategy the objective would no longer be to advance the Cuban Revolution as such but to help save Fidel—if necessary, from himself.[3] Now, on several occasions, García Márquez conceded—though he advanced it as an avant-garde intuition—that "we are in the first stages of a new and unpredictable era," but then specified, perhaps less convincingly, that this new era "seems destined to liberate our thinking."[4] What he did not acknowledge was that this new era represented the defeat of everything he had always believed in. He decided to make not a clean breast of it but the best fist of it, and to act as if all that was happening was exactly what he had been hoping for: it was the reactionaries, first among them the U.S. government, who did not grasp the enormity of what was happening in the world and the scale of the opportunities that now awaited mankind. This, he argued, required everyone to reconsider their political convictions.[5] It was, truly, a defining moment in his thinking.

Surely things could only get better? No, they immediately got worse. In late February, a few weeks after the example of Panama, the Sandinista government in Nicaragua, which had won power and held on to it in the teeth of American opposition, was voted out of office by a people weary of war and pessimistic about the future in a continent still dominated by the Colossus of the North. García Márquez was stupefied but managed to bluster that the Sandinistas would win the next election.[6] Fidel Castro would not have been surprised by the Nicaraguan reverse but he must have been bitterly disappointed and fearful for his own country's future. The truth was that Latin America as a whole was poorer at the end of the 1980s than it had been in the 1960s and most of its countries were heavily in debt. Economic backwardness and injustice were everywhere to be seen. *One Hundred Years of Solitude* was thought to have been a memorial to underdevelopment at the very moment when underdevelopment, thanks to the 1960s revolutions, was on its way out for ever. Far from it; in the 1980s Latin America seemed to be on its way back to Macondo.

Journalists pursued García Márquez everywhere in Colombia. As usual. He was already working on another historical drama about erotic passion to be entitled *Of Love and Other Demons* and now marked his return by announcing that he would be adapting Jorge Isaacs's *María* (1867), Colombia's best-known and most-loved novel before *One Hundred Years of Solitude*, for Colombian television, to be shown in October. He said it was a great challenge and a great responsibility but one he was looking forward to immensely. He was hoping to make the housewives of Latin America weep even more with the television version than their great-great-grandmothers—and his—had wept with the original novel in their laps back in the 1870s. "Love," he declared—for *María* is indeed the best-known love story in the history of Latin America—"is the most important subject in the history of humanity. Some say it is death. I don't think so because everything is connected to love."[7] He could not more succinctly have conveyed his own evolution in terms of a thematic centre of gravity.

Despite the announcement that he was "back"—viewed with inevitable scepticism by Colombians who had heard it many times before—García Márquez and Mercedes were soon on their way to Chile and Brazil, before returning temporarily to safe haven in Mexico. The visit to Chile was for the inauguration on 11 March of Patricio Aylwin, the first democratic President in Chile since 1973. Now García Márquez was finally able to get some satisfaction from seeing the back of Pinochet, who had also, like the Sandinistas, been voted out of office (though not out of Chile's political life). García Márquez had encountered him in Washington in 1977 when the Panama Canal treaty was signed during García Márquez's literary strike (due precisely to Pinochet being in power); now they were together again at a ceremony where the Chilean General must have felt much the less comfortable of the two. (The London *Financial Times*, appropriately, remarked that Pinochet was now "adrift in his labyrinth.")[8] García Márquez's most notable experience was taking part in the symbolic gesture of reopening Pablo Neruda's house at Isla Negra, a place of pilgrimage closed down by the dictatorship for seventeen years. He was accompanied by José Donoso, Jorge Edwards, the poet Nicanor Parra and Enrique Correa, General Secretary of the new government.

In August Gaviria, elected in May, came to power in Colombia at the age of forty-three. Almost his first policy initiative was to propose a National Constituent Assembly to reform the country's system of government—the current constitution dated back to the country's only *costeño* president, Rafael Núñez, in 1886—and this of course was exactly what García Márquez, who had always said that the old constitution was merely "theoretical," would have wished Gaviria to do. (On 4 September *El País* asked rhetorically if García Márquez was a "Gavirista."[9] Not yet, was the answer. But he soon would be.) A new constitution would redefine the country and might lead to an entirely different future. García Márquez was proposed on 27 August as a candidate for the Constituent Assembly, tasked with drawing up the new document; the press would discuss his possible participation endlessly for the next few months, taking great pleasure in exposing the contradictions of a man who was a "friend of dictators" and who had never voted in his entire life.

Despite his constructive beginning, Gaviria was given no honeymoon by the drug-traffickers, and politics as usual continued in the very month of his inauguration. On 30 August Diana Turbay, journalist daughter of ex-President Julio César Turbay, and five other journalists were abducted by gangsters working for Pablo Escobar. On 31 August bandits attempted to abduct radio journalist Yamid Amat. These events and other similar cases would form the basis for García Márquez's documentary novel *News of a Kidnapping* four years later, though at this moment the pattern of events was not clear even to him. On 3 September he found the second phrase of his new slogan. The first was already familiar: "The times are changing and we have to adjust." The second was new: "Only Fidel can change Cuba. But the United States always needs a bogeyman."[10] This was brilliantly ingenious but whether Fidel had been consulted about the need to change Cuba was in doubt. He was certainly not saying so publicly himself; but he would soon have to acknowledge Cuba's economic orphanhood without the Soviet Union and with the U.S. embargo still in place and the so-called "Special Period" of unparalleled austerity would shortly be proclaimed.

In 1991 García Márquez improved his Colombian operation and confirmed his long-term intention to divide his life between Mexico and Colombia by installing his cousin Margarita Márquez, daughter of his late uncle Juan de Dios, as his local secretary in the spacious Bogotá apartment he and Mercedes had bought for their hitherto mythical return. But the month of García Márquez's latest visit was another brutal one. Marina Montoya, a grandmother, was taken away from the other hostages captured by Escobar and murdered. The army attempted to rescue Diana Turbay on 25 January but she was killed as she attempted to flee her kidnappers. This provoked García Márquez—usually reluctant to make declarations in support of Colombian governments—to speak out. In a Radio Caracol interview on 26 January he said that the "Extraditables"—those liable to be arrested and sent to the United States for trial—should "respect the lives of journalists."[11] Hostage Beatriz Villamizar was released on 6 February, but Maruja Pachón and Pachito Santos, a member of the *El Tiempo* dynasty (and a future vice-president of the country), remained in captivity. To add to the chaos, there was also intense guerrilla activity around Bogotá itself. Meanwhile President Gaviria issued a statement in the United States declaring that on balance he still favoured extradition for drug-traffickers, a decision which ensured that the current levels of violence would continue or even increase. It seemed to be a war to the death between the drug cartels and civil society.

In July García Márquez returned briefly to Mexico to attend to his affairs and commitments there. Before he left, however, President

Gaviria, who had perhaps been listening to García Márquez, had negotiated a sensational but profoundly controversial deal with Pablo Escobar through which the master criminal gave himself up in return for a
reduced sentence and comfortable prison conditions—not in the
United States, as the drug-traffickers all feared, but near his home city
of Medellín. García Márquez described this agreement, which was certain to be condemned both by the Colombian right and by the USA, as
a "triumph of intelligence." He pointed out that the USA itself had
a long history of negotiating with gangsters when there were reasons
of state for doing so.[12] It would be difficult to support all the agonizing twists and turns government policy would be obliged to take over
the coming three years but García Márquez would do his best to be
helpful.

And Gaviria would be helpful to him. When García Márquez got
back to Colombia, he had important business to attend to which would
demonstrate to all the doubters—of whom there were many—that he
was committed not only to returning to the country on a long-term
basis but also to participating in political life. He had decided to buy
into the bid for a nightly television news bulletin, to be called QAP
(taxi-driver slang for "ready, at your service, over to you"). The idea
was Enrique Santos Calderón's; other journalists involved were María
Elvira Samper and María Isabel Rueda, and Julio Andrés Camacho,
owner of the magazine *Cromos*, was a significant shareholder; as was
García Márquez (though he would later claim that he was just "the
holy spirit" of the enterprise). Not surprisingly, the Gaviria government gave the QAP a licence to begin broadcasting on 1 January 1992.

Meanwhile García Márquez and Mercedes were showing their
commitment to the great return in the most tangible way of all. Following the purchase of the apartment in Bogotá they selected a location for a new house in Cartagena, a plot right on the seafront by the
old city walls and next to the derelict Santa Clara convent, one of the
city's most beautiful colonial buildings. Colombia's leading architect,
Rogelio Salmona, who had helped García Márquez out in Paris in
1957, would lead the project. It seemed that Cuba was no longer García Márquez's first priority. Or at least he was going to make it *seem* as
if Cuba were no longer his first priority.

In August 1991, as part of his ongoing process of adaptation to the
triumph of the liberal capitalist world, he at last entered the United
States on a normal visa, for the first time since 1961. The new laws on
communism and immigration had finally caused the name Gabriel

García Márquez to be removed from the prohibition list. He had been waiting thirty years for a regular visa and now he entered the country to open the New York Film Festival held between 16 and 30 August. The prohibition had irritated García Márquez even more than he had been prepared to admit. For one thing, like most people on the Costa, not least the other members of the Barranquilla Group, he had never felt the visceral hatred for the USA and the lordly contempt for its culture which was so common among Latin American intellectuals and which they shared, of course, with many Europeans, most notably the French. (Ironically enough, Fidel Castro was also unprejudiced against the U.S. people and their culture; his lifelong love of baseball is just one example.)

In fact García Márquez's objections to the USA had been overwhelmingly political in nature. He had been quick to notice that his American readers were significantly more enthusiastic than his European ones and much less troubled, surprisingly enough, by his extra-literary positions. His translations into English had always sold well and been well received by critics, and both his main translators, Gregory Rabassa and Edith Grossman, were Americans. In recent years he had been eager to build whatever links he could with progressive American film-makers, notably Francis Ford Coppola, Robert Redford and Woody Allen.[13] And he had begun to appreciate New York much more now that he was visiting as a high-profile tourist and not under constant siege from Cuban anti-revolutionaries. So it was a great relief to have got his situation regularized. While he was in New York the attempted coup against Mikhail Gorbachev took place in Moscow; this would lead to the Soviet leader's fall in December and the eventual disintegration of the USSR. García Márquez watched events on the television in his New York hotel room and discussed these and other world developments with none other than his former *bête noire*—only Pinochet had been a more hated figure—the ex–U.S. Secretary of State Henry Kissinger.[14] Cuba was high on the agenda.

In the late autumn, having made his peace with the United States, Latin America's most recent oppressor, García Márquez returned to its original colonizer, Spain. The year 1992 was fast approaching and with it the celebration of the 500th anniversary of the so-called "discovery of the New World." The Spaniards, not always fully aware of how patronizing they can seem to Latin Americans, were dismayed when Latin Americans fell over one another to declare that they had not needed "discovering," thank you very much—they, or their Indian forefathers and mothers, had discovered themselves many centuries before—and that it was by no means obvious to them that the arrival of the Spaniards in what they had mistakenly named the "Indies" in 1492 was a cause for celebration. The Spaniards hastily rebranded the forthcoming event the quincentenary of the "Encounter of Two Worlds" and engaged in some crisis diplomacy to get everyone back on board (so to speak). García Márquez had been one of the high-profile doubters. Yet secretly he must have been delighted at the prospect. His friend François Mitterrand had been in power for the celebration of the bicentenary of the French Revolution; now his Spanish friend Felipe González was in power for the organizing of the celebration of the half millennium since Europe's arrival in the New World.

Always closely attuned to history, García Márquez had been working on an appropriate literary project for the occasion. Ever since the 1960s, and in a sense since he had actually lived in Europe in the mid-1950s, he had been toying with stories which communicated the reverse experience to the one being commemorated by the Spanish, namely that of Latin Americans arriving in Europe and confronting what for them was, despite everything, an alien culture. In a sense it was what he had recently been talking about with regard to Hispanic immigration into the United States, a kind of symbolic reverse colonization—some might even say a return of the repressed. He had outlined literally dozens of plots over the years and now he had decided to select the most promising ones, those which survived his final cull, to produce a collection that could appear in 1992. Some of them had emerged as late as the period 1980–84 when, just as he had written chronicles that would eventually turn into film scripts for the *Difficult Loves* series, so he had also produced stories that could be slipped into this new literary collection. García Márquez was never in a hurry to publish but he rarely missed an opportunity either; many of his projects remained ongoing for decades but found their way into artistic form—and into book form—in the end, and often at the ideal moment. Thus he delayed the completion and publication of his new novel *Of Love and Other Demons* and attended to his Europe-based tales.

He travelled to Barcelona, where he now had a sumptuous apartment on the Passeig de Graça or Paseo de Gracia, one of the city's classiest addresses, in a block that had been refurbished by the prestigious architect Alfons Milà. After this he travelled round Europe, as if to stake his claim on the once-imperialist territory, part of which was busy recalling its adventures in his own region of the world, visiting

Switzerland and Sweden among other countries. The main reason was that he had decided to call his new story collection *Cuentos peregrinos*. In Spanish the primary meaning of the word *peregrino* is the noun "pilgrim" but there is a second, adjectival meaning: "strange," "surprising" or "alien"—hence the title of the English translation, *Strange Pilgrims*. He too was an alien pilgrim, less at home politically in the world than ever yet more determined than ever to put his best foot forward and think—or at least talk—positively. By now his projected short fiction collection was down to about fifteen stories but his visit to Europe, intended as a mere last-minute refresher course, more sentimental journey than practical update, put him in something of a panic. The Europe he remembered was not the Europe of today and neither of those Europes seemed to have been encapsulated in his book. He took hasty notes and then dedicated the next few months to an intense revision of the new book which, he had promised his agent and his publisher, would be ready in time to appear at the Seville Exposition the following July.

Unhappily, Cuba began the quincentenary year with another execution, that of an invading rebel Eduardo Díaz Betancourt. García Márquez himself made a public appeal for clemency, as did the leaders of even the countries most sympathetic to Cuba, but to no avail.[15] The Cuban authorities judged that in Cuba's circumstances deterring counter-revolution and terrorism was a matter of life and death. Mexico's leading intellectual, the poet Octavio Paz, and the Latin American right had a field day and García Márquez had to scramble yet again to justify his relationship with the Cuban leader by explaining his record of getting prisoners pardoned and released. His own popularity was undiminished, however, at least with the Latin American people. When, in February, he made a brief appearance at a conference at the National Autonomous University of Mexico, just a few blocks from his house, the entire audience stood up as soon as he entered the auditorium and gave him a two-minute standing ovation.[16] He was not even one of the participants. It happened everywhere he went. Latin America has not, historically, been a continent of winners but García Márquez was an undefeated and undisputed world champion.

Yet suddenly the champ was laid low by an unexpected enemy. He had been feeling tired for some time and had suddenly found it difficult to breathe when he got back into the thin air of Bogotá. He decided on a check-up. Doctors found a tumour a centimetre across in his left lung, due almost certainly to all the black tobacco he had smoked for all those years in front of all those typewriters. The doctors proposed an operation. He told the newsmen that both Fidel Castro and Carlos Salinas had called him before the surgery to wish him well. Castro offered him a private plane to Cuba with his personal doctor and Salinas lamented that he was not returning to Mexico for the treatment. García Márquez promised that Mexico would be his first stop after he recovered. He could have chosen to go to Cuba, Mexico or the United States but decided to have the surgery in Colombia. No metastasis was detected and the operation was deemed a complete success; he would have no breathing difficulties. His prospects were excellent and he was said to be in the best of spirits.

García Márquez had feared death all his life and had therefore also feared illness. Ever since he had become famous he had listened closely to doctors and had taken most of their advice about healthy living. Now, despite all his precautions, he had fallen ill. And almost nothing was more frightening than lung cancer. Yet he surprised himself and those who knew him. He took the challenge in hand, insisted on knowing all the facts about the illness and its likely prognosis, and was able to boast: "I mastered my life."[17] He was supposed to take six weeks of complete rest but on 10 June it was announced that he would be at the Seville Exposition in July, as scheduled, to launch not only the Colombian Pavilion but his own new book. By now it was known that there would be twelve "pilgrim stories," and that the book was ready.

There was indeed almost a García Márquez takeover of the Seville Exposition. He became lord of the Colombian exhibition hall after his arrival in the Andalusian city, despite having declared in Madrid that there would not be a "Macondo Pavilion" in Seville.[18] ("Macondo" was a word he had not used for many years and its use now was a sign of things to come.) Just as he had in Madrid, he advertised his new book, *Strange Pilgrims*, of which 500,000 copies had been printed, at every opportunity. And the public clamoured for his autograph wherever he went. The Colombian politician and future presidential candidate Horacio Serpa, waiting to enter the Colombian Pavilion, heard two Spaniards commenting on the picture of García Márquez presiding over the banner advertising the twenty-fifth anniversary of *One Hundred Years of Solitude*: "And who is that guy?" "Oh, he's the dictator of Colombia, he's been in power twenty-five years now."[19] In fact it was the first time García Márquez had ever been present at the launch of one of his own books—it was after all 1992, and on Colombia's national day!—and the crowds had to be controlled by the police. García Márquez even acted as President for a day because Pablo Escobar had escaped from prison and Gaviria had cancelled his journey to Spain. The Nobel Prize winner found himself opening a Colombian bottling plant in Madrid.

Strange Pilgrims brought together a collection of the first works by García Márquez set outside Latin America, and they all have a somewhat autobiographical air about them. The author states in his prologue that all except two of them ("The Trail of Your Blood in the Snow" and "Miss Forbes's Summer of Happiness") were completed in April 1992, though all were begun between 1976 and January 1982, in other words during the period when García Márquez was working for *Alternativa* and had resolved not to publish anything "literary" until Pinochet fell from power in Chile. It is, in retrospect, astonishing that he was working on these whimsical and in some cases rather slight creations at a time when he was interacting closely with Fidel and Raúl Castro and writing politically committed diatribes against the United States and the Colombian ruling class.

The stories are organized in no discernible order, whether chronological or thematic. The first, "Bon Voyage, Mr. President," narrated in the third person, is many readers' favourite, and is set in the 1950s in Geneva, the first place García Márquez went to in 1955, directly after landing in Paris. The protagonist, ex-President of the Caribbean republic Puerto Santo, has come from exile in Martinique to have medical tests in Switzerland. Like another story, "Maria dos Prazeres," and his last novel, *Memories of My Melancholy Whores*, it tells the story of someone who discovers that death can always be postponed and is best forgotten about—a story, then, that probably became more relevant to the author in the final stages of preparing the collection. Here a charming but deeply cynical member of the ruling class wins over two well-meaning proletarians, justifying his own manipulations by saying, "They're lies and they're not lies. When it has to do with a president, the worst ignominies may be both true and false at the same time."

García Márquez had decided to spend this quincentennial summer in Europe following his enforced stay in Bogotá. Strange pilgrimage. An invasion in reverse. Everyone who met him said he looked wonderful. "The doctors took out the only unhealthy things inside me," he declared.[20] Then he returned to Mexico. On 6 November Mercedes turned sixty and it was reported that she had received a huge floral tribute from President Salinas on her birthday.[21] She had a whole phalanx of admirers among men of power and influence, many of whom even envied García Márquez a companion who showed—but never showed off—such an array of qualities, such good judgement, such permanent support. She was a consummate diplomat. This was not long after her husband was asked what he expected in the twenty-first century and he said that he thought women should take over the world to save humanity.[22]

Then, continuing this diplomatic revisionism, he took his first-ever political step against those totemic representatives of the Colombian left, the country's guerrillas. He signed a letter sent to *El Tiempo* on 22 November by a long list of Colombian intellectuals, including the painter Fernando Botero. The letter was effectively in support of Gaviria's recent decision to wage all-out war on the guerrillas, who had shown no interest in his peace overtures.[23] The result, undoubtedly, would be to leave the guerrillas feeling isolated, especially by "petit-bourgeois intellectuals," and to cause them to take an even harder line, which continues to this day. For García Márquez it was a huge decision but undoubtedly one consonant with the other decisions he had taken as a result of the fall of the Berlin Wall. Probably, as much as anything, he was hoping to have a quieter time following his illness. He did not want to be constantly urged to support the almost insupportable. He would never again have quite the influence with the Colombian left that he had enjoyed until that moment; but then the Colombian left would not have the influence it had before. Inevitably rumours spread still more widely that he would soon be moving away from Castro too; after all Fidel was the originator and the symbol of most of the guerrilla movements which had swept Latin America ever since the early 1960s. García Márquez laughed the rumours off. He would never abandon Fidel.[24]

He had dissociated himself from the guerrillas at precisely the moment that a new president was about to enter the White House in Washington. It was reported that Bill Clinton, the first Democrat President for twelve years, was "an enthusiastic reader of García Márquez." Perhaps things were looking up at last: it had been widely reported that the Bush family had no books in their house and much preferred watching television.

García Márquez stayed on in Cartagena and on 11 January could be seen in a photo in *El Espectador* at the bullring talking with Augusto López Valencia, the President of Julio Mario Santo Domingo's multinational company, Bavaria.[25] The newspaper had no comment or

explanation of their encounter. In previous eras García Márquez would
have either ensured that such meetings were unknown to the world or
would have provided some explanation, including serendipity. Not any
longer. He too was now in the bourgeois world and was ready to commit himself to the market economy. As a socialist he had always been
opposed on principle to charity (though, privately, he had always been
generous to dependent individuals with his own money, whilst never
drawing attention to the fact); but in the absence of any other form of
income for causes in which he believed, he turned to a phenomenon
that was returning to the Western world on a scale not seen since the
last great triumph of monopoly capitalism at the time of the American
"Gilded Age" in the late nineteenth century: public philanthropy. (Bill
Clinton himself would eventually write a book on "Giving.")[26] He had
a Cuban film foundation to run. And he was beginning to think of
another major and similarly costly project, an institute of journalism.
The overt socialist war, both armed and intellectual, was over, the class
struggle was in abeyance, and he had become convinced that the cultural and political war of positions—acting as progressively as possible
in the circumstances—was all that he could aspire to. Thus he began to
cultivate the rich, famous and powerful more assiduously than before.

As part of his diplomatic self-redefinition, he had allowed his name
to go forward to a Unesco "Forum of Reflection," or forum of twenty-
one "Wise Men," as the Colombian press dubbed it, to discuss the
planet's growing problems within the so-called "new world order" at a
time when Unesco had been under heavy criticism by the USA and the
UK for just this kind of thing—costly international "junkets," mere
"talking shops" instead of concrete action. Of course talk had been
thought dangerous in the powerhouses of the liberal West, for the first
time in decades, since the advent of Thatcher and Reagan. Talk caused
trouble and was mainly indulged in by leftists; and after all, what was
the point of idle speculation when, as Thatcher herself had famously
declared, there was "no such thing as society." García Márquez was
nominated by Luis Carlos Galán's widow, Gloria Pachón, who was
Colombian ambassador to Unesco in Paris, and of course by her boss,
Gaviria. García Márquez said he was doing it as much for the sake of
his country as for the world.[27] Other members included Vaclav Havel,
Umberto Eco, Michel Serres and Edward Said. The first meeting was
held in Paris on 27 January 1993 and put García Márquez in touch
with the first-ever Hispanic director of Unesco, the Spaniard Federico
Mayor, who soon became a firm friend. As if to emphasise his

enhanced dignity and respectability, and perhaps to impress the folks back home in the "Athens of South America," he followed up his visit to Paris, home of the Academy mentality, with a broadside against the Spanish Royal Academy, author, he alleged, of "a geocentric dictionary."[28] Once again, in the past he would not have deigned to refer to academies. But this would turn out to be yet another extremely smart move in the longer term and would, again, put him in close touch with people—academicians, philologists, right-wing poets—on whom he would never previously have "wasted" his time. Before long he would be building links with the University of Guadalajara in Mexico, where he had recently developed a close relationship with its Rector, Raúl Padilla López, and he and Carlos Fuentes gave their support for Guadalajara's Chair in honour of Julio Cortázar. Fuentes and García Márquez were already talking about ways of approaching the new U.S. President, Bill Clinton, presumed to be much more moderate—as well as more cultured—than his recent Republican predecessors.

In June, ignoring all his own complaints about distractions from writing, he was in Barcelona electioneering with Felipe González, creating a sensation in front of forty thousand PSOE supporters at one of González's late rallies at Montjuïc. He would perhaps have done better to travel to Venezuela where another friend, Carlos Andrés Pérez, was entering a political crisis from which he would never recover. On 20 May Pérez was relieved of his functions as President of Venezuela, accused of stealing 17 million dollars of the nation's money when he came to power in 1989. García Márquez sent a public message of support stressing Pérez's courage in resisting several coup attempts against him—one by a soldier called Hugo Chávez, currently serving out a jail sentence—and his "magnificent sense of friendship" (what did that have to do with anything, many readers asked), though not exalting his great sense of integrity. Unfortunately García Márquez went still further and had the effrontery to criticize the institutions and representatives of the country and to imply that the accusations were a put-up job; he barely stopped short of criticizing the Venezuelan people.[29] He would never be quite so popular in Venezuela again. His personal relationships with the powerful were beginning to cost him dear.

In October García Márquez met Gloria Pachón's sister Maruja, by then Minister of Education in Colombia, and her husband Alberto Villamizar. The couple proposed that he should write a book about their experiences in 1990–91, when Maruja was kidnapped. He was still absorbed in the preparation of *Of Love and Other Demons* and asked for a year to think about it but to their astonishment he came back to them after just a few weeks and accepted. He was a man of sixty-six embarking on another demanding and exhausting project. The book would be called *News of a Kidnapping*. As it happened, by the time he had made his mind up two of the principal protagonists of the drama were dead: Father Rafael García Herreros, who had persuaded Pablo Escobar to give himself up, had died on 24 November 1992, and Escobar himself was gunned down by Colombian police in Medellín on 2 December 1993, only weeks after García Márquez's first conversation with his former victims, Maruja and Alberto.

But just before Escobar was finally tracked down by the police came the pay-off for all García Márquez's efforts with Gaviria. It was announced that Colombia was restoring its diplomatic links with Cuba. Castro, on his way back from attending the inauguration of a new president in Bolivia, had recently made a "private visit" to Cartagena—at last García Márquez had had the pleasure of greeting his friend on Colombian soil—and now, just a few weeks later, full relations were restored. Fidel in, Escobar out: this was a wonderful month both for Gaviria and for García Márquez.

At the end of the year the whole García Márquez family got together in Cartagena for the first time in many years. A historic photograph was taken of Luisa Santiaga and all her children. There would never be another such meeting.

García Márquez continued to keep busy; far too busy, surely. Almost no one knew it but, as usual, he was already at work on his next book before the last one was even published. But he needed to keep it secret for the time being. In March he travelled to Itagüí near Medellín in north-western Colombia with a number of American reporters, including James Brooke of the *New York Times*. Their objective was to visit the Ochoa brothers, the leading drug-traffickers after Escobar. Brooke recalled:

> Presidents come and go but the owlish writer, universally known by his nickname, Gabo, endures . . . A day spent with Mr. García Márquez quickly sketched the dimensions of the man. At the airport in Cartagena, where he lives, travelers recognized the author in his black-rimmed glasses and repeated his nickname in awe. At a prison in Itagüí, outside Medellín, three convicted cocaine traffickers known as the Ochoa brothers tripped over themselves vying for the honor of serving him lunch. At a bar-

racks in Neiva, uniformed helicopter pilots from Colombia's anti-drug police ignored the national police commander and jostled for position in souvenir photos with the writer.[30]

This was the only journey García Márquez would make while researching *News of a Kidnapping*. Two years later he revealed that he had given Brooke and other journalists the slip and talked to Jorge Luis Ochoa by himself. He didn't want his sources to be "burned" nor Ochoa to give a false version of their meeting.

Suddenly, just as García Márquez was looking forward to the publication of *Of Love and Other Demons*, Mexico, his refuge, his place of stability, began to implode, and Carlos Salinas, his great friend, began to move into difficulties that would eventually be greater even than those recently suffered by the hapless Carlos Andrés Pérez in Venezuela. First, down in Chiapas, in the Mexican south, a new indigenist movement, the Zapatistas, inspired by a mysterious and charismatic guerrilla leader known as "Comandante Marcos," began to catch world headlines and Salinas seemed to be caught off guard and to have little idea what to do. But then, even more dramatically, the governing PRI's official candidate for the upcoming elections, Luis Donaldo Colosio, a good friend of García Márquez's, was assassinated in the north of the country, the first politician of his stature to die in this way since the bloody revolutionary period in the 1920s. Salinas himself was suspected by many observers of having planned the murder of his own successor, placing García Márquez in a situation not entirely different from the one he had faced four years earlier in Havana when his friend Tony la Guardia was executed by his friend Fidel Castro. He had got very close to Colosio and had high hopes that the somewhat unorthodox candidate might take the country in a more progressive direction. For the first time García Márquez broke his personal rule—and Mexico's laws—by issuing a statement on the event and calling for calm in this country he loved.[31] Colombia, Cuba, Venezuela, now even Mexico, all his citadels were falling: it was back to Macondo with a vengeance.

And García Márquez himself was wondering whether he had started on a decline of his own. He was interviewed in March and April by David Streitfeld of the *Washington Post* as the last preparations were made for the publication of *Of Love and Other Demons*. Streitfeld noted that García Márquez's books were obsessed with death and so was their author, who felt that if he stopped writing he might die: "In more ways than the cancer, his body is beginning to betray him. 'It's curious,' he says, 'how one starts to perceive the signs of growing old. I first started to forget names and telephone numbers, then it became more encompassing. I couldn't remember a word, a face, or a melody.' "[32] No doubt this helped to explain why writing his memoirs had recently come to seem a much more pressing task than before.

On 22 April, in the midst of so much political chaos, *Of Love and Other Demons* was published. Its launch coincided with the Bogotá Book Fair, where his old friend Gonzalo Mallarino made an impassioned speech exalting his friend's new novel. García Márquez had reached the summit of his powers, he declared.[33] He had dedicated the novel to Carmen Balcells, "bathed in tears." Once again it was set in Cartagena: late in 1949 a young journalist, working for a newspaper whose editor is Clemente Manuel Zabala, is sent to investigate a story. The old convent of Santa Clara is to be converted into a de luxe hotel and some of the oldest tombs have been opened for relocation. (García Márquez was making his peace with Cartagena past by mentioning—acknowledging—Zabala; and he was imagining his way in to Cartagena present because his new house was to be built right across the street from the old convent.) In one of the tombs there has appeared a skull with a torrent of bright red hair that has continued growing for almost two centuries and is now more than twenty-two metres long. The young journalist decides to investigate the case. The result is this novel.

The novel imagines that one December, late in the colonial period, a rabid dog bites several people in the market at Cartagena, including a girl with long red hair called Sierva María, who is just about to celebrate her twelfth birthday. Although her father the Marquis of Casalduero is one of the wealthiest men in the city, he is also a weakling and has allowed Sierva María, unloved by her mother, to be brought up in the slave yard. Despite the fact that rabies does not develop, the Catholic Church believes that she is possessed by the devil—she has merely taken on African beliefs—and urges the Marquis to have her exorcised. She is taken to the convent of Santa Clara for supervision and the Bishop brings in one of the up-and-coming experts on possession and exorcism, Cayetano Delaura, a theologian and librarian destined, it is said, for the Vatican. The girl will never see the streets of Cartagena again.

Delaura, who has no experience or understanding of women, has a dream about the girl even before he meets her. She is in a room—

which in his dream is the room he had as a student in Salamanca—
looking out on a snow-covered landscape and she is eating grapes from
her lap that never run out; if they did she would die. The girl he meets
the next morning, tied hand and foot because of her rages, is exactly as
he dreamed her. His first reaction is to tell the Abbess that the treatment she is suffering would turn anyone into a devil. His second reaction is to become obsessed with the child and to begin to explore the
forbidden books in the library that only he is permitted to see. He finds
a secret entrance to the convent, and begins to visit Sierva María every
night, reciting poetry. Finally he declares his true feelings, embraces
her, and they sleep together without quite completing the sexual act.
But in April, nearly five months after she was bitten by the rabid dog,
the process of exorcism begins. Her hair is cut off and burned. The
Bishop officiates in front of all the authorities and nuns but collapses;
Sierva María naturally acts like one possessed. Delaura's misdeeds are
discovered and he is condemned by the Inquisition as a heretic—which
of course he is: indeed, he is guilty and Sierva María is innocent—and
he is condemned to spend many years in a lepers' hospital. Sierva
María waits for him in vain and after three days she refuses to eat. She
never understands why Delaura did not come back, but on 29 May she
in her turn dreams about the field of snow but now she eats the grapes
two at a time in her fever to get to the last one. Before the sixth exorcism she is dead but her shorn head is bursting with hair again.

This book is a further sign of García Márquez's engagement with
Cartagena. *Love in the Time of Cholera* may be interpreted as a re-
encounter with his father, and with Colombia's past, as well as an
exploration of the conflict between marriage and sexual adventurism;
above all, a book about the suburb of Manga, where his parents lived
and where he had recently bought his mother an apartment. *Of Love
and Other Demons* is about the old walled city, where García Márquez
was having a new "mansion" built as he wrote the book; thus both novels have to do in an oblique way with his properties and his power. This
time he was recovering the whole of Colombian history back to the
late colonial period. The work has a sort of bleak, heavy authority—
like some works by Alvaro Mutis—with few light features. *Love in the
Time of Cholera* was written before the historic disasters of 1989; *Of
Love and Other Demons*, though set in the colonial period, is conceived
from the world after 1989 and is a much darker work. For all his optimistic declarations about the future, there is little doubt that in his
deeper feelings García Márquez saw a world going backwards for the

first time in two hundred years: backwards, in some respects, before the French Revolution and the Enlightenment, backwards before Latin America's independence from Spain (now being reversed, at least in the economic sense), and backwards from the dreams of the socialist revolution of 1917. He was writing in a world where no revolution seemed conceivable and a Bolivarian conception that political action in Colombia is futile would again begin to dominate his thinking.

The use of dreams in this work—using elements of García Márquez's own adolescent experience (his exile from home to a school in icy climes, his trunk, his book without a cover, his terrifying nightmares)—is stunning. The end of the novel, like De Palma out of Hitchcock, makes the blood run cold and reminds the reader that when this writer is fully focused, his powers of evocation are second to none. The last pages give the work a retrospective brilliance which it has perhaps not entirely earned. In particular, perhaps the greatest miracle, as the reader also noticed on the last page of *The General in His Labyrinth*, is how the writer gives us what we have come to expect—the same themes, albeit arranged in a different design, the same subjects, same structure, same style, same narrative technique—including what, perversely and paradoxically, we want most of all: to be stunned by the manner in which, within the familiar, this writer can nevertheless surprise us yet again in ways we somehow expect yet can never entirely anticipate. Like a journey on a literary roller-coaster, with the biggest churn of the stomach at the very end of the ride.

The book was generally well received, not least by academics, who were pleased to see García Márquez rather deliberately taking up the academy's current "postmodern" preoccupations with feminism, sexuality, race, religion, identity and the legacy of the Enlightenment as it related to all these questions. Jean-François Fogel declared in *Le Monde* that García Márquez remained "one of the few novelists capable of evoking love without irony or embarrassment."[34] A. S. Byatt in the *New York Review of Books* described the novel as "an almost didactic, yet brilliantly moving, tour de force."[35] Peter Kemp in the London *Sunday Times* spoke of incredible events narrated in a calm style: "At once nostalgic and satiric, a resplendent fable and a sombre parable, *Of Love and Other Demons* is a further marvellous manifestation of the enchantment and the disenchantment that his native Colombia always stirs in García Márquez."[36] Despite everything, "Márquez," as most English-speaking reviewers insisted on calling him, had woven his "magic" yet again.

· · ·

AT THE TIME *Of Love and Other Demons* was published in Colombia, García Márquez made a visit to Spain to resume his practice of being elsewhere when a book of his was launched. He visited Seville again for the spring fair and attended some of the traditional early season bull-fights. Rosa Mora of *El País* caught up with him in April and he told her that he had been working on his memoirs, especially the story of his return to Aracataca with his mother: "I think that everything I am came out of that trip."[37] But the memoirs had come to a halt again and in any case he was resolved that his next book should be some kind of reportage. Not only was he missing journalism, he said, but he had Unesco backing for one of his most cherished projects, a journalism foundation which would challenge the work of modern schools of communication since these, in his perception, "mean to do away with journalism."

In recent years more journalists had been killed in Colombia than almost anywhere else in the world. There were also, unfortunately, many more spectacular and usually tragic stories to report in that country than almost anywhere else in the world. Nowhere had a higher murder rate; and almost nowhere else could boast Colombia's toxic and terrifying mixture of terrorism, drug-trafficking, guerrilla warfare and paramilitary activity, combined with police and military responses that at times were almost as violent as the ills they were seeking to eradicate. César Gaviria was at the end of his hallucinatory four years in government and had striven heroically to prevent the country from sliding into outright anarchy but the next government, due to be elected in May, also had a nightmarish challenge on its hands. And of course García Márquez was working, still secretly, on a book ("some kind of reportage") which would be based on the period just past. But he was not yet ready to make a full announcement because in this case it was absolutely crucial to conceal and protect his sources.

In June, back in Latin America, he was present at the 4th Ibero-American Summit of all the leaders of Latin America and the Iberian Peninsula, held in Cartagena. Gaviria had arranged the venue as out-going President of Colombia. The King of Spain, Felipe González, Carlos Salinas de Gortari and Fidel Castro, as well as Gaviria, were all present at the meeting in what was now effectively García Márquez's home town. All of them, even the King, were men García Márquez by now considered "friends"; though some Colombians sniped that García Márquez seemed to be a member of the Cuban delegation and indeed he offered himself as bodyguard to Fidel Castro: "I was there because it was rumoured they were going to try to assassinate Fidel. And Cuban security was not going to let Fidel take part in the parade, so I offered to accompany him in the horse-drawn carriage. I told them that here in Colombia, if I went with him, no one would dare to fire. So five of us got in the coach, all squeezed in together and joking about the situation. Just as I was telling Fidel I was sure nothing would happen, the horse reared up."[38] At this summit Carlos Salinas had proposed an "Association of Caribbean States," to include Cuba. Fidel said that since Cuba was always excluded from everything, "by the will of those who run this world," he much appreciated the invitation.[39] And García Márquez was gratified that he was able to show the Cuban leader some results from all his energetic diplomatic activity.

Two weeks later the final round of the Colombian elections was held. The two candidates were Liberal Ernesto Samper and Conservative Andrés Pastrana. It was revealing about Colombia that Pastrana, a former mayor of Bogotá, son of a former president, and a well-known television news anchor, had been thought a certain dead man when he was kidnapped by one of the drug cartels in 1988, while Samper, who had just finished a term as Colombian ambassador in Madrid, had barely survived a hail of bullets at the airport of El Dorado in Bogotá the following year. Samper should have been a natural ally of García Márquez. He was on the left of the Liberal Party, he was the brother of his old friend Daniel Samper (a journalist with *Alternativa* and *El Tiempo*), and García Márquez had invited him and his number two Horacio Serpa to meet Fidel Castro in Cuba in March 1987. But that meeting had not gone well.[40] As a populist Samper was more hostile to Castroism than a more conservative but also pragmatic politician such as Gaviria had proved to be. Samper was also a tough, sceptical, obdurate machine politician, very popular in the provinces despite his Bogotá background, with priorities that were different from those of García Márquez.

In the event Samper won the election but Pastrana cried foul immediately, having been passed a tape recording by the American secret services which seemed to suggest that Samper's campaign manager had received a significant contribution from parties connected directly to the drug-trafficking cartels. This provoked a political and indeed constitutional crisis such as even Colombia had rarely experienced in its history and it would dog Samper's entire four-year term as

President. As a matter of fact it was never certain that he would actually manage to complete his period in office. García Márquez would always deny that he was opposed to the new President at the beginning of his administration but he would never give his unconditional support to Samper and indeed was already building his relationship with younger politicians such as Juan Manuel Santos, another "dauphin" of the *El Tiempo* dynasty, who had been Minister of Foreign Trade during the Gaviria period and had been designated by the outgoing government to greet the distinguished guests when they arrived at the Ibero-American Summit. García Márquez considered Santos a future president of Colombia and began to cultivate him. Santos would become one of Samper's most formidable enemies—and from within his own party.

García Márquez took a team from *Paris Match* to see his new house being built in Cartagena and told them that he had been "waiting thirty years to build the perfect house in the perfect place."[41] Now at last his dream was coming true. Unfortunately a shadow, literally, had been cast over his plans. The Santa Clara convent, scenario of *Of Love and Other Demons*, had been converted into the five-star hotel the novel had mentioned fictionally when it was written in 1993, and all the rooms on the western side of the building directly overlooked García Márquez's new home, still under construction, notably the terrace and the swimming pool.

On 7 August 1994, the day of Samper's inauguration, García Márquez and Mercedes sent the new President a message of congratulations and best wishes, which was reprinted in the press, but it did not take a very suspicious mind to see that this was not an especially warm greeting and that it implicitly anticipated difficult times for the new government. Indeed, as the newspaper headlines revealed, it was a kind of warning: "Mr. President, take good care of your senses."[42] Events were taking on, undoubtedly, a Shakespearean turn. Things had been going so well for García Márquez recently, and they had started so badly for Samper almost from the day of his inauguration, that it is possible that the normally circumspect García Márquez began to overreach himself from the very beginning of Samper's term.

However in September, at last, he finally gained access to the very centre of power on the planet when he and Carlos Fuentes were invited by Fuentes's friend William Styron to meet Bill and Hillary Clinton at Styron's house at Martha's Vineyard. The owners of the *Washington Post* and *New York Times* were also present. García Márquez

was hoping to talk about Cuba—only the week before he had persuaded Fidel to allow dissident writer Norberto Fuentes to leave the
country—but unfortunately for him U.S.–Cuban relations were then
going through one of their worst phases and it is said that Clinton
refused to discuss Cuban affairs.[43] They did discuss the Colombian crisis, however, and García Márquez made some defence of Samper and
urged Clinton not to punish Colombia for Samper's possible misdemeanours. Something the American President and the three writers
were able to agree on, in a highly cordial meeting, was their shared
enthusiasm for the work of William Faulkner. Fuentes and García
Márquez were astonished to hear Clinton recite whole passages from
The Sound and the Fury entirely from memory. As for Cuba, Clinton
would find himself unable to resist the pressure from the Miami
Cubans and a virulently anti-communist Republican Senate and would
be forced to allow ever-harsher sanctions against the island state.
There is little evidence that García Márquez's future relationship with
the most powerful man on the planet brought positive results either for
Cuba or for Colombia, though there is no doubt that in terms of his
own glamour and prestige it was certainly good for García Márquez.

The following month César Gaviria became Secretary General of
the Organization of American States. Ironically enough Gaviria, a
right-of-centre neo-liberal, found it difficult to pursue his own inclina-
tion of liberalizing hemispheric relationships with Cuba in the face of
opposition from a Democrat President in the USA but he persisted in
the endeavour. So now García Márquez had important relationships
with the Secretary General of the Organization of American States,
the Director General of Unesco, and the leaders of the United States,
Mexico, Cuba, France and Spain. Only Colombia was missing. Meanwhile, on the occasion of Gaviria's inauguration as Secretary General,
Carlos Fuentes, always politically acute, said that Bill Clinton should
"lose Florida but gain the world" and that Fidel Castro should "lose
Marx but save the Revolution."[44] Neither man had any intention of
heeding his advice.

On 20 September Alfonso Fuenmayor, the last essential representative—and the very heart—of the Barranquilla Group, died in Barranquilla. (Germán Vargas had died in 1991 and Alejandro Obregón the
following year.) From the time his old colleague and mentor fell sick
García Márquez had kept away, saying that he was "too much of a
chicken" to confront his friend in such a crisis.[45] Perhaps his own illness had made him superstitious about coming too close to death.

Fuenmayor's son Rodrigo and Group members Quique Scopell and Juancho Jinete attended the wake alone, with two bottles of whisky standing between the three of them. This left as García Márquez's most prominent old friend Alvaro Mutis, who was still going strong.

In February García Márquez's son Rodrigo married Adriana Sheinbaum in a quiet ceremony at the Hall of Record in East Los Angeles. The couple's first child, Isabel, would be born on 1 January 1996 and the second, Inés, in 1998. The previous July García Márquez had assured *Paris Match*, "I have excellent relations with both my sons. They are what they wanted to be, and what I wanted them to be."[46] Rodrigo's career as a film-maker in Hollywood would go from strength to strength.

On 5 March García Márquez carried out his first-ever interview for television, with Jack Lang, in Cartagena. He chose Sergio Cabrera, director of the highly praised movie *The Snail's Strategy*, as his cameraman. Lang was in his last days as a minister. François Mitterrand, now a very sick man, had survived to the end of his two seven-year terms; he would die on 8 January 1996. The French Socialist Party was about to be voted out of office and would never be elected again during the rest of Jack Lang's political career. García Márquez's contact with politicians in France began to wane.

Now he formally launched his Foundation for a New Ibero-American Journalism, whose regular "workshops" would be held both in Barranquilla and Cartagena, though Cartagena would gradually assume precedence and become the operational centre. He loved the word "foundation," like the word "workshop," because, no doubt, they reminded him of his grandfather the Colonel, the man he always claimed had "founded" the town of Aracataca. This new foundation was García Márquez's present to his adoptive Colombian city and the strongest symbol of his renewed commitment to the country and its well-being. (However, the foundation's youthful director, Jaime Abello, was from Barranquilla, not Cartagena; the choice was certainly not accidental.) It would provide brief courses for young journalists from all over Latin America, with the incentive of García Márquez himself leading a significant number of them and other world-famous journalists such as Poland's Ryszard Kapuściński and the USA's Jon Lee Anderson also taking part.

By the time *Of Love and Other Demons* was published García Márquez had lost patience completely with the new Colombian President. In an interview with Mexican journalist Susana Cato in Mexico he barely concealed his frustration and contempt for Samper. She asked, "What are Colombians thinking of doing so as not to arrive at the twenty-first century in the same situation they are in today?" García Márquez replied:

> How do you suppose we can think about the twenty-first century when we're still trying to reach the twentieth? Just think that I've spent three years trying to make sure there is not a single false piece of information in a book about a country where we no longer know what is true and what is false. What future can there be for fiction if a presidential candidate does not realize that his sacred advisors are receiving millions of dollars of dirty money for his campaign? Where his accusers are not taken seriously because in the midst of the many truths they told, they also told a lot of lies. Where the President in turn sets himself up as the accuser of his accusers with the argument that they really did receive dirty money but didn't use it in their campaign because they stole it . . . In a country like that, goddammit, we novelists have no option but to look for another job.[47]

It was a return to old arguments from a man protesting that he just wanted to record everyday naturalistic reality but that Colombia's horrors went beyond ordinary notions of reportage. Macondo lived on.

Things went from bad to worse. García Márquez became concerned that his bodyguards, supplied by successive governments ever since the Betancur regime, were now poorly and inconsistently managed. They were changed so often that in the end more than sixty men had an intimate acquaintance with his lifestyle and personal details. This, in Colombia, was a highly dangerous situation in which to find oneself and made him wonder how safe he was in the country. He and Samper had continued to talk, with tension constantly increasing between them—some said García Márquez was even drinking more whisky—until they met, for the last time, over Easter 1996, in the apartment of the ex-Mayor of Cartagena, Jorge Enrique Rizo. García Márquez told Samper, who was about to be judged by Congress, that the constitutional reforms he was considering might be thought to be an advance payment to the congressmen for absolving him. Stung, Samper replied, "It must be those Gaviria supporters filling your head with stories." García Márquez then retorted, "Kindly pay me some respect. Why when I give an opinion that coincides with what you want to hear is it me that is thinking but when it doesn't it's the opposition brainwashing me?" Samper tried to smoothe it over but García Márquez was heard to mutter, "There's no more to be done here." From that moment he began to withdraw from active participation in the nation's affairs and he and Samper would not meet again for many years.[48]

The attacker could also be attacked, however. Cuban exile Norberto Fuentes, who had been a good friend of García Márquez, and whom he had only recently persuaded the authorities to release from the island, had recently written the first of several articles in which he not only showed that he felt no sense of gratitude to García Márquez but violently excoriated him for his role in the Cuban set-up whilst minimizing the extent of his influence and his achievements.[49] As usual García Márquez declined to reply. But in April he did something that astonished all who knew him by giving a talk at the Higher Military School in Bogotá. Amidst some uneasy jokes he told them, ominously, that "President Samper holds the future of this country in his hand." He also said, perhaps not very diplomatically, "We'd all be a lot safer if each one of you carried a book in your rucksack."[50] He spent Easter with the disgraced Carlos Andrés Pérez in Caracas. Did Samper reflect that García Márquez had criticized the Venezuelans for trying to get rid of their President as some Colombians were now trying to get rid of him?

On 2 April, just as excitement was growing about *Of Love and Other Demons*, whose launch was scheduled for the Bogotá Book Fair in May, a previously unknown group based in Cali, which called itself the Movement for the Dignity of Colombia, kidnapped ex-President Gaviria's brother Juan Carlos, an architect. It was not the first time Gaviria's relatives had been targeted. Colombia's problem, the group announced in a communiqué, was "not legal but moral." Although evidently a right-wing organization, they quoted García Márquez himself as saying that Colombia was "in the midst of a moral catastrophe" and asked him to take over as President from Samper because, they said, he was one of the few people in Colombia with "clean hands." They also demanded that César Gaviria should resign as Secretary General of the Organization of American States. Since García Márquez was only a month away from publishing his new book about the problems of contemporary Colombia, since one of the main subjects of that book was Gaviria's hard line in resisting the pleas from the families of kidnap victims, and since Gaviria himself was one of García Márquez's main informants, the ironies of the situation were overwhelming. Enrique Santos Calderón said in *El Tiempo*: "García Márquez has said in an interview with *Cambio 16* that he feels he is living through his own reportage. And indeed one shivers to see ex-President Gaviria in the same situation today as the families of the hostages were at that time, or to see the current 'kidnap tsar,' Alberto Villamizar, doing the same as he did five years ago when he was trying to free his wife Maruja Pachón."[51]

Villamizar and Pachón were the principal protagonists of García Márquez's next book, *News of a Kidnapping*. He had not written a work about contemporary Colombia since the time of *No One Writes to the Colonel*, *In Evil Hour* and *Big Mama's Funeral* in the 1950s. The most political of his historical novels, *The General in His Labyrinth*, had made him deeply unpopular with the Colombian ruling class at precisely the moment when he was considering returning to Colombia for the long term. He was never likely, ironically, to ingratiate himself with Cartagena upper-class society—an upper-class *costeño* was never going to respect one of lower-class origins—even though he had devoted three books in a row to their "Heroic City" and even though, and indeed partly because, he now had the biggest, most glamorous and expensive house in town.

No, Bogotá was his target in Colombia, even though he was always uncomfortable there. That was where the power in the country lay. In some respects his next book was written mainly about—possibly even for—the Bogotá-based ruling class. His old leftist supporters would mainly not find it to their taste, but the Bogotá bourgeoisie would find it impossible to reject. Since the death of Luis Carlos Galán, by no means the last but somehow the culmination and symbol of the wave of murders and kidnappings terrorizing the nation, many Colombians had begun at last to convince themselves that their country was indeed hopeless. Galán had repeatedly refused offers from Pablo Escobar to join his campaign and to fund it. García Márquez had not been an associate of Galán's nor indeed ever an admirer of those, like him, who seemed to feel themselves destined by some spiritual or providential mission. (Only Fidel was entitled to that pretension.) Galán's replacement César Gaviria also seemed too cool, too serious, too clean-cut, too straight for García Márquez; but both men had needed a powerful friend in 1990 and each had something to offer the other; moreover neither was from Bogotá.

In fact the new book was an astonishing achievement. It would have been a remarkable feat for any writer at any time and all the more so, therefore, for a man who was sixty-nine when he completed it. Critics had been saying for years that García Márquez's talents were better suited to dramas set in the distant past and that he—like most novelists—was perhaps not equipped to write about contemporary issues. Besides, most observers felt it was almost impossible for anyone to make sense of the chaos that was Colombia in those years and that to create a coherent plot and construct a compelling narrative about it seemed beyond the powers of anyone. Yet when the book appeared even those who disliked its attitudes and point of view agreed that the great story-teller had done it again and produced a top-class page-turner. Indeed, many said that they had not been able to go to bed without finishing the book and some even confessed to the feeling that if they did not complete the novel in one sitting the hostages who were its central characters might not be able to escape from their predicament: such was the power of the narrative. An obvious first question, then, is whether García Márquez sacrificed complexity for clarity in producing his X-ray of the country.

Certainly the author set out to encapsulate Colombia's labyrinthine complexity within the dramas of seven central characters. The first is the heroine, Maruja Pachón, journalist, director of the film foundation Focine, sister of Gloria Pachón (the widow of Galán and recent ambassador to Unesco). The second, the hero, is Maruja's husband Alberto Villamizar, brother of the second hostage, Beatriz Villamizar, who is Maruja's friend as well as her sister-in-law; Alberto does all he can to get his sister (released first) and his wife out of their nightmare predicament. Francisco Santos (generally known as Pachito) is the third major figure, a top journalist with *El Tiempo* and son of its director Hernando Santos. (Today he is the Vice-President of Colombia.) The fourth is Diana Turbay, a television journalist, daughter of ex-President Julio César Turbay; she is captured with several colleagues who are gradually released one by one; then, tragically, she is killed during the army's ill-fated operation to rescue her. The fifth is Marina Montoya, sister of a key member of the Barco government, the oldest of the hostages, the first to be taken, and the only one, eventually, to be murdered by the drug-traffickers. The sixth central character is President Gaviria, who perhaps ought to be the hero of the narrative and in some ways, given García Márquez's close relationship with him, it is surprising that he is not. And the seventh is Pablo Escobar, who hardly appears but is of course the villain of the piece and the evil genius behind the entire drama, a man for whom García Márquez undoubt-edly has extremely ambivalent feelings, not excluding admiration. Numerous family members and their servants, numerous minor drug-traffickers and their subordinates, and numerous government minis-ters and other public servants (including General Miguel Maza Márquez, head of the secret police and a cousin of the author's), also appear. García Márquez gathers them all together, organizes them and expertly orchestrates the re-telling of the appalling drama.

He states in his prologue that this "autumnal task" was the "most difficult and saddest of my life." It is surprising, then, that a book about something with no happy ending for either Colombia or many of the protagonists (Marina, Diana, an unnamed and quickly forgotten "mulatto" hostage) should have a contrived happy ending due entirely to its focus on certain protagonists and García Márquez's own desire to be a "bringer of good news." It is as if his brilliantly executed work of political journalism had been hijacked—kidnapped?—by another book with all the requirements and preconceptions of the Hollywood thriller and with a soap opera ending. We are persuaded to care des-perately whether Maruja survives, although her chauffeur is killed on the fourth page of the narrative—despatched as clinically by the narra-tor as the real driver was by his killers—and never mentioned again (the same goes for Pachito Santos's chauffeur). From the standpoint of narrative effectiveness, it seems not to matter how many other, inferior people die as long as the stars survive. Indeed, within the conventions of the thriller, the death of some makes a necessary contrast with the much-desired survival of the fittest. This is the cruel, even heartless art of the narrator of this book. He is, surely, a long way from Zavattini; or even the Fellini of *La dolce vita*.

The basic conception is an alternation between odd-number chap-ters dealing with the hostages and their kidnappers and even-number chapters dealing with the families and the government. In essence the drama of the story is, first, the ordeal of the hostages and their efforts to survive, negotiating daily life with their guards; second, the efforts of the families to negotiate both with the kidnappers and with the gov-ernment for the release of the hostages. At a deeper level of course the real struggle is between the "Extraditables" and the government, with the hostages and their families merely the pawns, but García Márquez turns it as far as possible into a "human-interest" story. He concen-trates above all on the four key figures out of the ten hostages: Maruja, Marina, Diana and Pachito. Of the four only Maruja and Pachito survive, being released within hours of each other on 20 May 1991 at the end of chapter 11; Marina and Diana die within two days of one another (23 and 25 January 1991), after many months in captivity, in chapter 6.

Conceived as a love story involving a crisis (a damsel in distress), a heroic struggle (a knight) and a successful homecoming, the book really ends at the conclusion of chapter 11, with Maruja's joyful return to her apartment block, greeted with euphoria by all her friends and neighbours, and then last, and ecstatically, by her husband. García Márquez evidently wanted to show that even in Colombia—perhaps even *for* Colombia—there could still be a happy ending. Escobar's sur- render and death is a mere postscript to this story, as is the return of Maruja's ring by the kidnappers which ends the narrative, and the final statement by Maruja herself that "All this has been something that should be written in a book." But the treatment of Escobar's death is intriguing. In soap operas and thrillers the demise of the villain, espe- cially a villain of Escobar's dimensions, is really the climax of the work. But here one senses that Escobar's death, treated cursorily, disrupts the very conventions it seems tailor-made to bring to a climax.

Like most of García Márquez's previous works, then, *News of a Kid- napping* is not about the lower orders (even as long ago as *In Evil Hour* the sudden appearance of the uprooted poor people in *el pueblo* came as a shock) but that absence matters more obviously and more crucially here. This is a book almost exclusively about upper middle-class peo- ple, including a number of significant right-wingers (the fathers of Diana Turbay and Pachito Santos are people García Márquez had pre- viously opposed and condemned). The columnist Roberto Posada García-Peña ("D'Artagnan") of *El Tiempo*, himself the servant of this ruling class, would launch a violent attack on García Márquez for "paying tribute to the Bogotá bourgeoisie."[52]

Almost as disconcerting, García Márquez entirely excludes the U.S. dimension from his book. It was the drug-traffickers' horror of extra- dition to the USA—Escobar's "better a grave in Colombia than a cell in the United States"—that determined the conflict which is the motor force of the events narrated in the book, and which of course requires some kind of anti-imperialist critique. But, in a work that even criti- cizes the guerrillas—despite his Cuban associations—for "all kinds of terrorist acts,"[53] the U.S. dimension is not dealt with at all, so that the entire causal-explanatory structure of the novel is distorted and unfo- cused. This is certainly not a book whose author would be embarrassed when, soon after publication, he presented it to Bill Clinton and it is not surprising that Clinton eventually appreciated its "human" side; there is no other side to this story. Which poses the hardest question of all: is this book actually written for the Bogotá bourgeoisie and Bill Clinton ("Us" and the U.S.) and not for "us" (the readers) at all? Or, to put it another way, is it written for "us" the readers, just as soap operas are written for us, in order to make us content with our station and to make us believe that the rich and famous are "just human beings . . ." "like us"?

And yet there is always more than one way of looking at a matter. It was of course García Márquez's first Bogotá-based book. It took stock of contemporary Colombia from the time he decided to "leave" Cuba around 1990 (though he never actually left) and he decided to "return" to Colombia (though he never fully "returned"). More than a taking of stock, however, it was also a taking of power. It was in a sense a display of sheer prowess and an implicit answer to all his Colombian critics. He didn't live there? Well, had any other contemporary Colombian been able to draw together all the complexities of the country's recent history and make them coherent and comprehensible, as he had? He was a vain courtier, fawning to power? Well, look what a direct relationship to power could do: here was a "journalist" who, thanks to his prestige, could reach any level of "contacts" and "sources," and those who couldn't reach them could never get the "full story" as he could. His writing was becoming hackneyed, self-repeating, self-quoting and self-indulgent? Well, this was what this elderly man—of nearly seventy—could do.

Snide editorials in *El Tiempo* like those that greeted *The General in His Labyrinth* would have been rather beside the point in the face of a work and a writer who had so patently taken symbolic possession of the country. So this time they were notable by their absence. García Márquez had not shown it but from the time *The General* was published he had waited seven years for his revenge, for the level of satisfaction which this book now gave him. There were no girlish interviews to the press expressing his "insecurity" about the new work, as there had been when *Of Love and Other Demons* was published. "Take that," said the *torero*. Surprising as it may seem, Colombia at last belonged to García Márquez, at the age of sixty-nine, in a way it never had before. *One Hundred Years of Solitude* had made Latin America belong to him, even the world; but not Colombia. *One Hundred Years of Solitude* was "Macondo," sure; but everyone in Bogotá and the other great cities of the interior (Medellín, Cali) knew that Macondo was the Costa and they did not include themselves among its referents. Now they themselves were less confident and complacent; and now García Márquez had finally taken in the whole of Colombia, not just the Costa. The backbiting would continue for ever—in the nature of political and social life—but with far less conviction. He was untouchable now. And he would be able to do almost anything he wanted.

The question can still be repeated: in writing *News of a Kidnapping* for the *cachacos* in part through *cachaco* eyes, did he, in effect, give in to them; did he undermine, at his moment of victory (or even because of the nature of that victory), his entire moral and political trajectory? Perhaps he had become conservative in that tired and depressing way that old men become conservative. Or perhaps he finally recognized "political reality" and in particular "political reality after the fall of the Wall." Or perhaps all he now wanted politically was to see Fidel and the Cuban Revolution symbolically resist the historical labyrinth until the great final labyrinth left them no further options. Or perhaps, still, he was refusing all those encircling realities, all those options and interpretations; perhaps, in the only way he knew how, García Márquez was maintaining his own dream all the way to the end. Perhaps. Certainly this is the question.

Naturally the book went to number one in the best-seller lists as soon as it was published. Although the reviews were overwhelmingly positive there were a few extremely aggressive and even abusive demolitions, especially from the United States, quite different in tone from even the *El Tiempo* reviews of *The General*.[54] But García Márquez had surveyed his options and he'd made his choice. We can be sure he was satisfied.

24

García Márquez at Seventy and Beyond: Memoirs and Melancholy Whores

1996–2005

N OW WHAT WAS he to do? The sixty-nine-year-old writer was still full of energy, still full of plans, still fascinated by politics and committed to "making a difference," as Americans would say. But was he any longer a writer of fiction? *The General in His Labyrinth* was a historical novel, brilliantly fictionalized but still a historical novel. *News of a Kidnapping*, similarly, was a documentary novel, more documentary, indeed, than novel. *The General*, obviously, was about "then," about how Colombia had started, two hundred years before; *News* was about "now," about what Colombia had become. Both had been written with undeniable verve. But did García Márquez have within him another ambitious work of the creative imagination or was that great world-historical wellspring now effectively dry? The world was his oyster, no doubt about it, but it was no longer the world that had made him. Could he respond to this new world, this post-communist, post-utopian, postmodern universe that now lay before the weary planet on the threshold of the twenty-first century?

Truth to tell, hardly anyone had been responding fully to the new era. It was a lot for the world to ask of an old man, though García Márquez was certainly asking it of himself. This was an age of good literature but not an age of great works. In fact, since as long ago as the

Second World War, there had been few writers—indeed few artists in any genre—about whom the public and the critics had been able to agree in the way that they had agreed, and still agreed, about most of the great artists of the modernist period between the 1880s and the 1930s. García Márquez was one of the few names, and *One Hundred Years of Solitude* one of the few titles, on everyone's list of great writers and great works in the second half of the twentieth century. And he had added *Love in the Time of Cholera*, which also regularly appeared in charts of the "top fifty" or "top hundred" novels of the twentieth century. Could he add another? Should he even try?

Certainly he wanted to go on. He had said he had "come out completely empty" after two of his books, *One Hundred Years of Solitude* and *Love in the Time of Cholera*.[1] Somehow he had always found the determination, and eventually the inspiration, to find new topics and new forms and come up with the next project, a book that first he wanted to write, then needed to write, then absolutely had to write. Now was no different; he was still looking. Indeed, he told his interviewers that he wanted to "go back to fiction." As usual he had a project. He had three short novels which together, he thought, might make an interesting book, another book about love; love and women. He told *El País*: "I'm surrounded by women. My friends are mainly women, and Mercedes has had to learn that that's my way of being, that all my relationships with them are just harmless flirtations. Everyone knows by now what I'm like."[2]

He added that he was beginning to lose his memory, on which his entire life and work had been founded. (This had happened to the autobiographically inspired protagonist of *The Autumn of the Patriarch*.) Yet ironically the shredder was the machine most used in his house. Lately, though, he had retrieved the drafts of *Of Love and Other Demons* and given them to Mercedes as a present. He seemed unaware that drafts had lost much of their magic—including financial—in the age of the computer because the computer conceals most genetic traces. Indeed, the evolution from handwriting to typewriting to computer production was one part of the explanation for the fading of the authorial aura in the mind of readers, and perhaps even for a loss of conviction in the mind of authors themselves. García Márquez had resisted this process better than most. And the destruction of most of his preparatory or unfinished works fitted his own strong conviction that it was the job of the artist to produce fully finished works on the classical model, though he would not have wanted to put it that way.

Retirement was a topic that was in the air and the omens were all bad. It was the autumn of all the patriarchs. Samper was obdurately refusing to resign, even though millions wanted him to do so. Carlos Andrés Pérez had been forcibly retired. Carlos Salinas had managed to see his term of office through but had been obliged to leave the country, threatened with jail or worse. No one had been able to force Fidel Castro into retirement but he would shortly be reaching three score and ten; the revolution itself was growing old and who could possibly replace him? Tellingly, García Márquez, instead of attending the launch of his book in Bogotá, went to visit another reluctant retiree, Felipe González, who, beset by allegations and scandals, had been voted out of office in Spain after thirteen years in the presidential Moncloa Palace in Madrid. García Márquez hastened to the Moncloa as soon as he arrived but the President was not at home and the writer found him alone with his bodyguards in the national park of Monfrague, like one more García Márquez character bereft of his power and glory.[3] The last time they had met González had said, as they embraced: "Heavens, man, I think you are the only person in Spain who wants to embrace the President." Now he declared himself relieved to be out of the job and on his way to retirement. He was about to be replaced by right-wing leader José María Aznar.

After an extended stay in Spain García Márquez travelled to Cuba to celebrate Fidel Castro's seventieth birthday with him. It was another autumnal event, not dissimilar to the visit to Felipe González. Fidel was not thinking of retiring but he was in an unusually reflective mood. He, who lived so much in the future and so, in order to get there, had to conquer the present minute by minute, was for once thinking about the past, his own past. He had said he wanted no special celebrations but Gabo had declared that he and Mercedes would travel to Cuba anyway. Prompted by this insistence Fidel, who could not celebrate his birthday officially on the actual day—13 August—due to pressure of work, nevertheless turned up at García Márquez's house that evening and was given his present, a copy of the new dictionary produced by Colombia's linguistic institute, the Instituto Caro y Cuervo. Then, two weeks later, Fidel revealed a surprise of his own: he took Gabo and Mercedes, a few close associates, a journalist and a cameraman to Birán, the tiny town where he was born, "a journey into his past, his memories, the place where he had learned to speak, to shoot, to breed fighting cocks, to fish, to box, where he had been educated and formed, where he had not been since 1969 and where, for the first time in his life, he could stand in front of the graves of his parents and offer them some flowers and a posthumous homage which until that moment he had been unable to carry out." Fidel escorted his guests around the town, went back to the old schoolhouse (he sat in his old desk), remembered his boyhood activities ("I was a cowboy, much more than Reagan because he was just a movie cowboy and I was a real one"), recalled his mother's and father's characters and eccentricities, and then, satisfied, declared: "I have not confused dreams with reality. My memories are free of fantasy."[4] García Márquez, who had been writing up his own memories lately—and in particular his return with his mother almost half a century before to the place where he was born—must have been given much food for thought.

In September, back in Cartagena, García Márquez spent some time at his new house. By now it was an open secret that he did not feel at home there, and not only because he and Mercedes were overlooked by the Hotel Santa Clara: they just didn't feel comfortable; in fact, they just didn't like it. An Argentinian journalist, Rodolfo Braceli, who had interviewed Maruja Pachón about her experiences in 1990–91 and about their representation in *News of a Kidnapping*, used his contact with her to find his way to an irritated but nonetheless forthcoming García Márquez, who was becoming increasingly reflective and philosophical in his interviews these days, like an old soldier out on a limb and at a bit of a loss: interesting and informative, even analytical but no longer focused on the one campaign that excluded all others—the next one—no longer as single-minded as in the past.[5] He mentioned again that he was beginning to forget things, especially phone numbers, even though he has always been a "professional of the memory." His mother now sometimes said to him, "And whose son are you?" Then other days she would get her memory back almost entirely and he would ask her about her recollections of his childhood.[6] "And now they come out more because she's not hiding them, she's forgotten her prejudices."

He told Braceli he had a lot of friends suddenly turning seventy and it had come as a surprise: "I'd never asked them how old they were." His personal feeling towards death, he said, was: "fury." He had never seriously thought about his own death until he was sixty. "I remember it exactly: one night I was reading a book and suddenly I thought, hell, it's going to happen to me, it's inevitable. I'd never had time to think about it. And suddenly, bang, hell, there's no escaping it. And I felt a kind of shiver . . . Sixty years of pure irresponsibility. And I solved it by killing off characters." Death, he said, was just like the light going off. Or being anaesthetized.

Clearly he was in a meditative, autobiographical mood—though the tendency had been evident, at least incipiently, since the end of *Alternativa* and the beginning of his weekly column in *El Espectador* and *El País*. Although he had destroyed most of the written traces of his private life and even of his professional literary activity, he had increasingly been thinking more about two particular aspects of his work. First, the how and the when, the technique and the timing. Clearly he was a master craftsman and increasingly aware that not everyone could tell stories the way that he or Hemingway could tell stories. Hence his script-writing "workshops" in Havana and Mexico City and now his journalism workshops in Madrid and Cartagena. Both were about story-telling: how to break reality down into stories, how to break stories down into their constituent elements, how to narrate them so that each detail leads on naturally to the next, and how to frame them in such a way that the reader or viewer feels unable to stop reading or watching. Second, the what and the why: he was averse, through his sense of "shame and embarrassment," to emoting and introspection. But for some years now he had been taking more interest in identifying the lived raw materials of his own experience, which had been processed in different ways and for different literary and aesthetic purposes in his works down the years. It was, in part, a way of controlling his own story, of making sure that no one else could shape it without accepting most of his own interpretation. He had been controlling his image for thirty years; now he wanted to control his story.

In October García Márquez travelled to Pasadena, California, for the 52nd Assembly of the Inter-American Press Association (SIP), where there were two hundred newspaper owners present, together with Central American Nobel Peace Prize winners Rigoberta Menchú and Oscar Arias, as well as Henry Kissinger. Luis Gabriel Cano of *El Espectador* was elected next president of the organization and it was agreed that the next meeting would be held in Guadalajara. García Márquez, very concerned to front his new journalism foundation, gave a keynote speech declaring that "journalists have become lost in the labyrinth of technology": teamwork had become undervalued and competition for scoops was damaging serious professional work. There were three key areas that needed attention: "Priority to be given to talent and vocation; that investigative journalism should not be considered a specialist activity because all journalism should be investigative; and ethics should not be an occasional matter but should always accompany the journalist as the buzz accompanies the fly."[7] (This last phrase would become the motto of his journalism foundation, the

FNPI. Its key slogan would be: "Not just to be the best but to be known to be the best." Very GGM.) García Márquez's speech, like his new foundation, was mainly concerned with what individual journalists should do to improve their professional and ethical standards, whereas in the 1970s he would have been concerned in the first instance with the ownership of the press. But he was moving now in a different world. Probably only he would have even tried to carry off this double life whereby he debated the problems of the bourgeois press in formally democratic countries whilst loyally supporting the one country in the hemisphere, Cuba, where there had never been a free press and never would be while Castro was in power. And García Márquez's syndicated articles were regularly reproduced in Havana in *Granma* and *Juventud Rebelde*. It was all much more difficult in an era in which he could no longer use the excuse of socialist objectives and the need to build a socialist economy. But if he had still been talking about all that, even supposing he had wanted to, he would not have been able to mix with magnates—one of his biggest donors would be Lorenzo Zambrano, a cement monarch from Monterrey—and would not have been able to persuade them to lay out their money.

Samper had announced before Christmas that he was bringing in a new television law which would set up a commission to decide whether channels were fulfilling their remit to be impartial. Everyone supposed that before long he would be cancelling QAP's licence to broadcast—QAP was one of Samper's most ferocious critics—and García Márquez would therefore be at the mercy of power for the first time since 1981. He went out of his way to announce that he would not be celebrating his seventieth birthday in Colombia. On 6 March he, Mercedes, Rodrigo and Gonzalo and their families would spend the day at a secret location away from the country.[8] Inevitably his seventieth birthday had been registered in all the Hispanic newspapers. Now *One Hundred Years of Solitude*'s thirtieth birthday was also registered. Any excuse to get the name García Márquez in the newspapers; because he sold newspapers just as he sold books. Now it turned out that despite his insistence that he did not want "posthumous homages while I'm still alive," he was intending to emphasize his absence from Colombia even more spectacularly by accepting a multiple anniversary celebration in Washington—of all places—in September, using the fiftieth anniversary of his first published story as the point of reference. Normally such celebrations in Washington would require cooperation, organization and ratification from the honoree's national embassy. But

García Márquez not only had an ongoing relationship with the man in the White House down the road but was also a close friend of the Secretary General of the Organization of American States, an institution in which even the USA, however hegemonic, was only *primus inter pares*. And it was Gaviria, by now disgusted with what he considered to be the embarrassment of Samper's government and infuriated at what he considered to be Samper's frittering of the inheritance that he, Gaviria, had left him, who used his contacts to arrange a series of events in honour of García Márquez which would culminate in a party at his own residence and a dinner at Georgetown University, with García Márquez and Toni Morrison, another Nobel Prize–winning novelist, as twin guests of the university Rector Father Leo Donovan.

The anniversary tendency had been developing down the years in Western culture as the great millennium approached. 1492, 1776, 1789: in the conditions of postmodernity these dates were becoming the temporal equivalents of theme parks. And in this sphere of things, García Márquez was well on his way to becoming a theme park all of his own, a monument without parallel in the literary world since Cervantes, Shakespeare or Tolstoy. He had become aware of it himself very soon after the publication of *One Hundred Years of Solitude*, a book which had changed the world for all those who read it inside Latin America, as well as for many outside. Little by little he became aware that it was he who was the golden goose; the "frenzy of renown" that surrounded him was so furious, so contagious that in the end, for all his plans and stratagems and manoeuvres, it really didn't matter what he did: he had entered the spirit of the age and he had also risen above and beyond the spirit of the age, into immortality, eternity. Marketing could work at the margins to increase it or diminish it but his magic was autonomous. He would be hard pressed to prevent the rest of his life from being one permanent celebration of his life, one long happy anniversary. How could he escape from this labyrinth? Did he any longer want to?

On 11 September he visited Bill Clinton for lunch at the White House. Clinton had already read *News of a Kidnapping* in manuscript but now García Márquez presented him with his personalized leather-bound copy of the English edition, "so it won't hurt so much." (Clinton had sent García Márquez a note when his publisher sent him the manuscript copy of *News*, "Last night I read your book from start to finish." One of García Márquez's publishers wanted to use this priceless puff on the cover when the book was eventually published. García

Márquez responded, "Yes, I'm sure he'd agree; but he'd never write me another note.") The two men discussed the Colombian political situation and, more generally, the problem of drug production in Latin America and drug consumption in the United States.[9]

And still Samper would not budge. A few weeks before the jamboree in Washington García Márquez had met up with the rising politician in the Santos family, Juan Manuel, to discuss the still-deteriorating Colombian situation. Santos had declared that he would be putting himself forward as a Liberal candidate for the next presidential elections in 1997. Whether they were conspiring, separately or together, to bring Samper down, only they could know, but they produced a "peace plan"—Santos, under pressure, would eventually say it was García Márquez's idea ("We have to do something daring, we've got to get everyone talking so as to share out the defeat, because we are all of us losing this war")—which would involve negotiations between all sectors of Colombian society: except the Samper government! Yet Santos denied, when the plan was unveiled in the second week of October, that he was trying to bring the government down. He and García Márquez flew to Spain—García Márquez went straight from Washington to Madrid—to talk to ex-President Felipe González (thereby snubbing the new right-wing President José María Aznar). However, Felipe González effectively killed the initiative by saying that he would only back it if Samper agreed to the negotiations and the United States and other powers gave their support.

In January 1998 Pope John Paul II, now old and sick, made his long-heralded visit to Castro's Cuba, the result of arduous and difficult negotiations. (García Márquez had assured me in 1997 that the Pope was "a great man" whose biography I should read.) It was of course Fidel's way of showing that Cuba, while maintaining its revolutionary principles, was capable of flexibility—he had even allowed Christmas to be reintroduced, on a one-off basis—and might be prepared to negotiate with the powerful of the earth. And who should be sitting at Castro's side during the events involved in the visit but Gabriel García Márquez. Despite his long and extremely successful record of anti-communist activism, the Pope was also known to be anti-capitalist in many respects and firmly against the decadent aspects of the new consumer societies, which made his visit seem a risk worth taking. Unfortunately for Cuba and Castro, the event, which looked as if it might give Cuba huge amounts of favourable publicity, not least in the United States, was blown off the world's television screens by the breaking scandal of Bill Clinton's affair with White House intern Monica Lewinsky. It was a double disaster: disastrous because the Pope's visit never did make the global impact it might have done; and disastrous because Clinton, García Márquez's friend, would be hugely weakened politically by the scandal and the subsequent moves to impeach him. Clinton would have to sit out the rest of his term, almost helpless, in just the way that Samper was doing. The ironies were unmistakable.

García Márquez decided not to return to Colombia for the first round of the elections in May. But he did send a televised message from his house in Mexico City explaining why he was supporting second-time Conservative candidate Andrés Pastrana and committing himself to "*camellar* con Andrés" ("*slog* with Andrés"). García Márquez supporting a Conservative! What would Colonel Márquez have said! The living members of his family viewed his gesture with disapproval and indeed stupefaction. But Pastrana was said to be close to the Miami Cubans and perhaps García Márquez thought that, in this and other ways, he might help with the Cuban situation. In return, García Márquez was supposed to be helping with education, officially Pastrana's principal policy concern after concern number one, a peace process with the guerrillas.

García Márquez was savagely though reluctantly criticized by the Liberal press. "D'Artagnan" wrote a coruscating piece in *El Tiempo* which was evidently intended as an epitaph to the García Márquez who had intervened in Colombian politics up to this moment but was now apparently deceased. How much influence he would really have upon Pastrana's administration is questionable. Neither he nor Andrés were seen "slogging," whether together or separately.[10] Gaviria, ever the clear-eyed pragmatist, tried to get Cuba voted back into the Organization of American States after a thirty-four-year absence but the resolution was vetoed, predictably enough, by the United States. This stymied Pastrana in advance—he was probably immensely relieved—and meant that García Márquez's strategy for Andrés's time in office was dead in the water before he even began, which no doubt explains why he would show such little interest in Colombian affairs over the next four years despite his promises of commitment. Clinton was interested not in improving relations with Cuba but in Pastrana's "peace process," with its promise of an end to the drugs trade, and in the autumn the President of the Inter-American Development Bank, a frequent visitor to García Márquez's house in Mexico City, made a huge loan to Colombia to produce "peace through development."[11] Over the next four years, in the midst of all the local and international dramas, Pastrana would be one of the most honoured and fêted guests in Washington. On 27 October he made the first state visit by a Colombian president in twenty-three years, with García Márquez in attendance, surrounded by an eclectic collection of American "Hispanics" and "Latinos," mostly musicians and actors.[12] Such ceremonial would be Pastrana's reward for his prior agreement to Clinton's "Plan Colombia," an anti-subversion policy reminiscent of Cold War strategies, a topic on which García Márquez made no explicit public statement at this time, though he must have been deeply embarrassed by it.

Having been deprived of his television slot at the end of 1997,[13] García Márquez made an almost immediate decision to purchase *Cambio*, a magazine originally connected to the Spanish magazine *Cambio 16*, so influential during the Spanish transition in the 1980s. *Cambio* ("Change"—which happened to be Andrés Pastrana's only slogan during his election campaign) was in direct competition with Colombia's most influential weekly political magazine, *Semana*; it was something like the competition between *Time* and *Newsweek*. García Márquez heard that Patricia Lara, a good friend and colleague of his brother Eligio, was prepared to sell the magazine and he and María Elvira Samper, ex-director of QAP, Mauricio Vargas, Germán Vargas's son (an ex-member of Gaviria's government and a known critic of Samper), Roberto Pombo, a journalist on *Semana*, and others decided to make a bid (one which included Mercedes in her own right). By Christmas the deal was done—the new company was called Abrenuncio S.A. after the sceptical enlightened doctor in *Of Love and Other Demons*—and by late January García Márquez was beginning to write long headline articles—mainly about big-name personalities like himself (Chávez, Clinton, Wesley Clark, Javier Solana)—in order to boost sales. Larry Rohter of the *New York Times* talked to him the following year and recorded that "the night in late January 1999 that *Cambio* held a party to celebrate its rebirth, he stayed at the event until midnight, greeting two thousand invited guests. He then returned to the office, working through the night to write a long article about Venezuela's new President, Hugo Chávez, which he finished as the sun was rising, just ahead of deadline. 'It's been forty years since I've done that,' he said, delight in his voice. 'It was wonderful.' "[14]

The Chávez issue of the magazine was particularly revealing. Colonel Hugo Chávez was the soldier who had tried to overthrow

García Márquez's friend Carlos Andrés Pérez. But he was also the man who, after coming to power in Venezuela, would come to the rescue of Castro's Cuba in the new millennium by holding Fidel's head above water through the sale of reliable cheap oil. Moreover he was a "Bolivarian" who argued for the independence and unity of Latin America and he was prepared to put Venezuela's money where his mouth was. Since García Márquez was also working behind the scenes to help Cuba and unify Latin America, Chávez might have been expected to receive his full, albeit discreet support. But García Márquez was never more than lukewarm about Chávez, perhaps because he was compromised by his prior relationship with Pastrana and Clinton—whereas Chávez's anti-Americanism was both permanent and virulent. García Márquez had met up with Chávez in Havana in January 1999 and had flown to Venezuela with him on his way back to Mexico. Afterwards he wrote a long article which was syndicated all over the world—making a lot of money for *Cambio*—and became very influential. It ended:

> Our plane landed in Caracas at about three a.m. I looked out of the window at that unforgettable city, a sea of light. The President took his leave with a Caribbean embrace. As I watched him walk away, surrounded by his guards with all their military decorations, I had the odd feeling that I had travelled and talked with two quite separate men. One was a man to whom obstinate good fortune had given the opportunity to save his country; the other was an illusionist who could well go down in history as yet another despot.[15]

In fact García Márquez had been in Cuba with Castro—and the now equally ubiquitous José Saramago, a Nobel Prize winner who had remained a communist and an outspoken revolutionary—celebrating the fortieth anniversary of the Cuban Revolution. Fidel, wearing glasses, read out a speech saying that the world, in the era of multinational capitalism (for the magnates) and consumer capitalism (for their customers) was now "a gigantic casino" and the next forty years would be decisive and could go either way, depending on whether people realized that the only hope for the planet to survive was to end the capitalist system.[16] Who knows what García Márquez thought of this, but his eyes looked those of a sick man, distant and distracted. Nevertheless he was putting in a huge effort to try to increase *Cambio*'s disappointing sales. An article even more widely distributed than the one on

Chávez was "Why My Friend Bill Had to Lie," which dismayed feminists around the world since instead of concentrating on the malign aspects of the Republican conspiracy to impeach Clinton, it cast him as just a typical guy pursuing sexual adventures—as all typical guys evidently did—and trying to conceal them from his wife and everyone else.

In Havana García Márquez had listened to Fidel calling for an end to capitalism, which was, he had said, entering the final stages of its devastation of the planet. Yet now, back in Europe in the last year of the twentieth century to meet yet another clutch of commitments and interview celebrities for his *Cambio* pieces, García Márquez became involved in a new organization, a strange *mélange* of intellectuals and magnates, which would be known as Foro Iberoamérica, whose ostensible purpose was to think about world development problems "outside of the box." A kind of preliminary meeting was organized by Unesco, the Inter-American Development Bank and the new Spanish government in Madrid. It was in part a continuation of the García Márquez–Saramago show. In his brief contribution García Márquez declared that Latin Americans had lived an inauthentic destiny: "We ended up as a laboratory of failed illusions. Our main virtue is creativity, and yet we have not done much more than live off reheated doctrines and alien wars, heirs of a hapless Christopher Columbus who found us by chance when he was looking for the Indies." He again mentioned Bolívar as a symbol of failure and repeated what he had said in his Nobel speech: "Let us get on quietly with our Middle Ages." Later he read out one of his new stories, "I'll See You in August," a tale about adultery surely quite inappropriate for such a forum.[17] Saramago, playing the role García Márquez used to play, proposed that everyone in the world "should become mulattos" and then there would be no need to argue about culture.

Weeks later García Márquez would find himself back in Bogotá attending the honorary enrolment of Carlos Fuentes and *El País*'s owner Jesús de Polanco in Colombia's Caro y Cuervo Institute of Philology. He sat on the platform looking older than he had ever looked before, but said nothing. And then, just as in 1992, he found that the Bogotá altitude had triggered a level of tiredness he had not been aware of in Europe. And he collapsed. He disappeared from the public radar for some weeks, while Mercedes denied rumours of cancer and asked the press to be "patient" for a while. At first it was reported that he had some bizarre malady called "general exhaustion syndrome." But everyone feared the worst. In the event the diagnosis was lymphoma, or cancer of the immune system.

Once again he had fallen ill in Bogotá and once again Bogotá had diagnosed his illness. This time however, given the gravity of the diagnosis, he went to Los Angeles, where his son Rodrigo lived, for a second opinion. Lymphoma it was. The family resolved that the treatment should take place in Los Angeles and García Márquez rented, first an apartment, then a bungalow in the hospital grounds. New treatments for lymphoma were constantly emerging and the prospects were quite different from the time when Alvaro Cepeda had to confront a similar challenge in New York. García Márquez and Mercedes called on Cepeda's daughter Patricia, a translator and interpreter who had already helped them on previous visits to the United States, most notably for the meetings with Bill Clinton. Patricia was married to John O'Leary, a Clinton associate and fellow lawyer who was a former ambassador to Chile. Each month García Márquez, following his treatments and subsequent tests, would, as he later said to me, "go off to see the doctor to find out whether I was going to live or die." But each month the reports were good and by the autumn he was back in Mexico City and making monthly visits to Los Angeles for check-ups.

In late November 1999 I flew to Mexico City to visit García Márquez. He was thinner than I had ever seen him and very short of hair. But he was full of vigour. I reflected again that throughout his life he had said that he feared death and yet he had shown himself one of the great fighters when the chips were really down. The meeting was emotionally charged because he knew that I had fallen sick with lymphoma four years before and survived.[18] He had done nothing for months, he told me, but now he was looking again at his notes for his memoirs, and he read out to me the narrative of his birth. Mercedes exuded calm and determination but I could see that the effort was straining even her resources. Still, she was made for this situation and was clearly surrounding her husband with normality, including the normality of not making a fuss. Gonzalo and his children visited, and Grandfather behaved just as he always did.

García Márquez had recently told *The New Yorker*'s Jon Lee Anderson that "Plan Colombia," agreed between Clinton and Pastrana, "could not work" and that the USA seemed to be moving back to an "imperial model."[19] In September he had threatened to sue the news agency EFE for 10 million dollars for reporting that he had "helped to negotiate U.S. military aid to Colombia."[20] Presumably this was his way of signalling his public separation from Pastrana and Clinton and their fateful "Plan."[21] Now he said to me: "As for Colombia, I think I've finally got used to it. I think you just have to accept it. Things are getting perceptibly better just at this moment, even the paramilitaries have realized that this can't go on. But the country will always be the same. There has always been civil war, there have always been guerrillas, and there always will be. It's a way of life there. Take Sucre. Guerrillas actually live in *houses* there, yet everyone knows they're guerrillas. Colombians come and visit me here or in Bogotá and they say, 'I'm with the FARC, how about a coffee?' It's normal." I took this to mean that he was finally renouncing the effort to change this incorrigible country through direct political activity, not to mention an implicit recognition that to place his own reputation in the hands of political conservatives—in this case Pastrana and the American Republicans who had taken Clinton as their political prisoner—had been a step too far, as most of his family and many of his friends could have told him. Ironically the illness now provided a cover for a discreet withdrawal from these unhappy alliances. Time to turn back to his memoirs, perhaps.

He wrote occasional articles and kept in contact with *Cambio* and the Cartagena journalism foundation but mainly he stayed in Mexico City, kept out of the limelight and concentrated on his recovery and his visits to Los Angeles, where he and Mercedes were able to spend more time with Rodrigo and his family. Gabo and Mercedes also developed a close relationship with *Cambio* journalist and investor Roberto Pombo, who had married into the *El Tiempo* dynasty and was currently posted in Mexico City. He would be like a third son to Gabo and Mercedes over the coming decade. García Márquez would write increasingly autobiographical articles for the magazine—as well as an interview with Shakira—and would have a "Gabo Replies" section where he would compose an article inspired by readers' questions. These articles would then be repeatedly advertised in the magazine and offered on a permanent basis to those who browsed the elecronic version on the Internet.

But of course his main activity would be the memoirs. He had often joked that by the time people got round to writing their memoirs they were usually too old to remember anything; but he had not mentioned that some people died before they even started the job. Completing the memoirs, now known as *Living to Tell It* (*Vivir para contarlo*), became his principal objective. Perhaps he remembered Bolívar's dilemma near the end of *The General in His Labyrinth*: "He was shaken by the overwhelming revelation that the headlong race between his misfortunes and his dreams was at that moment reaching the finish line. The rest was darkness. 'Damn it,' he sighed. 'How will I ever get out of this labyrinth!' "

He tried to keep out of politics but occasionally *Cambio* dragged him back in. It was edging perceptibly to the right in his absence, but so, the young journalists might have retorted, was he. Chávez was going from strength to strength as a populist leader of the Third World but García Márquez told me, "It's impossible to talk to him." Evidently Castro did not agree, since he and Chávez met and talked frequently. When I put this to him, García Márquez said, "Fidel's trying to control his excesses." Chávez would say in late 2002 that García Márquez had never made any contact with him since their meeting early in 1999 and that he much regretted this. Since Chávez was not so very different from Omar Torrijos of Panama—except that Chávez was much more powerful because he had oil and was democratically elected—it seems likely that beyond personal questions (including his friendships with Carlos Andrés Pérez and Teodoro Petkoff) García Márquez considered him too much of a loose cannon for the new era and for the behind-the-scenes diplomacy that he himself had been engaged in for the last decade.

One example of this was the news in November 2000 that the Mexican industrialist Lorenzo Zambrano of Monterrey, the king of Mexican cement (CEMEX), was to donate $100,000 for prizes to be awarded to winners of competitions organized by the Foundation for a New Ibero-American Journalism in Cartagena.[22] Weeks later it was announced that media giant Televisa was to work with *Cambio* to produce a Mexican edition directed by Roberto Pombo. This was García Márquez's world now. The inauguration of Mexico's new right-wing President Vicente Fox coincided with a meeting of the Foro Iberoamérica, which this time involved not only García Márquez and Carlos Fuentes again, as resident intellectuals, but also Felipe González, ex-President of Spain; Jesús de Polanco, the owner of *El País*; international banker Ana Botín; Carlos Slim, the richest man in Mexico and destined to be the richest man in the world, for a while, by mid-2007, another personal friend of García Márquez; and Julio Mario Santo Domingo, the richest man in Colombia, yet another friend of García Márquez, now the owner of *El Espectador* and another generous donor to the Cartagena foundation. Whether García Márquez, as the president of an independent journalism foundation, should really have been hobnobbing with monopoly capitalists who happened to own great newspapers and television stations as part of their other holdings was not clear and has certainly never been publicly addressed by him. He now normally refused all comment to the press but remarked that he'd had no idea what he or anyone else was doing at the forum until he heard Carlos Fuentes's excellent speech explaining the importance of an interface between the world of business and the world of ideas! As for Mexico, he hadn't the faintest notion what was going on. He further entertained journalists by declaring that he was now just "the husband of Mercedes," which some took as recognition of his new dependence on her and his gratitude for the way she had seen him through his recent and ongoing trials.[23] He had recovered most of his hair and fifteen of the twenty kilos he had lost, though observers whispered that he had not recovered his sharp wits and full powers of expression. Perhaps the chemotherapy had accelerated the process of memory loss which he himself had been complaining about for some years.

He was well out of Colombia. His old friend Guillermo Angulo had been kidnapped by the FARC on the way to his country house outside Bogotá. Angulo, a man in his seventies, would be released months later; he told me he was sure García Márquez had something to do with his release, which was an exceptional event: most FARC hostages remained in captivity for years, like presidential candidate Ingrid Betancourt.[24] By the end of 2000 it was widely agreed that Andrés Pastrana was perhaps the weakest Colombian President of the post-1948 era. When an open letter was sent to Pastrana and George W. Bush in February 2001 by luminaries such as Eric Hobsbawm, Ernesto Sábato and Enrique Santos Calderón, requesting that any joint Colombian–U.S. activity in Colombia should involve the United Nations and the European Community, the name of García Márquez was attached.[25] Once again he was signalling his opposition to "Plan Colombia": this meant burning his boats not only with Pastrana but also with Gaviria, who supported it.

In March Comandante Marcos led his unarmed Zapatista guerrillas into Mexico City as he had long been promising. García Márquez, with the help of Roberto Pombo, briefly escaped from retirement to carry out an interview for *Cambio*. The Zapatistas, who had attracted left-wing sympathy and support from all over the world, including many political pilgrimages by well-known intellectual and artistic figures down to Chiapas, were not the kind of organization García Márquez any longer spent time supporting. Indeed his silence about the sufferings of ordinary people, not least the displaced peasants of Colombia, caught in a nightmare world between the guerrillas, the paramilitaries, the landowners, the police and the army, is something that cannot fail to disconcert anyone observing his activities over the course of the years after 1980. But this was not a man who had ever made crowd-pleasing political statements for the sake of his own conscience: he had always been a deeply political and practical person who did what he thought was necessary and not—contrary to the assertions of his critics—what he thought would make him popular.

While García Márquez had been fighting his cancer his youngest brother Eligio had been fighting his own battles. Like Gabito he was struggling to finish a book, *Tras las claves de Melquíades: historia de "Cien años de soledad"* (*Following Melquíades's Clues: The Story of "One Hundred Years of Solitude"*), while suffering from a terminal brain tumour. He was unable to finish the book as he would have wanted but he and his family and friends decided that it should appear before he died. By the time it was published in May Eligio was in a wheelchair and scarcely able to speak. He was the last of the Buendías and would die shortly after deciphering the family's ancestral document, as had been uncannily predicted in *One Hundred Years of Solitude*. (Cuqui had been the first of the brothers and sisters to die, in October 1998.) Gabito did not find the strength to travel to Eligio's funeral at the end of June.

On 11 September the twin towers of the World Trade Center of New York were brought down by civil airplanes piloted by Al Qaeda jihadists and world politics changed dramatically, accelerating on the path to war that George W. Bush had already seemed determined upon, though this was not quite the script that Bush had envisaged. García Márquez had recently been to Cuba to see Fidel Castro, who was rumoured to be in declining health. Two weeks after the horrors in New York, and three weeks after the release of Guillermo Angulo, on 24 September 2001, Consuelo Araujonoguera, Colombian ex-Minister of Culture and wife of the Procurator General of the Republic, was kidnapped by FARC guerrillas near Valledupar; almost a week later, on 30 September, she was found dead, apparently caught in crossfire. Known to the whole of the country as "La Cacica" ("the chief"), she was the principal promoter of Valledupar and its *vallenato* festival, a friend of García Márquez, Alvaro Cepeda, Rafael Escalona (she was also his biographer), Daniel Samper (until they fell out over a television biography he wrote), and Alfonso López Michelsen. Bill Clinton had met her and would write about her in his memoirs. She was one of the last people anyone would have imagined being killed by those who claimed to be the defenders of the Colombian people and their culture.

By January 2002 it was clear that García Márquez was going to make it. He was gradually returning to public life. Those who met him noticed that he was more hesitant, sometimes confused, lacking in memory, but looking well. For a man of his age—he would soon be seventy-five—and continuing commitments—he was still contributing to both *Cambio* and his journalism foundation—it was a remarkable recovery which testified again to his extraordinary vitality. That said, the delay in bringing out the memoirs suggested that he was not working as effectively as in the past. He had sent a first version to Mutis at the end of July 2001 but something had delayed his progress and he eventually called on his son Gonzalo and Colombian writer William Ospina to check facts and help fill the gaps in his failing memory. He was putting the finishing touches to the book when his mother, Luisa Santiaga Márquez Iguarán, died in Cartagena at the age of ninety-six. Her husband and two of her sons had died before her. Once again Gabito failed to make the funeral.[26]

On 7 August Alvaro Uribe Vélez, a renegade Liberal, was inaugurated as President of Colombia on an anti-guerrilla ticket. FARC guerrillas—the FARC were alleged to have killed his father—fired rockets at him during his inauguration. Once again Horacio Serpa, the Liberal candidate and loyal servant of Ernesto Samper, had lost out. The country was glad to see the back of Pastrana but in Uribe it seemed to be taking a big risk. He was a landowner from Antioquia with rumoured links to paramilitary forces. Nevertheless he would govern with extraordinary, almost frenetic energy and with a style at once populist and authoritarian which would keep his ratings almost eerily high. His election left Colombia, in the era of Chávez, Lula of Brazil, Morales of Bolivia, Lagos and Bachelet of Chile, and the Kirchners of Argentina, as the country with the only significant right-wing government in South America—though Colombians were well used to being out of step. Uribe would be a close ally and supporter of George W. Bush.

The time approached at last for the publication of the memoirs, which covered the period from García Márquez's birth to 1955. At the last moment *"Vivir para contarlo"* (living to tell "it," masculine, living to tell the act of living itself) changed to *"Vivir para contarla"* (living to tell "it," feminine, living to tell "la vida," life, the contemplation of life).

The English translation, as usual, added an extra, romanticized dimension: "*Living to Tell the Tale*," that is, surviving great adventures and then relating them—but not planning to do so in advance and not doing so as a way of life.[27] Of course the English version had another point: these memoirs had been delayed by a drama, the drama of García Márquez's fight against death, against cancer, and his heroic victory. Everyone, above all his readers, was aware of this.

He had been talking about his memoirs ever since the publication of his great novel about Macondo. That should have given his readers the clue to his deepest motivation as a writer. Going back was all he ever wanted, writing about himself was all he ever wanted; Narcissus wanted to return to his own original face but even his face, lost in time, lost in all the times, was constantly changing, never the same, so even if he had found that original—eternal, oracular—face he would have seen it differently each time it appeared to him. But it was what he wanted. In 1967 people hearing him talk about his memoirs must have thought: this man hasn't lived enough. But Narcissus has always lived long enough to want to see if his face is still the same. Yet if he never had his own mother tell him his face was beautiful, then he was doomed always to look for her, find her, go back with her. And so the book would start with Luisa Santiaga's search for her lost son in Barranquilla in 1950, bringing poignant memories of another journey she had made some sixteen years before:

> My mother asked me to go with her to sell the house. She had come that morning from the distant town where the family lived, and she had no idea how to find me . . . She arrived at twelve sharp. With her light step she made her way among the tables of books on display, stopped in front of me, looking into my eyes with the mischievous smile of her better days, and before I could react she said:
> "I'm your mother."

Thus at the age of seventy-five, Gabriel García Márquez begins the story of his life with a scene in which, once again, his mother is afraid that he will not know who she is and has to introduce herself to him. That re-encounter, he would claim—it is the central theme of the memoirs—took place on "the day I was really born, the day I became a writer."[28] It was the day he had got his mother back. And they had gone back home together. Back to the beginning.

On the matter of his memoirs he had started to say a surprising thing to journalists as early as 1981: "García Márquez [has been] talking about his memoirs, which he hopes to write soon and which will really be 'False Memoirs' because they won't tell what his life actually was, nor what it might have been, but what he himself thinks his life was."[29] Twenty-one years later he would be saying exactly the same thing. What on earth did it mean? Well, now he had an epigraph to clarify it: "Life is not what one lived but what one remembers and how one remembers it in order to recount it."

Living to Tell the Tale turned out to be his longest book. Like all his others it falls neatly—less neatly than usual—into two halves but the structural proof that the exercise had caused him serious problems is that each of the two halves ends with the least interesting—to him and also, unfortunately, to us—section related to the land of the *cachacos*: firstly the Zipaquirá section, 1943–6, and secondly Bogotá and *El Espectador*, 1954–5.

Though much of the writing is extraordinary it must be admitted that it is writing as wish-fulfilment: it conceals all the hurt (which is extraordinary given the way it begins). There are occasional digs at his father simply because of the character that he "is," and not because Gabito himself feels any hostility or has any oedipal feelings or a world-view still shaped by the Márquez Iguarán side of the family. In general the book continues the sense of reconciliation—of making peace—initiated by *Love in the Time of Cholera*. Its author has been careful to send small—usually one-paragraph, sometimes one-line—compliments to all his friends and their wives or widows. There are no real intimacies or confessions. The book contains his public life and his "false," invented life, but it does not contain much of his "private" life and very little indeed of his "secret" life.

The central theme is the narrator becoming a writer through both a growing and irresistible vocation and an unusual and privileged experience of life. (And not, for example, the narrator becoming a writer who at the same time is developing a sophisticated and serious political consciousness which will inform and shape what he actually writes.) The irony, of which he seems unaware (by the time he finishes this book he has lost some of the acute awareness he used to have), is that the book—and his life—are formed by and dominated by the period *before* he became aware of the vocation and indeed, strictly speaking, by the period before he himself could even read and write. García Márquez is perhaps uncomfortable with the autobiographical genre itself. As a writer he is an extrovert, both declarative and a fabulist. But when relating his own life he has more of a psychic need to conceal than to exhibit. Moreover in a memoir it can be disastrous to claim to know what you don't know—from which much of the humour of *One Hundred Years of Solitude* itself, for example, derives—or to assert facts which are contradictory. Similarly the trademarks of the García Márquez style—hyperbole, antithesis, sententiousness, displacement—are far more problematical in an autobiographical work. When all is said and done, we are left with the irony of a García Márquez who exposed himself utterly in the barely penetrable *The Autumn of the Patriarch* and now conceals himself absolutely in the apparently transparent *Living to Tell the Tale*!

Of course it is obvious, on even the briefest of considerations, that García Márquez became obsessed by his memoirs not so much because of his alleged vanity but because it was the best way of combating his fame and his anguish by getting out his own story, his own version of his life and character. Despite the promise of the early pages, this was not a confessional work.

On 8 October 2002 *Vivir para contarla* was published in Mexico City, with extraordinary fanfare and truly staggering advance sales. The magician was back again. Back, indeed, this time, from the dead.

GARCÍA MÁRQUEZ WAS a great survivor by any definition. He had not only withstood the cancer treatments physically and mentally, he had completed the first volume of his memoirs—he really had lived to tell the tale—and had left an image of himself with which he personally was content and which, he knew, would also survive. The baby on the cover holding the biscuit was now a man of seventy-five and what a life he had led. It had taken him all those years to journey through the labyrinth we all of us have to travel, made up in part of the world and in part of our perception of it. García Márquez, looking back, had decided that he was born to invent stories and that he had lived more than anything else to tell the tale of existence as he himself had experienced it. The anxious child he had chosen to leave on that cover eternally looking for his mother had waited all those years to tell the world the story of how in reality he had found her again, got her back for ever, and how thereafter, born again as a writer, he had set out on the road that would make him a visionary who would enchant the world. It was tragically appropriate that it was at the very moment he started the final push to finish the work that she herself had lost her memory, and that at the moment he was putting the final touches to a book which was so much hers as well as his she should have passed on from the life he was there recording.

That first part of the memoirs, in which—as a matter of fact—his mother found *him* (not the other way round) and told him who she was and took him back to the house where he was born, the house she had left while he was growing from baby to boy, is, truly, an anthology piece, a great work of autobiographical creation by any measure, a story told by a great classical writer of modern literature. Really, it was that story above all that he had wanted to tell; all the others faded when held against the vivid colours of that journey and the passions that inspired its telling. The rest of the book was a pleasure to read, García Márquez talking directly, at last, about his remarkable life and times, but nothing in its nearly six hundred pages would equal the radiant triumph of the first fifty. Of course of all his books it was the one most certain to disappoint the expectations of its readers. But once they had adjusted to the realization that autobiographies—even the autobiographies of literary wizards—are rarely as magical as novels, most of them found it satisfying and agreeable and a book they would read again, even if the experience of reading it was like the experience of a warm, comforting bath which eased away all the hard knocks and bruises of life while growing colder, all too soon.

Within three weeks the book had sold an astonishing 1 million copies in Latin America alone. None of his books had ever sold faster. On 4 November García Márquez took a copy to President Fox in the palace of Los Pinos in Mexico City. Chávez of Venezuela had got hold of one and sent congratulations, waving it at the cameras during his weekly television broadcast and urging all Venezuelans to read it. On the 18th the King and Queen of Spain would land in Mexico City on an official visit; naturally they would make time for García Márquez. Presumably he gave them a copy.

In December he travelled once more to the Havana Film Festival and saw Fidel and Birri and his other friends. When he got back from the festival in January he gave what would prove to be his last personal one-to-one interview, not a sit-down affair but a kind of ramshackle amble through his Mexico City home and out across the garden and into the study with an American photographer, Caleb Bach. His secretary Mónica Alonso Garay was close at hand. She said her boss had a prodigious memory but it was notable that she frequently jumped in to answer questions on his behalf. He talked to Bach about the photograph of himself as a baby he had chosen for the cover of *Living to Tell the Tale*. He was pleased with the result. He said he had a twenty-seven-year-old parrot called Carlitos. And he revealed—having forgotten that he swore he would never do so—what his psychiatrist friend (Luis Feduchi) had told him in Barcelona in the 1970s that had made him give up smoking the same day he heard it: it would cause memory loss in later life . . .[30]

In March 2003 the United States and Great Britain invaded Saddam Hussein's Iraq without United Nations approval on the pretext that Iraq had weapons of mass destruction (as the invaders themselves did, of course, though it turned out that Iraq did not) and that it was harbouring Al Qaeda militants (which it was not; but after the invasion it would). Some said that 9/11 had changed the world for ever; others said that the U.S. response to 9/11, of which the Iraq invasion was merely the most far-reaching act, had changed the world much more, only not in the way that the invaders intended but in the way that the perpetrators of 9/11 had intended. Shock and awe for the Iraqis; stupefaction and disbelief for the rest of the world, not least García Márquez. The BBC Latin American website carried an article on the challenges of covering the war entitled "Living Not to Tell the Tale." The United States opened a new prison camp at Cuba's Guantánamo Bay, a zone it had occupied, like the Panama Canal, since the start of the twentieth century; there hundreds of alleged Al Qaeda militants arrested in Afghanistan and Pakistan were imprisoned for years and possibly tortured without any form of trial, on that island where, the United States had always insisted, Castro's government had jails where his opponents were imprisoned for years and possibly tortured without any form of trial. There were no human rights on the island of Cuba, they said. Newspeak. It transpired that the Bush government now had an official invasion plan for Cuba. Just as soon as they had dealt with North Korea, Iraq and Iran, the "Axis of Evil . . ."

On 19 July *El País* carried a photo of the old man in Mexico City with the caption: "García Márquez does not allow himself to be seen. It is increasingly rare to see García Márquez at any public event."[31] On the occasions when he did appear, he refused all comment to the press. Evidently what *El País* really meant to say was: "Is there something wrong with García Márquez? Why is he hiding himself away? Is he ill? Why won't he speak? Is he losing his memory? Is he finished?"

Meanwhile the memoir was published in English and French. Same cover. Same family photographs in the surrounding publicity. Not quite the success of the Spanish-speaking world but a very good reception in the English-speaking world, though much less so in France. To coincide with its publication, the New York PEN Club organized a special homage to García Márquez on 5 November 2003. Given PEN's traditions of protecting free speech and the human rights of authors, this was a surprising decision in view of the onslaught, not least from Americans, against García Márquez over his Cuba links earlier in the year. One of the main organizers was Rose Styron, who was not only a friend of ex-President Clinton—who made a video presentation—but had also been at the fabled "Camelot" dinner for artists and intellectuals put on by President Kennedy and Jackie in the early 1960s.[32] Many of New York's top glitterati, literati and illuminati were present and must have been extremely disappointed by García Márquez's failure to turn up even at this event. He was not entirely well, that was true; but he was also extremely disillusioned by developments in U.S. society and by U.S. policy both in Colombia and in the Middle East during George W. Bush's presidency. He sent a party-pooping message to the act of homage which was not only undiplomatic—and ungrateful—but also one of the most pessimistic declarations ever made by this relentlessly upbeat personality. It was not a time, he said, for celebrations. Despite this, in January 2004 *One Hundred Years of Solitude* became an "Oprah Book" recommended by Oprah Winfrey's mass-viewing television talk show in the United States. It leaped from number 3,116 in the sales list to number one.[33]

García Márquez felt unable to ignore big long-term commitments he had accepted in Mexico and attended most of them but still without any press declarations. He would just turn up like some benign old white-haired wizard and sit on the designated platform or hand over the appropriate prize. He still took part in such *Cambio* meetings as were held in Mexico, and Roberto Pombo looked after him there just as Carmen Balcells looked after him in Spain and Patricia Cepeda in the United States.

He had been hoping to be more energetic and adventurous. He and Mercedes had recently changed apartments in Paris. They had given up the small place in Rue Stanislas and bought a bigger one on the Rue du Bac, one of Paris's most sought-after streets—right under Tachia's. So now he owned the apartment beneath her in a curious kind of fidelity to an ill-starred love which had become a difficult and uncomfortable kind of friendship. He would have very few opportunities to visit the new apartment but his son Gonzalo and family set up there for a while when they moved from Mexico to Paris in 2003. (Gonzalo wanted to take up painting again.)

He had set aside the memoirs but he had been planning a novel entitled *Memoria de mis putas tristes* ("Memoir of My Sad Whores," though eventually translated into English as *Memories of My Melancholy Whores*) for many years, at least a quarter of a century. When I saw him in Havana in 1997 it was the book he was currently thinking about and when we talked a year later it was clear that the book was well advanced. It is most likely that a first version was completed long before he published *Living to Tell the Tale* and that few significant changes were made between autumn 2002 and autumn 2004 when it finally appeared. Conceived originally as a long short story, it is hardly more than a novella but was publicized and sold as a novel.

In October, as the new work was being anticipated all around Latin America, he returned to Colombia and press photos showed him walking the streets of Cartagena, looking lost and confused, with Mercedes, his brother Jaime, now working for the journalism foundation, Jaime's wife Margarita, and Jaime Abello, the long-term director of the foundation. Many people had predicted García Márquez would never return to Colombia again. They were confounded. And yet the old magician did not look entirely himself.

When the new novel finally appeared most of its readers were totally disconcerted. Simply told, it is the story of a man about to celebrate his ninetieth birthday who decides to have a night of passionate sex with an adolescent virgin and pays the madam of a brothel he used to frequent to arrange it for him. Although he does not take the girl's virginity he becomes obsessed with her, gradually falls in love with her, and decides to leave her all his property. The man presents himself as utterly mediocre, a bachelor newspaperman who has never done anything of interest in his entire life until, at the age of ninety, he finds love for the first time. Strikingly, it is García Márquez's only novel set in Barranquilla, though the city is not named.

It seems likely that instead of an image, the usual inspiration for García Márquez's novels, this one began with its striking title, which stuck in García Márquez's consciousness and waited down the years for the chance to become a novel. Yet the title is a problem. First, obviously, it is shocking (and presumably meant to be). "*Puta*," "whore," though more literary than "*prostituta*," "prostitute," is also less neutral and more derogatory. Some television and radio stations in Colombia refused to allow the word *puta* to be uttered by their presenters. Secondly, the title bears no precise relation to the content of the book: the novel itself insists that what we have here is a "love story" and the only "whore" with whom the narrator has any sexual relation is the fourteen-year-old girl with whom he becomes obsessed and who appears never to have had a previous sexual relationship of any kind, paid or unpaid. Nor, as far as can be divined, is she "melancholy." (Nor, come to that, is she ever awake.) The title is best understood as a line written embodying the distinctive poetic conceit, known as hyperbaton (the separation for effect of words that normally go together), of the influential Spanish Golden Age bard Luis de Góngora (1561–1627). If the line were by him the informed reader would deconstruct it as "My Sad Memories of Whores." Or even: "I, Sad, Remember Whores." Not that this resolves the problem of the plural: the only two whores in the main body of the novel are Delgadina, the girl, as mentioned, and Rosa Cabarcas, the madam (unless, and this would be profoundly significant, as we shall see, the title also includes a brief reference in the narrative to an ex-prostitute called Clotilde Armenta and, more specifically, the two-line reference to another madam, Castorina, at the very end of the book). A García Márquez on top of his form would have resolved the reader's perplexities: here he (the intended reader is probably a he) is left with the impression that he has been conned by a title that suggested an altogether racier book. Though many readers may reflect that this one is quite racy enough.

García Márquez always acknowledged that the book was inspired by Yasunari Kawabata's *The House of the Sleeping Beauties*, about an establishment where old men go to lie alongside drugged prostitutes whom they are not allowed to touch.[34] (The epigraph itself is from that novel.) Yet the effect of this acknowledgement may be to conceal the fact that sexual relations between mature men and inexperienced adolescents are a recurrent motif in García Márquez's work.

There are two social phenomena here which usually coincide but are analytically separate. The first is the attraction men feel for the woman as "girl," the adolescent barely old enough or even (in the case of Remedios in *One Hundred Years of Solitude*, for example) not old enough to have sexual relations. (On the whole the more conventional Don Juan character would prefer to seduce older females, not least those who, married or betrothed, belong to other men.) The second is the obsession with virginity. In *Chronicle of a Death Foretold* virginity, or the honour and shame syndrome associated with it, is the central focus of the drama; but the female protagonist, Angela Vicario, is not an adolescent. In *Love in the Time of Cholera*, however, Florentino Ariza, a man by then in his seventies, who manages to retain the affection of most readers, has a sexual relationship with his fourteen-year-old niece and ward, América Vicuña (the same initials as Angela Vicario), though—to be fair to him—he also has sexual relations with every other kind of woman imaginable.

The best-known exposition of this topic in all of literature is Nabokov's *Lolita*, a controversial work if ever there was one. But why is the theme so prevalent in Latin American literature? (Not that an obsession with schoolgirls is confined to Latin American men.) It is often used in Latin American fiction as a symbol of the discovery and conquest of the continent itself, as a taking possession of the unknown and unexplored, as a desire for newness, for all that has not yet been exploited and developed. But this can hardly explain the apparent strength of the impulse in Latin American men themselves, beyond any literary fancy. One possibility is that although young women have always been seduced, violated or bought by older, wealthier and more powerful men in all cultures, adolescent boys in Latin America have typically had their first sexual experience with an older woman, usually a servant or a prostitute, and that many of them go on yearning for the first experience with an innocent and untutored adolescent that they never had when they themselves were still innocent and untutored adolescents. Romeo and Juliet has not traditionally been a theme common in Latin American literature or indeed in Latin American society itself.[35]

García Márquez decided to marry his own wife when she was nine (or eleven, or thirteen, the age varies). Clearly he gets some ironic or even perverse pleasure out of the mere assertion that she was only nine (as does Mercedes herself). But perhaps the real instinct was neither ironic nor perverse; perhaps he wished to reserve her in advance, to keep her, pure and unsullied, all for himself and for always. (Dante, of course, was happy to leave Beatrice unsullied even by himself.)

When García Márquez first discussed this novel with me he was seventy. But María Jimena Duzán—a friend of García Márquez's who became a journalist as a teenager—remembers him telling her about the project in Paris when he was fifty.[36] By the time the book was published he was nearly eighty. And his protagonist was ninety. Almost uniquely in modern literature, this extraordinary novelist had been writing about old people since he was a very young man. And the older he has got the more he has written about the attractions of very young women. Perhaps it is not surprising that a boy for whom his grandparents were so very important should have become obsessed with contrasts of youth and age (the very stuff of fairy stories). There is a remarkable contrast between the cover of *Living to Tell the Tale*, with the photograph of one-year-old García Márquez in sepia used in all editions across the world, and the Spanish-language edition of *Memories of My Melancholy Whores*, which has a photograph of an old man dressed all in white shuffling away, possibly off-stage, perhaps into the great beyond: as if turning his back on life for the last time (though the novel itself defies such an interpretation). It is impossible not to think of the many retired colonels who appear down the years in García Márquez's fiction; but the picture also looks eerily like that same García Márquez, his body slimmed, his hair thinned, his powers waning, who had sat revising that novel before it was delivered to the press. Whether anyone had consciously planned this contrast we do not know.

Because the novel is written in the first person it has an interesting impenetrability quite foreign to most of García Márquez's novels. Here no irony—the distance between the narrator and the character—impels us towards a critique or even a reliable interpretation of the protagonist. When the narrator—let us call him by his nickname, Mustio Collado, since we never learn his real name—writes on the first page that for his ninetieth birthday he decided to give himself a night of wild love with an adolescent virgin, we seem to get no clue as to how to react. When he talks of his morality and the purity of his principles we do not know whether to judge him from where we are today or whether to begin to accept that in his society (1950s Barranquilla) there would have been no necessary contradiction for a middle-class journalist like him to speak in this way.

Collado has never in his life had sex without paying for it. He dislikes complications and commitments. The girl procured for him is just fourteen, seventy-six years younger than he is. She is working class, her father is dead, her mother an invalid; evidently she has no older brothers; she is very dark skinned, has a pronounced lower-class accent, and works in a clothing factory. Collado wishes to think of her as a fantasy lover, a living but unconscious doll. He calls her Delgadina—somewhat grotesquely, since the Spanish ballad of that name is about a perverse and ruthless king who wishes to violate his own helpless daughter; but Collado doesn't see the irony. One morning the girl leaves him a message on the mirror of their hotel room: "For the ugly papa."[37] He doesn't wish to know her real name (still less her real self).

Eventually, after a series of melodramas triggered only by the old man's needs and fantasies, he decides that he truly loves the girl and makes all his possessions over to her in his will. He does not die on his ninety-first birthday, as he has come to fear, and the next morning goes out into the street feeling radiant and confident that he will live to be a hundred. (Naturally the reader reflects that the best thing for the girl would be for him to die at once.) "It was, at last, real life, with my heart safe and condemned to die of happy love (not crazy love) in the joyful agony of any day after my hundredth birthday." It is the young who die for love in García Márquez's books: love keeps the old alive.

In fact there are two other possible readings not yet mentioned by critics. First, that the once invulnerable, exploitative and inhuman old man is now susceptible because of "love" and is taken for a ride, with or without the girl's knowledge, by the "malign" madam, Cabarcas, who has turned the impoverished Delgadina into a whore; and that she is still deceiving him between the end of the action of the novel (now most likely with the girl's knowledge) and its writing. The novel never addresses the fact that absolutely everything the protagonist knows about Delgadina (other than the fruits of his pornographic fumblings and paedophiliac fantasizings) comes through the mediation of the brothel-keeper, who may have made up the girl and her love for her customer like any writer of *romans roses* or Hollywood movies, giving her audience—Collado—exactly what he desires. And of course Collado rejects all real details about the girl; he simply and quite explicitly doesn't want to know. If this secondary plot is intended to be the primary—or corrective—plot, then the novel acquires a dimension of self-critique that is really very interesting. The least that can be said is that it converts the silly old fool into an object of contempt (though not pity), certainly for the reader and possibly for both the reader and the writer.

The other reading (not necessarily excluded by the first) is that Collado is a damaged personality. At the age of eleven he is introduced involuntarily to sex by an older woman who is also a prostitute, in the very building—in the book—where Collado's father worked (which happens to be the building—in reality—where García Márquez cohabited with prostitutes when he worked for *El Heraldo*: the "Skyscraper"). The experience first traumatizes the boy and then turns him into a sexual addict. Since it was, apparently, Gabriel Eligio who organized a similar and a similarly traumatic experience for Gabito at a similar age, and since García Márquez has chosen to situate this—explanatory, exculpatory?—episode close to the very end of the book, it is possible that it is meant to provide an explanation for the old man's inability to love or develop close relationships, for his obsession with prostitutes, and for his paedophiliac desire for that young virgin with whom, perhaps, he would like to have had his own first sexual experience if time could somehow be conjured anew and he could go back to his adolescence. If this were the case, it would inevitably induce the reader to ask himself whether the same analysis is to be applied retrospectively to the similar fantasies in all this author's earlier novels; in which case this one, narrated by a protagonist now "free at last of a servitude that had kept me enslaved since the age of thirteen,"[38] would be as ruthlessly self-exposing and self-critical as *The Autumn of the Patriarch*, written thirty years before. It would also suggest that the García Márquez who consciously forgave his father in the writing of *Living to Tell the Tale* continued, perhaps unconsciously (perhaps not), to blame him for childhood traumas whose effects were prolonged into adulthood. In short, just as in the memoir, written at the age of seventy-five, he had returned to the idea that Luisa Santiaga, who had abandoned him, feared he might not know her, so in *Memories*, written at the age of seventy-seven, he returns to the idea that the father who took his mother away when he was a baby subsequently perverted his sexual being when he was just beginning adolescence.

Memories is possibly García Márquez's least-accomplished novel. But, as in all of them, even through the relative flatness and banality of the narrative here, a radiance of the imagination, and occasionally of the poetic faculty, shines through as it were from behind the silver screen. By this writer's standards the book is weak, sometimes even embarrassing—in short, unfinished. But nevertheless, given the profundity of his underlying vision of the world, it has—because of its potential, which allows each reader to complete the story in the way that he or she desires—as many levels of ambiguity, ambivalence and complexity as any of his others—more than *Of Love and Other Demons*, for example; more also than *Chronicle of a Death Foretold*—because this book has both an unashamed and unattenuated flirtation with fantasy and a conventional moral dimension that most of the others quite deliberately lack. It is a fairy tale, albeit a disconcertingly lurid one.

One might say that in one way the ending takes García Márquez to the end of his literary and philosophical journey through life. When he realized, in his sixties, that he was going to die, he decided that he had to do everything fast, "without missing a strike." When he contracted lymphoma in his seventies the compulsion became even stronger but he had to prioritize: thus because writing his memoir *Living to Tell the Tale* was, not altogether ironically, his most urgent objective, he forsook all other activities for a time and completed that book. By then it had become obvious that his memory was fading frighteningly fast and so he went into reverse, deciding that after managing to complete the autobiography he had to take things as they came. The narrator of *Memories of My Melancholy Whores* is in no hurry whatever at the end—we hurry on only to death—but is determined to live as long as possible and to take each day as it comes. Though he too has lived to tell his tale. The poignant, or paradoxical, side of this is that García Márquez only came to this patient wisdom—if wisdom it is—when physical reality no longer gave him any other choice.

John Updike, reviewing the book in *The New Yorker* in 2005, retrieved its possible motivations with his usual ingenuity and eloquence:

> The instinct to memorialize one's loves is not peculiar to nonagenarian rakes; in the slow ruin of life, such memory reverses the current for a moment and silences the voice that murmurs in our narrator's ear, "No matter what you do, this year or in the next hundred, you will be dead forever." The septuagenarian Gabriel García Márquez, while he is still alive, has composed, with his usual sensual gravity and Olympian humor, a love letter to the dying light.[39]

It turned out that García Márquez had two big reasons for returning to Cartagena at the time the novel appeared. There was to be another meeting of the Foro Iberoamérica. (His contributions to Cartagena's conference and tourist income were by now considerable.) And before that the King and Queen of Spain were due in town. They arrived on 18 November and during their visit the old rascal engaged in social pleasantries with their Hispanic majesties and a possibly embarrassed President Uribe. If they asked him about the book he no doubt explained that it was inspired by the story of a Spanish princess sexually abused by her father the king. Of course he would have just been playing the fool. (Pictures of him sticking his tongue out at the proffered camera lens now regularly appeared in the newspapers.)

It seemed there were no more books to write. His new life—the end of his life, his retirement—could begin. In April 2005, after all the fears, and for the first time since he fell sick, he crossed the Atlantic, returned to Spain and France, and visited his apartments in Europe one more time. Again, the occasion of his journey was a meeting of the Foro Iberoamérica in Barcelona, a commitment that now seemed to outweigh all others. The press had been celebrating in advance that García Márquez was returning to Spain—this year was the 400th anniversary of the publication of *Don Quixote*—and particularly to Barcelona, where it was the Year of the Book. But when he arrived they reported that he seemed hesitant and even—it was implied—disorientated.

We had been out of contact for three years. I hesitated, then finally flew to Mexico City to talk to him in October. Mercedes had influenza so he came to visit me twice at my hotel. He looked quite different. He no longer had the appearance of the typical cancer survivor: he had still been shockingly slim and his hair was still short and thin when he completed *Living to Tell the Tale* in 2002. Now he looked as he always had; he was merely an older version of the man I had known between 1990 and 1999. But he was more forgetful. With suitable prompts he could remember most things from the distant past—though not always the titles of his novels—and engage in a reasonably normal, even humorous conversation. But his short-term memory was fragile and he was manifestly anguished about that and about the phase he seemed to be embarked upon. After we'd talked about his work and his plans for a while, he stated that he was not sure he would be doing any more writing. Then he said, almost plaintively: "I've written enough, haven't I? People can't be disappointed, they can't expect any more of me, can they?"

We were sitting in huge blue armchairs in a secluded hotel lounge which looked out on Mexico City's southern ring road. Outside was the twenty-first century, flying away. Eight lanes of traffic that never stopped.

He looked at me and said, "You know, sometimes I get depressed."

"What, you, Gabo, after all you've achieved? Surely not. Why?"

He gestured towards the world beyond the window (the great urban thoroughfare, the silent intensity of all those ordinary people going about their everyday business in a world no longer his), then he looked back at me and murmured, "Realizing that all this is coming to an end."[40]

Immortality—The New Cervantes

2006~2007

B
UT LIFE HAD NOT yet finished with Gabriel García Márquez.
Though a few weeks after our last meeting in Mexico City one
might have thought so. In January 2006 he gave a surprise
interview to Barcelona's *La Vanguardia* newspaper—a surprise at least
to those who were by then accustomed to the fact that he no longer
talked to the press. But this was no spur-of-the-moment matter. It
seemed possible that there had been a family meeting which had
decided, given the circumstances, on a formal "last statement" followed by withdrawal. Then silence.

Mercedes was present at the interview at the family home in Mexico City—at the previous one, three years before, it had been Mónica,
his secretary—and it was Mercedes who put an end to the conversation, as the reporters seemed to indicate in their piece. García
Márquez himself said little—the report was more a narrative than a
dialogue—and when he was asked a question about his past life he said,
"You will have to ask my official biographer, Gerald Martin, about that
sort of thing, only I think he's waiting for something to happen to me
before he finishes."[1] It was true that I was taking a long time. But such
"ardent patience," to quote the title of Antonio Skármeta's novel about
Pablo Neruda's postman, had now been rewarded by the discovery,
after fifteen years, that I was the great man's "official" biographer and
not just a "tolerated" one, as I was given to explaining. If only I'd
known!

It seemed to be a matter of working out how much longer he could appear in the public eye and under what conditions. He could not be relied upon to give clear or accurate answers to direct and unexpected questions and he was capable of forgetting what he had said five minutes before. I was no expert on the different forms and progressions of memory loss but my impression was that the condition was moving rather steadily. It was hard to see a man who had made memory the central focus of his entire existence beset by such a misfortune. "A professional rememberer," he had always called himself. Yet by the time his mother died she had been unaware of who she was and who her children were. His half-brother Abelardo had been suffering from Parkinson's disease for three decades. Their younger brother Nanchi was apparently developing it. Eligio had died of a brain tumour. Gustavo had returned from Venezuela with signs of memory loss. And now there was Gabito's condition. "Problems with the noddle," Jaime said to me. "It seems to be the family thing."[2]

García Márquez was now almost seventy-nine. (Ever since the spectacular celebrations for his seventieth birthday he had given up pretending that he had been born in 1928. One might say he had started to act his age.) Notwithstanding his uncertain condition, which no one in his inner circle was inclined to reveal and about which the media maintained a surprisingly discreet silence, the question of his eightieth birthday had to be confronted. As part of Spain's long-term programme of cultural diffusion the Spanish Royal Academy had begun, after 1992, to organize triennial congresses to celebrate the Spanish language and its literatures around the Hispanic world. At the first, much delayed congress, in Zacatecas, Mexico, in April 1997, García Márquez had famously suggested that traditional Spanish grammar and spelling should be "retired."[3] Although this had caused controversy, even affront, the academy, so authoritarian in the past, was by then far too diplomatic and strategic an institution to allow a writer of García Márquez's stature to become a renegade and he was invited to visit the academy itself and meet its officers during a visit to Madrid in November of that year. Still, in 2001 he declared that he would not be going to the second congress in Zaragoza, Spain, as a protest against Spain's policy of requiring visas from Latin Americans for the first time in its history. He said that Spain seemed to be declaring itself a European country first and a Hispanic one second. Controversy continued in 2004, when he was not invited to the third congress in Rosario, Argentina (a country he had always superstitiously avoided revisiting in any case). José Saramago, the Portuguese Nobel Prize winner, then declared that if García Márquez were not invited he would not go either, whereupon the academy declared that there had been an administrative oversight and of course the Colombian Nobel Prize winner was invited. García Márquez still did not attend. But the 2007 congress was scheduled for Cartagena de Indias, Colombia, the city where García Márquez now had his principal home in Colombia and which he had exalted in two memorable novels.

Moreover, in 2004 the academy had launched a mass-market edition of Cervantes's *Don Quixote* to celebrate the 400th anniversary of the publication of that most important book in the history of Spain and its various literatures. What an idea it would be if for 2007, in Cartagena, the academy could follow this up with a similar edition of *One Hundred Years of Solitude*, to coincide with the fortieth anniversary of its first publication and García Márquez's own eightieth birthday. First a Spanish genius, then a Latin American one. After all, many critics compared the Colombian novel to its illustrious predecessor and argued that it already held and would for the foreseeable future continue to hold the same significance for Latin Americans as Cervantes's work held, first for Spaniards, then for Spanish Americans as well. Of course some would disagree. But one critic who had not always been a devotee of García Márquez would shortly declare, using a very twenty-first-century analogy, that *One Hundred Years of Solitude* had tapped into the "DNA" of Latin American culture and had been inseparable from it since its first publication in 1967.[4] Like Cervantes, García Márquez had explored the dreams and delusions of his characters which, at a certain time in history, had been those of Spain during its great imperial period and had then, in a different form, become those of Latin America after independence. Moreover, like Cervantes, he had created a mood, a humour, indeed a sense of humour, which was somehow instantly recognizable and, once it came into existence, seemed to have always been there and was an integral part of the world to which it referred.

In April 1948 García Márquez had fled from Bogotá and travelled to Cartagena for the first time in his life. In that beautiful but decadent and run-down colonial city he had met newspaper editor Clemente Manuel Zabala and had been invited to become a journalist on a recently founded daily named, perhaps appropriately, *El Universal*. On 20 May 1948 the new recruit had been saluted in the pages of his new literary home. On 21 May, 358 years to the day after a certain Miguel de Cervantes wrote to the King of Spain asking for employment abroad, "possibly in Cartagena," the new recruit's first column had appeared.[5] Cervantes never made it to Cartagena, nor indeed to any part of the Indies: he never saw the New World, though he would help to create an even vaster new world—Western modernity—in his books and those books would travel to the new continent despite the Spanish prohibition against the reading and writing of novels in the recently discovered dominions. In April 2007, to coincide with the Royal Academy congress in Cartagena and the arrival of the King and Queen of Spain, a new statue of Cervantes was installed on the harbour-front in the old colonial port.

For most of his life Cervantes had been unappreciated and frustrated. Whereas García Márquez, as his eightieth birthday approached, was one of the best-known writers on the planet and a celebrity who could hardly have achieved more fame and recognition in his own continent had he been a footballer or a pop star. The Hispanic international establishment was planning to give him in life the kind of recognition that Cervantes only acquired, gradually and over centuries, after his death. When García Márquez won the Nobel Prize in 1982 there had been seven weeks of celebratory media coverage in Latin America from the moment the news was announced in October until the moment the King of Sweden presented him with the award in December. When he reached seventy in 1997 there had been a week of festivities in March, accompanied by extensive news items in the press, and then another week in September when the fiftieth anniversary of his first short story was celebrated in Washington, with a party organized by the Secretary General of the Organization of American States and a visit to the White House to see his friend Bill Clinton. Now he was about to celebrate reaching his eightieth birthday, the sixtieth anniversary of his public debut as a writer, the fortieth anniversary of the publication of *One Hundred Years of Solitude* and the twenty-fifth anniversary of the award of the Nobel Prize. And so his friends and admirers began to plan a period of eight weeks in March and April 2007 to match those seven unforgettable weeks in 1982.

Many steps had already been taken to turn García Márquez into a living monument. The Barranquilla Group's old haunt "The Cave" had been ingeniously relaunched as part museum and part bar-restaurant by a local journalist, Heriberto Fiorillo. There had been a move to rename Aracataca as Aracataca-Macondo on the model of

Proust's Illiers-Combray; unfortunately, although most residents appeared to be in favour, not enough of them had turned out for the referendum and the proposal fell. Now the local and national authorities agreed to convert Colonel Márquez's old house in Aracataca, where little Gabriel had been born, into a major tourist attraction—it was already a somewhat ramshackle though evocative museum—and it was resolved that the remains of the old house should be demolished and a carefully researched reconstruction carried out.

So March 2007 arrived. The annual Cartagena Film Festival was dedicated to García Márquez. And, appropriately enough, Cuba was the "highlighted country." (In April García Márquez would be the featured writer at the Bogotá Book Fair at the moment when Colombia began its year's reign as the "World's Capital of the Book." Circles within circles, everything coinciding, as in a dream.) Almost all the films based on García Márquez's books were shown and many of the directors who had made them were in attendance, including Fernando Birri, Miguel Littín, Jaime Hermosillo, Jorge Alí Triana and Lisandro Duque. But although the festival ran through his birthday García Márquez himself did not turn up. When he was asked why, he retorted, "Nobody invited me." It was not one of his most successful jokes; but how could he not be forgiven? On 6 March a birthday party accompanied by *vallenato* music was held in a top Cartagena hotel—appropriately enough, a hotel named "Passion"—without the principal guest, who celebrated more quietly with his family elsewhere. After this, tension began to mount. Many of the posters announcing the Royal Academy event—known in Spanish as the "Congreso de la Lengua" (Congress of the Language or—it is the same word—the Tongue) featured a photograph of García Márquez, the advertised guest of honour, sticking his tongue out at the viewer. This acknowledgement of the famous writer's well-known sense of humour was no doubt intended to signal that the academy itself had a sense of humour but even if that were true it was doubtful that it would extend to the possibility of the celebrity guest failing to turn up at the party they had so carefully prepared for him.

In the middle of the month yet another great event, the annual meeting of the Inter-American Press Association, was held in Cartagena. There were two guests of honour: Bill Gates, the computer magnate, who was the richest man in the world (though within a few months García Márquez's billionaire friend Carlos Slim of Mexico would overtake Gates), and Gabriel García Márquez himself, who, although not willing to speak, had promised to turn up. He did so only on the last day but his appearance, as usual, caused a sensation and, as usual, immediately put all other participants in the shade. It was a big moment for Jaime Abello, the Director of García Márquez's journalism foundation, and García Márquez's brother, another Jaime, by now the Assistant Director. It was also a big moment for the Spanish Royal Academy, which, along with all of Colombia, was able to breathe a discreet sigh of relief.

Witnesses reported that Gabo looked very well. Although somewhat hesitant, he was in good humour and seemed on good form. Contrary to my assessment a year before, he seemed to have stabilized his condition and had evidently resolved, while no longer giving interviews, to confront both the malady and his public with the optimism and gallantry that had characterized him in easier times. Friends and admirers were flying in to Cartagena from all over the world, as well as the hundreds of linguists and other academics attending the Royal Academy congress. There were huge concerts with international pop stars, smaller *vallenato* performances, a profusion of literary events and many other fringe activities. The weather was glorious. Just as, three years before, the academy had produced a new mass-market version of *Don Quixote* to accompany the previous congress, so now it launched its new critical edition of *One Hundred Years of Solitude*. It was no surprise that it included essays by two of his best literary friends, Alvaro Mutis and Carlos Fuentes; what got everyone talking was that there was also a long piece by—of all people—Mario Vargas Llosa. Had there been a reconciliation? Certainly for the essay to be included both men would have had to agree. Though what Mercedes Barcha felt about the decision was not known.

Days before the inauguration Julio Mario Santo Domingo, Colombia's richest and most powerful businessman, now the owner of *El Espectador*, hosted a special party—a kind of belated birthday party—at which the guests of honour were Gabo and Mercedes. It was held on the top floor of another of Cartagena's luxury hotels—in which the King and Queen of Spain would stay in the following week—and guests included Carlos Fuentes, Tomás Eloy Martínez, ex-President Pastrana, *The New Yorker*'s Jon Lee Anderson taking time out from the Iraq War, ex–Vice President of Nicaragua and novelist Sergio Ramírez, and many other luminaries and beautiful people from Bogotá, Cartagena and, especially, Barranquilla. Champagne, whisky and rum flowed in profusion to lubricate the sweetest of lives and the omnipresent rhythms of the *vallenato* throbbed deep into the night. In corridors and on balconies party-goers whispered the big question. Would Gabo be giving a speech at the ceremony to honour him on the first day of the congress? And if so . . .

The great day dawned: 26 March 2007. Several thousand people filed in to the Cartagena Convention Centre, on the site where García Márquez used to eat and drink late at night after working in *El Universal* in 1948 and 1949.[6] Many of his friends were there and most of his family, though not his sons. Ex-Presidents Pastrana, Gaviria and—astonishingly—Samper were all present, as was ex-President Betancur, who would be on the podium with the other speakers, which would include the current President, Alvaro Uribe Vélez. The day was asphyxiatingly hot but most men were wearing dark suits, Bogotá-style. Carlos Fuentes, generous as ever, was due to give the special eulogy of his friend; Tomás Eloy Martínez, recovering from a brain tumour, was also due to speak. So were the Director of the Royal Academy, Víctor García de la Concha, and the former Director of the Instituto Cervantes, Antonio Muñoz Molina. So were the President of Colombia and the King of Spain. So was García Márquez.

When García Márquez and Mercedes walked in the entire audience rose to its feet and applauded for several minutes. He looked happy and relaxed. The two groups on the podium, García Márquez and his entourage (Mercedes, Carlos Fuentes, the Colombian Minister of Culture, Elvira Cuerdo de Jaramillo) and the academy entourage on the other side of the stage, got themselves organized and seated. Members of the expectant audience could scarcely believe their luck to be there. On a huge screen behind the protagonists the television coverage showed the arrival of the King and Queen of Spain, Don Juan Carlos and Doña Sofía, and watched them mounting the stairways and striding along the corridors of the vast convention building until their arrival inside the auditorium was announced.

There were many speeches, including the King's, most of them more interesting than such occasions usually produce. The stand-out speech was that of García de la Concha, whose task it was to present García Márquez with the first copy of the Royal Academy edition of *One Hundred Years of Solitude*.[7] He told an indiscreet story, having previously asked King Juan Carlos's permission to do so. It transpired that when the academy first thought up the idea of honouring García Márquez at this congress García de la Concha had asked the writer's permission to go ahead with the organization of the event. García Márquez had said he was in agreement but "who I really want to see is the King." The next time García Márquez saw Juan Carlos he passed on the message himself: "You, King, what you have to do is come to Cartagena." (The "you" was conveyed in the Spanish familiar: "tú.") This double- or treble-edged anecdote brought a huge collective howl of laughter made up of different ingredients—depending on each person's interpretation and whether the listener was a Spaniard or a Latin American, a monarchist or a republican, a socialist or a conservative— followed by a protracted ovation. Did this Latin American not know his place? Worse, did he just not know how to speak to a king? Or, worst of all, did he feel superior to the King of Spain and had he thus talked down to him? Those close to the podium noticed that when García Márquez approached the monarch and shook his hand he did so with the Latin American student salute—one man's thumb entwined around the other's—which spoke rather of an encounter of equals. The Bourbons had lost Latin America in the early nineteenth century; now Juan Carlos was doing his best to make amends both diplomatically and economically.

The most dramatic moment for those who knew was the beginning of García Márquez's own speech. He started hesitantly and stumbled over the first sentences but gradually got into his stride. More than a speech, it was a sentimental reminiscence of the time, in Mexico, when he and Mercedes were living in poverty and hoping that one day he would hit the jackpot and publish a best-selling book. It was an authentic fairy story—"I've still not got over my surprise that all this has happened to me"—and also, the audience felt, a message of thanks and recognition to the companion who had seen him through those hard times and all the other times, good and bad, over the last half century. Mercedes looked on anxiously and sombrely and prayed that this man who had got through so many challenges would get through this one too. He did: he finished with the story of the two of them mailing half the manuscript from Mexico City to Buenos Aires in 1966 because they were too poor to mail the whole thing.[8] The ovation that greeted the speech's conclusion lasted many minutes.

Earlier, in the midst of the proceedings, another announcement had electrified the auditorium. "Ladies and gentlemen, Señor William Clinton, ex-President of the United States, has arrived in the building." The crowd rose as the most famous man on earth made his way down to the front of the hall. The King of Spain, five Presidents of

Colombia and now the most popular ex-President of the most powerful country in the world—some observers reflected that the only superstars missing were Fidel Castro, ailing in Cuba, and the Pope in Rome. Once again it had been demonstrated that if García Márquez was obsessed with—fascinated by—power, power was repeatedly, irresistibly, drawn to him. Literature and politics have been the two most effective ways of achieving immortality in the transient world that Western civilization has created for the planet; few would hold that political glory is more enduring than the glory that comes from writing famous books.

WE WERE ABLE to have only the briefest of conversations before I left Cartagena. It was the end of many things.

"Gabo, what a wonderful event," I said.

"Wasn't it," he said.

"You know, many people around me were weeping."

"I was weeping too," he said, "only inside."

"Well," I said, "I know that I will never forget it."

"Well, what a good thing you were there," he said, "so you can tell people we didn't make up the story."

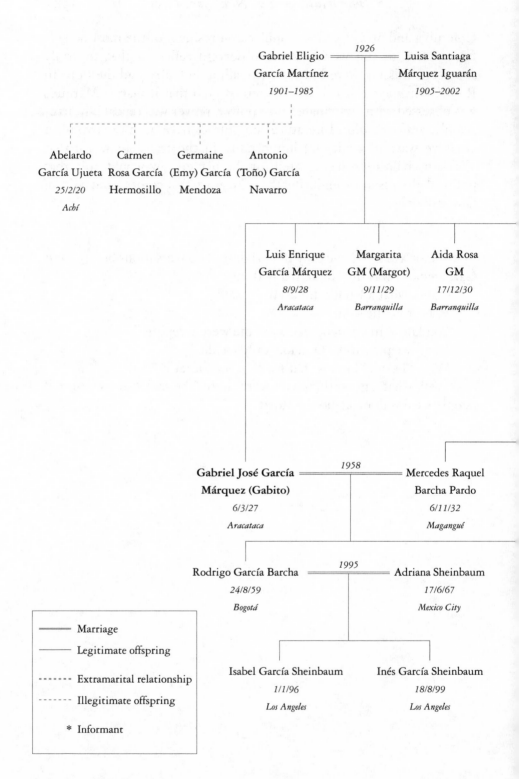

Gabriel Eligio ══════ 1926 ══════ Luisa Santiaga
García Martínez   Márquez Iguarán
1901–1985   *1905–2002*

Abelardo   Carmen   Germaine   Antonio
García Ujueta Rosa García (Emy) García (Toño) García
25/2/20   Hermosillo   Mendoza   Navarro
Achí

Luis Enrique   Margarita   Aida Rosa
García Márquez   GM (Margot)   GM
8/9/28   *9/11/29*   *17/12/30*
Aracataca   *Barranquilla*   *Barranquilla*

Gabriel José García ══════ 1958 ══════ Mercedes Raquel
Márquez (Gabito)   Barcha Pardo
6/3/27   *6/11/32*
Aracataca   *Magangué*

Rodrigo García Barcha ══════ 1995 ══════ Adriana Sheinbaum
24/8/59   *17/6/67*
Bogotá   *Mexico City*

Isabel García Sheinbaum   Inés García Sheinbaum
1/1/96   *18/8/99*
Los Angeles   *Los Angeles*

───── Marriage

───── Legitimate offspring

┄┄┄┄ Extramarital relationship

┄┄┄┄ Illegitimate offspring

   * Informant

The García Márquez (GM)
and Barcha Pardo (BP) Families

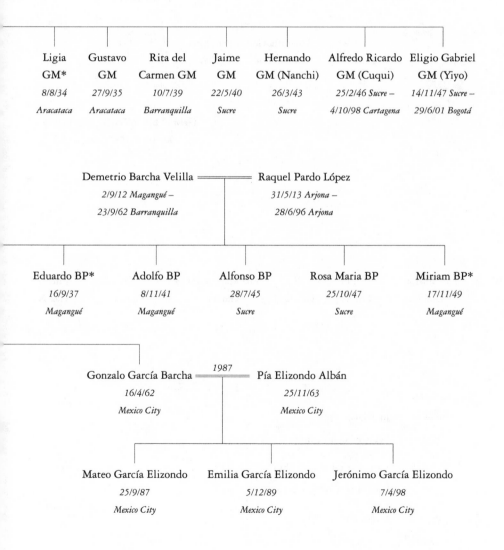

Ligia GM*	Gustavo GM	Rita del Carmen GM	Jaime GM	Hernando GM (Nanchi)	Alfredo Ricardo GM (Cuqui)	Eligio Gabriel GM (Yiyo)
8/8/34	27/9/35	10/7/39	22/5/40	26/3/43	25/2/46 Sucre –	14/11/47 Sucre –
Aracataca	Aracataca	Barranquilla	Sucre	Sucre	4/10/98 Cartagena	29/6/01 Bogotá

Demetrio Barcha Velilla ═══════ Raquel Pardo López

2/9/12 Magangué –   31/5/13 Arjona –

23/9/62 Barranquilla   28/6/96 Arjona

Eduardo BP*	Adolfo BP	Alfonso BP	Rosa Maria BP	Miriam BP*
16/9/37	8/11/41	28/7/45	25/10/47	17/11/49
Magangué	Magangué	Sucre	Sucre	Magangué

Gonzalo García Barcha ═══ 1987 ═══ Pía Elizondo Albán

16/4/62   25/11/63

Mexico City   Mexico City

Mateo García Elizondo	Emilia García Elizondo	Jerónimo García Elizondo
25/9/87	5/12/89	7/4/98
Mexico City	Mexico City	Mexico City

Pedro García Gordón

Late 1800s, Madrid (Spain)

Aminadab García ========================== María de los Ángeles

1834 Caimito (Sucre)   Paternina Bustamante

1855 Sincelejo

Argemira García Paternina ===============================

1887 Caimito – 1950 Sincé

Gabriel Eligio García Martínez

1901 Sincé – 1984 Cartagena

| Luis Enrique García | Benita García | Julio García | Ena Marquesita García | Adán Reinaldo García | Eliécer García |

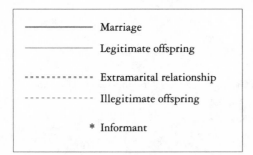

———————— Marriage

———————— Legitimate offspring

- - - - - - - - - Extramarital relationship

- - - - - - - - - Illegitimate offspring

* Informant

The García Martínez Family

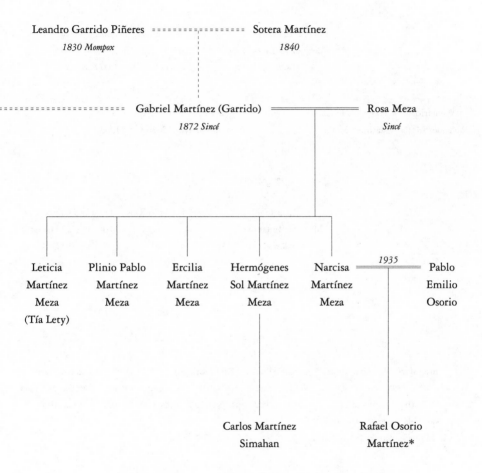

Leandro Garrido Piñeres — Sotera Martínez
1830 Mompox — *1840*

Gabriel Martínez (Garrido) — Rosa Meza
1872 Sincé — *Sincé*

| Leticia Martínez Meza (Tía Lety) | Plinio Pablo Martínez Meza | Ercilia Martínez Meza | Hermógenes Sol Martínez Meza | Narcisa Martínez Meza | *1935* | Pablo Emilio Osorio |

Carlos Martínez Simahan

Rafael Osorio Martínez*

The Márquez Iguarán Family

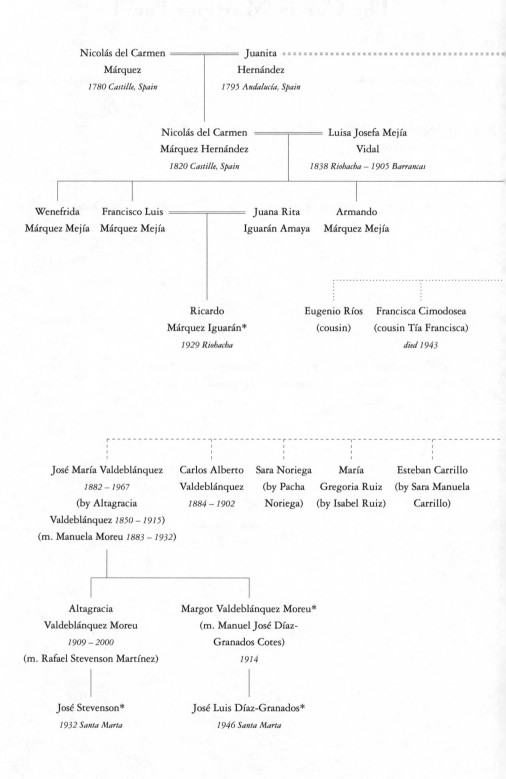

Nicolás del Carmen Márquez
1780 Castille, Spain
═══ Juanita Hernández
1795 Andalucía, Spain

Nicolás del Carmen Márquez Hernández
1820 Castille, Spain
═══ Luisa Josefa Mejía Vidal
1838 Riohacha – 1905 Barrancas

Wenefrida Márquez Mejía

Francisco Luis Márquez Mejía ═══ Juana Rita Iguarán Amaya

Armando Márquez Mejía

Ricardo Márquez Iguarán*
1929 Riohacha

Eugenio Ríos (cousin)

Francisca Cimodosea (cousin Tía Francisca)
died 1943

José María Valdeblánquez
1882 – 1967
(by Altagracia Valdeblánquez *1850 – 1915*)
(m. Manuela Moreu *1883 – 1932*)

Carlos Alberto Valdeblánquez
1884 – 1902

Sara Noriega (by Pacha Noriega)

María Gregoria Ruiz (by Isabel Ruiz)

Esteban Carrillo (by Sara Manuela Carrillo)

Altagracia Valdeblánquez Moreu
1909 – 2000
(m. Rafael Stevenson Martínez)

Margot Valdeblánquez Moreu*
(m. Manuel José Díaz-Granados Cotes)
1914

José Stevenson*
1932 Santa Marta

José Luis Díaz-Granados*
1946 Santa Marta

Blas Iguarán
1805 Riohacha

AC's other children
(including Petra
Cotes, Tranquilina's
half-sister), link
to the GM family
to Consuelo
Araujonoguera,
Alfonso López
Michelsen, José
Francisco Socarrás,
Poncho Cotes and
Ruth Ariza Cotes

Rosa Antonia
Iguarán Hernández
1827 Riohacha

Agustín Cotes
(or Silvestre)
1825 Fonseca

Nicolás Ricardo
Márquez Mejía
1864 Riohacha – 1937 Santa Marta

1885

Tranquilina
Iguarán Cotes
1863 Riohacha – 1947 Sucre

Rosa Antonia
Iguarán Cotes

José Antonio
Iguarán Cotes

Juan de Dios
Márquez Iguarán
1888 Riohacha – 1957 Botogá
(m. Dilia Caballero)

Margarita Miniata
Márquez Iguarán
1889 Riohacha – 1910

Luisa Santiaga
Márquez Iguarán
1905 Barrancas – 2002 Cartagena

Margarita Márquez Caballero*
1936 Santa Marta

Elvira Carrillo
(Tía Pa – by Sara
Manuela Carrillo)

Nicolás Gómez
(by Amelia Gómez)

Remedios Núñez
(Tía Meme –
by Jesusa Núñez)

Petronila Arias
Márquez

Others
unknown

Oscar Alarcón*

	Marriage
	Legitimate offspring
	Extramarital relationship
	Illegitimate offspring
	Cousin
*	Informant

The Buendía Family
in *One Hundred Years of Solitude*

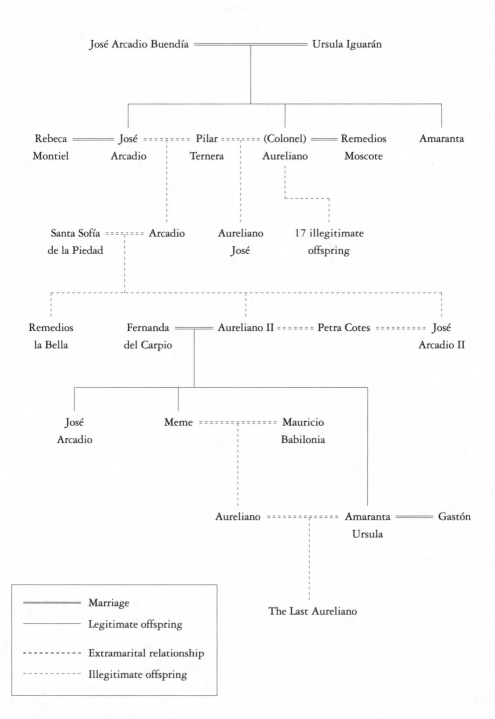

José Arcadio Buendía ═══════ Ursula Iguarán

Rebeca Montiel ═══ José Arcadio ╌╌╌╌ Pilar Ternera ╌╌╌╌ (Colonel) Aureliano ═══ Remedios Moscote   Amaranta

Santa Sofía de la Piedad ╌╌╌╌ Arcadio   Aureliano José   17 illegitimate offspring

Remedios la Bella   Fernanda del Carpio ═══ Aureliano II ╌╌╌╌ Petra Cotes ╌╌╌╌ José Arcadio II

José Arcadio   Meme ╌╌╌╌ Mauricio Babilonia

Aureliano ╌╌╌╌ Amaranta Ursula ═══ Gastón

The Last Aureliano

─────── Marriage

─────── Legitimate offspring

╌╌╌╌╌╌╌ Extramarital relationship

╌╌╌╌╌╌╌ Illegitimate offspring

Notes

Abbreviations

GM   García Márquez
GGM   Gabriel García Márquez
OHYS   *One Hundred Years of Solitude*

Prologue: From Origins Obscure (1800–1899)

1. This section, despite its somewhat literary style, is based directly upon conversations with Luisa Santiaga Márquez in Cartagena in 1991 and in Barranquilla in 1993; and on Gabriel García Márquez's (henceforth GGM's) and his sister Margarita's (henceforth Margot's) own recollections.

2. This prologue and the next three chapters are based upon conversations with all the members of the García Márquez (henceforth GM) family and many members of the extended family over the period 1991–2008, as well as many journeys around the Colombian Costa from Sucre to Riohacha and beyond, some of them with GGM's brothers. The most authoritative informants were Ligia GM, a Mormon, who considers it her duty to research her family's history (it is to Ligia above all that I owe the family trees); Margot Valdeblánquez de Díaz-Granados, who spent long periods in her grandfather Colonel Márquez's house in the 1920s and 1930s; Ricardo Márquez Iguarán, who in 1993 and 2008 gave me invaluable information on the family ramifications in the Guajira; and Rafael Osorio Martínez, who in 2007 gave detailed insight into Gabriel Eligio García's family background in Sincé. GGM himself never had more than a general and rather vague knowledge of the details of this family history but his understanding of the underlying structure and dynamic of the genealogy is extraordinary and the stories of specific relatives blessed or cursed with colourful or dramatic lives form the foundation of his fictional oeuvre. In general a biographer of GGM also depends heavily on random snippets of information which appear from time to time in the Colombian press. The only previous biographical works are Oscar Collazos, *García Márquez: la soledad y la gloria* (Barcelona, Plaza y Janés, 1983), helpful but brief, and, most substantially, Dasso Saldívar, *García Márquez: el viaje a la semilla. La biografía* (Madrid, Alfaguara, 1997), on GGM's life to 1967: its most useful contribution is the information it provides on the genealogical background to the two sides of the GM family and on his childhood and schooldays. Historically the first biographical study was Mario Vargas Llosa, *García Márquez: historia de un deicidio* (Barcelona, Barral, 1971), which is also a work of literary criticism: although factually unreliable, it is especially illuminating because most of Vargas Llosa's information came direct from GGM in the late 1960s. Equally important is the book by GGM's brother Eligio Gar-

cía, *Tras las claves de Melquíades: historia de "Cien años de soledad"* (Bogotá, Norma, 2001). GGM's own most considered autobiographical reflections before his brilliant but not always accurate 2002 memoir *Living to Tell the Tale* (London, Jonathan Cape, 1993) (its epigraph, "Life is not what one lived, but what one remembers and how one remembers it in order to recount it," must be taken as a warning) were those in Plinio Apuleyo Mendoza, *The Fragrance of Guava* (London, Faber, 1988), though, taken as a whole, GGM's weekly columns published in *El Espectador* (Bogotá) and *El País* (Madrid) between 1980 and 1984 were even more informative and illuminating but are unavailable in English. Juan Luis Cebrían, *Retrato de GGM* (Barcelona, Círculo de Lectores, 1989), is a biographical essay with excellent illustrations. Mendoza, *The Fragrance of Guava* and GGM, *Living to Tell the Tale* are the only key works on GGM's biography available in English but Stephen Minta, *Gabriel García Márquez: Writer of Colombia* (London, Jonathan Cape, 1987) and Gene Bell-Villada, *García Márquez: The Man and His Work* (Chapel Hill, University of North Carolina Press, 1990) are also helpful. Literary-critical analyses (see esp. Bell, Wood) can be found in the bibliography.

3. On "natural children" see GGM, "Telepatía sin hilos," *El Espectador* (Bogotá), 23 November 1980. See the family trees in the appendix for the way in which *OHYS* replicates the García Martínez and Márquez Iguarán family histories in their oscillation between legitimate and illegitimate unions.

4. See Guillermo Henríquez Torres, *El misterio de los Buendía: el verdadero trasfondo histórico de "Cien años de soledad"* (Bogotá, Nueva América, 2003; 2nd revised edition, 2006). Henríquez, a native of Ciénaga, believes that the Buendía family of *OHYS* is based on his own family, the Henríquezes, descended in part from Jews who migrated from Amsterdam to the Caribbean. While few readers will swallow Henríquez's thesis whole, his book provides invaluable background and atmospherics to a reading of *OHYS*.

5. See GGM, *Living to Tell the Tale*, pp. 66–7, for a revised version of this episode. None of Nicolás Márquez's "natural" children inherited his name: they all carried their mother's surname.

6. Interview, Barrancas, 1993.

7. José Luis Díaz-Granados explained his relation to Gabriel García Márquez as follows when I first met him in Bogotá in 1991: "Colonel Márquez, when he was eighteen, had had a son by Altagracia Valdeblánquez; he was called José María and carried the maternal surname, Valdeblánquez: he was my mother's father. Later Colonel Márquez married Tranquilina Iguarán Cotes, the aunt of my father, Manuel José Díaz-Granados Cotes, and had three more children, among them Luisa Santiaga Márquez Iguarán, mother of Gabriel García Márquez. In other words, I am the double cousin of Gabriel García Márquez." This personal story was typical of the entanglements I came across, not only in the admittedly "exotic" Guajira but everywhere else I travelled in Colombia in the 1990s. Indeed JLD-G married a cousin in 1972!

8. Ligia García Márquez, interview, Bogotá, 1991.

9. There is reason to believe Argemira was one of the prototypes for Pilar Ternera, a central character of *OHYS*.

10. I owe my information on Gabriel Martínez Garrido, who should have been called Gabriel Garrido Martínez, to his grandson Rafael Osorio Martínez. His evidence made me realise that GGM could easily have been called Gabriel Garrido Márquez (or, indeed, Gabriel Garrido Cotes); and this made me further realise just how far-reaching was GGM's decision to identify with his Liberal grandparents from the Guajira rather than his Conservative, landowning grandparents from Sincé (then in Bolívar department).

11. When Gabriel junior was married in 1958 and needed his birth certificate, the family would persuade the priest in Aracataca to change the names of his paternal grandparents so that they appeared as Gabriel García and Argemira Martínez.

1 / Of Colonels and Lost Causes (1899–1927)

1. See Ernesto González Bermejo, "GGM, la imaginación al poder en Macondo," *Crisis* (Buenos Aires), 1972 (reprinted in Alfonso Rentería Mantilla, ed., *GM habla de GM en 33 grandes reportajes* (Bogotá, Rentería Editores, 1979) pp. 111–17), where GGM says he wants Latin American revolutions to cease to be "martyrologies": he wants the continent and its people to start winning. His own life is a monument to this ambition.

2. See David Bushnell, *The Making of Modern Colombia. A Nation in Spite of Itself* (Berkeley and Los Angeles, University of California Press, 1993), Eduardo Posada-Carbó, *The Colombian Caribbean: A Regional History, 1870–1950* (Oxford, Clarendon Press, 1996), and Frank Safford and Marco Palacios, *Colombia: Fragmented Land, Divided Society* (Oxford, Oxford University Press, 2001).

3. "Aunt Margarita was sixteen years older than my mother and there were various other children in the years between, all of them dead at birth: one baby girl, then two twin girls, and others . . . Uncle Juanito was seventeen years older than my mother and she called him 'godfather,' not brother." Ligia quoted in Silvia Galvis, *Los García Márquez* (Bogotá, Arango, 1996), p. 152.

4. The Márquez Iguarán family's closest relationship of all was with Eugenio Ríos, Nicolás's nephew and business partner. His daughter Ana Ríos was only two when Luisa passed through but remembers everything her mother Arsenia Carrillo told her about those now legendary days. When her sister Francisca Luisa Ríos Carrillo was born on 25 August 1925 she was "baptized" by Luisa two weeks after her birth, and thus became her goddaughter.

5. I am grateful to Gustavo Adolfo Ramírez Ariza for a copy of the *Gaceta Departmental* of Magdalena for November 1908 which shows that Nicolás was imprisoned for "homicide" at Santa Marta on 7 November 1908 but had not yet been tried.

6. Saldívar, *GM: el viaje a la semilla*, p. 44.

7. See Mario Vargas Llosa and GGM, *La novela en América Latina: diálogo* (Lima, Milla Batres, 1968), p. 14. In *OHYS* the Nicolás role is played by José Arcadio Buendiá and Medardo becomes Prudencio Aguilar.

8. GGM in conversation, Mexico City, 1999.

9. See *Living to Tell the Tale*, p. 40, for GGM's version of this episode.

10. In *Leaf Storm*, pp. 51–4, GGM himself gives a romantic, Faulknerian version of what we could call the GM family founding myth, which blames the exodus on "the war" (and is indeed much less candid and "historical" than the still romanticized version he would give later in *OHYS*).

11. Henríquez, *El misterio*, contradicts Saldívar's version of events, which follows the GM family line.

12. Aracataca is forty metres above sea level, eighty-eight kilometres from Santa Marta, and its average temperature is twenty-eight degrees (which is why this is GGM's preferred working room temperature).

13. See Lázaro Diago Julio, *Aracataca . . . una historia para contar* (Aracataca, 1989, unpublished), an invaluable work of local history despite a tendency to consider GGM's literary works as historiographical evidence in their own right.

14. These two words are much disputed in Colombia and it is reckless for a for-

eigner to get involved. It is generally agreed that *costeños* are the inhabitants of the tropical lowlands in the Caribbean or Atlantic north of the country. The original *cachacos* were the upper-class inhabitants of Bogotá, but many *costeños* have come to consider all inhabitants of "the interior" (mainly Andean) of the country as *cachacos*, sometimes including even the *paisas* or inhabitants of Antioquia. See GGM, *Living to Tell the Tale*, pp. 41–2.

15. Judith White, *Historia de una ignominia: la UFC en Colombia* (Bogotá, Editorial Presencia, 1978), pp. 19–20. Nevertheless Colonel Márquez was undoubtedly one of the town's leading Liberals. (He had been President of the Liberal Club in Riohacha when still a young man.)

16. See Saldívar, *GM: el viaje a la semilla*, p. 50; White, *Historia*; and Catherine C. LeGrand, *Frontier Expansion and Peasant Protest in Colombia, 1850–1936* (Albuquerque, New Mexico University Press, 1986), p. 73.

17. See *Living to Tell the Tale*, p. 15, where GGM asserts—erroneously—that his grandfather was twice Mayor of Aracataca.

18. See *ibid.*, p. 42, for GGM's narration of this event.

19. See *ibid.*, pp. 44–60, on their courtship, a surprisingly lengthy narrative given that GGM had already told the story another way in *Love in the Time of Cholera* (1985).

20. Ligia GM, in Galvis, *Los GM*, pp. 151–2.

21. GGM does not directly mention his father's surname in his memoir, which is noteworthy, to say the least.

22. GGM himself would meet Pareja as a student in Bogotá, where Pareja was a law professor, had a bookshop and took a leading role in the 1948 *Bogotazo*.

23. Cited by José Font Castro, "El padre de GM," *El Nacional* (Caracas), July 1972. See also J. Font Castro, "Las claves reales de *El amor en los tiempos del cólera*," *El País* (Madrid), 19 January 1986.

24. This is the version GGM reconstructs in his first novel *Leaf Storm* (1955).

25. All can still be seen today, with the exception of the house, which was demolished early in 2007 to make way for a reconstructed version and a museum.

26. In Spanish: "La niña bonita de Aracataca." Both Vargas Llosa and Saldívar use this phrase.

27. People in Aracataca told me they never saw Luisa out in the street in the 1920s.

28. *Love in the Time of Cholera* is based to a significant extent, as mentioned above, on the courtship between Gabriel Eligio and Luisa Santiaga. García Márquez relates in *Living to Tell the Tale* that Aunt Francisca was an accomplice of the young couple; but Gabriel Eligio was always insistent that she was his worst enemy. He called her the "guard dog" ("la cancerbera").

29. Leonel Giraldo, "*Siete Días* en Aracataca, el pueblo de 'Gabo' GM," *Siete Días* (Buenos Aires), 808, 8–14 December 1982. Gabriel Eligio would never change. Many years later he and his wife were asked in an interview what was their best memory. Luisa answered, "When Gabriel Eligio gave me the ring." Gabriel Eligio answered, "My bachelor days, how I enjoyed them!"

30. Ligia GM, in Galvis, *Los GM*. Interview with Ruth Ariza Cotes, Bogotá, 2007.

31. Interview, José Font Castro, Madrid, 1997.

32. Vargas Llosa, *Historia de un deicidio*, p. 14.

33. See *Living to Tell the Tale*, pp. 59–60. In fact the house where they spent their honeymoon was the home of the Márquez Iguarán family next to the customs house in Riohacha. It was there, according to Ricardo Márquez Iguarán, who took me there in June 2008, where Gabriel Eligio's "excellent marksmanship" led to GGM's conception

on the night of 12–13 June 1926. After two weeks the couple moved to another, more modest house in the next street.

34. Clearly there are mysteries relating to the reasons why Nicolás reluctantly assented to their marriage and why García Márquez's birth date has always been such a problem. The most obvious explanation, here as everywhere else in the world, at all times and in all places, is that Luisa Santiaga got pregnant out of wedlock and (since the date of the wedding seems not to be in doubt) that Gabito was born well before 6 March (or on 6 March but well overdue) and for that reason was not baptized and registered (by what was after all a very respectable, official, law-abiding and God-fearing family) until he was three. Luisa Santiaga insisting on marrying the illegitimate, unqualified Gabriel Eligio despite parental opposition is a remarkable story. Since there seems no doubt of her love for Gabriel Eligio, it is possible that her only way of securing her parents' reluctant agreement was to get pregnant. However, there is no more than circumstantial evidence for this.

2 / The House at Aracataca (1927–1928)

1. Mendoza, *The Fragrance of Guava*, p. 17.

2. See John Archer, "Revelling in the fantastic," *Sunday Telegraph Magazine* (London), 8 February 1981. "One of the ways they kept me quiet at night was to tell me that if I moved dead people would come out of every room. So when darkness fell I would be terrified." And Germán Castro Caycedo, " 'Gabo' cuenta la novela de su vida," *El Espectador*, 23 March 1977: "I'm not afraid of darkness. I'm afraid of big houses because dead people only come out in big houses . . . I only buy little houses because dead people don't come out in them."

3. Aida GM, in Galvis, *Los GM*, p. 99: "So then the grandson just sort of stayed in my grandparents' house." In one interview the grandson himself would tell a journalist, "My parents gave me to my grandparents as a present, to please them," a version which reconciles contradictions in several of the others.

4. Luis Enrique GM, in Galvis, *Los GM*, p. 123.

5. See *Living to Tell the Tale*, pp. 32–6, for GM's evocation of the house. My description is based on careful comparison of GGM's memoirs, the architects' analysis quoted in Saldívar, *GM: el viaje a la semilla*, and the version established by the architects responsible for the 2008 reconstruction.

6. See *ibid.*, p. 34, where GM says the room had "1925" inscribed on it, which is the year it was completed.

7. Margot GM, in Galvis, *Los GM*, p. 65.

8. See *Leaf Storm*; and *Living to Tell the Tale*, p. 35.

9. GGM himself would later "remember" a visit from Uribe Uribe, although the General was assassinated fourteen years before he was born. See *Living to Tell the Tale*, p. 33.

10. Like the character in *Leaf Storm* based upon him, Nicolás was always wandering around the house looking for little odd jobs like tightening screws and touching up paint. GGM himself would adopt this practice in later years as a way of relaxing between bouts of writing; by that time he was wearing workman's overalls in order to write.

11. See *Living to Tell the Tale*, pp. 33 and 73–4: GGM says she was "my grandfather's older sister."

12. See GGM, "Watching the Rain in Galicia," *The Best of Granta Travel* (Lon-

don, Granta/Penguin, 1991), pp. 1–5, where GGM describes Tranquilina's ways with bread and hams, the like of which he never tasted again until he visited Galicia: though already eating something similar (*lacón*) in Barcelona in the 1960s had brought back the pleasures but above all the anxieties and solitude of his childhood.

13. Ligia GM, in Galvis, *Los GM*, p. 152.

14. GGM, "Vuelta a la semilla," *El Espectador*, 18 December 1983.

15. See "Growing Up in Macondo: Gabriel García Márquez," *Writers and Places*, transcript (BBC2 film, shown 12 February 1981, producer John Archer).

16. See Germán Castro Caycedo, " 'Gabo' cuenta la novela de su vida. 6," *El Espectador*, 23 March 1977, etc., for the image of the immobilized child, full of terror, and the obsession in his work with burials.

17. BBC2, "Growing Up in Macondo": "Everyone in the family is Caribbean and everyone in the Caribbean is superstitious. My mother still is today, there are still many African and Indian belief systems operating inside Catholicism . . . I myself believe in telepathy, premonitions, the power of dreams in ways we still don't under-stand . . . I was brought up in that world, am still profoundly superstitious and I still interpret my own dreams and operate largely through instinct."

18. From my discussions with Margot Valdeblánquez based on her memories and family photographs; see also Saldívar, *GM: el viaje a la semilla*, pp. 96–7, based on the recollections of Sara Emilia Márquez.

19. BBC2, "Growing Up in Macondo."

20. "Recuerdos de la maestra de GM," *El Espectador*, 31 October 1982.

21. Story told by Gabriel Eligio to José Font Castro.

22. See Mendoza, *The Fragrance of Guava*, p. 18.

23. See GGM, "La vaina de los diccionarios," *El Espectador*, 16 May 1982, in which he recalls his grandfather's misplaced respect for dictionaries and confesses his own pleasure in catching them out.

24. From my discussions with Margot Valdeblánquez based on her memories and family photographs; see also Saldívar, *GM*, pp. 103–4, based on the recollections of Sara Emilia Márquez.

25. White, *Historia*, pp. 19–20.

26. See Gabriel Fonnegra, *Bananeras: testimonio vivo de una epopeya* (Bogotá, Tercer Mundo, n.d.), pp. 27–8.

27. *Ibid.*, p. 191.

28. *Ibid.*, p. 26.

29. See Catherine C. LeGrand, "Living in Macondo: Economy and Culture in a UFC Banana Enclave in Colombia," in Gilbert M. Joseph, Catherine C. LeGrand and Ricardo D. Salvatore, eds., *Close Encounters of Empire: Writing the Cultural History of U.S.–Latin American Relations* (Durham, N.C., Duke, University Press, 1998), pp. 333–68 (p. 348).

30. GGM, *Living to Tell the Tale*, p. 18.

31. Saldívar, *GM: el viaje a la semilla*, pp. 54, 522.

32. There is no definitive history of this event and no consensus as to the number of civilians killed by the army. Inevitably most writers view it through their own ideo-logical prism.

33. Carlos Arango, *Sobrevivientes de las bananeras* (Bogotá, ECOE, 2nd ed., 1985), p. 54.

34. See María Tila Uribe, *Los años escondidos: sueños y rebeldías en la década del veinte* (Bogotá, CESTRA, 1994), p. 265.

35. See Carlos Cortés Vargas, *Los sucesos de las bananeras*, ed. R. Herrera Soto (Bogotá, Editorial Desarrollo, 2nd edition, 1979), p. 79.

36. Roberto Herrera Soto and Rafael Romero Castañeda, *La zona bananera del Magdalena: historia y léxico* (Bogotá, Instituto Caro y Cuervo, 1979), pp. 48, 65.

37. White, *Historia*, p. 99.

38. Herrera and Castañeda, *La zona bananera*, p. 52.

39. Arango, *Sobrevivientes*, pp. 84–6.

40. Fonnegra, *Bananeras*, pp. 136–7.

41. *Ibid.*, p. 138.

42. *Ibid.*, p. 154.

43. José Maldonado, quoted in Arango, *Sobrevivientes*, p. 94.

44. White, *Historia*, p. 101.

45. See GGM, "Vuelta a la semilla," *El Espectador*, 18 December 1983, in which he confesses that "it was only a few years ago I found out that he [Angarita] had taken up a very definite and coherent position during the strike and the killing of the banana workers." It is extraordinary to discover that GGM did not know most facts relevant to the strike—not excluding the actions of his grandfather, Durán, Angarita and others close to him—at the time of writing *OHYS*.

46. Cortés Vargas, *Los sucesos de las bananeras*, pp. 170–71, 174, 182–3, 201, 225. Did GGM ever learn about the writing of these letters?

47. Transcripts of the documents, including Angarita's testimony, can be found in 1928: *La masacre en las bananeras* (Bogotá, Los Comuneros, n.d.).

3 / Holding His Grandfather's Hand (1929–1937)

1. See *Living to Tell the Tale*, pp. 11–13, 80 and 122–5, for memories of these two visits.

2. In *ibid.*, p. 123, he has her saying "You don't remember me anymore," but this should probably be counted an example of poetic licence.

3. Margot was a disturbed child who would persist in eating earth until she was eight or nine years of age. She would inspire the characters of Amaranta and Rebeca in *One Hundred Years of Solitude*.

4. BBC2, "Growing Up in Macondo."

5. "El microcosmos de GM," *Excelsior* (Mexico City), 12 April 1971.

6. LeGrand, *Frontier Expansion*, p. 73.

7. Margot GM, in Galvis, *Los GM*, pp. 60–61. Evidently Margot and Gabito were thoroughly spoilt, as he acknowledges in "La conduerma de las palabras," *El Espectador*, 16 May 1981.

8. It is generally believed in Aracataca that Nicolás bought and then rented out premises in the zone known as Cataquita which were turned into one of the "academias" or dance halls where both liquor and sex were freely available. See Venancio Aramis Bermúdez Gutiérrez, "Aportes socioculturales de las migraciones en la Zona Bananera del Magdalena" (Bogotá, November 1995, Beca Colcultura 1994, I Semestre, unpublished ms.).

9. BBC2, "Growing Up in Macondo."

10. See *Living to Tell the Tale*, p. 82, on his lifelong fear of the dark.

11. See Carlota de Olier, "Habla la madre de GM: 'Quisiera volar a verlo . . . pero le tengo terror al avión,'" *El Espectador*, 22 October 1982: "'If my father were alive,' says Doña Luisa, 'he would be happy. He always thought that death would prevent him enjoying Gabito's triumphs. He intuited that in time Gabito would achieve an outstanding position and often said, "What a pity I won't be there to see how far this child's intelligence will take him."'"

12. See GGM, "Manos arriba?," *El Espectador*, 20 March 1983, which notes that most visitors to the house wore guns.

13. See Nicolás Suescún, "El prestidigitador de Aracataca," *Cromos* (Bogotá), 26 October 1982, pp. 24–7, which begins its portrait of GGM the child blinking like a movie camera and thus absorbing and processing the world and turning it into stories.

14. Margot GM, in Galvis, *Los GM*, pp. 64–5.

15. "La memoria de Gabriel," *La Nación (Guadalajara)*, 1996, p. 9.

16. Elena Poniatowska, "Los *Cien años de soledad* se iniciaron con sólo 20 dólares" (interview, September 1973), in her *Todo México* (Mexico City, Diana, 1990).

17. GGM told Germán Castro Caycedo, in " 'Gabo' cuenta la novela de su vida," *El Espectador*, 23 March 1977, that until he himself was waiting for money in Paris he had always considered this ritual something of a comedy.

18. Galvis, *Los GM*, p. 64. The Colonel also wrote frequently to his eldest son José María Valdeblánquez.

19. See GGM, "Vuelta a la semilla," *El Espectador*, 18 December 1983, where GGM speaks with great familiarity—for the first time—of General José Rosario Durán's house, which he and the Colonel must have passed, or even visited, on many occasions.

20. BBC2, "Growing Up in Macondo." See GGM, *Living to Tell the Tale*, p. 84, on Father Angarita.

21. See GGM, "Memoria feliz de Caracas," *El Espectador*, 7 March 1982; also *Living to Tell the Tale*, p. 43, on the Venezuelans in Aracataca.

22. See GGM, *Living to Tell the Tale*, pp. 24–32.

23. Saldívar, *GM: el viaje a la semilla*, pp. 67, 71–2.

24. Interview with Antonio Daconte (grandson), Aracataca, November 2006. See GGM, *Living to Tell the Tale*, pp. 18 and 87–8.

25. See GGM, *Living to Tell the Tale*, pp. 87–8 and 91–2.

26. GGM, "La nostalgia de las almendras amargas," *Cambio* (Bogotá), 23 June 2000. Also on Don Emilio, see "El personaje equívoco," *Cambio*, 19–26 June 2000.

27. BBC2, "Growing Up in Macondo."

28. See Henríquez, *El misterio*, pp. 283–4.

29. Interview with Margot Valdeblánquez de Díaz-Granados, Bogotá, 1993.

30. See *OHYS* and *Living to Tell the Tale*, pp. 66–7, on the arrival of the seventeen bastards with ash on their foreheads.

31. BBC2, "Growing Up in Macondo."

32. See GGM, *Living to Tell the Tale*, pp. 62–4.

33. See Galvis, *Los GM*, p. 59.

34. This was a traumatically confusing experience, to say the least. García Márquez has always said that he did not "meet" his mother until he was five years old. Clearly he must mean "remember," because he must have seen her on at least one of the two visits to Barranquilla. In any case his first recollection, however conditioned by memory and desire, was a defining moment of his life, later recorded in both *Leaf Storm* and *Living to Tell the Tale*. To awareness of his grandmother, his aunts and the servants, then, was now added a concrete awareness of this new personage: his mother.

35. GGM, "Cuánto cuesta hacer un escritor?," *Cambio 16*, Colombia, 11 December 1995. See *Living to Tell the Tale*, pp. 94–5, for GGM's recollections and attitude to the school.

36. According to Fonnegra, *Bananeras*, pp. 96–7, a Pedro Fergusson was Mayor of Aracataca in 1929.

37. See GGM, "La poesía al alcance de los niños," *El Espectador*, 25 January 1981.

38. Saldívar, *GM: el viaje a la semilla*, p. 120.

39. "Recuerdos de la maestra de GM," *El Espectador*, 31 October 1982.

40. Margot Valdeblánquez, interview, Bogotá, 1991.

41. Saldívar, *GM: el viaje a la semilla*, p. 120.

42. See Saldívar, "GM: 'La novela que estoy escribiendo está localizada en Cartagena de Indias, durante el siglo XVIII,'" *Diario 16* (Madrid), 1 April 1989.

43. See Rita Guibert, *Seven Voices* (New York, Vintage, 1973), pp. 317–20, for GGM on the relation between his early drawing of comic strips and his desire for public performance, which he was ultimately too self-conscious to carry off.

44. BBC2, "Growing Up in Macondo."

45. GGM, "La vaina de los diccionarios," *El Espectador*, May 1982.

46. Luis Enrique GM, in Galvis, *Los GM*, pp. 123–4.

47. Family births: Gabito, Aracataca, March 1927; Luis Enrique, Aracataca, September 1928; Margot, Barranquilla, November 1929; Aida Rosa, Barranquilla, December 1930; Ligia, Aracataca, August 1934 (she remembers the house in Aracataca in Galvis, *Los GM*, p. 152); Gustavo, Aracataca, September 1936; then Rita, Barranquilla, July 1939; Jaime, Sucre, May 1940; Hernando ("Nanchi"), Sucre, March 1943; Alfredo ("Cuqui"), Sucre, February 1945; and Eligio Gabriel ("Yiyo"), Sucre, November 1947.

48. Mendoza, *The Fragrance of Guava*, p. 21. (My translation.)

49. See GGM, "La túnica fosforescente," *El Tiempo*, December 1992; also "Estas Navidades siniestras," *El Espectador*, December 1980, in which he says he was five when all this happened. In *Living to Tell the Tale*, p. 70, he says that he was ten on this occasion, not seven, as chronological laws would suggest.

50. In *Leaf Storm*, pp. 50–54, Martín, the character based partly on Gabriel Eligio, is both sinister (he uses Guajiro witchcraft, including sticking pins in dolls' eyes) and bland; evidently he never loved Isabel (the character based partly on Luisa) but only wanted contact with the Colonel's influence and money; and he left before his child (the character partly based on GGM) could have any memories of him—which of course is true of GGM's own experience, except in that case Gabriel Eligio also took Luisa away; whereas in *Leaf Storm* GGM, in wish-fulfilment, has the mother to himself and sends the father away for ever.

51. "Recuerdos de la maestra de GM," *El Espectador*, 31 October 1982.

52. Margot GM, in Galvis, *Los GM*, p. 61.

53. See *Living to Tell the Tale*, p. 85.

54. See Leonel Giraldo, "*Siete Días* en Aracataca, el pueblo de 'Gabo' GM," *Siete Días* (Buenos Aires), 808, 8–14 December 1982.

55. GGM addresses this question in *Living to Tell the Tale*, pp. 82–4.

56. Margot GM, in Galvis, *Los GM*, p. 62. See *Living to Tell the Tale*, pp. 84–5, for GGM's reflections on the return of his parents; note in particular that although refusing overtly to criticize his father he immediately starts talking about beatings, thereby showing that he associates his father with violence (for which, he says, Gabriel Eligio later apologized). Of course most parents physically chastised their children in those days.

57. See Margot's recollections in Galvis, *Los GM*, p. 68.

58. GGM, *Los cuentos de mi abuelo el coronel*, ed. Juan Gustavo Cobo Borda (Smurfit Cartón de Colombia, 1988).

59. See *Living to Tell the Tale*, pp. 95–6.

60. Ramiro de la Espriella, "De 'La casa' fue saliendo todo," *Imagen* (Caracas), 1972.

61. See Luis Enrique's hilarious recollections of the journey to Sincé in Galvis, *Los GM*, pp. 124–5; also GGM, *Living to Tell the Tale*, pp. 96–7.

62. Interview with GGM, Mexico City, 1999.

63. I visited Sincé with GGM's brother-in-law Alfonso Torres (married to GGM's sister Rita, who had lived there) in 1998.

64. Margot GM, in Galvis, *Los GM*, p. 68.

65. Saldívar, "GM: 'La novela que estoy escribiendo está localizada en Cartagena de Indias, durante el siglo XVIII,'" *Diario 16*, 1 April 1989. These are clearly very important statements. GGM's stories and novels are obsessed with corpses but GGM himself seems never to have seen the corpses of people who were important to him until his father died in 1984. In his first story, "La tercera resignación" (1947), the narrator himself dies but his corpse does not decompose or get buried.

66. Guillermo Ochoa, "Los seres que inspiraron a Gabito," *Excelsior* (Mexico City), 13 April 1971. Of course he was not eight but ten when his grandfather died (in "El personaje equívoco," *Cambio*, 19–26 June 2000, he says it happened "when I was not much more than five"); but he was indeed eight when his grandfather had his fateful accident and it was then that the life he had led until that moment, already threatened by the return of his parents and siblings, effectively came to an end.

67. Luisa Márquez, interview, Barranquilla, 1993.

68. Margot GM, in Galvis, *Los GM*, p. 69.

69. Luis Enrique, in Galvis, *Los GM*, p. 130. Did the always mischievous Luis Enrique know more about the "academy" and its antecedents than he lets on?

70. GGM, "Regreso a la guayaba," *El Espectador*, 10 April 1983. On his relation to Aracataca, see also GGM, "Vuelta a la semilla," *El Espectador*, 18 December 1983.

4 / Schooldays: Barranquilla, Sucre, Zipaquirá (1938–1946)

1. GGM, *Living to Tell the Tale*, pp. 128–29.

2. *Ibid.*, p. 132.

3. *Ibid.*, pp. 142–3.

4. Mendoza, *The Fragrance of Guava*, p. 19.

5. GGM, *Vivir para contarla* (Mexico City, Diana, 2002), p. 173. (My translation.)

6. *Vivir para contarla*, p. 163. (My translation.) The fact that he did survive was always attributed by Luisa Santiaga to the fact that she gave him cod-liver oil every day: see Guillermo Ochoa, "El microcosmos de GM," *Excelsior* (Mexico City), April 12 1971: " 'The kid smelled of fish all day,' his father says."

7. The following sections on Sucre draw on my interviews with Señora Luisa Márquez de García in Cartagena and Barranquilla, 1991 and 1993, on a conversation with GGM himself in Mexico City in 1999, and on many conversations with all his brothers and sisters down the years—as well as on the published sources recorded in these notes.

8. Gustavo GM, in Galvis, *Los GM*, p. 185.

9. *Living to Tell the Tale*, p. 155.

10. *Vivir para contarla*, p. 188. (My translation.)

11. Juan Gossaín, quoted by Heriberto Fiorillo, *La Cueva: crónica del grupo de Barranquilla* (Bogotá, Planeta, 2002), pp. 87–8.

12. Saldívar, *GM: el viaje a la semilla*, is the best source on GGM's time in the Colegio San Juan. But see also José A. Núñez Segura, "Gabriel García Márquez (Gabo-Gabito)," *Revista Javeriana* (Bogotá), 352, March 1969, pp. 31–6, in which one of the Jesuit teachers at the school retrieves some of GGM's juvenile compositions.

13. Galvis, *Los GM*, p. 70.

14. GGM mentions this murder in *Living to Tell the Tale*, pp. 227–8.

15. The youngest, Yiyo, did not entirely agree: he once told me that all the younger children, the ones born in Sucre, were "hopeless," including him, precisely because they were the only ones his father had delivered!

16. See Harley D. Oberhelman, "Gabriel Eligio García habla de Gabito," in Peter G. Earle, ed., *Gabriel García Marquez* (Madrid, Taurus, 1981), pp. 281–3. Oberhelman interviewed Gabriel Eligio about his medical training and experience.

17. Guillermo Ochoa, "El microcosmos de GM," *Excelsior*, 12 April 1971.

18. *Living to Tell the Tale*, p. 224.

19. GGM in conversation, Mexico City, 1999.

20. Rosario Agudelo, "Conversaciones con García Márquez," *Pueblo*, suplemento, "Sábado Literario" (Madrid), 2 May 1981. In other versions GGM laughs this traumatic experience off; *Living to Tell the Tale* gives a kind of intermediate version; and *Memories of My Melancholy Whores* gives a fictionalized account.

21. Popular Caribbean musical genre whose style evolved out of the *cumbia*, Colombia's traditional national dance rhythm.

22. Roberto Ruiz, "Eligio García en Cartagena. El abuelo de Macondo," *El Siglo*, 31 October 1969.

23. Quoted by Gossaín in Fiorillo, *La Cueva*, p. 88. Gabriel Eligio later denied the intention to trepan.

24. See GGM, "El cuento del cuento. (Conclusión)," *El Espectador*, 2 September 1981, in which he recalls his adolescent days in Sucre (un-named) and states that they were "the freest years of my life." On his attitude to prostitutes, see Claudia Dreifus, "Gabriel García Márquez," *Playboy* 30:2, February 1983.

25. *Living to Tell the Tale*, p. 166.

26. My translation. See *Living to Tell the Tale*, pp. 168–71.

27. *Ibid.*, p. 174.

28. See GGM, "Bogotá 1947," *El Espectador*, 21 October 1981 and "El río de nuestra vida," *El Espectador*, 22 March 1981. The writer Christopher Isherwood visited Colombia in the 1940s and travelled on the *David Arango*. See his evocation of the journey in *The Condor and the Cows* (London, Methuen, 1949).

29. GGM, *The Autumn of the Patriarch* (London, Picador, 1978), p. 16.

30. *Living to Tell the Tale*, pp. 179–80.

31. The best evocation of this entire journey and the arrival in Bogotá is in Germán Castro Caycedo, " 'Gabo' cuenta la novela de su vida. 1 and 2," *El Espectador*, 23 March 1977.

32. GGM, "Bogotá 1947," *El Espectacdor*, 18 October 1981.

33. GGM, *Living to Tell the Tale*, pp. 184–5.

34. The best source on the school at Zipaquirá is Saldívar, *GM: el viaje a la semilla*. Much of my information is based on an interview with a schoolmate of GM, José Espinosa, Bogotá, 1998.

35. Rosario Agudelo, "Conversaciones con García Márquez," *Pueblo*, suplemento, "Sábado Literario" (Madrid), 2 May 1981.

36. See Aline Helg, *La educacíon en Colombia 1918–1957: una historia social, economíca y politica* (Bogotá, CEREC, 1987).

37. GGM, "'Estoy comprometido hasta el tuétano con el periodismo político.' *Alternativa* entrevista a GGM," *Alternativa* (Bogotá), 29, 31 March–13 April 1975, p. 3.

38. See Juan Gustavo Cobo Borda, "Cuatro horas de comadreo literario con GGM" (interview 23 March 1981), in his *Silva, Arciniegas, Mutis y García Márquez* (Bogotá, Presidencia de la República, 1997), pp. 469–82 (p. 475).

39. *Living to Tell the Tale*, p. 196.

40. Quoted by Carlos Rincón, "GGM entra en los 65 años. Tres o cuatro cosas que querría saber de él," *El Espectador*, 1 March 1992.

41. Margot García Márquez told me in 1993: "When Mamá was pregnant with Nanchi, it happened again. This time even Mamá got upset. She was in bed in the two-storey house in Sucre square and she wouldn't get up. That time she even screamed at him. And Mamá was always incredibly sick, vomiting, with each of her pregnancies, she always lost weight, it was amazing but true. And I got really upset for her and wanted to do something about it, but she wouldn't let me."

42. Luis Enrique GM, Galvis, *Los GM*, p. 146.

43. *Living to Tell the Tale*, pp. 217–18.

44. Saldívar, *GM: el viaje a la semilla*, p. 156.

45. Darío too came from a small Caribbean town, he too was brought up away from his own mother, and he too had listened to an old colonel telling tales of war. Thirty years later García Márquez's *The Autumn of the Patriarch* would be, among other things, a loving tribute to Darío's poetic language.

46. *Living to Tell the Tale*, p. 205.

47. "La ex-novia del Nobel Colombiano," *El País* (Madrid), 7 October 2002.

48. *Vivir para contarla*, p. 242. (My translation.)

49. See GGM, *One Hundred Years of Solitude* (London, Picador, 1978), pp. 29–30.

50. *Living to Tell the Tale*, p. 204.

51. *Ibid.*, p. 193.

52. *Ibid.*, p. 193.

53. See Saldívar, *GM: el viaje a la semilla*, p. 166; also GGM, *Living to Tell the Tale*, pp. 193–4.

54. See Germán Santamaría, "Carlos Julio Calderón Hermida, el profesor de GM," *Gaceta* (Bogotá, Colcultura), 39, 1983, pp. 4–5.

55. In interviews after he became famous he frequently denied ever having written poetry: see, for example, his conversation with María Esther Gilio, "Escribir bien es un deber revolucionario," *Triunfo* (Madrid), 1977, included in Rentería, ed., *GM habla de GM en 33 grandes reportajes*.

56. See *La Casa Grande* (Mexico City/Bogotá), 1:3, February–April 1997, p. 45, where the poem is published "thanks to Dasso Saldívar and Luis Villar Borda."

57. *Living to Tell the Tale*, pp. 205–6.

58. Ligia GM, in Galvis, *Los GM*, p. 165: "When Gabito fell in love with Mercedes she was a girl of eight in a pinafore dress with little ducks on."

59. See Beatriz López de Barcha, "'Gabito esperó a que yo creciera,'" *Carrusel*, Revista de *El Tiempo* (Bogotá), 10 December 1982.

60. This was republished by Héctor Abad Gómez, "GM poeta?," *El Tiempo, Lecturas Dominicales*, 12 December 1982. See also Donald McGrady, "Dos sonetos atribuidos a GGM," *Hispanic Review*, 51 (1983), pp. 429–34. The most popular *cumbia* in Colombia, composed years later, is called "Colegiala" ("Schoolgirl").

61. See GGM, "Memorias de un fumador retirado," *El Espectador*, 13 February 1983.

62. *Living to Tell the Tale*, p. 200.

63. *Vivir para contarla*, p. 281. (My translation.) See also GGM, "El cuento del cuento. (Conclusión)," *El Espectador*, 2 September 1981, where he recalls how he discovered that María Alejandrina Cervantes's brothel had become a convent school when he returned fifteen years later.

64. See *Living to Tell the Tale*, pp. 236–9.

65. *OHYS*, p. 301.

66. Interview, Cartagena, 1991.

67. In Mompox Mercedes had a close school friend called Margarita Chica Salas, who also lived in Sucre: she would shortly be involved in the drama surrounding the murder of Cayetano Gentile, a close friend of GM and his family.

68. Gertrudis Prasca de Amín, interview, Magangué, 1991.

69. GGM, *Crónica de una muerte anunciada* (Bogotá, Oveja Negra, 1981), p. 40. (My translation.)

70. GGM, "El río de nuestra vida," *El Espectador*, 22 March 1981, mentions the "irrecoverable José Palencia." See *Living to Tell the Tale*, pp. 239–43.

71. *Living to Tell the Tale*, pp. 243–4.

72. Saldívar, "GM: La novela que estoy escribiendo está localizada en Cartagena de Indias, durante el siglo XVIII," *Diario 16*, 1 April 1989.

73. Ligia GM, in Galvis, *Los GM*, p. 158.

74. See GGM, "Telepatía sin hilos," *El Espectador*, 16 November 1980, in which he states that Tranquilina died "almost one hundred years old."

75. Aida Rosa GM, in Galvis, *Los GM*, p. 99.

5 / The University Student and the *Bogotazo* (1947–1948)

1. This chapter draws on a wide range of sources and conversations but especially on interviews with Gonzalo Mallarino (Bogotá, 1991), Luis Villar Borda (Bogotá, 1998), Margarita Márquez Caballero (Bogotá, 1998), Jacques Gilard (Toulouse, 1999, 2004) and Gustavo Adolfo Ramírez Ariza (Bogotá, 2007).

2. In M. Fernández-Braso, *GGM: una conversación infinita* (Madrid, Azur, 1969), p. 102, GGM remarks that the Colombian Academy considers even the Spanish Royal Academy "progressive" and talks of "protecting" the language (even against Spain!).

3. Kafka, "Letter to his Father" (November 1919). Kafka's father never read this letter.

4. Interview, Bogotá, 1993. ALM was in fact a distant relation through a shared Cotes great-grandfather, as would later be discovered when they became friends.

5. Luis Villar Borda, interview, 1998. On this period see also GGM, "Bogotá 1947," *El Espectador*, 18 October 1981.

6. See Juan B. Fernández, "Cuando García Márquez era Gabito," *El Tiempo, Lecturas Dominicales*, October 1982. One of his key companions at this time was to be Afro-Colombian medical student Manuel Zapata Olivella, who would later intervene in his destiny in a decisive fashion on more than one occasion. Other important *costeño* students were Jorge Alvaro Espinosa, who introduced GGM to Joyce's *Ulysses*, and Domingo Manuel Vega, who lent him Kafka's *Metamorphosis*.

7. Alvaro Mutis, "Apuntes sobre un viaje que no era para contar," in Aura Lucía Mera, ed., *Aracataca/Estocolmo* (Bogotá, Instituto Colombiano de Cultura, 1983), pp. 19–20, describes Mallarino on the 1982 Nobel trip as "our dean," GGM's oldest *cachaco* friend from the Bogotá period.

8. For important details about Camilo Torres and his decision to be a priest and subsequent departure, see Germán Castro Caycedo, "'Gabo' cuenta la novela de su vida. 2," *El Espectador*, 23 March 1977.

9. Plinio Apuleyo Mendoza, *La llama y el hielo* (Bogotá, Gamma, 3rd edition, 1989), pp. 9–10.

10. The direct translation would be "cock-sucking" because the image is of the owner of a fighting cock gazing ironically and provocatively at his adversary over the cock's comb, while soothing it lovingly with his lips.

11. See GGM, "Bogotá, 1947," *El Espectador*, 18 October 1981; and "El frenesí del viernes," *El Espectador*, 13 November 1983, which recalls his desolate Sundays in Bogotá.

12. Gonzalo Mallarino, interview, Bogotá, 1991.

13. The second, "Celestial Geography," was published on 1 July 1947.

14. See Germán Castro Caycedo, "'Gabo' cuenta la novela de su vida. 2," *El Espectador*, 23 March 1977, on GGM's farewell to Camilo Torres.

15. *La Vida Universitaria*, Tuesday supplement of *La Razón*, Bogotá, 22 June 1947. See *La Casa Grande* (Mexico City/Bogotá), 1:3, February–April 1997, p. 45, where this poem is republished "thanks to Dasso Saldívar and Luis Villar Borda."

16. See Juan Gustavo Cobo Borda, "Cuatro horas de comadreo literario con GGM," in his *Silva, Arciniegas, Mutis y GM* (Bogotá, Presidencia de la República, 1997), pp. 469–82, for one of the many versions of this story. Borges would later say that "The Metamorphosis" was the only story from this collection that he did not in fact translate.

17. Of course it isn't the way *Kafka's* grandmother talked—that, precisely, was the difference!

18. See John Updike, "Dying for love: a new novel by GM," in *The New Yorker*, 7 November 2005: "A velvety pleasure to read, though somewhat disagreeable to contemplate; it has the necrophiliac tendencies of the precocious short stories, obsessed with living death, that GM published in his early twenties."

19. GGM, *Todos los cuentos (1947–1972)* (Barcelona, Plaza y Janés, 3rd edition, 1976), pp. 17–18. (My translation.)

20. *Ibid.*, pp. 14–15.

21. *Ibid.*, pp. 17–18.

22. GGM tells the whole story to Germán Castro Caycedo, "'Gabo' cuenta la novela de su vida. 3," *El Espectador*, 23 March 1977.

23. GGM, *Collected Stories* (New York, Harper Perennial, 1991), p. 24.

24. "La Ciudad y el Mundo," *El Espectador*, 28 October 1947.

25. *Living to Tell the Tale*, p. 271.

26. Gustavo Adolfo Ramírez Ariza is preparing a major revisionist work on García Márquez's relationship with and experiences in Bogotá.

27. GGM, *Collected Stories*, p. 19.

28. Luis Enrique GM, in Galvis, *Los GM*, pp. 132–3.

29. The ending *-azo* in Spanish conveys the idea of a violent blow by or against something.

30. See Gonzalo Sánchez, "*La Violencia* in Colombia: New research, new questions," *Hispanic American Historical Review*, 65:4 (1985), pp. 789–807.

31. Interview, Bogotá, 1998. In "Bogotá 1947," *El Espectador*, 18 October 1981, GGM states categorically that his papers disappeared in the fire which destroyed his *pensión* (with specific reference to "El fauno en la tranvía"). *Living to Tell the Tale*, p. 288, tells a different story.

32. See Herbert Braun, *Mataron a Gaitán: vida pública y violencia urbana en Colombia* (Bogotá, Norma, 1998), p. 326.

33. Ironically, his first revolutionary act was to help a looter smash a typewriter; García Márquez would later assure Castro that the typewriter was his!

34. See Arturo Alape, *El Bogotazo: memorias del olvido* (Bogotá, Universidad Central, 1983).

35. Interview, Margarita Márquez Caballero, Bogotá, 1998.

36. Rita GM, in Galvis, *Los GM*, p. 237.

6 / Back to the Costa: An Apprentice Journalist
in Cartagena (1948–1949)

1. *Living to Tell the Tale*, p. 304. This chapter draws on interviews with the GM family, with Ramiro de la Espriella (Bogotá, 1991), Carlos Alemán (Bogotá, 1991), Manuel Zapata Olivella (Bogotá, 1991), Juan Zapata Olivella (Cartagena, 1991), Jacques Gilard (Toulouse, 1999, 2004), Héctor Rojas Herazo (Barranquilla, 1998) and Marta Yances (Cartagena, 2007), among many others.

2. There are two excellent books on García Márquez's time in Cartagena: Gustavo Arango, *Un ramo de nomeolvides: García Márquez en "El Universal"* (Cartagena, El Universal, 1995) and Jorge García Usta, *Como aprendió a escribir García Márquez* (Medellín, Lealon, 1995), which appeared in a revised edition and with a slightly less inflammatory title in 2007: *García Márquez en Cartagena: sus inicios literarios* (Bogotá, Planeta, 2007). Both claim more for the impact of the city upon his development as a writer than the evidence can perhaps sustain, but they both write as correctives to the majority view that it was the subsequent period in Barranquilla (1950–53) which was decisive. They were reacting above all against the work of the French scholar Jacques Gilard, who, in the 1970s, gathered together all García Márquez's journalism in *El Universal* (Cartagena), *El Heraldo* (Barranquilla), *El Espectador* (Bogotá) and elsewhere. Whatever view is taken of this ongoing polemic Gilard's contribution to García Márquez studies is unsurpassed and his prologues to the volumes of GGM's *Obra periodística* are indispensable. No more than a handful of GGM's more than 1,000 articles, essays and brief literary pieces published in the press between 1948 and 2008 have ever appeared in English. Specifically on this period, see Jacques Gilard, ed., *Gabriel García Márquez, Obra periodística vol.I: Textos costeños 1* (Bogotá, Oveja Negra, 1983).

3. *Living to Tell the Tale*, pp. 306–16, tells the story of these days and weeks in great detail.

4. See profile of Rojas Herazo by GGM, *El Heraldo* (Barranquilla), 14 March 1950.

5. *Living to Tell the Tale*, pp. 313–14 and pp. 320–21. In *Living* GGM calls him "José Dolores."

6. See "Un domingo de delirio," *El Espectador*, 8 March 1981, in which GGM, back in Cartagena, talks about its magic and reveals that his favourite place used to be the wharf of the Bahía de las Animas, where the market used to be. See also "Un payaso pintado detrás de una puerta," *El Espectador*, 1 May 1982.

7. Although, in Cartagena, it is thought that García Márquez did not acknowledge Zabala precisely because he learned so much from him, in 1980 García Márquez said to a journalist, Donaldo Bossa Herazo, "Zabala is a gentleman to whom I owe much of what I am." (Arango, *Un ramo de nomeolvides*, p. 136.)

8. The two articles, both untitled, appeared in *El Universal* under the "Punto y Aparte" byline on 21 and 22 May 1948, six weeks after the *Bogotazo*.

9. These and all his other articles from this period can be found in Gilard, ed., *Textos costeños 1*.

10. See Gilard, ed., *Textos costeños 1*, pp. 94–5.

11. *Living to Tell the Tale*, pp. 324–5.

12. Ligia GM, in Galvis, *Los GM*, p. 169.

13. Arango, *Un ramo de nomeolvides*, p. 178.

14. García Usta, *Como aprendió a escribir García Márquez*, p. 49.

15. The phrase in Spanish was "tan modosito" (Arango, *Un ramo de nomeolvides*, p. 67).

16. *Ibid.*, p. 275.

17. Franco Múnera, quoted by *ibid.*, p. 178. The detail is significant: in the racist Colombia of the 1940s, above all in Bogotá, the drum was a coded sign for *costeño* culture in general and black culture in particular; García Márquez's explicit attachment to that instrument was, equally, a sign of an attachment to his regional culture and a gesture of defiance to the *cachaco* view of the world.

18. *El Universal*, 27 June 1948.

19. See GGM's article on Poe in *El Universal*, 7 October 1949. On his relation with Ibarra Merlano, see Cobo Borda, "Cuatro horas de comadreo literario con GGM," *op. cit.*

20. *El Universal*, 4 July 1948; see Arango, *Un ramo de nomeolvides*, p. 149. The article was republished in *El Heraldo* (Barranquilla), 16 February 1950, with the addition of the name Albaniña.

21. *El Universal*, 10 July 1948; republished with slight differences in *El Heraldo*, 1 February 1950.

22. Arango, *Un ramo de nomeolvides*, pp. 208, 222.

23. Luis Enrique GM, interview, Barranquilla, 1998.

24. Luis Enrique GM, interview, Barranquilla, 1993.

25. *Living to Tell the Tale*, pp. 333–9.

26. See GGM, "El viaje de Ramiro de la Espriella," *El Universal*, 26 July 1949, which mentions both writers.

27. See Virginia Woolf, *Orlando* (New York, Vintage, 2000), p. 176: "But love—as the male novelists define it—and who, after all, speak with greater authority?—has nothing whatever to do with kindness, fidelity, generosity, or poetry. *Love is slipping off one's petticoat* and—But we all know what love is. Did Orlando do that?" (My emphasis.)

28. The phrase was "mucha vieja macha": see Arango, *Un ramo de nomeolvides*, p. 220.

29. Rafael Betancourt Bustillo, quoted by García Usta, pp. 52–3.

30. Arango, *Un ramo de nomeolvides*, p. 231.

31. But this would have involved, again, inventing so-called "magical realism" all on his own, and writers more than twice his age such as Miguel Angel Asturias (*Men of Maize*, 1949) and Alejo Carpentier (*The Kingdom of This World*, 1949) were only just getting round to this idea as García Márquez began to wrestle with "The House," in a country whose fiction was painfully backward even by the Latin American standards of the time.

32. *Vivir para contarla*, p. 411. (My translation.)

33. See GGM's articles on La Sierpe in Gilard, ed., *Gabriel García Márquez, Obra periodística vol. II: Textos costeños 2* (Bogotá, Oveja Negra, 1983).

34. See Eligio García, *La tercera muerte de Santiago Nasar* (Bogotá, Oveja Negra, 1987), p. 61.

35. See GGM, "La cándida Eréndira y su abuela Irene Papas," *El Espectador*, 3 November 1982.

36. Fiorillo, *La Cueva*, p. 95.

37. In *Living to Tell the Tale*, p. 350, he says he *starts* it now! On p. 363 he says it was never more than "fragments" anyway!

38. Arango, *Un ramo de nomeolvides*, p. 266.

39. *Ibid.*, p. 243. Jaime Angulo Bossa recalls that in Cartagena in those days he and García Márquez always shook one another's left hand (*ibid.*, p. 302). Ironically enough, although critics have argued interminably as to whether García Márquez's reading of modernist novels originated in Cartagena or Barranquilla, none of them seem to have noticed that his active political education undoubtedly began right there in Cartagena,

due first to Zabala and then to Ramiro de la Espriella; politics was never the Barran-quilla Group's principal concern.

40. See Juan Gossaín, "A Cayetano lo mató todo el pueblo," *El Espectador*, 13 May 1981, in which Luis Enrique GM tells the extraordinary story of María Alejandrina Cervantes: her improvised brothel in Sucre was "a sort of office where we all met dur-ing the vacations . . . My mother never worried if it was late and Gabito hadn't got home because she knew he was at María Alejandrina's. I don't know if people can understand the way things were thirty years ago without being scandalized . . ."

41. GGM, "Viernes," *El Universal*, 24 June 1949. The book's importance to him was such that, no doubt exaggerating, he would later attribute his entire understanding of the nature of time both in life and in fiction to having read *Mrs. Dalloway*.

42. Gilard, ed., *Textos costeños 1*, pp. 7–10; Saldívar, *GM*, pp. 556–7.

43. GGM, "Abelito Villa, Escalona & Cía," *El Heraldo*, 14 March 1950.

44. Arango, *Un ramo de nomeolvides*, p. 237.

45. Both Arango and García Usta take this line.

7 / Barranquilla, a Bookseller and a Bohemian Group (1950–1953)

1. Arango, *Un ramo de nomeolvides*, p. 222.

2. *Ibid.*, p. 311. This chapter draws upon interviews with the GM brothers and sis-ters, Alfonso Fuenmayor (Barranquilla, 1991, 1993), Germán Vargas (Barranquilla, 1991), Alejandro Obregón (Cartagena, 1991), Tita Cepeda (Barranquilla, 1991), Susy Linares de Vargas (Barranquilla, 1991), Heliodoro García (Barranquilla, 1991), Guillermo Marín (Barranquilla, 1991), Quique Scopell (Barranquilla, 1993), Katya González (Barranquilla, 1991), Pacho Bottía (Barranquilla, 1991), Ben Woolford (London, 1991), Ramón Illán Bacca (Barranquilla, 1991, 2007), Antonio María Peñaloza Cervantes (Aracataca, 1991), Otto Garzón Patiño (Barranquilla, 1993), Alberto Assa (Barranquilla, 1993), Juan Roda and María Fornaguera de Roda (Bogotá, 1993), Jacques Gilard (Toulouse, 1999, 2004), Guillermo Henríquez (Barranquilla, 2007), Meira Delmar (Barranquilla, 2007), Jaime Abello (Barranquilla, 2007), and many others.

3. Conversation, Mexico City, 1993.

4. On the Barranquilla Group see especially Alfonso Fuenmayor, *Crónicas sobre el grupo de Barranquilla* (Bogotá, Instituto Colombiano de Cultura, 1978) and Fiorillo, *La Cueva*, which has outstanding illustrations. Fiorillo has produced several other invalu-able works on cultural matters surrounding the group. On Vinyes, see Jacques Gilard, *Entre los Andes y el Caribe: la obra americana de Ramón Vinyes* (Medellín, Universidad de Antioquia, 1989) and Jordi Lladó, *Ramon Vinyes: un home de lletres entre Catalunya i el Caribe* (Barcelona, Generalitat de Catalunya, 2006).

5. "What, you are Subirats? Subirats, the mediocre translator of Joyce?" (Fuen-mayor, *Crónicas sobre el grupo*, p. 43).

6. Fiorillo, *La Cueva*, pp. 46, 98.

7. See Alvaro Mutis, "Apuntes sobre un viaje que no era para contar," in Mera, ed., *Aracataca-Estocolmo*, pp. 19–20, for examples.

8. See Fiorillo, *La Cueva*, p. 108.

9. Daniel Samper, Prologue, *Antología de Alvaro Cepeda Samudio* (Bogotá, Bib-lioteca Colombiana de Cultura, 1977); also Plinio Mendoza, "Requiem," *La llama y el hielo*.

10. See GM, "Obregón, o la vocación desaforada," *El Espectador*, 20 October 1982.

11. "El grupo de Barranquilla," *Vanguardia Liberal*, Bucaramanga, 22 January 1956, quoted by Gilard in *GGM, Obra periodística vol. V: De Europa y América 1* (Bogotá, Oveja Negra, 1984), p. 15.

12. Fiorillo, *La Cueva*, p. 96.

13. *Ibid.*, pp. 136–7.

14. *Ibid.*, p. 58; in more recent times the singer Shakira's father had a jeweller's shop there.

15. The present writer was given an unforgettable tour of this zone by Alfonso Fuenmayor in 1993, not long before he died; Jaime Abello, director of GGM's Foundation for New Ibero-American Journalism, gave me a splendid update in 2006.

16. It may have been Rondón who first introduced GGM to the world of communism. See " 'Estoy comprometido hasta el tuétano con el periodismo político': *Alternativa* entrevista a GGM," *Alternativa* (Bogotá), 29, 31 March–13 April 1975, p. 3, where he mentions belonging to a communist cell "at the age of twenty-two."

17. See the first paragraph of *Living to Tell the Tale*.

18. Fiorillo, *La Cueva*, p. 74. Eufemia's brothel is another place given mythical status by references in García Márquez's story "The Night of the Curlews" and *One Hundred Years of Solitude*. Many of the group's escapades were later immortalized in both literature and local legend, such as the time when Alfonso Fuenmayor frightened a parrot down from a tree and it fell into the *sancocho* stew that is always boiling away in anecdotes about *costeño* brothels at this time; García Márquez, without thinking, picked up the saucepan's great lid and the parrot met its destiny as a substitute for chicken in the fragrant bubbling stew. On prostitution and literature in Barranquilla see Adlai Stevenson Samper, *Polvos en La Arenosa: cultura y burdeles en Barranquilla* (Barranquilla, La Iguana Ciega, 2005).

19. Fiorillo, *La Cueva*, p. 93.

20. GGM told me this in Havana in 1997.

21. See *Living to Tell the Tale*, p. 363. In *Memories of My Melancholy Whores* her fictional re-creation will be called Castorina.

22. In *Living to Tell the Tale* he is called not Dámaso but Lácides.

23. Faulkner said this in his famous *Paris Review* interview, which made a big impression on GGM. For an early description of the Skyscraper and its inhabitants see Plinio Mendoza, "Entrevista con Gabriel García Márquez," *Libre* (Paris), 3, March–May 1972, pp. 7–8.

24. "Una mujer con importancia," *El Heraldo*, 11 January 1950.

25. "El barbero de la historia," *El Heraldo*, 25 May 1951.

26. "Illya en Londres," *El Heraldo*, 29 July 1950.

27. "Memorias de un aprendiz de antropófago," *El Heraldo*, 9 February 1951.

28. "La peregrinación de la jirafa," *El Heraldo*, 30 May 1950.

29. Saldívar, *GM: el viaje a la semilla*, refutes GGM's story and asserts categorically that the visit to Aracataca with his mother was in 1952 and that GGM only said that it was in 1950 in order to make Barranquilla the place where *Leaf Storm* was first written and in order to make the journey with his mother its inspiration—whereas in fact, according to Saldívar, *Leaf Storm* was first written in Cartagena in 1948–9! Since at the time Saldívar asserted this GGM was planning to make the journey with his mother the point of departure for his entire memoir and the definitive confirmation of his literary vocation, Saldívar's hypothesis is especially reckless—and, in my judgement, entirely mistaken.

30. Later he would use this memory to create his story "Tuesday Siesta" about the mother and sister of a dead thief who have to walk through the hostile streets of Macondo to visit his grave. Those who have read Juan Rulfo's *Pedro Páramo* (1955),

which had an enormous influence on GGM, starting with the first line of *OHYS*, will have noted that both the style and the content of this section of *Living to Tell the Tale* are reminiscent of Juan Preciado's arrival in Comala at the start of Rulfo's book. On Aracataca at this time, see Lázaro Diago Julio, *Aracataca . . . una historia para contar* (Aracataca, 1989, unpublished), pp. 198–212.

31. Ironically enough, the local historian Diago Julio says that 1950 was Aracataca's most prosperous year since the 1920s (*ibid.*, p. 215).

32. *Living to Tell the Tale*, p. 26.

33. GGM, interviewed by Peter Stone for the *Paris Review* in 1981. See Philip Gourevitch, ed., *The "Paris Review" Interviews*, Vol. II (London, Canongate, 2007), pp. 185–6.

34. Said to me in 1999; and see Anthony Day and Marjorie Miller, "Gabo talks: GGM on the misfortunes of Latin America, his friendship with Fidel Castro and his terror of the blank page," *Los Angeles Times Magazine*, 2 September 1990, p. 33.

35. In *Living to Tell the Tale* GGM says he barely spoke to his mother on the return journey; but in Juan Gustavo Cobo Borda, "Cuatro horas de comadreo literario con GGM," he says that he immediately began to ask her about "the story of my grandfather, the family, where I'd come from."

36. GGM, "¿Problemas de la novela?," *El Heraldo*, 24 April 1950.

37. Fiorillo, *La Cueva*, pp. 20–21.

38. *El Heraldo*, 14 March 1950.

39. Escalona remains the best-known composer of *vallenatos* and a national institution. See Consuelo Araujonoguera, *Rafael Escalona: el hombre y el mito* (Bogotá, Planeta, 1988), a biography by the woman who would stage the now traditional *vallenato* festivals in Valledupar until she was killed, apparently in a firefight between the army and FARC guerrillas, in September 2001.

40. See Fiorillo, *La Cueva*, p. 36.

41. See *Living to Tell the Tale*, Fuenmayor, *Crónicas sobre el grupo*, and Gilard, ed., *Textos costeños* 1.

42. See Fiorillo, *La Cueva*, pp. 186–7.

43. On GGM and Hemingway, see William Kennedy, "The Yellow Trolley Car in Barcelona: An Interview" (1972), in *Riding the Yellow Trolley Car* (New York, Viking, 1993), p. 261.

44. GGM, "Faulkner, Nobel Prize," *El Heraldo*, 13 November 1950.

45. Eligio García, *Tras las claves de Melquíades*, pp. 360–61.

46. Carlos Alemán gave me a copy of the letter when we met in Bogotá in 1991. The Spanish version was later reprinted in Arango, *Un ramo de nomeolvides*, pp. 271–3.

47. Curiously, two years before, Gaitán had been buried in the courtyard of his house in Bogotá because it was feared that his tomb would attract unhealthy attention from both his admirers and his enemies.

48. "Caricatura de Kafka," *El Heraldo*, 23 August 1950.

49. Martín is both sinister (he uses Guajiro witchcraft, including sticking pins in dolls' eyes) and bland: a curious combination.

50. "El viaje a la semilla," *El Manifiesto* (Bogotá, 1977), in Rentería, p. 161.

51. GGM told Elena Poniatowska (interview, September 1973, in *Todo México*, p. 224), that he "has never been able to use Mercedes literarily because he knows her so well that he has no idea what she is really like."

52. I talked to Meira Delmar about those days in November 2006.

53. Ligia GM, in Galvis, *Los GM*, pp. 165–6. Mercedes said the same to me in 1991.

54. See Antonio Andrade, "Cuando Macondo era una redacción," *Excelsior* (Mexico City), 11 October 1970.

55. Aida GM, interview, Barranquilla, 1993.

56. See "El día que Mompox se volvió Macondo," *El Tiempo*, 11 December 2002. Margarita Chica died in Sincelejo in May 2003. The best source on the causes of this murder and its aftermath is Eligio García, *La tercera muerte de Santiago Nasar* (Bogotá, Oveja Negra, 1987).

57. See *Living to Tell the Tale*, pp. 384–6.

58. Ligia GM, in Galvis, *Los GM*, p. 154.

59. See Angel Romero, "Cuando GM dormía en *El Universal*," *El Universal*, 8 March 1983, which would become a key source for Arango's book.

60. Gilard, ed., *Textos costeños 1*, p. 7.

61. Gustavo GM, in Galvis, *Los GM*, p. 211; GGM mentions the incident in "El cuento del cuento," *El Espectador*, 23 August 1981.

62. *Living to Tell the Tale*, p. 390.

63. García Usta, *Como aprendió a escribir García Márquez*, pp. 34–5.

64. Arango, *Un ramo de nomeolvides*, p. 274.

65. *Ibid.*, p. 211.

66. Gustavo GM, in Galvis, *Los GM*, p. 194.

67. GGM, "Nabo. El negro que hizo esperar a los ángeles," *El Espectador*, 18 March 1951.

68. It is also manifestly "Faulknerian."

69. Saldívar says this visit was in 1949. This appears to be based on a false memory due to GGM having lived in Cartagena twice: in 1948–9 and in 1951–2. Mutis himself has always been clear that he used his position with the airline Lansa to travel to Cartagena to meet GGM and he did not work for Lansa until 1950.

70. GGM, "Mi amigo Mutis," *El País* (Madrid), 30 October 1993. The fact that he did not meet Mutis until 1951 does not inhibit GGM from stating that he used to tell Mutis and Mallarino his stories in Bogotá in 1947–8: see "Bogotá 1947," *El Espectador*, 18 October 1981.

71. See Santiago Mutis, *Tras las rutas de Maqroll el Gaviero* (Cali, Proartes, 1988), p. 366.

72. See Fernando Quiroz, *El reino que estaba para mí: conversaciones con Alvaro Mutis* (Bogotá, Norma, 1993), pp. 68–70.

73. *Vaina*. Colombianism: "whatsit," "thingumajig." A whole dissertation could be written on this word, which is an integral part of the Colombian national character. It is used, at first sight, when the speaker is unable or cannot be bothered to come up with a precise word. In a country, however, where speech is normally unusually precise, the use of *vaina* is almost always quite deliberate (while feigning spontaneity), a kind of national custom or even addiction, a way of leaving things imprecise, even a way of showing that one wishes to be free, un-pompous—or even, in the country where "the best Spanish in the world" is spoken, transgressive. And obviously, for *vaina* to mean "everything," as here, rather than, as is usually the case, some insignificant object unworthy of a name, shows a still more ironic and irreverent attitude. The word is used overwhelmingly by male speakers—possibly because women are aware that it comes from the Latin *vagina*.

74. *Vivir para contarla*, p. 481. (My translation.)

75. In a 1968 interview, GGM said Vinyes consoled him over the rejection: see Leopoldo Anzacot, "García Márquez habla de política y literatura," *Indice* (Madrid), 237, November 1968; but of course Vinyes had left in April of that year.

76. There were still some remarkable moments. One of the most memorable was "The Coca-Cola Drinker" ("El bebedor de Coca-Cola," 24 May 1952), his salute to

Ramón Vinyes following his death in Barcelona on 5 May, just before his seventieth birthday. It is a testament to the "wise old Catalan" but also to the vision and originality of Gabito himself, his last disciple, who found a way of saying goodbye which was at once irreverent, self-mocking and touching. It ended, "Last Saturday they called us from Barcelona to say that he's died. And I've sat down to remember all these things; just in case it's true."

77. I interviewed Poncho Cotes in Valledupar in 1993. See Rafael Escalona Martínez, "Estocolmo, Escalona y Gabo," in Mera, ed., *Aracataca-Estocolmo*, pp. 88–90, on their relationship.

78. Interview, Manuel Zapata Olivella, Bogotá, 1991. See Zapata Olivella, "Enfoque antropológico: Nobel para la tradición oral," *El Tiempo, Lecturas Dominicales*, December 1982.

79. See Ciro Quiroz Otero, *Vallenato, hombre y canto* (Bogotá, Icaro, 1983).

80. (My translation.) This song won the composition prize at the Vallenato Festival in 1977. García Márquez's knowledge of the virtually unknown *vallenato* genre in the 1940s had been deepened by Clemente Manuel Zabala and Manuel Zapata Olivella (both from the Bolívar side of the Costa) even before he met Escalona, but he had always loved the popular music of his region.

81. See GGM, "Cuando Escalona me daba de comer," *Coralibe* (Bogotá), April 1981.

82. See, for example, "La cercanía con el pueblo encumbró la novela de América Latina," *Excelsior* (Mexico City), 25 January 1988.

83. *Vivir para contarla*, p. 499. (My translation.)

84. Cobo Borda, *Silva, Arciniegas, Mutis y García Márquez*, p. 479.

85. See Plinio Mendoza, "Entrevista con Gabriel García Márquez," *Libre*, 3, March–May 1972, p. 9, where GGM quotes the line and confesses that it may be the inspiration for *The Autumn of the Patriarch*.

86. In *Chronicle of a Death Foretold* his fictionalized self would also become an encyclopedia salesman, "during an uncertain period when I was trying to understand something of myself" (London, Picador, 1983), p. 89.

87. See map of the Colombian Atlantic/Caribbean Coast.

88. See Gilard, ed., *Gabriel García Marquez, Obra periodística vol. III: Entre cachacos I*, p. 66.

89. Remembered in a letter from GGM Barcelona to Alvaro Cepeda Samudio Barranquilla, 26 March 1970. I am grateful to Tita Cepeda for sight of this letter.

90. *Vivir para contarla*, p. 504 (my translation); though Gilard was informed that GGM left first (*Textos costenos I*, p. 25).

91. This work won the National Short Story Prize for 1954. See *Living to Tell the Tale*, p. 454, where, as usual he affects indifference to both money and glory.

92. Cobo Borda, *Silva, Arciniegas, Mutis y García Márquez*, p. 480. GGM also says here that the novelist he most enjoys, who really sends his mind travelling, is Conrad—again, thanks to Mutis.

93. *Vivir para contarla*, pp. 506–7. (My translation.)

8 / Back to Bogotá: The Ace Reporter (1954–1955)

1. Interviews with Alvaro Mutis, Mexico City, 1992, 1994. For the purposes of this chapter I also talked with José Salgar (Bogotá, 1991; Cartagena, 2007), Germán Arciniegas (Bogotá, 1991), Juan Gustavo Cobo Borda (Bogotá, 1991), Ana María Bus-

quets de Cano (Bogotá, 1991), Alfonso and Fernando Cano (Bogotá, 1993), Alvaro Castaño (Bogotá, 1991, 1998 and 2007), Nancy Vicens (Mexico City, 1994), José Font Castro (Madrid, 1997), and Jacques Gilard (Toulouse, 1999, 2004), among many others. In 1993 Patricia Castaño guided me on an expert tour of all the GGM-related sites in central Bogotá.

2. See Alfredo Barnechea and José Miguel Oviedo, "La historia como estética" (interview, Mexico 1974), reproduced in Alvaro Mutis, *Poesía y prosa* (Bogotá, Instituto Colombiano de Cultura, 1982), pp. 576–97 (p. 584).

3. *Living to Tell the Tale*, p. 439.

4. Oscar Alarcón, *El Espectador*, 24 October 1982, p. 2A. I interviewed Oscar Alarcón, a cousin from Santa Marta whom GGM introduced into *El Espectador*, in 2007.

5. From my interview with Salgar, 1991.

6. "La reina sola," *El Espectador*, 18 February 1954.

7. Gilard, ed., *Entre cachacos 1*, pp. 16–17. Gilard's work is again indispensable for this period.

8. See Sorela, *El otro García Márquez*, p. 88. Sorela, a onetime journalist with Spain's *El País*, has a number of illuminating insights into GGM's journalism.

9. Gilard, ed., *Entre cachacos 1*, is particularly severe on GGM's film criticism.

10. Such consistency, reliability and—yes—humanity is what connects him so irresistibly to his immortal precursor, Cervantes.

11. Whereas he was more than happy to do so indirectly, much later in life, through film and journalism "workshops."

12. *Living to Tell the Tale*, p. 450. See also José Font Castro, "Gabo, 70 años: 'No quiero homenajes póstumos en vida,'" *El Tiempo*, 23 February 1997, for reminiscences of this period.

13. Interviews with Nancy Vicens, Mexico City, 1994 and 1997; on Luis Vicens, see E. García Riera, *El cine es mejor que la vida* (Mexico, Cal y Arena, 1990), pp. 50–53.

14. Quoted by Fiorillo, *La Cueva*, p. 262.

15. See Diego León Giraldo, "La increíble y triste historia de GGM y la cinematografía desalmada," *El Tiempo, Lecturas Dominicales*, 15 December 1982, both on *La langosta azul* and on his cinema criticism in Barranquilla and Bogotá. My friend Gustavo Adolfo Ramírez Ariza has pointed out that GGM's *costeño* friends made—even more—frequent visits to Bogotá.

16. *Living to Tell the Tale*, pp. 463–5.

17. Gilard, ed., *Entre cachacos 1*, pp. 52–3.

18. GGM, "Hace sesenta años comenzó la tragedia," *El Espectador*, 2 August 1954.

19. Published on 2, 3 and 4 August 1954 respectively.

20. GGM recalls this trip to "Urabá" in "Seamos machos: hablemos del miedo al avión," *El Espectador*, 26 October 1980. One of his most detailed accounts of his manipulations, however, is in Germán Castro Caycedo, " 'Gabo' cuenta la novela de su vida. 4," *El Espectador*, 23 March 1977. See also *Living to Tell the Tale*, pp. 444–50. Daniel Samper, "GGM se dedicará a la música," 1968, in Rentería, pp. 21–7, gives a particularly outrageous version of this anecdote: p. 26, "Y así fue como se salvó al Chocó." See "GGM: 'Tengo permanente germen de infelicidad: atender a la fama,'" *Cromos*, 1 January 1980, in which he goes even further ("we were modifying reality"), to the evident shock of some *El País* journalists.

21. "Hemingway, Nobel Prize," *El Espectador*, 29 October 1954. The article is unsigned but Gilard is surely right in believing that the author is GGM.

22. *Living to Tell the Tale*, p. 472, says it was in GGM's office in *El Espectador*.

23. GGM, talk given to *El País*, journalist's course, Universidad Autónoma de Madrid, 28 April 1994.

24. Interview with José Font Castro, Madrid, 1997.

25. See "La desgracia de ser escritor joven," *El Espectador*, 6 September 1981. Twelve years after its first appearance, when García Márquez was briefly back in Bogotá after the publication of *OHYS*, he found dozens of copies of this first edition for sale in second-hand bookshops at a peso each and bought as many as he could.

26. See *Living to Tell the Tale*, p. 482.

27. See Claude Couffon, "A Bogotá chez García Márquez," *L'Express* (Paris), 17–23 January 1977, pp. 70–78, especially p. 74.

28. See Dante, *Vita Nuova*, chapter II.

29. Mercedes was an excellent high-school student and had thought of studying bacteriology at university but it seems that the endless imminence of her hypothetical marriage to Gabito eventually made her shelve such plans.

30. See *Living to Tell the Tale*, pp. 467–8, 470.

31. See Juan Ruiz, Arcipreste de Hita, *El libro de buen amor* (fourteenth century), so influential in Spanish culture and psychology. The theme of "crazy love" is mentioned on both the first page and—implicitly, through reference to its opposite, "good love"—the last page of *Memories of My Melancholy Whores*, his last novel, which GGM published when he was seventy-seven years old.

32. Mexico City, 1997.

33. See for example Claudia Dreifus, "Gabriel García Márquez," *Playboy* 30:2, February 1983, where he states that Mercedes said it was best for him to go or he would blame her for the rest of their lives (p. 178).

9 / The Discovery of Europe: Rome (1955)

1. " 'Los 4 grandes' en Tecnicolor," *El Espectador*, 22 July 1955.

2. This chapter draws on interviews with Fernando Gómez Agudelo (carried out by Patricia Castaño, Bogotá, 1991), Guillermo Angulo (Bogotá, 1991, 2007), Fernando Birri (Cartagena, 2007, London, 2008), and Jacques Gilard (Toulouse, 1999, 2004), and discussions with many other communicants, including, notably, John Kraniauskas.

3. " 'Los 4 grandes' en Tecnicolor." For a different recollection of his journey see "Regreso a la guayaba," *El Espectador*, 10 April 1983, in which he states, once again, that his intention was "to return to Colombia a few weeks later."

4. Germán Castro Caycedo, " 'Gabo' cuenta la novela de su vida. 4," *El Espectador*, 23 March 1977. Castro Caycedo 4 and 5 give one of the best accounts of GGM's experiences in Geneva.

5. Again Gilard's work is essential: see *Gabriel García Márquez, Obra periodística vol. V: De Europa y América 1* (Bogotá, Oveja Negra, 1984), p. 21.

6. *Ibid.*

7. Sorela, *El otro García Márquez*, p. 115.

8. In fact the Pontiff's crisis, which had arisen when García Márquez was still in Bogotá, was already long past. But see "Roma en verano," *El Espectador*, 6 June 1982, where GGM insists on this story and goes into detail.

9. *Ibid.* In Germán Castro Caycedo, " 'Gabo' cuenta la novela de su vida. 5," *El Espectador*, 23 March 1977, he states that he was in Rome "eight months, or a year."

10. *Excelsior* (Mexico City), 19 March 1988, reported that *La Stampa* of Turin said that GGM's Montesi articles threw no new light on the case. More to the point, given García Márquez's handicaps, is whether the case was summed up better by any other journalist.

11. *El Espectador*, 16 September 1955, p. 1.

12. Karen Pinkus, *The Montesi Scandal: The Death of Wilma Montesi and the Birth of the Paparazzi in Fellini's Rome* (Chicago, Chicago University Press, 2003), p. 2.

13. See *ibid.*, p. 36, on Bazin's *What Is Cinema?*

14. GGM, "Domingo en el Lido de Venecia. Un tremendo drama de ricos y pobres," *El Espectador*, 13 September 1955.

15. "Roma en verano," *El Espectador*, 6 June 1982.

16. GGM, "Confusión en la Babel del cine," *El Espectador*, 8 September 1955. Over a quarter of a century later Rosi, by then a firm friend, would travel to Colombia, to make a movie of GGM's novel *Chronicle of a Death Foretold*.

17. See Gilard, ed., *De Europa y América 1*, pp. 5–8.

18. See GGM, "Me alquilo para soñar," *El Espectador*, 4 September 1983. Frida's story is similar to that of Rafael Ribero Silva in Rome (mentioned in this chapter)— she went to Europe to be a classical singer.

19. Cf. GGM, "El mar de mis cuentos perdidos," *El Espectador*, 22 August 1982, which relates GM's sudden superstition, many years later, about leaving Cadaqués and never returning for fear of dying.

20. But see "Polonia: verdades que duelen," *El Espectador*, 27 December 1981, in which, now that it was safe to do so, he stated categorically that his first and only journey to Poland was for two weeks in the autumn of 1955.

21. "90 días en la Cortina de Hierro. VI. Con los ojos abiertos sobre Polonia en ebullición," *Cromos*, 2,203, 31 August 1959.

22. *Ibid.*

23. "La batalla de las medidas. III. La batalla la decidirá el público," *El Espectador*, 28 December 1955.

24. GGM, "Triunfo lírico en Ginebra," *El Espectador*, 11 December 1955.

25. GGM, "Roma en verano," *El Espectador*, 6 June 1982. GGM characterizes the girl as one of the "sad whores" of the Villa Borghese: "sad whores" would appear in the title of his last novel over fifty years later.

26. See "La penumbra del escritor de cine," *El Espectador*, 14 November 1982, in which he gives a detailed appreciation of the role of script-writers, almost all of whom are anonymous, except for Zavattini.

27. Quoted by Eligio García, *Tras las claves de Melquíades*, pp. 408–9.

28. *Ibid.*, p. 432. García Márquez would remark, many years later, and not of Fellini but of Zavattini: "In Latin America art has to have 'vision,' because our reality is often hallucinatory and hallucinated. Has no one suspected that the most likely source for the Latin American novel's 'magical realism' is *Miracle in Milan?*"

29. Guillermo Angulo, interview, 1991. See also Guillermo Angulo, "En busca del Gabo perdido," in Mera, ed., *Aracataca-Estocolmo*, p.85.

30. Eligio García, *Tras las claves de Melquíades*, p. 408.

31. Claude Couffon, "A Bogotá chez García Márquez," *L'Express*, 17–23 January 1977, p. 75. GGM tells Couffon he went straight to the Hôtel de Flandre the first night.

10 / Hungry in Paris: *La Bohème* (1956–1957)

1. This chapter draws on interviews with Plinio Apuleyo Mendoza (Bogotá, 1991), Hernán Vieco (Bogotá, 1991), Germán Vargas (Barranquilla, 1991), Guillermo Angulo (Bogotá, 1991, 2007), Tachia Quintana Rosoff (Paris, 1993, 1996, 2004),

Ramón Chao (Paris, 1993), Claude Couffon (Paris, 1993), Luis Villar Borda (Bogotá, 1998), Jacques Gilard (Toulouse, 1999, 2004) and many other informants.

2. Paris being Paris, both hotels are still standing, though the Hôtel de Flandre is now called the Hôtel des Trois Collèges. GGM's stay there was recorded by a plaque in 2007. His son Gonzalo and Tachia Quintana were in attendance when the plaque was unveiled.

3. Plinio Mendoza, "Retrato de GM (fragmento)," in Angel Rama, *Novísimos narradores hispanoamericanos en "Marcha" 1964–1980* (México, Marcha Editores, 1981), pp.128–39.

4. *Ibid.*, p. 137. See also "GM 18 años atrás," *El Espectador*, 27 February 1974.

5. Plinio Mendoza, *La llama y el hielo*; Plinio Mendoza, "GM 18 años atrás," *op. cit.*

6. Incredibly, four years later, another great Latin American writer, GGM's future friend Mario Vargas Llosa, would end up in an attic let by Madame Lacroix, and for the same reason.

7. On Otero Silva, see GGM, "Un cuento de horror para el día de los Inocentes," *El Espectador*, 28 December 1980.

8. Mendoza, *La llama y el hielo*, pp. 49–51. (*La llama y el hielo* would cause a rift between Mendoza and GGM, and especially between Mendoza and Mercedes, who considered some of its revelations a betrayal of confidence and of their friendship.)

9. See Antonio Núñez Jiménez, "García Márquez y la perla de las Antillas (o Qué conversan Gabo y Fidel)" (Havana, 1984, unpublished manuscript). Núñez Jiménez gave me privileged access to this manuscript when I visited Havana in 1997. The story about Guillén is also told in GGM, "Desde París con amor," *El Espectador*, 26 December 1982. In fact Perón—not in any case a dictator—had fallen in September 1955 and so it seems likely that the shout was for Peru's Odría, who left power reluctantly on 28 July, or Nicaragua's Somoza, who was assassinated on 21 September.

10. GGM, "El proceso de los secretos de Francia. XII. El ministro Mitterrand hace estremecer la sala," *El Independiente* (Bogotá), 31 March 1956. These articles can be found in Gilard, ed., *De Europa y América 1*.

11. Mendoza, *La llama y el hielo*, pp. 19–20.

12. See Consuelo Mendoza de Riaño, "La Gaba," *Revista Diners* (Bogotá), no. 80, November 1980, which records that GGM wrote to Mercedes three times a week but "was said to have had a Spanish girlfriend in Paris."

13. Peter Stone, "García Márquez" (*Paris Review*, 1981), in Gourevitch, ed., *The "Paris Review" Interviews*, p. 188.

14. See Mendoza, *The Fragrance of Guava*, p. 56.

15. Quoted by Eligio García, *Tras las claves de Melquíades*, p. 403.

16. See Juan Goytisolo, *Coto vedado* (Barcelona, Seix Barral, 1985), pp. 209–12, on the Mabillon and other cafés and their connections.

17. This narrative is based on a long interview in Paris in March 1993.

18. Possibly the most complete version of GGM's sufferings in Paris is given in Jean Michel Fossey, "Entrevista a Gabriel García Márquez," *Imagen* (Caracas), 27 April 1969. But see also Germán Castro Caycedo, " 'Gabo' cuenta la novela de su vida. 5," *El Espectador*, 23 March 1977, for important details.

19. Agustín's three friends, all tailors, are called Alfonso, Alvaro and Germán, the names of GGM's best friends from Barranquilla.

20. Mendoza, *The Fragrance of Guava*, p. 26.

21. His uncle José María Valdeblánquez spent decades in the government bureaucracy in Bogotá; in 1993 I drank several large whiskies in Riohacha with García Márquez's sardonic cousin, Ricardo Márquez Iguarán, who worked for years with

Valdeblánquez in the pensions department in the late 1940s—"years and years, and we never paid out a single pension!"

22. The narrative of *No One Writes to the Colonel* takes place from early October to early December 1956—we know this because of the references to Suez. This means that it was written at the same time as the Colombian and Middle Eastern events it describes were taking place, not to mention during the period when GGM and Tachia Quintana were together—21 March to mid-December 1956.

23. My translation.

24. Sorela, *El otro GM*, p. 133.

25. The story is framed in the same way that *Chronicle of a Death Foretold*, its contemporary, would be: a narrator who sounds like GGM talks to Billy in Cartagena many years later and then, in Paris, he investigates the hospital records to see when Nena checked in and talks to a functionary Billy consulted in the Colombian embassy.

26. See GGM, "El argentino que se hizo querer de todos," *El Espectador*, 22 February 1984.

27. Gustavo GM, in Galvis, *Los GM*, p. 206.

28. Fuenmayor discusses this episode in *Crónicas sobre el grupo de Barranquilla*. GGM's first novel *Leaf Storm* had been dedicated to Germán Vargas; the friends in *No One Writes to the Colonel* are called Alfonso, Alvaro and Germán: all three men will appear in *OHYS*, together with Ramón Vinyes (and Mercedes . . .). No wonder GM would repeatedly tell journalists that he wrote "so that my friends will love me more." And who could be surprised that a man with his experience of family life in childhood would cling to the friends who had first made him feel that he belonged.

29. Quoted in Silvana Paternostro, "La mirada de los otros," *Página 12* (Buenos Aires), 5 May 2004.

30. GGM, "Georges Brassens," *El Espectador*, 8 November 1981.

31. GGM, "Desde París, con amor," *El Espectador*, 26 December 1982, in which he recalls working for the Algerian National Liberation Front. (Twenty-five years later, at the independence celebrations, he would say that it was the only struggle he'd ever been imprisoned for.)

32. GGM, "Desde París con amor," *El Espectador*, 26 December 1982.

33. Couffon, "A Bogotá chez García Márquez," *L'Express*, 17–23 January 1977, p. 76.

34. Plinio Mendoza, in Mera, ed., *Aracataca-Estocolmo*, pp. 100–1.

35. GGM, "Mi Hemingway personal," *El Espectador*, 26 July 1981.

11 / Beyond the Iron Curtain: Eastern Europe During the Cold War (1957)

1. Mendoza, *La llama y el hielo*, p. 21. This chapter draws on interviews with Plinio Mendoza (Bogotá, 1991), Luis Villar Borda (Bogotá, 1998), Guillermo Angulo (Bogotá, 1991, 2007), Hernán Vieco (Bogotá, 1991), Tachia Quintana (Paris, 1993), Manuel Zapata Olivella (Bogotá, 1991), Jacques Gilard (Toulouse, 1999, 2004) and others.

2. Even in the published articles about this journey, which he revised in 1959, García Márquez would still disguise Soledad as "Jacqueline," a French graphic artist originally from Indochina, and Plinio as "Franco," a nomadic Italian journalist. In the 1950s it was impossible for a Colombian even to travel beyond the Iron Curtain without risking the gravest political and personal consequences. See Gilard, ed., *De Europa y América 1*, p. 7.

3. GGM, "90 diás en la Cortina de Hierro. I. La 'Cortina de Hierro' es un palo pintado de rojo y blanco." *Cromos*, 2,198, 27 July 1959. All these articles are collected in Gilard, ed., GGM, *Obra periodística vol. V* and *vol. VI: De Europa y América 1 and 2*.

4. GGM, "90 diás en la Cortina de Hierro. VI. Con los ojos abiertos sobre Polonia en ebullición," *Cromos*, 2,199, 3 August 1959.

5. GGM, "90 diás en la Cortina de Hierro. II. Berlín es un disparate," *Cromos*, 2,199, 3 August 1959.

6. GGM, "90 días en La Cortina de Hierro. III. Los expropiados se reúnen para contarse sus penas," *Cromos*, 2,200, 10 August 1959.

7. Many years later Villar Borda would be the last Colombian ambassador to East Berlin.

8. In July 2004 Jacques Gilard told me, "On one occasion GGM said to me that he wasn't sure whether he was a communist in Bogotá but he thinks he was. Certainly when he arrived in Vienna in 1955 and met up with Jorge Zalamea, who was attending a communist conference, he definitely considered himself a communist." Which did not mean that he was a member of the party, of course.

9. GGM, "90 días en La Cortina de Hierro. III. Los expropiados se reúnen para contarse sus penas," *op. cit.*

10. GGM, "90 días en la Cortina de Hierro. I. Berlín es un disparate," *Cromos*, 2,199, 3 August 1959.

11. *Ibid.*

12. *Ibid.*

13. García Márquez stated in his articles that only "Jacqueline" went back to Paris and that he and "Franco" stayed in Berlin and left the car there, travelling on by rail to Prague. This is to facilitate not only the incorporation of the May 1957 visit to Germany but also the 1955 visit to Czechoslovakia and Poland into the forthcoming July–August 1957 visit to the USSR and Hungary. Thus did three separate trips get folded, eventually, into one supposed trip of "Ninety days behind the Iron Curtain."

14. Arango, *Un ramo de nomeolvides*, p. 88. The troupe was the Delia Zapata Folklore Group, about which García Márquez had written an article in Bogotá ("Danza cruda," *El Espectador*, 4 August 1954), and, as fate would have it, the troupe was short of an accordionist and a saxophonist.

15. GGM, Paris to Tachia Quintana, Madrid, summer 1957.

16. The journey is described in GGM, "Allá por los tiempos de la Coca-Cola," *El Espectador*, 11 October 1981.

17. GGM, "90 días en la Cortina de Hierro. VII. URSS: 22, 400,000 kilómetros cuadrados sin un solo aviso de Coca-Cola," *Cromos*, 2:204, 7 September 1959. The four articles on the USSR, which would be published in *Cromos*, Bogotá, in 1959, were first published as two articles, "Yo visité Rusia" 1 and 2 in *Momento*, Caracas, 22 and 29 November 1957. Both sets are published in Gilard, ed., *Gabriel García Márquez, Obra periodística vol. VI: De Europa y América 2* (Bogotá, Oveja Negra, 1984), but I quote here from the 1959 set because the articles are more complete and because they are integrated into an overall perspective.

18. Molotov would be ousted on 1 June 1957.

19. GGM, "90 días en la Cortina de Hierro. VIII. Moscú la aldea más grande del mundo," *Cromos*, 2,205, 14 September 1959.

20. *Ibid.*

21. *Ibid.*

22. GGM, "90 días en la Cortina de Hierro. IX. En el Mausoleo de la plaza Roja Stalin duerme sin remordimientos," *Cromos*, 2,206, 21 September 1959.

23. *Ibid*. Cf. GGM, "El destino de los embalsamados," *El Espectador*, 12 September 1982, in which the bodies of Lenin and Stalin are discussed, Evita Perón, Santa Anna and Obregón mentioned, and the delicate hands of Stalin, Fidel Castro and Che compared.

24. Mendoza, *La llama y el hielo*, p. 30.

25. Later GGM would meet another alleged dictator with exquisitely delicate hands, Comandante Castro, known to the world as "Fidel"—not even an uncle but everyone's friend and comrade. By that time GGM himself would be everyone's friend too: "Gabo."

26. GGM, "90 días en la Cortina de Hierro. IX. En el Mausoleo de la plaza Roja Stalin duerme sin remordimientos," *Cromos*, 2,206, 21 September 1959.

27. *Ibid*.

28. GGM, "90 días en la Cortina de Hierro. X. El hombre soviético empieza a cansarse de los contrastes," *Cromos*, 2,207, 28 September 1959.

29. GGM, "Yo visité Hungría," *Momento* (Caracas), 15 November 1957.

30. *Ibid*.

31. *Ibid*.

32. *Ibid*.

33. Mendoza, *La llama y el hielo*, p. 32.

34. GGM, London to Luisa Santiaga Márquez, Cartagena (via Mercedes in Barranquilla), 3 December 1957.

35. Claude Couffon, "A Bogotá chez García Márquez," *L'Express* (Paris), 17–23 January 1977, p. 76.

36. See Gilard, ed., *De Europa y América 1*, pp. 33–8.

37. See Anthony Day and Marjorie Miller, "Gabo talks: GGM on the misfortunes of Latin America, his friendship with Fidel Castro and his terror of the blank page," *Los Angeles Times Magazine*, 2 September 1990: " 'Between high school and my first trip to socialist countries I was somewhat a victim of propaganda,' he says. 'When I returned [from Eastern Europe in 1957], it was clear to me that, in theory, socialism was a much more just system than capitalism. But that in practice, this wasn't socialism. At that moment, the Cuban Revolution occurred,' he says" (pp. 33–4).

38. On 15 November 1957, GGM published "I Visited Hungary" in *Momento*, and on 22 and 29 November, "I Was in Russia" 1 and 2, also in *Momento*. Almost two years later, end of July to end of September 1959, eleven further articles appeared under the general heading, "90 Days Behind the Iron Curtain," in the weekly *Cromos*, Bogotá—three on Germany, three on Czechoslovakia, one on Poland and four on the USSR (effectively repeating the 1957 articles); curiously, he does not repeat the Hungarian article. For a detailed reconstruction of the sequence of writing and publication, see Gilard, ed., *De Europa y América 1*, pp. 33–8.

39. Tachia Quintana, interview, Paris, 1993.

40. GGM, London, to Luisa Santiaga Márquez, Cartagena (via Mercedes, Barranquilla), 3 December 1957.

41. Gilard, ed., *De Europa y América 1*, p. 44.

42. GGM, "Un sábado en Londres," *El Nacional* (Caracas), 6 January 1958.

43. GGM, Mexico City, to Mario Vargas Llosa, London, 1 October 1966.

44. GGM, London, to Luisa Santiaga Márquez, Cartagena (via Mercedes, Barranquilla), 3 December 1957. See Claudia Dreifus, "Gabriel García Márquez," *Playboy* 30:2, February 1983, pp. 65–77, 172–8: *Playboy*: "How did Mercedes react [to his departure for Europe]?" GM: "This is one of the mysteries of her personality that will never be clear to me—even now. She was absolutely certain I'd return. Everyone told

her she was crazy, that I'd find someone new in Europe. And in Paris, I did lead a totally free life. But I knew when it was over, I'd return to her. It wasn't a matter of honor but more like natural destiny, like something that had already happened."
45. Conversation, Mexico City, 1993.
46. Conversation, Mexico City, 1999.

12 / Venezuela and Colombia:
The Birth of Big Mama (1958–1959)

1. See GGM, "Caribe mágico," *El Espectador*, 18 January 1981. This chapter and the next one draw on conversations with Plinio Mendoza (Bogotá, 1991), Consuelo and Elvira Mendoza (Bogotá, 2007), José Font Castro (Madrid, 1997), Domingo Miliani (Pittsburgh, 1998), Alejandro Bruzual (Pittsburgh, 2005), Juan Antonio Hernández (Pittsburgh, 2004, 2008), who read this chapter in manuscript, Luis Harss (Pittsburgh, 1993), José Luis Díaz-Granados (Bogotá, 1991 and after), José ("Pepe") Stevenson (Bogotá, 1991, Cartagena, 2007), Malcolm Deas (Oxford and Bogotá, 1991), Eduardo Posada Carbó (Oxford, 1991), Eduardo Barcha Pardo (Arjona, 2008), Alfonso López Michelsen (Bogotá, 1993), Germán Arciniegas (Bogotá, 1991), Ramiro de la Espriella (Bogotá, 1991), Jacques Gilard (Toulouse, 1999, 2004), Rafael Gutiérrez Girardot (Barcelona, 1992), Jesús Martín Barbero (Pittsburgh, 2000), Luis Villar Borda (Bogotá, 1998), Rita García Márquez and many others.
2. Mendoza, *La llama y el hielo*, pp. 35–6. See also GGM, "Memoria feliz de Caracas," *El Espectador*, 7 March 1982.
3. Mendoza, *La llama y el hielo*, p. 89.
4. GGM, "No se me ocurre ningún título," *Casa de las Américas* (Havana), 100, January–February 1977, pp. 85–9.
5. See the conclusion of *The Autumn of the Patriarch*, which was undoubtedly inspired by these celebrations in Caracas.
6. See Mendoza, *La llama y el hielo*, pp. 40–41; GGM returns to this episode in "Los idus de marzo," *El Espectador*, 1 November 1981, and relates it to both *The Autumn of the Patriarch* and *Chronicle of a Death Foretold*.
7. Then as later, he would ignore Miguel Angel Asturias's *The President*, based on Guatemala's tyrant Manuel Estrada Cabrera, a novel which had been a sensation when it was published in Buenos Aires in 1948—by Losada, the publisher who had turned down *Leaf Storm*—and had won the same international book award when it appeared in French in 1952 that *OHYS* would receive eighteen years later.
8. See Mendoza, *The Fragrance of Guava*, pp. 80–90; and Ernesto González Bermejo, "García Márquez: ahora doscientos años de soledad," *Triunfo* (Madrid), 44, 14 November 1970 (see Rentería, pp. 49–64).
9. See Gilard, ed., *De Europa y América 1*, pp. 50–51.
10. GGM, "El clero en la lucha," *Momento*, 7 February 1958.
11. José Font Castro, interview, Madrid, 1997.
12. Eligio Garcia, *Tras las claves de Melquíades*, p. 232.
13. Rita GM, in *ibid.*, p. 243.
14. Fiorillo, *La Cueva*, p. 266.
15. Mercedes Barcha, interview, Cartagena, 1991. Cf. Beatriz López de Barcha, "'Gabito esperó a que yo creciera,'" *Carrusel, Revista de El Tiempo* (Bogotá), 10 December 1982: "In 1958 Gabito came from Paris to Caracas and 'one day he just turned up at the house.' Two days later they were married."

16. See Castro Caycedo, "Gabo cuenta la novela de su vida": includes brief exchange with Mercedes.

17. See Alfonso Fuenmayor, "El día en que se casó Gabito," *Fin de Semana del Caribe*, n.d. (see Fiorillo, *La Cueva*, pp. 265–7).

18. Rita GM, in Galvis, *Los GM*, pp. 46–47.

19. Eligio García, "Gabriel José visto por Eligio Gabriel, el benjamín," *Cromos* (Bogotá), 26 October 1982, pp. 20–21.

20. Germán Castro Caycedo, "'Gabo' cuenta la novela de su vida. 3," *El Espectador*, 23 March 1977.

21. Consuelo Mendoza de Riaño, "La Gaba," *Revista Diners* (Bogotá), November 1980.

22. Domingo Miliani, "Diálogo mexicano con GGM," *Papel Literario, El Nacional* (Caracas), 31 October 1965.

23. Mario Vargas Llosa, conversation, Stratford, England, 1990.

24. Mercedes Barcha, conversation, Mexico City, October 1993.

25. Mendoza, *La llama y el hielo*, p. 46.

26. Mercedes Barcha, interview, Cartagena, 1991.

27. María Esther Gilio, "Escribir bien es un deber revolucionario," *Triunfo* (Madrid), 1977 (see Rentería, pp. 141–5).

28. Eligio García, *Tras las claves de Melquíades*, p. 424.

29. Mendoza, *La llama y el hielo*, p. 44.

30. Domingo Miliani, "Diálogo mexicano con GGM," *Papel Literario, El Nacional* (Caracas), 31 October 1965.

31. See Consuelo Mendoza, "La Gaba," *Revista Diners* (Bogotá), November 1980; Beatriz López de Barcha, "'Gabito esperó a que yo creciera,'" *Carrusel, Revista de El Tiempo* (Bogotá), 10 December 1982; and Claudia Dreifus, "Gabriel García Márquez," *Playboy* 30:2, February 1983, p. 178.

32. Sorela, *El otro GM*, p. 185.

33. Eligio García, *Tras las claves de Melquíades*, p. 366.

34. GGM, "Mi hermano Fidel," *Momento* (Caracas), 18 April 1958.

35. Núñez Jiménez, "GM y la perla de las Antillas."

36. GGM, "No se me ocurre ningún título," *Casa de las Américas* (Havana), 100, January–February 1977.

37. Mendoza, *La llama y el hielo*, p. 60.

38. Antonio Núñez Jiménez, *En marcha con Fidel* (Havana, Letras Cubanas, 1982), reproduces this speech.

39. Mendoza, *La llama y el hielo*, p. 67.

40. See Gilard, ed., *De Europa y América 1*, p. 53; and Mendoza, *La llama y el hielo*, pp. 67–8.

41. Mendoza, *La llama y el hielo*, pp. 75–7.

42. Mendoza's account differs from GGM's; in the former it was all Mendoza's doing, in Bogotá not Caracas, and GGM was not in the picture. Mendoza agreed "on condition that the resourcing was right and that they also hire a friend of his in Caracas on the same salary." GGM gives a quite different account in Núñez, "GM y la perla de las Antillas."

43. Núñez Jiménez, "GM y la perla de las Antillas."

44. Mendoza, *La llama y el hielo*, p. 71.

45. Interview, José Stevenson, Cartagena, March 2007. I also talked to Eduardo Barcha Pardo, Mercedes's brother, in Arjona, in 2008. He was a student in Bogotá at the time, was drafted in to Prensa Latina, and stayed with his sister and her husband in their Bogotá apartment.

46. GGM, "Colombia: al fin hablan los votos," *Momento* (Caracas), 21 March 1958.

47. José Luis Díaz Granados, interview, Bogotá, 1991; see also Consuelo Mendoza, "La Gaba," *Revista Diners*, November 1980.

48. Mendoza, *La llama y el hielo*, p. 72.

49. GGM, "¿Nagy, héroe o traidor?," *Elite* (Caracas), 28 June 1958.

50. See Mendoza, "Entrevista con Gabriel García Márquez," *Libre*, 3, March–May 1972, pp. 13–14, where Mendoza and GGM reminisce about Torres.

51. Mendoza, *La llama y el hielo*, p. 74.

52. *Ibid.*, p. 71.

53. GGM, *Collected Stories*, p. 184.

54. *Ibid.*, p. 200.

55. See Hernán Díaz's portrait of GGM at the time he was working for Prensa Latina. The change of demeanour is evident and striking.

56. See Gilard, ed., *De Europa y América 1*, pp. 60–63.

57. *Ibid.*, pp. 53–4. See also Gilard, "García Márquez: un projet d'école de cinéma (1960)," *Cinémas d'Amérique latine* (Toulouse), 3, 1995, pp. 24–38, and "'Un carnaval para toda la vida,' de Cepeda Samudio, ou quand García Márquez faisait du montage," *Cinémas d'Amérique latine* (Toulouse), no. 3, 1995, pp. 39–44.

58. See Daniel Samper, "GGM se dedicará a la música," *El Tiempo*, December 1968, in Rentería, p.24; and Saldívar, *GM: el viaje a la semilla*, pp. 389–90.

13 / The Cuban Revolution and the USA (1959–1961)

1. Mendoza, *La llama y el hielo*, pp. 87–8.

2. See E. González Bermejo, "Ahora doscientos años de soledad . . .," *Triunfo*, November 1971 (in Rentería, ed., *García Márquez habla de García Márquez en 33 grandes reportajes*, p. 50); also Angel Augier, "GM en La Habana," *Mensajes* (UNEAC, Havana), I:17, 10 September 1970. Aroldo Wall would later be an important link between Julio Cortázar and the Cuban Revolution.

3. Mendoza, *La llama y el hielo*, p. 88.

4. Sixteen years later the indomitable Walsh would be tortured and murdered in Buenos Aires by the Argentine military for his courageous opposition during the so-called dirty war. Cf. GGM, "Rodolfo Walsh, el escritor que se le adelantó a la CIA," *Alternativa*, 124, 25 July–1 August 1977. See also GGM, "Recuerdos de periodista," *El Espectador*, 14 December 1981.

5. Núñez Jiménez, "GM y la perla de las Antillas." See also GGM, "Recuerdos de periodista," *El Espectador*, 14 December 1981, for different details.

6. Mendoza, *La llama y el hielo*, pp. 84–6.

7. *Ibid.*, p. 81.

8. Arango, *Un ramo de nomeolvides*, p. 179.

9. See Eligio García, *Tras las claves de Melquíades*, pp. 474–9.

10. See Orlando Castellanos, interview with García Márquez in *Formalmente Informal*, Radio Havana, reprinted in *Prisma del meridiano* (Havana), 80, 1–15 October 1976.

11. GGM, "Regreso a México," *El Espectador*, 23 January 1983.

12. Kennedy, "The Yellow Trolley Car in Barcelona," p. 258.

13. GGM, "Nueva York 1961: el drama de las dos Cubas," *Areíto*, 21, June 1979, pp. 31–3.

14. Miguel Fernández-Braso, *Gabriel Gárcia Márquez (Una conversación infinita)* (Madrid, Azur, 1969), p. 31.

15. GGM, "El fantasma para el progreso," *El Espectador*, 28 February 1982.

16. Núñez Jiménez, "García Márquez y la perla de las Antillas."

17. GGM, "Nueva York 1961: el drama de las dos Cubas," *Areíto*, 21, June 1979, p. 33.

18. CGM, New York, to Alvaro Cepeda, Barranquilla, 26 April 1961, mentions the "invasions" only at the very end of the letter.

19. Of course the counter-revolutionaries would accuse him anyway. See Guillermo Cabrera Infante, "Nuestro prohombre en La Habana," *El Tiempo*, 6 March 1983. He claims to be one of "those who know his true biography" and then inadvertently demonstrates that this is false (or else himself deliberately misleads) when he claims that GGM fled New York as soon as he heard about the Bay of Pigs invasion, fearing that it would be successful. This story has been circulated by other influential anti-revolutionary writers such as Carlos Franqui and Carlos Alberto Montaner and is demonstrably untrue.

20. Mendoza, *La llama y el hielo*, p. 104.

21. Núñez Jiménez, "GM y la perla de las Antillas."

22. Mendoza, *La llama y el hielo*, pp. 75–106.

23. GGM, New York, to Alvaro Cepeda, Barranquilla, 23 May 1961.

24. GGM, New York, to Plinio Mendoza, 29 May 1961.

25. *Ibid.*

26. Mendoza, *La llama y el hielo*, p. 106.

27. Ernesto Schóo, "Los viajes de Simbad," *Primera Plana* (Buenos Aires), 234, 20–26 June 1967.

28. GGM, "Regreso a México," *El Espectador*, 23 January 1983.

29. GGM, Mexico City, to Plinio Mendoza, Bogotá, 30 June 1961.

14 / Escape to Mexico (1961–1964)

1. See GGM, "Regreso a México," *El Espectador*, 23 January 1983, in which he declares that he will never forget his date of arrival (2 July 1961!), because a friend called him next day to tell him about Hemingway's death. However, a letter from GGM to Plinio Mendoza in Bogotá on 30 June 1961 disproves one of the best-loved legends about García Márquez, namely, that he arrived in Mexico City on the day Hemingway died. Not so. See also "Breves nostalgias sobre Juan Rulfo," *El Espectador*, 7 December 1980, in which again he gets most of his dates and calculations about his time in Mexico wrong. Even the best memories are fallible.

2. This chapter and the two following draw on interviews with Plinio Mendoza (Bogotá, 1991), Alvaro Mutis (Mexico City, 1992, 1994), María Luisa Elío (Mexico City, 1992), Carlos Monsiváis (Mexico City, 1992), Francisco ("Paco") Porrúa (Barcelona, 1992), Carmen Balcells (Barcelona, 1991, 1992, 2000), Berta Navarro (Mexico City, 1992), María Luisa ("La China") Mendoza (Mexico City, 1994), Carlos Fuentes (Mexico City, 1992), James Papworth (Mexico City, 1992), Gonzalo García Barcha (Mexico City, 1992, 1994, Paris, 2004), Berta ("La Chaneca") Hernández (Mexico City, 1993), Aline Mackissack Maldonado (Mexico City, 1993), Tulio Aguilera Garramuño (Pittsburgh, 1993), Manuel Barbachano (Mexico City, 1994), Margo Glantz (Mexico City, 1994), Augusto ("Tito") Monterroso and Barbara Jacobs (Mexico City, 1994), Elena Poniatowska (Mexico City, 1994), Jorge Sánchez (Mexico City, 1994), Juan and Virginia Reinoso (Mexico City, 1994), Luis Coudurier (Mexico City, 1994), Vicente and Albita Rojo (Mexico City, 1994), Nancy Vicens (Mexico City,

1994), Ignacio ("Nacho") Durán (Mexico City, 1994, London, 2005), Guillermo Sheridan (Guadalajara and Mexico City, 1997), among many others.

3. GGM, "Regreso a México," *El Espectador*, 23 January 1983.

4. GGM, "Un hombre ha muerto de muerte natural," *México en la Cultura, Novedades* (Mexico City), 9 July 1961; in the Núñez Jiménez conversation GGM says it was the *Novedades* people who told him Hemingway was dead, which is what he tells Plinio Mendoza in his letter of 10 July 1961.

5. On his feelings towards Hemingway see GGM's comments in Alejandro Cueva Ramírez, "García Márquez: 'El gallo no es más que un gallo,' " *Pluma* 52 (Colombia), March–April 1985. See also "Mi Hemingway personal," *El Espectador*, 26 July 1981.

6. GGM, Mexico City, to Plinio Mendoza, Bogotá, 9 August 1961. See "Breves nostalgias sobre Juan Rulfo," *El Espectador*, 7 December 1980, which gives a similar picture of the elevatorless building and apartment.

7. GGM, Mexico City, to Plinio Mendoza, Bogotá, 13 August 1961.

8. GGM, Mexico City, to Plinio Mendoza, Bogotá, 26 September 1961. GGM, Mexico City, to Alvaro Cepeda, Barranquilla, 4 December 1961, writes: "In May you have to come and baptize Alejandra, who will be born at the end of April. Don't miss the opportunity because this is the last godchild we can offer you. After this we're shutting up shop."

9. GGM, "Mi otro yo," *El Espectador*, 14 February 1982.

10. GGM, Mexico City, to Plinio Mendoza, Bogotá, 9 August 1961.

11. See GGM, "Breves nostalgias sobre Juan Rulfo," on Rulfo; also Eligio García, *Tras las claves de Melquíades*, pp. 592–9.

12. GGM, Mexico City, to Plinio Mendoza, Bogotá, 13 August 1961.

13. "The Sea of Lost Time," GGM, *Collected Stories*, p. 220.

14. GGM had recently been working in New York, mostly late at night, on Alvaro Cepeda's film about Barranquilla's annual carnival, financed by the Santo Domingo Aguila Beer firm.

15. See Darío Arizmendi Posada, "El mundo de Gabo. 4: Cuando Gabo era pobre," *El Mundo* (Medellín), 29 October 1982.

16. Fiorillo, *La Cueva*, p. 105.

17. And Juan García Ponce would later live with Elizondo's ex-wife, the mother of the daughter that García Márquez's son would one day marry.

18. Eduardo García Aguilar, "Entrevista a Emilio García Riera," *Gaceta* (Bogotá, Colcultura), no. 39, 1983.

19. GGM, Mexico City, to Plinio Mendoza, Bogotá, early December 1961.

20. GGM, Mexico City, to Plinio Mendoza, Barranquilla, April 1962.

21. See especially "La desgracia de ser escritor joven," *El Espectador*, 6 September 1981, in which he says that having accepted this prize and the earlier one for "One Day After Saturday" in 1954 are his only regrets from his career as a writer.

22. GGM, *Living to Tell the Tale*, p. 231.

23. See Bernardo Marques, "Reportaje desde Cuba (I). Gabriel García Márquez: pasado y presente de una obra," *Alternativa* (Bogotá), 93, 9–16 August 1976.

24. GGM, Mexico City, to Plinio Mendoza, Barranquilla, 16 June 1962. In a letter GGM, Mexico City, to Alvaro Cepeda, Barranquilla, spring 1963, he confesses to having crashed the car while blind drunk.

25. GGM, Mexico City, to Alvaro Cepeda, Barranquilla, 20 March 1962.

26. In Saldívar, *GM: el viaje a la semilla*, p. 429, Mutis is quoted as suggesting that GGM never worked on *The Autumn of the Patriarch* in Mexico; but GGM, Mexico City, to Plinio Mendoza, Barranquilla, 1 July 1964, puts the issue beyond doubt.

27. José Font Castro, "Anecdotario de una Semana Santa con Gabriel García Márquez en Caracas," *Momento* (Caracas), 771, April 1971, pp. 34–7, says that GGM read him the first part of *The Autumn of the Patriarch* in 1963 (p. 37).

28. GGM, Mexico City, to Plinio Mendoza, Barranquilla, late September 1962.

29. GGM, Mexico City, to Plinio Mendoza, Bogotá, 4 April 1962.

30. Not September 1963, as everyone, including Saldívar, recounts. See GGM, Mexico City, to Plinio Mendoza, Barranquilla, 17 April 1963.

31. Antonio Andrade, "Cuando Macondo era una redacción," *Excelsior* (Mexico City), 11 October 1970, gives a different view, saying that Alatriste sacked GGM and in response to desperate pleas paid him some money for *El Charro*.

32. Raúl Renán, "Renán 21," in José Francisco Conde Ortega et al., eds, *Gabriel García Márquez: celebración. 25° aniversario de "Cien años de soledad"* (México, Universidad Autónoma Metropolitana, 1992), p. 96.

33. *Ibid.*, p. 95.

34. Rodrigo García Barcha told me: "We always went to English-speaking schools. It's one of Dad's obsessions, he has a great complex about not being able to speak English and he was determined that we would be able to."

35. GGM, Mexico City, to Plinio Mendoza, Barranquilla, 8 December 1963: GGM says he finished the script "this morning."

36. GGM says he met Fuentes in 1961; Eligio García says 1962; Fuentes himself says 1963; Julio Ortega, *Retrato de Carlos Fuentes* (Madrid, Círculo de Lectores, 1995), p. 108, says 1964.

37. Carlos Fuentes, *El Nacional* (Mexico City), 26 March 1992. In Mexico, as elsewhere, GGM's close relationships would be with the most important writers (with the exception of Octavio Paz, who was generally hostile to him). His warmest relationships, among the leading authors, would be with Fuentes and with Carlos Monsiváis.

38. Miguel Torres, "El novelista que quiso hacer cine," *Revista de Cine Cubano* (Havana), 1969.

39. GGM, Panamá City, to Plinio Mendoza, Barranquilla, late October 1964.

40. GGM, Mexico City, to Plinio Mendoza, Barranquilla, late November 1994.

41. GGM, "Sí, la nostalgia sigue siendo igual que antes," *El Espectador*, 16 December 1980.

42. Emir Rodríguez Monegal, "Novedad y anacronismo de *Cien años de soledad*," *Revista Nacional de Cultura* (Caracas), 185, July–September 1968.

43. GGM, Mexico City, to Plinio Mendoza, Barranquilla, 22 May 1965, says he finished the script "a week ago" and it now has a definitive title, *Tiempo de morir*.

44. Miguel Torres, "El novelista que quiso hacer cine," *Revista de Cine Cubano* (Havana), 1969; Emilio García Riera, *Historia documental del cine mexicano* (Mexico City, Universidad de Guadalajara, 1994), 12 (1964–5), pp. 229–33.

45. See Plinio Mendoza, "Entrevista con Gabriel García Márquez," *Libre*, 3, March–May 1972, where he says that in Mexico he wrote film scripts ("very bad ones," according to the experts") and learned all there was to know about the industry and its limitations (p. 13). He stated that the directors he most admired were Welles and Kurosawa but the films he had most enjoyed were *Il Generale della Rovere* and *Jules et Jim*.

46. Emilio García Riera, *Historia documental del cine mexicano*, 12 (1964–5), pp. 160–5.

47. Miguel Torres, "El novelista que quiso hacer cine," *Revista de Cine Cubano* (Havana), 1969.

48. José Donoso, *The Boom in Spanish American Literature: A Personal History* (New

York, Columbia University Press/Center for Inter-American Relations, 1977), pp. 95–7.

49. His book would be called *Los nuestros* [*Our People*] in Spanish but the English title was more historically significant: *Into the Mainstream*.

50. Eligio García, *Tras las claves de Melquíades*, pp. 55–6, 469.

51. Luis Harss and Barbara Dohmann, *Into the Mainstream: Conversations with Latin-American Writers* (New York, Harper and Row, 1967), p. 310.

52. *Ibid.*, p. 317.

53. Eligio García, *Tras las claves de Melquíades*, pp. 68–9.

54. Carme Riera, "Carmen Balcells, alquimista del libro," *Quimera*, 27 January 1983, p. 25.

55. Eligio García, *Tras las claves de Melquíades*, p. 608.

56. He would tell Mendoza in a letter that he had the first sentence when he was seventeen!

57. Two examples: in *The Fragrance of Guava* GGM assures Plinio Mendoza categorically that he turned the car around ("It's true, I never got to Acapulco," p. 74) but in "La novela detrás de la novela," *Cambio* (Bogotá), 20 April 2002, he states that they did drive on to Acapulco for the weekend ("I didn't have a moment's peace on the beach") and got back to Mexico City "on the Tuesday."

15 / Melquíades the Magician:
One Hundred Years of Solitude (1965–1966)

1. GGM, "La penumbra del escritor de cine," *El Espectador*, 17 November 1982.

2. Mendoza, *The Fragrance of Guava*, p. 80.

3. Poniatowska, interview, September 1973, *Todo México, op. cit.*, pp. 218–19.

4. See Alastair Reid, "Basilisk's Eggs," in *Whereabouts. Notes on Being a Foreigner* (San Francisco, North Point Press, 1987), pp. 94–118. Reid is excellent on the question of veracity and verisimilitude in García Márquez.

5. Eligio García, *Tras las claves de Melquíades*, p. 59. In a letter Paco Porrúa told me: "Gabo's experience in Buenos Aires, lived in a kind of rapture of communion and enthusiasm, was undoubtedly very exceptional. The book in the street, the theatre in the street . . . Gabo was a popular personage in the streets and in the parties that took place night after night. There were scenes bordering on hysteria: it was surprising how many señoras from Buenos Aires said they had an uncle or grandfather identical to Aureliano Buendía" (Barcelona, 6 May 1993).

6. Carlos Fuentes, "No creo que sea obligación del escritor engrosar las filas de los menesterosos," "La Cultura en México, *¡Siempre!* (Mexico City), 29 September 1965.

7. Saldívar, *GM: el viaje a la semilla*, p. 433.

8. See José Font Castro, "Anecdotario de una Semana Santa con Gabriel García Márquez en Caracas," *Momento* (Caracas), 771, April 1971, pp. 34–7.

9. Eligio García, *Tras las claves de Melquíades*, p. 617.

10. Poniatowska, interview, September 1973, *Todo México, op. cit.*, p. 195.

11. I talked to María Luisa Elío about this in 1992 and to GGM in 1993.

12. Poniatowska, interview, September 1973, *Todo México, op. cit.*, p. 197.

13. Claude Couffon, "A Bogotá chez García Márquez," *L'Express*, 17–23 January 1977, p. 77.

14. José Font Castro, "Anecdotario de una Semana Santa con Gabriel García Márquez en Caracas," *Momento* (Caracas), 771, April 1971, p. 36.

15. Mendoza, *La llama y el hielo*, pp. 110–11.

16. Eligio García, *Tras las claves de Melquíades*, pp. 88–91. See also GGM, "Valledupar, la parranda del siglo," *El Espectador*, 19 June 1983.

17. Eligio García, *Tras las claves de Melquíades*, pp. 505ff.

18. *Ibid.*, pp. 570–71.

19. Carlos Fuentes, "García Márquez: *Cien años de soledad*," "La Cultura en México," *¡Siempre!* (Mexico City), 679, 29 June 1966.

20. Plinio Mendoza, *The Fragrance of Guava*, p. 77.

21. Fiorillo, *La Cueva*, pp. 105–6.

22. *Ibid.*, pp. 268–9.

23. As Jorge Ruffinelli has perceptively pointed out, the only way to tell the story of this book's writing, publication and reception (and the way it mainly has been told) is as a fairy tale (*La viuda de Montiel* [Xalapa, Veracruz, 1979]).

24. James Papworth, interview, Mexico City, 1994.

25. GGM, "Desventuras de un escritor de libros," *El Espectador, Magazín Dominical*, 7 August 1966.

26. GGM, Mexico City, to Plinio Mendoza, Barranquilla, 22 July 1966.

27. Claude Couffon, "A Bogotá chez García Márquez," *L'Express* (Paris), 17–23 January 1977, p. 77. In Mendoza, *The Fragrance of Guava*, however, GGM says Mercedes alone took it to the post office (p. 75) . . . (Perhaps this was the second package?)

16 / Fame at Last (1966–1967)

1. Alvaro Mutis, quoted by Saldívar, *GM*, p. 498. This chapter draws particularly on conversations with Mutis (Mexico City, 1992, 1994), Tomás Eloy Martínez (Washington, 1997, Warwick, 2006, Cartagena, 2007), Paco Porrúa (Barcelona, 1992 and by letter), Eligio GM, José ("Pepe") Stevenson, as well as many others.

2. Eligio García, *Tras las claves de Melquíades*, pp. 618–19.

3. See Claudia Dreifus, "Gabriel García Márquez," *Playboy* 30:2, February 1983, p. 174.

4. See Eligio García, *Tras las claves de Melquíades*, pp. 32–3.

5. As reprinted in A. D'Amico and S. Facio, *Retratos y autorretratos* (Buenos Aires, Crisis, 1973), which included photos of GGM taken in Buenos Aires in 1967.

6. Ernesto Schóo, "Los viajes de Simbad," *Primera Plana* (Buenos Aires), 234, 20–26 June 1967.

7. Mario Vargas Llosa, "*Cien años de soledad*: el Amadís en América," *Amaru* (Lima), 3, July–September 1967, pp. 71–4.

8. See GGM, "La poesía al alcance de los niños," *El Espectador*, 25 January 1981, where GGM, railing against literary critics, says that even Rojo doesn't know why he put the reverse letter on the cover.

9. "Cien años de un pueblo," *Visión*, 21 July 1967, pp. 27–9.

10. See, for example, "De cómo García Márquez caza un león," *Ercilla* (Chile), 168, 20 September 1967, p. 29.

11. GGM, Mexico City, to Plinio Mendoza, Barranquilla, 30 May 1967.

12. Saldívar, *GM: el viaje a la semilla*, p. 500.

13. Tomás Eloy Martínez, "El día en que empezó todo," in Juan Gustavo Cobo Borda, ed., *"Para que mis amigos me quieran más . . .": homenaje a Gabriel García Márquez* (Bogotá, Siglo del Hombre, 1992), p. 24.

14. *Ibid.*

15. Saldívar, *GM: el viaje a la semilla*, p. 501.

16. Martínez, "El día en que empezó todo," in Cobo Borda, *op.cit.*, p. 25.

17. *Ibid.*

18. José Emilio Pacheco, "Muchos años después," *Casa de las Américas* (Havana), 165, July–December 1987.

19. Quoted by Paternostro, *Paris Review*, 141, *op. cit.*

20. See Vargas Llosa, *Historia de un deicidio*, p. 80.

21. *Ibid.*

22. Emir Rodríguez Monegal, "Diario de Caracas," *Mundo Nuevo* (Paris), 17, November 1967, pp. 4–24 (p. 11).

23. *Semana* (Bogotá), 19 May 1987, notes that *OHYS* was scarcely mentioned in the Colombian press at this time.

24. Mendoza, *La llama y el hielo*, p. 111.

25. Eligio GM, in Galvis, *Los GM*, p. 257.

26. See, for example, Félix Grande, "Con García Márquez en un miércoles de ceniza," *Cuadernos Hispanoamericanos* (Madrid), June 1968, pp. 632–41.

27. Iáder Giraldo, "Hay persecución a la cultura en Colombia," *El Espectador*, 2 November 1967.

28. Alfonso Monsalve, "La novela, anuncio de grandes transformaciones," *Enfoque Internacional* (Bogotá), 8, December 1967, pp. 39–41; reprinted in *El Tiempo*, "Lecturas Dominicales," 14 January 1968, p. 4.

17 / Barcelona and the Latin American Boom:
Between Literature and Politics (1967–1970)

1. GGM, Bogotá, to Emir Rodríguez Monegal, Paris, 30 October 1967.

2. GGM, Barcelona, to Plinio Mendoza, Barranquilla, 21 November 1967.

3. This chapter and the two following draw on interviews with Juan Goytisolo (London, 1990), Luis and Leticia Feduchi (Barcelona, 1991, 2000), Paul Giles (Barcelona, 1992), Germán Arciniegas (Bogotá, 1991), Germán Vargas (Barranquilla, 1991), Margot GM (1993), Eligio GM (1991, 1998), Jaime GM (Santa Marta, 1993), Mario Vargas Llosa (Washington, 1994), Jorge Edwards (Barcelona, 1992), Plinio Mendoza (Bogotá, 1991), Nieves Arrazola de Muñoz Suay (Barcelona, 1992, 2000), Carmen Balcells (Barcelona, 1992, 2000), Rosa Regás (Havana, 1995), Beatriz de Moura (Barcelona, 2000), Juan Marsé (Barcelona, 2000), José María Castellet (Barcelona, 2000), Tachia Quintana (Paris, 1993), Ramón Chao (Paris, 1993), Claude Couffon (Paris, 1993), Jacques Gilard (Toulouse, 1999, 2004), Roberto Fernández Retamar (Havana, 1995), Víctor Flores Olea (Providence, R.I., 1994), Rafael Gutiérrez Girardot (Barcelona, 1992), Joaquín Marco (Barcelona, 1992), Annie Morvan (Paris, 1993), Paco Porrúa (Barcelona, 1992, and letter), Juan Roda and María Fornaguera de Roda (Bogotá, 1993), Alfonso López Michelsen (Bogotá, 1993), as well as many conversations with others.

4. On this and on Spain in general, see GGM, "España: la nostalgia de la nostalgia," *El Espectador*, 13 January 1982.

5. Note that as late as 1978 GGM declared to Angel Harguindey of *El País* that if he were a Spaniard he would be in the Spanish Communist Party. (See Rentería, ed., p. 172). It should be emphasized that he always stressed that such decisions depended on the specific circumstances of the case.

6. Rosa Regás, interview, Havana, January 1995.

7. Luis and Leticia Feduchi, interviews, Barcelona, 1992 and 2000.

8. Both Rodrigo and Gonzalo García Barcha told me this.

9. Paul Giles, interview, Barcelona, 1992.

10. Carmen Balcells, interview, Barcelona, 1991.

11. Francisco Urondo, "La buena hora de GM," *Cuadernos Hispanoamericanos* (Madrid), 232, April 1969, pp. 163–8 (p. 163).

12. Dislike of critics would become almost an obsession for this man who had himself been an occasional critic in his journalism from 1947 onwards, and sometimes a cruel one (his review of Biswell Cotes's book *Neblina azul* in *El Universal*, late 1949, is typical: see Gilard, ed., *Textos costeños 1*).

13. In 1973 the film director Pier Paolo Pasolini would agree with GGM about *OHYS* and its conception and would go even further in perhaps the most scathing attack ever launched against the writer and his book. See "GGM: un escritor indigno," *Tempo*, 22 July 1973, an article characteristic of Pasolini's fanaticism and exaggeration.

14. In the prologue to *Strange Pilgrims* (1992), GGM writes that after a few years in Barcelona he had a life-changing dream: he was at his own burial (Spanish *entierro*: it is important to remember that this concrete word is the one normally used in Spanish for "funeral") and had a good time chatting to his old friends until the moment when he realized that they were leaving after the ceremony and he could not.

15. GGM talked about this repeatedly after 1967, to the irritation of many critics (none of whom, needless to say, were as famous as him). But compare Bob Dylan, *Chronicles. Volume I* (New York, Simon and Schuster, 2004): "After a while you learn that privacy is something you can sell, but you can't buy it back . . . The press? I figured you lie to it" (pp. 117–18).

16. GGM's aversion to *OHYS* may to some degree have extended to Buenos Aires, where fame first beset him. In a letter, Paco Porrúa, the midwife to his celebrity, told me: "When I met Gabo again in Barcelona, I noticed some changes. Above all I had the impression that Gabo no longer spoke with the inspired spontaneity of before, and that in some way he was constructing a new persona. Years later, in 1977, I saw him again in Barcelona and had a conversation with him and Mercedes about those days in Buenos Aires. Well, I embarked on a monologue about how wonderful those days had been. Gabo and Mercedes listened reluctantly, almost with an air of disapproval. Later I thought that the famous dream he had had in Barcelona about attending his own funeral had evidently pointed on to other deaths" (Barcelona, 6 May 1993).

17. See Franco Moretti, *Modern Epic: The World System from Goethe to García Márquez* (London, Verso, 1996). Compare and contrast Pasolini's response, noted above, with Moretti's assessment of the book's transcendental importance.

18. Fernández-Braso, *Gabriel García Márquez. (Una conversación infinita)*, p. 27.

19. *París: la revolución de mayo* (Mexico, Era, 1968).

20. GGM, Barcelona, to Plinio Mendoza, Barranquilla, 28 October 1968.

21. *Ibid.*

22. GGM seems never to have made any comment on the Tlatelolco events even in his private correspondence. This is at first sight extraordinary given that he had lived in Mexico for six years (though probably explicable in the sense that he intended to return there), not least considering its similarity to the 1928 Ciénaga massacre, undoubtedly the best-known and most controversial episode alluded to in GGM's entire oeuvre.

23. Beatriz de Moura, interview, Barcelona, 2000.

24. Juan Marsé, interview, Barcelona, 2000.

25. Julio Cortázar to Paco Porrúa, 23 September 1968. See Julio Cortázar, *Cartas*, ed. Aurora Bernárdez, 3 vols. (Buenos Aires, Alfaguara, 2000).

26. GGM, "El argentino que se hizo querer de todos," *El Espectador*, 22 February 1984.

27. Carlos Fuentes, *Geografía de la novela* (Mexico, Fondo de Cultura Económica, 1993), p. 99. While they were in Prague Japanese writer Yasunari Kawabata received the Nobel Prize for Literature in Stockholm. García Márquez would be an enthusiastic reader of his works.

28. Carmen Balcells, interview, Barcelona, 1991.

29. Gonzalo's first child, Mateo, was born in 1987.

30. See Régis Debray, *Les Masques* (Paris, Gallimard, 1987) for a superb insight into the mind-set of the *bien-pensant* leftists of the 1970s.

31. Rodrigo García Barcha, interview, New York, 1996.

32. See "Memorias de un fumador retirado," *El Espectador*, 13 February 1983, in which GGM recalls giving up smoking "fourteen years ago."

33. See Eligio GM's chronicle in *Aracataca-Estocolmo* (pp. 22–4): "Feduchi, the analyst of the thousand pipes, the one who helped GGM with the motivation of the murderers in *Chronicle* and helped him give up smoking, though ironically he couldn't keep to it himself."

34. See E. González Bermejo, "Ahora doscientos años de soledad . . . ," *Triunfo*, November 1971, in Rentería, p. 50.

35. John Leonard, *New York Times Book Review*, 3 March 1970. The *New York Times* published a favourable review on 8 March which it later included in 1996 as one of the reviews anthologized to celebrate the newspaper's centenary.

36. See José Donoso, *Historia personal del "Boom"* (Barcelona, Seix Barral, 1983; 2nd revised edition with appendix by Ma. Pilar Serrano, "El boom doméstico"). English version, *The Boom in Spanish American Literature: A Personal History* (New York, Columbia University Press/Center for Inter-American Relations, 1977).

37. This relationship was a drama from start to finish. See Jacques Gilard and Fabio Rodríguez Amaya, *La obra de Marvel Moreno* (Viareggio-Lucca, Mauro Baroni, 1997); also Plinio Mendoza's novel *Años de fuga* (1985) and *La llama y el hielo*.

38. Mendoza, *La llama y el hielo*, p. 120. On Barcelona and GGM's relationships there, see especially pp. 120–25.

39. See Adam Feinstein, *Pablo Neruda: A Passion for Life* (London, Bloomsbury, 2004), p. 351.

40. GGM, Barcelona, to Plinio Mendoza, summer (August?) 1970.

41. "GGM evoca Pablo Neruda," *Cromos*, 1973 (quoted in Rentería), p. 95.

42. Julio Cortázar, letter to Eduardo Jonquières, 15 August 1970, *Cartas*, p. 1419.

43. María Pilar Serrano de Donoso, in José Donoso, *Historia personal del "Boom,"* p. 134.

44. Donoso, *The Boom in Spanish American Literature*, pp. 105–6.

18 / The Solitary Author Slowly Writes:
The Autumn of the Patriarch and the Wider World (1971–1975)

1. Fiorillo, *La Cueva*, p. 271.

2. Juan Gossaín, "Regresó García Márquez: 'Vine a recordar el olor de la guayaba,'" *El Espectador*, 15 January 1971.

3. It turned out that he was referring specifically to the trial of members of the

Basque separatist group ETA in Burgos, in which three alleged terrorists had been sentenced to death.

4. This phrase would be translated rather delicately in English as "the fragrance of guava" when a book of interviews with that title later appeared.

5. Juan Gossaín, "Ni yo mismo sé quién soy: Gabo," *El Espectador*, 17 January 1971.

6. Guillermo Ochoa, "Los seres que inspiraron a Gabito," *Excelsior*, 13 April 1971.

7. Gonzalo García Barcha, interview, Paris, 2004.

8. See Lourdes Casal, ed., *El caso Padilla: literatura y revolución en Cuba. Documentos* (Miami, Universal, and New York, Nueva Atlántida, 1972), p. 9; and Jorge Edwards, *Persona Non Grata* (New York, Paragon House, 1993), p. 220.

9. The protest was published in newspapers all over the Western world, including, for example, the *New York Review of Books* on 6 May 1971.

10. In 2007 he allowed the Spanish academy to include a fragment from the book in the special edition of *OHYS* published that year.

11. This interview appeared in *El Tiempo* on 29 May 1971. Its importance was recognized by it being reproduced immediately in *Prensa Latina* (though with "limited"/"non-publishable" status), where it must have stimulated very mixed reactions, and later in the first number of *Libre*.

12. See *Realms of Strife: 1957–1982* (London, Quartet Books, 1990), p. 153.

13. See Guibert, *Seven Voices*, pp. 330–32.

14. Interview with Julio Roca, *Diario del Caribe*, 29 May 1971.

15. " '*Cien años de soledad* es un plagio': Asturias," *La República*, 20 June 1971.

16. See Félix Grande, "Con García Márquez en un miércoles de ceniza," *Cuadernos Hispanoamericanos* (Madrid), 222, June 1968, pp. 632–41.

17. "Gabo pasea con *Excelsior* y come tacos," *Excelsior* (Mexico City), 12 July 1971.

18. Document in Casa de las Américas archive, Havana.

19. See Vargas Llosa's reading of this story in *Historia de un deicidio*, pp. 457–77.

20. In June 1973 "The Incredible and Sad Tale of Innocent Eréndira" would be published in *Esquire*. For a reading of *Eréndira*, see A. Benítez Rojo, "Private Reflections on GM's *Eréndira*," in *The Repeating Island: The Caribbean and the Postmodern Perspective* (Durham, N.C., Duke University Press, 1996), pp. 276–93.

21. See Jaime Mejía Duque, "La peste del macondismo," *El Tiempo*, "Lecturas Dominicales," 4 March 1973.

22. Juan Bosch, perpetual presidential candidate in the Dominican Republic, and overthrown by the Americans in 1965, also compared García Márquez with Cervantes in June 1971.

23. Poniatowska, interview, September 1973, *Todo México*, pp. 202–3.

24. Carmen Balcells, interview, Barcelona, 2000. Cf. Ricardo A. Setti, *Diálogo con Vargas Llosa* (Costa Rica, Kosmos, 1989), pp. 147–50.

25. Eligio García, *El Tiempo*, 15 August 1972.

26. Myriam Garzón, conversation, 1993.

27. See *Excelsior*, 5 August 1972: "En vez de yate, donativo político: García Márquez cedió su premio."

28. See 17 August 1972 interview in *Excelsior*: "GM es muy embustero, dice su padre. Lo era de chiquito, siempre inventaba cuentos."

29. See the interview given to *Cromos* after Neruda died, "GGM evoca a Pablo Neruda," *Cromos*, 1973 (in Rentería, *op.cit.*).

30. Even MAS leader Pompeyo Márquez, in his article for *Libre*, 3 (March–May 1972), "Del dogmatismo al marxismo crítico," pp. 29–34, had said that it was MAS's policy never to adopt "anti-Soviet positions" (p. 33).

31. Mendoza, *La llama y el hielo*, pp. 196–7.

32. Fiorillo, *La Cueva*, pp. 161–2.

33. GGM, Barcelona, to Fuenmayor, Barranquilla, early November 1972. (See Fiorillo, *La Cueva*, pp. 162–3.)

34. "GGM evoca a Pablo Neruda," *Cromos*, 1973, p. 96.

35. *Excelsior*, 13 May 1973. For a sober appraisal of the book's writing, objectives and achievements over a quarter of a century later, see GGM, "Hoja por hoja y diente por diente," *Cambio*, 2001.

36. In this respect it can be directly compared to Asturias's *The President* (1946).

37. See Emir Rodríguez Monegal, "Novedad y anacronismo de *Cien Años de soledad*," in his *Narradores de esta América, Tomo II* (Caracas, Alfadil, 1992).

38. Guillermo Sheridan and Armando Pereira, "GM en México (entrevista)," *Revista de la Universidad de México*, 30:6, February 1976.

39. *Ibid.*

40. GGM gives his best explanation of the timescale in Odete Lara, "GM," *El Escarabajo de Oro* (Buenos Aires), 47, December 1973–February 1974, pp. 18–21.

41. See Northrop Frye's concept of archetypal characters and seasons (symbolic phases) in *Anatomy of Criticism* (1957).

42. Sheridan and Pereira, "GM en México (entrevista)," *op. cit.*

43. Juan Gossaín, "El regreso a Macondo," *El Espectador*, January 1971. Cf. Conrad's *Nostromo* (of which GGM's book is a deliberately and grotesquely distorted descendant), in which the protagonist dies "from solitude."

44. GGM, *The Autumn of the Patriarch* (London, Picador, 1978), p. 45 (my emphasis).

45. *Ibid.*, p. 74.

46. *Ibid.*, p. 180.

47. *Ibid.*, p. 205.

48. *Ibid.*, p. 39.

49. *Ibid.*, p. 199.

50. *Ibid.*, pp. 200–2.

51. *Ibid.*, p. 203. Asturias had previously shown in *The President* that his dictator's (Estrada Cabrera's) character had been formed by a deprived childhood mitigated by the unceasing efforts of a devoted lower-class mother.

52. Carmen Balcells, interview, Barcelona, 2000.

53. Tachia Quintana (Rosoff), interview, Paris 1973.

54. The award had been announced in November of the previous year. See *Excelsior*, 19 November 1972.

55. Poniatowska, interview, September 1973, *Todo México*, p. 194.

56. *Excelsior*, 10 September 1973. It was around now that GGM seems to have formed an understanding with *Excelsior* journalists. They seem to have been tipped off about his movements from this time and he received more coverage from them than any Mexican writer and, indeed, more favourable coverage than any Mexican writer, over the next fifteen years.

19 / Chile and Cuba:
García Márquez Opts for the Revolution (1973–1979)

1. See Plinio Mendoza, "Fina," in *Gentes, lugares* (Bogotá, Planeta, 1986), where he tells the extraordinary story of his journey to Chile via Arica with Fina Torres, then a photographer, directly after the coup. Mendoza was the only foreign journalist who

got to Neruda's house and saw his body just four hours after his death, and Fina Torres's photographs were reproduced all over Latin America.

2. Reproduced in *Excelsior*, 8 October 1973.

3. Ernesto González Bermejo, "La imaginación al poder en Macondo," *Crisis* (Buenos Aires), 1975 (reproduced in Rentería, *op.cit*). In this interview, conducted in 1970, GGM had said, "I want Cuba to create a socialism which takes account of its own conditions, a socialism which resembles Cuba itself: human, imaginative, joyful, without any bureaucratic corrosion."

4. Juan Gossaín, "Ni yo mismo sé quién soy: Gabo," *El Espectador*, 17 January 1971.

5. Guibert, *Seven Voices*, p. 333. On p. 329, however, GGM says that he is greatly disillusioned by the USSR, whose system "is not socialism."

6. See Luis Suárez, "El periodismo me dio conciencia política," *La Calle* (Madrid), 1978 (in Rentería, pp. 195–200).

7. In a letter, GGM to Plinio Mendoza, April 1962, he expounds the theory that *El Tiempo* readers are the key to Colombian elections.

8. This chapter is based in part on interviews with each of these three journalists: Antonio Caballero (Madrid, 1991, Bogotá 1993), Daniel Samper (Madrid, 1991), and Enrique Santos Calderón (Bogotá, 1991, 2007); and also on interviews with José Vicente Kataraín (Bogotá, 1993), Alfonso López Michelsen (Bogotá, 1991), Belisario Betancur (Bogotá, 1991), Hernando Corral (Bogotá, 1998), Julio Andrés Camacho (Cartagena, 1991), José Salgar (Bogotá, 1991), José Stevenson (Bogotá, 1991, Cartagena, 2007), Fernando Gómez Agudelo (Bogotá, 1993), Felipe López Caballero (Bogotá, 1993), Laura Restrepo (Bogotá, 1991), Jaime Osorio (Bogotá, 1993), Luis Villar Borda (Bogotá, 1998), Jesús Martín Barbero (Pittsburgh, 2000), María Luisa Mendoza (Mexico City, 1994), Elena Poniatowska (Mexico City, 1994), and many others.

9. See Margarita Vidal, "GGM," 1981 *Cromos* interview reprinted in *Viaje a la memoria (entrevistas)* (Bogotá, Espasa Calpe, 1997), pp. 128–39.

10. Enrique Santos Calderón, "Seis años de compromiso: breve historia de esta revista y de las realidades que determinan su cierre," *Alternativa* 257, 27 March 1980 (last issue).

11. No. 1, 15–28 February 1974. No. 2, 1–15 March 1974, included GGM's "El golpe en Chile (II). Pilotos gringos bombardearon La Moneda."

12. From English version, "Why Allende Had to Die," *New Statesman*, London, 15 March 1974, p. 358.

13. Both would be published in 1975.

14. See Rafael Humberto Moreno Durán, *Como el halcón peregrino* (Bogotá, Santillana, 1995), p. 117. Moreno Durán says GGM was late for the party because he "had been at Miguel Angel Asturias's funeral in Madrid." I asked GGM about this in 2002 and he denied it. The timing would have been right but I was unable to ask Moreno Durán himself why he had stated this before he himself died in 2005. See also Julia Urquidi Illanes, *Lo que Varguitas no dijo* (La Paz, Khana Cruz, 1983).

15. See Donoso, *Historia personal del "boom,"* pp. 148–9.

16. "It seemed so strange, we had always travelled everywhere together" (Rodrigo García Barcha, interview, New York, 1996).

17. Núñez Jiménez, "GM y la perla de las Antillas."

18. "Gabriel García Márquez: de la ficción a la política," *Visión*, 30 January 1975.

19. Enrique Santos Calderón, interview, Bogotá, 1991.

20. The interview was reproduced in the *New York Review of Books* on 7 August

1975 in the form of a review of Agee's book (*Inside the Company: CIA Diary*, Harmondsworth, Penguin, 1975).

21. However, Sorela, *El otro García Márquez*, takes a very critical view of GGM's relationship with López Michelsen down the years.

22. One of the most violent reactions was from Colombian left critic Jaime Mejía Duque, in *"El otoño del patriarca" o la crisis de la desmesura*, published in Medellín in July 1975 by none other than Oveja Negra, GGM's own future publisher.

23. Lisandro Otero, *Llover sobre mojado: una reflexión sobre la historia* (Havana, Letras Cubanas, 1997), p. 208.

24. *Alternativa*, 40, 30 June–7 July, GGM, "Portugal, territorio libre de Europa"; 41, 7–14 July, "Portugal, territorio libre de Europa (II). ¿Pero qué carajo piensa el pueblo?; and 42, 14–21 July, "Portugal, territorio libre de Europa (III). El socialismo al alcance de los militares."

25. See *Excelsior*, 5 June 1975, quoting Lisbon's *Diário Popular*.

26. *Excelsior*, 30 June 1975.

27. *Excelsior*, 17 June 1975.

28. See *Alternativa*, 38, 16–23 June 1975, "GGM entrevista a Torrijos. 'No descartamos la violencia.'"

29. Núñez Jiménez, "GM y la perla de las Antillas." See also GGM, "Allá por los tiempos de la Coca-Cola," *El Espectador*, 11 October 1981, which is really also a blockade story concerning Che Guevara's attempts to find a substitute for Coke in the early days of the Revolution.

30. See *Alternativa*, 51, 15–22 September 1975, "Cuba de cabo a rabo (I)"; 52, 22–29 September 1975, "Cuba de cabo a rabo (II). La necesidad hace parir gemelos"; 53, 29 September–6 October 1975, "Cuba de cabo a rabo (III). Final, si no me creen, vayan a verlo."

31. Rodrigo García Barcha, interview, New York, 1997.

32. Enrique Santos Calderón, interview, Bogotá, 1991.

33. See, for example, María Luisa Mendoza, "La verdad embarazada," *Excelsior*, 8 July 1981.

34. This is the $64,000 question that most journalists and many readers wish to discuss with GM's unfortunate biographer as soon as they meet him.

35. Neither man has been willing to discuss the matter but I have discussed this incident with several eyewitnesses, including Mercedes Barcha, and with close associates of both men. In 2008 MVL himself published a play, *Al pie del Támesis*, in which the protagonist reflects on having punched his best friend thirty-five years before and never having seen him again.

36. See Perry Anderson, "A magical realist and his reality," *The Nation*, 26 January 2004, a virtuoso comparison of the two men based on a reading of their memoirs. Once again GGM comes out on top.

37. Núñez Jiménez, "GM y la perla de las Antillas."

38. *Ibid.*

39. See his personal testimony, *Y Fidel creó el Punto X* (Miami, Saeta, 1987).

40. Núñez Jiménez, "GM y la perla de las Antillas."

41. "Felipe González: Socialista serio," *Alternativa*, 129, 29 August–5 September 1977.

42. See "Felipe," *El Espectador*, 2 January 1983, in which GGM recalls this first meeting in Bogotá.

43. "GGM entrevista a Régis Debray: 'Revolución se escribe sin mayúsculas,'" *Alternativa*, 146–7, 26 December–20 January 1977–78.

44. GGM, "El general Torrijos sí tiene quien le escriba," *Alternativa*, 117, 5–12 June 1977.

45. GGM, "Torrijos, cruce de mula y tigre," *Alternativa*, 126, 8–15 August 1977.

46. See Graham Greene, *Getting to Know the General: The Story of an Involvement* (London, Bodley Head, 1984). Dedicated to "The Friends of My Friend Omar Torrijos in Nicaragua, El Salvador and Panama."

47. See GGM, "Graham Greene: la ruleta rusa de la literatura," *El Espectador*, 27 January 1982, and "Las veinte horas de Graham Greene en La Habana," *El Espectador*, 16 January 1983.

48. See Ramón Chao, "García Márquez: El caso Reynold González," *Triunfo* (Madrid), 29 April 1978, pp. 54–6.

49. Fidel Castro, interview, Havana, January 1997.

50. See for example *Alternativa* 94, 23–30 August 1978, "Turbay, el candidato enmascarado."

51. See Sorela, *El otro García Márquez*, p. 249, on GGM's relations with the Sandinista leadership.

52. See GGM, "Edén Pastora," *El Espectador*, 19 July 1981.

53. See GGM, "Locura maestra, tomar palacio," *Excelsior*, 1 September 1978: this was the lead article on the front page of the newspaper for that day.

54. GGM, "Edén Pastora," *El Espectador*, 19 July 1981.

55. *Excelsior*, 21 December 1978.

56. See "Habeas: de verdad por los derechos humanos," *Alternativa*, 194, 25 December 1978–22 January 1979.

57. In an interview in Paris with Ramón Chao and Ignacio Ramonet in October 1979, "La guerra de la información. Tres casos: Nicaragua, Vietnam y Cuba," *Alternativa*, 237, 1–8 November 1979. GM would note that Lolita Lebrón and her Puerto Rican comrades had now been released by Carter, "though only out of electoral considerations."

58. See "Habeas y los derechos humanos: despegue por lo alto," *Alternativa*, 201, 26 February 1979, which announces that GGM has met Pope John Paul II on 19 January and the King and Queen of Spain on 3 February.

59. Quoted by *El Tiempo* on 8 February 1979.

60. "Gobierno de post-guerra: GGM entrevista a Sergio Ramírez," *Alternativa*, 218, 21–28 June 1979.

61. This was around the time that GGM's film script *Viva Sandino*, later also known as *El secuestro* and *El asalto*, was published.

62. Chao and Ramonet, "La guerra de la información. Tres casos: Nicaragua, Vietnam y Cuba," *Alternativa*, 201, 26 February 1979.

63. On the McBride Report, see GGM, "La comisión de Babel," *El Espectador*, 2 November 1980. See also Sorela, *El otro García Márquez*, p. 250, who states that there were eight meetings in 1980–81: four in Paris and one each in Stockholm, Dubrovnik, Delhi and Acapulco.

64. At the end GGM and his Chilean colleague, Juan Somavía, later Secretary General of the International Labour Organization, dissatisfied with the compromise reached by the commission, sent in a joint minority commentary.

65. These comments were made at a lunch in Mexico City given by the Federación Latinoamericana de Periodistas to Mexican President José López Portillo.

66. GGM, "Del malo conocido al peor por conocer," *El Espectador*, 9 November 1980.

67. See "La Revolución Cubana me libró de todos los honores detestables de este

mundo," *Bohemia* (Havana), 1979, in Rentería, pp. 201–9: "I have no more ideas for books. Won't it be marvellous the day I start to get them again."

20 / Return to Literature: *Chronicle of a Death Foretold* and the Nobel Prize (1980–1982)

1. See GGM, "La comisión de Babel," *El Espectador*, 2 November 1980.

2. Carmen Galindo and Carlos Vanella, "Soy más peligroso como literato que como político: GM," second of two articles, *El Día* (Mexico City), 7 September 1981.

3. See GGM, "Georges Brassens," *El Espectador*, 8 November 1981, and "Desde París con amor," *El Espectador*, 26 December 1982. Many of the articles during this period have Parisian themes.

4. María Jimena Duzán, interview, Bogotá, 1991.

5. Enrique Santos Calderón, interview, Bogotá, 1991.

6. Consuelo Mendoza de Riaño, "La Gaba," *Revista Diners* (Bogotá), November 1980.

7. *Excelsior*, 20 March 1980.

8. "Gabriel García Márquez. ¿Esbirro o es burro?," *El Universal*, 17 May 1980.

9. Alan Riding, "For GM, revolution is a major theme," *New York Times*, 22 May 1980.

10. See Juan Gossaín, "A Cayetano lo mató todo el pueblo," *El Espectador*, 13 May 1981, p. 7a, an interview with Luis Enrique GM.

11. See Eligio García's *Crónica de la crónica*, which compares the original events with the novel, and the novel and the original events with the film and the events of its production.

12. See GGM, "El cuento del cuento," *El Espectador*, 23 August 1981, and "El cuento del cuento (Conclusión)," *El Espectador*, 30 August 1981.

13. See Sorela, *El otro García Márquez*, p. 255, on the 1980–84 articles.

14. GGM wrote a letter to Plinio Mendoza, 22 July 1966, in which he says—in 1966, immediately after completing *OHYS* but before it was published!—that he would like to do exactly this kind of journalism.

15. See John Benson, "Notas sobre *Notas de prensa 1980–1984*," *Revista de Estudios Colombianos*, 18 (1998), pp. 27–37.

16. The four articles appeared in *El Espectador* between mid-September and early October 1980.

17. The name and subtitle of a U.S. TV series of a subsequent era.

18. "Sí, la nostalgia sigue siendo igual que antes," *El Espectador*, 16 December 1980.

19. GGM, "Un domingo de delirio," *El Espectador*, 8 March 1981.

20. Cobo Borda, "Crónica de una muerte anunciada: García Márquez sólo escribió su nueva novela cuando su mamá le dio permiso" (1981: later published in Cobo Borda, *Silva, Arciniegas, Mutis y García Márquez*, pp. 419–27).

21. See Sorela, *El otro García Márquez*, pp. 259–62, on this incident: he says he knows for sure that GGM was right about the threat.

22. See *Cromos*, 31 March 1981, "El viaje de GM: crónica de una salida anticipada."

23. See Vidal, *Viaje a la memoria*, pp. 128–39.

24. "GGM y su nuevo libro vistos a través de su editor," *El Espectador*, 3 May 1981.

25. See *Excelsior*, 12 May 1981.

26. *Excelsior*, 7 May 1981.

27. See GGM, "Mitterrand, el otro: el presidente," *El Espectador*, 24 May 1981.

28. Felipe González, interview, Madrid, 1997.

29. *Excelsior*, 4 August 1981.

30. "Torrijos," *El Espectador*, 9 August 1981.

31. See Beatriz López de Barcha, " 'Gabito esperó a que yo creciera,' " *Carrusel*, Revista de *El Tiempo*, 10 December 1982.

32. Quoted by José Pulido, "No quiero convertirme en la estatua del Premio Nobel," *Muro de confesiones* (Caracas, El Libro Menor, Academia Nacional de la Historia, 1985), pp. 9–18.

33. See also "Habla GM: 'Votaré por primera vez en mi vida por López,' " *El Tiempo*, 23 May 1982.

34. GGM, "Crónica de mi muerte anunciada," *El Espectador*, 14 March 1982.

35. "Con las Malvinas o sin ellas," *El Espectador*, 11 April 1982.

36. "Otra vez del avión a la mula. . . ! Qué dicha!," *El Espectador*, 31 January 1982.

37. "Bangkok la horrible," *El Espectador*, 28 March 1982.

38. "Peggy, dame un beso," *El Espectador*, 4 April 1982.

39. "Como sufrimos las flores," *El Espectador*, 6 December 1981.

40. Claudia Dreifus, "GGM," *Playboy* 30:2, February 1983, pp. 65–77, 172–8.

41. Plinio Apuleyo Mendoza, ed., *El olor de la guayaba* (Barcelona, Bruguera, April 1982).

42. María Esther Gilio, "Escribir bien es un deber revolucionario," *Triunfo* (Madrid), 1977, in Rentería, ed., pp. 141–6.

43. This section is based on Núñez Jiménez, "GM y la perla de las Antillas," pp. 69–103.

44. *Ibid.*

45. "Beguin y Sharon, premios 'Nobel de la muerte' " *El Espectador*, 29 September 1982.

46. Alfonso Fuenmayor, "Transparencia de un Nobel," in Mera, ed., *Aracataca-Estocolmo*, pp. 30–33.

47. See "Gabriel José visto por Eligio Gabriel, el benjamín," *Cromos*, 26 October 1982, pp. 20–21.

48. See GGM, "William Golding, visto por sus vecinos," *El Espectador*, 9 October 1983, in which GGM remembers when he heard the news about his own award in 1982.

49. Eligio García, "Así se recibió el Nobel," *Revista Diners* (Bogotá), November 1982.

50. GGM, "Obregón o la vocación desaforada," *El Espectador*, 20 October 1982.

51. GGM, "USA: mejor cerrado que entreabierto," *El Espectador*, 7 November 1982.

52. See for example the *Latin American Times* for December 1982, cover story.

53. Joseph Harmes, "A spellbinding storyteller," *Newsweek*, 1 November 1982.

54. Salman Rushdie, "Márquez the Magician," *Sunday Times* (London), 24 October 1982.

55. See Mera, ed., *Aracataca-Estocolmo*, for the best insight into the Nobel experience and what it meant for Colombia.

56. Plinio Mendoza, "Postales de Estocolmo," in *ibid.*, pp. 96–103.

57. See Guillermo Cano, "Crónica anticipada de unas ceremonias," *El Espectador*, 5 December 1982.

58. Anthony Day and Marjorie Miller, "Gabo talks: GGM on the misfortunes of

Latin America, his friendship with Fidel Castro and his terror of the blank page," *Los Angeles Times Magazine*, 2 September 1990.

59. Mera, ed., *Aracataca-Estocolmo*, p. 30.

60. Mendoza, "Postales de Estocolmo," in *ibid.*, p. 96.

61. Eligio García, "Gabriel José visto por Eligio Gabriel," *Cromos*, 14 December 1982.

62. GGM, "Cena de paz en Harpsund," *El Espectador*, 19 December 1982.

63. Beatriz López de Barcha, "'Gabito esperó a que yo creciera,'" *Carrusel*, Revista de *El Tiempo*, 10 December 1982.

64. See *El Espectador*, 11 December 1982.

65. Mendoza, "Postales de Estocolmo," in Mera, ed., *Aracataca-Estocolmo*, p. 98.

66. Ana María Cano, "Para leer en la mañana: El arrugado liquiliqui," *El Espectador*, 13 December 1982.

67. Plinio Mendoza, "La entrega del Nobel: un día inolvidable," *El Tiempo*, 12 December 1982.

68. Mendoza, "Postales de Estocolmo," in Mera, ed., *Aracataca-Estocolmo*, p. 103.

69. "La cumbia del Nobel," *Gente* (Buenos Aires), December 1982.

70. See Tom Maschler, *Publisher* (London, Picador, 2005), pp. 128–9.

71. Nereo López, "Humanas y hermosas anécdotas de la delegación folklórica colombiana en Estocolmo," in Mera, ed., *Aracataca-Estocolmo*, pp. 91–5.

72. See Gloria Triana in *El Espectador*, 6 October 2002, "Hasta la Reina Silvia se divirtió."

73. GGM, "El brindis por la poesía," *El Espectador*, 12 December 1982.

74. Alexandra Pineda, "El Nobel Gabo piensa en *El Otro*," *El Espectador*, 12 December 1982.

75. *El Espectador*, 10 December 1982.

76. Rita GM, in Galvis, *Los GM*, p. 249.

77. Eligio García, "La entrega del Nobel: Estocolmo fue una fiesta y una rosa amarilla," *El Mundo al Vuelo*, Avianca, 64, February–March 1983.

78. Alvaro Mutis, "Apuntes sobre un viaje que no era para contar," in Mera, ed., *Aracataca-Estocolmo* pp. 19–20.

79. *El Tiempo*, 12 December 1982.

21 / The Frenzy of Renown and the Fragrance
of Guava: *Love in the Time of Cholera* (1982–1985)

1. GGM, "Felipe," *El Espectador*, 2 January 1983.

2. "Diálogo de Gabo con Felipe González," *El Tiempo*, 27 December 1982.

3. See Leo Braudy, *The Frenzy of Renown: Fame and Its History* (New York, Vintage, 1986; 1997).

4. Sorela, *El otro García Márquez*, p. 259.

5. Roberto Pombo, "El año de GM," *Semana* (Bogotá), January 1997.

6. David Streitfeld, "The intricate solitude of GGM," *Washington Post*, 10 April 1994.

7. Juan Cruz, "Relato de un tímido," *El País* (Madrid), 11 January 1993.

8. Rodolfo Braceli, "El genio en su laberinto," *Gente* (Buenos Aires), 15 January 1997.

9. GGM, "Las veinte horas de Graham Greene en La Habana," *El Espectador*, 16 January 1983.

10. Reproduced in Guillermo Cabrera Infante, *Mea Cuba* (London, Faber & Faber, 1994), p. 210.

11. GGM, "Regreso a México," *El Espectador*, 23 January 1983.

12. GGM, "Sí: ya viene el lobo," *El Espectador*, 30 January 1983.

13. See Alfonso Botero Miranda, *Colombia, no alineada? De la confrontación a la cooperación: la nueva tendencia en los No Alineados* (Bogotá, Tercer Mundo, 1995).

14. Núñez Jiménez, "GM y la perla de las Antillas."

15. GGM, "Regreso a la guayaba," *El Espectador*, 10 April 1983.

16. Very unusually GGM hit back in "Con amor, desde el mejor oficio del mundo," *El Espectador*, 24 April 1983.

17. GGM, "Cartagena: una cometa en la muchedumbre," *El Espectador*, 5 June 1983.

18. GGM, "Contadora, cinco meses después," *El Espectador*, 10 July 1983.

19. Tomás Eloy Martínez, "El día en que empezó todo," *Página 12* (Buenos Aires), 21 August 1988.

20. See GGM, "Bishop," *El Espectador*, 23 October 1983.

21. See María Teresa Herrán, "GM ante el mito de Gabo," *El Espectador*, 5 November 1983.

22. Laura Restrepo, interview, Bogotá, 1991.

23. GGM, "Vuelta a la semilla," *El Espectador*, 18 December 1983.

24. See Claudia Dreifus, "Gabriel García Márquez," *Playboy* 30:2, February 1983, p. 172.

25. Régis Debray, *Les Masques* (Paris, Gallimard, 1987), pp. 26–8.

26. See Arango, *Un ramo de nomeolvides*, p. 247.

27. *Ibid.*, p. 120.

28. See Marlise Simons, "The best years of his life: an interview with GGM," *New York Times Book Review*, 10 April 1988.

29. "GGM usa escritura computarizada," *Excelsior*, 16 October 1984.

30. *Chronicle of a Death Foretold*, p. 93.

31. Arango, *Un ramo de nomeolvides*, p. 136.

32. Eric Nepomuceno, "GGM afronta en su nueva obra los peligros de la novela rosa," *El País*, 28 August 1984.

33. Margot GM, in Galvis, *Los GM*, p. 67.

34. Eligio GM, in *ibid.*, pp. 285–6. Remarkably, Tía Pa was in attendance at the time. She would die herself a year later.

35. Jaime GM, in *ibid.*, p. 55.

36. Eligio GM, in *ibid.*, p. 286.

37. GGM, "La vejez juvenil de don Luis Buñuel," *El Espectador*, 1 August 1982. Not only *Love in the Time of Cholera* (1985) but also the seeds of *Memories of My Melancholy Whores* (2004) lie in this article.

38. Marlise Simons (of *New York Times*), "Sexo y vejez: una charla con GM," *El Tiempo*, 14 April 1985. In 1988 Simons would interview him again: Marlise Simons, "The best years of his life: an interview with GGM," *op.cit.*

39. Yasunari Kawabata, *La casa de las bellas durmientes* (Barcelona, Luis de Caralt, 2001), p. 79.

40. María Elvira Samper, "Habla Gabo," *Semana*, 13 May 1985.

41. The most obvious point of reference is Valéry Larbaud's *Fermina Marquez* (Paris, 1911), about a beautiful Colombian girl in France and the loves she inspires. Its title was bound to attract GGM's attention; then the plot also captured his imagination.

42. *Semana*, 9 December 1985.

43. Hernán Díaz, "Una historia trivial antes del huracán," *Revista Diners* (Bogotá), September 1985.

44. Belisario Betancur, interview, Bogotá, 1991. It is to these circumstances that GGM's later book *News of a Kidnapping* (1996) looks back, in order to set the political context for the events (1990–93) that he himself narrates.

45. "It's taken me half a century to write about love," *Excelsior*, 17 January 1986.

46. Thomas Pynchon, "The heart's eternal vow," *New York Times Book Review*, 10 April 1988.

47. GGM, in conversation, Mexico City, 1999.

22 / Against Official History: García Márquez's
Bolívar (*The General in His Labyrinth*) (1986–1989)

1. " 'Colombia está al borde del holocausto': GM," *Excelsior*, 28 July 1986.

2. In the Brazilian edition of *Playboy*, among other places; also in a debate with Günter Grass at the end of the 45th PEN Congress in New York in January 1986.

3. Núñez Jiménez, "GM y la perla de las Antillas."

4. Interviews with Fidel Castro, Tomás Gutiérrez Alea, Fernando Birri, Alquimia Peña, Cacho Pallero, María Luisa Bemberg, Eliseo Alberto, Jorge Alí Triana, Lisandro Duque, Jaime Humberto Hermosillo, Jorge Sánchez, Ignacio Durán, Mario García Joya, Berta Navarro; conversations with Julio García Espinosa, Dolores Calviño, Stella Malagón, Martha Bossío, Miguel Littín.

5. Littín was best known for *The Jackal of Nahueltoro*, 1971; but he had also filmed García Márquez's story *Montiel's Widow* in Mexico in 1978, with Geraldine Chaplin in the starring role.

6. GGM, *Clandestine in Chile* (Cambridge, Granta, 1989).

7. This issue had distanced GGM from Mitterrand. France was still testing in the South Pacific. In July 1985, Greenpeace's ship *Rainbow Warrior* had been sunk in Auckland harbour by French agents ordered—we now know—by Mitterrand himself.

8. "Con emotivo discurso de Gabo se instaló 'reunión de los 6,' " *El Tiempo*, 7 August 1986. See GGM's speech, "El cataclismo de Dámocles," Conferencia Ixtapa, 1986 (Bogotá, Oveja Negra, 1986).

9. Gonzalo and Pía would marry in 1987 and a son, Mateo, García Márquez's first grandchild, would be born in late September.

10. See Andrew Paxman, "On the lot with GGM" (interview), *Variety*, 25–31 March 1996.

11. Michel Brandeau, "Le tournage de 'Chronique d'une mort annoncée,' " *Le Monde*, July 1986.

12. See *La Razón*, Buenos Aires, 7 December 1986, for text of GGM's speech.

13. María Jimena Duzán, interview, Bogotá, 1991.

14. See espcially Marlise Simons, "GM on love, plagues and politics," *New York Times*, 21 February 1988.

15. See Hugo Colmenares, "El demonio persigue las cosas de mi vida," *El Nacional*, 22 February 1989, in Caracas.

16. See "Robert Redford es un admirador de GM," *Excelsior*, 15 October 1988.

17. Elías Miguel Muñoz, "Into the writer's labyrinth: storytelling days with Gabo," *Michigan Quarterly Review*, 34:2, 1995, pp. 173–93, on GGM's work at Sundance, August 1989.

18. See GGM, "Una tontería de Anthony Quinn," *El Espectador*, 21 April 1982.

19. Newell's previous films included *Four Weddings and a Funeral*, *Donnie Brasco* and *Harry Potter and the Goblet of Fire*.

20. See, for example, Larry Rohter, "GM: words into film," *New York Times*, 13 August 1989.

21. See *El coronel no tiene quien le escriba*, guión cinematográfico por Paz Alicia Garciadiego (México, Universidad Veracruzana, 1999).

22. *Excelsior*, 7 August 1990: *New York Times* reviews Salvador Távora's adaptation of *Chronicle of a Death Foretold* in the *Festival Latino*. Mel Gussow said it would need a director with Buñuel's genius to adapt GGM.

23. GGM, "Fidel Castro, el oficio de la palabra," *El País*, 6 March 1988. See "Plying the Word," *NACLA*, 2 August 1990.

24. GGM, *Diatriba de amor contra un hombre sentado* (Bogotá, Arango, 1994).

25. Osvaldo Soriano, "La desgracia de ser feliz," *Página 12* (Buenos Aires), 21 August 1988.

26. Osvaldo Quiroga, "Soledades de un poeta que no acudió a la cita," *La Nación* (Buenos Aires), 21 August 1988.

27. It was said at the time that Monica Vitti had considered staging the play in Rome that year. Later it would be produced in Bogotá with Laura García as Graciela; in 2005 actress-singer Ana Belén played the part in Spain and in January 2006 Graciela Dufau, despite all her sufferings, revived the play in Buenos Aires. Despite the reservations of the critics, it is clear that actresses have enjoyed playing the role.

28. "GM sólo quiere hablar de cine," *Occidente*, 3 December 1989.

29. "Cordial entrevista en Moscú de GM con Gorbachev," *El Espectador*, 11 July 1987.

30. *Excelsior*, 21 July 1987.

31. See his voluminous "gratitudes" or acknowledgements in the published editions.

32. See Susana Cato, "El Gabo: 'Desnudé a Bolívar,'" *Proceso* (Mexico City), 3 April 1989.

33. See GGM, "El río de la vida," *El Espectador*, 25 March 1981.

34. "'Me devoré tu último libro': López a Gabo," *El Tiempo*, 19 February 1989. On 29 July 1975, the 450th anniversary of the founding of Santa Marta, López Michelsen, the President of Colombia, met with Carlos Andrés Pérez of Venezuela and Omar Torrijos of Panama at San Pedro Alejandrino and paid homage to Bolívar, who had died there in 1830. A plaque commemorates the event. All three men would become close friends and allies of GGM over the next decade.

35. Belisario Betancur, *Página 12* (Buenos Aires), 2 April 1989.

36. *Excelsior*, 21 March 1989.

37. María Elvira Samper, "*El general en su laberinto*: un libro vengativo. Entrevista exclusiva con GGM," *Excelsior*, 5 April 1989.

38. See for example Oscar Piedrahita González, "El laberinto de la decrepitud," *La República* (Colombia), 14 May 1989; and Diego Mileo, "En torno al disfraz literario," *Clarín* (Buenos Aires), 22 June 1989.

39. "El libro" (editorial), *El Tiempo*, 19 March 1989.

40. *El Tiempo* editorial, "La rabieta del Nobel," 5 April 1989.

41. *Excelsior*, 28 March 1989. See also "'Mario ha ido demasiado lejos': GM. 'Admiro el valor de Vargas Llosa,'" *Excelsior*, 28 June 1989.

42. "GM no volverá a España," *El Espectador*, 28 March 1989.

43. *Excelsior*, 28 March 1989.

44. Comité de la Carta de los Cien, "Open Letter to Fidel Castro, President of the Republic of Cuba," *New York Times*, 27 December 1988.

45. *The General in His Labyrinth* (London, Jonathan Cape, 1991), p. 230.

46. The decision was a collective one, though Castro's enemies assumed that he took a leading role; they also alleged that Ochoa had to be killed to conceal Fidel Castro and Raúl Castro's own implication in the Caribbean drug trade.

47. 16 July, *Sunday Mirror* headline, "Shabby ghost at the feast," compared her to Marie Antoinette.

48. "El narco-escándalo cubano. Siguen rodando cabezas militares," *El Espectador*, 15 July 1989.

49. See Geoffrey Matthews, "Plague of violence scars land of magical beauty," *Guardian* (London), 3 September 1989.

50. See "GM: 'Hay que apoyar al Presidente Barco,'" *El Tiempo*, 20 August 1989.

51. "GM: 'Castro le teme a la Perestroika,'" *Excelsior*, 22 December 1989.

23 / Back to Macondo?
News of a Historic Catastrophe (1990–1996)

1. Most of these events are mentioned, whether briefly or at length, in GGM, *News of a Kidnapping* (London, Jonathan Cape, 1997).

2. "Condenada al fracaso, la guerra contra la droga: GM," *Excelsior*, 3 November 1989.

3. See Anthony Day and Marjorie Miller, "Gabo talks: GGM on the misfortunes of Latin America, his friendship with Fidel Castro and his terror of the blank page," *Los Angeles Times Magazine*, 2 September 1990, pp. 10–35, in which he states that the USA has an "almost pornographic obsession with Castro" (p. 34). If it were not for Castro, he adds, "the U.S. would be into Latin America all the way to Patagonia."

4. See *Excelsior*, 9 February 1989.

5. Day and Miller, "Gabo talks," p. 33.

6. *Excelsior*, 10 March 1990.

7. See José Hernández, "*María* es un texto sagrado," *El Tiempo*, 10 March 1990.

8. Imogen Mark, "Pinochet adrift in his labyrinth," *Financial Times*, 25 November 1990.

9. Reported in *La Prensa*, 5 September 1990.

10. "GM: sólo Fidel puede transformar a Cuba; EEUU siempre necesita un demonio," *Excelsior*, 3 September 1990.

11. *Excelsior*, 27 January 1991; also "Llamamiento de Gabo por secuestrados," *El Tiempo*, 27 January 1991.

12. "Gabo: 'Es un triunfo de la inteligencia,'" *El Tiempo*, 20 June 1991.

13. "Redford: 'Gabo es un zorro viejo,'" *El Espectador*, 3 March 1991.

14. Renato Ravelo, "El taller de GM," *La Jornada*, 25 October 1998.

15. "Pide GM perdonar la vida a los dos infiltrados," *La Jornada*, 18 January 1992.

16. *Excelsior*, 15 February 1992.

17. "GGM: 'L'amour est ma seule idéologie," *Paris Match*, 14 July 1994.

18. *Excelsior*, 31 July 1992.

19. *Semana*, 14 July 1992.

20. "GM descubre la literatura y le gusta," *El Nacional*, 10 August 1992.

21. *Semana*, 17 November 1992.

22. *Semana*, 29 September 1992.

23. "Nunca es tarde," *El Tiempo*, 23 November 1992.

24. "GM desmiente en Cuba el rumor de discrepancias con Castro," *El País*, 14 December 1992.

25. *El Espectador*, 11 January 1993.

26. Bill Clinton, *Giving: How Each of Us Can Change the World* (London, Hutchinson, 2007).

27. *El Espectador*, 28 January 1993.

28. *Excelsior*, 29 January 1993.

29. "GGM exalta 'el talento' de CAP," *Excelsior*, 18 June 1993.

30. James Brooke, "Cocaine's reality, by GM," *New York Times*, 11 March 1994.

31. 24 March 1994. The statement was issued as a press release.

32. David Streitfeld, "The intricate solitude of GGM," *Washington Post*, 10 April 1994.

33. Gonzalo Mallarino speech at Bogotá Book Fair in praise of GGM's new book (22 April 1994), published in *El Espectador*, 25 April 1994.

34. Jean-François Fogel, "Revolution of the heart," *Le Monde*, 27 January 1995.

35. A. S. Byatt, "By love possessed," *New York Review of Books*, 28 May 1995.

36. Peter Kemp, "The hair and the dog," *Sunday Times* (London), 2 July 1995.

37. Rosa Mora, "El fin de un ayuno," reproduced in *El Espectador*, 17 April 1994.

38. See Silvana Paternostro, "Tres días con Gabo," *Letra Internacional* (Madrid), May–June 1997, p. 13. Castro himself would recall this event in *Granma* in July 2008.

39. *Unomasuno* (Mexico City), 25 July 1994.

40. See Ernesto Samper, "Apuntes de viaje," *Semana*, 3 March 1987. I interviewed Samper in Bogotá in April 2007.

41. "GGM: "L'amour est ma seule idéologie," *Paris Match*, 14 July 1994.

42. "Querido Presidente, cuídese los sentidos," *El Tiempo*, 8 August 1994.

43. "Una charla informal," *Semana*, 6 September 1994.

44. *La Jornada* (Mexico City), 14 September 1994.

45. Fiorillo, *La Cueva*, p. 85.

46. "GGM: "L'amour est ma seule idéologie," *Paris Match*, 14 July 1994.

47. Susana Cato, "Gabo cambia de oficio," *Cambio 16*, 6–13 May 1996.

48. See "Por qué Gabo no vuelve al país," *Cambio 16*, 24 February 1997.

49. Norberto Fuentes, "De La Habana traigo un mensaje," 13 March 1996. Fuentes's *Dulces guerrilleros cubanos* would appear in 1999 and GGM would get a grim starring role in it.

50. Pilar Lozano, "Gabo da una lección a los 'milicos,'" *El País*, 16 April 1996.

51. Enrique Santos Calderón, "Noticia," *El Tiempo*, 5 May 1996. Santos Calderón notes that *Newsweek* has recently said that GGM is fixated on Pablo Escobar because he represents power, which is GGM's true obsession, not politics. See Virginia Vallejo, *Amando a Pablo, odiando a Escobar* (Mexico City, Random House Mondadon, 2007), for a remarkable X-ray of Colombian politics and society in the era of Escobar.

52. Roberto Posada García-Peña (D'Artagnan), "Las Cozas del Gavo," *El Tiempo*, 22 May 1998.

53. GGM, *News of a Kidnapping*, pp. 129–30. The FARC, in particular, would give credence to this statement with their practice of kidnapping for ransom over the following years. In 2008 they suffered a series of devastating blows, including the death of their leader, "Sureshot" Manuel Marulanda, the death through bombing of the second-in-command, Raúl Reyes, and the liberation of Ingrid Betancourt by the Colombian armed forces.

54. See, for example, Joseph A. Page, "Unmagical realism," *Commonweal*, 16, 26

September 1997; and Charles Lane, "The writer in his labyrinth," *New Republic*, no. 217, 25 August 1997. See also Malcolm Deas, "Moths of Ill Omen," *London Review of Books*, 30 October 1997.

24 / García Márquez at Seventy and Beyond: Memoirs and Melancholy Whores (1996–2005)

1. Darío Arizmendi, "Gabo revela sus secretos de escritor," *Cromos*, 13 June 1994.
2. "La nostalgia es la materia prima de mi escritura," *El País*, 5 May 1996.
3. Rosa Mora, "He escrito mi libro más duro, y el más triste," *El País*, 20 May 1996.
4. Ricardo Santamaría, "Cumpleaños con Fidel," *Semana*, 27 August 1996.
5. Rodolfo Braceli, "El genio en su laberinto," *Gente* (Buenos Aires), 15 January 1997.
6. Jean-François Fogel, "The revision thing," *Le Monde*, 27 January 1995.
7. *El País*, 9 October 1996.
8. Pilar Lozano, "Autoexilio de Gabo," *El País*, 3 March 1997.
9. "Clinton y GM en el Ala Oeste," *El Espectador*, 12 September 1997.
10. *El Tiempo*, 7 June 1998.
11. "Pastrana desnarcotiza la paz. Con apoyo del BID se constituye Fondo de Inversión para la Paz (FIP)," *El Espectador*, 23 October 1998.
12. "Salsa Soirée: fete for Colombian president a strange brew," *Washington Post*, 29 October 1998.
13. GGM and his colleagues withdrew their bid, convinced that Samper would turn it down. In an interview with me in April 2007 Samper denied that the decision had been taken but said flatly that "no government anywhere in the democratic world is obliged to favour its adversaries."
14. Larry Rohter, "GGM embraces old love (that's news!)," *New York Times*, 3 March 1999.
15. GGM, "El enigma de los dos Chávez," *Cambio*, February 1999.
16. "Castro augura el fin del capitalismo en el mundo," *El País*, 3 January 1999.
17. Rosa Mora, "GGM seduce al público con la lectura de un cuento inédito," *El País*, 19 March 1999.
18. I was in England and García Márquez called me from Bogotá on 28 June after the diagnosis. He knew that I had had lymphoma in 1995. He said, "I have never in my life been as exhausted as I was when this started. There was not a scrap of energy left in me." We talked about the course of the illness and what one could do to fight as effectively as possible; how to eat, how to think, how to live. "Well," he said, "now you and I are colleagues." I sensed that he was very shocked but determined to fight. But I was also aware that he was seventy-two years of age.
19. Jon Lee Anderson, "The Power of García Márquez," *The New Yorker*, 27 September 1999.
20. *El Tiempo*, 23 September 1999.
21. See this piece of clairvoyance in *The Autumn of the Patriarch* (1975), p. 181: "he stood up to the arguments of the sterile ministers who shouted 'bring back the marines, general, bring them back with their machines for fumigating plague-ridden people in exchange for whatever they want.' "
22. *Semana*, 14 November 2000.
23. Juan Cruz, "El marido de Mercedes," *El País*, 2 December 2000.

24. Guillermo Angulo, interview, Bogotá, April 2007.

25. 27 February 2001. The letter was circulated in newspapers around the world.

26. Freud was late for his father's burial and had a guilty dream about it; he then failed to attend his mother's funeral under the excuse of ill health.

27. See Richard Ellman on Joyce: "The life of an artist, but particularly that of Joyce, differs from other lives of other persons in that its events are becoming artistic sources even as they command his present attention" (*James Joyce*, new and revised edition [New York, Oxford University Press, 1983], p. 3).

28. Matilde Sánchez, "GGM presentó en México sus memorias: 'Es el gran libro de ficción que busqué durante toda la vida,'" *Clarín* (Buenos Aires), 24 March 1998.

29. *Excelsior*, 12 November 1981: "GM ends up talking about his memoirs, which he hopes to write quite soon and which will really be 'False Memoirs' because they won't recount his life as it was, nor as it might have been, but what he himself believes it to have been."

30. Caleb Bach, "Closeups of GGM," *Américas*, May–June 2003.

31. *El País*, 19 July 2003.

32. *Semana*, November 2003.

33. Later, *Love in the Time of Cholera* would also be adopted by the Oprah Winfrey show.

34. See GGM, "El avión de la bella durmiente," *El Espectador*, 19 August 1982, which was later adapted as a story for *Strange Pilgrims*.

35. Isaacs's *María* is a partial exception.

36. María Jimena Duzán, interview, Bogotá, 1991.

37. GGM, *Memories of My Melancholy Whores* (New York, Alfred A. Knopf, 2005), p. 74.

38. *Ibid.*, p. 45.

39. John Updike, "Dying for love: a new novel by García Márquez," *The New Yorker*, 7 November 2005.

40. When I got home, reflecting on this conversation, I opened *The General in His Labyrinth*, to see if its last lines were, as I remembered, another hymn to the radiance of existence. In them the dying Bolívar is dazzled by "the final brilliance of life that would never, through all eternity, be repeated again." Cf. GGM, "Un payaso pintado detrás de una puerta," *El Espectador*, 1 May 1982, in which GGM recalls the emotions of his own radiant youth as dawn approached each morning in Cartagena.

Epilogue: Immortality—The New Cervantes (2006–2007)

1. Xavi Ayén, "Rebeldía de Nobel. GM: 'He dejado de escribir,'" *La Vanguardia* (Barcelona), 29 January 2006.

2. Jaime GM, conversation, Cartagena, March 2007.

3. *La Jornada*, 8 April 1997, prints GGM's text, "Botella al mar para el dios de las palabras."

4. Ilan Stavans, "GM's 'Total' novel," *Chronicle of Higher Education*, 15 June 2007. Two years before Stavans's text, Christopher Domínguez, in Mexico's *Letras Libres* (December 2004), repeated an earlier statement that García Márquez was Latin America's "Homer." Similarly, Roberto González Echevarría, in a notable piece in *Primera Revista Latinoamericana de Libros* (New York), December 2007–January 2008, remarked that *OHYS* was immediately recognizable as "something perfect . . . a classic," a book which had marked both his life and his career. All three are rigorous, sceptical critics

not temperamentally inclined to write blank critical cheques nor indeed to give fulsome praise to left-of-centre writers.

5. Arango, *Un ramo de nomeolvides*, p. 91.

6. See GGM, "Un domingo de delirio," *El Espectador*, 10 March 1981, where he satirizes the idea of building a convention centre in Cartagena. Ironies abound.

7. GGM, *Cien años de soledad*. Edición conmemorativa (Madrid, Real Academia Española/Asociación de Academias de la Lengua Española, 2007; published in Colombia by Norma).

8. In this version he stated that he and Mercedes had mailed the second half first by mistake and that Paco Porrúa, the publisher, anxious to read the first half, had sent them the money they needed by return of post. Through its homage the academy had bound him definitively to the novel he had tried so hard to escape from, and his speech was not only a thank you to his wife but a kind of reconciliation with the book that had transformed both their lives forty years before.

Bibliography

WORKS BY GABRIEL GARCÍA MÁRQUEZ IN SPANISH

Journalism, Interviews, Memoirs, etc.:

Obra periodística vol. I: Textos costeños 1 [1948–50], ed. Jacques Gilard (Bogotá, Oveja Negra, 1983).

Obra periodística vol. II: Textos costeños 2 [1950–53], ed. Jacques Gilard (Bogotá, Oveja Negra, 1983).

Obra periodística vol. III: Entre cachacos 1 [1953–5], ed. Jacques Gilard (Bogotá, Oveja Negra, 1983).

Obra periodística vol. IV: Entre cachacos 2 [1955], ed. Jacques Gilard (Bogotá, Oveja Negra, 1983).

Obra periodística vol. V: De Europa y América 1 [1955–6], ed. Jacques Gilard (Bogotá, Oveja Negra, 1984).

Obra periodística vol. VI: De Europa y América 2 [1957], ed. Jacques Gilard (Bogotá, Oveja Negra, 1984).

Por la libre: Obra periodística 4 [1974–95] (Barcelona, Mondadori, 1999).

Periodismo militante (pirated political journalism; Bogotá, Son de Máquina, 1978).

Notas de Prensa 1980–84 (Madrid, Mondadori, 1991).

El secuestro (documentary film script, 1982, aka *Viva Sandino, El asalto*; Bogotá, Oveja Negra, 1984).

Relato de un náufrago (documentary narrative, 1970; Barcelona, Tusquets, 29th edition, 1991).

La novela en América Latina: diálogo (with Mario Vargas Llosa) (Lima, Milla Batres, 1968).

El olor de la guayaba. Conversaciones con Plinio Apuleyo Mendoza (Bogotá, Oveja Negra, 1982).

"La soledad de América Latina"/"Brindis por la poesía" (speeches at Nobel Prize ceremonies, Stockholm, December 1982).

"El cataclismo de Dámocles" (Conferencia Ixtapa, 1986) (speech on the dangers of nuclear proliferation, Bogotá, Oveja Negra, 1986).

La aventura de Miguel Littín clandestino en Chile (documentary narrative, 1986; Bogotá, Oveja Negra, 1986).

"Un manual para ser niño" (essay on children's educational needs; *El Tiempo*, Bogotá, 9 October 1995).

Noticia de un secuestro (documentary narrative; Bogotá, Norma, 1996).

Taller de guión de Gabriel García Márquez. "*Cómo se cuenta un cuento*" (scriptwriting workshop, EICTV Cuba/Ollero & Ramos, Madrid, 1995).

Taller de guión de Gabriel García Márquez. *"Me aquilo para soñar"* (scriptwriting workshop, EICTV Cuba/Ollero & Ramos, Madrid, 1997).

Taller de guión de Gabriel García Márquez. *"La bendita manía de contar"* (scriptwriting workshop, EICTV Cuba/Ollero & Ramos, Madrid, 1998).

Vivir para contarla (memoir; Bogotá, Norma, 2001).

Literary Works (date of first publication followed by edition used):

La hojarasca (1955; Madrid, Alfaguara, 2nd edition, 1981).

El coronel no tiene quien le escriba (1961; Buenos Aires, Sudamericana, 1968).

La mala hora (1962; Madrid, Alfaguara, 2nd edition, 1981).

Los funerales de la Mamá Grande (1962; Barcelona, Plaza y Janés, 1975).

Cien años de soledad (1967; Buenos Aires, Sudaméricana, 18th edition, 1970).

La increíble y triste historia de la cándida Eréndira y de su abuela desalmada (1972; Madrid, Mondadori, 4th edition, 1990).

El otoño del patriarca (1975; Barcelona, Plaza y Janés, 1975).

Todos los cuentos (1947–1972) (1975; Barcelona, Plaza y Janés, 3rd edition, 1976).

Crónica de una muerte anunciada (1981; Bogotá, Oveja Negra, 1981).

El amor en los tiempos del cólera (1985; Barcelona, Bruguera, 1985).

Diatriba de amor contra un hombre sentado (1988; Bogotá, Arango, 1994).

El general en su laberinto (1989; Bogotá, Oveja Negra, 1989).

Doce cuentos peregrinos (1992; Bogotá, Oveja Negra, 1992).

Del amor y otros demonios (1994; Bogotá, Norma, 1994).

Memoria de mis putas tristes (2004; New York, Alfred A. Knopf, 2004).

Works by Gabriel García Márquez in English

The Autumn of the Patriarch, trans. Gregory Rabassa (London, Picador, 1978).

Chronicle of a Death Foretold, trans. Gregory Rabassa (London, Picador, 1983).

Clandestine in Chile, trans. Asa Zatz (Cambridge, Granta, 1989).

Collected Stories, trans. Gregory Rabassa and J. S. Bernstein (New York, Harper Perennial, 1991).

The Fragrance of Guava: Conversations with Gabriel García Márquez, ed. Plinio Apuleyo Mendoza, trans. Ann Wright (London, Faber, 1988).

The General in His Labyrinth, trans. Edith Grossman (London, Jonathan Cape, 1991).

In Evil Hour, trans. Gregory Rabassa (New York, Harper Perennial, 1991).

Leaf Storm, trans. Gregory Rabassa (London, Picador, 1979).

Living to Tell the Tale, trans. Edith Grossman (London, Jonathan Cape, 2003).

Love in the Time of Cholera, trans. Edith Grossman (London, Jonathan Cape, 1988).

Memories of My Melancholy Whores, trans. Edith Grossman (New York, Alfred A. Knopf, 2005).

News of a Kidnapping, trans. Edith Grossman (London, Jonathan Cape, 1997).

No One Writes to the Colonel, trans. J. S. Bernstein (includes *Big Mama's Funeral*; Harmondsworth, Penguin, 1974).

Of Love and Other Demons, trans. Edith Grossman (Harmondsworth, Penguin, 1996).

One Hundred Years of Solitude, trans. Gregory Rabassa (London, Picador, 1978).

The Story of a Shipwrecked Sailor, trans. Randolph Hogan (New York, Vintage, 1989).

Strange Pilgrims, trans. Edith Grossman (Harmondsworth, Penguin, 1994).

"The future of Colombia," *Granta* 31 (spring 1990), pp. 87–95.

"Plying the Word" (portrait of Fidel Castro), *North American Congress on Latin America* 24:2 (August 1990), pp. 40–46.

"Watching the Rain in Galicia," *The Best of Granta Travel* (London, Granta/Penguin, 1991), pp. 1–5.

WORKS ON GABRIEL GARCÍA MÁRQUEZ

Bibliographical Works:

Cobo Borda, Juan Gustavo, *Gabriel García Márquez: crítica y bibliografía* (Madrid, Embajada de Colombia en España, 1994).

Fau, Margaret E., *Gabriel García Márquez. An Annotated Bibliography*, vol. 1 1947–1979, and vol. 2 1979–85 (Westport, Conn., Greenwood Press, 1980).

Klein, Don, *Gabriel García Márquez: una bibliografía descriptiva*, 2 vols. (Bogotá, Norma, 2003).

Sfeir de González, Nelly, *Bibliographic Guide to Gabriel García Márquez, 1986–1992* (Westport, Conn., Greenwood Press, 1994).

Biographical Works:

Alvarez Jaraba, Isidro, *El país de las aguas: revelaciones y voces de La Mojana en la vida y obra de Gabo* (Sincelejo, Multigráficas, 2007).

Anderson, Jon Lee, "The Power of García Márquez," *The New Yorker*, 27 September 1999, pp. 56–71.

Arango, Gustavo, *Un ramo de nomeolvides: García Márquez en "El Universal"* (Cartagena, El Universal, 1995).

Aylett, Holly, *Tales Beyond Solitude. Profile of a Writer: Gabriel García Márquez* (film documentary, London, ITV, *South Bank Show*, 1989).

Bell-Villada, Gene, *García Márquez: The Man and His Work* (Chapel Hill, University of North Carolina Press, 1990).

Billon, Yves, *García Márquez: A Witch Writing* (film documentary, Zarafa Films, France 3, 1998).

Books Abroad, 47:3 (Summer 1973) (on GGM's Neustadt Prize).

Bottía, Pacho, *Buscando a Gabo* (film documentary, Colombia, 2007).

Bravo Mendoza, Víctor, *La Guajira en la obra de Gabriel García Márquez* (Riohacha, Gobernación de la Guajira, 2007).

Cebrián, Juan Luis, *Retrato de Gabriel García Márquez* (Barcelona, Círculo de Lectores, 1989).

Collazos, Oscar, *García Márquez: la soledad y la gloria* (Barcelona, Plaza y Janés, 1983).

Conde Ortega, José Francisco, Mata, Oscar and Trejo Villafuerte, Arturo, eds, *Gabriel García Márquez: celebración. 25° aniversario de "Cien años de soledad"* (México City, Universidad Autónoma Metropolitana, 1991).

Darío Jiménez, Rafael, *La nostalgia del coronel* (Aracataca, 2006, unpubd).

Esteban, Angel and Panichelli, Stéphanie, *Gabo y Fidel: el paisaje de una amistad* (Bogotá, Espasa, 2004).

Facio, Sara and D'Amico, Alicia, *Retratos y autorretratos* (Buenos Aires, Crisis, 1973).

Fernández-Braso, Miguel, *Gabriel García Márquez. (Una conversación infinita)* (Madrid, Azur, 1969).

———. *La soledad de Gabriel García Márquez* (Barcelona, Planeta, 1972).

Fiorillo, Heriberto, *La Cueva: crónica del grupo de Barranquilla* (Bogotá, Planeta, 2002).

Fiorillo, Heriberto, ed., *La Cueva: Catálogo Reinaugural, 50 años 1954–2004* (Barranquilla, La Cueva, 2004).

Fuenmayor, Alfonso, *Crónicas sobre el grupo de Barranquilla* (Bogotá, Instituto Colombiano de Cultura, 1978).

Galvis, Silvia, *Los García Márquez* (Bogotá, Arango, 1996).

García, Eligio, *Son así: reportaje a nueve escritores latinoamericanos* (Bogotá, Oveja Negra, 1983).

———. *La tercera muerte de Santiago Nasar. Crónica de La crónica* (Madrid, Mondadori, 1987).

———. *Tras las claves de Melquíades: historia de "Cien años de soledad"* (Bogotá, Norma, 2001).

García Usta, Jorge, *Como aprendió a escribir García Márquez* (Medellín, Lealon, 1995).

———. *García Márquez en Cartagena: sus inicios literarios* (Bogotá, Planeta, 2007).

Gilard, Jacques, "García Márquez: un project d'école de cinéma (1960)," *Cinéma d'Amérique Latine* 3 (1995), pp. 24–45.

Guibert, Rita, *Seven Voices* (New York, Vintage, 1973).

Harss, Luis, *Los nuestros* (Buenos Aires, Sudamericana, 1968). English: L. H. and Barbara Dohmann, *Into the Mainstream: Conversations with Latin-American Writers* (New York, Harper & Row, 1967).

Henríquez Torres, Guillermo, *García Márquez, el piano de cola y otras historias* (2003, unpubd).

———. *El misterio de los Buendía: el verdadero trasfondo histórico de "Cien años de soledad"* (Bogotá, Nueva América, 2003; 2nd revised edition, 2006).

Leante, César, *Gabriel García Márquez, el hechicero* (Madrid, Pliegos, 1996).

Mendoza, Plinio Apuleyo, *La llama y el hielo* (Bogotá, Gamma, 3rd edition, 1989)

———. *Aquellos tiempos con Gabo* (Barcelona, Plaza y Janés, 2000).

Mera, Aura Lucía, ed., *Aracataca/Estocolmo* (Bogotá, Instituto Colombiano de Cultura, 1983).

Minta, Stephen, *Gabriel García Márquez: Writer of Colombia* (London, Jonathan Cape, 1987).

Moreno Durán, Rafael Humberto, *Como el halcón peregrino* (Bogotá, Santillana, 1995).

Muñoz, Elías Miguel, "Into the writer's labyrinth: storytelling days with Gabo," *Michigan Quarterly Review* 34:2 (spring 1995), pp. 171–93.

Núñez Jiménez, Antonio, "García Márquez y la perla de las Antillas (O 'Qué conversan Gabo y Fidel')" (Havana, 1984, unpubd).

Plimpton, George, *Writers at Work: The "Paris Review" Interviews. Sixth Series* (New York, Viking Press, 1984).

Rentería Mantilla, Alfonso, ed., *García Márquez habla de García Márquez en 33 grandes reportajes* (Bogotá, Rentería Editores, 1979).

Saldívar, Dasso, *García Márquez: el viaje a la semilla. La biografía* (Madrid, Santillana, 1997).

Sorela, Pedro, *El otro García Márquez: los años difíciles* (Madrid, Mondadori, 1988).

Stavans, Ilan, "Gabo in decline," *Transition* 62 (October, 1994), pp. 58–78.

Timossi, Jorge, *De buena fuente: reportajes alrededor del mundo* (Caracas, C & C, 1988).

Valenzuela, Lídice, *Realidad y nostalgia de García Márquez* (La Habana, Editorial Pablo la Torriente, 1989).

Vargas Llosa, Mario, *García Márquez: historia de un deicidio* (Barcelona, Barral, 1971).

Wallrafen, Hannes, *The World of Márquez* (intro. by GGM, London, Ryan, 1991).

Woolford, Ben and Weldon, Dan, *Macondo mío* (film documentary, London, 1990).

Writers and Places, "Growing Up in Macondo," transcript (BBC2, 11 February 1981).

Literary-Critical Works:

Barth, John, "The Literature of Exhaustion," *Atlantic Monthly*, 220:2, August 1967, pp. 29–34; "The Literature of Replenishment," *Atlantic Monthly*, 245, January 1980, pp. 65–71.

Bell, Michael, *Gabriel García Márquez: Solitude and Solidarity* (New York, St.Martin's Press, 1993).

Bell-Villada, Gene, *Gabriel García Márquez's "One Hundred Years of Solitude": A Casebook* (Oxford, Oxford University Press, 2002).

Benitez-Rojo, Antonio: *The Repeating Island: The Caribbean and the Postmodern Perspective* (Durham, N.C., Duke University Press, 1996), esp. "Private Reflections on García Márquez's *Eréndira*," pp. 276–93.

Benson, John, "Gabriel García Márquez en *Alternativa* 1974–79. Una bibliografía comentada," *Chasqui*, 8:3 (May 1979), pp. 69–81.

———. "Notas sobre *Notas de prensa* 1980–1984," *Revista de Estudios Colombianos* 18 (1998), pp. 27–37.

Bhalla, Alok, *García Márquez and Latin America* (New York, Envoy Press, 1987).

Bloom, Harold, ed., *Gabriel García Márquez* (New York, Chelsea House, 1989).

Bodtorf Clark, Gloria J., *A Synergy of Styles: Art and Artifacts in Gabriel García Márquez* (Lanham, Md./New York/Oxford, University Press of America, 1999).

Cobo Borda, Juan Gustavo, "Vueltas en redondo en torno a GGM," *Letras de esta América* (Bogotá, Universidad Nacional de Colombia, 1986), pp. 249–99.

———. *Silva, Arciniegas, Mutis y García Márquez* (Bogotá, Presidencia de la República, 1997).

———. *Para llegar a García Márquez* (Bogotá, Temas de Hoy, 1997).

———. *Lecturas convergentes* [GGM and Alvaro Mutis] (Bogotá, Taurus, 2006).

Cobo Borda, Juan Gustavo, ed., "*Para que mis amigos me quieran más . . .*": homenaje a *Gabriel García Márquez* (Bogotá, Siglo del Hombre, 1992).

———. *Repertorio crítico sobre Gabriel García Márquez*, vols 1 and 2 (Bogotá, Instituto Caro y Cuervo, 1995).

———. *El arte de leer a García Márquez* (Bogotá, Norma, 2007).

Deas, Malcolm, *Del poder y la gramática y otros ensayos sobre historia, política y literatura colombianas* (Bogotá, Tercer Mundo, 1993).

Debray, Régis, "Cinco maneras de abordar lo inabordable; o algunas consideraciones a propósito de *El otoño del patriarca*," *Nueva Política* 1 (January–March 1976), pp. 253–60.

Detjens, W. E., *Home as Creation. (The Influence of Early Childhood Experience in the Literary Creation of Gabriel García Márquez, Agustín Yáñez and Juan Rulfo)* (New York, Peter Lang, 1993).

Díaz Arenas, Angel, *La aventura de una lectura en "El otoño del patriarca" de Gabriel García Márquez, I Textos intertextualizados, II Música intertextualizada* (Kassel, Reichenberger, 1991).

Dolan, Sean, *Gabriel García Márquez* (Hispanics of Achievement) (New York, Chelsea House, 1994).

Donoso, José, *Historia personal del "Boom"* (Barcelona, Seix Barral, 1983). Appendix by María Pilar Serrano. English: Donoso, José, *The Boom in Spanish American Literature: A Personal History* (New York, Columbia University Press/Center for Inter-American Relations, 1977).

Fiddian, Robin, ed., *García Márquez* (London, Longman, 1995).

Fuentes, Carlos, *Myself with Others* (London, Deutsch, 1988).

———. *Valiente mundo nuevo: épica, utopía y mito en la novela hispanoamericana* (Mexico City, Fondo de Cultura Económica, 1990).

———. *Geografía de la novela* (Mexico City, Fondo de Cultura Económica, 1993).

García Aguilar, Eduardo, *García Márquez: la tentación cinematográfica* (Mexico City, UNAM, 1985).

Gilard, Jacques, *Veinte y cuarenta años de algo peor que la soledad* (Paris, Centre Culturel Colombien, 1988).

Giraldo, Luz Mary, *Más allá de Macondo: tradición y rupturas literarias* (Bogotá, Universidad Externado de Colombia, 2006).

González Bermejo, Ernesto, *Cosas de escritores: Gabriel García Márquez, Mario Vargas Llosa, Julio Cortázar* (Biblioteca de Marcha, n.p., n.d.).

Janes, Regina, *Gabriel García Márquez. Revolutions in Wonderland* (Columbia, University of Missouri Press, 1981).

Joset, Jacques, *Gabriel García Márquez, coetáneo de la eternidad* (Amsterdam, Rodopi, 1984).

Kennedy, William, *Riding the Yellow Trolley Car* (New York, Viking, 1993).

Kline, Carmenza, *Fiction and Reality in the Works of Gabriel García Márquez* (Salamanca, Ediciones Universidad de Salamanca, 2002).

———. *Violencia en Macondo: tema recurrente en la obra de Gabriel García Márquez* (Bogotá, Fundación General de la Universidad de Colombia, Sede Colombia, 2001).

Latin American Literary Review 25, Special Issue: "Gabriel García Márquez" (Pittsburgh, January–June 1985).

Levine, Suzanne Jill, *El espejo hablado. Un estudio de "Cien años de soledad"* (Caracas, Monte Avila, 1975).

Ludmer, Josefina, *"Cien años de soledad": una interpretación* (Buenos Aires, Trabajo Crítico, 1971).

Martínez, Pedro Simón, ed., *Recopilación de textos sobre Gabriel García Márquez* (Havana, Casa de las Américas, 1969).

McGuirk, Bernard, and Cardwell, Richard, *Gabriel García Márquez: New Readings* (Cambridge, Cambridge University Press, 1987).

McMurray, George R., *Gabriel García Márquez: Life, Work and Criticism* (Fredericton, Canada, York Press, 1987).

Mejía Duque, Jaime, *"El otoño del patriarca" o la crisis de la desmesura* (Bogotá, Oveja Negra, 1975).

Mellen, Joan, *Literary Masters, Volume 5: Gabriel García Márquez* (Farmington Hills, Mich., The Gale Group, 2000).

Moretti, Franco, *Modern Epic: The World System from Goethe to García Márquez* (London, Verso, 1996).

Oberhelman, Harley D., *The Presence of Faulkner in the Writings of García Márquez* (Lubbock, Texas Tech University, 1980).

———. *Gabriel García Márquez. A Study of the Short Fiction* (Boston, Twayne, 1991).

———. *The Presence of Hemingway in the Short Fiction of Gabriel García Márquez* (Fredericton, Canada, York Press, 1994).

———. *García Márquez and Cuba: A Study of Its Presence in His Fiction, Journalism, and Cinema* (Fredericton, Canada, York Press, 1995).

Ortega, Julio, ed., *Gabriel García Márquez and the Powers of Fiction* (Austin, University of Texas Press, 1988).

Oyarzún, Kemy and Magenny, William W., eds, *Essays on Gabriel García Márquez* (University of California, Riverside, 1984).

Penuel, Arnold M., *Intertextuality in García Márquez* (York, S.C., Spanish Literary Publications Company, 1994).

Rama, Angel, *Los dictadores latinoamericanos* (Mexico City, Fondo de Cultura Económica, 1976).

———. *García Márquez: edificación de un arte nacional y popular* (Montevideo, Universidad Nacional, Facultad de Humanidades, 1987).

Reid, Alastair, *Whereabouts. Notes on Being a Foreigner* (San Francisco, North Point Press, 1987). [See esp. "Basilisk's Eggs," pp. 94–118.]

Review 70 (Center for Inter-American Relations, New York), "Supplement on Gabriel García Márquez." [Reviews of translations of *OHYS*; 1971.]

Revista Iberoamericana 118–119, "Literatura colombiana de los últimos 60 años"/ "Homenaje a GGM" (Pittsburgh, July–December 1984).

Rincón, Carlos, *La no simultaneidad de lo simultáneo* (Bogotá, Editorial Universidad Nacional, 1995).

———. *Mapas y pliegues: ensayos de cartografía cultural y de lectura del Neobarroco* (Bogotá, Colcultura, 1996).

Rodman, Selden, *South America of the Poets* (New York, Hawthorn Books, 1970).

Rodríguez Monegal, Emir, *El Boom de la novela latinoamericana* (Caracas, Tiempo Nuevo, 1972).

Rodríguez Vergara, Isabel, *Haunting Demons: Critical Essays on the Works of Gabriel García Márquez* (Washington, OAS, 1998).

Ruffinelli, Jorge, ed., *La viuda de Montiel* (Xalapa, Veracruz, 1979).

Shaw, Bradley A. and Vera-Godwin, N., eds., *Critical Perspectives on Gabriel García Márquez* (Lincoln, Neb., Society of Spanish and Spanish American Studies, 1986).

Sims, Robert L., *El primer García Márquez. Un estudio de su periodismo 1948 a 1955* (Potomac, Maryland, Scripta Humanistica, 1991).

Solanet, Mariana, *García Márquez for Beginners* (London, Writers and Readers, 2001).

Stavans, Ilan, "The Master of Aracataca," *Michigan Quarterly Review* 34:2 (spring 1995), pp. 149–71.

Tobin, Patricia, "García Márquez and the Genealogical Imperative," *Diacritics* (summer 1974), pp. 51–5.

Von der Walde, Erna, "El macondismo como latinoamericanismo," *Cuadernos Americanos* 12:1 (January–February 1998), pp. 223–37.

Williams, Raymond, *Gabriel García Márquez* (Boston, Twayne, 1984).

Wood, Michael, *García Márquez: "One Hundred Years of Solitude"* (Cambridge, Cambridge University Press, 1990).

Zuluaga Osorio, Conrado, *Puerta abierta a García Márquez y otras puertas* (Bogotá, La Editora, 1982).

———. *Gabriel García Márquez: el vicio incurable de contar* (Bogotá, Panamericana, 2005).

OTHER WORKS

Agee, Philip, *Inside the Company: CIA Diary* (Harmondsworth, Penguin, 1975).

Alape, Arturo, *El Bogotazo: memorias del olvido* (Bogotá, Universidad Central, 1983).

Ali, Tariq, *Pirates of the Caribbean: Axis of Hope (Evo Morales, Fidel Castro, Hugo Chávez)* (London, Verso, 2006).

Arango, Carlos, *Sobrevivientes de las bananeras* (Bogotá, ECOE, 2nd edition, 1985).

Araujonoguera, Consuelo, *Rafael Escalona: el hombre y el mito* (Bogotá, Planeta, 1988).

Bagley, Bruce Michael and Tokatlian, Juan Gabriel, *Contadora: The Limits of Negotiation* (Washington, Johns Hopkins Foreign Policy Institute, 1987).

Balzac, Honoré de, *The Quest of the Absolute* (London, Dent, Everyman, n.d.).

Birri, Fernando, *Por un nuevo nuevo cine latinoamericano 1956–1991* (Madrid, Cátedra, 1996).

Braudy, Leo, *The Frenzy of Renown: Fame and its History* (New York, Vintage, 1986).

Braun, Herbert, *The Assassination of Gaitán: Public Life and Urban Violence in Colombia* (Madison, University of Wisconsin Press, 1985).

Broderick, Walter J., *Camilo Torres: A Biography of the Priest-Guerrillero* (New York, Doubleday, 1975).

Bushnell, David, *The Making of Modern Colombia. A Nation In Spite of Itself* (Berkeley and Los Angeles, University of California Press, 1993).

———. *Simón Bolívar: Liberation and Disappointment* (New York, Longman, 2004).

———. "What is the problem with Santander?," *Revista de Estudios Colombianos* 29 (2006), pp. 12–18.

Cabrera Infante, Guillermo, *Mea Cuba* (London, Faber & Faber, 1994).

Carter, Jimmy, *Keeping Faith: Memoirs of a President* (New York, Bantam, 1981).

Casal, Lourdes, ed., *El caso Padilla: literatura y revolución en Cuba. Documentos* (Miami, Universal and New York, Nueva Atlántida, 1972).

Castañeda, Jorge G., *Utopia Unarmed: The Latin American Left After the Cold War* (New York, Vintage, 1994).

Castrillón R., Alberto, *120 días bajo el terror militar* (Bogotá, Tupac Amaru, 1974).

Cepeda Samudio, Alvaro, *La casa grande* (English version: Austin, University of Texas Press, 1991).

Clinton, Bill, *Giving: How Each of Us Can Change the World* (London, Hutchinson, 2007).

Conrad, Joseph, *Nostromo*, ed., Ruth Nadelhaft (Peterborough, Canada, Broadview Press, 1997).

Cortés Vargas, Carlos, *Los sucesos de las bananeras*, ed. R. Herrera Soto (Bogotá, Editorial Desarrollo, 2nd edition, 1979).

Dante Alighieri, *Vita Nuova* (Oxford, Oxford University Press, 1991).

Darío, Rubén, *Autobiografía* (San Salvador, Ministerio de Educación, n.d.).

Debray, Régis, *Les Masques* (Paris, Gallimard, 1987).

———. *Praised Be Our Lords: The Autobiography* (London, Verso, 2007).

Diago Julio, Lázaro, *Aracataca . . . una historia para contar* (Aracataca, 1989, unpubd).

Díaz-Granados, José Luis, *Los años extraviados* (Bogotá, Planeta, 2006).

Donoso, José, *The Garden Next Door* (New York, Grove Press, 1991).

Duzán, María Jimena, *Death Beat* (New York, Harper Collins, 1994).

Edwards, Jorge, *Persona Non Grata: A Memoir of Disenchantment with the Cuban Revolution* (New York, Paragon House, 1993).

Ellner, Steve, *Venezuela's "Movimiento al Socialismo": From Guerrilla Defeat to Innovative Politics* (Durham, N.C., and London, Duke University Press, 1988).

Feinstein, Adam, *Pablo Neruda: A Passion for Life* (London, Bloomsbury, 2004).

Fluharty, Vernon L., *Dance of the Millions: Military Rule and the Social Revolution in Colombia, 1930–1956* (Pittsburgh, University of Pittsburgh Press, 1957).

Fonnegra, Gabriel, *Bananeras: testimonio vivo de una epopeya* (Bogotá, Tercer Mundo, n.d.).

Fuentes, Norberto, *Dulces guerreros cubanos* (Barcelona, Seix Barral, 1999).

Fundación del Nuevo Periodismo Iberoamericano, *La ética periodística; El reportaje; Ediciones dominicales* (Manizales, La Patria, 1999).

Gerassi, John, *Revolutionary Priest. The Complete Writings and Messages of Camilo Torres* (London, Jonathan Cape, 1971).

Giesbert, François, *Dying Without God: François Mitterrand's Meditations on Living and Dying*, intro. William Styron (New York, Arcade, 1996).

Gilard, Jacques, *Entre los Andes y el Caribe: la obra americana de Ramón Vinyes* (Medellín, Universidad de Antioquia, 1989).

Giraldo, Luz Mary, ed., *Cuentos y relatos de la literatura colombiana*, 2 vols. (Bogotá, Fondo de Cultura Económica, 2005).

Gleijeses, Piero, *Conflicting Missions: Havana, Washington and Africa, 1959–1976* (Chapel Hill, North Carolina University Press, 2002).

González, Felipe and Cebrián, Juan Luis, *El futuro no es lo que era: una conversación* (Madrid, Santillana, 2001).

González, Reinol, *Y Fidel creó el Punto X* (Miami, Saeta, 1987).

Gott, Richard, *In the Shadow of the Liberator: Hugo Chávez and the Transformation of Venezuela* (London, Verso, 2000).

———. *Cuba: A New History* (New Haven, Yale Nota Bene, 2005).

Goytisolo, Juan, *Realms of Strife: Memoirs 1957–1981* (London, Quartet, 1990).

Greene, Graham, *Getting to Know the General* (Harmondsworth, Penguin, 1984).

Guerra Curvelo, Weildler, *La disputa y la palabra: la ley en la sociedad wayuu* (Bogotá, Ministerio de Cultura, 2002).

———. *El poblamiento del territorio* (Bogotá, I/M Editores, 2007).

Guillermoprieto, Alma, *The Heart that Bleeds: Latin America Now* (New York, Vintage, 1994).

Gutiérrez Hinojosa, Tomás Darío, *Cultura vallenata: origen, teoría y pruebas* (Bogotá, Plaza y Janés, 1992).

Guzmán Campos, Germán, Fals Borda, Orlando and Umaña Luna, Eduardo, *La violencia en Colombia*, vols 1 and 2 (Bogotá, Tercer Mundo, 1961 and 1964).

Helg, Aline, *La educación en Colombia 1918–1957: una historia social, económica y política* (Bogotá, CEREC, 1987).

Herrera Soto, Roberto and Romero Castañeda, Rafael, *La zona bananera del Magdalena: historia y léxico* (Bogotá, Instituto Caro y Cuervo, 1979).

Hinckle, Warren and Turner, William, *The Fish Is Red: The Story of the Secret War Against Castro* (New York, Harper & Row, 1981).

Hudson, Rex A., *Castro's Americas Department* (Washington, D.C., Cuban American National Foundation, 1988).

Hylton, Forrest, *Evil Hour in Colombia* (London, Verso, 2006).

Illán Bacca, Ramón, *Escribir en Barranquilla* (Barranquilla, Uninorte, 2nd revised edition, 2005).

Independent Commission of Enquiry on the U.S. Invasion of Panama, *The U.S. Invasion of Panama: the Truth Behind Operation "Just Cause"* (Boston, South End Press, 1991).

Isherwood, Christopher, *The Condor and the Cows: A South American Travel-Diary* (London, Methuen, 1949).

Kagan, Robert, *A Twilight Struggle: American Power and Nicaragua 1977–1990* (New York, Free Press, 1996).

Kapuściński, Ryszard, *Los cinco sentidos del periodista (estar, ver, oír, compartir, pensar)* (Bogotá, Fundación para un Nuevo Periodismo Iberoamericano and Fondo de Cultura Económica, 2003).

Kawabata, Yasunari, *The House of the Sleeping Beauties and Other Stories* (New York, Ballantine, 1969). Spanish edition: *La casa de las bellas durmientes* (Barcelona, Luis de Caralt, 2001).

King, John, *Magical Reels: A History of Cinema in Latin America* (London, Verso, 2000).

Kissinger, Henry, *The White House Years* (New York, Little, Brown & Co., 1979).

La masacre en las bananeras: 1928 (Bogotá, Los Comuneros, n.d.).

Lara, Patricia, *Siembra vientos y recogerás tempestades: la historia de M-19* (Bogotá, Planeta, 6th edition, 1991).

Larbaud, Valery, *Fermina Márquez* (Paris, Gallimard, 1956).

LeGrand, Catherine C., *Frontier Expansion and Peasant Protest in Colombia, 1850–1936* (Albuquerque, NM, New Mexico University Press, 1986).

———. "Living in Macondo: Economy and Culture in a UFC Banana Enclave in Colombia," in Gilbert M. Joseph, Catherine C. LeGrand and Ricardo D. Salvatore, eds, *Close Encounters of Empire: Writing the Cultural History of U.S.–Latin American Relations* (Durham, N.C., Duke University Press, 1998), pp. 333–68.

Lemaitre, Eduardo, *Historia general de Cartagena, vol. II: la Colonia* (Bogotá, Banco de la República, 1983).

LeoGrande, William M., *Our Own Backyard: The United States in Central America, 1977–1991* (Chapel Hill, North Carolina University Press, 1998).

Libre, Revista de crítica literaria (1971–1972). Facsimile edition (nos. 1–4), with introduction by Plinio Apuleyo Mendoza (Mexico City and Madrid, El Equilibrista y Ediciones Turner, Quintocentenario).

Lladó, Jordi, *Ramón Vinyes: un home de lettres entre Catalunya i el Càrib* (Barcelona, Generalitat de Catalunya, 2006).

Llerena Villalobos, Rito, *Memoria cultural en el vallenato* (Medellín, Universidad de Antioquia, 1985).

López Michelsen, Alfonso, *Palabras pendientes: conversaciones con Enrique Santos Calderón* (Bogotá, El Ancora, 2001).

Luna Cárdenas, Alberto Luna, *Un año y otros días con el General Benjamín Herrera en las Bananeras de Aracataca* (Medellín, Bedout, 1915).

Lundkvist, Artur, *Journeys in Dream and Imagination*, prologue by Carlos Fuentes (New York, Four Walls Eight Windows, 1991).

Lynch, John, *Simón Bolívar: A Life* (New Haven, Yale University Press, 2006).

MacBride, Sean, *Many Voices, One World: Communication and Society, Today and Tomorrow. Towards a New, More Just and More Efficient World Information and Communication Order* (London, Unesco, 1981).

Martínez, José de Jesús, *Mi general Torrijos. (Testimonio)* (Bogotá, Oveja Negra, 1987).

Martínez, Tomás Eloy, ed., *Lo mejor del periodismo de América Latina: textos enviados al Premio Nuevo Periodismo CEMEX FNPI* (Mexico City, Fundación para un Nuevo Periodismo Iberoamericano and Fondo de Cultura Económica, 2006).

Maschler, Tom, *Publisher* (London, Picador, 2005).

Maya, Maureén and Petro, Gustavo, *Prohibido olvidar: dos miradas sobre la toma del Palacio de Justicia* (Bogotá, Casa Editorial Pisando Callos, 2006).

Mendoza, Plinio Apuleyo, *Gentes, lugares* (Bogotá, Planeta, 1986).

Miranda, Roger and Ratliff, William, *The Civil War in Nicaragua: Inside the Sandinistas* (New Brunswick and London, Transaction, 1993).

Mitterrand, François and Wiesel, Elie, *Memoir in Two Voices* (New York, Arcade, 1995).

Mundo Nuevo, Paris and Buenos Aires, 1966–1971.

Mutis, Alvaro, *Poesía y prosa* (Bogotá, Colcultura, 1981).

———. *The Adventures and Misadventures of Maqroll* (New York, New York Review Books, 2001).

Núñez Jiménez, Antonio, *En Marcha con Fidel* (Havana, Letras Cubanas, 1981).

Ortega, Julio, *Retrato de Carlos Fuentes* (Madrid, Círculo de Lectores, 1995).

Otero, Lisandro, *Llover sobre mojado: una reflexión sobre la historia* (Havana, Letras Cubanas, 1997; 2nd edition, Mexico City, Planeta, 1999).

Palacios, Marco, *Between Legitimacy and Violence: A History of Colombia, 1875–2002* (Durham, N.C., Duke University Press, 2006).

Pastrana, Andrés, *La palabra bajo fuego*, prologue by Bill Clinton, with Camilo Gómez (Bogotá, Planeta, 2005).

Paternostro, Silvana, *In the Land of God and Man: A Latin American Woman's Journey* (New York, Plume/Penguin, 1998).

Petras, James and Morley, Morris, *Latin America in the Time of Cholera: Electoral Politics, Market Economies and Permanent Crisis* (New York, Routledge, 1991).

Pinkus, Karen, *The Montesi Scandal: The Death of Wilma Montesi and the Birth of the Paparazzi in Fellini's Rome* (Chicago, Chicago University Press, 2003).

Poniatowska, Elena, *Todo México* (Mexico City, Diana, 1990).

Posada-Carbó, Eduardo, *The Colombian Caribbean: A Regional History, 1870–1950* (Oxford, Clarendon Press, 1996).

Quiroz Otero, Ciro, *Vallenato: hombre y canto* (Bogotá, Icaro, 1981).

Rabassa, Gregory, *If This Be Treason. Translation and its Dyscontents: A Memoir* (New York, New Directions, 2005).

Ramírez, Sergio, *Hatful of Tigers: Reflections on Art, Culture and Politics* (Willimantic, Conn., Curbstone Press, 1995).

———. *Adiós muchachos: una memoria de la revolución sandinista* (Mexico City, Aguilar, 1999).

Ramonet, Ignacio, *Fidel Castro: My Life. A Spoken Autobiography* (New York, Scribner, 2008).

Restrepo, Laura, *Historia de una traición* (Bogotá, Plaza y Janés, 1986).

Safford, Frank and Palacios, Marco, *Colombia: Fragmented Land, Divided Society* (Oxford, Oxford University Press, 2002).

Salinas de Gortari, Carlos, *México: un paso difícil a la modernidad* (Mexico City, Plaza y Janés, 4th edition, March 2002).

Samper Pizano, Ernesto, *Aquí estoy y aquí me quedo: testimonio de un gobierno* (Bogotá, El Ancora, 2000).

Santos Calderón, Enrique, *La guerra por la paz*, prologue by Gabriel García Márquez (Bogotá, CEREC, 1985).

Saunders, Frances Stonor, *Who Paid the Piper: The CIA and the Cultural Cold War* (London, Granta, 1999).

Setti, Ricardo A., *Diálogo con Vargas Llosa* (Costa Rica, Kosmos, 1989).

Stevenson, José, *Nostalgia boom* (Bogotá, Medio Pliego, 1977).

Stevenson Samper, Adlai, *Polvos en La Arenosa: cultura y burdeles en Barranquilla* (Barranquilla, La Iguana Ciega, 2005).

Tarver, H. Michael, *The Rise and Fall of Venezuelan President Carlos Andrés Pérez. II The Later Years 1973–2004* (Lewiston, N.Y., Edwin Mellen, 2004).

Tila Uribe, María, *Los años escondidos: sueños y rebeldias en la década del veinte* (Bogotá, CESTRA, 1994).

Tusell, Javier, *Retrato de Mario Vargas Llosa* (Barcelona, Círculo de Lectores, 1990).

Urquidi Illanes, Julia, *Lo que Varguitas no dijo* (La Paz, Khana Cruz, 1983).

Valdeblánquez, José María, *Historia del Departamento del Magdalena y del Territorio de la Guajira 1895–1963* (Bogotá, El Voto Nacional, 1964).

Vallejo, Virginia, *Amando a Pablo, odiando a Escobar* (Mexico, Random House Mondadori, 2007).

Vargas, Mauricio, Lesmes, Jorge and Téllez, Edgar, *El presidente que se iba a caer: diario secreto de tres periodistas sobre el 8,000* (Bogotá, Planera, 1996).

Vargas, Mauricio, *Memorias secretas del Revolcón: la historia íntima del polémico gobierno de César Gaviria revelada por uno de sus protagonistas* (Bogotá, Tercer Mundo, 1993).

Vázquez Montalbán, Manuel, *Y Dios entró en La Habana* (Madrid, Santillana, 1998).

Vidal, Margarita, *Viaje a la memoria (entrevistas)* (Bogotá, Espasa Calpe, 1997).

Villegas, Jorge and Yunis, José, *La guerra de los mil días* (Bogotá, Carlos Valencia, 1979).

Vindicación de Cuba (Havana, Editora Política, 1989).

Vinyes, Ramón, *Selección de textos*, ed. Jacques Gilard, 2 vols. (Bogotá, Instituto Colombiano de Cultura, 1981).

Wade, Peter, *Blackness and Race Mixture: The Dynamics of Racial Identity in Colombia* (Baltimore, Johns Hopkins University Press, 1993).

———. *Music, Race and Nation: "Música Tropical" in Colombia* (Chicago, University of Chicago Press, 2000).

White, Judith, *Historia de una ignominia: la UFC en Colombia* (Bogotá, Editorial Presencia, 1978).

Wilder, Thornton, *The Ides of March* (New York, Perennial/HarperCollins, 2003).

Williams, Raymond L., *The Colombian Novel, 1844–1987* (Austin, University of Texas Press, 1991).

Woolf, Virginia, *Orlando* (New York, Vintage, 2000).

Zalamea, Jorge, *El Gran Burundún-Burundá ha muerto* (Bogotá, Carlos Valencia, 1979).

Index

Credits are grouped according to their order in the insert, by page.

Colonel Nicolás R. Márquez. *(Family Archive–Margarita Márquez Caballero)*
Tranquilina Iguarán Cotes de Márquez. *(Family Archive–Margarita Márquez Caballero)*
Colonel Nicolás R. Márquez on a tropical day out in the 1920s. *(Family Archive–Margarita Márquez Caballero)*
Luisa Santiaga Márquez Iguarán. *(Family Archive–Margarita Márquez Caballero)*
Gabriel Eligio García and Luisa Santiaga, on their wedding day, 11 June 1926. *(Gustavo Adolfo Ramírez Ariza, GARA–Archive)*

GGM on his first birthday. *(Family Archive–Margarita Márquez Caballero)*
The Colonel's old house in Aracataca. *(GARA–Archive)*
Elvira Carrillo, "Aunt Pa." *(GARA–Archive)*
Aida GM, Luis Enrique GM, Gabito, cousin Eduardo Márquez Caballero, Margot GM and baby Ligia GM, 1936. *(Photo by Gabriel Eligio García, courtesy of Family Archive–Margarita Márquez Caballero)*

Gabito at the Colegio San José, Barranquilla, 1941. *(GARA–Archive)*
The Liceo Nacional in Zipaquirá, where GGM studied between 1943 and 1946. *(GARA–Archive)*
The GM brothers, Luis Enrique and Gabito, with cousins and friends, Magangué, c. 1945. *(Family Archive–Ligia García Márquez)*
Argemira García and her daughter Ena, early 1940s. *(Family Archive–Ligia García Márquez)*
GGM, mid-1940s. *(GARA–Archive)*
Berenice Martínez, mid-1940s. *(GARA–Archive)*

Mercedes Barcha at school in Medellín, 1940s. *(GM Family Archive)*
Steamship *David Arango*. *(Photo by William Caskey)*
Fidel Castro and other student leaders during the *Bogotazo*, April 1948. *(http://www.latinamericanstudies.org)*
Barranquilla, April 1950: farewell for Ramón Vinyes. *(GARA–Archive)*
Barranquilla, in the *El Heraldo* office, 1950. *(Photo by Quique Scopell, courtesy of El Heraldo)*
GGM, Bogotá, 1954. *(El Espectador)*

GGM, Paris, 1957. *(Photo by Guillermo Angulo)*
Tachia Quintana in Paris. *(Photo by Yossi Bal, courtesy of Tachia Rosoff)*
GGM and friends, Red Square, Moscow, summer 1957. *(GARA–Archive)*
The Soviet invasion of Hungary, Budapest, 1956. *(Hulton-Deutsch Collection/CORBIS)*
Caracas, 13 May 1958. *(Bettmann/CORBIS)*

GGM working for Prensa Latina, Bogotá, 1959. *(Photo by Hernán Díaz)*
Mercedes Barcha in Barranquilla. *(GARA–Archive)*
Cuba, December 1958: Che Guevara and comrades relax. *(Popperfoto/Getty Images)*
GGM and Plinio Mendoza working for Prensa Latina, Bogotá, 1959. *(El Tiempo)*
GGM and Mercedes, on Séptima in Bogotá, 1960s. *(GARA–Archive)*

Havana, January 1961. *(Getty Images)*
Havana, 21 April 1961. *(Bettmann/CORBIS)*
Mexico, 1964. GGM in glasses. *(GARA–Archive)*
GGM in Aracataca, 1966. *(GARA–Archive)*
Valledupar, Colombia, 1967. *(Photo by Gustavo Vásquez, courtesy María Elena Castro de Quintero)*
Camilo Torres. *(GARA–Archive)*

Wizard or dunce? GGM in Barcelona, crowned by the famous cabbalistic cover of *One Hundred Years of Solitude*, 1969. *(Colita/CORBIS)*
Mercedes, Gabo, Gonzalo and Rodrigo, Barcelona, late 1960s. *(GM Family Archive)*

The Soviet invasion of Czechoslovakia, August 1968. *(epa/CORBIS)*
GGM, Barcelona, late 1960s. *(GARA–Archive)*
GGM and Pablo Neruda, 1972. *(GARA–Archive)*
Boom couples, Barcelona, 1974. *(Photo by Colita)*

GGM, Barcelona, 1970s. *(Photo by Rodrigo García)*
GGM and Carlos Fuentes, Mexico City, 1971. *(Excelsior)*
GGM and Mercedes, 1970s. *(Excelsior)*
Cartagena, 1971: GGM visits his parents. *(Excelsior)*

Writers of the Boom. *(Photo by Silvia Lemus)*
Julio Cortázar, Miguel Angel Asturias and GGM, West Germany, 1970. *(GARA–Archive)*
Paris, 1973. The wedding of Charles Rosoff and Tachia Quintana. *(Tachia Rosoff, Personal Archive)*
Santiago de Chile, 11 September 1973. President Salvador Allende. *(Dmitri Baltermants/The Dmitri Baltermants Collection/CORBIS)*
Santiago de Chile, 11 September 1973. General Pinochet and his henchmen. *(Ullstein-bild—dpa)*

Cuban troops in Angola, February 1976. *(AFP/Getty Images)*
Castro, President of Cuba, 1980s. *(Excelsior)*
General Omar Torrijos, 1970s. *(AFP/Getty)*
GGM interviews Felipe González in Bogotá, 1977. *(Alternativa)*
Bogotá, 1977: GGM, Consuelo Araujonoguera ("La Cacica") and Guillermo Cano, editor of *El Espectador*. *(El Espectador)*
GGM, Carmen Balcells and Manuel Zapata Olivella, 1977. *(GARA–Archive)*

Mexico City, 1981: GGM buried by press attention following his self-exile from Colombia. *(Bettmann/CORBIS)*
Alvaro Mutis chauffeurs GGM. *(GARA–Archive)*
Stockholm, December 1982: Jaime Castro, Germán Vargas, GGM, Charles Rosoff,

Alfonso Fuenmayor, Plinio Mendoza, Eligio García and Hernán Vieco. *(GM Family Archive)*

Stockholm, December 1982: GGM in *costeño "sombrero vueltiao." (Photo by Nereo López, courtesy of the Biblioteca Nacional de Colombia)*

Stockholm, December 1982: GGM in the chalk circle. *(GARA–Archive)*

Cartagena, 1993. Luisa Santiaga and her children. *(Family Archive–Ligia García Márquez)*

GGM and Fidel Castro, by the Caribbean, 1983. *(Photo by Rodrigo Castaño)*

Havana, 1988: GGM and Robert Redford. *(Excelsior)*

Bogotá, mid-1980s: GGM and Mercedes with President Betancur and his wife. *(GARA–Archive)*

Bogotá's Palacio de Justicia in flames, 6 November 1985. *(http://alvaroduque.wordpress.com)*

Berlin, November 1989. *(Regis Bossu/Sygma/Corbis)*

Bogotá, 1992: GGM salutes his admirers in the Jorge Eliécer Gaitán Theatre. *(GARA–Archive)*

GGM and Mercedes, October 1993. *(GARA–Archive)*

GGM, 1999. *(GARA–Archive)*

Barcelona, *c.* 2005: Carmen Balcells in her office. *(© Carlos González Armesto)*

Havana, 2007: GGM and Fidel Castro. *(Diario El Tiempo/epa/Corbis)*

Cartagena, March 2007: GGM and Bill Clinton. *(Cesar Carrion/epa/Corbis)*

Cartagena, March 2007: GGM and King Juan Carlos I of Spain. *(AFP/ Getty Images)*

Cartagena, March 2007: GGM waves to admirers during his eightieth birthday celebrations. *(STR/AFP/Getty Images)*

TEXT PERMISSIONS

The author and publishers gratefully acknowledge Gabriel García Márquez and the Agencia Literaria Carmen Balcells, S.A., and Alfred A. Knopf, a division of Random House, Inc. for permission to quote extracts from copyright material by Gabriel García Márquez throughout this book, and also acknowledge Latimer, S.A., for the English translations of the original Spanish-language editions of various of his works, as follows: *One Hundred Years of Solitude* (1970); *No One Writes to the Colonel* (1971); *The Autumn of the Patriarch* (1977); *Leafstorm* (1979); *In Evil Hour* (1980); *The Story of a Shipwrecked Sailor* (1986); *Love in the Time of Cholera* (1988); *Clandestine in Chile* (1989); *The General in His Labyrinth* (1991); *Collected Stories* (1991); *Strange Pilgrims* (1993); *Of Love and Other Demons* (1995); *News of a Kidnapping* (1997); *Living to Tell the Tale* (2003) and *Memories of My Melancholy Whores* (2005).

In addition, the author and publishers gratefully acknowledge the copyright holders of the following texts: Plinio Apuleyo Mendoza (ed.), *The Fragrance of Guava: Conversations with Gabriel García Márquez* (London, Faber & Faber, 1998); Plinio Apuleyo Mendoza, *La llama y el hielo* (Bogotá, Gamma, 1989). Gustavo Arango, *Un ramo de nomeolvides* (Cartagena, El Universal, 1996). Guillermo Cabrera Infante, *Mea Cuba* (London, Faber & Faber, 1994); José Donoso, *The Boom in Spanish American Literature: A Personal History* (© Columbia University Press, 1977). Claudia Dreifus, "Gabriel García Márquez" (*Playboy*, February 1983), copyright © *Playboy* 1983. Reprinted by permission of *Playboy*; excerpt from "Cocaine's Reality, by García Márquez" by James Brooke (*The New York Times*, March 11, 1995), copyright © 1995 by *The New York Times*. All rights reserved. The printing, copying, redistribution, or retransmission of the material without express written permission is prohibited. Reprinted by permission of PARS International, on behalf of *The New York Times*; Heriberto Fiorillo, *La Cueva: crónica del grupo de Barranquilla* (Bogotá, Planeta, 2002). Silvia Galvis, *Los García Márquez* (Bogotá, Arango Editores, 1996). By permission of the author. Eligio García, *Tras las claves de Melquíades* (Bogotá, Normal, 2001). Rita Guibert, *Seven Voices* (New York, Vintage, 1973); Luis Harss and Barbara Dohmann, *Into the Mainstream: Conversations with Latin-American Writers* (New York, Harper and Row, 1967); Antonio Núñez Jiménez, "García Márquez y la perla de las Antillas (o 'Qué conversan Gabo y Fidel')" (unpublished manuscript, Havana, 1984). Gabriel García Márquez, *Paris Review* Writers at Work interview by Peter H. Stone, Issue 82, winter 1981, and "Solitude and Company: An Oral Biography of Gabriel García Márquez" by Silvana Paternostro, *Paris Review*, no. 166, summer 2003. Reprinted by permission of the Wylie Agency; Elena Poniatowska, "Los *Cien años de soledad* se iniciaron con sólo 20 dólares" (interview, September 1973), in *Todo México*, 1 (Mexico City, Diana, 1990).

A NOTE ON THE TYPE

THIS BOOK was set in Janson, a typeface long thought to have been made by the Dutchman Anton Janson, who was a practicing type-founder in Leipzig during the years 1668–1687. However, it has been conclusively demonstrated that these types are actually the work of Nicholas Kis (1650–1702), a Hungarian, who most probably learned his trade from the master Dutch typefounder Dirk Voskens. The type is an excellent example of the influential and sturdy Dutch types that prevailed in England up to the time William Caslon (1692–1766) developed his own incomparable designs from them.

Composed by North Market Street Graphics,
Lancaster, Pennsylvania
Printed and bound by Berryville Graphics,
Berryville, Virginia
Designed by Virginia Tan